America's Virgin Islands

America's Virgin Islands

A History of Human Rights and Wrongs

SECOND EDITION

William W. Boyer

CAROLINA ACADEMIC PRESS
Durham, North Carolina

Library of Congress Cataloging-in-Publication Data

Boyer, William W.
  America's Virgin Islands : a history of human rights and wrongs / William W.
Boyer. -- 2nd ed.
    p. cm.
  Includes bibliographical references and index.
  ISBN 978-1-59460-687-8 (alk. paper)
  1. Virgin Islands of the United States--History. I. Title.

F2136.5.B69 2010
972.97'22--dc22

                                2010012038

CAROLINA ACADEMIC PRESS
700 Kent Street
Durham, North Carolina 27701
Telephone (919) 489-7486
Fax (919) 493-5668
www.cap-press.com

To my daughter
Helen Hoy Boyer

We cannot enjoy half slavery and half freedom. We want it all or nothing. We don't want to be revolutionists; we don't want to be communists; we don't wish to be branded against organized government. We want to be the same as every member of this American nation, and we are entitled to that privilege.

I am told you cannot oppose government, but, by God, government can hear us cry, and must hear us protest, and we are going to protest until we get the form of government we wish.

Casper Holstein, 1934

Contents

List of Tables xi

List of Illustrations xiii

Preface to the Second Edition xv

Preface to the First Edition xvii

Introduction xxiii

Part I
Roots: 1492–1917

Chapter 1 · Columbus, Colonialism, and Captivity 3
  Settlement of St. Croix 5
  Danish Colonization 8
  Company Rule 11
  Plantation Agriculture 12
  The Slave Trade 15

Chapter 2 · Repression and Rebellion 21
  Slave Systems 21
  Slavery in the Virgin Islands 24
  Rebellion 31
  Slave Conspiracies 33

Chapter 3 · Slavery to Serfdom 35
  End of the Slave Trade 35
  The Free Colored 38
  The Moravians 44
  Peter von Scholten 48
  Emancipation 53
  Serfdom 58

Chapter 4 · Purchase of a People   61
The White Minority   62
Restricting the Franchise   64
Revolt of the Laborers   67
Economic Decline   71
Treaty of 1867   77
Treaty of 1902   80
The Transfer   83

Chapter 5 · American Antecedents   89
Northwest Ordinance   90
Continental Expansion   92
Spanish-American War   94
Puerto Rico   98
Insular Cases   101
Caribbean Imperialism   106

Part II
Freedom Struggle: 1917–1954

Chapter 6 · Prejudice and Poverty   111
A Legacy of Neglect   111
Federal Indifference   112
Infusion of Racism   114
Naval Autocracy   120
Americanization   123
Navy Justice   126
Repression of Native Leaders   128
The Francis Case   133
The Issue of Citizenship   139

Chapter 7 · Reform and Relief   143
Political Peonage   143
Agitation for Reform   146
Withdrawal of the Navy   149
"An Effective Poorhouse"   151
Pearson and His Critics   153
A New Deal   161
A Paradox   164

Chapter 8 • **Progress and Politics**   167
Personality and Culture   167
The Virgin Islands Company   176
A Constitution for the Islands   183
Parties and Politics   188
Judges and Justice   191
The Islands at War   195
The First Black Governor   203
The First Native Governor   209

Part III
Tourism Syndrome: 1954–1980

Chapter 9 • **Penury to Prosperity**   229
Persistence of Poverty   229
Organic Act Revision   231
Revised Organic Act of 1954   236
Archie Alexander   238
Charges and Countercharges   242
Tourism to the Rescue   247
Rockefeller's Resort   250

Chapter 10 • **Development Decade**   255
Paiewonsky's Progress   258
Condemnation without Representation   260
Impact of Tourism   263
Harvey and Hess   267
Donkeycrats and Unicrats   272
Pressure from the Press   280
Toward More Self-Rule   282
Ominous Signs   287

Chapter 11 • **Aliens and the Alienated**   293
Influx of Aliens   296
Last Appointed Governor   302
First Elected Governor   305
Roundup of Illegals   307
Alienation of the Land   313
Fountain Valley   321
A Crescendo of Crime   328
A King for Governor   331

Chapter 12 · Political Culture 335
    Affinity with the East 337
    "Concerned Virgin Islanders" 341
    Social Infrastructure 342
    Economic Infrastructure 351
    Economic Development 358
    Fiscal Uncertainty 365
    Personalistic Politics 372
    The Status Issue 378
    A Community in Trouble 381

Part IV
Persisting Problems: 1980–2010

Chapter 13 · Constitutional Conundrums 389
    The Fourth Constitutional Convention 389
    Virgin Islands Nonimmigrant Alien Adjustment Act of 1982 390
    The Political Status Referendum of 1993 393
    The Fifth Constitutional Convention 398
    Failure of the Fifth Attempt 400
    Natives versus Down-Islanders 403

Chapter 14 · Cacophony of Conflicts 407
    Crime and Law Enforcement 407
    Health 411
    Public Education 414
    Politics and Government 417
    Tourism 423

Epilogue 427

Appendix · Letter from Governor Hastie to the Author 431

Selected Bibliography 435

Index 445

List of Tables

Table 1. Total Number of Slaves in the Virgin Islands, 1733–1846　　25

Table 2. Composition of Free Colored in Christiansted, 1791–1811　　39

Table 3. Total Number of Free Colored in the Virgin Islands, 1789–1835　40

Table 4. Church Affiliation in the Virgin Islands, 1835　　49

Table 5. Population of the Virgin Islands, 1773–1911　　53

Table 6. Estimated Composition of Virgin Islands Population by
　　　　　Groups, 1950, 1960, 1965　　265

List of Illustrations

United States Virgin Islands 2

Plan for a British slaving ship 19

Governor-General Peter von Scholten 51

Sugar mill driven by water power 54

Ruins of St. Croix sugar plantation 55

Natives coaling steamers, St. Thomas, 19th Century 74

In the canefields, circa 1905 75

Worker's family in St. Croix, circa 1910 77

Group of natives, St. Thomas, between 1890 and 1901 80

Transfer ceremony, St. Thomas, March 31, 1917 84

Secretary Lansing handing Constantin Brun, the Danish Minister in Washington, a Treasury Warrant for $25 M. At right is Rear Admiral James H. Oliver, first appointee to the Governorship of the V.I. of the U.S.A. 87

President Herbert Hoover's visit to St. Thomas, 1931 166

Governor Lawrence Cramer of the Virgin Islands, standing, discussing pending legislation in Washington, D.C., 1938 183

Governor Charles Harwood of the Virgin Islands speaking at a Red Cross meeting, 1941 201

President Harry Truman and Governor William Hastie at Emancipation Garden, St. Thomas, February 22, 1948 204

Women in a northern St. Croix village, 1941 215

A Farm Security Administration borrower and his wife in their homestead house constructed with FSA aid in Christiansted, 1941 216

At the health clinic in Frederiksted, St. Croix, 1941 217

Cultivating sugar cane on Virgin Islands Company land, St. Croix, 1941 218

A French fisherman and his wife in "Frenchtown," St. Thomas, 1941   219

Puerto Rican family in a St. Croix village reconditioned by the
    Virgin Islands Company, 1941   219

Class in Christiansted high school, 1941   219

The police chief of St. John, 1941   219

Court day in Frederiksted, St. Croix, 1941   219

The St. Croix Municipal Council in session, Christiansted, 1941   220

In the Government House rum distillery of the Virgin Islands
    Company near Christiansted, 1941   220

Cooking dinner on coal pots in a district of Charlotte Amalie, 1941   221

Alton Adams directing his U.S. Navy Virgin Islands band, 1941   221

The slaughterhouse in Charlotte Amalie, 1941   222

Collecting garbage from an open sewer in Christiansted, 1941   223

In the men's section of the Christiansted hospital, 1941   224

An alien inmate of the insane asylum at the Charlotte Amalie
    hospital, 1941   225

An inmate of the insane asylum, St. Thomas, 1941   226

Governor Ralph Paiewonsky congratulates arrival of first jet airline,
    June 9, 1962   254

Trunk Bay, St. John   261

Dr. Melvin H. Evans, President Nixon's nominee to be last appointed
    Governor, July 1, 1969   295

Desalination plant, St. Croix   353

Market Place, Charlotte Amalie, St. Thomas   359

Cruise Ships in St. Thomas harbor   385

Former Governor Turnbull with the author in St. Thomas, 2009   402

The author with Governor Farrelly at Government House, St. Thomas   421

Preface to the Second Edition

In October 2008, the publisher of the first edition of this book, Keith Sipe, asked me to consider researching and writing a second edition to update the book for the period 1980 to 2010. I accepted this challenge and spent several weeks during June and July 2009 in the Virgin Islands to conduct the necessary research. I found very few of those still alive who helped me in my research during the late 1970s. Among others, they were: Emerita Professor of History Dr. Marilyn Krigger; former governor and historian Dr. Charles Turnbull; long-time leader of down-islanders George Goodwin; and retired linguist, social scientist and historian Emeritus Professor Dr. Arnold Highfield who, though he was then vacationing in Vermont, nevertheless offered me valuable advice. I will always be indebted to Krigger, Turnbull, Highfield, and Goodwin for helping me conduct research for both editions. Although I missed those who had passed on, I shall never forget their past contributions.

During my 2009 research visit, I found my first edition had been well received, a fact that facilitated meeting many gate-keepers of knowledge who were forthcoming and generous in helping my research for this second edition. They were: Patricia Abbott, Madeleine Anduze, Julie Bederman, Dr. Lawrence Benjamin, Dr. Ingrid Bough, Annice Canton, Dr. Carlyle Corbin, Gerard Emanuel, Wilfredo Geigel, Robert Johnson, Rudolph Krigger, Edgar Lake, Susan Lugo, Dr. Frank Mills, Mario Moorhead, Judith Rogers, Dr. Malik Sekou, Lawrence Sewer, Oswin Sewer, Rachelle Shells, Beverly Smith, Dr. Gilbert Sprauve, Dr. Tibor Toth, Joel Turnbull, and George Tyson.

My greatest debt of gratitude is owed to Emerita Professor Marilyn Krigger who taught Virgin Islands history for many years at the University of the Virgin Islands, and who read and critiqued my drafts of both editions of this book. I am especially indebted also to: Professor Edward Ratledge of the University of Delaware for providing me an office and resources to write this second edition; Dr. Dan Rich, former Provost of the University of Delaware, who arranged for the University to fund, in part, my 2009 research visit to the Virgin Islands; and my wife, Dr. Nancy Boyer, and my daughter, Helen Hoy Boyer, who supported and assisted my research.

My research for this second edition was greatly facilitated by the resources and staffs of: the von Scholten Collection of the Enid M. Baa Public Library and Archives in Charlotte Amalie; the Ralph M. Paiewonsky Library of the University of the Virgin Islands on the St. Thomas campus; the Caribbean Collection and Archives of the Florence Williams Public Library in Christiansted; the Library of the University of the Virgin Islands on the St. Croix campus; and the Morris Library of the University of Delaware.

Regardless of all the help I have received, I alone am responsible for any errors or shortcomings in this second edition.

W.W.B.

Newark, Delaware

March 2010

Preface to the First Edition

Ever since I wrote a master's thesis in 1949, entitled *Civil Liberties in the Virgin Islands of the United States*, I harbored the intention of updating that work and publishing it as a book. Accordingly, I returned to the Islands for this purpose. Knowing that a scholarly history of the Islands, that emphasized or adequately treated the American period, had yet to be written, I abandoned the effort of updating my thesis* and decided to write that history of the Islands from the time of their discovery by Columbus in 1493 to the present, but with emphasis on the American period since 1917. The following is the fruit of that decision.

Columbus named them the "Virgin Islands," and although Denmark called them the "Danish West Indies" while they were under that country's rule, the term "Virgin Islands" is generally retained throughout this work and refers to those Caribbean islands purchased by the United States in 1917, and are not to be confused with the nearby British Virgin Islands.

A number of difficulties confronts one bent on writing a serious history of the Virgin Islands. Foremost, of course, is the expense, especially for a mainlander. Besides round-trip airfare; the cost of living in the Islands substantially exceeds that of the mainland. By avoiding the tourist season—roughly December through May—and living frugally, I was able to maximize my expenditures during seven research visits over a three-year period. Newly-made friends in the Islands were great money-saving helpers. A special debt of gratitude is owed to the late Dr. Charles P. Messick who had provided for a special fund to cover my professional expenses to supplement the Charles P. Messick Professorship I hold at the University of Delaware. My research in the Islands was also supported by a grant from the Penrose Fund of the American Philosophical Society, and I am particularly grateful in this respect to George W. Corner, Chairman of the Society's Committee on Research. Finally, a grant from the Dean's office of the College of Arts and Science, University of Delaware, supported the typing of this book manuscript.

---

* The thesis, nevertheless, was published in 1982 by Antilles Graphic Arts, Inc., Sunny Isle, St. Croix.

Another difficulty for scholars is the paucity of reliable statistics and historical records in the Islands. Here the situation is not only deplorable, but it is sad. Despite frequent declamations of Virgin Islanders of the need to protect and preserve the culture of the Islands, in point of fact few Islanders are interested in establishing a well organized and professionally administered, government supported, territorial archives service that would bring together copies—if not originals—of those documents concerning the history of the Islands that are known to repose in the national archives of Denmark, The Netherlands, Germany, England, France, Portugal, Spain, a number of African countries, and the United States. Of these, the archives of Denmark and the United States are the most important.

Assuming availability of necessary research funds, it is not enough for a researcher to have linguistic facility in the Danish language to research the archives in Copenhagen. The researcher must also be competent to transcribe the old Gothic script in which Danish documents are written, or be provided with translator service. Some Virgin Islanders believe that some of those documents that reflect adversely on Danish rule have been purged from the Danish archives. This may be true, but apparently more than three thousand linear shelf feet of historical documents relating to the Islands still remain untapped in the Royal Archives of Denmark. Most of these materials, which pertain to the history of the Virgin Islands prior to 1917, are unregistered, unmicrofilmed, and, therefore, simply unavailable to scholars.

Only one scholarly study of the Islands under Danish rule, based on research of Danish archival material, has ever been published in English, namely Waldemar Westergaard's *The Danish West Indies Under Company Rule, 1671–1754* (1917). Scholars interested in undertaking Danish archival research would be required to spend several years in Denmark, to learn the Danish language and archaic Gothic script, and to spend much money. Hopefully, this problem in time may become resolved, but it will require considerable funding by the United States Government under an agreement with the Government of Denmark.

In 1977, the U.S. National Endowment for the Humanities (NEH) modestly funded a feasibility study for planning the microfilming of documents in the Danish and other archives relating to the history of the Virgin Islands, undertaken by George Tyson of the controversial Island Resources Foundation (IRF) of St. Thomas, and resulting in his paper *The Historical Records of the U.S. Virgin Islands: A Report and Program Plan* (1977). This plan called for establishment of a Virgin Islands Historical Records Program and suggested that the Virgin Islands government contract with the nongovernmental IRF to implement, coordinate, and administer it. Lieutenant Governor Henry Millin of the Virgin Islands, among others, charged that this proposal was an attempt to usurp government functions in establishing an archival service in the Islands in violation of UNESCO standards. IRF's subsequent proposal to NEH for funding Mr. Tyson to write a pre-1917 history of the Virgin Islands, largely based on Danish archival research, was not approved.

Meanwhile, the Virgin Islands government has no archives, except in name only, having changed the name of the St. Thomas Public Library in 1978 to the Enid M. Baa Library and Archives. The Government of the Virgin Islands has no filing or records system, no records retention system, and no archives system. Each government official decides what records under his or her jurisdiction should be retained or destroyed. As each Governor has left office, he has taken his files with him. The scholar, given such anarchy, is thus denied access to important public records.

After Governor Melvin Evans took office in 1971, he acquired an old ship that formerly served as a navy prison on the Great Lakes. Some government files since 1972 are stored in cardboard boxes in the hold of this decrepit ship, which is located on the western end of St. Thomas Harbor, under lock and key and without any staff or supervision. No directory of their location exists, and access to these records requires the written permission of the Lieutenant Governor. The boxes of files are stacked haphazardly in this damp, unlighted hold exposed to rot and rodents. A worse place for housing public records could not exist. In St. Croix, all public safety records were allegedly destroyed in 1974 because they were stored in mahogany file cases that someone wanted. Other public records said to have been stored in the old fort in Frederiksted—site of the emancipation of slaves in 1848—are rumored to have been burned to make the fort usable for the 1976 bicentennial celebrations.

The records in the National Archives in Washington, D.C., pertaining to the Virgin Islands have been quite useful. Record Group 55, Records of the Government of the Virgin Islands, totals 190 cubic feet and covers the period of U.S. administration of the Islands from 1917 to 1943, but a few documents date as late as 1950. There are additional records in other record groups in the National Archives relating to the governing of the Virgin Islands by the United States Government. Most of these represent records of agencies in Washington that have had supervisory responsibilities of one kind or another over the Islands. Of particular significance are records of the Interior Department's Office of Territories and its predecessor, the Division of Territories and Island Possessions, relating to the supervision of the insular government from 1931 to 1951. I express my gratitude to Richard C. Crawford of the National Archives, who served as my contact archivist.

Charles F. Reid edited in 1941 his comprehensive and annotated *Bibliography of the Virgin Islands of the United States* (New York: H. W. Wilson Co.), which has proven a quite usable indicator of sources for me. Professor Arnold R. Highfield of the St. Croix branch of the College of the Virgin Islands is in the process of updating Reid's bibliography. He is also engaged in translating the works of the Moravian missionary Oldendorp, which should shed considerable light on the history of slavery in the Islands. I am indebted to Dr. Highfield for his suggestions regarding sources, for insights he has shared, and for his edited volume, *A Bibliography of Articles on the Danish West Indies and the United States Virgin Islands in the New York Times 1867–1975* (Gainesville: University Presses of Florida, 1978) on which I relied.

I am also indebted to history Professor Marilyn F. Krigger of the College of the Virgin Islands in St. Thomas. Professor Krigger directed me to many sources and read the entire manuscript. Her prudent observations and constructive comments have proven very helpful and I thank her for her generosity, encouragement, and interest.

I wish, too, to especially acknowledge: Blanca Ropes, former Deputy Clerk of the U.S. District Court in St. Croix, for facilitating my research and helping me gain access to court records and other documents; George Goodwin, President of the Alien Interest Movement in St. Thomas, for his many kindnesses that enhanced my understanding of the problems of foreign workers and their dependents in the Islands; and Attorney Gustav A. Danielson, CPA, for imparting to me understanding of many complexities of public finance and utilities regulation in the Islands as well as directing me to various sources that would otherwise have remained undiscovered.

My greatest debt of gratitude is owed to John P. Collins, whose rare empathy and altruism prompted him to share with me his extensive personal files on public affairs in the Islands and to introduce me to anyone he thought could help me. Knowing him has enriched this book and my life.

There are many others whose help of one kind or another evokes my grateful acknowledgement. Listed alphabetically, they are: George Alexis, Attorney Edwin Armstrong, Enid M. Baa, Ulrich Benjamin, Attorney James A. Bough, Attorney Robert Bowles, Commissioner Milton C. Branch, Omar Brown, Anvil Browne, Annamaria Carrera, Senator Hector Cintron, Vincen M. "Beef" Clendinen, Luc Cuadrado, Attorney Mario N. de Chabert, Delegate Ron de Lugo, Dr. Peter P. de Zela, Professor Isaac Dookhan, Chuck Downs, Professor Thomas Drake, Attorney Thomas Elliot, Gerard Emanuel, Governor Melvin H. Evans, Jeffrey Farrow, Janet Foster, Comptroller Darrell E. Fleming, Geraldo Guirty, the late Governor William H. Hastie, James E. Henry, Elroy Hill, Delita Jacobs, Larry Kavanaugh, Professor Paul Leary, June Linqvist, Senator John

Maduro, Attorney Michael Marden, Professor Jerome L. McElroy, Ariel Melchior, Sr., Professor Mark J. Miller, Lieutenant Governor Henry Millin, Liston Monsanto, Dr. Patricia Gill Murphy, Attorney Sharon L. Nolan, Consul Henry O'Neal, Flavius Ottley, Isidor Paiewonsky, Senator Michael Paiewonsky, Felix Pitterson, Gordon "Specs" Powell, George Richards, Senator Ruby Rouss, Eugene Tyson, Bertha S. Vasquez, Ronald Walker, Wendell Walker, Mildred C. Wallace, Leona Watson, Attorney James Wisby, Professor Raymond Wolters, and the late Judge Warren H. Young.

I am indebted, too, for the helpful assistance of the staffs of the Public Libraries of St. Thomas and St. Croix, the Library of Congress in Washington, and the Morris Library of the University of Delaware.

This book would not have been written without the encouragement of my wife, Barbara Massey Boyer, who read the entire manuscript and offered many perceptive criticisms and suggestions.

Regardless of all the help I have received from many different quarters and persons, I alone remain responsible for the errors and shortcomings in this book.

W. W. B.
Newark, Delaware
May, 1982

Introduction

When most Americans think about the Caribbean, they may think of Fidel Castro's Cuba, because it was the Castro regime that brought them the Bay of Pigs, the missile crisis, the Soviet presence in the Caribbean and the flood of refugees into Florida. Relatively few Americans think of the U.S. territory of Puerto Rico, and still fewer think of the little noted Virgin Islands of the United States—represented as tiny specks on the map. This last condition, however, is changing, for the U.S. Virgin Islands are rapidly beginning to rival Florida and California as a popular tourist mecca.

Most continental Americans can be forgiven for not knowing about their American microcolony—the U.S. Virgin Islands. After all, this island group has been given slight attention in history books, by scholars, or even by the contemporary press. Indeed, the American news media—whose job it is to know about such places—is woefully ignorant about the American Virgin Islands and the surrounding Caribbean. For example, while a filmstrip on television's ABC evening news of April 6, 1979, was depicting a volcanic eruption on the British Windward Caribbean island of St. Vincent, commentator Frank Reynolds wrongly informed a nationwide audience of millions that St. Vincent was one of the U.S. Virgin Islands.

The United States Virgin Islands are a small group of islands, constituting the easternmost point of U.S. territory, located midway in the great curving archipelago of Caribbean islands—stretching from Cuba to Trinidad—between the Greater Antilles to the west and the Lesser Antilles to the east and south. The U.S. Virgin Islands consist of three main islands—St. Thomas, St. John, and St. Croix—and about fifty small islets and cays, the largest of which are: Hassel Island and Water Island guarding the harbor of St. Thomas; Outer Brass, Inner Brass, Hans Lollik, and Thatch Cay surrounding St. Thomas; Loango off the coast of St. John; and Buck Island immediately to the north of St. Croix.

Located at a latitude of 18 degrees north of the equator and a longitude of 64 degrees west of Greenwich, St. Croix lies completely within the Caribbean, while the southern shores of St. Thomas and St. John are washed by the Caribbean Sea and their northern shores by the Atlantic Ocean.

The Virgin Islands are approximately 1,400 miles southeast of New York City, 990 miles east-southeast of Miami, and 1,035 miles northeast of the Panama Canal. St. Thomas is about 40 miles east of Puerto Rico and 40 miles north of St. Croix, while St. John is 3 miles east of St. Thomas and immediately adjacent to the British Virgin Islands, most prominent of which is Tortola. The three main islands total an area of about 132 square miles only. St. Croix is the largest, St. Thomas second, and St. John the smallest. At their greatest extremities, St. Croix is about 22 miles long and 6 miles wide with an area of about 84 square miles; St. Thomas is about 13 miles long and 2 to 3 miles wide with an area of about 28 square miles; and St. John is about 9 miles long and 5 miles wide with an area of about 20 square miles.

Volcanic in origin, the Islands are hilly, with St. Thomas and St. John having the highest peaks, and with St. Croix's northwest quadrant being a rugged, rain-forested area rising sharply from the water's edge, and its eastern promontory beyond its main port, Christiansted, consisting of a rough, arid, hilly tract. St. Croix, however, is topographically more diverse and is dominated by a broad rolling coastal plain covering its central and southern portions. Otherwise, the Islands are devoid of flat land. Innumerable bays, fringed by white sandy beaches, dent their coasts, especially those of St. Thomas and St. John, offering protection through the years for ships, smugglers, and pirates and, more recently, offering relaxation to tourists. St. Thomas Harbor, Coral Bay in St. John, and Christiansted Harbor in St. Croix are the most outstanding of these indentations.

Except for a few streams on St. Croix, the Islands have no rivers. Together with a relatively low rainfall and low moisture-holding capacity of the soils, the Islands have been plagued with frequent droughts and water shortages. Lying directly in the hurricane track, the Islands have also suffered occasionally from the destructive winds and floods wrought by hurricanes and tropical storms, most notably in the years of 1765, 1772, 1785, 1819, 1837, 1867, 1916, 1928, 1979, 1989, and 1995.

The Virgin Islands, however, are appropriately called "America's Paradise," and enjoy a near-perfect climate with an average temperature of 78 degrees throughout the year. Each island has something unique to offer the visitor— the Old World charm, architecture, and ruins of St. Croix, the most Danish of the Islands; the incomparable panoramic view from the mountain tops of St. Thomas of one of the most beautiful enclosed harbors in the world; and the unspoiled, natural, relaxed setting of forested mountains and valleys of St. John which boasts the most beautiful beaches in the Caribbean.

The Virgin Islands are rich in Native American lore and artifacts; the Islands having been inhabited successively by three main Indian groups—the Ciboneys, the Arawaks, and the Caribs. It was allegedly at Salt River in St. Croix, on Columbus' second voyage in 1493, that the Spaniards had their first reported hostile action with New World Indians—the Caribs. As the Virgin Islands became colonized, the last of the Caribs vanished.

At present, the population of the Islands comprises a diverse mixture of peoples, including descendants of African slaves and of European (Danish, Spanish, Portuguese, and Scottish) settlers, as well as immigrants from the Eastern Caribbean, Puerto Ricans, and people from the mainland of the United States. Virgin Islanders, themselves, distinguish between native Virgin Islanders, "down-islanders" from other Caribbean islands, Puerto Ricans, continentals, French, Jews, Arabs, and persons from the Dominican Republic.

Natives, continentals, and Puerto Ricans include both black and white residents, and there are many Virgin Islanders of mixed blood, but blacks comprise the great majority. In addition, many continentals—including condominium dwellers, students, etc.—are itinerant residents living in the Islands for only part of a year. Not included are upward to 2 million tourists who visit the Islands each year.

Since the 2000 census does not break down these groups, it is not possible to know their numbers. The census fixed the total population at 108,612, with St. Croix numbering 53,234, St. Thomas at 51,181, and St. John at 4,197. The racial makeup of the territory was 76.19 percent Black or African descent, 13.09 percent White, and 7.23 percent from other races. Hispanic or Latino of any race was 13.99 percent of the population.

In many respects, the American Virgin Islands are a microcosm of the human family. The diversity of their physical environment is matched by the diversity of their people. This is a history of the Virgin Islands of the United States. It is a record of the people of the Virgin Islands and the struggles of their greater number as slaves, serfs, and citizens to gain control of their own destiny. This is a history, broadly conceived, of human rights and human wrongs.

Part I

Roots:
1492–1917

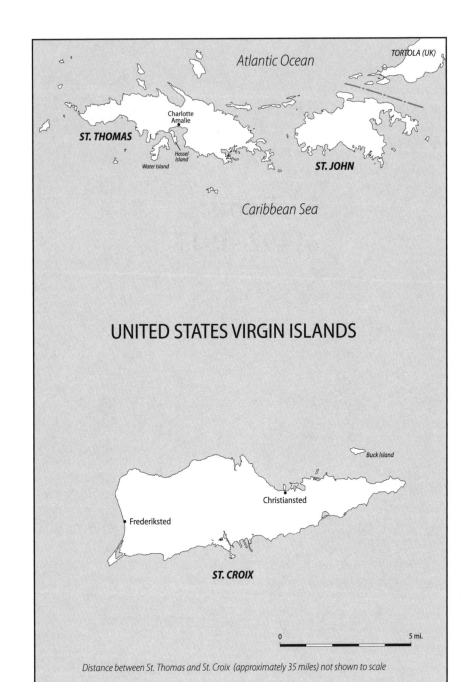

Atlantic Ocean

TORTOLA (UK)

Charlotte
Amalie

ST. THOMAS

Hassel
Island

Water Island

ST. JOHN

Caribbean Sea

UNITED STATES VIRGIN ISLANDS

Buck Island

Christiansted

Frederiksted

ST. CROIX

0   5 mi.

Distance between St. Thomas and St. Croix (approximately 35 miles) not shown to scale

1

Columbus, Colonialism, and Captivity

For "God, Glory, and Gold," the advent of empire began with the voyages of Columbus in the last decade of the fifteenth century. Although Vikings had already "encountered" America in the north of the Western Hemisphere, and Africans may have had contact with the south prior to 1492, it was Columbus' achievements that began the almost five centuries of Western imperialism.

His encounter of what he mistakenly thought was Asia marked the end of the Middle Ages and the rise of the nation state with its concomitants of nationalism and colonialism—a colonialism that was to expand over most of the earth and to enslave many of its inhabitants. The Crusades, Marco Polo, and the Portuguese opening of Africa had set the stage for the adventures of Columbus and his contemporary, Vasco da Gama, that were to kindle such momentous world change.

The end of empire was not to come all at once but was to be protracted over the centuries. Indeed, remnants still persist. The American Revolution of 1776, not the Russian Revolution of 1917, was to provide the dynamism for a waking world. Not until the second half of the twentieth century, however, were empires to be rapidly liquidated. Paradoxically, it remained for Americans to nearly complete the process with their final exit from Vietnam in 1975.

Historians, generations hence—motivated perhaps by a new ethic—may assess this era of empire as the most barbaric and inhuman in the millennia of recorded history. The islands of the Caribbean stood at center stage during the overture of empire and played important parts in the ensuing scenes over the next five centuries—colonialism, slavery, emancipation, war, decolonization, and the so-called East-West and North-South struggles.

The metropolitan powers of Europe competed to exert dominion over the Caribbean, but none was able to achieve dominance. They were able, however, to destroy almost totally the Indians. Except for a few Caribs in Dominica, there are no indigenous people left in the islands. In the process of colonization, they were destroyed during the sixteenth and seventeenth centuries by Spaniards, Englishmen, Dutchmen, Scotsmen, Normans, and Bretons.[1] Then, over three centuries, millions of Africans came and were enslaved on continental and West Indian plantations, providing the labor for the cultivation of cotton and cane and the production of sugar.

The Caribbean islands, therefore, became properties of European states—as subsequently did most of the Afro-Asian world—but, unlike the latter, they became colonial possessions without colonized peoples.[2] The inhabitants were colonists and slaves in the Virgin Islands as elsewhere in the West Indies.

The Virgin Islands group was encountered by Columbus during his second voyage in 1493. On November 14 of that year, he came upon an island, which he named "Santa Cruz," subsequently to be renamed "St. Croix" by the French. A well-manned boat was sent ashore, the crew of which was fiercely attacked by a group of Carib Indians.[3]

It was recorded by Dr. Chanca, who accompanied Columbus, that a few days later the fleet sailed through a cluster of many smaller islands to the north on which Columbus bestowed the pretentious name "Las Once Mil Virgines" (the 11,000 virgins) in honor of the legend of St. Ursula and her 11,000 mar-

---

1. The destruction of the indigenous Caribbean population was rapid and total. "The results are to be seen in the best estimates that have been prepared of the trend of population in Hispaniola. These place the population in 1492 at between 200,000 and 300,000. By 1508 the number was reduced to 60,000; ... in 1514, 14,000.... In 1570 only two villages survived of those about whom Columbus had assured his Sovereigns, less than eighty years before, that 'there is no better nor greater people in the world.'" Eric Williams, *From Columbus to Castro: The History of the Caribbean 1492–1969* (New York: Harper & Row, Publishers, 1970), p. 33.

2. Michael M. Horowitz, "Introductory Essay" in his edited *Peoples and Cultures of the Caribbean, An Anthropological Reader* (Garden City, NY: The Natural History Press, 1971), p. 1.

3. The story of this violent skirmish, as told by Washington Irving who had examined the letters and diaries of Columbus, is quoted by Theodoor de Booy and John T. Faris in their *The Virgin Islands, Our New Possessions and the British Islands* (Westport, CT: Negro Universities Press, 1970), pp. 37–40, as reprinted from its original publication in 1918 (by J. B. Lippincott Co., Philadelphia and London). See, also, Samuel Eliot Morison's *Second Voyage of Christopher Columbus from Cadiz to Hispaniola and the Discovery of the Lesser Antilles* (Oxford: Clarendon Press, 1939), pp. 81–88; and his *Journals and other Documents on the Life and Voyages of Christopher Columbus* (New York: Limited Editions Club, 1963), p. 212. But Morison's contention that Columbus' landing site was Salt River on the North shore of St. Croix is convincingly disputed by a St. Croix historian: Wilfredo A. Geigel, *Salt River in St. Croix: Columbus' Landing Site?* (Santurce, Puerto Rico: El Libro Inc., 2005).

tyred virgins,[4] because of their number and, it is claimed, "to exaggerate his find" in the eyes of his royal patrons, Ferdinand and Isabella of Spain.[5]

Columbus did not encounter Indians in the northern group, where he did not land, but archeological researchers have established the presence of Indian settlements in all major islands of the group prior to his visit.[6] Although Spain asserted its exclusive right to settle these islands, the Spanish neglected to colonize the smaller islands of the Lesser Antilles in favor of the larger and more lucrative Greater Antilles, thus leaving the former for settlement by other European nations.

When European settlement of the Virgin Islands eventually began during the seventeenth century, few Indians were to be found. Various explanations have been advanced. Some may have been captured by the Spanish to replace the rapidly dying Indian workers in Spanish mines of the Greater Antilles. Others may have fled southeastward to the Lesser Antilles. Whatever the causes, their absence when the Virgin Islands were colonized spurred the early introduction of African slavery into the Islands.[7]

Settlement of St. Croix

Santa Cruz (later known as St. Croix) became the first of the Virgin Islands to be colonized, although at that time it was not considered one of the Virgin Islands. Most historians agree that the Dutch and the English settled in Santa Cruz about the same time, around 1625, the Dutch settling in the harbor area of Bassin, the future Christiansted, and the English establishing their presence on the southwestern shore near present-day Frederiksted. Some French Protestant refugees from the Catholic-dominated half of St. Christopher (now known as St. Kitts) joined the Dutch colonists on Santa Cruz.[8]

As both the English and Dutch settlements expanded, quarreling between them over territory, jurisdiction, and authority increased. Finally, in 1645, the

---

4. *Select Documents Illustrating the Four Voyages of Columbus* (London: Hakluyt Society, 1930), vol. I, pp. 38–39.

5. Norwell Harrigan and Pearl I. Varlack, "The U.S. Virgin Islands and the Black Experience," *Journal of Black Studies*, 7, 4 (June 1977), p. 387.

6. See Theodoor de Booy, *Archeology of the Virgin Islands* (New York: Museum of the American Indian, 1920).

7. Isaac Dookhan, *A History of the Virgin Islands of the United States* (College of the Virgin Islands, St. Thomas: Caribbean Universities Press, 1974), pp. 28–29.

8. See, *e.g.*, Florence Lewisohn, *St. Croix Under Seven Flags* (Hollywood, FL: The Dukane Press, 1970), pp. 20–25; this is the most detailed history of St. Croix.

English Governor was killed by the Dutch Governor. The contemporary French writer, du Tertre, recounted:

> Immediately both people ran for their weapons; they clashed, and in a furious battle the Dutch Governor was so grievously wounded that he died of his wounds a few days later. After this confrontation both of the two parties were satisfied that enough blood had been shed and retired to their respective parts of the island. Upon the death of their governor, the Dutch elected a new one. Under the pretext of a settlement, he was cleverly lured to the house of the Englishman who was bent on revenge. The former, having come under the protection of the word of the latter, was arrested by the Englishman and condemned to be executed as punishment for the death of his predecessor; this was done.[9]

The weaker Dutch inhabitants decided to abandon the island and departed for St. Eustatius and St. Martin. Fearing ill treatment from the English, the French settlers also left the island for the French island of Guadeloupe.

The English alone remained masters of the island. As their colony was strengthened and their number increased, however, the nearby Spaniards on Puerto Rico became alarmed. In 1650, five ships bearing 1,200 Spanish soldiers descended on Santa Cruz by night, caught the English by surprise, killed about 120 of them, and forced all the remaining English to leave the island. Having been informed of the overthrow of the English, the Dutch attempted to regain their possessions by landing a small force on the island, but the remaining garrison of sixty Spaniards easily killed and captured these misadventurers.

The French who occupied half of St. Christopher, also having heard of the overthrow of the English, seized upon the opportunity to expand their dominion. Philippe de Lonvilliers de Poincy, strongman official of the Knights of Malta on St. Christopher, dispatched 160 of his best troops to Santa Cruz. After losing thirty to forty men in a Spanish ambush, the French succeeded in deceiving the Spanish garrison to capitulate and to sail for San Juan. The success of the venture elated de Poincy and he promptly sent 300 of his planters to establish the renamed new colony of St. Croix.

---

9. Aimery Caron and Arnold R. Highfield, *Jean-Baptiste DuTertre on the French in St. Croix and the Virgin Islands: A Translation with Introduction and Notes (St.* Thomas: Bureau of Libraries, Museums and Archeological Services, Occasional Paper no. 4, 1978), pp. 21–22. See, also, Aimery Caron, *Inventory of French Documents Pertaining to the U.S. Virgin Islands 1642–1737* (St. Thomas: Bureau of Libraries, Museums and Archeological Services, Occasional Paper no. 3, 1978).

De Poincy spared no effort or expense to develop this fertile island. He required, however, that all exports and imports be routed through St. Christopher so that he could exact his percentage of profits. This trading prohibition, and the fact that "the air was so infected by the vapors from the ground that two-thirds of all those sent there died,"[10] caused the remaining colonists to despair and revolt, encouraged some to engage in illegal trading, smuggling, and piracy, and generally contributed to a lack of progress.

In the third year after St. Croix was settled by the French, de Poincy formally deeded his islands to the Knights of Malta.[11] The Knights were given the rights of governing—to appoint judges and officers—but the King of France retained sovereignty over all French islands in the West Indies. Nothing much changed on St. Croix. De Poincy was still ruling the colony from his St. Christopher headquarters. It was not until de Poincy appointed the remarkably effective M. du Bois to be Governor of St. Croix, and to give tax relief and free trade rights to the settlers, did St. Croix begin to prosper. It was Governor du Bois who successfully urged the planters gradually to convert their coffee, ginger, indigo, and tobacco plantations to the more profitable sugar.

The system of bonded labor provided the labor for the plantations. Bonded persons (men and women) were Europeans who agreed to serve their masters for five to seven years after which they would be given their liberty. Meanwhile, they were carried from island to island and traded in much the same manner as African slaves. In St. Croix, the vast majority of bondmen came from the lowest class of French society, a fact commonly viewed as justification for their servitude. According to Arnold Highfield:

> In the final analysis, the lot of these people was quite severe. Overworked, underfed, and poorly clothed and sheltered, many of these unfortunate souls struggled daily to survive. Having no capital investment in them, their masters often cared little whether they lived or died, especially near the end of their bond term when they might well become tomorrow's competition in the competitive world of plantation agriculture.[12]

---

10. Caron and Highfield, *Jean-Baptiste DuTertre*, p. 33.

11. The Knights of Malta, also known as the Knights of St. John of Jerusalem and the Knights Hospitalers, were a rich and powerful order of the Roman Catholic Church. Founded in Jerusalem in the early 1000s, the order moved first to Cyprus, then to Rhodes, and finally in the 1500s to Malta.

12. Arnold R. Highfield, "Bondmen and the Labor Problem," *The St. Croix Avis*, June 12, 1978, p. 11.

As the labor-intensive crop of sugar replaced tobacco and other crops during the late seventeenth century, and as the armies of Louis XIV required increasing numbers of soldiers, bonded European labor was gradually replaced by African slavery.

De Poincy died in 1660 and was succeeded as Governor of St. Christopher by Chevalier de Sales who concluded an agreement that year with the Dominican Order to establish a mission on St. Croix. Besides other references to the presence of African slaves in St. Croix, du Tertre relates that this agreement called for the colonists to provide land, tax exemption, and "ten Negroes to each Dominican Father," among other provisions.[13]

At this time, the Knights of Malta held only those islands de Poincy had given them, namely St. Croix, St. Bartholomew, and their halves of St. Christopher and St. Martin. The other French islands (Guadeloupe and Martinique) were governed by their private owners. Seeking to exert a stronger French presence in the Caribbean, Louis XIV decided that the Crown should take over the government and commerce of the islands through a new commercial company. Accordingly, a contract to indemnify the Knights and the owner-governors was concluded in 1665, and the King sent emissaries from the new French West India Company to secure the islands. Thus ended colonial rule of St. Croix by the Knights of Malta and the beginning of Company rule under the Crown.

Company rule fared badly and lasted only nine years, until 1674, when the King dissolved the Company and replaced it with Crown rule. These decades were interspersed with illegal trading, wars, privateering, piracy, and religious conflicts. Indeed, the English and French were more often at war than at peace. Deciding that maintaining St. Croix as a French colony was no longer militarily feasible or economically profitable or desirable, the Crown acted in 1695 on a recommendation to move the St. Croix colony to St. Domingue (later Haiti), the French part of Hispaniola. In January, 1696, a total of 1,200 persons including slaves were removed to St. Domingue, thus marking the end of French colonization of St. Croix.[14]

Danish Colonization

The expansion of European empires in Asia, Africa, and the Western Hemisphere usually was achieved either through direct conquest and settlement by

---

13. Caron and Highfield, *Jean-Baptiste DuTertre*, p. 57.
14. Caron, *Inventory of French Documents*, p. 37.

European governments or through government charters granted to companies or merchants who subscribed capital for trade and settlement beyond the seas. Spain and Portugal resorted to direct expansion under royal authority while other countries—notably Great Britain, the Netherlands, France and Denmark—generally pursued their imperial designs through chartered companies.[15]

As early as 1625, Christian IV (1588–1648) of Denmark gave permission to Dutch merchants in Copenhagen to promote trade between Denmark and the West Indies, but a colonizing expedition was not commissioned until forty years later. By the 1660s, Denmark had established an absolute monarchy which led to the chartering of national joint stock companies in which the King himself held shares. A plan for colonizing St. Thomas was approved by Frederik III (1648–1670) in 1665. The first settlement of St. Thomas was ravaged by sickness, causing the death of Danish Governor Erik Nielson Smit, among others, and by English privateers and a devastating hurricane. After nineteen perilous months, the surviving Danes abandoned the island.[16]

The second attempt to colonize St. Thomas was to prove more ambitious and successful. Denmark established a Board of Trade in 1668, and among the first acts of Christian V upon his accession to the throne in 1670 were conclusion of a treaty of alliance with Britain (thus neutralizing her privateers) and the chartering of the Danish West India Company, directing it to prepare for the resettlement of St. Thomas.

The charter authorized the Company to occupy and take possession of St. Thomas "and also such other islands thereabouts or near the mainland of America as might be uninhabited and suitable for plantations, or if inhabited, then by such people who have no knowledge concerning us."[17] The charter, similar to the usual seventeenth century commercial company charters, conferred very broad powers. Under this charter and the "reglement" accompanying it, preparations for the settlement of St. Thomas began in the summer of 1671.

Among the powers conferred upon the Company by its charter were all powers of colonial government, except the conduct of foreign relations reserved to the Danish Crown and the allowance of appeals to the Danish Supreme

---

15. H. Morse Stephens, "Introduction" in Waldemar Westergaard, *The Danish West Indies Under Company Rule (1671–1754)* (New York: The Macmillan Company, 1917), p. xx.

16. Dookhan, *A History of the Virgin Islands*, pp. 32–37. Larsen states that "the breaking point" came in 1668 when "most of the remaining Danes left St. Thomas and returned to Denmark." Jens Larsen, *Virgin Islands Story* (Philadelphia: Muhlenberg Press, 1950), p. 13.

17. Westergaard, *The Danish West Indies*, pp. 32–33.

Court from Company decisions in the administration of justice. The Company was given a monopoly of all trade with the West Indies, and its colonies could import duty-free all goods from Denmark, but their exports to Denmark were subject to a 2.5 percent duty if they remained in Denmark or one percent if re-exported from Denmark.

To populate the colonies, the charter empowered the Danish West India Company to recruit its soldiers, skilled workers, and artisans by taking two enlisted men from each company of the Danish military forces "from among the strong, industrious men who are married and know some trade...." In addition, to provide plantation and other workers, the Company was authorized to take as many as necessary "of those who have been condemned to prison or put in irons" as well as many women "as may be desired from among those whose unseemly lives have brought them into prison or a house of correction."

The conduct of the business of the Company was vested in the Company directors and their appointed officers, subject to its assembly of shareholders and the Danish government including the Board of Trade.[18]

The Company directors selected George Iversen to be Governor of the new colony. He and 189 others departed on the *Ferö* for St. Thomas on February 26, 1672, arriving there on May 25, 1672. The passenger list included 116 bondmen or indentured servants, who had bound themselves to Company employment, plus 61 convicts who were in reality white slaves.

A total of 89 persons died aboard the *Ferö*, and 75 more were to die soon after landing. Of three succeeding Danish ships arriving at St. Thomas over the next three years, 46 of a total of 134 persons died enroute with more dying soon after landing. Indeed, of a total complement of 324 persons departing from Denmark in the first three years, including those on the *Ferö*, 263 died en route or soon after landing, resulting in a survival rate of less than 19 percent.

To replenish these grievous losses, more Danish convicts were sent whom the Governor was later to characterize variously as "uncontrollable," "lazy, shiftless louts ... of no use," and "vagabonds and idlers." Fortunately, other colonists began arriving, including French, Germans, English, Jews, and, comprising the greater number, Dutch who were seeking a safe haven from the English. Accordingly, Dutch became the prevailing language from the beginning. The town established on the north side of St. Thomas' harbor was first called "Tap Huis" or "Hus," meaning "Rum Shop" or "Pub" because of the revelry of the

---

18. For the contents of the Danish West India Company charter, see Westergaard, *The Danish West Indies*, pp. 294–302.

town's people. Later it was named "Charlotte Amalie" for the wife of King Christian V.[19]

Company Rule

To control this "motley throng," Governor Iversen gained such notoriety for severity as to move the directors to declare his brutal management as having given the Company "such a bad reputation among the common people in Denmark that they are of the opinion that if they should serve in the West Indies they would be worse off than if they served in Barbary."[20]

Among Governor Iversen's first laws was his repressive ordinance, proclaimed two and one-half months after the *Ferö* landed, which set forth stringent measures "for the honor of God and the good of the government." Severe penalties were provided for any person missing Sunday service at Christian's Fort and for any servant who "leaves his master … and if it is his custom to run away, his master may put him in irons until he is broken of bad habits.…" It was further provided that no man may let his "negro" leave the estate after sunset, and "whoever at night observes a strange negro on his estate, shall catch him, and carry him in the morning to the fort, where he shall be punished." Other provisions pertained to the defense measures each person was obliged under penalty to perform "if (and God forbid it) an enemy should come unexpectedly." Fines for breaking any of these rules were to be divided into three parts, "one for the king, one for the church, and one for the complainant."[21]

Although the Company directors were solely responsible for conducting Company business, the distance and communication difficulties between them in Denmark and the Virgin Islands required extensive delegation of authority to the Governor in whom—together with his Privy Council of a merchant, bookkeeper, treasurer, and secretary—the active administration of colonial government was vested. The Governor was responsible to return profits to Copenhagen which, in turn, required colonial expansion to other islands.

---

19. *Ibid.*, pp. 35–39.

20. *Ibid.*, pp. 37, 38.

21. The complete text of this proclamation of August 8, 1672 appears in John P. Knox, *A Historical Account of St. Thomas, W. I.* (New York: Charles Scribner, 1852), pp. 48–51. This book was reprinted by Adolph Sixto in St. Thomas in 1922, and again by the College of the Virgin Islands in 1966. Fort Christian, especially in its early years, was the center of all community life in St. Thomas. Any gathering of consequence was held there, whether legal, social, religious, or ceremonial. Jno. Lightbourn, *The Story of Fort Christian, 1672—* (St. Thomas: Bureau of Libraries and Museums, Museum Leaflet Series No. 1, 1973).

The Danish had asserted sovereignty over uninhabited St. John as early as 1684, but the hostility of the English—who had established a colony on nearby Tortola in 1666—prevented the Danes from settling St. John until 1717. Because of its close proximity to St. Thomas and its small population, St. John was destined always to be administered as an appendage of St. Thomas, never separately.

Meanwhile, the much larger island of St. Croix—some forty miles to the south of St. Thomas with which it had conducted much illegal trade—had already experienced a checkered history under five flags. Although the French had abandoned St. Croix in 1696, the island was still claimed by France. Amidst reports that the English were illegally settling on St. Croix, and pirates were using the island as a rendezvous, the French King first considered selling St. Croix to the English or exchanging it for the English half of St. Christopher. He next considered selling it to the Brandenburg Trading Company which enjoyed treaty-backed commercial privileges on St. Thomas.[22] Finally, on June 15, 1733, France sold St. Croix to the Danish West India and Guinea Company with the stipulation that the Danes would not resell the island without French approval. The Danes discovered a settlement in St. Croix of 150 Englishmen and 456 slaves.[23]

Caribbean anarchy and the rapaciousness of European powers posed continuing threats to Denmark's expanded domain in the area. Governor Mathias de Abadia of Puerto Rico, refusing to recognize Denmark's newly proclaimed sovereignty over St. Croix, claimed the island for the Spanish government. He also refused to return ten slaves who had escaped St. Croix, because they had become Catholic converts. This prompted the King of Denmark to request the King of France in 1735 to demand that the King of Spain order the Governor of Puerto Rico to leave the Danish colonies in peace.[24] Had it not been for Denmark's neutral position during most of the European wars of the seventeenth through the nineteenth centuries, the security of the Virgin Islands could not have been assured.

Plantation Agriculture

From soon after the beginning of Danish rule until its end in 1917, the Danes formed only a small proportion of the population. The Company had found convict labor ill-suited and unreliable for plantation cultivation, and the indentured servants accompanying Iversen in 1672 died faster than they

---

22. See: Caron, *Inventory of French Documents,* pp. 43–48.
23. Lewisohn, *St. Croix,* pp. 82, 84.
24. Caron, *Inventory of French Documents,* pp. 55, 56.

could be replaced. Accordingly, the colony encouraged immigration through various tax-free incentives. In 1688, there were 90 surveyed plantations on St. Thomas with a total white plantation population of 148 distributed as follows: 66 Dutch, 31 English, 17 Danes and Norwegians, 17 French, 4 Irish, 4 Flemish, 3 Germans, 3 Swedes, and one each of Scottish, Brazilian, and Portuguese. The first slave ship arrived in 1673 with 103 slaves. Early reliance on Company importation of African slaves was considered necessary to assure a continuing and adequate labor supply.

In 1673, the population of St. Thomas numbered about 100 whites and 100 slaves; by 1733, whites on St. Thomas had increased to 565 while slaves numbered 4,187. Meanwhile, the population of St. John increased from 20 whites and 16 slaves in 1718, when that island was occupied, to 208 whites and 1,087 slaves in 1733. In other words, there were nearly seven slaves for every white after the first sixty years of the colony.[25]

Despite a steady increase in population, the Company was unable to profit enough by 1690 to have paid any dividends to its shareholders. Bankruptcy was averted, however, mainly through rapid strides in the cultivation of sugar which replaced tobacco in 1684 as the medium for paying fines. By 1715, there were 40 estates on St. Thomas devoted to sugar of which 32 had their own wind-powered sugar mills.

Compared with St. Thomas, plantation agriculture in St. John—mostly in sugar cane—developed rapidly after its settlement. There were 109 plantations in St. John in 1733, the year that Denmark acquired St. Croix. St. Croix reached a maximum of 264 plantations in 1742, equally divided between cotton and sugar cane, with an average size of 120 acres compared to approximately 60 to 70 acres in St. Thomas and 80 to 90 acres in St. John.[26]

The Danes wanted rapid settlement and development of St. Croix. Surveys between 1735 and 1754 finally established the boundaries of the plantation estates according to a logical and uniform plan. The island was divided into nine quarters with each estate approximating 2,000 by 3,000 Danish feet totaling 150 Danish acres. A road through the center of the island, later known as Centerline Road, was first surveyed and used as a base for establishing the pattern of estates, the names of many of which are still in use. The Danish West India and Guinea Company offered plantation sites cheaply to the first newcomers, who consisted mostly of British and Dutch islanders plus some Jews originating from Brazil, Portugal, and Spain, Huguenots from the French islands, and

---

25. Westergaard, *The Danish West Indies*, pp. 41, 126, 130.
26. Dookhan, *A History of the Virgin Islands*, pp. 73–75.

a few Germans. Surprisingly, few Danes chose to become planters, preferring instead to accept government assignments in the Islands.

By 1748, all the flat land in St. Croix was under cultivation. The 1751 census listed 120 sugar estates and 122 cotton estates, with a total of 1,900 slaves. The planters of St. Croix frequently complained about the monopolistic practices of the Company. In response, the Company eased some of its trade restrictions and, in 1747, gave St. Croix its own governorship and administration separate from that of St. Thomas-St. John.

The planters, however, did not long remain assuaged. Although commerce and plantation agriculture of the Islands had continued to develop, particularly with the cultivation of St. Croix, the Company nevertheless found itself beset with constant financial difficulties. In 1753, the planters petitioned the King to buy out the Company. In 1754, the Crown offered the Company very generous terms, purchased the Company's shares, and assumed its obligations. Company rule thus came to an end, and the Danish West Indies became a royal colony under a new form of government. The Crown designated the most lucrative of the three islands—St. Croix—as the new capital for all three islands which would be represented by a joint governing council in Christiansted presided over by the new Governor-General. In addition, two municipal councils, one for St. Croix and the other for St. Thomas and St. John, were established to administer their internal affairs.[27]

The inception of Crown rule generally is considered as the beginning of the most prosperous period for the Danish islands. The replacement of Company rule with Crown rule, however, did not mean that the Danish Government decided to go into business in the Company's stead. Rather, it signaled the Government's decision "to the great joy of its West Indian colonists" to throw open "all of the trade formerly enjoyed by the Company to all its subjects, whether they lived in Denmark, Norway, the duchies, or in the West Indies."[28]

After the end of Company rule, the inhabitants of St. Thomas turned increasingly toward trade and commerce and away from plantation agriculture which gradually declined in importance in St. Thomas and St. John after 1754. On the other hand, the second half of the 18th century was a period of increasing prosperity for St. Croix planters. With the monopoly of the Company ended, new markets were created and the planters were able to secure higher prices for their produce. Cotton and sugar production on St. Croix flourished and the population of the Islands steadily increased.

---

27. Lewisohn, St. *Croix*, pp. 89–91, 101–104.
28. Westergaard, *The Danish West Indies*, p. 240.

Previous Company trade restrictions were progressively relaxed by the Danish Government. In 1764, the trade of St. Thomas with other European colonies in America was thrown open to the ships of all nations, and St. Thomas became an important shipping center and point of distribution for West Indian trade and for trade with the British American colonies.[29] None of this new-found prosperity, however, could have been possible without extensive reliance on the slave trade.

The Slave Trade

The failure of Indian slavery in much of the New World followed by the limited servitude extracted from poor Europeans, including indentured servants and convicts, laid the historic base for the construction of African slavery. The African slave was cheaper; the money required to procure a European's service for ten years could buy an African for life, whose offspring would also be enslaved. African labor, moreover, was found to be eminently superior to Indian and European labor. A Darwinian "survival-of-the-fittest" rationale explains the preference for African labor. The reason for the origin of African slavery, therefore, was primarily economic, although a growing school of thought argues that African slavery, partially at least, had a racial basis from the beginning. Later rationalizations of white racial superiority were concocted to justify the economic fact that the New World colonies needed African labor because it was the cheapest and the best.[30]

---

29. In 1815, the trade of St. Thomas and St. John was freed of all restrictions, a status that St. Croix was not to achieve until 1833 on the hundredth anniversary of Denmark's possession of that island. For trade relations between the Danish West Indies and the British American colonies, see: Jean Louise Willis, *The Trade between North America and the Danish West Indies, 1756 to 1807 With Special Reference to St. Croix* (unpublished Ph.D. dissertation, Columbia University, 1963); Westergaard, *The Danish West Indies*, pp. 250–251; and Dookhan, *A History of the Virgin Islands*, pp. 91–93. At the start of the American Revolution, St. Croix was providing 13 percent of all rum imported into the thirteen colonies. George F. Tyson, Jr., *Powder, Profits & Privateers, A Documentary History of the Virgin Islands During the Era of the American Revolution* (St. Thomas: Bureau of Libraries, Museums and Archeological Services, Occasional Paper no. 1, 1977), p. 14, n. 3. See, also, Florence Lewisohn, *"What So Proudly We Hail," The Danish West Indies and the American Revolution* (St. Croix: Prestige Press, 1975).

30. Eric Williams, *Capitalism and Slavery* (Chapel Hill: University of North Carolina Press, 1944), pp. 7–29; reprinted under the title "The Origin of Negro Slavery" in Horowitz, ed., *Peoples and Cultures of the Caribbean*, pp. 47–74.

The demand for slaves tied together Europe, Africa, and the Americas in mercantilism's drama of tragedy, greed, and enterprise, and the so-called triangular "slave trade" became the link among the various Europeans, coastal peoples of West Africa, and those of the interior. "The Americas had plantations, Africa had the labor for them, and Europe, with its industries and ships, absorbed their raw products, did the carrying, and found markets in all continents."[31]

The first reliable evidence of Europeans on the Gold Coast of Africa is the account of the Portuguese in 1471, but no permanent settlement was founded until 1482. They were followed by the English in 1553 and the Dutch in 1593 whom the Swedes and Danes sought eventually to emulate. The concern with the elimination of foreign competition was one of the dimensions of mercantilism whereby colonies were forbidden to trade with nations other than their parent countries—a restriction frequently evaded, but one that led to conflicts among the colonizing powers. Thus, the Dutch ended the Portuguese presence on the Gold Coast, in 1641, having conquered the Portuguese forts and territories. Indeed, it was unlikely that the Dutch, during their period of supremacy, would have permitted the English and Danes to conduct trade on the Gold Coast had they not been compelled to do so by the Africans who were well aware of the value of competition.[32]

The Danes had been engaged in trade along the West African coast since 1649 when they first sent a ship to Guinea. Once Danish colonization commenced in the West Indies and plantation agriculture was undertaken, demands for greater numbers of African slaves far exceeded available supplies. Accordingly, a triangular trade was established by which ships with Danish merchandise sailed to Guinea where African slaves were purchased and carried onward to the Virgin Islands, the produce of which was then taken back to Denmark.

Although the Danish West India and Guinea companies merged in 1673 to become the West India and Guinea Company that assumed control of the Guinea trade in 1674, the Company relied on concessions to private slave traders—such as the Brandenburg Trading Company—until 1696 when St. Thomas Governor Johan Lorentz successfully urged the Company, itself, to take up the Guinea slave trade "since all other trade is as nothing compared with this slave trade."[33] Thereafter, the Danish West India and Guinea Company

---

31. Daniel F. McCall, "Introduction" in Georg Norregard, *Danish Settlements in West Africa 1658–1850* (Boston: Boston University Press, 1966), p. xxiv.

32. Norregard, *Danish Settlements*, pp. 3–5.

33. Quoted in Westergaard, *The Danish West Indies*, p. 145, and in Norregard, *Danish Settlements*, p. 84. Lorentz was remarking about the tremendous profits enjoyed by Brandenburgers' slave trade. In 1685, a 30-year treaty between Denmark and the Brandenburg

traded in slaves until 1734 when the trade was opened to all residents. The large profits earned by private traders, however, induced the Company quickly to resume its slaving operations.

The Company could not maintain a slaving monopoly, simply because it could not keep more than two ships at a time on the Copenhagen-Guinea-West Indies run—hardly sufficient to meet the growing demand for more slaves, particularly after the settlement of St. Croix in 1734. By contrast, the English and Dutch between them had hundreds of ships at their disposal. Accordingly, it is oversimplification to characterize the Danish slave trade as a simplistic triangular trade. The multinational character of the Danish slave trade must be considered.

The Danish slave trade comprised slave exports on Danish ships from both Danish and foreign forts and centers on the West African coast, slave exports on foreign ships from Danish forts on the coast, as well as transshipment of slaves imported into the Danish Islands to other destinations. Indeed, Dutch interlopers supplied far greater numbers of slaves for the St. Thomas slave market than did the Danish Company during its existence.[34] Portuguese, French, and English traders also arrived at the Danish West African forts to collect slaves.

The historian Svend Green-Pedersen estimates that, between the years 1733 and 1802, of a total of about 123,000 slaves imported into the Danish West Indian colonies, about 70,000 were re-exported and only some 53,000 slaves were retained for use in the Islands. He concludes, therefore, that "the Danish slave trade was centered in the West Indies and not in Africa."[35] Philip Curtin—whose estimates are lower—agrees that the Danish Islands "functioned more

---

Trading Company granted the latter extraordinary use of St. Thomas harbor for transshipment of slaves and other trade and the right to establish a large plantation on St. Thomas. From 1692 to 1694, the Brandenburgers transported 2,413 slaves to St. Thomas, many of whom were sold to local planters while the remainder were transshipped to other islands, principally the French colony of St. Croix. The Brandenburgers dominated St. Thomas until 1699 when their activities ceased. Svend Erik Green-Pedersen, "The Scope and Structure of the Danish Negro Slave Trade," *The Scandinavian Economic History Review*, 19, 2 (1971), 157. See, also, Enid M. Baa, *The Brandenburgers at St. Thomas or The Bordeaux Plantation 1685–1973*, unpublished paper presented at the Tenth Conference of Caribbean Historians, March 26–April 1, 1978 (xeroxed, St. Thomas: College of the Virgin Islands), pp. 56ff.

34. For the Dutch slave trade, see, Johannes Postma, *The Dutch Participation in the African Slave Trade: Slaving on the Guinea Coast, 1675–1795* (unpublished Ph.D. dissertation, Michigan State University, 1970).

35. Svend Erik Green-Pedersen, "The History of the Danish Slave Trade, 1733–1807," *Revue Française d'Histoire d'Outre-Mer* (Paris: Societe Française d'Histoire d'Outre-Mer, Librarie Orientaliste Paul Guenthner, 1975), p. 209.

as trading posts than as true centers of the South Atlantic System."[36] Even if Green-Pedersen's higher estimates are accepted as more accurate, the evidence still does not support Jens Larsen's claim that "St. Thomas was for many years the world's largest slave market."[37] Curtin estimates, for example, that 387,000 slaves were imported into the English island of Barbados, alone, for the period of 1640 to 1807, and that the Danish Islands accounted for only 0.3 percent of total slave imports during the whole period of the Atlantic slave trade.[38]

Contrary to some perceptions, Europeans did not often venture into the African hinterland to hunt down and kidnap those to become enslaved. Rather, representatives of European companies and governments negotiated with coastal African chiefs to establish sites for forts along the African coast, usually near the mouths of rivers for convenient anchorage and inland transportation. The Danes initially established two such forts—Fort Frederiksberg and Fort Christiansborg—on the coast of Guinea. Deals were made with chiefs to make captures, generally from rival tribes, in return for tribute, to transport the captives downstream to the forts where they would be held for the ships that would carry their human cargoes to the West Indies.

Sometimes, the captives had to await the arrival of ships or were too many to be housed inside the forts. In either case, they were housed outside the forts and extra precautions were required to prevent runaways. Male slaves frequently were put in irons, with rings of iron encircling their necks and ankles connected by iron chains. Sometimes they were chained in pairs when they were required to move from one place to another; long lines of slaves would be made by chains connecting the rings around their necks. Still, escape attempts were made, but the African chiefs in league with the slavers undertook to capture and return runaways. After having killed their slave overseer, or "bomba," one night in 1727 at Fort Christiansborg, of those slaves who managed to escape, half were caught, and the ringleader was broken on the wheel and then beheaded.[39]

When a ship arrived, the ship's doctor would inspect and help sort the captives. Men, women, and children were selected for enslavement on the basis of their general health and strength. It was in the interest of slave merchants and ship captains, of course, to select and safely transport as large a human cargo as possible. For the sake of greater profits, the temptation to overcrowd the

---

36. Philip D. Curtin, *The Atlantic Slave Trade: A Census* (Madison: University of Wisconsin Press, 1969), p. 85.

37. Jens Larsen, *Virgin Islands Story* (Philadelphia: Muhlenberg Press, 1950), p. 55.

38. Curtin, *The Atlantic Slave Trade*, pp. 55, 88–89.

39. Norregard, *Danish Settlements*, p. 86.

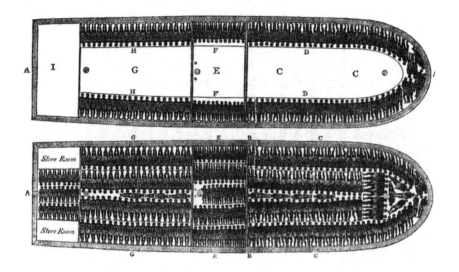

Plan for a British slaving ship

vessels was equally great, and though the conditions of the journeys varied, generally they were deplorable.

Aside from the wretchedness and misery of the depressed and terrorized captives, they were usually packed in chains as close as possible within the holds of the ships, lying side by side. Poor sanitation and ventilation, bad water, and foul food were combined with disease, epidemics, suffocation, and even suicide to reduce drastically the number of survivors. In some instances, when ships foundered, whole slave cargoes perished. Between 1698 and 1754, vessels of the Danish West India and Guinea Company had taken over ten thousand slaves from Africa of whom over one quarter perished at sea, a much larger loss than that suffered by other slavers. The estimated loss from a normal slave cargo during the crossing was expected to average about 15 percent.[40] Many of the survivors died within a few days after landing in the Danish colonies.

---

40. *Ibid.*, pp. 88–89. See, also, Westergaard, *The Danish West Indies*, ch. 7.

Upon arrival, slaves were either sold on board the ship or on shore. If sold on board, prospective buyers—including agents for other islands—by right of prior purchase were permitted to select those they wanted. If the slaves were sold on shore, an auction was held until all were purchased. Once purchased, they were branded by their owners.

Slave traders and merchants often made huge profits. Some St. Thomas fortunes were made this way. Generally, slaves were sold at prices ranging between 25 and 100 percent higher than the buying prices, with able bodied men commanding the highest prices. For computing the prices of others, a woman was valued at three-fourths a man, a boy at two-thirds, and a girl at one-half. Children were frequently sold separately from their parents, and planters preferred to buy slaves from different tribes.[41]

The costs of the slave trade in terms of human misery and death are incalculable. Perhaps, Georg Norregard came close to quantifying these costs with this comment:

> If we consider how many ... deaths among the Africans were caused by the slave trade, the sum total is ... very depressing. Many lives were lost in the battles or surprise attacks whereby native kings and traders procured their slaves. Some fell by the wayside during the endless marches along the narrow paths through forest and bush down to the coast. Next, some died at the forts, and many died on board the ships. Finally, after landing ... quite a few died from exhaustion due to the sufferings they had undergone. It seems fairly safe to say that, for every able-bodied slave put to work in the New World, at least one African life had been sacrificed on the way.[42]

This, then, was the slave trade upon which the Danish colonies and slave system in the West Indies were constructed.

---

41. Westergaard, *The Danish West Indies*, pp. 149–150.
42. Norregard, *Danish Settlements*, p. 89.

2

Repression and Rebellion

A theory of social change can be constructed from the history of slavery. The slave systems in the Western Hemisphere generally were based on terror and repression of the slaves in order to maintain a disciplined, efficient, and productive labor force. Nevertheless, significant differences in the severity of the slave systems did exist, possibly reflecting institutional differences among the European powers.

Slave Systems

The institution of slavery was alien to England, the Netherlands, Denmark, and France when they acquired their colonial possessions. They had no tradition of slave law and, accordingly, they either had to devise legal codes to govern slavery or accommodate that institution within their legal systems. In either case, the slave was regarded as chattel property rather than a human personality.

In the case of France, however, the French *Code Noir*—promulgated in 1685—was somewhat temporized by the spirit of Roman Catholicism which, from the time of Thomas Aquinas (1225–1274), recognized the slave as having a soul. Although the French Code made the slave a chattel, it accorded milder treatment than the laws governing English, Dutch, and Danish slaves. The *Code Noir* called for baptism of all slaves; only Roman Catholics could have charge of them; they were not to be worked on Sundays or holy days; and they could marry without the consent of their owners.[1]

Spain and Portugal, on the other hand, were not strangers to slavery. When they acquired colonial possessions, a long legal as well as moral tradition already existed in both countries with respect to slavery. The fusion of Church and State was reflected in their slave laws in terms of an inherent belief in the

---

1. Williams, *From Columbus to Castro*, p. 183. For differences in the severity of the slave laws in the West Indies, and their antecedents in Europe, see, E. V. Goveia, *The West Indian Slave Laws of the 18th Century* (Barbados: Caribbean Universities Press, 1970).

equality of men under the law of nature, and the belief, therefore, that slavery was against both nature and reason. The doctrine of the equality of human nature had long before been asserted by Cicero, applied to slavery by Seneca,[2] and passed down the centuries through the Justinian Code to the Spanish and Portuguese. Consequently, when African slaves arrived in Spanish and Portuguese colonies, a body of law already existed—protective of them as human beings—which long before had been elaborated from Roman law.

Under Roman law, masters who ill treated slaves were compelled to sell them, and the sick or aged slave who had been abandoned was freed as a matter of course. Slaves had other rights that could be redressed against their masters, and the law specified the multiple means by which they could gain their freedom through manumission.[3]

These features were much elaborated in the Spanish slave code, known as *Las Sieta Partidas*, which in addition set forth the right of a slave to marry a free person and the conditions by which slaves could appeal to the courts and be witnesses, even against their masters. In the Spanish possessions, moreover, a slave could gain his freedom by law as soon as he could repay his purchase price to his master. As a consequence, by 1790 the number of free blacks in all the Spanish possessions exceeded the number of slaves.[4]

Within the Western Hemisphere there were three types of slave systems, according to the historian Frank Tannenbaum. The British, American, Dutch, and Danish were the most severe, and the Spanish and Portuguese were the least severe. In between these two extremes were the French. The Northern European group had no effective slave tradition or slave law, "and their religious institutions were little concerned about the Negro." At the other extreme, Tannenbaum observed, were the Spanish and Portuguese with both a slave law "and a belief that the spiritual personality of the slave transcended his slave status." While the French had the same Roman Catholic religious principles as the Spaniards and Portuguese, they lacked a slave tradition and slave law.[5]

---

2. R. W. Carlyle and A. J. Carlyle, *A History of Medieval Political Theory in the West* (Edinburgh and London: W. Blackwood and Sons, 1903), vol. I, 8.

3. See, *e.g.*, J. Declareuil, *Rome The Law-Giver* (New York: Alfred A. Knopf, 1927).

4. Zachary Macauley, *Negro Slavery* (London: Hatchard and Son of Picadilly and J. Arch of Cornhill, 1823), p. 109. "In the British West India islands ... manumissions ... can only be effected by a will in writing, executed and attested with due solemnities, or by a solemn deed under the hand and seal of the master, accompanied in both cases with registration in a public office." James Stephen, *The Slavery of the British West India Islands* (London: Joseph Butterworth and Son, 1824; New York: Kraus Reprint Co., 1969), vol. I, 389–390.

5. Frank Tannenbaum, *Slave and Citizen, The Negro in the Americas* (New York: Alfred A. Knopf, 1947), 65n, see also pp. 45–53.

In assessing the total experience of slavery in the Western Hemisphere, Tannenbaum propounded the following thesis:

> Wherever the law accepted the doctrine of the moral personality of the slave and made possible the gradual achievement of freedom implicit in such a doctrine, the slave system was abolished peacefully. Where the slave was denied recognition as a moral person and was therefore incapable of freedom, the abolition of slavery was accomplished by force—that is, by revolution. The acceptance of the idea of the spiritual equality of all men made for a friendly, an elastic, milieu within which social change could occur in peace. On the other hand, where the slave was denied a moral status, the law and the *mores* hardened and became stratified, and their historical outcome proved to be violence and revolution.[6]

The many slave rebellions among Northwest European and French colonies of the West Indies during the eighteenth and nineteenth centuries might be cited in support of Tannenbaum's analysis. Similarly, in the predominantly Protestant United States—inheritors of the English common law—freedom of the slaves was occasioned by one of the bloodiest civil wars in world history.

Other scholars appear to agree with Tannenbaum. For example, Gilberto Freyre, Stanley Elkins, and Herbert Klein have claimed a relatively mild slave system for Latin America, attributed to Iberian colonists and their distinct cultural heritage, as contrasted with the more severe slave systems maintained by Northwest European colonists derivative from their quite different cultural heritage.[7] Indeed, it was Freyre's earlier description of the position of the "Negro" in Brazil that intrigued Tannenbaum, who compared it with the harsh situation in the U.S. South, and moved him to find an explanation for the difference.

Tannenbaum, however, has had strong critics, including Eric Williams, Robert Brent Toplin, and Harry Hoetink.[8] Williams, for example, attributed differences in slave systems to economic—rather than religious or legal—fac-

---

6. *Ibid.*, pp. viii–ix.

7. Gilberto Freyre, *The Masters and the Slaves: A Study in the Development of Brazilian Civilization* (New York: Alfred A. Knopf, 1946); Stanley Elkins, *Slavery, A Problem in American Institutional and Intellectual Life* (Chicago: University of Chicago Press, 1959); and Herbert Klein, *Slavery in the Americas: A Comparative Study of Virginia and Cuba* (Chicago: University of Chicago Press, 1967).

8. Eric Williams, "Race Relations in Caribbean Society," in *Caribbean Studies: A Symposium* (Jamaica: 1957); Robert Brent Toplin, ed., *Slavery and Race Relations in Latin America* (Westport, CT: Greenwood Press, 1974); Harry Hoetink, *Caribbean Race Relations: A Study of Two Variants* (London, Oxford, and New York: Oxford University Press, 1967);

tors. Accordingly, he pointed to the cruelty of the plantation system in France's Haiti of 1789 as contrasted with the liberal slave systems found at that time in England's Trinidad and Spain's Cuba. Hoetink also criticized Tannenbaum for ignoring economic and "somatic" factors.

That the religion of Thomas Aquinas and the law of Justinian were both alien to Denmark may or may not have influenced its slave system in the Virgin Islands. Whatever the explanations, however, the experience with slavery in these Danish islands by any measure was marked by severe repression and violent rebellion.

Slavery in the Virgin Islands

The total number of slaves in the Virgin Islands continued to increase through the eighteenth century until a peak was reached in 1803 of 35,727, of whom 27,161 were claimed by St. Croix, after which the number steadily declined in all three islands.

A rigid social caste system differentiated slaves of the Virgin Islands. The main distinctions were between the higher status native-born slaves and the lower status African-born slaves, and between occupational groups. Division of labor was rigidly enforced and jobs were not interchangeable. Accordingly, for most slaves occupational or upward mobility was hopeless. Most were field slaves, comprising 82 percent of St. Croix slaves in 1797, and their work from sunrise to sunset was the most arduous. At the top of the slave hierarchy were the houseservants or domestics, many of whom were mulattoes and served as concubines or mistresses of their masters and estate managers. At the bottom were the field laborers and other menial workers. In between were the skilled artisans, whose numbers increased particularly in St. Thomas as commerce and trade replaced agriculture on that island. Whatever their work and status, the slaves of the Virgin Islands were chattel property and could be bought and sold and even exchanged for payment of debts.[9]

---

and Harry Hoetink, *Slavery and Race Relations in the Americas: Comparative Notes on Their Nature and Nexus* (New York: Harper & Row, 1973).

9. See, *e.g.*, Lawrence P. Spingarn, "Slavery in the Danish West Indies," *American Scandinavian Review*, 45, 1 (March 1957), 39–40; and Lionel Vallee, *The Negro Family on St. Thomas, A Study of Role Differentiation* (unpublished Ph.D. dissertation, Cornell University, 1964), pp. 44–45.

Table 1. Total Number of Slaves in the Virgin Islands, 1733–1846

Year	St. Thomas	St. John	St. Croix	Total
1733	3,741	1,087	425	5,253
1755	3,949	2,031	8,897	14,877
1775	3,979	2,355	23,384	29,718
1792	4,279	1,917	22,240	28,436
1803	5,968	2,598	27,161	35,727
1815	4,848	2,445	24,339	31,632
1826	4,548	2,206	21,356	28,110
1835	5,032	1,971	19,876	26,879
1846	3,494	1,790	16,706	21,990

Sources: Jens Vibaek, Dansk Vestindien 1755–1848: Vestindiens Storhedstid (Denmark: Fremad, 1966), pp. 102–103, 327; and Svend Erik Green-Pedersen, "The History of the Danish Negro Slave Trade, 1733–1807," Revue Française d'Histoire l'Outre-Mer (Paris, 1975), p. 204.

The proportion of slaves in the Virgin Islands exceeded 88 percent in 1789. Although the percentage gradually declined thereafter, slaves still comprised over 65 percent of the population in 1835. Slavery in the Virgin Islands contrasted sharply with slavery in nearby Puerto Rico, where slaves never exceeded 14 percent of the population because the labor needs of its self-sufficient economy were satisfied by free men. The Virgin Islands, on the other hand, had plantation economies on St. Croix and St. John. Their slave systems were different, "not because Puerto Rico was under Spanish rule and the Virgin Islands Danish, but because of their differing economies," according to Eric Williams. "The plantation economy was notoriously harsher on the slave."[10]

Drawn from all classes of West African society, some slaves were of noble or even royal lineage whose pride on occasion prompted a preference for death through suicide rather than for forced labor. Harsh regulations prescribing severe punishment were promulgated in 1684.

> Slaves were forbidden to hold feasts and "drum dances," heathenish customs brought with them from Africa. They were also forbidden to carry knives or clubs, and were ordered to be at home on Sundays by sunset, and on other evenings at drum-beat. A slave transgressing these laws was "for the first offense to be whipped, for the second to have his ears cut off, and for the third to be hung, and his head placed on a stake."[11]

10. Eric Williams, "Race Relations in Puerto Rico and the Virgin Islands," Foreign Affairs, 23 (January 1945), pp. 308–309.

11. Knox, A Historical Account of St. Thomas, pp. 55–56.

In 1685, Governor Gabriel Milan introduced to St. Thomas a form of punishment known as "impalement" which entailed piercing the slave with a spear through the body from below, then erecting the spear to exhibit the victim to passersby until death came. Runaway slaves became the most constant difficulty of the planters. Many disappeared into the "bush" and the more venturous escaped to Puerto Rico where the Spanish worked them for a year before freeing them and giving them land to cultivate. For 1745 alone as many as 300 slaves escaped to Puerto Rico. Despite frequent entreaties to Spanish authorities, no fugitives were returned until after 1767 when the Governor of Puerto Rico extracted a promise "for more religious toleration to Roman Catholics" in the Virgin Islands. And no Spanish slave escaping to the Virgin Islands is recorded, doubtlessly because the Virgin Islands planters "treated their slaves far more harshly than the Spanish planters."[12]

In light of the cruel treatment of the slaves of the Virgin Islands, one might question the assertion "that some truth resides in the claim that slaves were better treated in the Virgin Islands than elsewhere in the West Indian colonies."[13] The British and other North Europeans were also architects of bestial brutality. The British, for example, in nearby Antigua nipped in the bud the slave conspiracy of 1736—involving "some of the most trusted and valuable slaves"— by burning seventy-seven slaves alive, breaking five on the wheel, gibbeting six, and banishing thirty-six.[14] But it is difficult to characterize any slave system as more repressive than that of the Virgin Islands.

In 1698 Governor Johan Lorentz of the Virgin Islands proclaimed amnesty for all runaways returning within a certain period, but he added that those not returning would be shot on sight. And in 1706 the death penalty was imposed on leaders of runaways, while other fugitives would lose a foot. From 1720 onwards, moreover, a special tax was levied on planters to indemnify those among them for any legally killed or injured slaves, thus removing a powerful economic constraint against the maiming and killing of slaves. The Governor's privy council, itself a body of slave owners, always could be expected to resolve any master-slave issue in favor of the master.[15]

---

12. Westergaard, *The Danish West Indies*, pp. 160–161; Dookhan, *A History of the Virgin Islands of the United States*, pp. 164–165.

13. Dookhan, *A History of the Virgin Islands*, p. 166.

14. Williams, *From Columbus to Castro*, p. 197. See, also, Paul Blanshard, *Democracy and Empire in the Caribbean* (New York: The Macmillan Company, 1947), pp. 185–186.

15. Dookhan, *A History of the Virgin Islands*, p. 164. During the severe drought of 1725–1726, a number of planters let their slaves starve to death, and "seventeen slaves distributed among thirteen planters had been executed," for stealing, "and were debited to the community at a price of about 120 rdl. each." Westergaard, *The Danish West Indies*, p. 165. Notices of runaway slaves frequently appeared in the local press and, according to George

With the ratio of blacks to whites—and the tension between them—increasing, Governor Philip Gardelin on September 5, 1733 promulgated a new mandate that may remain unparalleled in world history as one of the most barbarous and oppressive measures ever imposed on a people. In its entirety, the mandate provided the following:

1. The leader of runaway slaves shall be pinched three times with red-hot iron, and then hung.

2. Each other runaway slave shall lose one leg, or, if the owner pardon him, shall lose one ear, and receive one hundred and fifty stripes.

3. Any slave being aware of intention of others to run away, and not giving information, shall be burned in the forehead, and receive one hundred stripes.

4. Those who inform of plots to run away, shall receive ten dollars for each slave engaged therein.

5. A slave who runs away for eight days, shall have one hundred and fifty stripes; twelve weeks, shall lose a leg; and six months, shall forfeit his life, unless the owner pardon him with the loss of one leg.

6. Slaves who steal to the value of four rix-dollars, shall be pinched and hung; less than four rix-dollars, to be branded, and receive one hundred and fifty stripes.

7. Slaves who receive stolen goods, as such, or protect runaways, shall be branded, and receive one hundred and fifty stripes.

8. A slave who lifts his hand to strike a white person, or threatens him with violence, shall be pinched and hung, should the white person demand it, if not, to lose his right hand.

9. One white person shall be sufficient witness against a slave; and if a slave be suspected of crime, he can be tried by torture.

10. A slave meeting a white person, shall step aside and wait until he passes, if not, he may be flogged.

11. No slave will be permitted to come to town with clubs or knives, nor fight with each other, under penalty of fifty stripes.

12. Witchcraft shall be punished with flogging.

13. A slave who shall attempt to poison his master, shall be pinched three times with red-hot iron, and then be broken on a wheel.

Tyson, "give lie to the claim that the slaves passively accepted their servitude." Tyson reprinted a representative selection of such notices for 1772–1778 in *Powder, Profits & Privateers*, pp. 100–103.

14. A free negro who shall harbour a slave or thief, shall lose his liberty, or be banished.

15. All dances, feasts, and plays are forbidden unless permission be obtained from the master or overseer.

16. Slaves shall not sell provisions of any kind without permission from their overseers.

17. No estate slave shall be in town after drum-beat, otherwise he shall be put in the fort and flogged.

18. The King's Advocate is ordered to see these regulations carried into effect.[16]

In referring to the Danish background in his 1972 book on the Virgin Islands, Gordon Lewis of the University of Puerto Rico observed: "Much has been made of the liberal quality of Danish rule. To some extent, that was so."[17] Such an observation could seriously be advanced only with respect to certain ameliorative developments during nineteenth century Danish rule, certainly not with respect to the eighteenth century.

The eighteenth century slave laws of the Virgin Islands comprised Gardelin's code of 1733, the Reglement of 1755, and many local proclamations. Historian Neville Hall closely analyzed these codes and characterized them as reflecting "an overwhelmingly negative view of the African."[18] Gardelin's code was elaborated by Governor Frederik Moth's articles of 1741, which sought to even further restrict social and sexual relations between slaves and free. Moth's successor, Governor Lindemark, sought to prevent slave enterprise of any sort and to forbid slaves to be seen with dogs outside their masters' estates. Not until the Reglement of 1755 was any consideration given to the welfare of slaves. This act prescribed minimum food rations and clothing material to be allotted each slave, and acknowledged for the first time certain minimum rights of slaves. These rights included the availability of religious instruction, the right

---

16. Quoted from Charles E. Taylor, *Leaflets from the Danish West Indies* (London: Wm. Dawson and Sons, 1888; reprinted New York: Negro Universities Press, 1970), pp. 101–102. See, also, Knox, *A Historical Account*, pp. 69–71, and Westergaard, *The Danish West Indies*, p. 167.

17. Gordon K. Lewis, *The Virgin Islands: A Caribbean Lilliput* (Evanston, IL: Northwestern University Press, 1972), p. 28. That penalties imposed on slaves in the Virgin Islands generally were more severe than penalties imposed for the same offenses in French and British West Indian colonies, see, *e.g.*, Williams, *From Columbus to Castro*, p. 192.

18. Neville Hall, "Slave Laws of the Danish Virgin Islands in the Late Eighteenth Century," in *Comparative Perspectives on Slavery in New World Plantation Societies*, ed. Vera Rubin and Arthur Tuden (Annals of the New York Academy of Sciences, vol. 292; New York: New York Academy of Sciences, 1977), p. 174.

not to work on Sundays and holy days, the prohibition of sexual exploitation of slave women, the prohibition of separation of marriage partners and minors from their parents, and recognition of the principle of manumission whereby a slave could be granted freedom at the owner's discretion either during the owner's lifetime or after his death by will or testament. There was no provision comparable to that found in the Spanish slave code permitting freedom by self-purchase, because Virgin Islands slaves were still chattel property and could own nothing.

In terms of its restrictive features, the Reglement appeared almost as punitive as the Gardelin code. Slaves belonging to different masters were forbidden to assemble at weddings or other events, under pain of whipping and branding for the first offense and death for subsequent offenses. Slaves were forbidden access to the courts, except in cases brought against them, and neither in civil nor criminal cases could a slave give testimony or evidence. The Reglement prescribed branding and castration for theft, whereas Gardelin had prescribed death, although violence or bodily assault against a white person was punishable by death. Runaways absent for a month or less would lose both ears and be branded. Those absent a second time would lose both legs, and a third time meant death. Thus, the punishments for marronage were more severe than those of 1733.

Compared with the Gardelin code, therefore, the Reglement of 1755 was both more liberal and more harsh than Gardelin's 1733 code. No amelioration of the slave system, however, was forthcoming, for the Reglement was not implemented. Authorities in Denmark devolved upon Governor Christian von Prock, the first royal governor, discretion to publish and enforce those provisions of the Reglement as he saw fit. Because planters opposed a code that acknowledged that slaves had certain rights, von Prock chose to ignore the Reglement, thus leaving in force Gardelin's infamous code in which the slave had no legal rights.

The Moravian missionary, Oldendorp, found Gardelin's code still in force and virtually unchanged in 1767. At that time, an owner could still inflict upon his slave practically any punishment he wished except death. And, according to Oldendorp, any offense by a slave against a white person, whether from his household or not, would result in punishment of the slave, the severity of which depended on the status of the offended white person. The chopping off of a hand or foot was still not uncommon, and flogging was customary, the resulting wounds of which were then washed with a brine and pepper solution. Torture was still commonly used to obtain confessions.[19]

---

19. C. G. A. Oldendorp, *Geschichte der Mission der evangelischen Breuder auf den caraibischen Inslen S. Thomas, S. Croix and S. Jan*, trans.: *History of the Mission of the Evangelical Brethren on the Caribbean Islands of St. Thomas, St. Croix and St. John* (Leipzig: Barby, 1777), pp.

New restrictions continued to be promulgated. Governor Peter Claussen in 1774 raised the punishment for slaves gambling on the streets from 50 to 150 lashes, and the Burgher Council of St. Croix proposed in 1778 that mourning parties at slave funerals be limited to twelve participants apart from the pall-bearers. There was some evidence in the 1770s that the slave laws were not being uniformly enforced and that certain masters colluded in this laxity. No improvements in the essential categories of food, clothing, and shelter were observed, however. Roasted sweet potatoes and brackish water was the standard fare for slaves. Many went without clothing. Housing featured straw roofs, earthen floors, and bare boards as beds. These conditions remained essentially unaltered by the end of the eighteenth century. Efforts to replace the Gardelin code and subsequent proclamations with a more liberal slave code were unavailing. The result was that by the beginning of the nineteenth century, there were still no legal protections of the slave's welfare, and the question of the degree of discretion possessed by an owner in the severity of punishing his slaves remained unresolved. Concluding his analysis of the eighteenth century slave laws of the Virgin Islands, Neville Hall of the University of the West Indies, has commented:

> By 1801, the year of the first brief British occupation, the extant police code of Gardelin's was not being enforced in all its rigor. Custom had tempered its administration, but this by no means eradicated instances of rank brutality.... Nor could they be removed until the metropolitan and colonial governments had the will and the energy to delimit with precision the boundaries of the slave master's discretion in relation to punishment and to devise appropriate machinery for the administration of a police code. None of this was to be achieved before the 1830s and the administration of Peter von Scholten, the last governor general of the Danish Virgin Islands.[20]

Gardelin's code of 1733, was not to be replaced for another hundred years.

299–307, 379–393. For reference to C. G. A. Oldendorp's observations in translation, see: Albert A. Campbell, *St. Thomas Negroes—A Study of Personality and Culture* (Psychological Monographs, vol. 55, no. 5; Evanston, IL: The American Psychological Association, Inc., Northwestern University, 1943), pp. 4–14, esp. p. 11; and Pauline Holman Pope, *Cruzan Slavery: An Ethnological Study of Differential Responses to Slavery in the Danish West Indies* (unpublished Ph.D. dissertation, University of California, Davis, 1969).

  20. Hall, "Slave Laws," p. 184.

Rebellion

Aside from the extremely restricted opportunity of being given their freedom through the unlikely generosity of their masters, the only ways of escape open for the slaves of the Virgin Islands were through suicide, which was not unusual, through flight, which was frequent, or through armed uprising, which was very rare. Even under the worst possible conditions, slaves would not readily resort to rebellion. The risks were too high. Eric Williams lists fourteen slave revolts in the West Indies between 1733 and 1776. None were in Spanish colonies. Two were in French possessions, and the remaining twelve were in Northern European possessions.[21]

One of the most famous West Indian slave rebellions was the revolt in St. John in 1733, soon after Governor Gardelin's new slave code was announced. At the time there were 208 whites and 1,087 slaves distributed among the 109 plantations of the island. Most of the slaves recently had arrived from Africa. Some were drawn from West African royalty, and these became the leaders of the rebellion. The rebellion had been preceded by a severe drought, a devastating hurricane, a plague of insects, and yet another hurricane. All crops, including foodstuffs, were wiped out. Already faced with starvation, the promulgation of Gardelin's slave code became the last straw for the slaves. Meanwhile, many of the plantations on St. John were managed by overseers hired by owners who resided in St. Thomas. The difficulty of securing honest and capable overseers led some owners to rely on former convicts or "free colored" as plantation managers, whose dependability for maintaining discipline and for suppressing the slaves was unreliable. St. John was ripe for rebellion. Few events during Danish rule of the Virgin Islands have received more published attention than the St. John slave revolt.[22] In recent years, these accounts

---

21. Williams, *From Columbus to Castro*, pp. 195–196. Throughout the history of slavery in the Virgin Islands, fears of slave uprisings abounded, dating from 1694 when "precautions were taken against a possible rising of slaves" on St. Thomas. In 1702, Governor Hansen complained also of "repeated attacks of pirates and privateers who had taken off slaves." Jno. Lightbourn, *The Story of Fort Christian* (St. Thomas: Bureau of Libraries and Museums, Museum Leaflet Series No. 1, 1973) unpaginated, reprinted from Walloe's *St. Thomas Almanac and Commercial Advertiser* of 1881.

22. See, *e.g.*, Westergaard, *The Danish West Indies*, pp. 168–178; Dookhan, *A History of the Virgin Islands*, pp. 165–170; Williams, *From Columbus to Castro*, pp. 196–197; Taylor, *Leaflets*, pp. 102–103; Darwin D. Creque, *The U.S. Virgins and the Eastern Caribbean* (Philadelphia: Whitmore Publishing Co., 1968), p. 21; Theodoor de Booy and John T. Faris, *The Virgin Islands: Our New Possessions and the British Islands* (Philadelphia: J. B. Lippincott, 1918), pp. 127–133.

have become romanticized through fictionalized versions of that historic tragedy.[23]

Carefully planned by its leaders, the rebellion began with a small group of slaves who captured the only fort on the island by killing seven Company soldiers. With the fort secured, the rebels fired three cannon shots prearranged to signal the island-wide uprising. Most of the whites encountered by the rebels were slain and their homes were robbed and burned. Reinforcements from St. Thomas were unable to capture the rebel slaves who, scattered in the "bush" all over the island, repeatedly ambushed their pursuers. A similar fate befell British contingents from St. Kitts and nearby Tortola who intervened at the behest of the beleaguered Governor Gardelin. Finally, Gardelin was able to move the French Governor of Martinique to send two ships of 228 soldiers under an experienced commander.

During April and May, 1734, the French force finally was able to find and destroy most of the "marons," as they were called, thus bringing the rebellion nearly to an end. For six months, the rebels had controlled the island. Those not surrendering or killed committed suicide. Finally, in August 1734 a last remnant of fourteen unarmed slaves surrendered on promise of a free pardon, most of whom were thereupon executed.

Those unfortunate enough to be captured by the French were transported to St. Thomas where twenty-seven were publicly executed. According to one account, the men were pinched in the customary way with red-hot tongs. Then their arms and legs were smashed, and finally their bodies were stretched on wheels where they were left to die slowly in the sun, a death far more painful than crucifixion of Biblical times. Women rebels were not tortured; they were merely beheaded with an ax, and their heads were then stuck up on poles.[24]

Only 146 of St. John's 1,087 slaves were reported to have been involved in the uprising. About fifty whites were reported killed. Planters were remunerated for only thirty slaves, who had either been condemned to death or to work in irons, plus six others who had been killed while fighting for their owners. There is no record that owners were indemnified for the many slaves killed or driven to suicide during the rebellion. Thus ended the insurrection of 1733–1734 on St. John that "greatly delayed the prospect for

---

23. See, *e.g.*, John L. Anderson, *Night of the Silent Drums. A Narrative of Slave Rebellion in the Virgin Islands* (New York: Charles Scribner's Sons, 1975); and Eleanor Heckert, *Muscavado* (New York: Dell Publishing Co., 1968).

24. Anderson, *Night of the Silent Drums*, pp. 376–377; see, also, Westergaard, *The Danish West Indies*, p. 176.

more normal and human relations between master and slave in the Danish islands."[25]

Slave Conspiracies

After the insurrection of 1733 on St. John, the planters of the Virgin Islands became ever more vigilant against the possibility of another slave uprising. The authorities reacted by adopting certain preventive measures that even further restricted the slaves, if that were possible. The gathering of slaves was limited to a certain number only after specified hours of the day. Owners were required, moreover, to keep white managers on their plantations at all times.

A free black, Mingo Tamarin, captain of the "Free Negro Corps" since 1721, had distinguished himself in leading 300 loyal slaves and free blacks in hunting down some of the St. John rebels. In 1746, he and his Corps hunted down a large number of runaways in St. Croix, thus possibly preventing another uprising on that island.[26] Details of this episode, however, remain sketchy.

Details do exist of a so-called planned insurrection on St. Croix in 1759, albeit a one-sided account, because one of the "trial" judges, Englebret Hesselberg, wrote a report "in accordance with orders issued to him" to Copenhagen authorities justifying the severe measures taken.[27] Hesselberg's report is a remarkable document because in his zeal to justify the actions of St. Croix authorities, including himself, he unwittingly betrayed a complete lack of even a most elementary sense of justice—this during the period of "Enlightenment," the era of Voltaire, Rousseau, and Beccaria. Ordinarily accepted rules of evidence were completely ignored. Chance remarks and idle rumors among desperately frightened black witnesses were solemnly treated as evidence. And torture was recognized as the legitimate method of procuring the truth.

Hesselberg reported that a "free negro" was induced to "confess" to the planning of the alleged slave conspiracy on the promise of mere banishment as "the worse" of his punishment. After he named those supposedly involved, however, he slit his throat and, before he died, retracted all to which he had previously

---

25. Westergaard, *The Danish West Indies*, p. 177.

26. *Ibid.*, p. 246.

27. Hesselberg's frightful report is translated and reprinted by Waldemar Westergaard in his "Account of the Negro Rebellion on St. Croix, Danish West Indies, 1759," *Journal of Negro History*, 11, 1 (January 1926), 50–61.

"confessed." Hesselberg stated that, nevertheless, "he was made an example of:" "His dead body was dragged through the streets by a horse, by one leg; thereafter hanged on the gallows by a leg, and finally taken down and burned at the stake."

Those judged guilty of conspiracy could be certain of public execution. The most merciful death was to be burned alive at the stake, because the agony could only last fifteen minutes at the most. The "wheel" and the "gibbet" (a form of slow death by hanging in irons) were reserved for "ring-leaders." Hesselberg candidly listed in his account the horrible punishments meted out to the alleged conspirators, none of whom confessed even after enduring the most excruciating pain. Of those accused of being involved in the conspiracy, thirteen suffered from one and one-half minutes to nine days of torture before they died. Two were broken on the wheel. Hesselberg wrote of one of them: "He was broken on the wheel with an iron crowbar, laid alive on the wheel, where he survived 12 hours. The head was then set on a stake, and the hand fastened on the gallows." Four others were burned alive; they lived from one and one-half minutes to fourteen minutes. Four were pinched with hot tongs and then hanged, some by the legs, others by the neck; one lived one-half hour but another lived twelve hours before he died by strangling. Three were "gibbeted," one living for 42 hours, another for 91 hours, and the third for almost nine days.

Hesselberg concluded that for ten others, "there is so great a suspicion that they are condemned to be sold out of the land." Fifty-eight were acquitted, and six were reported "free as birds and not yet captured. For each one seized alive, the captor will receive 50 rixdollars; 25 rd. will be paid for each one killed."[28]

From Hesselberg's own account, there is at least a reasonable doubt that any slave conspiracy to rebel ever existed on St. Croix in 1759. Such was the paranoiac temper of white society and Danish rule on St. Croix that a single retracted confession could be used to establish the guilt of so many so-called conspirators. The ratio of 11,807 slaves to only 1,690 whites, according to the 1758 census, was seven to one in St. Croix.[29]

Describing "the cruel and detestable slavery" in St. Croix in a letter to a friend in 1776, the poet, Philip Freneau, wrote: "If you have tears prepare to shed them now.... no class of mankind in the known world undergo so complete a servitude...."[30]

---

28. *Ibid.*, pp. 58–61.

29. *Ibid.*, p. 52. A petition of the English residents of St. Croix in 1765 to the British House of Commons recorded that "the Island of Santa Cruz is supposed to have a resident Stock of Negroes, to the Number of 16,000; 12,000 of which are computed to have been bought, within Seven Years past, of the British merchants: 1100 is the annual Supply required to repair and keep up the original Stock...." Tyson, *Powder, Profits & Privateers*, p. 12.

30. Tyson, *Powder, Profits & Privateers*, p. 20.

3

Slavery to Serfdom

With some difficulty, Denmark was able to preserve its neutrality during the American Revolutionary War.[1] Generally the last quarter of the 18th century was a time of economic prosperity for the Virgin Islands. It was also a time of rising protests in both Europe and the New World about slavery and the slave trade. "All over the Christian world the antislavery protests were beginning to be heard."[2] The very brutality of the Danish slave system fostered the forces of amelioration and—though the end of slavery in the Virgin Islands was to take a long time—together these forces would provide a social mix that would make emancipation inevitable. Contributing to gradual amelioration were the end of the slave trade, the rise in status of the so-called "free-colored," the influence of the Moravians, and the towering figure of Peter von Scholten.

End of the Slave Trade

One reason slavery in the Virgin Islands has been represented by some authors as more humane or less severe than the institution appeared elsewhere is the fact that Denmark was the first European nation to end its participation in the slave trade. Ernst Schimmelmann, a prominent Danish nobleman and Minister of Finance in Copenhagen, who owned slaves and was engaged himself in the slave trade, is usually given credit for the Royal Ordinance of March 16, 1792 ending the Danish slave trade.[3] Ernst was the son and heir of H. C. Schimmelmann, wealthy absentee owner of St. Croix plantations and of sugar refineries in Copenhagen, who had died in 1782. The Schimmelmanns were well known for the rare humanity and compassion with which they treated their slaves in St. Croix. There was no denying Ernst Schimmelmann's humane

---

1. See, Lewisohn, *St. Croix Under Seven Flags*, p. 187, and Chapter 1 of this book, n. 29.
2. Lewisohn, *St. Croix Under Seven Flags*, p. 190.
3. Norregard, *Danish Settlements in West Africa, 1658–1850*, p. 172.

philosophy and his desire to prohibit the slave trade. The fact remains, however, that the Danes ended the slave trade not for humanitarian but for other reasons.

Slavery within England had been outlawed in 1772. In the 1780s, William Wilberforce and other Englishmen aroused widespread discontent with slavery, and in 1787 they formed an abolition lobby to concentrate all their energies on ending the British slave trade as a matter of strategy, rather than to attack directly the institution of slavery itself.[4] Ernst Schimmelmann closely followed the debate in Britain and, although the British Parliament had rejected a proposal in April 1791 to abolish the slave trade, he considered it imminent that the British would act to end their participation in the slave trade. That Britain would delay banning the slave trade until 1807 was not apparent in 1791. Although Denmark had emancipated its serfs in 1788, the Danes, unlike the English or French, had no organized movement to abolish the slave trade or slavery. Nevertheless, Schimmelmann attached great weight to his belief that Britain—the dominant slave trading nation—would soon abolish this trade. The Danish historian Green-Pedersen has conjectured that Schimmelmann "realized quite well that the Danish slave trade was an integral part of the Atlantic slave trade, and so, in 1791–92, it was natural to wonder whether it would be possible and/or desirable for Denmark to continue her slave trade alone."[5] Accordingly, at Schimmelmann's suggestion, the Great Negro Trade Commission was established in the summer of 1791 to study, and report on, the Danish slave trade, and Schimmelmann himself became its chairman and most influential member.

Another Danish historian, Georg Norregard, has linked efforts by Paul Isert and other Danes to establish plantations in Guinea—as an economically feasible alternative to the slave trade—to the actual ending of the Danish slave trade. In his chapter entitled "Plantations and the Abolition of the Slave Trade," Norregard asserted that reports reaching Copenhagen "that it was possible to cultivate the African soil ... profoundly influenced the renewed discussion of the slave traffic between Africa and America."[6]

Both Norregard and Green-Pedersen, however, cited the unprofitability of the Danish slave trade as the primary reason for banning it. Not only had the Danes suffered much larger losses of slaves than losses incurred by slavers of other nations, but the high death rate among Danish sailors engaged in the

---

4. Roger Anstey, *The Atlantic Slave Trade and British Abolition, 1760–1810* (Atlantic Highlands, New Jersey: Humanities Press, 1975), p. 255.

5. Green-Pedersen, "The History of the Danish Negro Slave Trade," p. 217.

6. Norregard, *Danish Settlements*, p. 175.

trade also strongly influenced the Great Negro Trade Commission. Of 2,004 Danish sailors who sailed in the Danish slave ships in the twelve-year period of 1777 to 1789, a total of 691, or more than one-third, died during the voyages.[7]

The Commission issued its report in December 1791. The greater part of the report consisted of an economic analysis of the impact of ending the slave trade upon future sugar production in the Virgin Islands. Because the brutality of slavery in the Islands resulted in a far higher death rate than birth rate among the slaves, the slave population required constant replenishment of about 2,000 imports yearly. According to Green-Pedersen:

> Through demographic calculations the Commission reached the conclusion that after a transitional period the slave population could be maintained by "natural reproduction" provided that some social improvements were made for the negroes. Because of this, the report looks more like a politico-economic programme for Danish colonialism than a declaration of human rights.[8]

Acting on the Commission's recommendations, the King's edict of March 16, 1792 projected the end of the slave trade ten years later on December 31, 1802 in order to permit the planters time to stock up on the number of slaves. The Danish treasury was authorized to advance loans at five percent interest to the planters so that they could purchase these extra slaves. Meanwhile, all nations were to be allowed to import slaves into the Virgin Islands and to export 2,000 pounds of raw sugar for each adult slave they imported. To encourage slave reproduction, female slaves could be imported duty-free, while the export of slaves from the Islands was strictly prohibited. The King's decree also expressed interest in promoting marriage among the slaves and urged they be given moral instruction.

The decree caused a great deal of protest from the planters in the Virgin Islands. Despite the fact that the slave population had increased to an all-time high of 35,727 in 1803—having increased from 22,240 in 1792 to 27,161 on St. Croix—the planters repeatedly petitioned for a postponement during the intervening years but to no avail. Although the slave trade was to officially end on January 1, 1803, illegal import of slaves into St. Croix continued, spurred principally by the avarice of St. Croix planters. British occupation of the Virgin Islands between 1801 and 1802 and again between 1807 and 1815 prevented Copenhagen from enforcing the 1792 decree. Illegal slave traders were

---

7. *Ibid.*, p. 152.
8. Green-Pedersen, "The History of the Danish Negro Slave Trade," p. 217.

encouraged by the commandants of the Guinea forts. "There is a great deal of evidence to support the fact that slave trade at the Danish forts continued, even if on a smaller scale than before," according to Norregard. "It was only in the 1820s, apparently, that a real effort was made to end the slave trade."[9]

One reason why illegal slave trading continued after 1803 was a worsening of the condition, and depletion of the number, of plantation slaves in St. Croix. After the British occupation ended in 1815, P. L. Oxholm took over as Governor General of the Virgin Islands. He reported to Copenhagen in 1816 that many slaves had suffered badly from hunger and starvation causing 1,654 deaths to only 726 births among slaves of St. Croix for 1814 and 1815 and a precipitous decline in the slave population.[10]

Sugar production had increased, most slaves had been converted to Christianity, and an increasing number were being married, Oxholm reported. "The better treatment of Negroes requires higher imports of foodstuffs and plantation tools and implements." He also reported an increase in the number of imported mules. "Many of the burdens, hitherto carried on the Negroes' heads, could now be transported in mule carts or on mule back." Finally, Oxholm reported that the number of "free colored" had doubled since 1792, thus further depleting the slave population, because:

> During the past twenty years freedom had been granted in a careless and easy way without first having arranged how the slaves could support themselves when emancipated. The white man's ever-increasing immoral habit to co-habit with colored concubines, who, when given their freedom or were bought free, contributed to the increase of this class. I have tried to stop this kind of emancipation by ordering the owners to support their emancipated slaves as long as they live, but this is a very difficult thing to control.[11]

The Free Colored

Contributing to the gradual amelioration of the system of slavery in the Virgin Islands was the emergence and growth of the so-called "free colored" who were intermediate between the dominant white minority and the slave major-

---

9. Norregard, *Danish Settlements*, p. 184.

10. Eva Lawaetz, ed. and trans., *Oxholm's Report of 1816: A Report from Governor General P. L. Oxholm to the Royal Westindian Chamber in Copenhagen (Det Kongelige Vestindiske Kammer) Dated May 4, 1816, St. Croix* (Christiansted, St. Croix: 1977), pp. 1–2.

11. *Ibid.*, pp. 4–5.

ity and included racially mixed persons as well as free blacks.[12] The free-black population emerged from slaves who gained their freedom through purchase or by action of their owners. Unlike the Spanish slave system, the rigid slave system of the Danes did not foster manumission by purchase, and comparatively few were able actually to buy their freedom until late in the 18th century. "Interbreeding," on the other hand, "which relaxed the tensions of servitude, had taken place on a large scale."[13] Accordingly, there were many more racially mixed persons than free blacks among the free-colored population of the Virgin Islands.

An important factor explaining the emergence of the free-colored class was the numerical disproportion between white males and white females and between white and black populations. The presence of relatively few European women among the settlers encouraged the slave owners to sexually exploit their female slaves, who, increasingly, were given their freedom by their owners. This explains why women far outnumbered men among the free-colored population, as the following illustrates:

Table 2. Composition of Free Colored in Christiansted, 1791–1811

Year	Women	Men	Girls	Boys	Total
1791	342	140	141	152	775
1795	381	151	172	183	887
1797	440	187	215	219	1,061
1805	609	230	290	285	1,414
1811	747	281	301	314	1,643

Source: Eva Lawaetz, ed., trans., comp., *Free Coloured in St. Croix, 1744–1816* (Christiansted, St. Croix, 1979), pp. 44–45.

Many of the freed women had been housekeepers and/or common-law wives of white males. The Ordinance of March 16, 1776 had established that the

---

12. The term "free colored" is used here instead of terms preferred by some Caribbean historians, such as "freemen" or "freedmen," because "free colored" was used in Danish official documents and referred to non-whites who were not slaves. "In the Danish West Indies the term *Negro* was reserved for persons of full African ancestry and was never applied to persons of mixed race who were known as colored or mulattoes. The term *colored* was seldom used to include Negroes except in the combined form of *Free Colored*." Jens Larsen, *Virgin Islands Story*, p. 162. "The word 'Negro' is seldom used in the Caribbean, and, when used, is not a 'fighting' word. All over the Caribbean it is either synonymous with 'slave,' or is a term of endearment, used colloquially by both whites and Negroes." Eric Williams, "Race Relations in Puerto Rico and the Virgin Islands," *Foreign Affairs*, (January, 1945), 23:313.

13. Williams, "Race Relations," p. 310.

child followed the mother and that, therefore, children of free-colored women were born free.

Besides natural increase as a factor, the free-colored class was augmented by immigration of free-colored persons, particularly into St. Thomas from other islands and from troubled areas such as from St. Domingue (now Haiti) and later from Hispanic America. Certain developments enhanced the attraction of St. Thomas as a booming commercial emporium offering increasing opportunities for free-colored immigrants. Charlotte Amalie became a free port in 1767, and all restrictions on foreign ships were removed in 1815. Steamships became common in the 1820s and 1830s, with establishment in St. Thomas of two banks in 1837, the coaling station in 1841, and the Caribbean headquarters of the Royal Mail Steam Packet Company by 1842.[14]

When the Moravian missionary Oldendorp visited the Islands in 1767–1768, he found that slaves worked only half days on Saturdays which permitted many to produce provisions, such as vegetables, fruit, chickens, and fish, that could be sold in the Sunday Market. In this way, some slaves were able to buy their freedom by earning the necessary amount, which varied with age and qualifications. Oldendorp sharply condemned the practice of some owners who sometimes sold a slave to another owner after having received money given by the slave toward the purchase of her or his freedom.[15]

Data on the number of free colored before 1835 are scattered and fragmentary, but the period of greatest growth of this class, 1789 to 1835, is evident from the following:

Table 3. Total Number of Free Colored in the Virgin Islands, 1789–1835

Year	St. Thomas	St. John	St. Croix	Total
1789	160	16	953	1,129
1797	239	15	1,164	1,418
1829	4,349	158	3,006	7,513
1835	5,204	202	4,913	10,319

Source: N. A. T. Hall, "The 1816 Freedman Petition in the Danish Virgin Islands: Its Background and Consequences" (unpublished paper presented at the Eleventh Conference of Caribbean Historians, April 5–11, 1979, xeroxed, Curacao: 1979), p. 27.

The phenomenal growth of the free-colored population is apparent, having grown on St. Thomas from 1600 in 1789 to 5,204 in 1835, which exceeded

---

14. Dookhan, *A History of the Virgin Islands of the United States*, pp. 100–103.

15. Eva Lawaetz, ed., trans., comp., *Free Coloured in St. Croix, 1744–1816* (Christiansted, St. Croix: 1979), p. 2.

that island's slave population of 5,032. The total of 10,319 free colored in 1835 for all three islands represented 25 percent of the entire population of the Virgin Islands.

The white elite, according to Albert Campbell, encouraged the development of a free-colored class and a rigid stratification along class lines of the entire non-white population.

> In following this tactic they necessarily yielded a considerable degree of equality to the favored members of the colored group, but they succeeded in maintaining their own minority in a position of social and political domination.[16]

"These free people of color were usually, but not exclusively, light skinned," wrote Eric Williams.

> Offspring of white fathers and black mothers, they were generally treated with indulgence by their fathers, often educated, and customarily left some property on the death of the father. In a society in which life, liberty and the pursuit of happiness were the inalienable rights of a white skin, it was inevitable that they despised the distaff-side of their ancestry. Too light to work in the fields, as the saying went, they regarded themselves as superior to the black slaves. Official policy sanctioned this differentiation.[17]

The free-colored population, nevertheless, was regulated by severe restrictions, which were only gradually relaxed over time. The most extensive research of the free colored in the Virgin Islands has been completed by Professor Neville Hall of the University of the West Indies, who cites a long list of "disabilities" suffered by this "free non-white group, neither wholly free nor yet slaves."[18]

Among the disabilities imposed on the free colored were: residential segregation in Christiansted and Frederiksted in houses and grounds not to exceed thirty Danish square feet each; legislation effectively preventing the free colored from becoming a rural population or owning rural land; outlawing free-colored participation in the tavern or rum business; establishment of a 10 p.m. curfew for free colored under penalty of arrest and fine or corporal punish-

---

16. Campbell, *St. Thomas Negroes—A Study of Personality and Culture*, p. 18.

17. Williams, "Race Relations," p. 309.

18. N. A. T. Hall, "The 1816 Freedman Petition in the Danish Virgin Islands: Its Background and Consequences" (unpublished paper presented at the Eleventh Conference of Caribbean Historians, April 5–11, 1979, xeroxed, Curacao), p. 27.

ment; prevention of their participation in unauthorized dances under penalty of 100 lashes in public; the requirement that all free colored wear on the breast or head dress a cockade, or badge, of red and white linen as a means of distinguishing the free colored from slaves at all times; the requirement that every free-colored person possess a certificate of freedom approved and signed by the Governor-General to be produced on demand under penalty of banishment or forfeiture of freedom; and regulations forbidding the free colored from wearing clothing made of silk, chintz, lace, linen, velvet, and gold and silver brocade, and from using gold and silver braid, expensive jewelry, ornaments of precious stones, and elaborate coiffures. No evidence from a free-colored person, moreover, was admissible against any white person, and no public offices for which any white persons qualified could be held by the free colored.[19]

The highest office to which a free-colored person could aspire was Captain of the Free-Colored Militia, who was the government's representative in everything concerning the free colored in his jurisdiction. According to instructions issued in 1771, each captain was responsible "to have his people under constant control, as it is his responsibility that they behave themselves in a quiet, decent, and inoffensive manner." He was responsible for the selection, training, supervision, and arming of the militia, which served as a police or security force for patrolling the towns, for quelling slave uprisings, and pursuing slave runaways and escaped prisoners. In addition, his instructions included maintaining an annual list of all free-colored persons in his district, administering punishments of free-colored violators of not more than 100 lashes with a thin cane ("crimes deserving more punishment must be reported to the Commandant"), and arranging for all free-colored males to "be entered in the militia roster as soon as they have completed their 16th year, and that they receive religious instruction and be apprenticed as craftsmen as well as participate in the drill exercises."[20]

According to Neville Hall, two circumstances in the early 19th century contributed to the free-colored's growing resistance to their oppressive condition.

---

19. *Ibid.*, pp. 6–10.

20. The "Instructions for the Captain of the Free Coloured" were issued by the local government on October 8, 1771 and are quoted here from the translation by Eva Lawaetz in her *Free Coloured in St. Croix, 1744–1816*, pp. 6–8. The first captain in the Virgin Islands was Mingo Tamarin who was appointed in 1721 and whose militia played an important role in suppressing slave revolts. Upon his death in 1765, he was succeeded by his son, Peter Tamarin. Kay Larsen, *Dansk Vestindien, 1666–1917* (Copenhagen: C. A. Reitzel, 1928), p. 87.

First was the remarkable increase in the free-colored population. The other circumstance was the second British occupation of 1807–1815, during which the British "paid very little attention" to the laws and customs regulating the free-colored class. By 1815, residential segregation was not being observed, and many free colored themselves had become property and slave owners. Upon the resumption of Danish rule in 1815, a number of free-colored men refused to serve in the militia, whereupon the authorities imprisoned all the participants, except one who was deported, and tightened enforcement of regulations particularly regarding the authentication of freedom certificates.[21]

Reaction to this renewed oppression was soon forthcoming. In 1816, a petition signed by 331 free-colored men from all three islands was addressed to the King of Denmark requesting removal of all free-colored disabilities and the granting of full citizenship and equality with the whites, principally by replacing their hated freedom certificates with "that distinguished badge of fealty, conferred on your Majesty's other subjects, called Burgher Briefs." They further urged removal of all forms of discrimination including that grossest insult to their dignity, the cockade, as they had already proved their worthiness for equal respect by providing 1,000 militia effectives, by owning lands, tenements, and slaves, and by paying taxes on their possessions.

> The petitioners also raised the delicate but deeply felt issue of the sexual exploitation of their women, particularly young women. It was common practice among white men, they asserted, to seduce and corrupt the morals of young freedwomen, habituating them to prostitution and loose living. This was not only in clear violation of the law, but was also taking place with impunity. The illegitimate children from these liasons (sic!) commonly rejoined the viciously circular ranks of their prostituted mothers, if girls; or were condemned to a future of low status, if boys.[22]

Although no immediate gains were realized as a result of the petition, the period after 1816 was one of general advance for the free-colored community, with increasing exceptions to their harsh regulation being permitted. Portending removal of their inferior legal status was the British Order in Council of 1829, which removed all legal disabilities of the free colored in the nearby British West Indies.[23]

---

21. Hall, "The 1816 Freedman Petition," pp. 12–15.

22. *Ibid.*, pp. 18–19.

23. *Ibid.*, pp. 19–23. The Petition of 1816 was taken to Denmark by two free-colored men, William de Windt and William Purcell, and presented to the Danish King, Frederik VI. See, Lawaetz, *Free Coloured in St. Croix*, pp. 37–38.

The ruling authorities in the Virgin Islands, however, were not yet quite ready to grant to the free colored equal status with the whites. They considered it very important that slaves who became free have employable skills and be able to support themselves. Under a local ordinance of 1831, a status tantamount to that of a serf's was imposed on those free-colored persons not then otherwise gainfully employed. This law would become a model for former slaves after emancipation.

The ordinance required all free-colored persons "not having a competence, a permanent profession or trade or other lawful means of gaining a livelihood" to engage themselves as servants or field laborers. A system of tenant farming and contract labor was thus created, whereby those free colored who became field laborers bound themselves to terms of one-year service renewable the first of each August.[24] Clearly, the freedom struggle of the free colored of the Virgin Islands was not yet over.

The Moravians

Also contributing to the setting for eventual emancipation of the slaves in the Virgin Islands was the work of Moravian missionaries for over a century. Inheritors of the teachings of John Hus of Prague, the Moravians had shared the persecution directed toward reformists by Roman Catholic authorities from the 12th through the 17th centuries. Often finding refuge in flight and worshipping in any place they could, they eschewed elaborate ritual and insisted they study the Bible—as the infallible word of God—and worship in the simplest kind of dwelling. Through the influence of John Amos Komensky, known by his Latin name of Comenius, education was considered by Moravians as a means of survival. Comenius believed that learning should not depend on coercion, but on acceptance through "learning by doing," by example, and by use of the senses of sight, touch, and hearing.

The fortunes of the Moravians took a turn for the better in 1722 when Count Nicholas von Zinzendorf offered them a portion of his estate in Germany. About six hundred Moravian men and women made up this first permanent colony which became the Moravian center of Herrnhut.[25]

---

24. Campbell, *St. Thomas Negroes*, p. 14.

25. For elaboration of the influence of the Moravians on education in the New World, see: Patricia Gill Murphy, *The Education of the New World Blacks in the Danish West Indies/U.S. Virgin Islands: A Case Study of Social Transition*, unpublished Ph.D. dissertation (xeroxed, University of Connecticut, 1977), pp. 22–71.

While attending the coronation in 1731 of his distant relative, Christian VI of Denmark, Zinzendorf met Anthony Ulrich, a slave from St. Thomas, who described to him the oppressive conditions of the Danish system of slavery. Upon Zinzendorf's invitation, Ulrich later traveled to the Herrnhut community to describe in person the conditions of the slaves. The Moravian leaders became convinced they should undertake missionary work for the first time by sending missionaries to St. Thomas. Ulrich warned them that

> nobody could preach to slaves in St. Thomas without becoming as a slave himself, since, after working all day on the plantations they were kept by a strict curfew to their huts by night, and only by working alongside them in the sugar cane fields could anyone hope to have a chance of preaching the Gospel.[26]

Leonard Dober, a potter, was chosen as the first of the Moravian Brethren to become a missionary, to be accompanied by David Nitschmann, a carpenter, as his temporary companion.

Despite opposition of the Danish West India Company, the plan to send Moravian missionaries to St. Thomas had the support of certain members of the royal court in Copenhagen, including Princess Charlotte Amalie. The two missionaries arrived in St. Thomas on December 13, 1732. Their initial success in proselytizing the slaves induced many more missionaries to follow, including seventeen who began mission work in St. Croix in 1735.

Three circumstances, however, posed formidable obstacles. The first was the high mortality rate among the missionaries: "the murderous climate had, before the end of 1736, killed nineteen of the thirty-nine missionaries."[27] The second circumstance was the opposition of the planters who forbade their slaves to attend Moravian preaching. "Even the Rev. J. Borm, pastor of the Reformed Dutch Church, was induced by prejudices ... to present a memorial to the Danish government against the Brethren."[28] A third circumstances stalled Moravian efforts on St. Thomas. Friederich Martin, who became director of Moravian work for all three islands in 1736, solemnized the marriage of one of his Moravian co-workers to a free-colored woman, an act that "contravened the law at that time and strengthened the whites in their opinion that the Brethren were not only fanatical visionaries but were also seriously planning to carry through a social revolution."[29] Both Martin and his co-worker were

---

26. *Ibid.*, p. 42.
27. Jens Larsen, *Virgin Islands Story*, p. 66.
28. Knox, *A Historical Account of St. Thomas*, p. 149.
29. Larsen, *Virgin Islands Story*, p. 66.

imprisoned until the intervention of Count Zinzendorf, who visited St. Thomas briefly in early 1739 and secured their release.

Count Zinzendorf found over 800 slaves were regularly attending the religious services, a success far beyond his expectations. As initiator of the Moravian movement in the Virgin Islands, however, he did not escape the sting of retribution. One night, an armed mob of whites attacked him and the slaves with him, flogging severely the slaves they found at New Herrnhut and destroying all the furniture of the mission house. Upon Zinzendorf's departure, the planters—whose memories of the slave revolt of 1733 on St. John were still fresh—petitioned Governor Frederik Moth expressing their conviction that "when the Moravians got permission to spread their harmful doctrine" it was to be feared "that our slaves might revolt against us and murder us."[30] The unswervable and influential Count, however, successfully importuned King Christian VI to issue an order on August 7, 1739 "that liberty and protection should be given to the Brethren."[31]

After Crown rule replaced Company rule in 1755, and particularly after the alleged slave conspiracy in St. Croix of 1759, Moravian missionary activity among the slaves flourished and increasingly became accepted among the planters and local authorities. The Moravian missionaries had made their first converts in 1736 when they baptized three slaves. By 1786, the missionaries had baptized 8,833 adult slaves and 2,974 slave children. Almost all St. Thomas slaves were church members at the end of the 18th century.[32]

One of the reasons for the change of attitude by the white minority toward the Moravians concerned the nature of their instruction of the slaves, namely, that slaves should obey their masters just as they should obey the commandments of God. For example, the Moravian missionary, Oldendorp, wrote the following in 1777:

> The religion of our Savior, Jesus Christ, indicates to Christian slaves their duties toward their masters very clearly, very specifically, and very completely. It advises those duties on the basis of reasons which are independent of the character of the master and his harsh or kindly treatment of his slaves. Christianity makes it a duty to the slaves to serve their masters with the same faithfulness and humbleness with which they feel themselves obliged to serve Christ, their Savior.[33]

---

30. Quoted in *ibid.*, pp. 67–68.
31. Knox, *A Historical Account of St. Thomas*, p. 151.
32. Campbell, *St. Thomas Negroes*, p. 10.
33. Quoted in *ibid.*

Thus the religious instruction imparted by the Moravians served the interests of the planters. The Moravian Church itself, moreover, acquired plantation estates in the Virgin Islands and purchased slaves to work on them. It was for this reason that the Anti-Slavery Society of England on one occasion reportedly "snubbed" Moravian elders. Not until 1844 did the Moravians free their slaves.

Notwithstanding their accommodation with elites, Moravians were theologically and educationally committed to accepting the equality of all peoples—whites, slaves, and Indians alike—and treating them as human beings. Establishing their first permanent North American colony at Bethlehem, Pennsylvania in 1740, they were already committed to the education of boys and girls of all faiths and of American Indians. Count Zinzendorf and his daughter were in Bethlehem in 1742 establishing Moravian schools, and in time these schools were to presage the equalitarianism that was to characterize the public school movement in the United States. Bethlehem mission schools became the center for training Moravian missionaries who were to go to the West Indies. Indeed, most missionaries who served in the West Indies in the 18th and 19th centuries had American training and experience. They were to become a link between the United States and the Virgin Islands.[34]

Transplanted to the Danish islands, the educational methods of Moravian teachers proved very effective in ameliorating the condition of the slaves, principally by contributing to their literacy and sense of self-worth, thereby preparing them for emancipation. Although Danish was the official language, and English and Dutch were the most common languages, most slaves spoke a Negro Dutch Creole dialect. The Moravians learned Creole, taught the slaves in Creole, and as early as 1761 translated the liturgy, hymnal, and Bible into Creole and followed these with Creole spelling books and readers. The use of their own language as printed vehicles for learning "undoubtedly afforded the slaves a sense of dignity."[35]

In the meantime, the Lutheran, Catholic, Anglican, and Presbyterian churches also began preaching the Christian gospel to the slaves during the latter half of the 18th century. In 1713, Lutheran Pastor Christian Fischer baptized the first slave in the Virgin Islands, 19 years before the Moravians arrived and 44 years before the Danish Lutheran State Church itself undertook missionary work among the slaves in the 1750s when nine Lutheran missionaries arrived in the Virgin Islands. From the outset, their mission was ill-fated. Half the popula-

---

34. Murphy, *The Education of New World Blacks*, pp. 68–70.

35. Ezra A. Naughton, *The Origin and Development of Higher Education in the Virgin Islands*, unpublished Ph.D. dissertation (Catholic University of America, 1973), p. 78.

tion was ill from hunger, and many slaves died of starvation in 1759 when drought, an earthquake, epidemics, and crop failures were experienced. Drought, crop failures, and hunger continued, and in 1765 a hurricane was followed by floods and more epidemics and hunger. Completely separate from the established Danish Lutheran clergy, the missionaries received tense and hostile treatment and little support from them. Moreover, too much was expected from each Lutheran missionary whose impractical instructions required a work day far longer than that of the slave. The consequence was a high incidence of mortality among the Lutheran missionaries. Still another difficulty was the failure of most of them to learn the Creole dialect of the slaves. This obstacle, plus the brutal Danish system which treated slaves "like animals," produced "a slackening influence."[36]

Finally, in 1796, Governor E. F. Walterstorff reported to Copenhagen that the mission was a failure and urged that the Lutheran missionaries be gradually withdrawn. "It was this failure of the Danish mission," according to Neville Hall, "that strengthened the claims of the Moravians, whom the Danish government itself identified in 1793 as best suited for the task of educating the slaves."

> The Moravians for their part continued unobtrusively with their work, speaking from their mission stations.... Unlike the Lutherans, they were not culture-bound and felt no sense of compulsion to teach slaves Danish. Yet literacy was high on their agenda and the success of their efforts in this connection was evidenced by the increasing number of slaves who could read in the first three decades of the nineteenth century.[37]

A significant result of Moravian endeavors was the fact that the Moravians could claim a greater church membership of slaves in the Virgin Islands by 1835 than any other church, as illustrated in Table 4.

Peter von Scholten

Perhaps no figure in the entire history of the Virgin Islands equals the stature of Peter Carl Frederik von Scholten (1784–1854). After his first appointment

---

36. Larsen, *Virgin Islands Story*, pp. 30, 36, 74–81. See, also, Eva Lawaetz, *Address Delivered by Rev. E. V. Lose on July 25, 1884 About the History of the Lutheran Church in Christiansted* (Christiansted, St. Croix: Christiansted Public Library, 1976), pp. 9–10.

37. Neville A. T. Hall, "Establishing a Public Elementary School System for Slaves in the Danish Virgin Islands, 1732–1846," (unpublished paper presented at the Tenth Conference of Caribbean Historians, March 27–April 1, 1978, xeroxed, St. Thomas: College of the Virgin Islands), pp. 6, 11.

Table 4. Church Affiliation in the Virgin Islands, 1835

Church	St. Croix Free	St. Croix Slave	St. Thomas Free	St. Thomas Slave	St. John Free	St. John Slave	Totals Free	Totals Slave
Moravian	276	6244	447	1895	237	1369	960	9508
Catholic	916	6433	4056	2265	19	46	4991	8744
Anglican & Presby.	3363	5111	1534	398	146	118	5043	5627
Lutheran	2120	1904	1748	461	80	86	3948	2451
Others*	43	0	483	28	1	3	527	31
None	87	184	66	251	6	307	159	742
Totals	6805	19876	8334	5298	489	1929	15628	27103

Source: Neville A. T. Hall, "Establishing a Public Elementary School System for Slaves in the Danish Virgin Islands, 1732–1846," (unpublished paper presented at the Tenth Conference of Caribbean Historians, March 27–April 1, 1978. (Xeroxed, St. Thomas, College of the Virgin Islands, 1978), pp. 17–18.

* Includes 8 Quakers (all Free), 83 Methodists (52 Free, 31 Slaves), and 467 Jews (all Free).

as Superintendent of Weights in St. Thomas in 1814, he rose successively in the colonial bureaucracy to Acting Commandant, Postmaster, Director of Customs, Governor of St. Thomas in 1823, and finally Acting Governor-General of all three Danish islands in 1827—a post he was to hold (with the "Acting" designation deleted eight years later) until his abrupt resignation in 1848. A gregarious, dynamic man, von Scholten was yet a humanist whose unrelenting efforts as Governor-General were directed to preparing the way for the emancipation of the free colored and the slaves. As he, himself, after his resignation, were to put it: "all my endeavors have been concentrated on slowly and systematically, through education, to prepare the free colored and the slaves for their rights and obligations as citizens and for their freedom."[38]

Although von Scholten was married, his wife had not accompanied him from Denmark except for a few years after 1815. Shortly following his move to Christiansted—then the capital of the Virgin Islands—to assume office as Governor-General, he shared his household with a free-colored woman, Anna Heegaard, who was to serve as his mistress and first lady in an unbroken association of over twenty years. Von Scholten's recent predecessor in office, Governor-General Adrian Bentzon, was known to have developed a second family

---

38. Eva Lawaetz, trans., "Peter von Scholten's letter of December 22, 1849, to Liebenberg, Counsel for the Defense, concerning the Negro Rebellion in St. Croix on July 3, 1848," in *Emancipation in the Danish West Indies, Eye Witness Accounts II* (St. Thomas: Bureau of Libraries and Museums, Government of the Virgin Islands of the United States, n.d.), p. 10.

with his free-colored housekeeper, a common practice at the time among the white elite including government officials, planters, and priests. "In these alliances it was often customary for young women to become not just housekeepers or mistresses but to progress to the accepted position and social duties of unofficial wives."[39]

Anna Heegaard's grandmother, Charlotte Amalie, was a St. Croix slave who was given her freedom in the 1790s when she was legally listed as a "sambo," or the daughter of a Negro and a mulatto. In 1774, Charlotte Amalie had given birth to a daughter, Susanna, whose father was the son of a white planter. In 1790, to Susanna and a Danish clerk was born Anna who at the age of 14 was listed as a "mustee," or a one-fourth colored person. From the age of 19 until she began her liaison with von Scholten, Anna is known to have lived as a mistress successively with at least three men—an attorney, a merchant, and a planter—with whom she apparently bore no children. From these associations and her inheritance, Anna became an owner of slaves and property, which accorded her the status of a quite wealthy woman by contemporary standards.[40]

Even in the absence of hard evidence, the juxtaposition in time of her alliance with von Scholten, together with his initiatives, strongly suggest, according to Neville Hall, "Anna Heegaard's influence on the issues of free coloured equality, amelioration and eventual emancipation."[41] Also a factor was the British Order in Council of 1829 which removed the disabilities of the free colored in the nearby British West Indies. In any event, von Scholten in 1830 proposed his "Plan for an Improved and more distinct organisation for Your Majesty's Free Coloured Subjects in the West India Colonies," which was approved by the King in 1831.

Von Scholten's plan abolished "free briefs" (freedom certificates) and substituted a new classification of all free-colored persons based on two divisions. The first, or upper, division consisted of three classes—ranking officers of the Free-Colored Militia, all other free-colored officers, and the remaining free-colored soldiers, respectively. Others could be included in the first division by the Governor-General if they merited "distinction ... on account of superior education, mental capacity, good conduct, situation in life, or from other considerations." Assigned to the second division were all others registered as free-colored persons.[42]

---

39. Lewisohn, *St. Croix Under Seven Flags*, p. 228.
40. *Ibid.*, pp. 228–230.
41. N. A. T. Hall, "Anna Heegaard—Enigma," *Caribbean Quarterly*, 22 (June–September 1976): 67.
42. Campbell, *St. Thomas Negroes*, p. 16.

Governor-General Peter von Scholten

Assignment to the first division had many advantages. Some few could be granted a "burgher's brief" (merchant's license), and all in the first division would be treated equally with whites while traveling, in prisons, or in hospitals. One paragraph of the plan, furthermore, gave the Governor-General the God-like power to change free-colored persons into whites, by directing the names of such persons to be "struck off the registry of the free-coloured population, and to be entered, as white inhabitants, in the congregation to which they belong." Eligibility depended on the pigmentation of one's skin, for the following distinction was made:

> Where free persons of colour, of both sexes, assimilate in colour to white, and they otherwise, by a cultivated mind and good conduct render themselves deserving to stand according to their rank and station in life, on an equal footing with the white inhabitants, all the difference, which the colour now causes ought to cease.[43]

A popular West Indian belief among some persons of color held that they could enter the gate to Heaven only when St. Peter, waving a magic wand, would change them into white persons.[44] Now, however, under this paragraph, the Governor-General of the Virgin Islands could change them into whites during this life. While this provision of changing racial status by decree was seldom carried out, it suggests, according to Eric Williams:

43. Quoted in *ibid.*

44. This was expressed as a long-held belief to this writer by some natives of Antigua, then of the British West Indies, during the writer's stay on that island in 1943–1944.

the way in which the free people of color formed a flexible caste that served as a convenient buffer between whites and blacks. As the saying goes…, the colored people were the "ham in the sandwich." … Under the Danes, prominent colored people received invitations to official functions to which many whites were not invited. Thus was established the Caribbean tradition of race relations. Emphasis was on color, not race; and color was closely associated with class, and even determined by class.[45]

For all its shortcomings, von Scholten's plan was a long step forward in unleashing the forces of freedom for the nonwhite population of the Virgin Islands—both the free colored and slaves. Although the plan was initially approved by King Frederik VI, it went through several subsequent redrafts and, finally, the Royal Ordinance of April 18, 1834 granted all "free people of color" in the Virgin Islands "full participation of every civil right" and removed "hitherto existing regulations … which drew a distinction between the white and colored population." The only qualifications were provision for a three-year probationary period for those to be manumitted from slavery in the future, free-colored children over fifteen, and recently arrived foreign free-colored persons.[46]

Thus, by the Royal decrees of 1831 and 1834, the free-colored population of the Virgin Islands gained full legal equality with whites, and their free-colored class status was abolished, leaving only two remaining population segments—free and unfree.

Apparently committed after 1834 to the inevitability of emancipation, von Scholten next turned his attention to preparing the unfree for their freedom. This he sought to accomplish through a program to ameliorate their condition, including establishment of a public school system. Although it is not possible to assess the degree to which Anna Heegaard influenced these endeavors, there is no doubt that "she was at the very least a sleeping partner, but partner nonetheless, in an enterprise of major magnitude," thereby offering constant support to von Scholten "to work with a fixity of purpose towards the day when the program of amelioration would justify a total and general emancipation."[47]

---

45. Williams, "Race Relations," p. 310.

46. For the English translation of the 1834 Royal ordinance, see, Campbell, *St. Thomas Negroes*, pp. 16–17.

47. Hall, "Anna Heegaard—Enigma," p. 70.

Emancipation

Insofar as population may be an indicator of the changing prosperity of a people, the following population figures for the three islands are revealing.

Table 5. Population of the Virgin Islands, 1773–1911

Year	St. Thomas	St. Croix	St. John	Total
1773	4,371	21,809	2,402	28,582
1796	4,734	28,803	2,120	35,657
1835	14,022	26,681	2,475	43,178
1850	13,666	23,720	2,228	39,614
1880	14,389	18,430	944	33,763
1911	10,678	15,467	941	27,086

Source: Luther H. Evans, *The Virgin Islands from Naval Base to New Deal* (Ann Arbor: J. W. Edwards, 1945), p. 21.

These figures reveal that the peak population year for the Danish Virgin Islands was 1835, after which the total population declined steadily until 1911, the year of the last Danish census, when it was only 63 percent of the 1835 population. After 1835, the population declined as plantation agriculture generally declined, hence the decline of plantation slavery, as indicated by the figures for St. Croix. In 1841, of 151 plantations on St. Croix, sixteen had been taken over by the colonial government because their owners had defaulted on loans, and sixty others were in the hands of creditors.[48]

Prosperous conditions generally prevailed until 1835 when the trade and sugar economy of the Islands began to decline. Sailing ships were being replaced by steam vessels, which found it less necessary to transship at St. Thomas when plying between European ports and the British and Spanish possessions in the West Indies. The consequent decline of the harbor, especially after mid-century, deprived many of the inhabitants of the three islands a place from which to distribute their wares and produce. Indeed, the degree of prosperity at the harbor of St. Thomas was an indicator of planter prosperity throughout the islands.

Several factors accounted for the slow slide of plantation agriculture in the Virgin Islands. Among them were: the decline of prices for plantation produce, thus putting Virgin Islands high-cost producers at a competitive disadvantage with low-cost producers elsewhere; the heavy debt burden of planters; the general exhaustion of the soil; inefficient agricultural methods; uneco-

---

48. Williams, *From Columbus to Castro*, p. 282.

Sugar mill driven by water power

nomic milling operations; excessive absentee-landlordism, particularly in St. Croix; the development of the process in Europe of making sugar from beets instead of from cane; hurricanes and droughts; and, of course, the abolition of the slave trade, and later of slavery, itself. When these factors are considered, in addition to the influence that steam vessels were to gradually make in the decline of St. Thomas harbor over the years, it is not difficult to understand the slackening economy of the Virgin Islands after 1835.[49] From the viewpoint of Denmark, the days of mercantilism in the Virgin Islands were over. The colony was becoming unprofitable and a liability.

Meanwhile, the European proletariat was involved in a general movement toward democracy. Serfdom had already been abolished in Denmark in the 1780s, and the abolitionists were gaining strength in Denmark and throughout Europe. When Britain abolished slavery in 1833, this event had a seismic effect in the Danish Virgin Islands, as well as within the Danish government and its colonial administration. Suddenly the blacks of nearby Tortola and the other British Virgin Islands were free, which presented a strange contrast with the continuing slavery in St. Thomas and St. John with which the British Virgins had such close historical interchange.

The abolition of slavery by Britain in 1833 prompted Governor-General Peter von Scholten to move immediately toward amelioration and gradual emancipation of slaves in the Danish colony. Largely from his efforts, a Royal

---

49. Westergaard, *The Danish West Indies*, pp. 252–253; Dookhan, *A History of the Virgin Islands*, p. 158.

decree of 1834 granted important concessions. Manumission was expressly permitted whereby slaves could purchase their freedom. The right of a slave to his plot of land was granted. Compulsory Sunday labor was prohibited. Public sale of slaves and the separation of slave children from their parents were forbidden. Pregnant women, furthermore, were exempted from hard labor.[50]

Fired by his ambition to prepare the slaves for freedom through education, von Scholten was convinced that the schools should be under Moravian direction, permission for which he obtained from Moravian authorities in Herrnhut, Germany, during his visit there in 1838. Also in 1838, a local committee he appointed recommended the erection of eight public schools to be paid for in part by planters and the remainder from public funds subscribed by the government. The Country School Ordinance of June 4, 1839 provided for free and compulsory education in the Danish Virgin Islands for the unfree as well as the free, and authorized the erection of eight schools in St. Croix, five in St. Thomas, and four in St. John. Instruction was to be in English under the direction of the Moravians.

Ruins of St. Croix sugar plantation

---

50. Williams, *From Columbus to Castro*, p. 302; Dookhan, *A History of the Virgin Islands*, p. 158.

A considerable number of planters objected to the new school plan. Not only did they regard the plan as "the first of a series of suggestions for the gradual extinction of slavery ... to the inevitable ruin of the Planter,"[51] but they considered the slave as essentially uneducable and unfitted for any other career. In a letter to King Christian VIII, von Scholten responded to these claims.

> we in fact *have* proof abundant that he is fitted with every sense and facility, which have raised the white Man to the elevated stand, which he now holds in the scale of creation; that the same thirst after knowledge, the same inventive genius is his, and that in no Case, we assert has it been observed, that placed in parallel circumstances of advantage for Education the Black Man has ever failed to keep pace with the white Man; but on the contrary we can say, that well known instances have occurred, in which he has surpassed *him*, who had been early taught to look on himself as superior to the *Negro Race*.[52]

Von Scholten was a determined man who had the King's support, and by January 1842, all eight schools in St. Croix were functioning.

Construction of public elementary schools in St. Thomas and St. John was to be much delayed. In his 1852 book on St. Thomas, Reverend John P. Knox complained:

> Good common schools are much needed at St. Thomas. None are at present sustained, either by government or the community. Our children would thus grow up in ignorance and vice, were it not for the little knowledge they obtain at the Sabbath school. Funds were once ordered by His Majesty to be appropriated for common schools in the islands. They were, however, unjustly employed in building expensive school-houses in Santa Cruz, and thus St. Thomas was deprived of its share.[53]

Beyond a few private schools, St. Thomas was to be without any educational facilities until public elementary schools were opened in 1878.[54] Von Scholten, however, was much more concerned with the imminent establishment of schools

---

51. Quoted in Hall, "Establishing a Public Elementary School System," p. 25.

52. *Ibid.*, p. 27.

53. Knox, *A Historical Account of St. Thomas*, p. 132.

54. Taylor, *Leaflets from the Danish West Indies* (1888), p. 35. "St. Thomas to-day stands almost alone in the West Indies as having no high school for the children of its taxpayers and respectable citizens. The consequences are sad to anticipate for those who are not rich enough to send their children to Europe." *Ibid.*, p. 4.

in St. Croix where plantation slavery exacted greater suffering and despair among the largest number of the "unfree"—as he called them—in the Virgin Islands.

Meanwhile, the Governor-General proposed another plan in 1840 under which slaves would purchase their freedom, but the planters refused to make the necessary payments to slaves by which they could purchase their freedom. Finally, a Royal decree of 1847 provided that all children thereafter born to slaves were to be free, but present slaves would be free only after twelve years, or in 1859.

The slaves of St. Croix were unwilling to wait twelve more years for their freedom. Led by an able young black man, known as Buddhoe, slaves in St. Croix secretly organized a revolution in July 1848. In Frederiksted, the houses of the police assistant, town bailiff, and a wealthy merchant were sacked. Most whites took refuge on vessels in the harbor. The slaves besieged the fort demanding immediate emancipation. When, finally, Governor-General von Scholten arrived cross-island from Christiansted, the assembled slaves demanded freedom in one hour or they would burn down the town. The Governor-General capitulated and read out his famous Proclamation of Emancipation as follows:

1.   All unfree in the Danish West India Islands are from to-day free.
2.   The estate negroes retain for three months from date the use of the houses and provision grounds of which they have hitherto been possessed.
3.   Labour is in future to be paid for by agreement, but allowance of food to cease.
4.   The maintenance of the old and infirm, who are not able to work, is, until further determined, to be furnished by the late owners.
The General Government of the Danish West India Islands,

St. Croix, the 3rd July, 1848.

P. v Scholten.[55]

Thus did the slaves of the Virgin Islands emancipate themselves. Plundering and burning by blacks continued for several days. Although no whites were killed, a number of blacks were killed and wounded, and eight were later executed. Meanwhile, the planters severely reproached von Scholten for "consecutive innovations" which sowed "the seeds of the tumultuous scenes which ensued and served as a pretext for emancipation."[56] Ill and despondent, von Scholten resigned and departed July 14 for Denmark. Although a Royal proclamation of September 22, 1848 confirmed his declaration of emancipation, he

---

55. *Ibid.*, p. 136. For Taylor's report of eyewitness accounts of these events, see, *Ibid.*, pp. 125–140.

56. Quoted in Campbell, *St. Thomas Negroes*, p. 21.

nevertheless was court-martialed and found guilty of dereliction of duty, but this decision was reversed unanimously by the Danish Supreme Court in 1852.

Over one hundred years after emancipation, William Hastie, then Governor of the Virgin Islands, wrote to this author his assessment of von Scholten, as follows:

> I believe the verdict of history will be that Governor Von Scholten seized the events of early July 1848 as a justification for the emancipation which he had wished to accomplish for a considerable period. He had been Governor for nearly twenty years and undoubtedly sided with the faction in Denmark, including the Queen, which had urged emancipation strongly. Von Scholten's arrest and conviction following the emancipation also strongly indicates that the course he followed was deliberate.[57]

Meanwhile, "General" Buddhoe was banished to Trinidad. His role in the history of the Virgin Islands has been assured, and a number of books feature him as a heroic figure. Today, portraits of Buddhoe hang in classrooms all over the Virgin Islands.[58]

Serfdom

In the years following emancipation, the planters sent numerous petitions to Denmark requesting compensation for the losses of property in the form of slaves, but unlike the British, who had granted adequate compensation for slave losses occasioned by emancipation in the British West Indies, Denmark refused to acknowledge the claims of the planters of the Virgin Islands until after 1853 when they received only 50 Danish West Indian dollars for each of their freed slaves.

Compounding the planters' frustrations was the fact that, although most blacks remained on the estates after emancipation, many refused to work.[59] Accordingly, within a month after emancipation, the local government on St.

---

57. Letter from William H. Hastie, Governor of the Virgin Islands of the United States, Charlotte Amalie, St. Thomas, to William W. Boyer, dated June 2, 1949. See Appendix for the full text.

58. See, *e.g.*, Pat Gill, *Buddhoe, The Man Who Shaped the History of St. Croix* (New York: Wentworth Press, 1976). In reference to this book, see, Jere Maupin, "Buddhoe Memorialized in New Book," *The Daily News* (St. Thomas, V.I.), July 2, 1977, p. 9.

59. Writing in 1852, Reverend Knox observed: "They feel deeply and justly the stain of slavery—subjection, dependence upon another's will, toiling for others; this has been the iron that has entered into their very soul; and it is not strange that they should consider freedom from such a condition the greatest good to be desired.... Another evil ... is the

Croix adopted regulations proposed by planters designed to force the blacks to continue their plantation labor on a yearly contract basis. These regulations were followed by a more elaborate and detailed law issued on January 26, 1849, having the imposing title: "Provisional Act to Regulate the Relations between the Proprietors of Landed Estates and Rural Population of Free Labourers."[60]

The 1849 act was interpreted by the blacks as an attempt to force them back into slavery. They had no bargaining power and no place to go. Some did manage to gain employment in the towns, and a number of workers migrated from St. Croix to St. Thomas, but the authorities soon put a stop to this by imposing an internal compulsory passport system between the islands.[61] The great majority of the newly-freed blacks were to remain unfree on the estates with no recourse open to them but to submit to the bondage imposed by the 1849 Labor Act.

The Labor Act of 1849 amended the previously discussed 1831 labor ordinance that forced many idle free-coloreds to become laborers. The new law institutionalized a system of serfdom based on contract labor, in place of slavery, some characteristics of which were to mark the legal relations between alien workers and their employers during the 1960s and 1970s in the Virgin Islands.

The law fixed the contract year from October to October, renewable each August. As during slavery, the work week was to consist of five days from sunrise to sunset, with Saturdays and Sundays free. Workers could work for extra wages on Saturdays or be required to work that day without wages as punishment for absences or idleness. Engagements made by heads of families were to include their children. Laborers were to be divided into three classes with wages of fifteen, ten, and five cents a day to be paid, respectively. From their earnings, twenty-five cents a week would be deducted for rations, should they choose to receive them. No laborer could refuse the work he might be ordered to do. To assure that a laborer remain in bondage to his former owner, the law placed him in a "no-win" predicament by providing:

> The laborer shall have given, or received, legal notice of removal from the estate where he serves, before any one can engage his services; otherwise the new contract to be void, and the party engaging in tampering with a laborer employed by others, will be dealt with according to law.

The contract was inviolable except by mutual agreement between the master and laborer, or by order of a magistrate. Many other provisions governed every

---

idea that labor is degrading.... [The black] connects work with slavery, for it was the exclusive province of the slave." Knox, *A Historical Account of St. Thomas*, pp. 127–128.

60. This Act is quoted in its entirety in *Ibid.*, pp. 248–255.
61. Dookhan, *A History of the Virgin Islands*, pp. 225–226.

detail of work, and punishment was liberally provided for violations. For example, parents would be fined for keeping their children from work. Estate owners or managers, moreover, could levy fines for trifles.

In commenting on this system Valdemar Hill, Sr. wrote in 1971:

> The name of the game was human exploitation, and Emancipation did not in any way alter the ulterior motives. The black people, who were "promoted" from slaves to "Danish subjects" remained a landless proletariat still dependent upon white colonists for economic survival. So ... the free blacks in the Danish West Indies were simply shunted from the status of chattels to the just as unbearable status of economic slaves.[62]

The black people of the Virgin Islands had found that liberty did not mean freedom. They found that their freedom struggle, far from being over, was just beginning. They found that changes in form, words, and labels did not mean change in substance.[63] Their bondage and penury continued. They had traveled a long and painful road of hopelessness—a road from slavery to serfdom.

---

62. Valdemar A. Hill, Sr., *Rise to Recognition, An Account of Virgin Islanders from Slavery to Self-Government* (St. Thomas: Printed by St. Thomas Graphics Inc., 1971), p. 47.

63. That laborers were still treated by local police much as they had been under slavery is illustrated by an incident of December 23, 1852 in St. Croix. A riot took place in Christiansted on the occasion of a militia raid on a house occupied by a woman who had assembled a group for the still forbidden "drum dancing," customary at Christmas time. The militia cut the skins of the drums and when they returned to the street they were met by a stone-throwing mob. An "over zealous" militia officer ordered his men to fire a volley which killed three persons and wounded seven. "The governor did not find it easy to convince the laborers that the act was unauthorized. The officer was severely punished and the militia corps was disbanded." De Booy and Faris, *The Virgin Islands, Our New Possessions*, pp. 194–195; and "Today in History," *Daily News*, December 23, 1977.

4

Purchase of a People

Throughout the history of the Danish West Indies, the white minority had held a position of dominance. The non-white population sought to emulate the life-styles of whites, and "raising the color," according to Albert Campbell, became an accepted method of improving status.[1] After emancipation, the central features of the transitional and complex society of the Danish Virgin Islands continued to be social stratification and status awareness.

Fieldwork was associated with blackness and was held in contempt by those with lighter skins, who usually had better jobs or worked less but earned more. It was difficult, therefore, to distinguish class prejudice from race prejudice. The idea that labor was degrading—that work was connected with slavery—was prevalent in the Virgin Islands after emancipation, an unfortunate legacy from the past. This linkage of color with class was commented upon by a local newspaper of St. Croix in 1882, as follows:

> From the time of slavery it was the habit when a fair-skinned slave was born and reared, to bring up the same as house-servant or tradesman. Among the owners themselves the saying was current, "Too light to work in the field;" the result of this peculiar notion has been that our field hands, up to this day, are almost exclusively black, that fieldwork is considered a disgrace, an imposition on the black race, and that parents consequently do all they can to withhold their children from this occupation. We do not believe that in the other West India islands the above circumstance is so peculiarly marked. Poor whites here would rather starve than work in the field, such occupation being considered beneath them.[2]

---

1. Campbell, *St. Thomas Negroes—A Study of Personality and Culture*, p. 24.
2. *Ibid.*, quoting *The St. Croix Avis*, July 19, 1882.

The White Minority

The whites of the Danish Virgin Islands had long comprised a peculiarly cosmopolitan group. On St. Thomas and St. John in 1765, the Dutch were the most numerous, but the English were to become predominant in the 19th century. The Danes were next and numbered about half the Dutch population. In descending order, then, were the French, Germans, English, and Irish.[3] It is likely that the Danes, who were chiefly officials and soldiers, never exceeded ten percent of the total population. On St. Croix, most of the white community was English, and many were Irish. During the second half of the eighteenth century, roughly half of the population of St. Thomas, and three-fourths of St. Croix, lived in rural areas. As plantation agriculture declined, the trend was toward urbanization on both islands.[4]

Highest on the social ladder were the Governor and his senior officials, followed by the planters and merchants. Individual members of the elite were themselves differentiated by the number of slaves and the amount of land owned, and the ostentatiousness of their life styles. Lowest in the white hierarchy were the lower officials, small-scale traders, soldiers, sailors, bookkeepers, and plantation overseers.

Only whites, of course, held government offices. Until 1754, the government was the Company itself. The Governor and his privy council were all-powerful, subject only to the Company directors in far away Copenhagen. In actual practice, however, planters from an early date were consulted in the selection of governors.

In 1703, the Company permitted the organization of a burgher council of six of the most prominent planters selected by the planters themselves, whose sole function was to consider disputes that the Governor was unable to settle. Efforts of the planters meanwhile to gain a measure of representative government were unsuccessful. After the cession of St. Croix, however, the Company in 1734 was granted a new charter under which all burgher council members were to be appointed by the Governor. The judicial function of the burgher council was replaced, moreover, with the council's right to confer with the Governor and the privy council whenever the burgher council had matters to propose concerning the common interest. The burgher council became, therefore, the main instrument by which the planters made known their grievances.[5]

---

3. Westergaard, *The Danish West Indies under Company Rule*, p. 247.

4. Dookhan, *A History of the Virgin Islands of the United States*, pp. 141–143.

5. Westergaard, *The Danish West Indies*, pp. 185, 215, 232. "In the Danish colonies all decisions respecting local government were made in Denmark. Local assemblies, known as

From the beginning of colonization, only the Lutheran Church (the official Danish state church) and the Dutch Reformed Church were permitted to hold public worship. The ministers of both churches were confirmed by the Danish King. Only after the Crown replaced Company rule in 1754 were Catholics, Jews, and Anglicans permitted to build places of worship, but the Catholics were at first forbidden to make any converts of whites.[6] As discussed previously, the various Protestant denominations—except for the ill-fated Lutheran missionaries—served the white minority rather than the black majority, who were served primarily only by the Catholics and Moravians. Although a measure of religious liberty was enjoyed by whites, "no utterances against the authorities were allowed publication."[7]

The changes of government instituted under the Company's new charter in 1734 were to remain intact until 1852 with only minor changes effected under Crown rule after 1754, such as changes in the system of taxation and some improvements in the judicial system.

In 1852, a description of the government of the Islands was written by Reverend Knox. He reported that the Governor still maintained supreme control over civil and military affairs, and supervised all proceedings. Occasionally, the Governor would visit St. Thomas and St. John (the seat of government since 1755 being at Christiansted, in St. Croix), but these islands were mostly under the authority of the Commandant and his council. Their government officials consisted of a secretary, a treasurer, a bookkeeper, judges and the police.[8] According to Knox, the white islanders still had little enjoyment of civil rights. It was true they had the right to appeal in certain instances, and the right to gain redress for their grievances in the courts. They also had the right of religious belief, but public worship was still restricted on St. Thomas and St. John to the Lutheran and Dutch Reform Churches, and "trial by jury is still unknown under the government of Denmark." Referring to the press on St. Thomas, Knox wrote: "the 'St. Thomas Times' (a small sheet) is the only paper published in the island. Until recently it was under a severe censorship." Furthermore, he related, there were no places of amusement in St. Thomas, and no "common schools" were sustained, either by the government or the com-

---

Burger Councils, did exist in both St. Thomas and St. Croix, but their role was advisory and administrative, and subordinate to the Governor-General. For the most part the islanders suffered silently under authoritarian rule." Tyson, *Powder, Profits & Privateers*, p. 14.

6. Dookhan, *A History of the Virgin Islands*, p. 184.
7. Westergaard, *The Danish West Indies*, p. 248.
8. Knox, *A Historical Account of St. Thomas*, pp. 166–167.

munity.[9] There were only five physicians on St. Thomas for a population in 1850 of 13,666, and they were generally employed by the year on estates by private families.[10]

Despite the fact that field work was indelibly stamped with the onerous conditions of slavery, the 1849 Labor Law was effective in virtually forcing most former slaves to continue working on the plantations. Now that they were emancipated from slavery, it remained for the white community to assure continuing white political dominance. Political repression must match economic repression. This was to be done by restricting the franchise exclusively to whites.

Restricting the Franchise

The Colonial Law of 1852, proclaimed by the King, was to be the instrument to politically repress the colored population of the Virgin Islands. The Law created a Colonial Council "invested with deliberative co-operation in the exercise of the legislative power." This phrasing meant that the Council would have no law-making power, but merely be advisory by making "representations" to the Governor about "any alterations in the laws" or about "the manner in which the laws are administered."

The Council was to consist of sixteen elected members, including eight from St. Croix, six from St. Thomas, two from St. John, and in addition, four members appointed by the King. Council meetings were to be held in secret. The key provision concerning the franchise was the following:

> The elective franchise is the right of every male of unblemished character, who is a native, or has resided 5 years in the Islands, is above 25 years of age, is in uncontrolled possession of his estate, and either has a yearly income of 500 Westindia dollars, or contributes to the States' Chest an amount of at least 5 Westindia dollars in ground and building tax. He must besides have resided one year in the elective district at the time the election takes place.[11]

---

9. *Ibid.*, pp. 170–178.

10. *Ibid.*, p. 202.

11. The initial draft of the Colonial Law of 1852 was made by the Governor and appears in Knox, *A Historical Account of St. Thomas*, pp. 263–268. The Law as proclaimed appears in James A. Bough and Roy C. Macridis, eds., *Virgin Islands, America's Outpost— The Evolution of Self Government* (Wakefield, Mass.: Walter F. Williams Publishing Co., 1970), pp. 11–14; all references herein to the 1852 Law are to this volume.

No secret ballot was provided; one had to declare openly those for whom one was voting, and their names were then registered in the protocol along side the names of the voters.[12]

The 1852 Colonial Law did not work well. All sessions of the Colonial Council were to be held in St. Croix, but the members from St. Thomas refused to voyage to St. Croix with the result that the Council did not even meet from 1856 to 1859. This early rift between the two islands, deriving principally from the differences in their economies, was to persist to the present day. St. Thomas was predominantly commercial in its economy, and its representatives wanted to create their own council to look after their commercial interests. St. Croix, on the other hand, was predominantly agricultural, and was the more populous of the two. This rivalry was not helped by the fact that at the time the plantation economy of St. Croix was declining while the commerce of St. Thomas was more prosperous. St. Thomians, moreover, resented the fact that St. Thomas' and St. John's annual budget surpluses were used to erase or reduce the annual deficits incurred by St. Croix.[13]

Accordingly, the Colonial Law of 1863 sought to remedy the shortcomings of its predecessor. It created two municipalities, each with its own Colonial Council, one for St. Croix, and the other for St. Thomas and St. John. The Council for St. Croix was to consist of thirteen elected and five appointed members, whereas the Council for St. Thomas and St. John was to consist of eleven elected members plus four appointed. Unlike the Colonial Council created by the 1852 Law, which was advisory only, the Colonial Councils of the two municipalities were given power to pass local ordinances which, if sanctioned by the King, were to be promulgated by the Governor. Also included in the 1863 Law was a bill of rights.

The franchise provision of the 1863 Law was even more restrictive than that of the 1852 Law. Voting rights were still restricted to "every man of unblemished character" who was at least 25 years of age, and lived at least five years in the Virgin Islands. While he had to have earned an annual income of at least $500 Danish West Indian (D.W.I.) or paid at least $5 D.W.I. property tax under the 1852 Law, he now had to have a minimum yearly income of $500 D.W.I. or owned property producing a yearly income of at least $75 D.W.I. in St. Croix and St. John, or $150 D.W.I. in St. Thomas. Under the 1852 Law, further-

---

12. Bough and Macridis, eds., *Virgin Islands*, p. 13. The Islands, in addition, continued to have their respective burgher councils, which were required by the Colonial Law of 1852 to maintain the lists of all eligible voters. *Ibid.*, p. 12.

13. Dookhan, *A History of the Virgin Islands*, pp. 208–209.

more, the voter should have lived at least one year in his electoral district; this was increased to two years residence in his municipality by the 1863 Law.

With only slight modification, the 1863 Colonial Law was to remain in effect until 1936, for almost two decades after the Islands came under American administration. The 1863 division of the Virgin Islands into two municipalities, moreover, each with its own treasury and legislature, was to remain in effect until 1954.

Between 1863 and 1936, the colonial governments of the Virgin Islands were marked by an extreme apathy of the voters. This pattern was established at the outset. In St. Thomas, for example, of a population of approximately 13,000, only 88 persons voted in 1865, and in 1868 of approximately 650 qualified voters only 268 were registered of whom only 35 actually voted. Isaac Dookhan attributed this continuing apathy to the belief among Virgin Islanders in the eventual take-over of the Islands by the United States.[14]

The franchise was carefully restricted to those males of "unblemished character," which meant those who held positions of economic consequence, namely white planters and merchants, not coloreds and blacks who comprised the mass of the people of the Virgin Islands. It is quite evident, therefore, that the post-emancipation political system continued to foster the rigid social stratification and status differentiation carried over from the days of slavery.

The Colonial Law of 1906, the last under the Danes, was a virtual re-enactment of the 1863 Law with only minor modifications. Voting by secret ballot was introduced for the first time. A modest bill of rights was included, providing for freedom of religion (although the Danish Lutheran Church was to receive public funds), freedom of assembly and association, freedom of the press, and the right to instruction in the public schools.

The 1906 Law extended the franchise by lowering the financial qualifications of voters, but only slightly. With regard to property qualifications to vote, for those who had property on St. Croix and St. John, the minimum yearly income therefrom was reduced from $75 D.W.I. to $60 D.W.I., and on St. Thomas the minimum was reduced from $150 D.W.I. to $140 D.W.I. Or, if one chose to qualify by his total annual income, the minimum therefor was reduced from $500 D.W.I. to $300 D.W.I. All other qualifications remained unchanged, however, and the overall effect was the continuance of restricting the franchise to the economically privileged.[15]

---

14. *Ibid.*, pp. 213, 216; see, also, Campbell, *St. Thomas Negroes*, p. 25.

15. The Colonial Law (No. 124-1906) for the Danish West India Islands is reproduced in Bough and Macridis, eds., *Virgin Islands*, pp. 15–29, and in W. Evans, *The Virgin Islands, A General Report by the Governor* (Washington: Navy Department, 1928), pp. 36–45.

Revolt of the Laborers

The consequences of the Labor Law of 1849 did not produce an adequate labor force for the needs of the St. Croix estates. Many of the former slaves drifted away from the estates over time and took up jobs in the towns and St. Thomas. Accordingly, the planters sought to import laborers to supplement the work of their former slaves, and a special tax was levied to support an immigration fund for this purpose. The labor shortage became acute in 1861 when extraordinarily favorable weather presaged unprecedented bountiful cane crops. The planters urged the Danish Government to enter forthwith into an agreement with the British Government to import labor from India as had been done in the French West Indies in 1860. Thus began one of the most sordid episodes in St. Croix's history, illuminating for revealing the debasing labor conditions of St. Croix and the maleficence of its planters.

For its part, the British Government was influenced by testimony of the Bishop of Antigua, dated March 3, 1861, which spoke favorably of the treatment of St. Croix's laborers:

> ... perhaps, nowhere are labourers so comfortably domiciled as in the Danish Island of St. Croix; there the labourer is invariably under annual contract, his dwelling being provided for him on the Estate. The Labourer's houses are under the inspection of the government which is equally careful to provide for them medical attendance in sickness, education for the children, and the asylums for the aged and infirm ... there is no denying that a parental care is exercised by the government over the labouring class whose rights are jealously guarded at any rate; they nowhere present to the eye of the stranger such a picture of domestic comfort and healthiness as in that picturesque little island.[16]

Unfortunately, as the British Consul's despatches were later to prove, the Bishop's picture of St. Croix was fantasy.

After complex negotiations between the Copenhagen and London governments, with subsidiary roles played by authorities in St. Croix and India, 321 people were hastily recruited, brought to Calcutta, sent off by steamship on February 29, 1863, which arrived in St. Croix June 15, 1863, five having died during the crossing. Upon arrival, they were allotted to planters on a quota basis.

---

16. Quoted in K. K. Sircar, "Emigration of Indian Indenture Labour to the Danish West Indian Island of St. Croix, 1863–68," *The Scandinavian Economic History Review*, 19 (1971): 137–138.

The despatches of the British Consul in St. Croix told of widespread cheating on the part of planters. The Indian "coolies" were regularly overcharged for food rations, and were supplied less than stipulated in the contract. Medical attention, to be provided free, was denied. Housing facilities were "totally inadequate," with as many as six Indians in one room and men and women lodged indiscriminately. In no case were penalties for breach of the contract or law imposed on the planters. The result was a higher incidence of disease and mortality and a much lower birth rate among the Indians than for the general population. Disobedience and minor offenses by Indians evoked harsh punishment from the police, and on several estates the Indians often received cruel and brutal treatment.

At the end of the five-year contract period in 1868, of 304 surviving adults, 233 refused reindenture at a $40 bonus and were sent back to Calcutta, where the Danish Government defaulted on returning their savings and paying them severance pay. The Government of Bengal issued a statement that "no emigration to any Danish colony should in future be permitted."[17] This ended the recruitment of Indian labor for St. Croix.

Since 1733, when the Danes acquired St. Croix, the outward tranquility of the Virgin Islands has been shattered from time to time by social unrest. Almost always the trouble has started in the western part of St. Croix in and around Frederiksted. This has been true from 1733 to the present. It was true in 1759, 1848, and 1878. If one puts a cauldron of water on a low simmering fire, and stops all outlets, sooner or later the cauldron will burst. Apparently this is what happened in Frederiksted on October 1, 1878.

The 1878 outbreak was a great surprise to everyone. The setting did not appear ripe for disorder. Indeed, so peaceful had life on St. Croix seemed that in 1877 the Colonial Council of St. Croix as an economy measure abolished all military forces outside of Christiansted, leaving only sixty soldiers in Christiansted with a few police to look after the rest of the Island.

The Danish Government, moreover, had constructed the Central Factory that was supposed to revolutionize the processing of sugar from cane. The Factory had just recently been opened for business in 1878 and employed laborers at thirty to thirty-five cents a day. This was much more than the ten cents a day average wage of plantation workers. Accordingly, many laborers looked forward to contract day, October 1, 1878, for the expiration of their labor contracts in anticipation of either higher wages from the planters or employment

---

17. *Ibid.*, p. 144. As many as 1,700 immigrant laborers had arrived by 1864 from Barbados and St. Eustatius alone. Dookhan, *A History of the Virgin Islands*, p. 226.

at the Factory. It was customary for plantation laborers to congregate in the towns on contract day to negotiate their next year's service, and many were in Frederiksted that fateful day.[18]

The contentment that seemed to pervade St. Croix, however, was misleading. The colonial master class of St. Croix, unmindful of the winds of change, still shuffled along under the old class legislation—the Labor Act of 1849 and the Colonial Law of 1863. One contemporary writer predicted in 1875 "eventual resistance," as one of the "sure consequences" of this "class legislation," as follows:

> Forced labour, under whatever name disguised, apprenticeship or other, always odious, becomes doubly so, when applied to a special caste or race of men. Scarcely less odious or less foolish, are the laws by which the terms and duration of agreement between workmen and their employers are fixed and limited beforehand; above all where differences of blood and colour tend inevitably to render irritating the very semblance of constraint, and exaggerate every difficulty of class and position. And hence the injudicious interference of artificial regulations, however seemingly well intentioned and, to use a cant phrase, "paternal," like those yet existing, the remnants of a best forgotten past in some West Indian Colonies—the Danish, for example, can only, as the result has already proved in those same Danish Islands, blight instead of foster, stunt, not promote development, besides giving rise to deep ill-feeling, mistrust, and eventual resistance; the sure consequences of class legislation, whatever its pretext.[19]

Police, judges, and prison officials, furthermore, acted in collusion to "intimidate" the workers through various ordinances against begging, vagrancy, and trespassing. Arbitrary imprisonment could be imposed simply on complaint of an employer, and life imprisonment was possible upon successive convictions for stealing cane. Gordon Lewis, in his pungent 1972 book, described this repressive atmosphere as follows:

> The mass of statutory legislation ... that sought to control public behavior—from conspiracy and disobedience to masters to whistling

---

18. For a detailed description of the atmosphere preceding, and events during, the "Laborers' Riot" of 1878, see, Taylor, *Leaflets from the Danish West Indies*, pp. 147–166; Dookhan, *A History of the Virgin Islands*, pp. 227–231; and Irene Armstrong, *Robert Skeoch: Cruzan Planter* (Christiansted, St. Croix: Armstrong, 1971), pp. 22–36.

19. Quoted from the *Quarterly Review*, July, 1875, in Taylor, *Leaflets from the Danish West Indies*, p. 148.

and loud singing on the streets, not to mention the innumerable police regulations for the supervision of weddings, funerals, and concerts—suggests the continuing existence of a sort of social civil war between a resentful populace and a strait-laced alien bureaucracy.[20]

The Labor Act of 1849, that continued those conditions of slavery most debasing of human dignity—servility and degradation, was the prime reason for the 1878 revolt. Among complaints voiced by laborers immediately before the revolt, according to a contemporary observer, were the following:

> Firstly, the low rate of wages given to the estate labourers in comparison to the larger amount given to those of the Central Factory, viz., ten cents against thirty-five cents. Secondly, the annual contract, which they pronounced to be a slavery, inasmuch as if the slightest mistake were made in the date of giving notice for a termination of the contract, they were compelled to remain on that estate for another year contrary to their will. Thirdly, the power given by law to a manager to fine for certain offences, and their frequent abuse of that prerogative, and lastly the difficulties thrown in the way of labourers leaving the island by the police authorities, such as compelling them to exhibit what money they had when they wanted a passport.[21]

An apparently joyful crowd of laborers had assembled in Frederiksted on contract day, October 1, 1878, when suddenly their mood turned to anger. A minor disorder evoked a response by police, which they interpreted to be an act of police brutality—an oft-made allegation in the subsequent history of St. Croix. The course of events moved swiftly. The crowd besieged the fort, where they were held off by the few police on hand. Then they turned to burning and pillaging the shops and houses of the town, while the white residents took refuge in local churches and on board a ship in the harbor.

Soldiers arrived from Christiansted the next morning and dispersed the rioters to the countryside where they proceeded to burn and ravage plantation houses and cane fields. Despite the appearance of warships from Britain, France and the United States—summoned from the area by their respective consuls in St. Croix—disorders continued for several days. It was a spontaneous and disorganized rebellion, with independent groups, each engaged in their own

---

20. Lewis, *The Virgin Islands*, p. 34.
21. Taylor, *Leaflets from the Danish West Indies*, p. 154.

forays under a number of separate leaders, one of whom was Mary Thomas, otherwise historically touted as "Queen Mary."

Much of Frederiksted was laid waste; 53 plantations suffered losses, and a total of 879 acres were burned. Only three whites were killed, as compared with 74 blacks. Not included were 12 laborers who were executed by shooting, as distinguished from death on the wheel, by burning, or by gibbeting of the previous century. In addition, 403 prisoners were taken of whom, after a trial of nearly eighteen months, 67 were sentenced to imprisonment. According to Isaac Dookhan:

> The trial revealed active participation of the newly arrived immigrants from the other West Indian islands. Of the so-called leaders, two were from Barbados, and one each from St. Eustatius, Antigua, St. Kitts and Jamaica. Among the other participants imprisoned, eleven were from Barbados, nine from Antigua and four from other islands.[22]

From this time onward, many crimes and disorders in the Virgin Islands would be attributed, rightly or wrongly, to alien laborers — "down islanders" or "off-islanders" — from other Caribbean islands.

Economic Decline

The Labor Act of 1849 came to an end on October 1, 1879. Thirty years of serfdom had ended. New ordinances were adopted to perpetuate the old system, but now that labor contracts could be negotiated individually for various terms at will, instead of on a yearly basis for all, laborers gained a greater measure of freedom and mobility. Accordingly, many emigrated to other Caribbean islands in search of better employment opportunities. Indeed, emigration became the most persistent cause of population decrease in the Virgin Islands, from a total population of 33,763 in 1880 to 26,051 in 1917.[23]

There was no alteration in the political system, meanwhile, to afford any opportunity for the overwhelming majority of the people to participate in the political system. The franchise remained reserved exclusively for the economically privileged. This was not the only means employed by the elite, however, to assure continued repression of the majority class. By keeping the benefits of

---

22. Dookhan, *A History of the Virgin Islands*, p. 231.
23. *Ibid.*, pp. 232, 237.

education beyond their reach, the majority would remain economically and socially subservient and dependent. Thus, Leon Bramson has observed about St. Croix:

> The educational system which emerged under Danish rule appears to have been very well suited to maintaining the *status quo* under plantation slavery and its aftermath, a kind of serfdom, while at the same time permitting the rise of a very small group among the mulatto elite who were facilitated in their efforts to occupy positions of authority and responsibility in both commercial and professional life....
>
> But for the ordinary resident of the island, the black countryman rather than the mulatto townsman, the Danish educational effort appears to have been dominated by an unwillingness to take their colonial responsibilities after emancipation very seriously.[24]

One could argue with Bramson that the Danes did take their colonial responsibilities seriously, through their minimal educational effort, if one defines the essence of colonialism as being the economic and political exploitation of a subject people for the benefit of a ruling elite.

Despite Governor von Scholten's efforts to introduce a system of free, compulsory, and universal public instruction in the Virgin Islands during the 1840s, the only education available to the lower classes was provided by the little church schools run by the Moravian brothers. Not until 1878 were "communal" schools opened on St. Thomas. No secondary schools were available under Danish rule. The children of the economically privileged were commonly sent to private schools for primary education and to Europe or elsewhere for post-primary education, practices that are still common among the elite of the Virgin Islands. The school report of 1899 for St. Thomas showed over 90 percent attendance with 556 children in the public schools and 655 in private schools, causing Albert Campbell to remark:

> While there was no definite segregation on the basis of color, the private schools tended to be made up of white and light-skinned chil-

---

24. Leon Bramson, "Society and Education in St. Croix: The Danish Period," unpublished paper presented at the American Sociological Association Annual Meeting, August 1975, San Francisco, pp. 116–118, as quoted in Margaret Alison Gibson, *Ethnicity and Schooling: A Caribbean Case Study* (unpublished Ph.D. dissertation, University of Pittsburgh, 1976), p. 108.

dren. The dark-skinned parents were found for the most part among the economically underprivileged, and their children necessarily went to the communal schools.[25]

The educational system, therefore, reinforced political and social class distinctions based on distinctions in pigmentation and property.

Because English was the dominant language in the Virgin Islands, from 1850 onwards the medium of instruction in the schools was also English. Most of the trade of the Islands for a long time had been with English-speaking peoples. The English were predominant in St. Croix. Finally, the propinquity of the British Virgin Islands to St. Thomas and St. John also helped explain the pervading influence of the English language in the Danish-ruled islands.

The Royal Danish Commission, appointed in 1902 to investigate conditions in the Islands, recommended more education and better health facilities, "but nothing was done to improve the education and public health standards of the black inhabitants."[26]

Expansion of educational facilities and opportunities in the Virgin Islands did not accompany any corresponding expansion of the economy. Unlike the experience in other developing polities, improved and expanded education in the Islands was not a springboard for economic development, perhaps because educational progress was too little and too late to stimulate development. The Virgin Islands was a regressing rather than a developing polity. The decline of its economy was already well under way, a trend that could neither be reversed nor arrested by educational development. Mass education did have the effect, however, of producing in due course a literate and articulate populace ever more impatient for opportunities for self-fulfillment, a decent standard of living, and political and social equality.

Regardless of various attempts to boost the economy, nothing seemed to work. The Central Factory on St. Croix yielded only six pounds of sugar for

---

25. Campbell, *St. Thomas Negroes*, p. 26.

26. Hill, *Rise to Recognition*, p. 55. Sister Caroline Jensen, a Danish nurse who served in St. Croix from 1909 to 1919, found on her arrival an infant mortality rate of 70 percent and the prevalence of leprosy. However, three leprosy hospitals were built by the Odd Fellows of Denmark in St. Croix. But the worst thing for the patients was that they were committed to the hospital. The whole area was enclosed by a barbed-wire fence, and if a patient once had been committed to the hospital, he could never come out again.... This was a great human tragedy." Eva Eawaetz, translator, *Sister Caroline About Her Work in St. Croix* (multilithed; Christiansted, St. Croix: Public Library, 1975).

Natives coaling steamers, St. Thomas, 19th Century

every hundred pounds of cane, by use of an expensive process, far below economically needed levels. It never produced a return to the shareholders, who voted to dissolve the company in 1887.[27]

The colonial government initiated the "parcelling-out" system in 1883, especially on St. Croix, by which plantations were subdivided for sale on generous terms to laborers. Although sugar cane production as a result increased for a time, drought, soil exhaustion, absentee landlordism, declining sugar prices, and other conditions combined to contribute to the general decline of plantation agriculture in the Virgin Islands.[28]

Similarly, various other efforts met with disappointing results, such as establishment in St. Croix of a Botanical Experiment Station in 1895, the Danish Plantation Company in 1903, the Bethlehem Central Factory in 1904, and a Department of Agriculture and an Agricultural Experiment Station in 1910. Important development projects on St. Thomas, directed to improvement of trade and commerce, included establishment of the National Bank of the Danish West Indies in 1904, a St. Thomas harbor authority in 1904, and the Danish West India Company in 1912. Whatever success these projects enjoyed was inadequate to thwart continuing economic decline. The economy was even

---

27. Taylor, *Leaflets from the Danish West Indies*, p. 174.
28. Dookhan, *A History of the Virgin Islands*, pp. 233–234.

more adversely affected by World War I, which occasioned reduced shipping and commerce together with increased inflation and unemployment.[29]

Had the Virgin Islands comprised profitable possessions for Denmark, then the Danes might not have sold them to the Americans. Instead, the declining economy—involving increasing expenditures, declining revenues, rising indebtedness, and recurrent budgetary deficits—caused the Virgin Islands to become a liability to Denmark. Accordingly, the very purpose of colonialism, namely, economic gain for the colonizing power, no longer existed for Denmark.

The people of the Virgin Islands, meanwhile, continued to be distressed. Part of the general economic malaise was the continuation of labor unrest in the Virgin Islands, an ominous development for planters, merchants, and Danish rulers, alike.

In 1915, first-class agricultural workers earned a maximum of 20 cents per nine-hour clay, a condition that moved a fiery young black man of St. Croix, David Hamilton Jackson, to give up his ambition of becoming a Moravian missionary and, instead, to dedicate his life to arousing the workers of the Vir-

In the canefields, circa 1905

---

29. See, *e.g.*, Luther Evans, *The Virgin Islands from Naval Base to New Deal*, pp. 29–31; and Dookhan, *A History of the Virgin Islands*, pp. 235–237.

gin Islands to improve their lives. His followers raised funds to send him to Copenhagen in 1915 where, at the age of 31, he was well received and won from the Crown a Royal decree granting freedom of the press. He returned and established the first free newspaper of the Virgin Islands, *The Herald*, in which were recited all the wrongs suffered by the black majority, including police brutality, frequent abuses of the work contract system, and the repression of the authoritarian political system. "This newspaper became the voice of the oppressed and the laboring class."[30]

A short time later, together with Ralph Bough, he organized the first labor union in the Virgin Islands. In January 1916, Jackson called a general strike, numbering about 10,000 plantation workers of St. Croix. The planters retaliated with a lockout and moved their families to Frederiksted and Christiansted where, as in 1878, they again took refuge in the churches. The Danes landed marines from a Danish cruiser and machine guns and cannons were placed to guard the approaches to government buildings. Martial law was declared and the sale of liquor stopped.[31]

The strike was successful, with wages of first-class workers increased to 30 to 35 cents a day. Not only were laborers "entitled to receive any visitor to their houses," according to the agreement, but their employers were enjoined "not to use any offensive language against the labourers or their institutions."[32]

Following Jackson's example, about 2,700 coal carriers—mostly black women—were organized in 1916 into the St. Thomas Labor Union by George A. Moorhead. The union staged a successful strike for higher wages in October 1916, compelling the Danish West India Company to capitulate. Thereafter, Jackson turned his attention to marshalling popular support for the transfer of the Islands from Denmark to the United States, and headed a local delegation to Copenhagen for that purpose. Jackson's reasons for favoring transfer were, according to one of his followers, that "he foresaw greater opportunity for all the people, more and higher free schooling, and a more flourishing economy in which islanders could be shareholders."[33]

---

30. Hill, *Rise to Recognition*, p. 62. The St. Croix Labor Union, originally organized by Jackson, still exists; *Ibid.*, p. 63. "Liberty Day," November 1st, is anually celebrated in the Virgin Islands in observance of freedom of the press. Known in local history as "Black Moses," Jackson was born in Christiansted on September 28, 1884, served as judge of the police court of Christiansted from 1931 to 1941, and died on May 30, 1946.

31. *The New York Times*, February 23, 1916, p. 16, col. 2.

32. Hill, *Rise to Recognition*, p. 63.

33. G. James Fleming, "The Hamilton Jackson I Remember." *Daily News* (St. Thomas), October 29, 1975, p. 24.

Worker's family in St. Croix, circa 1910

Treaty of 1867

Negotiations between the United States and Denmark concerning purchase of the Virgin Islands commenced during the American Civil War and continued intermittently over half a century. During the Civil War, the British government was decidedly hostile to the government in Washington, while Denmark was more friendly than almost any other European country. It granted many favors to the United States Navy at St. Thomas. But Denmark was involved at the time in a severe conflict with Austria and Prussia over the duchies of Schleswig and Holstein, making it vulnerable to the acquisitive designs of a number of European powers.

As early as October, 1863, Secretary of State Seward had been warned by one of his consuls in Denmark that Great Britain might covet the Virgin Islands. In July 1864, another consul in Denmark, George P. Hansen, sent Seward a dispatch about "a rumor" that Austria might take the Islands as repayment for her expenses of the Danish war, and ended with this admonition:

> The West India Islands, in the possession of Denmark, are of not much danger to us, but it seems to me we cannot very well afford to let a powerful European nation get possession of them. If they ever change ownership, the ownership should be in the U. States.[34]

---

34. Quoted in Halvdab Koht, "The Origin of Seward's Plan to Purchase the Danish West Indies," *The American Historical Review*, 50 (July 1945): 765. During the final negotiations in 1864 for the conclusion of peace between Denmark and the German powers, the Danish King instructed the Danish representatives "to use their utmost efforts to rescue for Den-

The Civil War demonstrated to the United States the danger of having an unprotected Atlantic coastline and the fact that all the important naval powers except the United States had possessions in the Caribbean. Convinced of the necessity of securing a naval station in the Caribbean, President Lincoln and Secretary Seward summoned Vice-Admiral Porter for consultation. According to the account of this meeting written by Olive Risley Seward, an adopted daughter of Secretary Seward, Admiral Porter stated the following:

> St. Thomas lies right in the track of all vessels from Europe, Brazil, the East Indies, and the Pacific Ocean, bound to the West Indian Islands or to the United States. It is the point where all vessels touch for supplies when needed, coming from any of the above stations. It is a central point from which any or all of the West Indian Islands can he assailed, while it is impervious to attack from landing parties, and can be fortified to any extent. The bay on which lies the town of St. Thomas is almost circular, the entrance being by a neck guarded by two heavy forts, which can be so strengthened and protected that no foreign power can ever hope to take it. St. Thomas is a small Gibraltar of itself, and could not be attacked by a naval force. There would be no possibility of landing troops there, as the island is surrounded by reefs and breakers, and every point near which a vessel or boat could approach is a natural fortification, and only requires guns with little labor expended on fortified works. There is no harbor in the West Indies better fitted than St. Thomas for a naval station. Its harbor and that of St. John, and the harbor formed by the Water Island, would contain all the vessels of the largest navy in the world, where they would be protected at all times from bad weather, and be secure against an enemy. In fine, St. Thomas is the keystone to the arch of the West Indies. It commands them all. It is of more importance to us than to any other nation.[35]

In January 1865, Secretary Seward initiated secret negotiations to acquire the Islands through Denmark's ambassador in Washington. Denmark sought postponement to give it time to consider reactions of other Western powers. Meanwhile, President Lincoln's assassination and the wounding of Seward himself, together with certain European developments, caused delay of negotiations until 1867.

---

mark the Danish-speaking districts of Slesvig, and they were authorized, if no other arguments could prevail, to suggest the Danish West Indies as a compensation." *Ibid.*, pp. 766–767.

35. Olive Risley Seward, "A Diplomatic Episode," *Scribner's Magazine* 2 (November 1887): 586–587.

The resumed negotiations concerned cession of St. Thomas and St. John only. France was cool to inclusion of St. Croix, and under the treaty by which France sold St. Croix to Denmark in 1733 its permission for cession was necessary. Seward's main interest, moreover, was in the harbor of St. Thomas.

The negotiations became almost deadlocked on an "only point of difference," namely Denmark's insistence that any final agreement be preceded by a plebiscite in the Islands "in order that the inhabitants could signify their approval or disapproval of the cession," and Seward's equally obdurate opposition to a referendum.[36]

The custom was well established in Europe, having originated with Bonaparte, to allow the people affected to express a preference in questions of this sort. Under the Treaty of Prague, moreover, the people of North Schleswig at that moment were preparing to vote whether to return to Danish allegiance, a subject of keen interest in Denmark.

> It became consequently a question of national dignity and political import that the king should allow an equally frank expression of his West Indian subjects before consenting to an irrevocable disposition of their fealty.[37]

It is not clear just why Seward was so strongly opposed to a vote by Virgin Islanders. It is known that he felt that a plebiscite was "not important," that it would "prove inconvenient and unnecessary," and that he wished "to avoid jealous intrigues." But these were hardly reasons sufficient to jeopardize negotiations. In the end, Seward finally agreed to the stipulation by sending a last cablegram: "Concede popular vote."[38]

The Treaty of 1867 provided: Danish cession of St. Thomas and St. John for $7.5 million; an opportunity for "the people ... of freely expressing their wishes in regard to this cession"; protection of their liberty, religion, property, and private rights; and their choice of citizenship within two years between retention of Danish allegiance or acquisition of United States citizenship, with those not expressing a preference thereafter "considered to have elected to become citizens of the United States."[39]

The vote in St. Thomas and St. John was taken on January 9 and 10, 1868, resulting in a vote of 1,244 in favor and 22 against the Treaty. If the com-

---

36. Charles C. Tansill, *The Purchase of the Danish West Indies* (Baltimore: The Johns Hopkins Press, 1932), pp. 50–71.

37. Seward, "A Diplomatic Episode," p. 590.

38. Tansill, *The Purchase*, pp. 52, 61n., 71.

39. For the text of the Treaty of 1867, see Tansill, *The Purchase*, Appendix A, pp. 517–520.

bined population of the two islands in 1868 is regarded as that reported in the 1870 census, namely 15,061, then less than 12 percent of "the people" voted.[40]

The Treaty was promptly ratified by the Danish Rigsdag, but because of the animosities and political passions surrounding the impeachment of President Johnson, the United States Senate failed to ratify the Treaty, a fact that impugned the good faith of the United States and caused the downfall of Denmark's Liberal government.

Treaty of 1902

The last third of the 19th Century was filled with intermittent rumors and denials of Denmark's desire to sell the Virgin Islands to the United States or to

Group of natives, St. Thomas, between 1890 and 1901

---

40. Dookhan, *A History of the Virgin Islands*, p. 253. Although only 12 percent of the population voted, Dookhan nevertheless concluded: "As far as the islanders were concerned, the transfer was settled." *Ibid.*

a European power, most persistently to Germany. The fate of the Islands continued to be connected with the vexing Schleswig-Holstein question, whereby Denmark clung to the hope of trading the Islands to Germany for North Schleswig in return, a prospect concerning which "the great majority" of Virgin Islanders were reported to be "bitterly opposed."[41] At various times, even Britain and France were rumored to be in the market for the Islands. Indeed, in defiance of America's Monroe Doctrine, France had acquired in 1877 the Caribbean island of St. Bartholomew from Sweden.[42]

There were other reasons why the government of Denmark was anxious to sell the Virgin Islands. The laborers' revolt of 1878 on St. Croix had required the Danish Government to increase expenditures considerably to support a strengthened garrison on that island. The Islands incurred deficits "from the time of the abolishment of slavery," amounting by the end of the century to a total indebtedness of nearly $3 million.[43]

During 1900, the United States and Denmark again engaged in secret negotiations marked, according to a report leaked to the press, by disagreement over the insistence by Denmark that "the inhabitants of the islands, after the sale, shall have full rights as American burghers, a concession which Denmark has hitherto not succeeded in inducing America to grant." This revelation caused *The New York Times* to editorialize "that at least their white inhabitants could be made good Americans," a clear inference that the majority of Virgin Islanders would not qualify to become "American burghers."[44]

Virgin Islanders were reported to be bitterly divided over transfer, with antagonists raising racial issues. For example, *The St. Croix Avis*—forgetful of the bloody history of the Islands—mythicized:

> We have all lived and worked together in the Danish Islands in a peaceful and amicable manner. Why risk the continuance of that harmony? The race question has never been a burning question in these islands. Why now import and scatter here the red-hot embers from those lands where it is a burning question?

In reference to this quote, *The New York Times* accused opponents of the sale of dangerously exciting the "black islanders" about "every lynching story they could get from the United States, the desire being to create in the minds of

---

41. Tansill, *The Purchase*, pp. 154–285, esp. pp. 156, 158, 166.
42. *Ibid.*, pp. 178, 180–182.
43. *Ibid.*, pp. 177, 218, 232.
44. *The New York Times*, Editorial, September 18, 1900, p. 6, col. 4.

their hearers the belief that death by fire or rope would be the inevitable fate of the Danish negroes under the new regime."[45]

The Treaty of 1902 differed in a number of respects from the 1867 Treaty. It was considered by the United States Senate before it was considered by the Danish parliament. A plebiscite of the Islanders was neither provided nor conducted. All three of the Islands were to be sold for $5 million, as against the 1867 provision for sale of only St. Thomas and St. John for $7.5 million.

Perhaps the most significant departure from the 1867 Treaty, which would have given the inhabitants a choice of retaining their allegiance to Denmark or becoming "citizens of the United States," was the omission in the 1902 Treaty of any mention of citizenship. Instead, it provided a choice between "Danish allegiance" and "allegiance to the United States," and otherwise left to Congress determination of the civil rights and the political status of the Islanders. One caveat included, however, was that all inhabitants were to retain all rights then in force. "If the present laws are altered," furthermore, "the said inhabitants shall not thereby be placed in a less favorable position in respect to the above mentioned rights and liberties than they now enjoy."[46]

The Treaty of 1902 met the same fate as that of the Treaty of 1867; neither was approved. Unlike the 1867 agreement, it was easily ratified by the United States Senate and failed ratification in Denmark's upper house—the Landsthing—by virtue of a tie vote. The switch of one vote would have given the United States possession of the Virgin Islands fifteen years earlier than their acquisition in 1917, but then Denmark would not have gained retribution of a sort for the humiliation it had suffered from the United States' rejection of the Treaty of 1867.

Among possible reasons Denmark failed to ratify the Treaty was the fact that once again the United States opposed—this time successfully—a plebiscite in the Islands.[47] Reasons for American opposition to such a vote still were not clear. Laurits S. Swenson, the American Minister to Copenhagen during the negotiations, reported a "minority" Danish opinion against Virgin Islanders having a right to vote on the cession inasmuch as they were generally "unmoneyed and have heretofore been excluded from all influence on or participation in the public affairs of the islands." If any vote were to be taken, it ought to be re-

---

45. *The New York Times*, Editorial, December 21, 1900, p. 8, col. 4.

46. For the text of the Treaty of 1902, see Tansill, *The Purchase*, Appendix B, pp. 521–526. In 1903, a committee of the House of Representatives conducted an investigation of allegations of bribery of members of Congress to ratify the Treaty of 1902, but the charges were unsubstantiated and discredited. *The New York Times*, August 1, 1916, p. 12, col. 2.

47. Tansill, *The Purchase*, p. 430.

stricted to "only that part of the population which has real economic interests in the islands."[48]

Whether American authorities shared such an elitist view as a reason for opposing a plebiscite is uncertain. Such a view was consistent with the spirit of imperialism then pervading the United States, corollaries of which were expansion at the expense of other nations and a disregard for the rights of "backward" peoples.

The Transfer

American statesmen had long viewed Germany as a threat to the Monroe Doctrine by which the United States opposed further acquisition of territory in the Western Hemisphere by any European power. Many Americans believed, moreover, that Denmark's rejection of the Treaty of 1902 was a result of German intrigue or influence. Historian Charles Tansill, however, after examining all available evidence including Germany's Foreign Office archives, repudiated any contention that Germany desired to challenge American hegemony in the Caribbean or to thwart American acquisition of the Virgin Islands.[49]

Although the evidence was lacking, the fear of German expansion in the Caribbean nevertheless was real enough to persuade American authorities to renew their efforts to acquire the Virgin Islands. Accordingly, in 1907 President Theodore Roosevelt sent Dr. Maurice Francis Egan to Copenhagen as United States Minister to restore good relations with the Danes and thus "pave the way" for American purchase of the Islands. After the outbreak of the World War, Egan feared the absorption of Denmark by Germany and hence a German take-over of the Danish West Indies.[50]

The opening of the Panama Canal in 1914 and the possibility that the United States might be drawn into the war against Germany heightened

---

48. Swenson to Hay, April 14, 1902, quoted in Tansill, *The Purchase*, p. 357.

49. See *ibid.*, pp. 373–453.

50. Maurice Francis Egan, *Ten Years Near the German Frontier* (New York: Hodder and Stoughton, 1918), pp. 203–258. Stephan Bonsal in 1912 wrote: "Should the Germans ever seek land as well as commerce in the West Indies, there are many indications that they would take St. Thomas and Curacao." *The American Mediterranean* (New York: Moffat, Yard and Company, 1912), p. 225. Westergaard similarly observed: "The rapid development of the great German shipping lines, such as the Hamburg-American, gives the observer no reason to doubt that Germany would welcome the chance to acquire St. Thomas or any other suitable port or coaling station in the neighborhood of the Panama Canal." *The Danish West Indies under Company Rule*, p. 260.

Transfer ceremony, St. Thomas, March 31, 1917

America's security interests in acquiring the Islands. The acquisition of Puerto Rico had lessened the attractiveness of St. Thomas' harbor as an American naval base. The sinking of the *Lusitania*, however, plus the strong anti-German sentiments of President Woodrow Wilson and the fear of German designs in the Caribbean (which led to American intervention in Haiti), induced Secretary of State Robert Lansing to seek the immediate purchase of the Islands.

Lansing first broached the subject to the Danish Minister in Washington in October 1915. Denmark's immediate response was negative to which Lansing retorted that the United States "would never permit the group to become German." This "plain-spoken threat" prompted the Danish Minister a few weeks later to ask whether the United States would feel it necessary to occupy the Islands in the event Denmark refused to sell them. Lansing replied that he "could conceive of circumstances which would compel such an act," such as the possible absorption of Denmark by "one of the Great Powers of Europe." That, said Lansing

> would create a situation which it would be difficult to meet other than by occupation of the islands, in view of the fact that Danish possessions would come under a different sovereignty in Europe and in case it did, the result might be very serious. The other circumstance was that if Denmark voluntarily, or under coercion, transferred title to the islands to another European power, which would seek to convert them into a naval base.[51]

---

51. Robert Lansing, "Drama of the Virgin Islands Purchase," *The New York Times Magazine*, July 19, 1931, vol. 80, sec. 5, p. 4.

Lansing's threat had the desired effect. Denmark promptly began negotiations. Although the American threat was secret at the time, *The New York Times* reported from Copenhagen in August 1916, that "if the proposed sale should be rejected ... an occupation of St. Thomas was thoroughly expected to be a consequence."[52]

There was considerable opposition to the sale in Denmark. Many Danes, including the Queen, were fearful that the American treatment of blacks, including the practice of lynching, would be extended to the Virgin Islands were they to become American possessions. Others opposed the sale as a matter of patriotism and national pride.[53] Some Danes, furthermore, still harbored a hope of giving the Islands to Germany in exchange for North Schleswig.

The Danish Government, goaded by Lansing's threat, nevertheless proceeded to negotiate, but with some strong concerns about what should be provided in the treaty. The Danish Government favored a provision that would specifically confer American citizenship upon the inhabitants of the Islands. It desired, moreover, a condition of free trade between the Islands and the continental United States. Finally, the Danish Government expressed its wish that a plebiscite on the transfer be held in the Virgin Islands.[54]

Secretary of State Lansing rejected each of these Danish conditions. He replied that it would be impossible to confer citizenship by treaty on the inhabitants because this was a matter for Congress which had not yet accorded full citizenship to Puerto Ricans. "Danish West Indians, however, will be regarded as nationals of the United States and entitled to its full protection, and will receive every possible political liberty." As to free trade between the Islands and the continental United States, this also was within the province of Congress. Concerning a plebiscite in the Islands, Lansing wrote that the American Government could not favor submitting "the question of transfer of the islands to a vote of the inhabitants."[55]

Denmark also wished included in the treaty a provision that Danish citizens in the Islands should retain the rights possessed under the laws then in force, and that if the laws are altered they should not be placed in a less favorable position with respect to those rights than they enjoyed at that time. Although Secretary of State John Hay had assented to this provision in the Treaty of 1902, Lansing now opposed it because "it creates a preferred class of aliens in the islands." Before Lansing could effect deletion of this "objectionable provision" in the draft

52. *The New York Times*, August 18, 1916. p. 1, col. 5.
53. Egan, *Ten Years*, pp. 215–220.
54. Tansill, *The Purchase*, p. 491.
55. *Ibid.*, pp. 491–492.

treaty, as well as other wording that seemingly conferred American citizenship on the inhabitants, President Wilson pressed for immediate signature of the treaty.

On August 4, 1916, the treaty was signed in New York City by Secretary Lansing and the Danish Minister, providing for the purchase of the Islands by the United States for the sum of $25 million, by far the most expensive land purchase the United States had ever made. With little opposition, the United States Senate formally ratified the treaty on September 7, 1916. On August 14, meanwhile, the Danish lower house approved the treaty by the fairly close vote of 62 in favor and 44 against, whereas it easily passed the upper house (the Landsthing whose tie vote defeated the 1902 Treaty) by a vote of 42 to 8. On December 14, a national plebiscite in Denmark approved the treaty by a vote of 283,694 to 157,596. This paved the way for favorable votes in favor of the transfer of the Islands in both Danish houses by votes of 90 to 16 and 40 to 19, respectively, followed with ratification by the King. On January 16, 1917, President Wilson signed the treaty, and ratifications were exchanged the following day. The Islands were formally transferred to the United States on March 31, 1917.[56]

It is difficult to gauge the opinion of the Virgin Islanders concerning the sale. On the one hand, it is known that the two Colonial Councils unanimously passed resolutions endorsing the transfer,[57] and that *The New York Times* reported from Copenhagen on August 17, 1916, the following:

> The Danish Government today received a cablegram from the Governor of the Danish West Indies, stating that at two meetings called there 4,727 persons, women and white residents included, voted in favor of the sale to the United States, and that only seven voted against it.[58]

On the other hand, no plebiscite in the Islands was authorized in the Treaty, Lansing having rejected it; the Islands' Governor, Christian Helweg-Larsen was

---

56. *Ibid.*, pp. 497–516. Two sources state that Denmark's upper house, the Landsthing, at first rejected the Treaty of 1917, but Tansill provided no evidence to support this contention, which is asserted in: Helen M. King, *The Transition from Danish Colony to American Territory, 1865–1917* (St. Thomas: Bureau of Libraries and Museums, 1975), p. 13; and Creque, *The U.S. Virgins and the Eastern Caribbean*, p. 67. Where the cost per acre for the Virgin Islands approximated $295, the cost was only $36 in the Canal Zone, 14 cents in the Philippines, 4 cents in the Louisiana Territory, 3 cents for the Mexican Cession, and 2 cents for Alaska. William H. Haas, ed., *The American Empire* (Chicago: University of Chicago Press, 1940), p. 116.

57. King, *The Transition*, p. 13.

58. *The New York Times*, August 18, 1916, p. 1, col. 5. Luther Evans also stated, without attribution, that "The inhabitants of the Islands voted overwhelmingly for the transfer." *The Virgin Islands from Naval Base to New Deal*, p. 44.

Secretary Lansing handing Constantin Brun, the Danish Minister in Washing-
ton, a Treasury Warrant for $25 M. At right is Rear Admiral James H. Oliver,
first appointee to the Governorship of the V.I. of the U.S.A.

reported to have been "strongly opposed" to the sale of the Islands;[59] and the same newspaper reported from St. Thomas on August 11, 1916 that opinion there on the transfer was "divided," and that

> So far there has been little public discussion of the subject, although not a little astonishment or resentment is freely expressed because the inhabitants were not consulted by the authorities in Copenhagen before the negotiation had progressed so far.[60]

Had a plebiscite in the Islands been made a condition of transfer, the vote might well have been overwhelmingly favorable because the inhabitants fully expected from the Treaty provisions thereby to be accorded American citizenship.

---

59. Tansill, *The Purchase*, p. 472. Gordon K. Lewis commented that "almost on the eve of transfer, Governor Helweg-Larsen could be popularly viewed as a 'Negro hater' who had advised the planters not to pay a daily wage above twenty-five cents." *The Virgin Islands*, p. 37.

60. *The New York Times*, August 23, 1916, p. 3, col. 6.

The 1902 provision was retained (President Wilson having waived objection to it) that those Danish citizens choosing to remain "shall not thereby be placed in a less favorable position" with respect to their rights by any subsequent alteration of the laws. Perhaps even more important to the inhabitants, however, was the Treaty stipulation that persons not choosing to elect Danish citizenship would be deemed to have accepted "citizenship in the United States." As provided in 1867 and 1902, Congress would otherwise determine "the civil rights and political status of the inhabitants."[61]

It will be recalled that the Treaty of 1867 gave inhabitants a choice of becoming "citizens *of* the United States," and that the Treaty of 1902 gave them a choice of "allegiance to the United States," whereas the Treaty of 1917 gave them a choice of becoming "citizens *in* the United States"—the difference between the 1867 and 1917 wording being a change from one two-letter word to another, from "of" to "in." This seemingly minor change of phrasing was later to be tortuously interpreted to deny American citizenship to the inhabitants, much to their dismay.

The conclusions are inescapable, therefore, that the United States induced Denmark to sell the Islands under a threat of force, that it took possession of the Islands without gaining the consent of their inhabitants, and that it deceived them into believing they were being accorded American citizenship when in fact the United States intended to deny them that status.

---

61. Article 6, *Convention between the United States and Denmark for the Cession of the Danish West Indies*, ratified by the United States, January 25, 1917; 39 Stat. 706. For the text of the Convention see Tansill, *The Purchase*, Appendix C, pp. 527–537; and Bough and Macridis, *Virgin Islands*, pp. 30–39.

5

American Antecedents

The American threat to use force to compel Denmark to sell the Virgin Islands to the United States represents merely a relatively minor and ignored chapter in the grand sweep of the history of American expansionism, beginning with the wars between the British, French, and Spaniards[1] and followed by the waves of westward migration[2] that ultimately pushed the United States across the Pacific.[3] This westward movement was marked by a record of broken treaties and unfulfilled promises to native Americans and the annexation of their lands.[4]

Simply put, Americans were not to be restrained. From the incipiency of the American nation, until the Vietnam War was to engrave on the national consciousness the limits of American power,[5] there seemed to be something about the psyche of Americans that propelled them toward ever continuing expansion.[6]

---

1. See, *e.g.*, Samuel Eliot Morison and Henry Steele Commager, *The Growth of the American Republic* (New York: Oxford University Press, 1942), vol. 1, pp. 85–91, 119–127.

2. See *e.g.*, Frederick Jackson Turner, *The Frontier in American History* (New York: Henry Holt and Co., 1953).

3. See, Kenneth Scott Latourette, *The United States Moves Across the Pacific* (New York: Harper and Brothers, 1946); Amaury de Riencourt, *The American Empire* (New York: Dell Publishing, 1970); Ronald Steel, *Pax Americana* (New York: The Viking Press, 1967).

4. See, *e.g.*, Helen Hunt Jackson, *A Century of Dishonor, A Sketch of the United States Government's Dealings with Some of the Indian Tribes* (Boston: Roberts Brothers, 1895).

5. See, *e.g.*, Townsend Hoopes, *The Limits of Intervention* (New York: David McKay Company, 1969); William W. Boyer, *The Agony of Vietnam* (Newark, Delaware: The University of Delaware, 1969).

6. Thus, the Governor of Virginia in 1772, Lord Dunsmore, wrote the following to the British Colonial Secretary: "I have learnt from experience that the established Authority of any government in America, and the policy of Government at home, are both insufficient to restrain the Americans; and that they do and will remove as their avidity and restlessness incite them. They acquire no attachment to Place: But wandering about Seems engrafted in their Nature; and it is a weakness incident to it, that they Should for ever immagine the Lands further off, are Still better than those upon which they are already Settled But to be more particular … In this Colony Proclamations have been published from time to time to

Northwest Ordinance

The earliest American colonial policy was formed under the Articles of Confederation by "Congress assembled," before the Constitution was adopted. The Northwest Ordinance of 1787[7] established the basic model for United States policy toward territories. It laid a permanent foundation for the American territorial system and colonial policy that enabled the United States to expand westward to the Pacific, and to add Hawaii and Alaska to the Union, with relatively little difficulty.

An ordinance of 1784, framed by Thomas Jefferson, would have permitted self-government by the settlers from the outset, but it was superseded by the Ordinance of 1787.[8] The essence of the new policy was to provide for colonies to evolve from the status of a dependent territory to statehood equal in every respect with the status of the original thirteen states. The principle of equality with the mother country was established, but the equality of full statehood was to be achieved only after a period of territorial evolution.

"Any status less than eventual statehood" according to Robert Berkhofer, "would have been a betrayal of the very principle upon which Americans had fought the Revolution."[9] A basic issue between the colonies and England was their claim that they were being ruled without their consent and without representation in the Parliament. The United States could not now repudiate that principle in the governance of its own territories.[10]

---

restrain them: But impressed from their earliest infancy with Sentiments and habits, very different from those acquired by persons of a Similar condition in England, they do not conceive their Government has any right to forbid their taking possession of a Vast tract of Country, either uninhabited, or which Serves only as a Shelter to a few Scattered Tribes of Indians. Nor can they be easily brought to entertain any belief of the permanent obligation of Treaties made with those People, whom they consider, as but little removed from the brute Creation." Quoted by Morison and Commager, *The Growth of the American Republic*, vol. 1, p. 144.

7. 1 *Stat.* 51. Organic acts of American territories prior to 1898 are printed in *Senate Doc.* 148, 56th Cong., 1st sess.

8. Merrill Jensen, *The New Nation: A History of the United States during the Confederation, 1781–1789* (New York: Alfred Knopf, 1950), pp. 350ff.

9. Robert F. Berkhofer, Jr, "The Northwest Ordinance and the Principle of Territorial Evolution," in John Porter Bloom, ed., *The American Territorial System* (Athens: Ohio University Press, 1973), p. 46.

10. The influence of Jefferson on this policy and its consistency with the philosophy of the Declaration of Independence, *viz.*, that governments derive their legitimate authority from the consent of the governed, is discussed by Arthur Bestor in his "Constitutionalism and the Settlement of the West: The Attainment of Consensus, 1754–1784," in Bloom, *The*

If the Northwest was to be settled entirely by native Anglo-Americans from the east, they would not have needed a period of tutelage on how to exercise their basic rights and how to form a republican government. It was anticipated, however, that many people of French descent and other non-English settlers would inhabit the West and, therefore, they would need a period of initiation into the mysteries of republicanism.[11]

Accordingly, the Northwest Ordinance provided for three stages of political development that roughly paralleled the stages of development the American colonies had passed through. The first stage of the Ordinance provided a period of strong executive control, the second stage a period of representative government, and the third consisted of provision of statehood. Thus, James Monroe wrote to Thomas Jefferson that the Ordinance would provide for "a colonial government similar to that which prevailed in these States previous to the Revolution."[12] Although only Congress could admit new states, the Northwest Ordinance "clearly indicated that ... statehood was to be regarded as a right rather than as a privilege which might be denied without cause by Congress."[13]

During the first stage, all of the area north and west of the Ohio River was to be governed as a single territory by a governor and three judges appointed by Congress. In the second stage, when the territory numbered five thousand free male inhabitants, Congress would authorize a two-house legislature, elected by freeholders owning fifty acres, which would share power with the governor who would have an absolute veto. The legislature would elect a delegate to Congress who would have the right to speak but not to vote. After the Constitution went into effect in 1789, the Ordinance was amended to substitute the President for the Congress as the appointing authority, with the requirement of the advice and consent of the Senate.[14]

American Territorial System, pp. 13–44. "With the end of the war ... discussion centered more and more upon prospective large-scale settlements in the West by Revolutionary soldiers, whose lands were a compensation for services rendered their country. Viewed in this light, self-government and eventual statehood for western settlements began to be regarded not as a risk but as a reward." *Ibid.*, p. 26.

11. Jack Ericson Eblen, *The First and Second United States Empires* (Pittsburgh: University of Pittsburgh Press, 1968), pp. 44–45.

12. Quoted by Whitney T. Perkins, *American Policy in the Government of its Dependent Areas—A Study of the Policy of the United States toward the inhabitants of its Territories and Insular Possessions* (unpublished Ph.D. dissertation, Fletcher School of Law and Diplomacy, 1948), p. 3.

13. Whitney T. Perkins, *Denial of Empire, The United States and its Dependencies* (Leyden: A. W. Sythoff, 1962), p. 15.

14. 1 *Stat.* 50.

No more than five nor less than three states were to be formed out of the territory, and whenever any one reached sixty thousand free inhabitants, the final status of statehood with admission in the Union would be attained. Meanwhile, at all stages, civil liberties were to be guaranteed in accordance with a bill of rights, but it was not clear after 1789 whether such rights rested on the will of Congress or on the Constitution. The Ordinance also proclaimed: "Religion, morality, and knowledge, being necessary to good government and happiness of mankind, schools and the means of education shall forever be encouraged." Furthermore, "There shall be neither slavery nor involuntary servitude in the said territory."

At first, people of French descent outnumbered other inhabitants in certain parts of the Northwest Territory, but settlers from the seaboard states soon became the most numerous.[15] The Ordinance was applied almost exactly as Congress had intended. Ohio became a state in 1802, Indiana in 1816, Illinois in 1818, Michigan in 1836, and Wisconsin in 1848.

Continental Expansion

The Northwest Ordinance of 1787 became regarded as one of the great historical documents of the United States. "Next to the Constitution itself," according to one authority, "it is the most important organic act of the Federal Government."[16] It furnished the model upon which subsequent legislation for other territories was based. In 1790, an act was passed providing that the Southwest Territory should have a form of government in all respects similar to that provided by the Northwest Ordinance, except for the clause excluding slavery.

The Louisiana Purchase of 1803 brought under American control two regions—one sparsely settled and the other populated by those of French descent already under an established government. The Treaty with France of that year ceded the vast Louisiana Territory for $15 million, or $10 million less than the United States paid for the tiny Virgin Islands in 1917. The Treaty outlined broadly the policy already being followed in the Northwest Territory, namely:

> that the inhabitants of the ceded territory shall be incorporated into the Union of the United States and admitted as soon as possible ac-

---

15. For patterns of settlement in the "Old Northwest," see: Turner, *The Frontier in American History,* pp. 222–236.

16. William Franklin Willoughby, *Territories and Dependencies of the United States. Their Government and Administration* (New York: The Century Co., 1905), p. 28.

cording to the principles of the Federal Constitution to the enjoyment of all the rights, advantages and immunities of citizens of the United States, and in the meantime they shall be maintained and protected in the free enjoyment of their liberty, property and the religion they profess.[17]

Despite this liberal provision, no bill of rights was provided for the first stage, and it was inferred that the Constitution and the laws of the United States were not extended to the Louisiana Territory of their own force, but only insofar as they would be extended by Congress. The principle of territorial evolution to statehood through three stages was again provided. Congress was later to extend specifically certain of its acts to the Louisiana Territory, implying that acts not so extended did not apply. The question whether the Constitution extended of its own force to the Louisiana Territory was not decided by the Supreme Court.

To the extent that Congress assumed by its actions that the Constitution did not follow the flag, the philosophy of the Declaration of Independence (that government derives its powers from the consent of the governed, and that all men are created equal and possess inalienable rights) was not observed. Thus, Whitney Perkins has referred to the Louisiana policy as "a plan which would curtail freedom in the name of freedom," and he cited the first governor of New Orleans as having written of its inhabitants: "I am convinced of their unfitness for a representative Government."[18] But the governor's lack of faith in Louisianans did not prevent Congress from developing the area according to the pattern of the Northwest Territory, a process ultimately completed with the admission of Idaho and Wyoming as states in 1890.

No new precedents were established in the acquisition of continental territories until 1848 when President Polk decided to treat the areas acquired from Mexico as part of the United States from the date of cession—a precedent at variance with the territorial evolution policy previously followed. Accordingly, Secretary of State Buchanan instructed the post-office agent in California that

> the constitution of the United States, the safeguard of all our civil rights, was extended over California the 30th May, 1848, the day on which our late treaty with Mexico was finally consummated. From that day its inhabitants became entitled to all the blessings and benefits of the best form of civil government ever established amongst men.[19]

---

17. Quoted in *ibid.*, pp. 37–38.
18. Perkins, *Denial of Empire*, pp. 20, 21.
19. Quoted by Perkins, *Denial of Empire*, p. 24.

In the *Dred Scott* decision of 1857, the Supreme Court maintained that the United States had no power to acquire territory except with the Constitution in full effect, and with the purpose of admission to statehood as soon as conditions would warrant admission.[20]

During the first century of American expansion, following the Northwest Ordinance of 1787, Congress established the concept that the territories were infant states, to be admitted into the Union as soon as conditions warranted. Thus, Congress generally extended local self-government, guarantees of fundamental rights of the Constitution, and the right to elect a non-voting delegate to Congress. Territorial status was merely a bridge between annexation and incorporation into the Union as co-equal states. Variations appeared, according to differences among some of the territories, but the essential pattern remained unchanged during the century of continental expansion. Indeed, it appeared that the Constitution was intended to follow the flag. This, then, was the established policy confronting American policy-makers when they faced the problem of governing areas acquired in 1898 from the Spanish-American War.

Spanish-American War

To understand the causes of the Spanish-American War, one must understand the changed national temper of the time. The period from 1865 to 1895 was one in which the American people on the whole had little interest in foreign affairs or further expansion. It is clear, however, that the long dormant "Manifest Destiny" was once again abroad in the land, and that certain forces and values were developing which were to produce a new kind of American imperialism as part of a world-wide imperialism movement.

On the naval side, Captain Alfred Thayer Mahan emphasized in his writings the importance of sea power, which inevitably portended a policy of expansion beyond the American continent. There were academicians such as John W. Burgess and Frank H. Giddings, and clergymen such as Josiah Strong, who popularized America's mission to civilize peoples of backward areas, as a sort of "white man's burden." There were politicians—particularly Republicans— such as John Hay, Theodore Roosevelt, and Henry Cabot Lodge, who avowedly supported imperialism and reserved their choicest epithets for "anti-imperialists." "Small states are of the past, and have no future," wrote Senator Lodge. As one of the great nations, the United States must for its future expansion

---

20. *Dred Scott v. Sanford*, 19 Howard 393, 446–448 (1857).

and present defense absorb some of these "waste places of the earth," in order to extend civilization and, he reasoned, for "the advancement of the race."[21]

Furthermore, there were the practitioners of "yellow journalism," such as Hearst and Pulitzer, who competed in the *New York Journal* and the *New York World*, respectively, in sensationalizing the events leading to the Spanish-American War.[22] Historians Morison and Commager attributed this "yellow press" campaign of propaganda between 1895 and 1898 as having brought the American people to demand intervention in Cuba on behalf of "humanity." A second explanation for the change in the national temper was the enormous increase in America's economic stake in Cuba, particularly in trade. Finally, "the United States had developed a new set of world interests which made it seem necessary that the entire Caribbean area be under American control."[23]

It was the bitter revolution for independence in Cuba, beginning in 1895, that unleashed all the chauvinism of the changed national mood and provided a focus for American imperialistic ambitions. Americans with property interests in Cuba clamored for intervention, supported by the yellow press which brazenly fabricated incidents to excite American opinion against Spain. The *Washington Star* editorialized about "the anarchical and barbarous condition of the Spanish so-called government in Cuba," which it is the "duty of the

---

21. Quoted by Morison and Commager, *The Growth of the American Republic*, vol. 2, p. 323. For U.S. developments leading to war with Spain, see Ernest R. May, *Imperial Democracy, The Emergence of America as a Great Power* (New York: Harcourt, Brace & World, 1961).

22. Allan Nevins, *American Press Opinion, Washington to Coolidge, A Documentary Record of Editorial Leadership and Criticism, 1785–1927* (New York: D. C. Heath and Company, 1928), p. 307. For a similar assessment of "the national temper" in the late 1890s, see Dexter Perkins, *The United States and the Caribbean*, revised edition (Cambridge: Harvard University Press, 1966), pp. 93–94; and Hugh Thomas, *Cuba: The Pursuit of Freedom* (New York: Harper & Row, 1971), pp. 310–315, 339–355.

23. Morison and Commager, *The Growth of the American Republic*, vol. 2, p. 326. Meanwhile, the Hawaiian Islands had become by 1890 "an American commercial appendage" which prompted the sons of American missionaries, with the connivance of the United States minister and the intervention of American marines, to depose the hapless Hawaiian Queen in 1893. President Harrison immediately accepted a treaty of annexation, but before the Senate could ratify it, anti-imperialist Grover Cleveland became President and withdrew it on the ground that the United States had improperly participated in the overthrow of the monarchy. After hostilities with Spain began, with McKinley then President, Congress approved annexation on July 7, 1898. An organic act in 1900 recognized the Islands as a fully organized territory of the United States, to which all provisions of the Constitution and laws of the United States were extended (with special exceptions), and to the inhabitants on whom citizenship in the United States was conferred. See, *e.g.*, Willoughby, *Territories and Dependencies*, pp. 60–63.

American Republic" to expel from the Island.[24] The *Kansas City Times* echoed that "the Spaniards are incapable of ruling a people in this hemisphere."[25]

William McKinley had been elected in 1896 on a Republican platform calling for Cuban independence. The explosion of the American battleship *Maine* in Havana harbor in February 1898 with the loss of two hundred and sixty men was to provide the pretext for war. "It was an accident, they say," Hearst's editorial stated. "Perhaps it was, but accident or not, it would never have happened if there had been peace in Cuba, as there would have been had we done our duty."[26] Officially blaming a submarine mine or some external cause, the United States demanded reparation and presented Spain with an ultimatum calling for an immediate armistice. The Spanish Government refused, blaming an internal explosion, but sought desperately to appease the United States even to the point of suspending hostilities against the Cuban rebels. The effort failed. McKinley, guided by prayer and in the name of "a Christian, peace-loving people," delivered his war message to Congress. Congress' joint Resolution of April 20, 1898 authorized the use of the "entire" armed forces of the nation to liberate Cuba, but added the so-called "Teller Amendment":

> That the United States hereby disclaims any disposition or intention to exercise sovereignty, jurisdiction or control over the said Island, except for the pacification thereof, and asserts its determination, when that is accomplished, to leave the government and control of the Island to its people.

After three months of what Secretary of State John Hay termed "a splendid little war," Spain sued for peace, the terms of which were dictated by McKinley: relinquishment of Spanish sovereignty over Cuba, outright cession of Puerto Rico and Guam, and United States occupation of the city, harbor and bay of Manila pending final disposition of the Philippines. In agreeing to these terms, Spain responded plaintively: "This demand strips us of the very last memory of a glorious past and expels us ... from the Western Hemisphere, which became peopled and civilized through the proud deeds of our ancestors."[27]

The Treaty of Paris, signed December 10, 1898, formalized the cession of the Philippines, Guam, and Puerto Rico to the United States. The United States

---

24. *Washington Star*, Editorial, April 8, 1898.
25. *Kansas City Times*, Editorial, April 12, 1898.
26. *New York Journal*, Editorial, February 17, 1898.
27. Quoted by Morison and Commager, *The Growth of the American Republic*, vol. 2, pp. 334–335.

thereby acquired non-contiguous and extra-continental territories populated by peoples of alien culture, language, and political heritage.

The growth of the American republic theretofore, spurred by the emotion of "Manifest Destiny,"[28] consisted of the acquisition of contiguous mainland territory as integral parts of the United States to be admitted to the Union as co-equal states.[29] Now, however, for the first time in American expansionist history, no promise was made of either statehood or citizenship for newly acquired territory.[30]

Article 9 of the Treaty of Paris stated that "The civil rights and political status of the native inhabitants of the territories hereby ceded to the United States shall be determined by the Congress." The only right guaranteed was freedom of religion.[31] Accordingly, the issues of statehood and citizenship for the new territories were postponed by the Treaty for later consideration by Congress.

Already, however, anti-imperialists were gathering their forces. Four days before the signing of the Treaty, Senator George C. Vest of Missouri introduced a joint resolution asserting that the Constitution gave no power to the United States to acquire territory except with the purpose of ultimately organizing such territory into states suitable for admission into the Union.[32] Citing the *Dred Scott* case, he denied that territory could be acquired "to he held as colonies, peopled by millions of subjects not citizens, with no hope or prospect of its ever becoming a state of the Union." The colonial system could not be maintained in a free country, he argued, "because it uproots and eliminates the basis of all republican institutions, that governments derive their just powers from the consent of the governed."[33] Debate on the Vest resolution continued day after

---

28. See, *e.g.*, Albert K. Weinberg, *Manifest Destiny* (Baltimore The Johns Hopkins Press, 1935).

29. See, *e.g.*, Julius W. Pratt, *America's Colonial Experiment* (New York: Prentice Hall, 1950), p. 1. Alaska was the only exception, having been ignored by Congress during the early decades of American rule. By the Act of May 17, 1884, Alaska had been left in the indistinct status of a "district." Willoughby, *Territories and Dependencies*, pp. 74–76.

30. American citizenship was given to the inhabitants of non-contiguous, but mainland, Alaska by the treaty of cession of 1867, "with the exception of the uncivilized native tribes." 15 *Stat.* 542 (1867). And Congress extended citizenship to the inhabitants of the non-contiguous Hawaiian Islands in 1900.

31. 30 *Stat.* 1759–1760 (1899).

32. 32 *Congressional Record* 20.

33. Quoted by Carl Brent Swisher, *American Constitutional Development* (Cambridge, Mass.: Houghton Mifflin Company, 1943), p. 468, citing 32 *Congressional Record* 96. For an understanding of the spirit of the anti-imperialist movement, see, also, Robert L. Beisner, *Twelve Against Empire: The Anti-Imperialists, 1898–1900* (New York: McGraw Hill Book Co., 1968).

day, but no vote on the resolution was ever taken. The sentiments of the Senate were revealed, however, when on February 6, 1899, it ratified the Treaty of Paris by the narrow margin of one vote over the two-thirds required.

Puerto Rico

Soon after American military forces occupied Puerto Rico, President McKinley appointed Dr. Henry K. Carroll to make an independent survey and report on the Island. In his report, Carroll summarized the hopes and aspirations of Puerto Ricans as follows:

> They expect under American sovereignty that the wrongs of centuries will be righted; that they will have an honest and efficient government; the largest measure of liberty as citizens of the great republic under the Constitution; home rule as provided by the Territorial system; free access to the markets of the United States and no customs duties on goods coming from our ports.[34]

Despite their lack of experience and education, Carroll was convinced that Puerto Ricans were ready for self-government in local affairs with an unrestricted suffrage because of their habit of obedience and respect for law and their native intelligence and industriousness. Accordingly, he recommended that the Constitution and laws of the United States be extended to Puerto Rico, their inhabitants be granted American citizenship, and that they be given the traditional territorial form of government so that they could learn under the pressure of responsibility.[35] General George W. Davis, head of the military government of Puerto Rico, rejected self-government in view of the profound illiteracy of 85 percent of the people, of their total unfitness to exercise the elective franchise and of the misuse of political power that would almost certainly be made by those seeking to secure it.[36]

In 1899, President McKinley appointed Elihu Root as Secretary of War specifically for the purpose of administering the newly acquired Spanish islands.[37] Neither then nor in later years did Root support statehood or citizen-

---

34. Henry K. Carroll, *Report on the Island of Porto Rico* (Washington: U.S. Government Printing Office, 1899), p. 56.

35. *Ibid.*, p. 57ff.

36. *Report of Brigadier General George W. Davis, U.S.V., on Civil Affairs of Porto Rico, 1899* (Washington: U.S. Government Printing Office, 1900), p. 76.

37. "President McKinley sent word to Elihu Root, prominent New York lawyer, that he wanted him to come to Washington as head of the War Department. When Root replied that he knew nothing about war or about the army, he was told that the President was not look-

ship for Puerto Rico. He believed that the Constitution extended no rights to Puerto Ricans because the full sovereign power of the United States over the new possessions was limited only by the treaty of cession. He conceded, however, that Puerto Ricans should have as much self-government as feasible and that they should be trained meanwhile for the exercise of further freedoms.[38]

A bill to provide a temporary civil government for Puerto Rico was sponsored by Senator Joseph B. Foraker of Ohio, chairman of the newly created Senate Committee on Pacific Islands and Porto Rico. As introduced, the Puerto Ricans were to be made citizens of the United States, the Constitution was to be extended to the Island, Puerto Rico was to be entitled to a non-voting delegate in the House of Representatives, and free trade was to exist between the mainland and the Island.

The legislators, however, were contemporaneously considering impending legislation for the Philippines, and when protectionist Republicans saw the significance of Puerto Rican legislation as a precedent for the Philippines they quickly decided to eliminate the free trade provision by providing a tariff of 25 percent (later reduced to 15 percent in the bill as passed) of the prevailing rates on goods traded between the United States and Puerto Rico.[39] The prevailing rates of duties actually paid upon dutiable imports to the United States government, from 1867 to that time, exceeded those of any other country in the world.[40] Protectionism was the dominant value of the Republican majority in Congress who feared that the principle of free trade in the relations with Puerto Rico might lead to free trade with the Philippines and perhaps later with Cuba.[41]

It could not be maintained, therefore, that the Constitution was in full force in Puerto Rico, because the tariff provision would have been in violation of Article I, section 8 of the Constitution providing that "all duties, imports, and excises shall be uniform throughout the United States." Since the Constitution

---

ing for anyone who knew about these subjects, but that he had to have a lawyer to direct the government of the Spanish islands and that Root was the lawyer he wanted. Root accepted the position, and, since for the time being all the possessions were under military control, he supervised generally their management." Swisher, *American Constitutional Development*, pp. 472–473. See, also, Philip C. Jessup, *Elihu Root* (New York: Dodd, Mead and Company, 1938), vol. 1, p. 215.

38. Lyman Jay Gould, *The Foraker Act, The Roots of American Colonial Policy* (unpublished Ph.D. dissertation, University of Michigan, 1958), pp. 72–74.

39. *Ibid.*, pp. 75–76. Gould's dissertation extensively treats the legislative history of the Foraker Act.

40. Franklin Pierce, *The Tariff and the Trusts* (New York: Grosser & Dunlap Publishers, 1907), p. v.

41. Perkins, *Denial of Empire*, pp. 118–119.

did not follow the flag, the provision of the original bill granting citizenship was also eliminated. Thus, the Senate's Democratic minority leader correctly observed that "Every feature of a free Territorial government has been sacrificed in order that a tariff may be enforced against Porto Rico."[42] Of all the original provisions excluded, Senator Foraker fought hardest to retain the grant of citizenship. "They must be either citizens, aliens, or subjects," he reasoned. "We have no subjects, and should not make aliens of our own."[43]

Most Puerto Ricans had assumed falsely that the Treaty of Paris had made them United States citizens. For example, a handbill distributed in San Juan on February 7, 1899 proclaimed that by the ratification of the previous day Puerto Rico became "definitely incorporated" into the Union. "We are, then, with legitimate pride, citizens of that great nation—the finest, most democratic and prosperous of the civilized world."[44] Over a year later, the United States Senate decided otherwise.

> The Democrats taunted the Republicans on the citizenship issue, accusing them of treating the Puerto Ricans as "quasi-alien." Repeated efforts were made to amend from the floor so as to extend the Constitution to Puerto Rico, but every attempt was checkmated by the presence of a Republican majority.[45]

The Foraker Act established a temporary civil government "of the old crown colony type,"[46] to replace military rule, by providing for appointment by the President with Senate confirmation of the governor and executive council, the election of an assembly by an electorate to be defined by the government in Puerto Rico, and the presence in the House of Representatives of a non-voting "resident commissioner."

Most Congressional attention was focused on the tariff issue, with little attention given to the civil government provisions, prompting one member of the House of Representatives to charge: "Not one line of the civil government feature of this bill has been discussed or even read in this House."[47] The main criticism was reserved for the executive council, to consist of eleven members

---

42. 56 *Congressional Record* 3685 (1900).
43. Quoted by Gould, *The Foraker Act*, p. 77.
44. 56 *Congressional Record* 3686 (1900).
45. Gould, *The Foraker Act*, pp. 79–80.
46. Morison and Commager, *The Growth of the American Republic*, vol. 2, p. 345; Gordon K. Lewis, *Puerto Rico: Freedom and Power in the Caribbean* (New York: MR Press, 1963), pp. 107–108.
47. Quoted by Gould, *The Foraker Act*, p. 84, citing 56 *Congressional Record* A 233 (1900).

to be appointed by the President, six of whom could be outsiders, and to be vested with control of the suffrage qualifications and the granting of franchises. Thus another House member commented:

> if I were asked to name the feature most glaringly obnoxious and most repugnant to my own sense of justice, I would unhesitatingly say it was that which puts into the hands of a carpetbag executive council, with only the approval of a carpetbag governor, the power to grant and dispense of every franchise, right, privilege, and concession of a public or quasi-public nature in the island.[48]

Insular Cases

Having made a review of the Supreme Court decisions prior to the American acquisition of extra-continental territories as a result of the Spanish-American War, W. W. Willoughby concluded that, from the first, the doctrine was held by the Court that Congress, when legislating on the civil rights of inhabitants of the territories, was governed by all those expressed and implied limitations which rest upon it when dealing with the same subjects within the States.[49] The question of the status of civil rights in the new possessions of Puerto Rico and the Philippines was related to the larger question of whether the Constitution follows the flag.

The issue was raised in *Downes v. Bidwell*[50] in 1901 when Downes brought an action against Bidwell, the collector of the port of New York, to recover duties exacted and paid under protest upon certain oranges consigned to Downes at New York. The oranges were brought to New York from San Juan, Puerto Rico, after the enactment of the Foraker Act.

The "conclusion and judgment" of the Court was announced by Justice Brown. He stated the issue of the case:

> This case involves the question whether the merchandise brought into the port of New York from Porto Rico since the passage of the Foraker Act, is exempt from duty, notwithstanding the third section of that act, which requires the payment of "fifteen per centum of the duties

---

48. *Ibid.*, p. 85, citing 56 *Congressional Record* A 234 (1900).

49. W. W. Willoughby, *The Constitutional Law of the United States*, 2nd edition (New York: Baker, Voorhis and Company, 1929), vol. 1, p. 476.

50. 182 U.S. 244 (1901).

which are required to be levied, collected and paid upon like articles of merchandise imported from foreign countries."

The question concerned, therefore, the status of Puerto Rico in relation to the United States. If Puerto Rico was part of the United States, the Foraker Act in consequence would be unconstitutional, violating Article I, section 8, clause 1, which provides that "all duties, imposts and excises shall be uniform throughout the United States," and section 9 of that Article, which provides that "vessels bound to or from one State" cannot "be obliged to enter, clear or pay duties in another."

Justice Brown cited *De Lima v. Bidwell*,[51] decided just previously, in which the Court held that Puerto Rico ceased to be a foreign country upon the ratification of the treaty of peace with Spain. The whole question of the civil rights of the inhabitants rested upon the question here before the Court, namely, the status of Puerto Rico. Justice Brown stated this view for the majority of the Court:

> We are therefore of the opinion that the Island of Porto Rico is a territory appurtenant and belonging to the United States, but not a part of the United States within the revenue clauses of the Constitution; that the Foraker Act is constitutional, so far as it imposes duties upon imports from such island, and that the plaintiff cannot recover the duties exacted in this case.[52]

A concurring opinion of great length was written by Justice White, with whom two other justices concurred. Thus, the Court was badly split, five to four, with five separate opinions written, three for the majority and two for the dissenters. Of all these various opinions, including that of Justice Brown, the concurring opinion written by Justice White was the most important because it established a new theory that ultimately became the doctrine of the Court with respect to the constitutional status of the territories acquired by the United States from Spain. Justice White developed the doctrine of "incorporation,"

---

51. 182 U.S. 1 (1901).

52. *Downes v. Bidwell*, 182 U.S. 244, 287 (1901). "The question which posed itself was whether or not all of the rights and privileges enumerated in the Constitution extended *ex proprio vigore* to the inhabitants of the non-contiguous territories. The question was disposed of by abandoning those fundamental principles such as government shall rest upon the consent of the governed, taxation with inherent right of representation, and trial by jury— principles which lie at the very basis and constitute the very essence of American political life." William M. Boyd, *The Administration of Territories and Island Possessions by the United States* (unpublished Ph.D. dissertation, University of Michigan, 1944), p. 3.

which was entirely without precedent, a doctrine that was to play such an important part in respect to the rights of the inhabitants of the extra-continental territories, including the American Virgin Islands. To develop the theory of incorporation, Justice White went into a most elaborate and tortuous historical review of the various documents of territorial acquisition. The treaty for the purchase of Louisiana, he noted, provided that " 'The inhabitants of the ceded territory shall be incorporated in the Union.' Observe how guardedly the fulfillment of this pledge is postponed," he continued, "until its accomplishment is made possible by the will of the American people, since it is to be executed only 'as soon as possible according to the principles of the Federal Constitution.' "[53] If the term "incorporated" as used here seemed a promise of ultimate statehood to the annexed population of Louisiana, such a meaning was not read by Justice White. With regard to the clause of the Louisiana treaty, the "minutest analysis" fails to disclose any reference to a promise of statehood, and thus the only pledges made referred to "incorporation into the United States." The closest Justice White came to defining incorporation was the following:

> In accordance with this view the territory acquired by the Louisiana purchase was governed as a mere dependency, until, conformably to the suggestion of Mr. Jefferson, it was by the action of Congress incorporated as a Territory into the United States and the same rights were conferred in the same mode by which other Territories had previously been incorporated, that is, by bestowing citizenship and the rights and immunities which pertained to the Northwest Territory.[54]

Some years later, however, the bestowal of citizenship and certain privileges and immunities listed in the Ordinance of 1787 upon the people of Puerto Rico and the Virgin Islands was not considered sufficient to "incorporate" those possessions into the Union. It may have been, although by no means is it clear, that Justice White thought incorporation as a territory implied a promise of ultimate statehood.

Returning to the question of whether Puerto Rico had been incorporated, Justice White continued his judicial exegesis by citing the provision of the Treaty of Paris to the effect that "The civil rights and political status of the native inhabitants hereby ceded to the United States shall be determined by the Congress."[55] This provision, he declared, made any intention to incorporate Puerto Rico inconse-

---

53. 182 U.S. 244, 325.
54. Ibid., 326.
55. Ibid., 333.

quential, and he concluded that the uniformity clause of the Constitution was not applicable to Congress in legislating for Puerto Rico; hence the tariff on Puerto Rican goods entering the United States was not in violation of the Constitution.

Unfortunately for the clarity of constitutional law, Justice White did not explain what constituted incorporation despite his extraordinary effort to rewrite American history. Congress gained considerable power from its very vagueness, and it is paradoxical that the principles of the Declaration of Independence and the basic human rights of the Constitution could be denied through the application of such an obscure doctrine.

The import of White's opinion was so significant and his reasoning was so laborious and mystic that the question is inevitably raised of what were his motives for conjuring this doctrine. W. W. Willoughby stressed the "character" of the population of these territories as having been the most important factor in influencing the doctrine.[56] Frederic R. Coudert suggested that Justice White was concerned with "racial" questions and that constitutional rights should not extend automatically to non-white populations of the new possessions. Coudert, counsel for the plaintiffs in the case, writing some years later, noted that Justice White had been born on a Louisiana plantation and served as a private in the Confederate Army during the Civil War.

> It is apparent that Mr. Justice White feared a decision in this case ... in favor of the plaintiffs might be held to confer upon the citizens of the new possessions rights which could not be taken away from them by Congress. I may say that in a conversation subsequent to the decision he told me of his dread lest by a ruling of the Court it might have become impossible to dispose of the Philippine Islands and of his regret that one of the great parties had not adopted his doctrine of incorporation in its platform as providing the solution for the then much mooted matter of the ultimate disposition of the Philippine Islands. It is evident that he was much preoccupied by the danger of racial and social questions of a very perplexing character and that he was quite desirous ... that Congress should have a very free hand with the new subject populations.[57]

In his dissent, Justice Harlan was constrained to say that "this idea of 'incorporation' has some occult meaning which my mind does not apprehend. It is enveloped in some mystery which I am unable to unravel."[58]

---

56. Willoughby, *The Constitutional Law of the United States*, vol. 1, p. 476.

57. F. R. Coudert, "Evolution of the Doctrine of Incorporation," *Columbia Law Review*, vol. 36, p. 832 (1926).

58. *Downes v. Bidwell*, 182 U.S. 244, 389–391.

The *Downes* case did not end the battle among the Justices whose fundamental differences continued for some years to come. In 1903, the Court held that the Constitutional rights of indictment by a grand jury and trial by a petit jury did not extend to the Hawaiian Islands and that only Congress could extend such rights.[59] In 1904, the Court held that jury trial likewise did not extend to the Philippines.[60] The same conclusion was reached with regard to Alaska in 1905.[61] Again, in 1914 the Constitutional requirement of indictment by grand jury was held by the Court as not applying "of its own force" to the Philippines.[62] It was not until 1922, however, that the doctrine of incorporation was unequivocally adopted by a unanimous Supreme Court.[63]

The doctrine of incorporation was invented by a Supreme Court Justice to deny the application of the Constitution to the noncontiguous territories including the insular possessions acquired by the United States as a result of its imperialist war with Spain. The doctrine found formal lodgment in American public law through the judicial debate of these insular cases. It has been used to declare, in effect, that the Constitution does not follow the flag, and that trial by jury is not a fundamental right, but only one of practice and convenience, a wholly new principle in American jurisprudence.[64] Blackstone had spoken of the right to trial by jury as "the most transcendental privilege which any subject can wish for"; Kent affirmed it as a "fundamental doctrine"; and Story declared it to be "a sacred and inviolable palladium."[65] The inhabitants of these possessions could only wait for civil liberties to be extended to them according to the will of Congress.

The doctrine of incorporation is clearly contrary to the principle of equality set forth in the Declaration of Independence and the Northwest Ordinance of 1787. The rights extended to the inhabitants of the Northwest Territory by the Ordinance of 1787, moreover, are strikingly like the rights guaranteed in the Bill of Rights of the Constitution. The representatives composing the Congress under the Articles of Confederation, which enacted the Ordinance, and those of the Constitutional Convention were not, in most instances, the same persons. The same states were represented in both, however, and only four

---

59. *Hawaii v. Mankichi*, 190 U.S. 197 (1903).
60. *Dorr v. United States*, 195 U.S. 138 (1904).
61. *Rasmussen v. United States*, 197 U.S. 516 (1905).
62. *Ocampo v. United States*, 234 U.S. 91 (1914).
63. *Balzac v. Porto Rico*, 258 U.S. 298 (1922).
64. Willoughby, *The Constitutional Law of the United States*, vol. 1, p. 497.
65. Quoted by J. W. Garner, "The Right of Jury Trial in the Dependencies," *American Law Review*, vol. 36, p. 340 (1909).

years expired between the passage of the Northwest Ordinance and the date that the Bill of Rights went into effect. If these facts suggest that it was the intent of the framers of the Constitution that the Constitutional rights and liberties should extend equally to all United States territories, such an argument was neither acknowledged nor supported by a majority of the Supreme Court.[66]

Caribbean Imperialism

Despite the Teller Amendment, by which the United States disclaimed sovereignty over Cuba, the Platt Amendment of 1901, which was to govern American relations with Cuba until 1934, constituted a severe impairment of Cuban sovereignty and independence. Formulated by Theodore Roosevelt's Secretary of War, Elihu Root, its chief provisions were those giving the United States an ultimate veto over the diplomatic and financial relations of Cuba with other nations, and recognizing the right of the United States to "intervene for the preservation of Cuban independence, the maintenance of a government adequate for the protection of life, property, and individual liberty, and for discharging the obligations with respect to Cuba imposed by the Treaty of Paris on the United States." The United States also received the right to build a naval base at Guantanamo for an initial annual rent of $2,000. The United States refused to withdraw its military forces until Cuba agreed to add these provisions to its constitution.

Under the Platt Amendment, the United States first intervened in restive Cuba in 1906 and reimposed its military rule until 1909. But this was merely the first of a series of American interventions in Cuba. President Taft sent marines to Cuba in 1912, and President Wilson did the same in 1917. Meanwhile, American advocates of annexation of Cuba were active, and Theodore Roosevelt wrote to a friend: "I am so angry with that infernal little Cuban republic that I would like to wipe its people off the face of the earth."[67]

American military presence in Panama in 1903 helped Panamanians to revolt successfully against Colombia and to establish the Republic of Panama, as a prelude to the 1904 treaty under which the United States leased the Panama

---

66. John W. Davis said of these Insular Cases that "there may be found in these opinions the most hotly contested and long continued duel in the life of the Supreme Court." Quoted by Henry Steele Commager, *Documents of American History* (New York: F. S. Crofts, 1944), 3rd edition, vol. 2, p. 193.

67. Quoted by Oscar T. Barck, Jr., and Nelson M. Blake, *Since 1900, A History of the United States in Our Times* (New York: the Macmillan Company, 1947), p. 86.

Canal Zone in return for its guarantee of Panama's independence. While the negotiations for the Canal were proceeding, the United States intervened in the Dominican Republic in 1904 under Theodore Roosevelt to collect Dominican duties and to pay its creditors. Roosevelt justified this action by developing the so-called Roosevelt (or "Big-Stick") Corollary of the Monroe Doctrine, namely, that inasmuch as the United States permits no European nation to intervene in the affairs of Latin American countries, the United States must itself assume the responsibility of preserving order and protecting life and property in those countries. Although there was no necessary connection between this principle of moral and police responsibility and the original Monroe Doctrine, it was used to justify American interventions in the Dominican Republic, Haiti, Cuba, Nicaragua, Mexico, and Honduras.

These interventions during the early years of the twentieth century comprised what came to be called dollar diplomacy, which started with Roosevelt, reached its zenith under Taft, and was continued by Wilson. Dollar diplomacy meant, in short, that an unstable and bankrupt country, facing possible intervention by a European nation potentially unfriendly to the United States, had to be saved from such intervention by the United States, using the Roosevelt Corollary as justification. Dollar diplomacy in Latin America was promoted under the guise of safeguarding the Panama Canal.

The Caribbean was to be regarded as within the power and protection of the United States. It was to become America's closed sea, the "American Mediterranean." Thus, Assistant Secretary of State Loomis stated in 1904 that "no picture of our future is complete which does not contemplate and comprehend the United States as the dominant power in the Caribbean Sea."[68]

In 1917, while arrangements for a government, and the formal transfer, of the Virgin Islands were being made, the Congress contemporaneously was considering revision of the Foraker Act. The result was the Jones Act of 1917,[69] which changed Puerto Rico's executive council into a completely elected senate and made the suffrage universal among adult Puerto Rican males. Most important, however, was the grant of United States citizenship to Puerto Ricans by the Jones Act, which Elihu Root called a "stupid ... performance on the part of Congress."[70] Practically, this meant that those moving to the mainland could claim title to the full protection of American citizenship and that Puerto Ricans became subject to the draft. But they remained without any cloak of

---

68. Quoted by Williams, *From Columbus to Castro*, p. 423.
69. 39 *Stat.* 951 (1917).
70. Quoted by Jessup, *Elihu Root*, vol. 1, p. 479.

protection of the United States Constitution, which still did not follow the flag.[71] In short, the Jones Act of 1917 "did not make clear just what Puerto Rico would become in the middle ground thus allotted to it."[72]

The decision to build the Panama Canal had an important effect on American policy. That policy became known as the Caribbean or big-stick diplomacy. It was consonant with imperialism, expansionism, and protectionism. It was aggressive and militant and based on the assumption that since the United States was to construct and maintain a canal, it must protect it. No possibly dangerous foreign power could be permitted to obtain a foothold near the approaches to the canal, nor could any republic of the Western Hemisphere be permitted to reach a stage of political and economic instability that might invite foreign intervention. The Monroe Doctrine should not permit that; it must be reinterpreted and applied to meet such situations.

This, then, was the Caribbean context within which the United States made its decisions to control completely the destiny of Puerto Rico and to acquire and hold the hapless Virgin Islands.

---

71. *Balzac v. Porto Rico*, 258 U.S. 298 (1922).
72. Perkins, *Denial of Empire*, p. 129.

Part II

Freedom Struggle: 1917–1954

6

Prejudice and Poverty

Colonialism may be defined as the economic and political exploitation of a subjugated people for the benefit of a ruling power. The Europeans who settled in the West Indies had no interest other than monetary; they were in the Caribbean purely for business reasons. Their sole ambition was "to make their fortunes by fair means or foul and return in triumph to their homelands."[1] This was particularly true of the Danes, probably because they never constituted more than a small minority of the European population of their colony.

A Legacy of Neglect

In the case of the Virgin Islands, the Danes evinced "almost no feeling of responsibility for the social problems," and their "lack of interest in anything beyond personal fortune persisted throughout the remaining years of Danish occupation."[2] The harshness of their slavery system, one of the most severe in the Western Hemisphere, was transformed after emancipation into an almost complete neglect of the social and economic uplift of the poor.

No Danish governor, subsequent to Peter von Scholten, demonstrated any personal interest in the welfare of the Virgin Islanders. In effect, Denmark was too concerned with internal problems. In the aftermath of slavery, according to Patricia Murphy, "there is little data to indicate schooling received much attention from either Denmark or the local government."[3] Clearly, the Danes

---

1. Campbell, *St. Thomas Negroes—A Study of Personality and Culture*, p. 62.
2. *Ibid.*, p. 63.
3. Patricia Gill Murphy, *The Education of the New* World *Blacks in the Danish West Indies/U.S. Virgin Islands: A Case Study of Social Transition* (unpublished Ph.D. dissertation, University of Connecticut, 1977), p. 90. It should be emphasized, however, that the Danes' enforcement of compulsory education in the Islands from the late 1870s was unusual for the Caribbean at that time. In his first report, Henry C. Blair, the Navy's school director for St. Thomas and St. John, found conditions at eleven schools (1,052 pupils and 37 teachers) to be "inefficient and antiquated." Blair reported: "No list of teachers and amounts of their

bequeathed to the Americans a legacy—borne of centuries of neglect—of a destitute people who eagerly anticipated social, economic and political benefits they never enjoyed under the Danes.

In August 1917, four months after he became the first American governor, Rear Admiral James Oliver summarized the dire conditions of the Islands, as including very high death and infant mortality rates; unhealthful hospitals, sanitation, water supply, sewerage, and fire prevention systems; woefully inadequate public instruction; and no proper family life. "The islands are incapable of self-support," Oliver reported. "This unfortunate situation is the natural inevitable result of centuries of neglect."[4]

Federal Indifference

Unlike other Western powers, which had long colonizing experiences in distant lands, the United States had only limited experience and no colonial machinery to activate in the Virgin Islands. The Islands were purchased solely for their strategic value, certainly not for economic or altruistic reasons. The simplest way to administer them, therefore, was to put them under military rule and to postpone any consideration of their status and their economic and political development. This decision was made easier by the fact that the Islands were transferred just one week before the United States entered the First World War.[5]

By the Act of March 3, 1917, Congress appropriated the purchase money of $25 million and provided for "a temporary government for the West Indian Islands acquired ... from Denmark."[6] Debate in the House of Represen-

---

salaries, no records of bonuses, honorarium.... No rules for governing the schools, teachers or pupils; No account of supplies, or purchases; No record of janitors not even a copy of the Municipal Ordinance under which the schools are conducted.... All were found lacking in everything pertaining to furniture and equipment.... no paper for classes in writing, drawing or composition.... Children are classed not according to their knowledge, but according to age.... Children are punished with so many lashes for specified offenses." *Report of the School Director for the Virgin Islands of the United States for the Year Ending July 1st 1918*, June 17, 1918, pp. 2–3; United States National Archives and Records Services in Washington, D.C. (hereafter cited as: NARS), Record Group (hereafter cited as: RG) 55/2, File 62.

4. Quoted by Evans, *The Virgin Islands, From Naval Base to New Deal*, p. 265.

5. The impending American entry into the War was clearly the context of the decision to place the Islands under the U.S. Navy, a decision which was first reported by *The New York Times* (March 24, 1917, p. 7, col. 3) under the headline: "War for the Defeat of Germany Now Favored by Wilson Cabinet."

6. 39 *Stat.* 1132 (1917). At a mass meeting held in St. Thomas, March 3, 1917, it was decided to suggest to Washington that the Islands be named the "American Virgin Islands"

tatives on the proposed bill[7] clearly indicated confusion concerning the contemplated status of the Islands, illustrated by the following exchange in the House of Representatives:

> MR. CALDWELL. There is a constitutional provision that prevents the levying of an export duty in the United States, is there not?
>
> MR. FLOOD. This [the Virgin Islands] is not a part of the United States yet.
>
> MR. CALDWELL. It will be as soon as we take possession of it, will it not?
>
> MR. FLOOD. No. It will be a possession....
>
> MR. FESS. While the temporary government is in operation, will it be under the Executive Department of the United States?
>
> MR. FLOOD. Absolutely.[8]

Debate in the Senate—as in the case of the Foraker Act concerning Puerto Rico seventeen years earlier—concentrated on the constitutionality of the export duty on sugar which, in turn, depended on the status of the Islands. The debate ended with Senator Underwood registering disappointment that the bill failed to clarify the constitutional status of the Islands:

> I had hoped, Mr. President, that the committee had investigated this subject and could give us some direct light upon it. I recognize the importance of the bill passing at an early date; and even if the tax should be subsequently decided to be unconstitutional, that portion of the bill which seeks to pay for the islands, if we live up to our contract, of course, ought to become a law. The only question is that if we pass this bill and there is doubt as to whether or not we can properly levy this tax, we may find the citizens of those islands and the government of the islands in a very embarrassed condition.[9]

The bill became law without any clarification of this issue. Practically no attention, moreover, was given to the bill's provisions by the general membership of either the Senate or House.

Congress was content by the Act of March 3, 1917 to confer upon the President of the United States the power to direct policies, to regulate insular of-

---

instead of the "Dewey Islands," in honor of Admiral Dewey, or other names being considered. *The New York Times*, March 4, 1917, 1, p. 5, col. 4.

7. H.R. 20755, 64th Cong., 2d sess. (1917).

8. 54 *Congressional Record* 3649 (1917).

9. 54 *Congressional Record* 3688 (1917).

ficials and federal appropriations, and to appoint a military official as governor in whom otherwise were vested "all military, civil and judicial powers."

All local laws including the Colonial Law of 1906—itself a virtual re-enactment of the Colonial Law of 1863—were to remain in force, "in so far as compatible with the changed sovereignty," until otherwise provided by Congress. "Nothing can be clearer ... than the intention of Congress to continue the whole governmental system practically as it then existed."[10]

This so-called "temporary" Presidential government, provided by the 1917 Act, not only perpetuated the Danes' repressive laws virtually unchanged for fifty-four years, since 1863, but it continued their authoritarian system—albeit under American suzerainty—for nineteen more years, until 1936 when Congress finally overcame its indifference to the extent of providing an organic act for the Islands. Although the Act of 1917 anticipated that the President would be active in initiating policy for the Islands, "there is little evidence that any president," prior to Franklin Roosevelt, "ever took the initiative in a matter of great importance to the Virgin Islands."[11]

Meanwhile, Virgin Islanders mistakenly thought that United States citizenship had been automatically bestowed on those among them who had not chosen Danish citizenship under the terms of the treaty of purchase. They mistakenly thought they would be given the right to vote and a large measure of self-government. And they mistakenly thought that American sovereignty would result in greater employment, higher wages, and an end of their poverty. On all counts, they were wrong. None of these aspirations were to be fulfilled for years to come.

Infusion of Racism

A number of commentaries have maintained that the United States Navy brought racial and color prejudice to the Virgin Islands. Political scientist Gordon Lewis observed that the "Annapolis mentality" was unsuited for a colonial civil service, and that the Navy's completely segregated service based on its policy of total racial exclusion, adopted in 1920, produced an all-white service that ruled over an overwhelmingly Negro population.[12]

---

10. Evans, *The Virgin Islands*, p. 53.

11. *Ibid.*, p. 99. "No executive order was ever issued concerning the relationship of the Navy Department to the government of the Virgin Islands." Dookhan, *A History of the Virgin Islands of the United States*, p. 206.

12. Lewis, *The Virgin Islands, A Caribbean Lilliput*, p. 51.

In his oft-cited study of the personality and culture of "St. Thomas Negroes," psychologist Albert Campbell claimed that although there was considerable discrimination between classes and different shades of color during the last eighty years of Danish rule, there was a minimum of overt discrimination against colored persons because of their race.

> The transfer in 1917 brought ... a group of administrators and merchants who were for the most part thoroughly imbued with the characteristic American credo regarding race. Many of the early naval and civilian officials were of southern origin.... The marines who policed the streets during the first few years of the American occupation were on occasion highly offensive ... There is no doubt ... that the fourteen years of naval rule greatly increased the consciousness of race in St. Thomas and gave added emphasis to the importance of being white.[13]

In commenting about how the increased racial emphasis during the Navy's regime affected sexual relationships, local historian Darwin Creque wrote: "Almost always black women of the lowest income groups preferred white bastard children to black ones."[14]

Geraldo Guirty has recounted an incident he witnessed in St. Thomas on the first Christmas eve under naval rule, in 1917, when he was eleven years old:

> There was a commotion on Main Street involving marines and natives. The marines came out with rifles, fired shots, and frightened the people who feared lynchings.... I ran as fast as I could to get home. That was just one major incident. There were many others that were minor, as, for example, also during that Christmas season, when a young native man was made to kneel at the command of a marine on Main Street and to recite the Lord's Prayer.[15]

---

13. Campbell, *St. Thomas Negroes*, pp. 80–81.

14. Creque, *The U.S. Virgin Islands and the Eastern Caribbean*, p. 76. "A feeling of identification with white persons is undoubtedly an important source of ego-gratification for many lower-class people who cannot fulfill their status ambitions in more direct ways. This process of raising the color takes many forms, of which the most obvious is the willingness of many lower-class women to serve as temporary sexual partners of white men.... In most cases these associations do not involve any monetary consideration; the principal motivation of the women appears to be a desire to be known as the intimate of a white man and if possible to bear a child lighter in skin-color than herself." Campbell, *St. Thomas Negroes*, p. 56.

15. Interview of Geraldo Guirty, Charlotte Amalie, St. Thomas, July 26, 1977. J. Antonio Jarvis wrote of the "race prejudice of the 'leathernecks'" in his *Brief History of the Virgin Islands* (St. Thomas: The Art Shop, 1938), p. 141.

Similar incidents involving U.S. sailors and marines on Christmas eve of 1918 provoked a letter to Governor Oliver, published in a New York City newspaper and signed by four St. Thomians. Calling his attention to "an outrage on our defenceless people hitherto unknown in this island," the letter read in part:

> Batches of these men paraded our streets with automatic revolvers, bottles, knives, sticks and stones.... Civilians were chased off the streets, some beaten, some searched, while others were fired at.... Why were these men not ordered off the streets? Would the civic rights of the people on the mainland have been so disrespected? Is this Democracy? This outrage is race hatred pure and simple.... We demand that all available measures be adopted and assurances given that such an outrage will never be made real again.[16]

Publication of the letter led the Director of Naval Intelligence in Washington to request Governor Oliver to conduct an investigation of these charges. Oliver's response attributed the trouble to "the worst element of the colored population" and claimed that his investigation found the statements in the letter to be untrue. "Generally speaking the St. Thomas negro is a very peaceable citizen," wrote Oliver, "but it does not take much to arouse him if he feels that he has been wronged, and unfortunately there are agitators constantly at work trying to make him dissatisfied with his position."[17]

Most of Governor Oliver's response to the Director of Naval Intelligence consisted of a scurrilous attack on the character and reputation of those who signed the letter, including revelations from local police files about their sex lives. He characterized Rothschild Francis as "a sort of half-witted negro ... apparently without an occupation ... constantly causing agitation amongst the ignorant class...." Octavius C. Granady was depicted "a negro" whose license to practice law was cancelled because "he defrauded the native population," and was adjudged by a local court as being "demented." Charles A. Emanuel was represented as being "a negro" who "has twice been reported to the police office for obtaining money under false pretenses." And Randolph A. Innis was reported to be "a negro without occupation, and is always with Rothschild Francis." Oliver's defamatory report also identified three "other agitators here that

---

16. NARS, RG 55/2, File 62. Director of Naval Intelligence to the Governor of the Virgin Islands, January 16, 1919, with copy of letter to the Governor in *New York News*, January 9, 1919.

17. NARS, RG, 55/2, File 62. Governor of the Virgin Islands to Secretary of the Navy via Director of Naval Intelligence, February 3, 1919, pp. 1–2.

are more troublesome ... causing much dissatisfaction by agitating the question of their citizenship status and the rights of the native born to govern themselves." They were: James C. Roberts, "the negro editor" of a St. Thomas newspaper, the "Bulletin," and a school teacher until "all of his pupils left him"; August Burnet, "an unlicensed attorney ... guilty of sharp practice and ... preying upon the old and feeble"; and, in St. Croix, D. Hamilton Jackson, "who has since forming a labor union been instrumental in causing a great deal of unrest amongst the natives," and whose "followers ... stand by him in his crookedness." Oliver concluded:

> It has been the policy of this Government carefully to avoid any action that would antagonize the natives in any way.... It must be borne in mind that these islands, like the Isthmus of Panama, are a nest and focus of intrigue and although it has not been possible, up to this time, to connect any of the disturbances that have occurred with German propaganda, it is considered not unlikely that they have such connection.... I, therefore, earnestly recommend that this matter be taken up with the Attorney General and he be requested to send a capable, trusted, and energetic representative here who is familiar with Federal laws, who would be qualified to carry on prosecutions, and who would act directly under the Federal Department.[18]

Other disturbances between marines and inhabitants followed as, for example, an altercation of the evening of March 30, 1921 in St. Thomas resulting in a severe injury to one marine and lesser injuries to two citizens.[19] More serious was the stabbing of a boy by a marine in St. Croix following which a crowd of about one hundred natives assembled at the home of R. E. Barrett, Despatching Secretary of St. Croix. In his letter of April 5, 1924 to Governor Philip Williams, Barrett blamed such incidents on the fact that the Marines without difficulty could obtain "an unlimited quantity of liquor."[20]

---

18. *Ibid.*, pp. 5–6.

19. NARS, RG; 55/2, File 62-1. Gaffney to the Governor of the Virgin Islands, March 31, 1921. "In 1921, inhabitants of Savanna and Back-of-All in St. Thomas were thrown in a state of terror through a party of Marines armed with rifles firing in all direction. Many houses were pierced by bullets and the Salvation Army was forced to flight during a revival meeting. Governor Oman appointed a Board of Enquiry to investigate the disturbance." "Today in History," *Daily News*, March 30, 1978.

20. NARS, RG, 55/2, File 89-1. Barrett to the Governor of the Virgin Islands, April 5, 1924.

By 1927, before ten years of Navy rule had expired, the Islands had already experienced six governors, among whom were those who unmistakenly were white supremacists. For example, Navy Governor Sumner Kittelle wrote President Warren Harding in 1922: "I cannot too strongly urge that there be no change made in the organic law until a full generation has elapsed ... and above all the white element must remain in the lead and in supreme control."[21] Noting "this uninterrupted succession of Southern Caesars," Casper Holstein, a leader of Virgin Islanders in New York City, complained: "Surely there must be some Northern white men in the Navy Department. Why this insistence on Southern whites for the governorship of the islands?"[22] Navy governors held themselves aloof from those who sought to influence them, seldom answering letters or petitions themselves, preferring instead to direct their seconds-in-command — with whom racist values were shared — to respond. Thus Government Secretary C. C. Timmons betrayed his racism by opposing the widening of the suffrage for fear it would presage all-black juries, and, therefore, "a person of the Caucasian race might not be entirely safe before such a jury."[23]

Memories of those days still "rankle" Virgin Islands oldsters, according to Edward O'Neill:

> To most of the navy, it was a strange world into which they had been transported, where, under old Danish social habits, men of color moved in the highest circles and were invited to Government House, while whites of lower station could only envy them.... Then, as now, the Virgin Islander was supersensitive about being treated as a lesser breed, and his pride was severely lacerated by the newcomers' attitude.[24]

---

21. NARS, RG 55/2, File 62-1. Governor Kittelle to President Harding, February 27, 1922. Harding replied: "I am more than glad to have this detailed information about conditions in the Islands." *Ibid.* Harding to Kittelle, March 20, 1922.

22. Casper Holstein, "Shell Game in the Virgin Islands Exposed by Mr. Casper Holstein," *The Negro World* (New York City), September 19, 1925; NARS, RG 55/2, File 95-1.

23. NARS, RG 55/2, File 62-1. C. C. Timmons, Government Secretary, to Elizabeth Harrington, May 27, 1921.

24. Edward A. O'Neill, *Rape of the Virgin Islands* (New York: Praeger Publishers, 1972), p. 43. For other commentaries about the increase of race consciousness under Navy rule, see, *e.g.*: Norwell Harrigan and Pearl I. Varlack, "The U.S. Virgin Islands and the Black Experience," *Journal of Black Studies*, 7, 394–398; Ezra A. Naughton, *The Origin and Development of Higher Education in the Virgin Islands* (unpublished Ph.D. dissertation, Washington, D.C.: Catholic University, 1973), p. 191; and Valdemar A. Hill, Sr., *Rise to Recognition* (St. Thomas: St. Thomas Graphics, 1971), pp. 72–73.

The racism of the Navy was institutionalized to the extent of preserving an all-white service by a policy of racial exclusion of black or colored persons. The only exception to this rule was the recruitment of Virgin Islands musicians into a colored brass band at the St. Thomas Naval Station—under local bandmaster Alton Adams—which was sent by Governor Kittelle on a tour of American public schools "as a publicity gimmick in defense of the Navy record in the islands."[25]

White supremacy was imposed on the predominantly black population of the Virgin Islands through military occupation manifested by the intimidating presence of armed marines in both St. Thomas and St. Croix. In response to those demanding civil government, the Navy government maintained that it constituted a civil government "in every particular," and that the Navy officers administering the civil affairs of the Islands were merely doing what they were assigned to do,[26] at a considerable saving to the inhabitants.[27] In his 1926 letter to former Governor Philip Williams, Governor Martin E. Trench unwittingly came close to assuming a posture of Naval indifference toward the Islands:

> As you perhaps know, the Navy Department has never declared any policy with regard to its relations to the Government of these islands. As I understand it, the Navy is perfectly willing to go ahead and send officers to administer affairs here and give them the help that they are giving now, provided Congress desires it. On the other hand the Navy Department is willing to move out if Congress desires to put somebody else in charge.[28]

Apologists for the Navy included portions of the continental press. For example, Henry S. Whitehead, who had resided in the Islands, claimed in a magazine article that the typical agitator against the government is a "bad darky"

25. Gordon K. Lewis, "Orphan Islands, The Early American Years," *Virgin Islands View* (St. Thomas), (September 1967): 21.

26. NARS, RG 55/2, File 62-1. C. C. Timmons, Government Secretary, to Elizabeth Harrington, May 19, 1921.

27. "… the combined salary of those officers performing civil duty only together with those officers who perform both naval and civil duty, aggregate for this municipality about $55,000 … annually." NARS, RG 55/2, File 108-1. William S. Zane, Government Secretary, to George A. Mena, Secretary, The Republican Club of St. Thomas and St. John, December 8, 1924.

28. NARS, RG 55/2, File 89-2. Governor Martin E. Trench to Philip Williams, August 5, 1926.

and dishonest. "He is in no sense a menace to white women and girls, as his confrère in the American South," Whitehead wrote. "He dreams of a Virgin Islands future when black shall rule in black's interest."[29]

Naval Autocracy

The Virgin Islands were formally transferred to the United States on March 31, 1917 and were placed under the rule of the United States Navy. During the first years of Navy rule, the hospitals were reorganized and improved, nurses were trained, sanitation projects were started, the entire population was vaccinated against smallpox, infant and maternal welfare was improved, and a mosquito control program to abate malaria was implemented. One result of these measures was the fall in the death rate from 35.4 per thousand during the period 1911 to 1917, to 25.0 during the period 1918–1922, and 19.5 in 1926.[30]

Otis Browne, a St. Croix educator during the naval administration, has commented:

> I'm not sorry the Americans came. I remember the barefoot students with chiggers between their toes. And the trachoma. And the lice. I remember how the Navy doctors cleaned up those diseases. I'm not sorry. They've done too much good.[31]

Other notable accomplishments during Navy rule (1917–1931) were construction of concrete reservoirs and catchments for improved water supply, introduction of a night-soil sewage removal and disposal system, organization of native police and fire departments, installation of salt water pumping systems, and improvements in education.

By any standard, this catalog of Navy achievements was impressive, leading Luther Evans to conclude that "it is obvious that in general the obligations of the United States to the people of the Virgin Islands have been satisfied in full measure."[32] Other assessments of Navy rule have been much less charitable.

---

29. Henry S. Whitehead, "The Grievance of the Virgin Islands," *The Independent*, September 4, 1926, p. 273; NARS, RG 55/2, File 99-1.

30. Knud Hansen, *From Denmark to the Virgin Islands* (New York: Dorrance and Company, 1947), pp. 103–109.

31. Otis Browne, Oral History with Patricia Gill Murphy, Christiansted, St. Croix, January 11, 1977, p. 38, in Murphy, *The Education of the New World Blacks*, p. 109.

32. Evans, *The Virgin Islands*, p. 320.

The Navy did little to improve the economy. Shortly after transfer, the governor requested the United States Department of Agriculture to take over the agricultural experiment station on St. Croix, established by the Danes in 1911, but its appropriations were reduced from a meager annual average of $3,938 during the period 1910–1917 to only a pittance of $632 during 1918–1931. In response to the colonial councils, the governor created in 1924 a department of agriculture, commerce and labor, but this department—as well as all public welfare activities—was put under the charge of the Navy chaplain.

Cultivated areas declined from 12,220 acres in 1916 to only 4,686 acres in 1932, and sugar production likewise declined from an average annual production of 13.5 million pounds during the period 1910–1917 to only 3.57 million pounds by 1931. Economic depression in the Islands, beginning in 1922, was marked by these developments: extension to the Virgin Islands in 1921 of the Prohibition Act which forbade the manufacture and sale of rum in the Islands, long periods of severe drought, a drop in sugar prices, increasing unemployment, an inadequate revenue system, larger recurring budget deficits, and substantial emigration of Virgin Islanders. Despite some immigration from Puerto Rico and the mainland, and rapidly declining mortality rates, the population of the Virgin Islands decreased from 26,051 in 1917 to 22,012 in 1930, a decline of 15.5 percent largely accounted for by emigration wrought by economic regression under Navy rule.[33]

Rothschild Francis, in a letter to *The New York Times* in 1923, charged that economic conditions in the Islands were marked by rampant unemployment,

---

33. See: Dookhan, *A History of The Virgin Islands of the United States*, pp. 268–271, and Evans, *The Virgin Islands*, pp. 274–275. Dookhan elsewhere claims that prohibition "destroyed the islands' thriving rum industry. Even the bay-rum industry suffered when the bay-rum was denatured with alicylic acid to prevent its use as beverage." Isaac Dookhan, *The Search for Identity, The Political Aspirations and Frustrations of Virgin Islanders under the United States Naval Administration 1917–1927* (unpublished, xeroxed, College of the Virgin Islands, August 1977), p. 34. Also, "Volsteadism hit at the heart of the shipping trade of St. Thomas." Isaac Dookhan, *Volsteadism or National Prohibition in the Virgin Islands: An Aspect of Administration Control, 1917–1934* (unpublished, xeroxed, College of the Virgin Islands, October 1978), p. 4. According to the Colonial Councils, prohibition caused curtailment of the Islands' exports by approximately 73 percent. *The New York Times*, April 10, 1923, p. 24, col. 3. But Luther Evans, staunch defender of the Navy's rule, argued just the opposite: "One of the most widely accepted falsehoods is that the application of the prohibition law plunged the Virgin Islands … into abject economic depression…. But not for a century has rum been more than a minor factor in the economic life of the Virgin Islands. The fallacy regarding bay rum is even more vicious … bay rum production in the last years of prohibition was more than double its highest pre-prohibition figure." Evans, *The Virgin Islands*, p. 5.

undernourished children, merchants unable to pay taxes, and threatened whole-
sale starvation.[34] Seven years later, as Navy rule was coming to an end, economic conditions were reported by Herbert D. Brown, chief of the United
States Bureau of Efficiency, to have grown "constantly worse" since 1917, because the Islands had been "the victims of a series of calamities."[35] Nevertheless, at no time during the fourteen years of Navy rule did any of the seven
governors take "the initiative in developing a program of either political or
economic reform and development."[36]

Under the Act of March 3, 1917 to provide a "temporary government" for
the Virgin Islands, the governor was authorized, until otherwise provided by
Congress, to exercise all military, civil, and political powers necessary to govern the Islands. By virtue of the Danish laws continued in effect by the 1917
Act, moreover, the governor could issue regulations, orders, and provisional
laws and dissolve the colonial councils. Four of the fifteen members of the
Colonial Council for St. Thomas and St. John, and five of the eighteen members of the Colonial Council for St. Croix, were to be appointed by the governor. He could also approve legislation subject only to Presidential override,
and he could appoint and remove judges of the police courts at will.

---

34. *The New York Times*, July 31, 1923, p. 16, col. 6. Letter to the Editor from Rothschild Francis, Chairman, Publicity Committee, St. Thomas, July 23, 1923.

35. *The New York Times*, June 22, 1930, sec. 2, p. 1, col. 3. "Nowhere under the American flag is the system of feudalism so strongly entrenched as it is in the Virgin Islands.
Nowhere is the price for maintaining it being exacted so inexorably." Thomas H. Dickinson, "The Economic Crisis in the Virgin Islands." *Current History*, (December 1927), 378–381.

36. Whitney T. Perkins, *Denial of Empire, The United States and its Dependencies*, pp.
170–171. A review of hearings before congressional subcommittees, dealing with federal
appropriations to the Islands, reveals that seldom if ever did an insular official testify in behalf of the insular budget during the period of naval administrations. Moreover, a review
of the annual reports of the Navy governors reveals that they did not urge policies upon
their superiors in Washington. On one occasion when a Navy governor did exercise initiative, he was thwarted by the Navy's chain-of-command bureaucracy in Washington. In April
1924, Governor Philip Williams wrote to Secretary of Labor James G. Davis requesting him
to send a group of experts to arbitrate or conciliate a dispute "between labor and capital."
Davis acknowledged receiving Williams' letter and stated that the matter was under review.
But the Secretary of Navy intervened with a radiogram to Williams: "Do you desire this
commission sent and will the Government of the Islands defray expenses to do so?" Williams
promptly responded: "Thank Secretary of Labor ... for his present offer. Tell him that con-
ditions have changed so that a commission of conciliation is not needed." Williams to Davis,
April 19, 1924; Davis to Williams, May 13, 1924; Secretary of Navy to Williams, radiogram,
May 20, 1924, Williams to Secretary of Navy, radiogram, May 21, 1924; NARS. RG 55/2,
File 59-3.

These powers, according to Isaac Dookhan, made the governor, "a veritable autocrat,"[37] and he acted as such. "Naval officers of the first American regime," wrote Jarvis, "were popes in the Vatican of Government Hill. They resided there in seclusion, venerated by all faithful employees."[38]

Americanization

At the time of transfer of the Islands, in 1917, the United States Supreme Court had accepted the doctrine of incorporation sufficiently to make it controlling in regard to the Virgin Islands. It was not until 1921, however, that a federal court declared that the Constitution did not extend, of its own force, to the Islands.[39] Accordingly, the Danish Colonial Law of 1906 remained in force.

Much of the power of the colonial councils over local administration was granted by the Colonial Law of 1906, which conferred upon them the authority to create administrative commissions. These commissions were guaranteed their existence until suspended by the councils. Practically all major activities of local government depended on these commissions, much to the consternation of the first American governor, Admiral Oliver. "He simply wouldn't put up with such 'un-American' governmental practices." Soon after the transfer in 1917, therefore, he persuaded the councils to suspend the commissions for five years, by "resorting to the far-fetched argument of the stress-of-war circumstances." The councils abolished the commissions and vested their executive powers in the governor. At the end of the five years, the commissions were abolished entirely. Thus were the Navy governors able to concentrate the powers of government in their own hands far more than did their Danish predecessors.[40]

Except for their efforts to exert greater control over the Islands, the Navy governors were intent on keeping intact the authoritarian political system they inherited from the Danes. Otherwise, the naval administrations followed a basic policy "to Americanize the people of the Virgin Islands and raise them to American standards of life,"[41] or—as expressed by Governor Oliver—to ad-

---

37. Dookhan, *The Search for Identity*, p. 6.

38. J. Antonio Jarvis, *The Virgin Islands and Their People* (Philadelphia: Dorrance and Company, 1944), pp. 91–92.

39. *Soto et al. v. United States*, 273 F. 628 (C.C.A. 3rd 1921).

40. Evans, *The Virgin Islands*, pp. 105–106.

41. *Ibid.*, p. 272.

vance this ignorant and uneducated people "in the scale of civilization."[42] The way to do this was "to Americanize the schools and thus the students."[43]

No thought was given to the possibility of offending the cultural norms or attitudes of the people. "We had 'dignity' in the Danish times," said one St. Croix resident.[44] "When the Americans came," recalled another, "they seemed to think that a child here could not think."[45] "Americanization," stated Patricia Murphy, "appears to have reinforced the concept of racial superiority/inferiority and corroded the self-pride inherent in the previous Moravian religious education."[46]

No effort was made to adapt a school system to the indigenous culture. Instead, an American director of education was imported from the States to revamp the educational system. In 1922, he introduced into the elementary grades courses in spelling, writing, drawing, manual training, and home economics "taken almost verbatim from the 1919 edition of the Course of Study of New Mexico." In 1923, a junior high school curriculum was adopted "based very largely upon the Utah course of study for secondary schools." Nothing was done during Navy rule to improve the curriculum.[47]

Asserting the purpose of the schools to be the acculturation to the standards of the ruling power, the director sought to recruit American teachers, as witness his report to the governor:

> The value of the American teacher cannot be overstated. They possess a command of the English Language and American ideals and standards that are very useful in the classroom. One of the objects of the public school is to make the pupils good prospective Americans. No one can do this better than the American teacher.[48]

The effort to recruit state-side teachers was not successful. With few exceptions, teachers were local persons.

---

42. Quoted by Dookhan, *The Search for Identity*, p. 5.

43. Gibson, *Ethnicity and Schooling: A Caribbean Case Study*, p. 108.

44. Elena Christian, Oral History with Patricia Gill Murphy, Christiansted, St. Croix, January 6, 1977, p. 28, in Murphy, *The Education of the New World Blacks*, p. 117.

45. Eulalie Rivera, Oral History with Patricia Gill Murphy, Christiansted, St. Croix, January 5, 1977, p. 35, in *ibid.*, p. 114.

46. *Ibid.*, p. 104.

47. Charles F. Reid, *Education in the Territories and Outlying Possessions of the United States* (New York: Bureau of Publications, Teachers College, Columbia University, 1941), p. 480.

48. Department of Education of the Virgin Islands, Annual *Report, 1925*, quoted in Gibson, *Ethnicity and Schooling*, p. 109, and in Pearl I. Varlack, *Teacher Education in the Virgin Islands: A Strategy for Curriculum Design* (unpublished Ph.D. dissertation, University of Pittsburgh, 1974), p. 74.

Not until 1931 did the first high school class in the Virgin Islands—in St. Thomas—graduate. And it was not until 1933 that a tenth grade was added in St. Croix. Since the Navy failed to offer Virgin Islanders opportunity for full secondary education, one could not say that local teachers on the whole were well qualified. Indeed, a 1928 educational survey reported:

> The educational standards of teachers ... are ... incredibly low. In St. Thomas, where the standards seem to be the best, the median teacher is a ninth grade product; 6 out of 47 teachers ... have seventh grade schooling or less; 9 have gone through eighth grade; 18 are ninth grade products; 9 have some senior high school work; 5 have had some college work. In St. John 4 of the teachers have gone as far as twelfth grade, 3 have been through ninth grade, and 2 through seventh. In St. Croix, where the evidence seems to be that the better qualified teachers have been leaving the system and less qualified ones have been substituted, 6 out of 42 teachers studied had had seventh grade schooling or less, 6 had been through the equivalent of eighth grade, 10 through ninth, 5 through tenth, 3 through eleventh, and 7 through twelfth, while 5 had had college work. No permanently valuable educational results can be hoped for until these standards are raised.[49]

No effort was made under Navy rule to raise the standards of St. Croix teachers, or to formulate any policy for the guidance of public education in the Virgin Islands. Among the Navy's educational achievements were: an increase of total annual expenditures for education from less than $20 million in 1917 to an annual average of $100 million from 1922 to 1931, a substantial reduction of illiteracy, and a reduction of the percentage of those enrolled in private schools from 33 to 26 percent during the period of 1921 to 1930. At the end of Navy rule, however, over 21 percent of the adult population remained illiterate, and the standard of work in the private schools remained higher than that in the public schools.[50]

---

49. Quoted by Reid, *Education in the Territories*, p. 484.

50. *Ibid.*, pp. 464–473. "When the Danish West Indies became the United States Virgin Islands in 1917, a literacy level of more than 98 percent had been reached." Pearl Varlack, "Teacher Education in the United States Virgin Islands: A Historical Profile," *Microstate Studies*, (Caribbean Research Institute, College of the Virgin Islands), 1 (1977): 73.

Navy Justice

The Colonial Law of 1906 authorized a "town court" and designated the Supreme Court of Denmark as the highest appellate authority for the Islands. After transfer to the United States, the town court became known as the "district court." The jurisdiction of the local courts was extended by the Act of March 3, 1917 to all cases on the Islands "to which the United States or any citizen thereof may be a party," and the Circuit Court of Appeals in far-off Philadelphia was given the appellate jurisdiction[51] formerly exercised by the court in Denmark. Otherwise the court structure continued unchanged together with practically all the Danish colonial laws.

The respective colonial councils enacted local "codes of laws" in 1920 and 1921, embodying almost all the provisions of the Alaskan Code simply because the lawyer commissioned by the Navy to draft the codes was imported from Alaska for that purpose. The respective codes for the two municipalities continued the political division and, confusingly, contained differences between them. The codes also continued the existing judicial structure with a district court having jurisdiction over both municipalities, three inferior or "police" courts, and juvenile courts.[52]

A number of rights equivalent to those in the Constitution of the United States were accorded the people of the Virgin Islands by the colonial laws carried over from the Danish period, including freedom of religion and the press and the right of peaceable assembly. The codes of 1920–1921, furthermore, added most of the rights of the accused of the American legal system, including trial by jury, except that provision was made for indictment by information rather than by grand jury. The codes provided that even when a defendant waived his right to a jury, the judge could still order a jury trial.[53] Although the Constitution did not follow the American flag to the Virgin Islands—because the doctrine of incorporation of the Insular Cases so applied to the "unincorporated" Virgin Islands—the Circuit Court of Appeals nevertheless held in 1921 that "the natural or personal rights" of the Fifth and Sixth Amendments of the United States Constitution did apply to the Islands, and thus an accused had the right to be confronted with witnesses against him and the right to he heard in his own defense.[54]

---

51. The Court held that its jurisdiction extended to review of both facts and law in all cases appealed to it from the Islands. *Clen v. Jorgensen*, 265 F. 120 (1920).
52. For discussion of the codes of 1920–1921, see Evans, *The Virgin Islands*, pp. 207–212.
53. *Ibid.*, p. 210.
54. *Solo et al. v. United States*, 273 F. 628 (1921).

The expressly stated purpose of the codes of 1920–1921 was to effect "an early Americanization" of local jurisprudence. But, wrote Luther Evans, the codes gave "no recognition of common-law marriage, a fact which should be taken into account in connection with the record of the natives in matters of irregular unions and illegitimacy."[55] Despite the codes' provisions for Americanization of the legal system and for the many rights of the people, the Navy's administration of the judicial system in the Islands was described by Darwin Creque as "deplorable … atrocious and un-American,"[56] and as a "farce" by one colonial council member, who added: "If we protest this rule in the newspapers, we are held for libel."[57] These were judgments with which many concurred.

Among the abuses of the Navy administration were the appointment of police judges for brief terms and permitting them to act also as government prosecutors, often in the same case, and the fact that some judges displayed "contempt for the Negro race." Even Navy apologist Luther Evans was moved to disgust. "To be designated 'niggers' and treated with disdain," wrote Evans, "is exceedingly distasteful to these proud people. Instead of inculcating in them a feeling of respect for the court it creates a feeling of distrust."[58]

Perhaps the most egregious abuse of power was the practice of executive interference in the judicial process. Lucius J. M. Malmin, appointed by President Wilson as the first district court judge, resisted in 1920 an attempt by Rear Admiral Joseph Oman, the Islands' second governor, to dictate a judicial decision of a case being tried before Malmin who, by order of the Governor, was thereupon "deprived of his court officials" appointed by the Governor. To escape possible arrest and the Governor's warrant that he not leave the Islands, Malmin took refuge on a British ship to the States, whereupon the Governor acted to remove him from office. Malmin then obtained a writ of mandamus from the Circuit Court of Appeals in Philadelphia, which had appellate jurisdiction over the Islands, ordering his reinstatement, but Governor Oman—backed by President Harding—ignored the writ and Malmin resigned.[59] After Judge

---

55. Evans, *The Virgin Islands*, p. 212.

56. Creque, *The U.S. Virgin Islands*, p. 79.

57. John B. Hestres quoted in *The New York Times*, July 30, 1925, p. 2, col. 6.

58. Evans, *The Virgin Islands*, p. 213.

59. Malmin later told his story before the American Bar Association meeting, September 1, 1925, at Detroit, after having failed in his attempt to see President Coolidge to tell him what Malmin termed the "unbearable and undemocratic conduct" of the Navy governors who were guilty of "maladministration of justice." *The New York Times*, August 25, 1925, p. 26, col. 3. See, also, Dookhan, *The Search for Identity*, p. 7, and the reprint of Malmin's ABA speech in "Autocracy in the Virgin Islands." *The Nation*, October 21, 1925, pp. 470–473.

Malmin's illegal removal, the codes of 1920–1921 vested appointment of all judges in the governor, which erased any remaining vestige of judicial independence and made it easier for the Navy governors to interfere in the judicial process by virtue of their appointment of more pliable judges. One such judge, a successor to Malmin on the district court, was a white continental, George Washington Williams of Baltimore, whose attitude was that "the Navy administration was above criticism and the local malcontents almost beneath contempt."[60] Prior to his appointment as judge of the district court, Williams had served the governor as government attorney, police judge, police chief, and member of the local board of parole and pardons—all at the same time!

Navy justice sometimes was devoid of any semblance of due process, as, for example, the summary deportation of a young woman teacher, who had incurred the displeasure of the Navy government, and her subsequent incarceration in a mainland insane asylum before her release.[61]

Repression of Native Leaders

During the last months of Danish rule, D. Hamilton Jackson had organized a labor union and general strike of the agricultural laborers of St. Croix, which ended in an agreement that raised wages from 20 to 35 cents for a nine-hour day for first-class workers. The Agreement of August 15, 1917 raised the scale to 50 cents and called for a daily task system based on actual measured field trials of the principal kinds of work. Shortly after the transfer, Governor James Oliver borrowed the services of Edward Enright, an assistant to the Governor of Puerto Rico, to supervise the field trials. Enright spent about a month in St. Croix, at the conclusion of which he reported to Governor Oliver concerning the Crucian workers that

---

60. Evans, *The Virgin Islands*, p. 211. Roger Baldwin, Director of the American Civil Liberties Union, vehemently protested the pending appointment of George Washington Williams to the District Court judgeship because of "his bias against labor unions," his opposition to self-government for the natives, and for misrepresentation of the Islands in his published articles; NARS, RG 55/2, File 95-1. Baldwin to Governor Philip Williams, June 25, 1924. That local authorities had already formed the opinion that the American Civil Liberties Union was "a supporter of all subversive movements," see, J. J. Gaffney, Government Secretary, to C. E. Rappollee, Despatching Secretary for St. Croix, February 23, 1923; NARS, RG 55/2, File 59.

61. Judge Malmin's speech before the American Bar Association, as reprinted in *The Nation*, October 21, 1925, p. 472.

it seems to be universally conceded that the present St. Croix laborer is not the equal of the laborer to be had in the island twenty five years ago.... the people are idling and not rendering half the usual amount of day's labor ... and ... they are showing a spirit of contentious caprice and even unwillingness to work at all.... The majority of planters I talked with consider that there is simply more drinking and gambling as a result of the higher wage and more money spent in finery and other extravagance.... Many planters advocate prohibition, at least of the sale of intoxicants.... To put drink beyond the reach of the laborer should be an unmixed good....

While a surprisingly large percent of them are literate this literacy carries no standard of decent living. The almost universal squalor is accompanied by ... a promiscuity of sexual relations that cannot fail to lower the standard of living in every way. There is almost no home life. Marriages are very rare, and the children—all these by one mother often claiming each a separate father appear to be held to be the concern of the woman alone.[62]

Enright saved his greatest vitriol, however, for the head of the labor union, D. Hamilton Jackson.

I had an interview with him and found him to be too ignorant of the subject matter and too inclined to discuss the world at large to warrant spending any further time with him.... He gave no evidence of possessing any information or experience that would entitle his opinion to any consideration. His propaganda ... has been marked ... by an active stirring up of race and class prejudice.[63]

Labelling Jackson "totally unfitted" for president of the union, Marine Major Jesse F. Dyer recommended in 1918 that the insular government refrain from dealing with the union.[64] In January 1919, R. G. Williams, Despatching Secretary for St. Croix, went a step further by recommending that "D. H. Jackson be deported from the island" and that two companies of marines be assigned to St. Croix for "general patrol, thereby keeping themselves foremost in the

---

62. NARS, RG 55/2, File 59. Edward Enright to the Governor of the Virgin Islands, August 16, 1917.

63. *Ibid.*

64. NARS, RG 55/2, File 59. Jesse F. Dyer to the Governor of the Virgin Islands, November 1, 1918.

eyes of the public."[65] As a matter of fact, Jackson did leave St. Croix for the mainland, but on his own volition to study for a law degree. During his absence, R. de Chabert served as president of the union. In January 1920, de Chabert negotiated a standard wage of $1.00 per day. When the planters association unilaterally reduced the day's wage to 50 to 65 cents for 9 hours work in August, 1921, because of "the world-wide economic depression also ... reflected upon our island," the union called a general strike which ended on November 21, 1921, but not until Jackson returned and found the laborers and especially their children on the estates "on the verge of starvation." The standard wage of 60 cents was agreed upon, and Despatching Secretary C. C. Timmons wrote the Governor: "Jackson has learned a lot during his stay in the States and he ... is the only leader now in the field ... capable of leading."[66]

St. Thomas laborers meanwhile were becoming organized and assertive. A 1919 agreement engineered by labor leader Morris Davis provided wages from 10 to 20 cents per hour for cargo handling and a normal working day from 6 a.m. to 6 p.m. with double pay for work at night and on holidays. Longshoremen and others were organized by Rothschild Francis into the Virgin Islands Federation of Labor which received its certificate of affiliation as "Federal Labor Union No. 17261" from the American Federation of Labor in March, 1920. Francis promptly called a "walkout" in April, 1920, to protest "a wanton, willful, malicious, and premeditated boycott" of the Union's longshoremen by the local shipping agent, Emile Berne.[67]

It was only a matter of time before authorities would subject Davis and Francis to similar abuses suffered by Jackson. Referring to Morris Davis, R. E. Barrett, Despatching Secretary for St. Croix, wrote Governor Philip Williams in 1924: "If it were not for the fact that he is so ridiculously ignorant and that it would make a martyr out of him in the eyes of his few followers, I would urgently recommend that he be denied the privilege of speaking in public."[68]

Following the lead of Hamilton Jackson, Rothschild Francis organized a mass meeting in Charlotte Amalie in July 1920 to solicit funds for a printing press with which he intended to eradicate "ignorance and superstition."[69] After

---

65. NARS, RG 55/2, File 59. R. G. Williams to the Governor of the Virgin Islands, January 29, 1919.

66. NARS, RG 55/2, File 59-1. C. C. Timmons to the Governor of the Virgin Islands, November 19, 1921; and Gaffney to Axel Holst, November 21, 1921.

67. Correspondence in NARS, RG 55/2, File 59 (1920).

68. NARS, RG 55/2, File 89-1. Barrett to Governor Williams, April 22, 1924.

69. "Synopsis of the Proceedings of Mass Meeting Convened on 'Athletic Field' Tuesday, July 13th, 1920, by Working Peoples' Committee": NARS, RG 55/2, File 59.

obtaining the press, Francis became editor and publisher of *The Emancipator*. The Navy sought to intimidate local labor leaders by assisting planters and merchants to import foreign workers from British islands and paying them lower wages.[70] United States immigration laws were not made applicable to the Islands until 1925.[71] Francis irately opposed the import of laborers. In 1922, protesting the presence of workers from Tortola for erection of two oil tanks on St. Thomas, Francis wrote:

> There is no immigration law between St. Thomas and Tortola, hence these exploiters can import cheap labor over night. Such people not only usurp the inalienable rights of natives but they enjoy many privileges free of charge that American workers are taxed to maintain.[72]

Francis' published views—so much at variance with those of the local elite—were bound to bring him into conflict with the military government.

Given the Navy's infusion of racism into the Islands, and the open contempt toward native people displayed by some judges, it was not surprising that the local editors were critical of the government and that the Navy administrators would use the local courts for press repression. What was surprising, however, was the extent to which the Navy went to stifle dissent, as illustrated by the following chronology.

In August 1921, police court judge and prosecutor George Washington Williams imprisoned for five days George E. Audain, editor of the *St. Thomas Mail*, for criminal libel for his editorial accusing the St. Croix police commissioner, Michael Dolan, of inefficiency. It did not matter that Dolan might, indeed, have been inefficient, a condition to which later he unwittingly came close to admitting. "I have a guilty conscience every time that I take my salary,"

---

70. See, *e.g.*, correspondence between C. C. Timmons, Government Secretary, June 2, 1921, and J. C. Watson, American Consul, Barbados, B.W.I., July 5, 1921; NARS, RG 55/2, File 59. The Navy government denied it was "in any was connected" with inducing the introduction of Puerto Rican laborers into St. Croix. J. J. Gaffney, Acting Government Secretary, to The Editor, *La Correspondencia*, San Juan, Puerto Rico, November 4, 1921; NARS, RC, 55/2, File 59.

71. From 1925 to 1941, the immigration laws were administered laxly by local police under authority first of the Governor and later the Immigration and Naturalization Service, but the INS did not assume full jurisdiction for their enforcement until 1941. Mark J. Miller and William W. Boyer, "Foreign Workers in the USVI: History of a Dilemma," *Caribbean Review*, Vol. 11, No. 2 (Winter 1982), n. 8.

72. Rothschild Francis, "The Class War in the Virgin Islands," *The New Day*, (Socialist Weekly), March 21, 1921, in NARS, RG 55/2, File 59.

Dolan said. "The islands are so law abiding that there is no need for a Police Commissioner. The only trouble that we have is with a small number of Red agitators."[73]

The terms "agitators," "Reds" and "Bolsheviks" were used frequently by government officers to refer to the dissenting editors, particularly to Hamilton Jackson, editor of the St. Croix *Herald*, and to Rothschild Francis, editor of the St. Thomas *Emancipator*. In 1922, Jackson, after mildly criticizing the St. Croix road commissioner in an editorial, was cited for contempt of court and imprisoned for six days. While serving his sentence, he was elected to the colonial council by overwhelmingly defeating the government's candidate.[74] Also in 1922, Francis was threatened with censorship by local officials because of his article criticizing the conduct of United States Marines not in the Virgin Islands but in Santo Domingo. His newspaper thereafter received no government advertising.[75]

Charging the dissenting editors as being "self-seeking leaders" and "professional malcontents" who set the "unthinking masses" against the insular government, and who "carry no weight with the good thinking people," Navy Governor Sumner Kittelle complained in his annual report for 1922 that:

> The leaders and their sub-leaders teach that the insular government is inefficient and oppressive, that the rights of the people are tramped upon, that free speech and a free press are inhibited, that the courts are conducted with prejudice.... They are un-American in thought and action and actively foment race hatred.[76]

While Hamilton Jackson was visiting the States in 1922, the acting editor of the *Herald* and minister of the African Methodist Church on St. Croix, Reverend Reginald G. Barrow, a native of Barbados, was summarily deported as an "undesirable alien" for an editorial critical of the insular government, after

---

73. *The New York Times*, August 1, 1926, p. 30, col. 5.

74. Eric D. Walrond, "Autocracy in the Virgin Islands," *Current History*, (October 1923): 121–122.

75. Arthur Warner, "Bayonet Rule for Our Colonial Press," *The Nation*, March 7, 1923, p. 267.

76. *Annual Report of the Governor of The Virgin Islands for the Fiscal Year ended June 30, 1922*, quoted in Dookhan, *The Search for Identity*, p. 22, and in Evans, *The Virgin Islands*, p. 221. In a 1924 letter to President Calvin Coolidge, Secretary of the Navy Denby quoted from a Governor's report that "Francis is the editor of a radical sheet called 'The Emancipator' which quotes from the vicious and radical (generally Negro, but sometimes white) press of New York City. He is a bad influence in his union and teaches anti-government, socialistic, semi-bolshevik and race hatred stuff." Quoted in Evans, *The Virgin Islands*, p. 223.

having served a prison term for another.[77] Then in 1923, while Rothschild Francis was in the United States, his associate editor of the *Emancipator*, Thomas Morenga-Bonaparte, a native of Grenada, was also deported by Navy Governor Henry Hough after questioning by the local police commission. No judicial process was involved in either case, and Hough justified these actions on an 1827 Danish law, which authorized deportation as "a police measure against aliens" on account of their "behavior."[78]

In 1924, Rothschild Francis—himself now a member of the colonial council—wrote a letter to the editor of *The New York Times* protesting the many "intrusions upon the civil liberties of the natives."[79] Shortly thereafter, Judge George Washington Williams retorted with his own letter to the same editor stating that "such agitators" as Francis "were doing incalculable harm." And Williams had the audacity to add: "Whatever grievances the natives may have are being handled in an orderly and almost entirely satisfactory way."[80] It appeared only a matter of time before Williams would try to jail Francis.

The Francis Case

In *Francis v. People of the Virgin Islands* (1926),[81] Rothschild Francis was convicted of criminal libel, and was later found guilty of contempt, in a proceeding instituted by Judge Williams of the District Court of the Virgin Islands. The testimony in the libel proceeding revealed these facts, briefly stated: Matthias, a policeman, was endeavoring to quiet a disturbance in Charlotte Amalie, with the result that men ran in different directions, and either they or some boys threw stones at him, whereupon he fired his pistol, the bullet

---

77. Walrond, "Autocracy in the Virgin Islands," p. 122. In a letter dated August 10, 1921 to U.S. Senator William S. Kenyon, Governor Sumner Kittelle referred to Barrow as "an ex-episcopal clergyman unfrocked by the Bishop for his Bolshevistic attitude and his agitation on the color question." NARS, RG 55/2, File 62-1.

78. Warner, "Bayonet Rule for Our Colonial Press," p. 267.

79. Letter to the Editor from Rothschild Francis, Member of the Colonial Council of St. Thomas and St. John, New York, February 1, 1924, in *The New York Times*, February 10, 1924, sec. 20, p. 14, col. 7.

80. Letter to the Editor from George Washington Williams, St. Thomas, February 24, 1924, in *The New York Times*, March 9, 1924, sec. 10, p. 12, col. 4.

81. 11 F.2d 860 (1924): *Same v. Williams, District Judge*. Although the contempt and libel cases were separately tried and decided in the District Court and went to the Third Circuit Court of Appeals on separate appeals, the appellate court disposed of them in one opinion.

from which lodged in the bathtub of a private residence. To obtain a witness to the affair, he arrested and later released a bystander, and then became involved in an effort to take home "an unruly negress" whom he struck with his club. Francis published an editorial in his *Emancipator* as follows:

A Native Batesko!

Something is wrong with our Police Force, everybody is saying. Recently a Policeman fired a shot which lodged in the tub of a private citizen. Then he attempted a false arrest and before we were about to go to press, he used his club in a brutal manner on a woman he was ordered to take home, we understand.

Merchants and other citizens are indignant. How long, oh justice! How long![82]

Matthias regarded himself as the person referred to and complained to the government attorney, who filed against Francis an information for criminal libel, based on the Compiled Code of the Municipality of St. Thomas and St. John, which defined a libel as

a malicious defamation, expressed either in writing, printing, or signs or pictures, ... tending ... to impeach the natural or alleged defects of one who is alive ... and thereby exposes him to public hatred or ridicule.[83]

On being arraigned before the District Court, Francis asked Judge Williams for a trial by jury, which Williams refused on the grounds that the Compiled Code gave the defendant the right to demand a jury only in cases of felony,[84] and that the right of trial by jury guaranteed by the Sixth Amendment of the Constitution of the United States did not extend to unincorporated territories, including the Virgin Islands.

Judge Williams tried the case and adjudged Francis guilty and sentenced him to thirty days imprisonment. The opinion rendered by Judge Williams was extraordinary in that he elaborately expressed the view that the court is an agency for the regulation of the public press. He justified this assumption by quoting at length from Joseph Pulitzer's *The Windows of Westminister*, Sir Thomas More's *Utopia*, and Anthony Trollope's *The Warden*. Then, speaking of the newspapers, he said:

---

82. *Ibid.*, p. 862.

83. *Compiled Code* of *the Municipality of St. Thomas and St. John*, Section 36 of Chapter 5, Title 4 (1921).

84. The Compiled Code defined a felony as a crime which is punishable by imprisonment for more than one year; *ibid.*, Section 5 of Chapter 12. Title 4.

In their superior wisdom and the plenitude of their powers, they presume to direct the activities of the Government and mercilessly to vilify and abuse any public official who happens to cross the path of their interest or whatever course they may be pursuing. This is particularly characteristic of this community, at least respecting a portion of the press. Half-baked opinions and ill-considered thoughts are brought to bear upon partial facts, resulting in a totally misinformed public, many of whom are only too credulous or too willing to believe the worst that may be said about a public official.

Many newspaper editors ... think that under the great panoply of "freedom of the press" they can find umbrage for their ulterior motives and spurious actions. Liberty of the Press! Oh, Liberty, what crimes are committed in thy name!

Referring to the passages he had quoted from the writings named, Judge Williams continued:

Their implication clearly is that great, even irreparable, harm may, and will, come through this powerful instrumentality if in ignorant or corrupt hands, and it is against the trade of such people—that the law should ever hold a deterring hand and keep a vigilant eye to prevent the people from being anaesthetized and responding to their diabolical influence. It is the Court's business to stop this; if not, whose is it assuming that the legislative branch of the Government has placed it within their power.[85]

Francis appealed from this conviction to the Circuit Court of Appeals in Philadelphia, which reversed Judge Williams on two grounds: (1) proof of the essential fact that the publication pointed to Matthias was lacking, and (2) it was not the function of the trial judge to exercise a control over the press. Concerning this latter point, Circuit Judge Woolley, for the Court, stated:

Clearly, the trial judge in reaching his judgment did not confine himself to the defendant's publication criticizing police conduct, but availed himself of the publication to exercise control over the press ...; ... it is ... clear such is not his function. Moreover, it is evident that in arriving at his judgment the judge was not influenced by the offending article alone but by the desire to curb what he regarded ... as bad practices of the defendant in his press comments on public officers

---

85. 11 F.2d 860, 863.

and public affairs. In all this we are constrained to say the trial judge … was wrong. The courts of the Virgin Islands are not instrumentalities for the regulation of the public press. Nor is it the function of a judge, when trying a libel action and on being confronted with a question of freedom of the press, to do anything than decide the matter in hand. He is not concerned with the public morals, nor charged with elevating the standard of the community, nor is he permitted to engage in, or even touch matters political. His duty is to remain within his own independent and entirely separate department of the government and administer justice between parties conscious they will be rightly and impartially decided.[86]

This unusual rebuke of Judge Williams has been often cited, and Francis obviously won a great victory for freedom of the press in the Virgin Islands, a victory still celebrated by the lively local press of the Islands.[87] But, unfortunately for Francis, the vendetta between Williams and himself was not ended. After taking his appeal from his conviction in the libel proceeding and before the Circuit Court had reversed that conviction, Francis published a long article in his *Emancipator*, which, without mentioning names, claimed a judge had convicted and imprisoned a man without a jury trial, a proceeding that caused a powerful "organization" to consider "an outrage." The editorial concluded:

Is this judge afraid that his decision will be reversed and remanded through a trial de novo?

Judges are not supermen.…

Now get the idea. The same judge that railroaded the accused to jail sought to block his chance to further an appeal. Not upon recognized process of law—not from a sense of justice—but from solely racial and political prejudices.

When the facts in this story are made public, and they have been ordered, those responsible for the appointment of this "Sir Oracle" in question will have to explain much.

The old saying "Truth, should be possessed by a juror, justice and judgment by a judge," comes afresh to memory, hence we concur with

---

86. *Ibid.*

87. The local newspapers annually recognize each June 7th as Freedom of the Press Day. See, *e.g.*, Editorial, *Daily News*, June 7, 1977. But "Liberty Day," celebrated annually on November 1st, was also initiated in observance of freedom of the press. See also, William W. Boyer, "Rothschild Francis and Freedom of the Press in the U.S. Virgin Islands," *Caribbean Affairs* (Trinidad), Vol. 4, No. 4, 1991, pp. 129–143.

our legal friends that trials per testes in certain instances carry with them dangerous, if not humiliating aftermaths.[88]

The "organization" that Francis was referring to was the American Civil Liberties Union, directed by Roger Baldwin, which had retained A. A. Berle, Jr. as counsel for Francis.

Based on the publication of this stinging article, Judge Williams, pursuant again to the Compiled Code, instituted against Francis a proceeding for contempt of court and, after hearing, adjudged him guilty and imposed a sentence of imprisonment for thirty days and a fine of $100. Francis moved for an allowance of an appeal, which Williams denied. Francis then moved for the allowance of an appeal from the order denying an appeal, which Judge Williams allowed.

Upon appeal to the Circuit Court from this conviction, Francis raised the question of the power of the District Court to prosecute him for contempt. Francis challenged this power on the grounds: (1) that the relevant section of the Compiled Code was invalid, (2) no such proceeding was recognized under Danish law, and (3) the Act of Congress of March 3, 1917 authorized no such proceeding.

Circuit Judge Woolley, again speaking for the Court, replied that inherent in every United States court is the power to enforce and protect the administration of justice within its jurisdiction. Then addressing himself to the question whether the District Court erred in convicting Francis for contempt, Judge Woolley found that the publication identified the judge and the court to which it was directed. He asserted that the right of free speech is not unlimited but should be exercised with regard to other rights accorded the people; hence, all are to be exercised under restraints imposed by law.[89]

The publication in question doubtlessly constituted a contempt of court, according to Judge Woolley. "Pending the determination of his appeal, the judgment of the District Court was law," Woolley reasoned, "and by that law he was bound until it was changed by orderly process. Instead of awaiting the decision on the appeal he attacked the court by the publication in question."

> On the principle that everyone is presumed to intend the natural and probable consequences of his acts, it is plain that the defendant intended to prejudice and did prejudice, the court in the public mind and particularly in the mind of the race constituting the major part of

---

88. 11 F.2d 860, 864.
89. *Ibid.*, p. 865.

the local population. For this hurt to the administration of justice the defendant is answerable.[90]

The Circuit Court affirmed the conviction of Francis for contempt. Accordingly, Francis won his case on the charge of criminal libel and lost his case on the charge of contempt of court. From his conviction on the latter charge, Francis petitioned the United States Supreme Court for a writ of certiorari, which was denied.[91] Even so, the case still was not over, at least so far as it concerned Judge Williams.

Williams was promptly summoned to appear before the United States Senate Committee on Territories and Insular Possessions, which at the time was engaged in holding hearings on bills providing a constitution for the Islands. Judge Williams was questioned intensely for several days in regard to the Francis proceedings, an excerpt from which follows:

> *SENATOR PITTMAN.* Judge, you said you did not believe that the man could get a fair trial from a jury.
> *JUDGE WILLIAMS.* Yes, sir.
> *SENATOR PITTMAN.* What do you think the jury would do? ...
> *JUDGE WILLIAMS.* We are getting into deep water.
> *SENATOR PITTMAN.* I understand you are in deep water, but that does not change the question any....
> *SENATOR ROBINSON.* Do you think there can be cases and that there are cases where a judge is actually prejudiced, where he has the discretion to grant or deny jury trials?
> *JUDGE WILLIAMS.* I suppose sir, that is possible on the ground that most anything is possible. But I say in practical experience it has not been harmful, and it certainly has conduced, in my judgment, to fair trials.[92]

Judge Williams remained, however, in his position as Judge of the District Court of the Virgin Islands. Rothschild Francis, apparently unaware of the legacy of liberty he had already forged, left the Islands as a disillusioned man to reside in New York City. Thus ended one of the most significant episodes in the history of Virgin Islands' jurisprudence.

---

90. *Ibid.*
91. 273 U.S. 693 (1926).
92. *Hearings before the Senate Committee on Territories and Insular Possessions on S. 3228, S. 4005, and S. 4550*, 69th Cong., 2d sess., Part I, 25–29 (1926).

The Issue of Citizenship

The facts that the Jones Act of 1917, discussed previously, granted United States citizenship to the people of unincorporated Puerto Rico, and that the treaty of cession of 1917 granted "citizenship in the United States" to those Virgin Islanders not choosing to retain Danish citizenship, led Virgin Islanders unequivocally to assume that the transfer of the Islands conferred on them American citizenship. Washington administrators, the Congress, and the local Navy government all appeared to have shared this assumption.

In January 1918, for example, Louis F. Post, Assistant Secretary of Labor, announced arrangements for meeting war-time "requirements for common labor" by the importation "of American citizens from Porto Rico and the Virgin Islands."[93] Congress, moreover, by the Act of March 3, 1917, extended the jurisdiction of the local courts to all cases in the Islands to which the United States "or any citizen thereof" may be a party. Had Congress intended to exclude Virgin Islanders from this category of "citizen" few cases would have arisen in the local courts. Finally, even the local codes of 1920–1921, formulated by the Navy government to Americanize the legal system of the Virgin Islands, assumed that the transfer brought American citizenship to the Islanders. A juror was required by the codes, for example, to be either a citizen of the municipality in which he resided, or a citizen of the United States. Luther Evans observed that this provision "was based on the assumption that the treaty of cession granted United States citizenship to the inhabitants of the Virgin Islands," except when the choice of retaining Danish citizenship was exercised.[94]

The constitutional status of the Islands was ignored by Congress, however, in framing and passing the Act of March 3, 1917, and even eight years later "the best experts consulted" were "not prepared to say whether the islands are a possession of or a part of the United States."

> Congress applied an export tax of $6 a ton on sugar shipped from the island of St. Croix, not only to foreign countries, but also to New York, where all the St. Croix sugar goes. Export duties are unconstitutional in the United States, and if the Virgin Islands are "a territo-

---

93. *The New York Times*, January 20, 1918, sec. 1, p. 1, col. 6.

94. Evans, *The Virgin Islands*, p. 216, at n. 6. Article 6 of the Treaty of Cession provided that Danish citizens remaining in the Islands who did not opt to retain their Danish citizenship would be held "to have accepted citizenship in the United States." This phrase was interpreted by the inhabitants to mean that they had been granted full citizenship in the United States.

rial part of the United States," as specifically designated by Congress, this provision would seem to be incompatible with the changed sovereignty. Some authorities say that the Constitution does not extend to the Virgin Islands. The Eighteenth Amendment does, however. Furthermore, Hawaii, Porto Rico and the Philippines all ship sugar to the continental United States entirely free from any export or import duty.[95]

The United States State Department soon disabused Virgin Islanders of any assumption that they were American citizens. In a letter dated March 9, 1920 to Senator Kenyon, Acting Secretary Frank L. Polk stated that the State Department was issuing passports

> to inhabitants of the Virgin Islands entitled to the protection of the United States.... They have American nationality and are entitled to the protection of the government, but have not the civil and political status of citizens of the United States.[96]

To substantiate the curious reasoning by which the State Department denied the American citizenship which nearly everyone assumed had been conferred, Richard W. Flourney, Jr., former acting chief of the Citizenship Bureau of the State Department, employed strained semantics and a tortuous exegesis of the English language. In an interview with Luther Evans in 1933, Flourney's memory of the arguments persuasive in 1920 were summarized by Evans as follows:

> He placed emphasis on the point that the treaty speaks of citizenship "in" the United States rather than citizenship "of" the United States, the former expression merely connotating United States nationality, and the latter expressly denoting full United States citizenship. Likewise, the provision that Congress was to determine "the civil rights and political status" of the inhabitants was viewed as clear evidence that the whole matter of citizenship, as distinguished from nationality, was intended to be left to the discretion of Congress. This provision was viewed by the State Department in 1920 as strong enough to be "controlling over" the provision regarding "citizenship in the United States,"

---

95. *The New York Times*, June 14, 1925, sec. 9, p. 11, col. 3.
96. Quoted by Evans, *The Virgin Islands.*, p. 62.

despite the fact that the right of determining civil and political status was made subordinate to the other provisions of the treaty.[97]

Thus, for the want of a two-letter word—"of" instead of "in"—Virgin Islanders were denied American citizenship. The State Department decree "created much dissatisfaction in the islands," reported the governor, "the islanders feeling that as the Virgin Islands were acquired by purchase, and not captured in war, their inhabitants should have been given the privilege of enjoying full United States citizenship."[98] The Virgin Islands were in the anomalous position of belonging to America without their people knowing just how American they were.

---

97. *Ibid.*, pp. 62–63. As discussed previously, Secretary of State Lansing, during treaty negotiations in 1916, rejected a Danish condition that the inhabitants of the Islands be granted American citizenship.

98. Waldo Evans, *The Virgin Islands of the United States, A General Report by the Governor* (Washington: U.S. Government Printing Office, 1928), p. 62.

7

Reform and Relief

At the very least, most Virgin Islanders were disappointed with American suzerainty over the Islands. They were unprepared for the worsening of the already slackening economy and for Washington's indifference. Their initial enthusiasm for transfer to American rule was dampened further by Washington's alleged reneging on the grant of citizenship together with the Navy's infusion of racism, repression, autocracy, and Americanization—all interrelated features of insular life under Navy rule. The Navy's achievements, particularly in health and education, paled in comparison with the growing discontent of Virgin Islanders. Most grievous, perhaps, was the postponement of any semblance of self-government and political democracy.

Political Peonage

It simply was not true that the Act of March 3, 1917, was in any respect, as reported by *The New York Times*, "liberal in its allowance for self-government."[1] Nor was it true, as assumed by American suffragists, that women of the Virgin Islands were to be enfranchised by that Act.[2] Under Navy rule, the franchise remained just as restricted as it was under Danish rule. It was still restricted to males of at least twenty-five years of age, who were either natives or residents for at least five years, and who had an annual income of $300 or owned property producing an annual income of $40 in St. Thomas and $60 in St. Croix and St. John—restrictions little changed since 1863 and virtually unchanged

---

1. *The New York Times*, February 21, 1917, p. 6, col. 3.

2. Mrs. Norman de R. Whitehouse, chairwoman of the New York State Committee of the Women Suffrage Party, expressed "satisfaction that the bill providing a plan of government for the Danish West Indies ... provides for continuing under American rule the equal suffrage established in the islands by the Danes." *The New York Times*, February 28, 1917, p. 10, col. 6.

since 1906. So impoverished were most Islanders under Navy rule that only about 5.5 percent of the total population of approximately 26,000 were qualified to vote for members of the colonial councils.[3]

The Navy did nothing to extend the franchise, even though the greater number of Virgin Islanders were law-abiding and could read and write, and though the Colonial Law of 1906 provided for revision of its franchise provisions within ten years.[4] Indeed, Navy governors actively opposed extension of the franchise or other political reforms to increase political democracy in the Islands. For example, the first governor, Admiral James Oliver, opposed extension because of the "large number of undesirables from other islands," and Governor Sumner Kittelle in 1922 argued that universal suffrage would put "power in the hands of self-constituted leaders who are unfitted and unworthy to hold such power."[5]

Because of the restrictive franchise, the two colonial councils were unrepresentative of most Virgin Islanders, the councils comprising for the most part merchants and planters together with the appointees of the governor—often government functionaries—who were expected to support the insular administration. Nevertheless, a few dissidents managed to be elected to the colonial councils, most notably Hamilton Jackson and Rothschild Francis, who became the principal local agitators for political reform. They could not expect, however, that the conservative composition of the colonial councils would allow for any local legislative initiative for political reform. The councils and governors were one when it came to maintaining the existing political system. The Colonial Council of St. Thomas and St. John, for example, in 1926 endorsed the following petition:

> The merchants, proprietors, tax payers and other citizens of St. Thomas petition Congress, through the local legislative assembly, and the President, through the Governor of the Virgin Islands, to suspend all national legislation which may cause withdrawal of the naval officers now administering the government of the Virgin Islands until a

---

3. Evans, *The Virgin Islands*, p. 82.

4. See Letter to the Editor from Rothschild Francis, Member of the Colonial Council of St. Thomas and St. John, New York, February 1, 1924 in *The New York Times*, February 10, 1924, sec. 20, p. 14, col. 7. The Colonial Law of 1906, section 18, stipulated that "Within 10 years from the entering into operations of this law the provisions concerning franchise contained in this section are to be revised."

5. *Annual Reports of the Governor of the Virgin Islands for the Fiscal Years of 1917 and 1922*, as quoted by Dookhan, *The Search for Identity*, pp. 30–31.

thorough investigation of the peculiar conditions here has been made and adequate measures for their improvement have been provided.[6]

Two months later, the Council recommended a ten-year delay in political reform, to which—wittingly or not, as events would prove—Congress acceded.[7] This is not to say that the political unity of councils and governors precluded executive-legislative differences. Whereas governors did little to relieve economic distress, the councils were very much concerned with removing restrictions on economic development, such as relief from the coastwise laws, repeal of prohibition, reduction of the export duty on sugar, and repeal of the federal income tax.[8]

Of the two colonial councils, the Colonial Council of St. Croix—forty miles distant from the seat of government in St. Thomas—was more at odds with the insular government. Crucians particularly found objectionable the practice of naval governors to appoint candidates, already defeated at the polls, to membership on the Colonial Council. On two occasions, moreover, governors used their power inherited from the Danes to dissolve colonial councils, the first occasion being dissolution of the Colonial Council of St. Thomas and St. John in 1922 when a quorum could not be obtained to pass government-sponsored legislation. The second occasion was in 1925 when Governor Philip Williams dissolved the Colonial Council of St. Croix because it refused to seat two of his appointees on the ground that they were neither citizens of the United States nor of the Virgin Islands. The Council did not reconvene until a year later after the Attorney General of the United States ruled it lacked authority to refuse to seat appointees of governors.[9]

---

6. *The New York Times*, May 30, 1926, sec. 2, p. 2, col. 8.

7. Dookhan, *The Search for Identity*, p. 32.

8. When the Islands were transferred from Denmark to the United States in 1917, they came under the U.S. coastwise laws, the Eighteenth Amendment, etc. Under the coastwise laws, no foreign ship could carry a passenger from one port to another American port. Under the Eighteenth Amendment, no ship carrying liquor was allowed to enter a Virgin Islands' port, and the local rum, including bay rum, could no longer be exported. St. Thomas was virtually put out of business, because that island depended almost entirely on commerce and shipping, while the rum produced on St. Croix and the bay rum produced on St. John could not be exported. Later, the prohibition laws were modified to admit liquor-laden ships under seal and to allow the export of bay rum provided its alcohol was denatured. Also, the President periodically suspended the operation of the coastwise laws to permit foreign ships to carry passengers from another American port to the Virgin Islands. See, Isaac Dookhan, *Volsteadism or National Prohibition in the Virgin Islands* (1978).

9. *The New York Times*, July 13, 1925, p. 2, col. 4; and Dookhan, *The Search for Identity*, p. 8.

Agitation for Reform

As early as 1919, the problem of bestowing upon the Virgin Islands a government more in accord with local needs and democratic self-government was given attention by some members of Congress. Expressing the opinion that the Islands seemed "almost to have been forgotten," a Senate committee recommended the appointment of six members of Congress to report on conditions in the Virgin Islands. The Senate report stated:

> The people of the islands feel they have been neglected by the United States; that when the American flag went up in the Virgin Islands it should have been followed by American laws ... and ideals as soon as possible.... There are great possibilities in these islands. They should not be neglected.[10]

A joint commission was appointed, and on February 5, 1920, it arrived at St. Thomas. The commission examined sixty-seven witnesses in the Islands, whose testimony covered 626 typewritten pages. The report of the commission stated that:

> The laws in the Virgin Islands date back three centuries and to a large extent are inapplicable to our form of government.... The laws are antiquated Danish laws. The judge of the court is police master, a member of the colonial tax commission, a member of the colonial council, also is in charge of deeds and mortgages of record. As police master he institutes cases which are tried before him. This is an un-American policy. There is a great need of an entire new code of laws.[11]

In February 1924, a federal commission of "Negroes" from the mainland, appointed by the Secretary of Labor, spent two weeks in the Islands investigating industrial and economic conditions. Among its recommendations, the commission reported:

> A new organic act should be passed, so as to authorize the adoption of a new code of laws based upon American ideals and calculated to insure an administration and enforcement of the laws in keeping with American practices.... The new organic act should provide for such reforms of the present legislative system that the municipal governments

---

10. Senate Report No. 160, 66th Cong., 1st sess. (1919).

11. H. R. Doc. No. 734, 66th Cong., 2nd sess. (1920). The Navy governor recommended in 1922 that any alteration of the government by an organic act be postponed for "at least a generation to come." Quoted in Evans, *The Virgin Islands*, p. 221.

of the several islands may be more centralized and the amended whole brought into closer touch and harmony with the masses and be more largely responsive to their peculiar needs.[12]

In the winter of 1923–1924, on the initiative of Rothschild Francis and the American Civil Liberties Union, the first draft organic act was prepared. On March 10, 1924, Senator McLean of Connecticut introduced "A Bill to Provide a Civil Government for the Virgin Islands, and for Other Purposes."[13] The proposed measure provided for wide legislative powers and a bill of rights. A. A. Berle, Jr., counsel for the American Civil Liberties Union and the New York City-based Virgin Islands Committee, testified that the system of government since the purchase had been inadequate, the lack of citizenship regrettable, and the judicial procedures open to grave reservations. Objecting to the property qualifications for voting, while permitting voting by Danish aliens, he asserted that successful government depended too largely upon the personality of the governor. "The same qualities that make a man a splendid and excellent naval officer," he said, "may make him a very bad administrator of civil government; and the Virgin Islands have had some unfortunate experiences."[14]

Rothschild Francis, the only other person to testify in support of the bill, asserted that governors had been "imperialistic or even autocratic." Even the Danish King could not discharge the judge, he observed, but under Navy rule the governor appointed and discharged the judge at will. The natives, moreover, were "political peons" under the aristocratic domination of two hundred foreigners (i.e., Danes) and an autocratic governor.[15]

---

12. *Report of the Federal Commission … to Investigate Industrial and Economic Conditions in the Virgin Islands U.S.A.* (Washington: U.S. Department of Labor, 1924), p. 26.

13. S. 2786, 68th Cong., 1st sess. (1924). Introduction of this bill took the Virgin Islands' government and people by surprise. "The governor radioed a strong protest against it, and on April 4 the councils in joint session called upon Congress to give the bill no further consideration." Evans, *The Virgin Islands*, p. 227.

14. *Hearings before Senate Committee on Territories and Insular Possessions on S. 2786,* 68th Cong., 1st sess., Part 1 (1924).

15. *Ibid.* On January 28, 1926, Mr. Cordova, delegate to the House of Representatives from Puerto Rico, introduced a bill to provide a permanent civil government for the Virgin Islands. H. R. 7183, 69th Cong., 1st sess. (1926). At the hearings on this bill, Dr. Rufus Tucker, having just returned from a study of economic conditions in the Islands for the Treasury Department, listed six points that he thought important in providing a civil government: (1) the extension of citizenship to the inhabitants of the Virgin Islands, (2) the elimination of appointed members of the municipal councils, (3) the transfer of jurisdiction over the Islands to the Bureau of Insular Affairs of the Army—("The Navy is not organized, and I do not believe it cares much for the job."), (4) the reorganization of the judiciary with

More bills were subsequently introduced, in 1926, with hearings on each, but little resulted from the efforts of various interested individuals, except the exchange of opinions. There were those who expressed the belief that the people were incapable of exercising self-government, that Navy government was, in reality, a sound civil government, just, impartial, and economical, needing little or no change. On the other side, there were those who pointed to the deplorable conditions in the Islands, the need for a civilian administration with a permanent government, and the necessity of conferring upon the people citizenship and the rights that attend self-government. A substantial bill of rights was provided in each of the 1926 bills, one of which included the following subjects:

> due process of law, equal protection of the laws, all the familiar rights of the accused, obligation of contracts, forced labor for debt, habeas corpus, ex post facto laws, just compensation, titles of nobility, excessive bail, warrant for arrest or search, press and religion, polygamous or plural marriages, child labor, universal manhood suffrage.[16]

None of the 1926 bills was acted on by Congress.[17]

Agitation for reform continued, nevertheless, aided principally by local dissidents such as Rothschild Francis and Hamilton Jackson, by the American Civil Liberties Union, and by various civic organizations formed among Virgin Islands' immigrants in New York City under the rival leaders Ashley L. Totten and Casper Holstein, the able and wealthy brother-in-law of Hamilton Jackson. In commenting on the pivotal role of the American Civil Liberties Union during this period, Isaac Dookhan has written:

> Broadly speaking, the ACLU served to bring the case of the Virgin Islands to the attention of the congressmen mainly through a regular

---

the functions of the District Court of the Virgin Islands transferred to the federal district judge in Puerto Rico, (5) the suspension or reduction of the sugar tax of $8 a ton export duty by vesting such authority in the councils, and (6) the abolition of the coastwise shipping laws of the United States so far as the Virgin Islands are concerned. *Hearings before House Committee on Insular Possessions on H. R. 7183*, 69th Cong., 1st sess. (1926), pp. 44–49.

16. *Hearings before Senate Committee on Territories and Insular Possessions on S. 3228*, 69th Cong., 1st sess., Part I (1926), pp. 1–9.

17. For a summary chart of the seven reform bills introduced in Congress in 1926, see: Dookhan, *The Search for Identity*, p. 28. At the time, Congress apparently felt its information about the Virgin Islands was too inadequate to provide an organic act for the Islands. See, *e.g., The New York Times*, March 18, 1926, p. 22, col. 4 (Editorial); April 8, 1926, p. 22, col. 1; June 6, 1926, sec. 2, p. 7, col. 6.

representative in Washington and other emissaries from time to time. More particularly, it introduced Virgin Islands politicians such as Jackson and Francis to the intricacies of political maneuvering in the national capital, served as an intermediary between Virgin Islanders and congressmen, and assisted in effecting a unity of purpose toward Virgin Islands problems among Virgin Islanders in the islands and in the United States.[18]

Although entreaties of the reformers were not immediately effective, they did serve to elicit federal interest, in place of indifference, in the plight of Virgin Islanders and the justice of their various complaints. Thus Congress was moved to reduce the export duty on sugar from $8 to $6 per ton and at last to grant United States citizenship to most Virgin Islanders in 1927, ten years after the transfer.[19] It was paradoxical that this grant of citizenship was announced with great fanfare on the occasion of the inauguration of Captain Waldo Evans— as seventh Navy governor in ten years—the reputed former autocrat of American Samoa.[20] Subsequently, a 1932 Act of Congress granted American citizenship to all natives of the Virgin Islands, regardless of their place of residence on January 17, 1917.[21]

Withdrawal of the Navy

After the devastation wrought by the hurricane of 1928, followed by the stock market crash of 1929, agitation for a new constitution shifted to eco-

---

18. Dookhan, *The Search for Identity*, p. 16. Dookhan provides a fairly complete account of the political activities of the ACLU and the various Virgin Islands' organizations in the United States during the period 1917–1927. *Ibid.*, esp. pp. 16–20.

19. 44 *Stat.* 1234 (1927). This Act also conferred upon the District Court of the Virgin Islands the authority to naturalize aliens in the Virgin Islands. Political demands of dissident Virgin Islanders, including the demand for citizenship, were expressed through three loosely organized political associations: the Progressive Party, the Republican Club, and the St. Croix-based People's Party. Dookhan, *The Search for Identity*, p. 12. Thus, a campaign to obtain citizenship for Virgin Islanders was begun in 1925 by the Republican Club of St. Thomas and St. John, with appeals made to leading Republicans in Washington and elsewhere. *The New York Times*, July 22, 1925, p. 21, col. 5.

20. See, *e.g.*, Samuel S. Shipley, "Our Naval Autocracy in Samoa," *The Nation*, March 15, 1922, pp. 309–311. For an eyewitness account of "the rejoicing and emotion of the people on this occasion," see Letter to the Editor from Adolph Gereau, St. Thomas, March 3, 1927, in *The New York Times*, March 20, 1927, sec. 9, p. 16, col. 3.

21. 47 *Stat.* 336 (1932).

nomic rehabilitation in the Islands to prevent the greater calamity of actual starvation. Replacement of Navy rule with a civil government was finally accomplished in 1931. Local reformers, however, could not claim much credit for this change. Withdrawal of the Navy was brought about principally by the intervention of a strong-willed and influential Washington bureaucrat, Herbert D. Brown, chief of the federal Bureau of Efficiency. The desire of Congress to end annual appropriations by rehabilitating the flagging economy of the Virgin Islands toward eventual self-sufficiency led Brown to undertake a survey of the Islands in the winter of 1929–1930.[22]

On Brown's recommendation, Congress appropriated an initial $141,000 to be used for the following purposes: (1) a homesteading plan, particularly in St. Croix, whereby land could be purchased and subdivided for resale to cultivators; (2) remodeling of the Grand Hotel in St. Thomas to promote tourism; (3) development of the bay-rum industry in St. John; (4) establishment of an industrial and agricultural school in St. Croix; (5) reorganization of the agricultural experiment station; (6) remodeling the poor farm; and (7) a reforestation program. Top priority was assigned to the homestead plan.[23]

In June, 1930, Brown returned to the Islands to supervise the distribution of the $141,000 special fund.[24] His desire to have control of the rehabilitation program brought him into inevitable conflict with Navy Governor Waldo Evans. The Navy, after all, had never done anything to arrest economic decline in the Islands, and its custodial role was not consonant with Brown's interventionist program. "Questions arose concerning authority over the money, and rumors became current that the Islands had two governors."[25] As a result of his quarrel with Governor Evans, Brown returned to Washington and asked President Hoover to withdraw the Navy from the Islands.

President Hoover acceded to Brown's suggestion and charged him with finding a competent person to become the Islands' first civil governor. Dr. Paul M. Pearson of Swarthmore, Pennsylvania, was selected by Brown, and on January 30, 1931 the President announced his appointment and transfer of the government to the Department of the Interior.[26] The transfer was made effec-

---

22. *The New York Times*, January 19, 1930, sec. 2, p. 6, col. 3.

23. Evans, *The Virgin Islands*, pp. 282–283. After only five weeks in the Islands, Brown, in March, 1930, issued his unpublished report of over 900 typewritten pages. *Ibid.*, pp. 159 and 187 at n. 7.

24. *The New York Times*, June 22, 1930, sec. 2, p. 1, col. 3.

25. Evans, *The Virgin Islands*, p. 162.

26. *The New York Times*, January 31, 1931, p. 1, col. 2.

tive by President Hoover's executive order of February 27, 1931, thus ending fourteen years of Navy rule.[27]

A number of influences present at the time may help explain President Hoover's decision to transfer the Islands to civilian control. One influence was the decline of the emphasis on naval power, especially as it related to the coastal defense of the United States, which was contemporaneous with the rise of air power and trends toward naval disarmament. With the defeat of Germany in World War I, moreover, the fears of hostile occupancy of the Islands, that motivated their acquisition for defense purposes in 1917, had disappeared. Civil rights and racial groups, together with local agitators, may have had some influence in inducing the transfer, but the key reason was the Navy's resistance to change in the face of continuing economic deterioration in the Islands. In any event, Congress provided the immediate setting for change, and the initiative for transfer was finally supplied by Herbert Brown.[28]

"An Effective Poorhouse"

When Brown returned to the Islands in the summer of 1930, he found appalling conditions. The drought had continued unabated. The two major sugar factories on St. Croix had financially collapsed. Masses of field workers were

---

27. Executive Order No. 5566, February 27, 1931. Naval and marine personnel in the Islands, at the time of transfer to the Interior Department, numbered 282 officers and men. *The New York Times*, February 3, 1931, p. 19, col. 6. President Hoover's executive order is reprinted in Bough and Macridis, eds., *Virgin Islands, America's Caribbean Outpost, Evolution of Self Government* (1970), pp. 40–41.

28. Reasons for the transfer are explored at length by John Frederick Grede, *The New Deal in the Virgin Islands, 1931–1941* (unpublished Ph.D. dissertation, University of Chicago, 1963), pp. 60–67. Grede cites a 1935 letter from George Foster Peabody to Mrs. Franklin D. Roosevelt in which Peabody, a wealthy New York banker friend, claimed credit for inducing transfer of the Islands to civilian control. *Ibid.*, pp. 64–65. Navy apologist Luther Evans attributed the transfer to the desire to cover-up the Brown-Waldo Evans feud and "allegations of poker-playing and drinking in Government House." Governor Evans opposed Brown's homesteading plan because he did not think the federal government should go into the "real estate business." According to Luther Evans, the Governor believed: "If the land of St. Croix were bought up and then turned over to the colored people 'they would make a mess of it as they are not qualified to handle such affairs independently.' The Governor did not believe 'for a moment' that Mr. Brown's 'fool scheme' would 'make the people self-supporting.'" Evans, *The Virgin Islands*, p. 277, 280. But whereas Luther Evans retrospectively sided with Governor Waldo Evans (no relation), President Hoover sided with Herbert Brown.

unemployed. The standard wage rate of those employed was 40 cents per day. The economy was near a standstill. Many were threatened with starvation. The Red Cross provided the only relief. Infant mortality was frightfully high.[29]

With the end of Navy rule, Brown's rehabilitation plan, and the onset of civil government, despair of the destitute turned to hope. Their aspirations, however, were soon dashed by President Hoover himself. Eight days after Governor Pearson's inauguration as the first civilian governor, Hoover became the first president to visit the Islands, ostensibly to bolster rehabilitation. Accompanied by Interior Secretary Wilbur, the President spent only five hours on St. Thomas. In the midst of a torrential downpour, he retired quickly to the battleship *Arizona* where he held a press conference. After expressing optimism about the future of Puerto Rico, which he had visited enroute, he made this ill-fated statement:

> The Virgin Islands may have some military value some time. Opinion upon this question is much divided. In any event, when we paid $25,000,000 for them, we acquired an effective poorhouse, comprising 90 per cent of the population.
>
> The people cannot be self-supporting either in living or government without discovery of new methods and resources.
>
> The purpose of the transfer of administration from the naval to a civil department is to see if we can develop some form of industry or agriculture which will relieve us of the present costs and liabilities in support of the population or the local government from the Federal Treasury or from private charity.
>
> Viewed from every point except remote naval contingencies, it was unfortunate that we ever acquired these islands. Nevertheless, having assumed the responsibility, we must do our best to assist the inhabitants.[30]

Richard Oulahan of *The New York Times* reported on March 30, 1931 that though the President realized that the economic depression in the Islands was attributable to causes beyond the control of Islanders, such as steamships abandoning St. Thomas as a coaling station and the decline of the sugar industry because of prolonged drought, he was nevertheless critical of the Islanders, according to Oulahan, for making "no effort to find employment in other directions." He had little faith, moreover, that they "will react favorably to the

---

29. Whereas the 1930 crude death rate was 22 per 1,000, or 2.2 percent, the infant mortality rate was 119 per 1,000, or 11.9 percent. For discussion of economic conditions in the Virgin Islands in 1930, see: Charles F. Reid, *Education in the Territories and Outlying Possessions of the United States* (New York: Columbia University, 1941), pp. 452–457.

30. *The New York Times*, March 27, 1931, p. 1, col. 3, and p. 23, col. 3.

principle of self-help." That the President's derision of Virgin Islanders might have been motivated by racial or ethnic considerations is evident from his concern over "the immigration question." Unrestricted emigration of Virgin Islanders and Puerto Ricans to New York, according to Oulahan, gave "the administration food for thought, in the light of the quota limitations placed on the immigrants from certain European countries who make especially desirable citizens."[31]

Whatever motives prompted Hoover to make his "poorhouse" comments, no Presidential statement could have been more calculated to offend the pride and dignity of Virgin Islanders and to degrade the poor among them. The *St. Thomas Mail Notes*, a local newspaper, attributed the Islands' poverty to "the application of stupid laws," and added: "Any American insultingly alluding to the Virgin Islands today as a poorhouse can only appear devoid of decency, even though that individual be the President of the United States."[32] From Copenhagen, former Danish Governor Helwig-Larsen interjected: "The main reason for the crisis is that the Americans have prohibited the production of rum, which in former times was a fine source of income."[33] St. Thomas merchants expressed their fear that Hoover's "unfortunate" remarks would ruin their business and further "injure the economic life of the islands."[34]

Pearson and His Critics

Governor Pearson thus began his tenure under a cloud cast by Hoover's skeptical pronouncement. More serious, however, was the Governor's immediate break with Herbert Brown, the architect of the rehabilitation program, just as Pearson's predecessor—Waldo Evans—had broken with Brown. Pearson was a humanist and wanted culturally to uplift Virgin Islanders. Having been a Chautauqua leader, he appointed a dramatics director who promptly produced a Gilbert and Sullivan operetta, much to the dismay and chagrin of Brown who considered an operetta incongruous with the appalling economic conditions. Although Pearson approved Brown's rehabilitation plan, he regarded it as a guide rather than a precise blueprint. Brown wrathfully questioned certain minor expenditures, which Pearson covered out of his own pocket. Finally, just one month after Pearson's inauguration, Brown wrote an

---

31. *The New York Times*, March 30, 1931, p. 10, col. 2.
32. *The New York Times*, April 8, 1931, p. 1, col. 2.
33. *The New York Times*, May 2, 1931, p. 10, col. 3.
34. *The New York Times*, April 2, 1931, p. 10, col. 6.

eleven-page letter to Interior Secretary Wilbur—a chronicle of Pearson's alleged misdeeds. Two weeks later, he followed with a seventy-five page confidential report to President Hoover denouncing, and proposing dismissal of, Pearson whose appointment Brown had originally recommended a few months before.[35]

Brown's demands were ignored, but he continued to criticize Pearson throughout most of his administration, even to the extent of giving wide publicity to his recommendation of Pearson's removal, and even after his Bureau of Efficiency was abolished by President Roosevelt.[36]

---

35. Grede, *The New Deal*, pp. 89–90; Evans, *The Virgin Islands*, pp. 291–292. A series of articles authored by Robert B. Smythe, critical of Pearson, appeared in *The Washington Post*, July 12, August 4, and August 5, 1931, making charges—among others—that Pearson's director of public entertainment (locally regarded as the "court jester") as well as other "absurd" high-priced positions were filled by friends from Pearson's home town of Swarthmore. The Department of Interior defended Pearson (see, *e.g.*, *The Evening Star*, Washington, August 4, 1931), despite its foreknowledge that almost "all administrative positions ... are filled by Swarthmore men and women." NARS, RG 126, File 9-11-12 (Part 1); R. A. Kleindienst to Assistant Secretary of Interior John H. Edwards, April 27, 1931. Pearson was to spend much of his tenure answering charges circulating in the Islands and the mainland. In answering the question—"why should Brown undertake to have me removed?"—Pearson claimed Brown "had given nearly a year to the preparation of the plans ... and yet I was given the publicity.... he is concerned only with saving his plans." NARS, RG 126, File 9-10-12 (Part 1); Pearson to Edwards, August 11, 1931.

36. See, *e.g.*, *The New York Times*, August 4, 1931, p. 22, col. 3, which reported that Brown termed "the appointment of a man to direct operettas in a community struggling to buy bread as 'absurd.'" In 1933, Brown was reported as "making strenuous efforts to be named to succeed Governor Paul Pearson." *The New York Times*, January 17, 1933, p. 40, col. 7. Over three years after Brown had been in the Islands, and almost two years after Franklin Roosevelt won election to the Presidency, Brown continued to wage a virulent campaign against Pearson. "Herbert D. Brown," wrote Pearson, "seems to have plenty of time to coach anybody to try to make a case against me. He has been trying to do this for nearly four years, one would think he would be weary of it. Not he.... Mr. and Mrs. Brown have several times gone to see my Swarthmore friends in an attempt to align them against me on one charge or another." NARS, RG 126, File 9-11-2 (Part 3); Pearson to Ernest Gruening, Director, Division of Territories and Island Possessions, Department of Interior, October 27, 1934. On November 25, 1934, Brown spoke at a mass meeting of the Virgin Islands Congressional Council and Allied Virgin Islands Societies at the Frederick Douglas High School in New York City, with Casper Holstein presiding. Brown related how Pearson came to be appointed Governor, declared Pearson unfitted for the post, that Brown had long urged Pearson's removal, but President Hoover had refused to act. He now urged Virgin Islanders to campaign for his removal, saying he was confident President Roosevelt will act when he realizes the real state of affairs in the Islands. NARS, RG 126, File 9-11-2 (Part 3). Of Pearson, Holstein wrote: "he is the wrong man in the wrong place." NARS, RG 126, File 9-11-2 (Part 4); Holstein to Secretary of Interior Harold L. Ickes, December 26, 1934. Roth-

Despite his troubles with Brown, Governor Pearson and his lieutenants vigorously pressed economic reform of the Islands, the first governor in a century—since von Scholten—to exhibit such compassion for the Islanders. Unlike his naval predecessors, Pearson besieged his superiors in Washington and the Congress with demands for new legislation to permit bond issues and increased taxes, to form a new bank, to exempt the Islands from the coastwise laws, and to fund public improvements. Directing attention to the lack of local capital and the extreme poverty of the residents, he declared in January 1932:

> Suffrage in the Virgin Islands includes a property qualification of about $300, or an annual income of $300. As there is an average of 908 voters out of 22,000 population, it is clear that few people have any money. For the calendar year 1930 income taxpayers in the Virgin Islands numbered 101, paying a total of $16,766.75.[37]

As early as April 1931 Pearson clashed with the local colonial councils.[38] A year later, the clashes became bitter. Some councilmen secretly cabled the United States Senate urging that Congress pass no laws affecting the Virgin Islands without the councils' consent, pursuant to the Colonial Law of 1906.[39]

---

schild Francis, however, continued to support Pearson from his residence in New York. "I am much interested in the copy of letter you send from Rothschild Francis. I have met him. He writes a convincing letter. He is somewhat of a bore in conversation. His exile from St. Thomas is because of his being short in his accounts. He was looked upon here as a ruthless, dishonest and dangerous agitator. I have had his ardent support it seems from the beginning. Of course, I am glad to have it but I am not misled by what he says." Pearson to Gruening, October 30, 1934; NARS, RG 126, File 9-11-2 (Part 3).

37. *The New York Times*, January 28, 1932, p. 7, col. 3. Virgin Islanders still were impoverished two and one-half years later. "We are giving food now to 48.24% of the families and 47% of the persons" on St. Thomas. NARS, RG 126, File 9-11-12 (Part 1); Alonzo G. Moron, Commissioner of Public Welfare, to Governor Pearson, August 21, 1934.

38. Evans, *The Virgin Islands*, p. 291.

39. *The New York Times*, June 7, 1932, p. 7, col. 3. Further clashes between Pearson and the colonial councils were reported in editions of *The New York Times* over the budget and taxes, June 27, 1933, p. 9, col. 2, and over a local police chief, June 3, 1933, p. 4, col. 2. Pearson was capable of strong counterattack. For example, Lionel Roberts, a member of the Colonial Council of St. Thomas, wrote Secretary of Interior Ickes, September 5, 1933 criticizing certain practices of Pearson's administration. Pearson retaliated by sending Roberts' police record (*viz.*, 1898—receiving stolen goods; 1908—violation of police regulations; 1921—slander; 1930—assault and battery) to the Interior Department. Roberts, nevertheless, was granted an interview with President Roosevelt in 1934 (Editorial, *Daily News*, May 25, 1934), and was later appointed a director of the Virgin Islands Company in which capacity he was an active member with whom Ickes carried on frequent correspondence. NARS, RG 126, File 9-11-2.

After the Democrats came to power in Washington in 1933, and Franklin Roosevelt replaced President Hoover, and Harold Ickes replaced Interior Secretary Wilbur, local demands for removal of Hoover-appointed Pearson became many-sided and vociferous. But Ickes, with Roosevelt's concurrence, was adamant in keeping Pearson in office.

The local colonial councils, still conservative in their predominant representation of planters and merchants, opposed increased taxes of any kind. The twenty men who owned 80 percent of St. Croix strongly opposed government sugar-growing schemes in competition with private sugar growers. When prohibition ended in 1934, and with their eyes on a vast rum market, they increased their opposition to any government involvement in the rum business. Meanwhile, some St. Thomas merchants wanted Roosevelt to remove Pearson to make way for a return to Navy rule and their profitable experience. These demands represented the right-wing opposition to Pearson—the opposition of the economic elite who felt threatened by Pearson's efforts to help the poor.[40]

There was also a more broadly-based and vituperative left-wing opposition to Pearson, spearheaded by the Roosevelt-Garner Democratic Club. Headed by labor leader Morris Davis, it was dedicated to ousting Pearson's Republican administration to make way for deserving Democrats. Other reasons for broad opposition to Pearson included Pearson's moralistic opposition to illegitimacy,[41] and the popular equation of the less authoritarian civilian government with ineffectiveness.

> Many of the public demonstrations against the Pearson administration were based on this new-found freedom to be openly critical, and the natives indulged themselves freely in the activity without really much of substance to complain about.[42]

The combined right and left-wing opposition to Pearson claimed that 1933 plebiscites in St. Croix and St. Thomas showed a total of 7,366 against his re-

---

40. But Hanson Baldwin viewed opposition to Pearson as essentially "a struggle between different philosophies of government, between the economy of capitalism and private ownership and so-called planned economy and public ownership." *The New York Times*, April 5, 1935, p. 6, col. 2. Local Catholics also feared the effect on their parochial school system of Pearson's greatly extended public education program. Grede, *The New Deal*, p. 153.

41. Grede, *The New Deal*, p. 39. The prevailing anti-marriage attitudes of Virgin Islanders and their conflict with Pearson's efforts to curb illegitimacy were fictionalized in a New Deal period novel of St. Croix by Du Bose Hayward in his *Star Spangled Virgin* (New York: Farrar and Rinehart, 1939).

42. Grede, *The New Deal*, p. 43. See, also, Joanna C. Colcord, "West Indies—American Style," *Survey Graphic*, 24 (April 1935): 165–170.

tention and only one hundred and fifty favoring him, but Pearson charged the votes were "a fraud."[43]

The Roosevelt-Garner Club was sometimes joined by other local groups, such as the Suffragist League, the Civic Betterment Club, and the Young Peoples Democratic Club. Increasingly, during Pearson's administration, their combined memberships held mass meetings and demonstrations of reported four to five thousand natives and, at times, would march on government buildings demanding Pearson's resignation. A near riot occurred in St. Croix in June 1934, at a meeting "under the surveillance of a squad of police armed with shotguns and rifles, as a result of reports a serious outbreak might occur."[44] In August, Morris Davis led another protest march in St. Croix that was stopped by police.[45] Finally, on the evening of October 16, 1934 Davis and his followers staged a protest march in St. Thomas without a police permit. Violence

---

43. Grede, *The New Deal*, p. 121. "You should know that this so-called referendum was conducted by a ghost organization, calling itself the 'Civic Betterment Association' the membership of which has not been disclosed but which is commonly supposed to consist of two white men, the one a dismissed Government Attorney, and the other a disappointed job seeker. This so-called referendum was so manifestly a fraud that the Colonial Council of St. Croix passed a Resolution condemning it and giving the Governor a vote of confidence." NABS, RG 126, File 9-11-2 (Part 2); Pearson to Rt. Rev. Edward D. W. Jones, October 26, 1934.

44. *The New York Times*, June 26, 1934, p. 15, col. 4. Concerning the Roosevelt-Garner Club and the Suffragist League, Pearson wrote Rev. Jones: "You say that there was a cablegram from citizens asking for my removal. Such a cable was signed by the Roosevelt-Garner Club, whose 'President-General' is Morris Davis, who has a prison record with a dozen counts. The Treasurer of this Club was recently committed to the penitentiary for life because of murder, and the Vice-President is a man with a half dozen counts on the police record. The other organization signing this cablegram ... was the Suffragist League, another ghost organization, with one known member, who was the leading bootlegger under the Navy Administration, and who has vigorously demanded the return of the Navy and the change from Civil to Naval Government.... The Suffragist League has no standing here, and its one known member has no reputation for veracity or regard for truth." *op. cit.*, n. 43. An internal unaddressed memorandum of the Interior Department stated: "Mr. George H. Ivins, Director of Education, Government of the Virgin Islands, informed me today that the Suffragist League of St. Thomas, V.I. is a very small and non-influential organization locally. It has a dozen or so members and its organizer Mrs. Ella Gifft is a small merchant who is interested in the return of the Navy solely for reasons of personal profit to be derived by sale of her produce in the generally expanded market thus created. It is evident that the agitation for the return of the Navy is led by the merchants, property owners, etc. who would stand to personally benefit by the presence of an unnecessarily large Navy personnel." NARS, RG 126, File 9-11-12 (Part 1). Memorandum signed by R. A. Kleindienst, March 14, 1933.

45. *The New York Times*, August 18, 1934, p. 3, col. 4.

broke out when police attempted to arrest Davis. Police were beaten and the acting police director sustained a fractured skull.[46]

Meanwhile, Pearson's success in eliciting continuing media support from both the Islands and the mainland[47] and political support from Washington[48] served only to increase the frustration and resistance of his opponents.

---

46. Jarvis, *Brief History of the Virgin Islands*, pp. 178–179; Dookhan, *A History of the Virgin Islands*, p. 279. After this incident, Pearson wrote: "It appears that Davis puts on a good show, in that he always has somebody up for denunciation. As we all know, the crowd likes that. They are not particularly interested in the truth of what is said. They just want to see somebody socked in the jaw. It is no worse here than in Washington, or New York, or Chicago, or Boston, or any other town, large or small. It is true, no doubt, that such a show gets a larger percentage of the population than elsewhere because we have little to entertain us. Those who attend the Davis show do not have the price of the movies, although that is limited to 10¢ minimum." NARS, RG 126, File 9-11-2 (Part 3); Pearson to Gruening, October 26, 1934. In a second letter, Pearson wrote: "In sending a report of the Morris Davis lecture in St. Croix, Harry Taylor, the Acting Lieutenant Governor, writes to me personally: 'Here's Davis' latest, indicating legal advice on the point of inciting a riot, and turning viciously to personalities, threats, etc. How long is this to continue? What is underway to stop it? Some say it will wear itself out. It won't. It will result in blood shed unless it is soon curbed and even if the prophecy proves fortunately wrong, it is wrecking the rehabilitation plans and prospects for the Islands, and demonstrating that a hand of an ignorant, malicious agent, with certain small but strategic backing can hamstring the accredited authorities of Government and make a mess of the Federal rehabilitation plans.' I can only say to Mr. Taylor that now that we have a Government Attorney and that another charge is imminent, we shall be able to rout the hand of little fellows, who are important only because they think they are immune." *Ibid.*; Pearson to Gruening, November 1, 1934.

47. Governor Pearson, father of the well-known columnist Drew Pearson, displayed considerable journalistic skill, himself, in publicizing his successes as the "Experimental Quaker" in the Virgin Islands. Much of the local press remained supportive of Pearson. See, *e.g.*, editorials in: *The St. Croix Avis*, October 18, 19, 22, 23, 1934; *The St. Croix Tribune*, October 22, 23, 1934; *The St. Thomas Mail*, October 20, 1934; and the *Daily News*, October 16, 1934. *The West End News* of St. Croix remained an exception. For national media support of Pearson, see, *e.g.*, Ralph Thompson, "The Promise of the Virgin Islands," *Current History*, March, 1935. NARS, RG 126, File 9-11-2 (Part 1).

48. Dookhan, *A History of the Virgin Islands*, p. 278. Pearson continually wrote to Gruening defending his administration. See, *e.g.*, Pearson to Gruening, January 11, 1935; March 9, 1935; and April 10, 1935. To one of Pearson's critics, Gruening replied: "The fact ... is that no administration has ever done more for the masses in the Virgin Islands than the present one." Gruening to Dr. R. A. Farley, President, Ministerial Alliance, Washington, D.C., June 5, 1935. Similarly, Secretary Ickes wrote to a Pearson critic: "That certain elements in the Islands are opposed to Governor Pearson is understandable, but, so far as I am informed, the opposition simmers down to personal dislike, political ambitions, or other superficial motives. Such arguments are not very impressive." Ickes to Jose I. Gimenez, St. Thomas, July 18, 1924; NARS, RG 126, File 9-11-2 (Part 1).

The Roosevelt-Garner Club, claiming to represent four thousand members at a mass meeting, communicated on February 2, 1935 a series of charges to Washington, demanding the impeachment among others of Ickes and Pearson, and claiming the Pearson government discriminated in favor of wealthy merchants and the West India Company and against the poor natives, and wasted most of the relief food and federal P. W. A. funds.[49] Reporting from St. Thomas, Hanson Baldwin wrote:

> Bitterness, rancor, passion and prejudice to an almost unbelievable degree are rampant in the islands ... a drama of political and personal hatred.
>
> The charges and vituperations that are hurled, seemingly indiscriminately, ... are worthy of the best efforts of Tammany mudslingers....
>
> Because of the bitterness of the feud the pleasant and peaceful social life of St. Thomas has been largely disrupted. Men have been expelled from the Tennis Club, allegedly because of their political views, and others have lost their jobs. There have been minor riots, personal assaults and open denunciations of all and sundry. Fear, suspicion and hatred are real here, despite the surface calm and apparently somnolent quiet of this onetime pirate rendezvous.[50]

Opposition to Pearson was exacerbated by the patronage appointment of T. Webber Wilson by Attorney General Homer Cummings to the district court judgeship in the Virgin Islands in the summer of 1934. Wilson, a Mississippian, rapidly became "probably the most popular white man in the islands,"[51] and the most

---

49. Grede, *The New Deal*, pp. 122–123. Thus, Pearson was charged with unduly favoring the "Blue Ticket" organization, "This organization has been able to perpetuate itself in office, and holds all the principal and elective and appointive jobs, by reason of the limitation on the suffrage ... where the great majority of the people cannot vote. It is charged that these Blue Ticket officeholders run affairs in the islands to suit their own financial advantage." Harold B. Hinton, "New Rule Forecast in the Virgin Islands," *The New York Times*, July 14, 1935, sec. 4, p. 12, col. 2. A petition to Senator Millard Tydings, Chairman of the Senate Committee on Territories and Insular Possessions, dated January 8, 1935, stated that the people of St. Thomas at a mass meeting of 4,000 natives, on January 8, 1935, charged the Pearson administration with "fraud, graft, corruption, and maladministration ... calumny, misrepresentation, lies, and double-dealing," and concluded: "An investigation into the affairs of the Virgin Islands will reveal a situation existing which is almost unbelievable in its prostitution of liberty and Democratic Government and comparable only to Russia in its darkest days under the Czar." NARS, RG 126, File 9-11-2 (Part 1).

50. *The New York Times*, March 18, 1935, p. 6, col. 1.

51. Hanson W. Baldwin, "Majority Opposes Pearson's Regime," *The New York Times*, April 9, 1935, p. 22, col. 1.

prominent leader of the opposition to Pearson. One of few government officials in the Islands not appointed by Interior Secretary Ickes, Wilson—charging the Pearson administration was attempting to dictate to the judicial branch—declared: "I am answerable only to Attorney General Cummings and to God Almighty."[52]

A case appeared for trial in Judge Wilson's court in January 1935 that was to kindle a Congressional investigation that would result in Pearson's replacement.[53] Leonard W. McIntosh, chief clerk of Pearson's Public Works Department, admitted having used $11 worth of government lumber and $27.49 worth of government cement in building his own house. When Pearson's government attorney, George Robinson, refused to prosecute, Judge Wilson fined Robinson for contempt and proceeded to try the case himself, allegedly sitting as prosecutor, judge, and jury. In a courtroom crammed with natives, Wilson found McIntosh guilty and fined him two hundred dollars. On imposing sentence, Wilson told McIntosh; "You have become a Judas and Benedict Arnold to your country."[54]

The McIntosh case outraged Pearson and Secretary Ickes, who fully supported Pearson and publicly denounced Judge Wilson.

> The lines were now clearly drawn and they cut across geographical, political, and governmental divisions. On the one hand was the Department of Interior represented by Pearson and Ickes. Ranged in implacable opposition was Judge Wilson ... supported in Washington directly by Senators Harrison and Tydings and indirectly by cabinet members James Farley and Homer Cummings.[55]

---

52. Hanson W. Baldwin, "Rule of Pearson Series of Storms," *The New York Times*, April 7, 1935, p. 33, col. 3.

53. Paul C. Yates, executive assistant to Pearson for five months, meanwhile resigned in protest and, denouncing Pearson, charged: "I, together with other loyal Democrats, have been abused and crucified by a gang of reactionary and thieving Hoover Republicans." Raymond Gram Swing, "Storm Over the Virgin Islands," *Nation*, July 24, 1935, p. 95. Whistleblower Yates then filed charges of corruption against the Pearson administration with both houses of Congress. *Time*, July 15, 1935, pp. 20–21. For Yates' criticisms, and Pearson's responses, see NARS, RG 126, File 9-11-2 (Part 3).

54. Baldwin, *The New York Times*, April 7, 1935, p. 33, col. 4; Grede, *The New Deal*, pp. 114–115; *Time*, February 4, 1935, p. 22. See, also, Raymond Gram Swing, "Justice in the Virgin Islands," *Nation*, January 23, 1935. The Court of Appeals in Philadelphia later upheld McIntosh's conviction. Referring to Judge Wilson's conduct of the trial, Judge Buffington, for the Court, stated: "We do not feel he acted as prosecutor, but in accord with judicial duty and in keeping with the standards laid down in many cases." *The New York Times*, March 15, 1935, p. 3, col. 5.

55. Grede, *The New Deal*, p. 116. A close working relationship developed between the Roosevelt-Garner Club and Judge Wilson and his supporters. In May, 1935, the Club or-

By the summer of 1935, unrest in the Islands had become serious enough to provoke Senator Millard Tydings, Chairman of the Senate Committee on Territories and Insular Possessions, to undertake a Congressional investigation of the Pearson administration.[56] The investigation committee convened on July 2, and the whole matter now became an affair of state and a well-publicized controversy within the New Deal administration. A series of anti-Pearson witnesses testified and various documents were admitted as evidence, including an affidavit signed by a Virgin Islands clergyman in which Pearson was called "a liar, a thief, a crook, and a son of a bitch."[57] Before any rebuttal witnesses could be heard, and about one week after the hearings opened, President Roosevelt intervened and persuaded Tydings to recess the hearings, after which the President simultaneously transferred Governor Pearson to a new post, especially created for him, of Assistant Director of Housing for the Public Works Administration, and Judge Wilson to the Federal Parole Board. To make room on the Parole Board for Wilson, Attorney General Cummings had to obtain the resignation of Dr. Amy Stannard, an able psychiatrist, an action which Cummings justified on the ground that women were not suitable for parole work.[58]

A New Deal

On July 24, 1935, Paul Pearson's tenure as the first civilian governor of the Virgin Islands came to an end. How may one assess his administration? Any estimate must take into account the deplorable conditions in the Islands, partly revealed by statistics, that confronted Pearson at the beginning of his administration.

---

ganized its most brazen demonstration of all. "When Judge Wilson returned to the Virgin Islands, after having been summoned to Washington for consultation, he was greeted at the wharf by a large crowd and escorted to his home in a grand parade led by Morris Davis." *Ibid.*, p. 124.

56. "It was symptomatic of what was wrong with the American conduct of colonial affairs that the first really important congressional investigation of the insular problem since 1917 was, in effect, a fierce intra-administration battle combined with a Senate-Interior conflict in which the real problem, by default, never was touched upon." Lewis, *The Virgin Islands*, p. 79.

57. Grede, *The New Deal*, p. 129.

58. Raymond Gram Swing, "Corruption, Sacred and Profane," *Nation*, August 7, 1935, pp. 155–156; *Newsweek*, August 3, 1935, pp. 8–9.

In 1930, of a total population of 22,012, ninety-one people owned the one hundred and ninety-three estates, seventy-seven owned farms of less than ten acres each, and six hundred renters of one-to-five acre plots paid $7 to $12 an acre cash rental. More than 80 percent of the land in St. Croix was owned by twenty men, and 90 percent of all cultivated land of the three islands was in the hands of one percent of the families. This meant that less than five percent of the people, that were engaged in agriculture, owned their own land.[59]

The serious obstacles to economic development presented by the plantation system and the deterioration of the agricultural economy were largely a heritage of the Danish period and resulted in a system of unregulated farm tenantry. Nothing was done to alleviate the situation under the Navy. Once a laborer became a tenant, he was seldom able to find the means or the opportunity to become a landowner. Of 2,944 persons recorded in 1930 as gainfully employed in agriculture, 2,440 or 83 percent were classified as farm laborers. Since the days of slavery these laborers formed a pool from which plantation owners and sugar factories drew their labor when needed. Since twice as many laborers are required to harvest a sugar crop as are needed for planting and cultivating, few laborers could hope for employment for more than one hundred to one hundred and twenty days in the year. A pay rate of 40 cents a day during the harvesting season was standard in 1930, when they could obtain employment. The early years of the New Deal under Pearson succeeded in raising wages, and by 1940 wage rates had increased to 80 cents and $1 per day.[60] Farm laborers were often tenant farmers in their spare time, cultivating areas of from one to three acres. Some of them were permitted to occupy estate or factory village houses without payment of rent, but these were usually dilapidated and without sanitary facilities. Other less fortunate laborers were required to pay rental of 25 cents per room per week for dwellings located at distances of two to five miles from the scene of their labor. Subsistence garden plots of 1/8 to 1/4 an acre were given to those who occupied village houses; they had to be worked during spare time.[61] "Farm laborers consequently were a landless, dispossessed class with little hope of improving their lot."[62]

---

59. *Annual Report of the Governor of the Virgin Islands, 1934*, pp. 18–19.

60. *Annual Report of the Governor of the Virgin Islands, 1940*, pp. 12–15. In 1944, from a visit to the sugar factory on the island of Antigua, British West Indies, this writer found that semi-skilled factory laborers received the meager rate of 40 to 60 cents a day during the harvesting season.

61. *Ibid.*

62. *Ibid.*, p. 13.

When Governor Pearson came to the Virgin Islands in 1931, he was completely surprised by the desperate conditions he found. Navy governors had not sounded any alarms in their annual reports, and even these were filed away and forgotten. In St. Croix, Governor Pearson found most of the laborers out of work, with 25 percent of the population being kept alive by the Red Cross. No sugar factories were then working. The Danish Company had collapsed the year before from the first impact of the depression. "Depression was general, serious, and complete."[63] In St. Thomas, decreased harbor activities had caused wide unemployment. In St. John, "the people were almost desperate." Whereas St. Croix had been exporting cotton, "none has been exported during the past three years." The death rate was three times that of the United States, and in St. Croix it exceeded the birth rate. "The standards of life are so low that 65 percent of the burials are pauper burials." The most productive men and women, between fifteen and forty-five years of age, were emigrating. "The nutrition of the people is poor."[64]

Governor Pearson sought to accomplish six objectives.[65] The first was to increase responsibility by the Islanders for their own government. This he sought to accomplish by appointing Islanders to administrative and executive positions. He increased the percentage of such positions filled by natives from 10 percent in 1931 to 75 percent in 1935.

Pearson's second objective was to increase self-support by the local government. He claimed that in 1934 the combined revenues of the three municipalities had increased 13.5 percent since 1931, while federal contributions to municipal deficits had decreased 31.5 percent since 1931.

Much more extensive were Pearson's claimed accomplishments with respect to his third objective—improvement of economic conditions. Income tax assessments by 1935 were five times those of 1931. Ship tonnage entering St. Thomas had increased, and some sixteen ships carrying tourists visited in 1934 compared to only three in 1930. For tourists, the Bluebeard's Castle Hotel was built and run by the government. Handicraft sales through cooperatives had expanded 600 percent in four years. The Virgin Islands Company had been created and invested $700,000 in the local economy, including the operation of two sugar mills, two rum distilleries and the rehabilitation of five others. Employment of public works projects had increased four times that of 1931, and at one time since then had peaked at fourteen times. Fifty units of low-cost

---

63. *Annual Report of the Governor of the Virgin Islands, 1931*, p. 3.
64. *Ibid.*, pp. 3–4.
65. For the following assessment of Pearson's accomplishments, see: Grede, *The New Deal*, pp. 132–134.

housing were built or under construction. As a result of homesteading, four times more small farmers were tilling their own land as in 1931. And, finally, the Virgin Islands National Bank had replaced the old Danish Bank.

Even in comparison with the Navy's notable achievements, Pearson was able to claim progress in improvement of health and sanitation, his fourth objective. The crude death rate of 22/1,000 of 1930 fell to 19/1,000 in 1934, while the infant mortality rate of 119/1,000 live births in 1930 was reduced to 97/1,000 in 1935. In addition, facilities were increased for hospitals and the leprosarium.

Improvement of education, Pearson's fifth objective, was marked by salary increases for teachers, summer institutes for teacher training, scholarships for study abroad, operation of the first senior high school, and a total enrollment of fifteen hundred persons in adult education by 1935.

Accomplishments with respect to Pearson's final objective, the improvement of social conditions, included recreational facilities, food relief for nearly one-half the population, work relief for a peak of another 20 percent, and public parks and beach improvements.

A Paradox

Given these admirable achievements of the Pearson administration, the question arises why most Virgin Islanders were not content during Pearson's tenure as Governor. They betrayed no gratitude for American attempts to advance economic emancipation of the Islands. Indeed, with the Islands being a focus of so much unprecedented ferment and activity, Virgin Islanders of every station responded with malevolence and vituperation toward their would-be benefactors. Reasons for this apparent anomaly are speculative, but certain factors are possibly suggestive of explanation.

Perhaps a distinctive insular psychology, borne of isolation and alienation from the mainland, enlarged or distorted dissent into misanthropic mass demonstrations. After all, Virgin Islanders had no experience with American politics and its elements of compromise, free expression, give-and-take, and the corollary of an extraordinary toleration of political differences. Indeed, the mass of Virgin Islanders still could not vote. They could not feel any sense of participating in the making of decisions about their destiny. They were still being ruled by Washington. They had always been put down by others. How could they now be expected to trust the wisdom of the white men who had replaced the naval officers?

Perhaps, also, they had been repressed so much for so long, that now they were letting off steam, and conditions had changed under civil rule permitting them to vent their long-time, pent-up, discontent. Every governor succeeding Pearson was to feel the steam of popular discontent, probably attributable to some if not most of the factors at work in the 1930s.

One must also be mindful that, despite their location, Virgin Islanders have always been strongly influenced by developments and events elsewhere featuring popular assertiveness and political participation—in the United States, the Caribbean, and the world. Bonus armies, civil rights movements, anti-colonialism, the new nationalism, and the so-called new international economic order have all influenced Virgin Islanders. However compassionate and noble were the motives behind it, Pearson's new deal may have heightened the sense of the people's dependency, counter to their quest for dignity and integrity. It certainly made them early participants in the coming revolution of rising expectations that was to sweep the Third World. In this sense, only a political system of self-determination and an economic system of self-sufficiency ultimately could ever fulfill their rising expectations—expectations kindled by the achievements of the Pearson administration.

Paul Pearson died in April 1938. His famous columnist son, Drew Pearson, some years later recalled:

> The problem of reviving those bankrupt islands eventually broke my father. He left the islands ... criticized and reviled. The white plantation owners conspired against him. The Negro politicians lampooned him. He was even accused of stealing 4 bags of cement.[66]

---

66. "Drew Pearson on the Washington Merry-Go-Round," as reprinted in *Hearings before House Subcommittee on Territories and Insular Possessions on H. R. 2644*, 83rd Cong., 2nd sess. (1952), p. 123.

President Herbert Hoover's visit to St. Thomas, 1931

8

Progress and Politics

The post of Governor, now vacated by Paul Pearson, was filled by his force-
ful and outspokenly liberal fellow-academician, Lawrence Cramer, who had
come to the Islands with Pearson in 1931 and had served ably as Lieutenant Governor and Administrator for St. Croix.

The beginning of the New Deal in the Virgin Islands could not be attributed
to the onset of the presidency of Franklin Roosevelt. Its inception properly
dates from Herbert Hoover's transfer of the Islands in 1931 from the Navy to
the Interior Department. The New Deal program had gone through trial and
experiment for three years under Governor Pearson. It was then reformulated
and amplified beginning in 1934 with the chartering of the Virgin Islands Company, Roosevelt's brief visit to the Islands, and the establishment of America's
first colonial office—the Interior Department's Division of Territories and Island Possessions—under Dr. Ernest Gruening. Reaching its fullest development under Governor Cramer between 1936 and 1938, the New Deal began to
disintegrate until by World War II it came to an end. The patronage appointment of Charles Harwood in 1941 as the successor to Governor Cramer was
to mark the capitulation of the New Deal in the Islands.

Meanwhile, the unpopularity of the Pearson administration, and the tribu-
lations of Pearson's successors that were to end in failure of the New Deal, were
not easily explainable. The factors were many, but prominent among them
was the inability of New Deal actors—both on the mainland and in the Islands—to fully comprehend the complexities of the personality and culture
of Virgin Islanders.

Personality and Culture

The total population of the Virgin Islands at the beginning of the New Deal
was little more than half the population of a century before. Commensurate
with the steady economic decline, the total decreased from 43,178 in 1835 to
26,051 in 1917—the year of transfer to American rule—a decline of 39.7 per-

cent. The total further declined to 22,012 in 1930. The average annual decrease in the last six years of Danish rule was 6.3 per thousand, and during the first thirteen years of American rule it was 11.4 per thousand.[1]

Many factors operated to explain the depopulation of the Islands. Foremost was the economic decline, itself, caused by factors over which Virgin Islanders had no control, such as the mid-nineteenth century shift from sailboats to steamships, followed by the increasing substitution of beet sugar on the world market for cane sugar, and the more recent constitutional prohibition of the production and sale of alcoholic beverages including rum. Despite marked reduction in the death rate under American health and sanitation programs, the population continued to decline because of the increase of outmigration.

Movement to the mainland of the United States, available to Virgin Islanders since 1917, was made easier after the granting of U.S. citizenship in 1927. Job opportunities were greater and wage rates higher on the mainland, attracting many of the able-bodied young adults, of the best workers, and of the most ambitious Virgin Islanders, most of whom migrated to New York City. Those left behind were predominantly children, women, and the elderly. The average St. Croix farmer during the New Deal period was 51.8 years old.[2]

It is not surprising, therefore, that those Virgin Islanders remaining behind became the subject of frequent derision and invidious characterization by white continentals. Thus Harry A. Franck commented in 1920 that the women were more industrious than the men. "The loose-kneed stroll of the Virgin Islander is typical of all his processes, mental, moral or physical," he wrote.[3] In his 1925 report on economic conditions in the Islands to the Secretary of Treasury, Dr. Rufus S. Tucker stated that employers rated the workingman in the Islands as one-fifth to one-half less efficient than the average laborer on the mainland, and much less efficient than the Puerto Rican laborer.[4]

Writing of the period 1917 to 1935, Luther Evans lamented that the failure to improve economic conditions, including homesteading, was "largely attributable to the unwillingness of natives to work," and added that "Cruzans,"

---

1. Evans, *The Virgin Islands*, p. 312.

2. Grede, *The New Deal in the Virgin Islands*, p. 37.

3. Harry A. Franck, "The Virgin Islands," *Century Magazine*, September 1920, pp. 616–630.

4. Rufus S. Tucker, *Report on Economic Conditions in the Virgin Islands*, 69th Cong., 2d sess., Sen. Doc. No. 41, (1925), pp. 6–9. Similarly, Robert Morss Lovett cited an estimate of a mainland private contracting firm that St. Thomas labor was only 25 percent as efficient as Georgia Negro labor. Robert Morss Lovett, "The Virgin Islands—Problem Children," *New Republic*, March 3, 1937, pp. 105–107.

particularly, "are of an ungracious and ugly disposition."[5] And Hanson Baldwin, writing in *The New York Times* in 1935, characterized native Virgin Islanders as follows:

> They are warm-hearted, simple, indolent from long centuries in the tropic sun, with little initiative and ambition because of decades of slavery and the later years of a paternalistic Danish Government, and they are the most of them probably more anxious to be helped than to help themselves.[6]

Such simplistic and stereotyped evaluations of Virgin Islanders failed to take account of the estimated twenty thousand Virgin Islanders who by 1930 were residing in the Harlem section alone of New York City—a number almost equal to the total population of those who remained behind. Many of these migrants worked as laborers, servants, and in other servile occupations—work that they would never have undertaken at home because of its association with low social status in the Islands. Many regularly remitted money to their kinfolk in the Islands. Their leaders were "conscientious patriots" who commanded sources of influence and money not available to those at home. Among the leaders were Ashley L. Totten, Secretary of the International Union of Sleeping Car Porters, and Casper Holstein who used his wealth to help finance college scholarships for young Virgin Islanders and to lobby in Washington for self-government for the Islands.[7]

In his eight-month study of St. Thomians in 1940, psychologist Albert A. Campbell of Northwestern University confirmed that local high school graduates were very reluctant to take any position which involved menial work, that St. Thomians could not be driven, and that employers found it increasingly difficult to employ servants from among them. Campbell refrained, however, from ascribing such attitudes wholly to the legacy of slavery. They were more properly associated with status awareness and social stratification within St. Thomas society. St. Thomians are always on their guard against appearing inferior, he explained. "This sensitivity, so characteristic of St. Thomians in their role of employee, is only the expression of a general attitude which pervades all of their social relationships."[8]

---

5. Evans, *The Virgin Islands*, p. 315.

6. Hanson W. Baldwin, "Virgin Isles Held Back by Poverty," *The New York Times*, April 6, 1935, p. 5, col. 2.

7. Lewis, *The Virgin Islands*, p. 113.

8. Campbell, *St. Thomas Negroes*, pp. 33–54.

The attitudes of Virgin Islanders toward work during the New Deal comprised a complex cultural phenomenon. To have described Virgin Islanders as "shiftless," "indolent," and "unwilling to work" was in error. Not only were those who migrated to the mainland willing to work, many in menial jobs, but so also were many who stayed in the Islands, provided they worked for the United States government—the only large-scale employer. Campbell found the U.S. government employed approximately one thousand of the eleven thousand inhabitants of St. Thomas. "In March, 1940, there were 654 persons working on WPA projects, 169 men were in the CCC camps, and 104 persons were employed by the PWA."[9]

For the most part, Virgin Islanders were content to leave manual work outside of government to immigrants from other Caribbean islands. Early in the century there was considerable immigration to St. Croix from the British West Indies, principally from St. Kitts and Barbados.[10] Marked economic improvement, reported by Governor Cramer in 1936,[11] followed by national defense construction in the late 1930s and early 1940s, spurred immigration from nearby Puerto Rico and the British Virgin Islands in numbers exceeding outmigration.[12] Most became laborers in the cane fields of St. Croix. Native Virgin Islanders preferred white-collar jobs and had an aversion to manual labor, particularly agricultural work. Although immigrants from the British islands also could associate such work with their ancestral slave status, Campbell observed that the English colonial policy in those islands did not foster "any illusions regarding equality" and had produced "a degree of servility among the lower class" which one did not often find among Virgin Islanders.[13]

Attitudes toward the newcomers were mixed. A survey of St. Thomas press opinion over the period 1936 to 1942 by local historian Marilyn Krigger revealed a greater acceptance of British Virgin Islanders than of Puerto Ricans. The former were perceived as well-mannered and very similar in culture to U.S. Virgin Islanders, whereas Puerto Ricans were regarded as "far more alien

9. *Ibid.*, p. 36.

10. Edwin A. Weinstein, *Cultural Aspects of Delusion: A Psychiatric Study of the Virgin Islands* (New York: Free Press, 1962), p. 46.

11. *Annual Report of the Governor of the Virgin Islands, 1936* (Washington: U.S. Govt. Print. Off., 1936), p. 1.

12. Marilyn F. Krigger, *Attitudes and References to Immigrants in the St. Thomas Press 1936–1942*, unpublished paper presented at the Tenth Conference of Caribbean Historians, March 27–April 1, 1978 (xeroxed, College of the Virgin Islands, St. Thomas, V.I.), pp. 2–3. Between 1927 and 1937, over 4,000 Puerto Ricans were estimated to have moved to the Virgin Islands. *Daily News*, August 7, 1937, p. 3, as quoted in Krigger, *ibid.*, pp. 7–8.

13. Campbell, *St. Thomas Negroes*, p. 54.

in habits, physique, language, traditions, race and color."[14] The fact that over sixty percent of St. Thomians themselves were alien born or of alien parent-age,[15] and that Puerto Ricans were bona fide U.S. citizens, did not alter this view. On the contrary, Puerto Ricans, precisely because they were citizens el-igible for government posts, represented a political threat to Virgin Islanders in contrast to aliens from the British islands.[16] Not only did American immi-gration authorities foster immigration of British islanders, but their laxity in enforcing immigration laws permitted many to enter illegally.[17]

Work attitudes of Virgin Islanders constituted only one major difficulty that bewildered New Deal actors. Equally distressing were the social consequences of a high rate of illegitimacy. Because of outmigration, females in the 1930s ex-ceeded by sixteen percent the number of males. The pattern of family organ-ization was "strongly reminiscent of the conditions prevailing under slavery ... when neither masters nor slaves bothered ... with legal ties."[18] Reliable assess-ment of sexual behavior was, of course, difficult for New Deal authorities. Caribbean writers, moreover, differed in their conceptions of "the family" and in the nomenclature they employed to denote varying attachments between males and females. Whether one described such relationships as "consensual," "extra-residential," or "common-law," the law of most Caribbean polities con-sidered children born outside of wedlock as illegitimate.[19] Characterizing the Negro lower-class family of the Virgin Islands as traditionally a part of West In-dian matricentric societies with typically a working mother and absentee father, Gordon Lewis explained this type of family to be inimical to family pride and

---

14. *Daily News*, August 3,1936, p. 3, as quoted by Krigger, *Attitudes and References*, p. 6.

15. Krigger, *Attitudes and References*, pp. 5–6.

16. *Ibid.*, p. 15. "The matter of distinguishing Virgin Islanders from British islanders is complicated by the fact that almost all Virgin Islands natives have relations in other Caribbean areas as a result of the many migrations that have occurred." Weinstein, *Cultural Aspects of Delusion*, p. 46.

17. See, *e.g.*, Krigger, *Attitudes and References*, and Miller and Boyer, *Foreign Workers in the U.S. Virgin Islands*, n. 8.

18. Campbell, *St. Thomas Negroes*, p. 41. "As a matter of policy, the masters did ... scat-ter around the newly arrived ... fellow villagers, kin, spouses, and their children were sep-arated.... By design, the African family was dismembered.... Polygamy was not unusual; but since no cultural patterns regulated these unions, they were ... unstable." Lionel Vallee, *The Negro Family on St. Thomas: A Study of Role Differentiation* (unpublished Ph.D. dis-sertation, Cornell University, 1964), pp. 41–43.

19. See, *e.g.*, James W. Green, *Social Networks in St. Croix, United States Virgin Islands* (unpublished Ph.D. dissertation, University of Washington, 1972), p. 357, n. 2, and p. 358, n. 4; and Vallee, *The Negro Family*, pp. 2–5.

unity, having very weak parent-child ties and its roots in slavery when pater-nity counted for little and planters were promiscuous. The female slave, how-ever, was "the linchpin" of this system and inheritance was through the female line. These conditions, Lewis explained, combined "to grant the colored woman an independent status denied to her male partner."

> This background produced at least two features of cardinal impor-tance: (1) the low prestige of the marriage tie, as compared to the Western monogamous tradition, and (2) an excessively liberal (to American continental eyes) attitude in native Virgin Islanders to sex-ual life in general, including as it does the distinct pattern of serial monogamy in which a woman will live with and bear children to sev-eral men, apparently without any real conflict emerging from the plu-ral relationship. Both of these features ... managed to survive the various attacks launched on them by American puritan morality since 1917.[20]

An inevitable result of such sexual mores was the high illegitimacy rates, ranging from 53 percent of births on St. Thomas to 64 percent on St. Croix; the continuing search for and apprehension of fathers filled local courts with child-support cases.[21] That New Deal authorities viewed this aspect of Virgin Islands culture adversely is understatement. Governor Pearson evoked much local enmity by announcing steps to improve the morals of Virgin Islanders who were "producing an abnormal increase of population without the proper assumption of responsibility for that increase."[22] In 1943, Government Secre-

---

20. Lewis, *The Virgin Islands*, p. 240. Lionel Vallee has noted certain similarities in the social structure of the African tribes represented in St. Thomas around 1769, the period when the slave trade was nearing its peak. Whereas five of the tribes were matrilineal, nine were patrilineal in structure, but even the latter had a matrilineal rule of descent. Marriage, on the other hand, was everywhere polygamous among all nine tribes in Africa, but it is doubt-ful polygamy or any particular pattern existed under slavery. "Thus," concludes Vallee, "any attempt at interpreting the present 'matrifocal' family structure, cannot rest solely on the basis of African survivals, nor exclusively as a product of slavery." Vallee, *The Negro Fam-ily*, pp. 203–204.

21. Grede, *The New Deal*, p. 39.

22. Quoted by Robert Morss Lovett in his autobiography, *All Our Years* (New York: The Viking Press, 1948), p. 282. One federal commission had called for the abolition of con-sensual marriages as "above all else requisite for the civil and industrial salvation" of the Virgin Islands. *Report to the Secretary of Labor of the Federal Commission to Investigate In-dustrial and Economic Conditions in the Virgin Islands*, U.S.A., February 29, 1924, as quoted by J. Antonio Jarvis, *Brief History of the Virgin Islands* (St. Thomas: The Art Shop, 1938), pp. 138–139.

tary Robert Morss Lovett confided in a private letter his view that "the weakness of the family" constituted "the greatest single obstacle to the attainment of a higher standard of living" in the Islands.[23] Later, he publicly explained:

> The support of the children born outside the family fell chiefly upon the women.... I felt it infinitely pathetic when a girl came with her baby and replied to my question, "Fatherless." ... The most serious aspect ... was the children.... With no responsible guardianship they fell into delinquency of various types. Petty thieving was common. Little boys, as well as adolescent girls, became the willing victims of sailors and Marines.[24]

To his credit, New Deal chronicler Luther Evans called for a greater measure of equality "to solve the colonial aspect of the problem"—equality that would not only eliminate race hostility ("it is essential to have dignity and to treat others with dignity"), but also would recognize "the possible validity of a different standard of morality."

> To Virgin Islanders the common practice of living with a woman or a man to whom one is not married is not particularly blameworthy.... The administrator must not scoff at these different practices as "inferior." He must accept them and show clearly that he is not contemptuous of those who participate in them. The governed must feel that their governors are sympathetic.[25]

The fact that Virgin Islands women generally found it necessary to raise children without the help of husbands led James Green to emphasize the prevalence of female exploitation and their subservience to men. "Women are expected to submit to the wishes of men," he wrote, "not only sexually but in day-to-day life generally."[26] In sharp contrast, Gordon Lewis emphasized the independence and "remarkably free status" of the Virgin Islands woman. Women are likely to gain status through their own accomplishments, he observed, rather than through husbands.[27] In the 1930s, the proportion of gainfully em-

---

23. Robert Morss Lovett to Benjamin W. Thoron, May 26, 1943, Lovett Papers, as quoted and cited in Grede, *The New Deal*, p. 39.

24. Lovett, *All Our Years*, pp. 282–283.

25. Evans, *The Virgin Islands*, pp. 322–323. But note that Evans' book has been severely criticized by others, as, for example, Gordon Lewis who considered it an apology for colonialism, and "an astonishing hodgepodge of ingenuousness, racism, and character assassination." Lewis, *The Virgin Islands*, pp. 90–91.

26. Green, *Social Networks in St. Croix*, p. 359, n. 6. A Crucian woman gains "recognition and esteem ... from the character of her domestic life." *Ibid.*, p. 257.

27. Lewis, *The Virgin Islands*, pp. 241, 242.

ployed women was 43.4 percent in the Virgin Islands compared to only 22 percent in the United States mainland.[28] That Virgin Islands women were not willing to be cast in a subservient role is illustrated by their victory at the polls in 1935. The local electoral board had refused the application of twenty-three women to vote on the ground that they were neither eligible under the Danish Colonial Law of 1906 nor under the Act of Congress of 1917. Three St. Thomas school teachers among them thereupon petitioned the local federal district court for a writ of mandamus. Judge Albert Levitt, after extensive research into the Danish codes, granted the writ. He held that the term "person" in the Danish Colonial Law of 1906 could not be interpreted as meaning only "man" without invalidating the entire Colonial Law. He also held that the Nineteenth (Women suffrage) Amendment to the United States Constitution applied to the Islands, even though Constitutional rights were not extended to Virgin Islanders under the Act of Congress of 1917.[29]

Most American New Deal officials were victims of their own cultural ignorance of the Virgin Islands. Of the total population of 24,889 in 1940—an increase of 2,877 since 1930—the U.S. census classified 2,236 or 9 percent as "white," 17,176 or 69 percent as "Negro," and 5,477 or 22 percent as "mixed and other."[30] The color-class hierarchy of the Islands was far too complicated to be accommodated within census classifications, or within the mainland black-white bifurcation with which New Deal officials were acculturated. Paul Blanshard wrote of "the most obvious fact of Caribbean life," namely "a basic causal connection between color, class, and ownership." The Caribbean social pattern, according to Blanshard, simply stated was this: the lighter skin a person had, the more wealth he was likely to possess, and the less work he was likely to perform.[31] Albert Campbell's 1940 study of St. Thomians essentially confirmed this pattern's existence in the Virgin Islands, with some specifically local modifications.[32] Most white continentals simply were unprepared to understand a

---

28. Grede, *The New Deal*, p. 40.

29. Hanson W. Baldwin, "Virgin Islands are Quieting Down," *The New York Times*, January 12, 1936, sec. 4, p. 5, col. 6.

30. *Sixteenth Census of the United States: 1940, Virgin Islands of the United States* (Washington: Govt. Print. Off., 1940), p. 9.

31. Paul Blanshard, *Democracy and Empire in the Caribbean* (New York: The Macmillan Company, 1947), pp. 51–59.

32. Campbell, *St. Thomas Negroes*, pp. 45–61. "Through a long and uninterrupted historical process white values have become established prestige values and, since throughout this period there has never been a white lower class…, the white upper class has become the model from which all prestige-seeking behavior takes its inspiration." But Campbell footnotes this assertion with this exception: "The French colony, which would seem to con-

highly stratified society marked by gradations of class and color. Perhaps Gordon Lewis expressed this phenomenon most saliently, as follows:

> American officials had to learn to come to terms with an amazingly complicated set of class-color correlates rooted in constitutive principles and historical background quite different from those of their parent society. A system of color classification based on the subtle gradations of skin pigmentation contained grievous pitfalls for the American who mistakenly applied the North American simplistic black-white dichotomy; similarly, he could easily overlook the fact that the social and economic cleavage between the Negro masses and the tiny propertied mulatto group with whom any mainland administrator naturally dealt was almost as sharp as that generally found elsewhere between black and white.[33]

The greater individual freedom and liberty afforded Virgin Islanders under ten years of civil administration, according to Albert Campbell, was not matched by greater social equality. Indeed, the question of race and color was brought into sharper focus. As native Virgin Islanders were receiving more education, and economic and political privileges, more resentment and antagonism was expressed by whites in the form of anti-Negro feeling. Conversely, Campbell found St. Thomians were beginning "to refuse to accord them deference because of their white skins." Authority attaching to white supremacy was eroding. Some whites were adamant. "Now that power is beginning to change hands," Campbell wrote, "the question of race has become vitally important to the white minority."[34]

The pronounced increase in tourism after 1935, moreover, only exacerbated the problem. One commercial hotel made a short-lived attempt to exclude colored guests. And other evidence of Jim Crow policy began to appear. Intelligent young natives, according to Campbell, "are sufficiently sophisticated to recognize the larger implications of the infiltration of American race practices, and they have begun to offer organized resistance."[35]

In many respects, the Virgin Islands consisted of a heterogeneous, transitional society beset with the intrusion of radical, exogenous, forces by conti-

---

stitute an exception to this statement, has always been isolated from the colored inhabitants and is not regarded by them in the same racial category as the other white residents." *Ibid.*, p. 51.

33. Lewis, *The Virgin Islands*, p. 85.
34. Campbell, *St. Thomas Negroes*, p. 82.
35. *Ibid.*, p. 83.

nental architects bent on economic reconstruction for altruistic reasons. Had New Deal actors pressed rehabilitative enterprise in a manner completely consonant with, and responsive to, the personality and culture of the Virgin Islands—that in itself would not have assured success of the New Deal in the Islands. Their lack of cultural empathy, however, probably assured, if not hastened, the demise of rehabilitative efforts, and helped forge, in their stead, a permanent dependency relationship with the metropolitan government in Washington. A radical New Deal invention—the Virgin Islands Company—was to provide a telling example of Fred Riggs' later description of negative development in a transitional society as a consequence of the heavy weight of bureaucratic power.[36]

The Virgin Islands Company

Naval rule had chiefly benefited St. Thomas, where activities had been concentrated around the naval station. "St. Croix was never enthusiastic about gold braid and marine guards."[37] Since the economic conditions were most desperate in St. Croix, it was there that New Deal rehabilitation was most needed. President Roosevelt was the initiator of the new policy. In 1934 he visited the Islands.[38]

Despite repeated attempts, the local government had been unable to interest private business to undertake the rehabilitation of the sugar industry.[39] As a consequence, on the initiative of the federal government, the Colonial Council of St. Thomas and St. John chartered the Virgin Islands Company (VICO) "to aid in effecting the economic rehabilitation of the Virgin Islands."[40] The

---

36. Fred W. Riggs, *Administration in Developing Countries, The Theory of Prismatic Society* (Boston: Houghton Mifflin Company, 1964).

37. Baldwin, "Virgin Islands are Quieting Down."

38. "When the President arrived yesterday at St. Thomas he was greeted by 18,000 persons." *The New York Times*, July 15, 1934, sec. 4, p. 8, col. 4. Dr. Ernest Gruening, director of the new Division of Territories and Island Possessions, announced that it became President Roosevelt's policy "to discover the 'new methods' and to develop the 'new resources' which would tend to transform the Virgin Islands into a self-sustaining, increasingly self-reliant, economically stable community." Ernest Gruening, "America's Dominion—Over Palm and Pine," *The New York Times*, September 20, 1936, sec. 7, p. 6.

39. *Annual Report of the Governor of the Virgin Islands, 1935*, p. 19.

40. *Annual Report of the Governor of the Virgin Islands, 1934*, p. 16. If "socialism" is defined as "the public ownership of the means of production," then VICO could represent one of the most extreme examples of socialism in American history. Initially, the Colonial Council of St. Croix had refused to charter VICO, principally because the twenty sugar estate owners "who owned 80 per cent of the island … did not like the government moving into the rum business.… Many saw Franklin D. Roosevelt swinging too far toward the col-

Company received an initial grant of $1,000,000, plus other funds from federal agencies. Concerning the story behind this initial grant, Governor William Hastie some years later wrote:

> Governor Pearson, Secretary Ickes and others had worked vigorously for a long time in an attempt to get the money necessary to start the Virgin Islands Company program. They were not successful. Several appeals direct to the President failed. Finally they convinced him that he should act, and he scribbled in longhand on a piece of note paper addressed, as I remember, to Harry Hopkins, the words "Give Virgin Islands one million dollars."[41]

In his 1934 annual report, Governor Pearson described the new Company as "a partnership program" between the U.S. Government and the Virgin Islands in a long-range development program.

> It will include a development of the winter vegetable crop during the off season for the United States, the improvement of handicraft industries, the development of the tourist trade, the improvement of the educational system to provide for adults and children of preschool age, a system of old age and unemployment compensation somewhat along the lines of those discussed by President Roosevelt, and extension of the homesteading and housing programs already initiated.[42]

President Roosevelt appointed three top-level incorporators to guide the operations of the Company—Secretary of the Interior Ickes, Assistant Secretary of the Interior Oscar Chapman, and Governor Pearson. Each incorporator held a $10 share of stock, and was bound to pass it on in trust to his successor in office. Appointed to sit with the incorporators on the Company's board of directors were D. Hamilton Jackson of St. Croix and Lionel Roberts of St. Thomas. To advise on Virgin Islands policies, particularly those relating to the development of the Company, Roosevelt appointed an advisory council of leading figures: Joanna C. Colcord, Harold Ickes, Dr. Mordecai W. Johnson,

---

lectivist state." Grede, *The New Deal*, pp. 152–153. See, also, R. G. Woolbert, "Rehabilitation in the Virgin Islands," *Foreign Affairs*, 17 (July 1939): 799; and Isaac Dookhan, "The Virgin Islands Company and Corporation: The Plan for Economic Rehabilitation in the Virgin Islands," *The Journal of Caribbean History*, 4 (May 1972): 58–59, 64.

41. Letter from William H. Hastie, Governor of the Virgin Islands of the United States, Charlotte Amalie, St. Thomas, dated June 2, 1949, to William W. Boyer. See Appendix for the full text.

42. *Annual Report of the Governor of the Virgin Islands, 1934*, p. 16.

George Foster Peabody, Charles W. Taussig, Henry Wallace, and Walter White.[43] Of the charter members of the advisory council, sugar expert Charles Taussig, President of the American Molasses Company, was perhaps the most important. Taussig had already accepted appointment as assistant to Governor Pearson to investigate the feasibility of reviving the rum industry in the Islands, and it was he who had conceived VICO. With repeal of the Eighteenth Amendment on December 5, 1933, the development of St. Croix cane lands and the operation of sugar mills and a rum industry—on a profit-sharing basis—became the heart of the Virgin Islands Company. Pearson's older rehabilitation programs and self-sufficiency objectives were integrated within VICO. Thus, homesteading became a part of the Company's program, and the number of individual homesteads in VICO projects increased to 828 units by 1940.[44]

During its years of operation, the Company gave permanent employment to about 500 people, and twice that number during the four to five months crop season. VICO grew sugar cane, ground cane, produced and sold sugar, distilled rum, supplied electric power to rural St. Croix, and performed other functions to develop the economy of the Islands. By 1940, the federal government had allocated nearly $3,500,000 for the Company's capital and operating expenses. With these funds, VICO acquired two sugar mills, a distillery, five thousand acres of land, villages, estate houses, farm and industrial structures, equipment, cattle and other farm animals. The Company rehabilitated and improved the sugar mills, distillery, and industrial buildings, procured industrial and farm equipment, restored workers' homes, and built many new houses, besides clearing, draining, and improving land that was put into cultivation or pasturage.[45]

Many New Dealers viewed VICO as an experiment which, if successful, could not only alter the national economy but also the American philosophy of government.[46] Others were less enthusiastic. "The Virgin Islands Company,"

---

43. *Ibid.* Walter White, national secretary of the National Association for the Advancement of Colored People (NAACP), resigned in 1935 from this little-used advisory council to signal his dissociation from Roosevelt because of Roosevelt's failure to publicly oppose a Southern filibuster against the Costigan-Wagner Anti-Lynching Bill led by Senate Majority Leader Joseph Robinson. William Hastie, then national NAACP chairman, was appointed. Rexford Tugwell replaced Henry Wallace in 1936. Grede, *The New Deal*, p. 48, n. 1 and p. 148, n. 1.

44. Grede, *The New Deal*, p. 157.

45. *Annual Report of the Governor of the Virgin Islands, 1940*, p. 16.

46. "President Hoover's 'effective poorhouse' has become a Roosevelt laboratory, or experiment station, and prosperity has already begun to succeed." *Literary Digest*, May 12, 1934, p. 36.

according to one observer, "is really an attempt to constitute a planned economy in an island where some say there is no economy to plan."[47] Among other critics were those who felt that history showed that St. Croix could never compete with other West Indian islands in cane production or rum making, and those mainlanders—including members of the Anti-Saloon League, the Methodist Episcopal Church, and the Women's Christian Temperance Union—who felt government ought not be in the rum business.[48]

Despite opposition to government rum-making, the first VICO-produced rum from St. Croix was sold in New York City in early 1937 with the confident prediction that "Within two years the production of the Virgin Islands will entirely relieve Congress of annual appropriations for St. Croix."[49] It is true that by the end of 1937 VICO showed a profit for the first time, of $5,195.85. Deficits, however, returned with the 1938–1942 drought. Then, with limitations of liquor imports to the United States from abroad during World War II, the demand for Virgin Islands rum, and sugar also, put VICO on a profitable basis for 1943–1945. The rum market collapsed with peace and another drought in 1946, and Virgin Islands rum exports declined 60 percent. Meanwhile, small homestead projects on St. Croix faltered. Increasingly, St. Croix natives left the cane fields for urban areas "hastened by their deep down distaste for farm labor," by droughts, by the attraction of war work, and by the economic necessity to increase size of holdings "to cope with the vagaries of climate."[50] By 1954, over three-fourths of cultivable land was in large holdings of two hundred and fifty acres or more.[51]

In his annual report for 1947, Governor Hastie stated that "The Virgin Islands Company continues to stand between the people of St. Croix and destitution." He reported a current wage rate for the Company's farm labor of $2 per 8-hour day, "the highest in the history of the Virgin Islands," and called for rechartering the Company as a federal corporation.[52]

---

47. Hanson W. Baldwin, *The New York Times*, April 12, 1935, p. 26, col. 2.

48. See, *e.g.*: Olive D. Shelley, President of the Women's Society First Presbyterian Church of Oak Ridge, Illinois to Secretary of Interior Harold Ickes, December 17, 1935, in NARS, RG 126, File 9-11-2 (Part 4); "Government Rum," *Literary Digest*, March 20, 1937, pp. 7–8. "Protected and financed by the nation which is recognized as the chief defender of private enterprise and initiative, the Virgin Islands have been thrust into an experiment in public enterprise which is socialistic in virtually all points and communistic in many." W. B. Courtney, "Rum, Romance, and Riches," *Colliers*, September 22, 1934, pp. 55–56.

49. *The New York Times*, March 10, 1937, p. 25, col. 4.

50. Grede, *The New Deal*, p. 157.

51. U.S. Senate, Committee on Interior and Insular Affairs, *Report Relative to Investigation and Hearings in the Virgin Islands*, 83rd Cong., 2d sess., 1954, p. 109.

52. *Annual Report of the Governor of the Virgin Islands, 1947*, p. 11.

Rechartering had been made necessary by the Government Corporation Control Act of 1945 which provided that all corporations supported by federal funds and not chartered by the U.S. Government must obtain a federal charter by June 30, 1948.[53] Failing to meet this deadline, Congress was forced to extend the life of the Company for another year—a failure that evoked sharp censure from President Truman.[54] Concerning Truman's personal and active interest in this and other Virgin Islands matters, Governor Hastie wrote on June 2, 1949 of Truman's two-days visit in February of the previous year and the possibility of yet another visit in 1949.

> His interest in the Virgin Islands Company as a development agency for this territory has been very keen. In his budget message to Congress this year he dealt with the subject specifically. Last June in approving a bill temporarily continuing the existence of the Virgin Islands Company he wrote quite sharply to Congress concerning the failure of the legislature to set the company up in such a manner as to carry out a long-range development program. The White House has on several occasions made specific representations to the Bureau of the Budget or to leaders of Congress with reference to Virgin Islands matters. During recent months the President invited the new Chairman of the House Sub-committee on Territories to the White House, and it is understood that the President expressed his personal concern that Congress act upon pending legislation concerning the political status of several of our possessions as well as the still pending Virgin Islands Company legislation.[55]

With Truman's prodding, Congress finally established the Virgin Islands Corporation (VICORP) on June 30, 1949.[56]

All assets and property of VICO were transferred to VICORP. The new Corporation was given probably the broadest grant of powers ever held[57] by a U.S. government corporation. Specifically, the new Corporation was authorized to:

1. Conduct studies, research, and experiments in the factors related to marketing of products and resources of the Virgin Islands.
2. Promote the investment of private capital in economic enterprises in the Islands.

---

53. 59 *Stat.* 597 (1945).
54. *The New York Times*, July 1, 1948, p. 1, col. 8.
55. Hastie to Boyer, June 2, 1949. See Appendix for the full text.
56. 63 *Stat.* 285 (1949).
57. Grede, *The New Deal*, p. 169.

3. Encourage and engage in land-use planning to promote the most beneficial use of the Islands' soil.
4. Help provide transportation between and around the Islands.
5. Promote the tourist trade.
6. Assist in the development of small farms and communities.
7. Make loans to private individuals for industrial, commercial, or agricultural undertakings in the Virgin Islands, when the money cannot be obtained privately.
8. Promote or engage in activities for the development of the industrial, commercial, mining, agricultural, livestock, fishery, or forestry resources of the Islands.

The Virgin Islands Corporation also was authorized to continue all VICO programs except the manufacture of alcoholic beverages. Thus, the two most important activities of VICORP were the continuing production of sugar and the production and distribution of electric power.[58] Under the new charter, therefore, it became necessary for VICORP to divest itself of its rum distillery which it first leased and later sold to A. H. Riise Distillery.[59] The major interest in this firm was held by Isaac Paiewonsky and his family. The now privately-run rum business and distillery—destined to become immensely profitable—was subsidized by VICORP's guarantee that 70 percent of its molasses would be purchased by A. H. Riise Distillery at less than market prices. Not entirely coincidental were the facts that Isaac Paiewonsky's son, Ralph, was the territory's national committeeman in the Democratic Party during these transactions, and that VICORP was the product of a Democratic administration in Washington.[60]

---

58. U.S. House of Representatives, Committee on Public Lands, *Incorporating the Virgin Islands Corporation*, H. R. Rept. 304, 81st Cong., 1st sess., 1949, pp. 3–4.

59. "Due to the fact that the Federal law charterizing the Virgin Islands Corporation prohibits it from manufacturing or selling rum, arrangements were made during the year to dispose of the corporation's rum and molasses stocks, and for the leasing of the distillery to private enterprise." *Annual Report of the Governor of the Virgin Islands, 1950*, p. 10. This is the only reference in annual reports of the governors to this transaction.

60. Grede, *The New Deal*, pp. 169–170. The Paiewonsky family fared well in dealing with prominent Democrats of the federal and insular governments. In a letter to Secretary of Interior Julius Krug of March 10, 1948, Isaac Paiewonsky offered to purchase a parcel of land, approximately 120 by 140 feet near the entrance of St. Thomas' scenic harbor on Hassel Island (most of which was already owned by Mr. Paiewonsky) for $500, on which, he wrote, "We expect to build about 25 cottages with a central building to serve as a Commissary and Dining Room with an outdoor swimming pool." He also promised to restore at his expense the small old Fort "so that it could take on value and interest as a historic

During 1951, VICORP inaugurated its loan program to promote local business and agriculture.[61] In 1954, the Secretary of Interior transferred to VICORP the management of the former Marine Corps Air Facility and Naval Submarine Base on St. Thomas—property including an airport, golf course, two water systems, transportation equipment, power generating facilities, hotels, piers, buildings, and seventy-five housing units.[62] Other VICORP activities included programs for water and soil conservation, promotion of tourism, reforestation, and livestock development.[63]

VICORP's sugar industry survived without rum profits, but only because of federal subsidies to cover VICORP losses. During the period 1935–1953, the total income of VICO/VICORP was reported to have been over $13 million, but expenses were over $15 million, causing an overall loss for the period of over $2 million.[64] To have kept the economy of the Virgin Islands from sinking, federal subsidy—hence Virgin Islands dependency—had to become institutionalized, perhaps on a permanent basis. It seemed that the objective of self-sufficiency was never to be reached.

---

relic." In a memorandum to the Secretary of March 15, 1948, Governor William H. Hastie recommended approval of the sale. "I believe the proposed development of tourist cottages in this area," stated Hastie, "will be a substantial asset to the community, and that the owner has the intention and financial ability to go forward with the project outlined in his application." Accordingly, the Secretary approved the sale and a deed of conveyance was executed by the Secretary, dated July 8, 1948, in which it was stipulated that Paiewonsky "shall maintain the old fort situated adjacent to the premises herein conveyed as a historical landmark." In a letter of August 7, 1948 to Governor Hastie, D. V. Starosselsky of Estate Wintberg, St. Thomas wrote: "I read in the local papers that the Government sold to Mr. Paiewonsky a parcel of land on Hassel Island at the Powder Magazine and Fort for $500.00. May I state that I have been interested in that parcel for several years, and am prepared to offer a considerably higher price. I also wish to state that I consider the sale of public property by private negotiations, without public bids, a policy which easily lends itself to charges of favoritism and collusion. In view of the above, I request that the sale be canceled and proper bids be put out so that all interested individuals may submit their bids." Governor Hastie's letter in reply to Starosselsky of August 19, 1948 refused his request and stated: "The parcel is of such size and location that it would have small utility except in connection with Mr. Paiewonsky's adjacent land." See, NARS, RG 126, File 9-11-7, Box No. 1201, "Hassel Island" (1948).

61. U.S. Senate, Hearings, Subcommittee of Committee on Appropriations, *Interior Department and Related Agencies Appropriations for 1955*, 83rd Cong., 2d sess., 1954, p. 435.

62. U.S. House of Representatives, *Report on Audit of the Virgin Islands Corporation for the Fiscal Year Ended June 30, 1954*, House Doc. 130, 84th Cong., 1st sess., 1955, pp. 15–16.

63. *Ibid.*, p. 11.

64. U.S. Senate, *Report Relative to Investigation*, p. 11.

Governor Lawrence Cramer of the Virgin Islands, standing, discussing pending legislation in Washington, D.C., 1938

A Constitution for the Islands

A development contemporaneous with the establishment of the Virgin Islands Company in 1934 was the creation within the Department of Interior of the new Division of Territories and Island Possessions under the directorship of Dr. Ernest Gruening. Before the creation of the Division, the Virgin Islands had relations with every federal executive department and many other federal agencies. Despite the Interior Department's overall responsibility for the Islands, these multiple agencies posed problems of policy coordination. After 1934, however, the general coordination of relations between the Islands and the federal government improved and became more stable under Gruening's new Division. Governor Lawrence Cramer—with the feuding surrounding Pearson now ended—was better able, therefore, to pursue the objective of political development of the Islands.

When Cramer became Governor in July 1935, the Virgin Islands government was still the "Temporary Government of the Danish West Indies Acquired by the United States," and the basic law was still the Danish Colonial Law of 1906 which had left unchanged most of the provisions of the Colonial Law of 1863. Indeed, the local legislative bodies were still known as "Colonial Councils" nineteen years after transfer from Denmark. During those nineteen years of "Temporary Government," there emerged certain major areas of political controversy—each a legacy from the Danish period.[65]

One area of controversy was the lack of local governmental coordination among the three islands. There were two local legislative bodies, one for St. Croix and the other for St. Thomas and St. John, with no provision for joint action. Each of the two jurisdictions had its own administrative machinery, including its own treasury, taxes, and collection systems. Inter-island rivalry became magnified by the continuation of this bifurcated Danish system.

Another area of controversy was also a remnant of Danish rule—of the long-time conflict between the governor representing the metropolitan power and the colonial councils representing planters and merchants. There were no clear lines of demarcation between the three branches of government—executive, legislative, and judicial. Besides the frequent disputes between governors and judges, there was the question of the governor's power of veto of colonial council bills, a question that became more important as federal funding increased. Should the governor or councils control federal funds? Should local tax rates be affected by federal funds? Prior to 1936, the governor's power of veto was absolute. The bill died with no override; he could veto any bill in whole or in part. If he approved a bill, it went to the President of the United States for approval or rejection. In addition, the governor still appointed four of the fifteen council members for St. Thomas and St. John and five of the eighteen members of the Colonial Council for St. Croix. The exercise of these

---

65. For extended discussion of these controversial areas, see, Grede, *The New Deal*, pp. 172–183.

gubernatorial powers practically guaranteed the continuing hostility of the councils.

A third area of controversy, of course, was the severely limited suffrage. Of twenty-five thousand Islanders in 1935, only twelve hundred were eligible to vote. Without popular government, Governor Cramer doubted that "any social program that requires action by the local legislatures, which also adds a burden in cost of government, has any chance of being enacted."[66]

When Governor Pearson went to Washington in the fall of 1932, he carried with him a draft of a constitution for the Islands prepared by then Lieutenant-Governor Cramer. Introduced into both houses of Congress, this bill was important for two reasons: (1) it was the first draft of a constitution drawn up by administrative authorities of the insular government; and (2) its provisions substantially became law in 1936 as the constitution of the Virgin Islands. Congress held joint hearings on this draft, which received the following endorsement of the American Civil Liberties Union:

> It is high time that the Congress of the United States should accord to the 25,000 islanders an opportunity to maintain a civil form of government with the greatest possible degree of autonomy.... We regard as untenable the theory that islands can be best ruled by so many officials appointed from Washington, most of whom doubtless will be, as in the past, white men, who are unfamiliar with the problems of the islands and too often moved by assumptions of the superiority of the white race.[67]

The conflicts surrounding Pearson's tenure as Governor created a climate too charged with controversy to permit passage of an organic act. Finally, in the summer of 1935, during the Senate's acrimonious investigation of affairs of the Islands, Senator Tydings requested that another bill be drafted, "which would meet with approval of the local people," for presentation at the next Congress.[68] The local legislatures thereupon appointed a joint committee which drafted another bill, while the Interior Department's Division of Territories and Island Possessions framed its own draft. These two bills were reconciled

---

66. U.S. House of Representatives, Committee on Insular Affairs, *Hearings on H. R. 11751 to Provide a Civil Government for the Virgin Islands of the United States*, 74th Cong., 2d sess. (1936), p. 11.

67. U.S. Congress, Senate Committee on Territories and Insular Affairs and House Committee on Insular Affairs, *Joint Hearings on S. 5457 and H. R. 14319 to Provide a Civil Government for the Virgin Islands of the United States*, 72d Cong., 2d sess., (1933), pp. 5–6.

68. U.S. House, *Hearings on H. R. 11751*, p. 1.

by Senator King, Chairman of the Senate Committee on Territories and Insular Affairs, and this compromise version closely resembled Cramer's original draft. By his own statement on the Senate floor, it is evident that both bills were well considered. Senator King stated that the people of the Virgin Islands were "literate and loyal citizens ... capable of managing their local affairs." Since the Islands were not yet self-supporting, however, federal control over local affairs was to be continued, "commensurate with continuing expenditures of federal funds to subsidize local government."[69]

On June 22, 1936, after nearly a score of years of intermittent pressure for Congress to end the "Temporary Government," President Roosevelt finally approved "The Organic Act of the Virgin Islands of the United States."[70] The Organic Act continued two legislatures, to be known as municipal councils, of nine elected members for St. Croix and seven elected members for St. Thomas and St. John. Although the Act perpetuated the two municipal subdivisions that existed under the Danish government, members were to be elected for two-year terms, all from representative districts with the exception of two elected at large; there were to be no appointed council members. Provision was made, moreover, for a Legislative Assembly of the Virgin Islands comprising at least one annual joint session of the two municipal councils to be called by the governor, limited to the matters specified by him, and requiring a two-thirds vote for passage of bills.

As before, the President was given the power to appoint the governor and the government secretary, with the consent of the Senate. The Secretary of the Interior was now given the power to appoint the administrator for St. Croix and other federally-funded executive and administrative officers, "and in making such appointments the secretary shall give due consideration to natives of the Virgin Islands." Appointment of all locally-funded officers and employees of the two municipal governments was vested in the governor with the approval of the respective municipal councils.

The Organic Act provided for the appointment by the President of the district judge for an eight-year term and the district attorney for a four-year term, and the Attorney General was authorized to appoint other officers necessary to carry on the business of the district court. The judicial branch of government was to consist of "The District Court of the Virgin Islands," to include extraordinary jurisdiction over federal as well as local issues, and such inferior courts as might be established by local law.

---

69. 80 *Congressional Record* 6607 (1936); *The New York Times*, May 5, 1936, p. 6. col. 4.

70. 49 *Stat.* 1807 (1936). The Act is reprinted in Bough and Macridis, eds., *Virgin Islands, America's Caribbean Outpost: The Evolution of Self Government* (1970), pp. 42–58.

The governor's power to veto a bill in whole or in part (his item veto was now restricted to money bills only) could now be overridden by a two-thirds vote of "the legislative body having jurisdiction," in which case the bill, if still disapproved by the governor, was then to be forwarded to the President for approval or rejection. Should no action be forthcoming from either the governor or President within ninety days, the bill automatically would become law, provided that Congress would not act to disallow or otherwise supersede local legislation. The governor could introduce bills in the councils and either he or his deputy was required to attend all council sessions. But the power of the governor to dissolve local legislatures was abolished, and each municipal council was empowered to "exclude from membership therein persons receiving compensation from the Government of the United States or from either of the municipal governments of the Virgin Islands."

The most sweeping change effected by the Organic Act concerned the suffrage. Gone were the restrictive property, income, and sex requirements. The right to vote was extended to all residents of the Virgin Islands who were citizens of the United States, twenty-one years of age or over, and able to read and write English. Although the franchise provision specifically forbade any discrimination based upon "difference in race, color, sex, or religious belief," the literacy requirement obviously was designed to exclude the increasing number of Spanish-speaking Puerto Rican immigrants, albeit also citizens of the United States, from participation in the political process of the Virgin Islands.

The Organic Act also included a bill of rights extending all the guarantees to the people of the Virgin Islands set forth in the Constitution of the United States except indictment by grand jury. In addition, slavery, child labor, imprisonment for debt, and polygamy were specifically prohibited.

In some ways, the most important part of the Organic Act was that concerning tax support of the Virgin Islands. The Act provided that all federal taxes collected in the Virgin Islands, including customs duties (minus administrative costs), income taxes, and other United States taxes on Virgin Islanders, "and all quarantine, passport, immigration, and naturalization fees collected in the Virgin Islands," were to be held for the respective municipal governments.

These last provisions could be interpreted as reflecting either the United States Government's acceptance of permanent financial dependence or expectation of future financial independence of the Virgin Islands.[71] The increased

---

71. Thus John F. Grede commented that the Act's "built-in subsidy would either pave the way for financial independence from the United States, if Lawrence Cramer's hopes materialized, or, herald the only other recourse—permanent dependence." Grede, *The New Deal*, pp. 196–197.

checks and balances, together with a separation of powers that circumscribed the governor with increased legislative and judicial powers, introduced a more American-type governmental system. Hostilities between the three branches were to continue, however, and the continuation of the two municipal jurisdictions would contribute nothing to reduction of inter-island rivalry. The Organic Act, however, did represent an historic and unprecedented advance toward democratic self-government.

Parties and Politics

Passage of the Organic Act of 1936 proved one of the great landmarks in the history of the Virgin Islands. Universal suffrage opened the political process to all classes and broke the long-time monopoly of political power of the planters and merchants. "After 1936, with the advent of popular suffrage, politics took on a new mass base, giving rise to the emergence of real political parties with their rationale in popular support."[72]

The suffrage provisions of the Organic Act were not to take effect until 1938, providing an interim period to prepare the people for political participation. A group of young St. Thomians organized in 1937 a civic organization, The Virgin Islands Progressive Guide, for this purpose of political education. Among its charter members were those who would figure prominently in Virgin Islands politics, including Carlos Downing, Valdemar Hill, Henry Richards, and Omar Brown.

The Progressive Guide resembled a social club more than a political organization. "People were completely unaware, and it became our job to go out and tell them," recalled Omar Brown. "We had to let them know about this Organic Act, what it would mean, what it would accomplish. In Market Square, we told them: 'You have a right to demand what you want. That is democracy!' "[73] The group distributed mimeographed messages and held numerous public lectures. According to Brown's description:

---

72. Lewis, *The Virgin Islands*, p. 321.

73. Suzanne Monsalud, "A Politician of the Past on Then and Now," *Daily News*, July 24, 1977, p. 2. Membership in the Progressive Guide required endorsement by two members "in good financial standing," followed by a committee's investigation and endorsement by a majority of members present at a general meeting. "Following this system, the Progressive Guide in many ways resembled a social club. This screening method was designed to prevent 'spies' from infiltrating into the Party and taking out its 'secrets' to the opposition: the merchants and land owners." Valdemar A. Hill, Sr., *Rise to Recognition: An Account of Virgin Islanders from Slavery to Self-Government* (1971), pp. 93–94. By 1939, the Party had 278 members in St. Thomas. *Ibid.*, p. 95. In 1944, J. Antonio Jarvis wrote: "Once the or-

We started lecturing on every nook and corner making people aware of their civic responsibilities. We pointed out the many issues, mainly the poor wages. We had been in a depression since 1909 when I was born. Wages were 12 cents per hour, or 96 cents for 8 to 9 hours a day, morning to night, Monday through Saturday. A teacher was paid only 30 dollars per month, and a nurse much less. We had to be radical because of those wages.[74]

It soon became apparent to Omar Brown and his friends that, to bring about their desired changes, they would have to stand for elective office themselves.

We knew that we would not be making much of a dent in the system by merely talking. So we decided to form the Progressive Guide Party. We had some good counsel from behind the scenes, such as from Judge William Hastie because of his continental experience, and from James A. Bough who was district attorney. We were charged with being everything, from "communists" to "giddy-boys," because the things we were saying were so foreign to the status quo. But Bough told us that "people don't throw stones at trees that don't bear fruit"— and we knew that we were inviting criticism only because we were being effective.[75]

In 1938 the Progressive Guide Party ran candidates for all seven seats of the Municipal Council of St. Thomas and St. John, and elected three including Omar Brown.[76] The other seats went to candidates of the more conservative People's Civic League including Lionel Roberts and Ralph Paiewonsky. Neither local party at that time had any alliance with national parties on the mainland.

In 1940 Omar Brown led a successful fight before the local public utilities commission to lower electricity rates, resulting in Brown becoming secretary,

---

ganization had obvious Fascist leanings. Now it tends toward New Deal socialism." Jarvis, *The Virgin Islands and Their People*, p. 155.

74. Interview of Omar Brown, Charlotte Amalie, St. Thomas, July 20, 1977.

75. *Ibid.*

76. "Whereas in 1936 there were 1,498 voters registered under the old restrictive requirements, now in 1938 there were double that number. This figure climbed to 5,374 a decade later, an increase from a bare 6 per cent of Virgin Islanders able to vote in 1936 to 21 per cent in 1948. This latter figure placed the Virgin Islands in a position comparable to Virginia or Arkansas in relation to registered voters. The per cent of registered voters who actually appeared at the polls, interestingly enough, remained about the same as before the Organic Act. Between 65 per cent and 70 per cent of those on the rolls actually voted, a performance that compared not unfavorably with the continental United States." Grede, *The New Deal*, pp. 202–203.

and future governor Morris de Castro becoming chairman, of the commission. Ralph Paiewonsky, another future governor, switched his allegiance to the Progressive Guide Party which won all seven seats of the Municipal Council in 1940, with Governor Cramer's support.[77]

"The major objective of the Progressive Guide," according to Valdemar Hill, "was to break the economic shackles of the working masses of black people once and for all." In 1941 Hill introduced a bill in the Municipal Council of St. Thomas and St. John to fix minimum wages and maximum hours which "created one of the greatest social and political struggles between the vested interest class and the masses of the people ever experienced in the Islands." Having passed the Council unanimously, the bill was hotly opposed by St. Thomas merchants. The Progressive Guide leaders organized a march of workers and housewives on Government House to urge Governor Harwood to sign the bill. In an unprecedented move, the Governor called a public hearing on the bill after which he signed it, stating that "existing wage standards are not adequate."[78]

With the power of the business element thus broken, the way was paved for more social legislation in the Municipality of St. Thomas and St. John. Accordingly, municipal ordinances were passed establishing rent and price controls, free secondary public education for adults, scholarships for college training in the United States, improved health services, and a workmen's compensation program paying up to fifteen dollars a week for various injuries (foot lost—52 weeks; arm lost—78 weeks; penis lost—75 weeks; little finger lost—4 weeks).[79] A bill introduced by the local administration providing for punishment for prostitution, fornication, and adultery was strongly rejected as "very drastic, dictatorial, and criminal in effect, and short of all respect for the rights of men and women in this cultured community."[80]

In his 1940 study of St. Thomians, psychologist Albert Campbell wrote that "recently certain social and political groups have begun to cut across class lines to some degree."[81] Because agriculture was still the basis of the economy of St. Croix, and wealthy businessmen and land owners continued to dominate the political and economic life of that island, universal suffrage did not foster as sud-

---

77. "We won over Ralph Paiewonsky to the Progressive Guide after that fight. We won everything. Governor Cramer was a liberal who sat in the legislature at that time and supported us." Interview of Omar Brown, July 20, 1977.

78. Hill, *Rise to Recognition*, pp. 96–97. The Virgin Islands had not been included in the Fair Labor Standards Act of 1938, which established continental minimum wages and maximum hours.

79. Jarvis, *The Virgin Islands and Their People*, p. 149.

80. *Daily News*, March 17, 1941.

81. Campbell, *St. Thomas Negroes*, p. 79.

den and dramatic change in St. Croix as it had in St. Thomas. The Progressive Guide Party did not organize a St. Croix branch until 1941. Although Jarvis was able to report in 1944 that "The Guides are also gaining a foothold in St. Croix where nearly half of the legislators are party members,"[82] most social legislation in St. Croix had to await the period following the Second World War.

Judges and Justice

The New Deal brought judicial change to the Virgin Islands as well as economic and political change. George A. Mena became in 1930 the first native to be appointed judge of the police court of St. Thomas and St. John, serving in that position until 1935.[83] Meanwhile, Albert Levitt had replaced the well known Judge Wilson as district court judge. Concerning Levitt's questionable application of the law, John Grede has written:

> In Government Secretary Herrick's view he stirred up the Negro-white issue by giving a suspended sentence to Wolf Zalinski, a white man, who, after repeated attempts, raped his thirteen year old stepdaughter. Levitt's claim that he had "private evidence" that the man was insane did not seem to offset the fact that the judge simultaneously sentenced a St. Croix Negro to five years in the penitentiary for attempted rape. Furthermore, in this and other cases, Levitt discussed in advance the matters likely to come before him.[84]

The Organic Act of 1936 converted the district court created by the municipal codes into a federal district court with all the jurisdiction conferred upon fed-

---

82. Jarvis, *The Virgin Islands and Their People*, p. 154.

83. Mena was admitted to the Virgin Islands bar in 1922 after having studied law through correspondence courses from Hamilton Law College in Chicago. He was a member of a committee appointed by the Colonial Council of St. Thomas and St. John to consider the question of an organic act. In 1925, Mena prepared a draft act to provide a permanent civil government, known as "the Mena draft." See, Evans, *The Virgin Islands*, pp. 228–231, and Lewis, *The Virgin Islands*, p. 49. In 1978, the Virgin Islands Legislature named the new criminal justice complex to be built in St. Thomas in honor of Mena. Act No. 4091, approved February 15, 1978.

84. Grede, *The New Deal*, p. 224, citing Robert Herrick to Ernest Gruening, January 25, 1936, Herrick Papers, Vol. XXVIII. On March 23, 1936, Judge Levitt charged Acting Governor Herrick with contempt of court for failing to appear in response to a subpoena, a charge which Levitt cancelled the next day. On July 17, Levitt resigned protesting the local administration illegally interfered with the functioning of his court. *The New York Times*, July 18, 1936, p. 11, col. 8.

eral district courts as well as the jurisdiction it previously exercised under the local codes.[85]

In 1937 William Hastie was appointed by President Roosevelt to replace Levitt as federal district court judge of the Virgin Islands, the first black to serve as a federal judge in the nation's history.[86] In 1939, Hastie resigned to become dean of Howard University Law School, and Roosevelt named another black lawyer as his successor—Herman E. Moore of Chicago. In exercising the extraordinary jurisdiction of the Virgin Islands District Court, Judge Moore often found it necessary "to turn in one day from a case involving domestic relations and support of children to one in admiralty."[87]

The character of Judge Moore's administration of justice was reflected in a classic case involving freedom of the press on an appeal in 1945 from a judgment by Moore at the district court in Christiansted, St. Croix, *People of Virgin Islands v. Brodhurst*.[88] Moore found Canute Brodhurst, black editor and publisher of the newspaper *The St. Croix Avis* (founded in 1844), guilty of criminal contempt in a summary proceeding and sentenced him to ten days in prison. To understand the issues raised by Brodhurst's appeal, it is necessary to detail the background to the alleged contempt.

Harry A. Beatty, a white man, had been charged with murder for having shot and killed Andrew Thompson, a black man, in St. Croix. The case aroused intense interest and feeling in the community. Beatty waived his right to a trial by jury, and Judge Moore tried the case himself. Beatty and two witnesses who were his friends, both white men, testified that Beatty shot Thompson in self defense, a version that remained uncontradicted. Accepting the facts as estab-

---

85. The U.S. Court of Appeals for the Third Circuit in Philadelphia was given appellate jurisdiction over the District Court of the Virgin Islands.

86. Hastie, a graduate of Harvard Law School, had been serving as assistant solicitor in the Department of Interior where he was credited with breaking down the Department's racially segregated lunch room facilities an event ultimately emulated in other federal agencies. Robert C. Weaver, "William Henry Hastie, 1904–1976," *Daily News*, March 1, 1977, p. 1.

87. "Often within one session of court the jurisdiction of the District Court may run the gamut, beginning at the opening of the session with the admission of new citizens to the United States in naturalization cases, and the hearing of Federal cases, then turning to a local appeal from the police courts, and from police court appeal to domestic relations, from domestic relations to an insanity hearing; and from civil hearings to criminal, from criminal to probate, from probate to chancery, and from chancery to admiralty, and then back to a local paternity charge." Herman E. Moore, "The Virgin Islands and Its Judicial System," *National Bar Journal* 3 (1945): 356. "The provision which vested such unusual power in the court, apparently was made because of the smallness of the population." *Ibid.*

88. 148 F.2d 636 (1945).

lished by this evidence, Judge Moore acquitted Beatty. Thus a black judge acquitted a white man for the murder of a black man. In rendering this judgment, Moore expressed his duty with respect to the case. For example, in speaking of the two witnesses, he stated:

> I have taken into consideration ... these two witnesses live in the same house with the defendant; that their home is in Louisiana where the life of Negroes is cheap; that the defendant may have had the same feeling about the life of a Negro. However, there is nothing in the evidence to contradict this testimony, and certainly this Court would not be warranted under any theory of law to throw out the testimony of witnesses merely because of the section of the country from which they came.... I was born in the heart of Mississippi. I know well the injustices against colored people there, but if Senator Bilbo ... or Congressman Rankin of Mississippi had a case in this Court, they would receive justice according to the evidence, and not according to the action of white people in Mississippi against Negroes. That is the way it must be in a Court of Justice, and no mob hysteria should ever make it otherwise.[89]

On appeal, Circuit Judge Maris commented that Judge Moore's opinion "reflects great credit upon his character and demonstrates his ability to administer the law impartially and justly in an atmosphere of intense public excitement and under circumstances which doubtless compelled him to subordinate his own natural feelings."[90]

Shortly after Beatty's acquittal, Brodhurst published in his newspaper an unsigned letter calling attention to public "cries of discontent and indignation" arising from the decision.

> What have we left they said? "Justice even is against us." We are the masses of this island but we are trampled under heels of the Hitlerites and bribe and injustice rule our reason. Our legislators tax us, we pay willingly and gladly, but when jobs are available with any decent salary we are forgotten, and a white continental is either sent for, or given the job that a native could have taken and done better with....
>
> Our Nurses, Teachers, Policemen, Janitors, Street Cleaners all have to toil doubly hard but they are of the masses, and must accept a pittance of a salary, and if they squawk for more they are automatically ousted....

---

89. *Ibid.*, note 3 at pp. 637–638.
90. *Ibid.*, p. 637.

This is not a race quarrel.... Here in St. Croix the trend is Justice versus Poverty.[91]

After a hearing, Judge Moore convicted Brodhurst and Paul E. Joseph, Editor of the *West End News*, for contempt, and delivered the following opinion:

I was born in Mississippi. I am a member of the Negro race, and I know and feel injustice to Negroes as much as anyone.... Here are two men that are riding upon a wave of discontent in Saint Croix and instead of directing that discontent in the channels where it would do these people some good, they are maliciously placing it upon this Court when they, as leaders, ought to know that this is wrong. As intelligent men and leaders in this community, you ought to know that this Court has nothing to do with the political life ... with the administration of the Islands economic problems.... You should know that this Court is trying to maintain law and, order and that this Court will not be governed by mob rule.[92]

On appeal, Judge Maris for the Third Circuit Court, held that although the St. Croix Code authorized Brodhurst's summary conviction of contempt, such authority was repealed by section 34 of the Organic Act of 1936 providing, that "No law shall be passed abridging the freedom of speech or of the press."[93] Even judges, Maris reasoned, could not use contempt in response to "merely defamatory criticism because of the constitutional free speech and press guarantees."

For these guarantees are but an expression of the belief of the founders of our nation that the preservation of freedom to criticize the acts of public officials is essential to the maintenance of democratic control over the processes of government.[94]

The case of *Francis v. People of Virgin Islands* (1926) was distinguished because that case was decided prior to the passage of the Organic Act and, therefore,

---

91. *Ibid.*, pp. 638–639.

92. *Ibid.*, note 4 at pp. 639–640.

93. 49 *Stat.* 1815 (1936). Concerning this provision of the Organic Act, Circuit Judge Maris said: "The Organic Act guarantees to the inhabitants of the islands in the very language of the First Amendment to the Constitution of the United States the same freedom of speech and of the press which is safeguarded to the inhabitants of the United States by the First and Fourteenth Amendments. The construction which has been placed upon these amendments is, therefore, determinative as to the interpretation and effect of the language of the Organic Act."

94. 148 F.2d 636, at p. 653.

before the constitutional guarantees of free speech and a free press had been extended to the Islands. Accordingly, the Circuit Court reversed Moore's conviction of Brodhurst for contempt.

Not reported in the case was the fact that Harry A. Beatty was a native Virgin Islander, having been born in St. Croix in 1902, the son of a conservationist and planter. Beatty had already received some distinction as a zoologist and was destined to become a world-known natural scientist.[95] Writing to a friend in 1976, Beatty observed: "My name has been given by fellow scientists to many earth creatures and that … is an honor that will last as long as civilization. So who cares about public sentiments?"[96]

The Islands at War

According to Robert Morss Lovett, who had served as Government Secretary of the Virgin Islands from 1939 to 1944, "Governor Cramer was devoted to the interests of the Virgin Islands, always thinking and working to those ends."[97] Lovett, along with Cramer's many other supporters, was shocked, therefore, when Secretary of Interior Harold Ickes, in December 1940, asked Cramer to resign. The rift between Cramer and Ickes had been precipitated by a disgruntled member of the Municipal Council of St. Thomas and St. John, Jacques Schiffer.

In the fall of 1940, Schiffer went to Washington and informed Ickes that the Virgin Islands were on the verge of a race war, that the whites were arming, and

---

95. Government of the U.S. Virgin Islands, *Profiles of Outstanding Virgin Islanders* (St. Thomas: Department of Education, 1976), pp. 44–47.

96. Harry A. Beatty to Enid M. Baa, St. Thomas, September 23, 1976, as quoted in interview of Ms. Baa, July 25, 1977, St. Thomas.

97. Robert Morss Lovett, *All Our Years* (New York: The Viking Press, 1948), p. 293. Governor Cramer was also concerned about Jewish refugees from Nazi persecution. In November, 1938, the Legislative Assembly of the Virgin Islands suggested the Islands serve as a temporary haven for such refugees. Lovett supported the proposal and President Roosevelt raised no objection, but jurisdictional questions between the Justice, Interior, and State Departments blocked action. As one of his last official acts, Governor Cramer thereupon signed an order in November, 1940, permitting European refugees to enter under the Alien Registration Act, an action opposed by Ward Canaday, a wealthy Virgin Islands property owner, and also by columnist Westbrook Pegler who warned that such refugees would probably include Communists as well as Nazi and Fascist spies and saboteurs. Finally, President Roosevelt put an end to the matter by insisting that a governor of an insular possession could not take action involving foreign policy without State Department or Presidential approval. Grede, *The New Deal*, pp. 242–245.

that he, himself, had engaged a body-guard. Schiffer's sensational story alarmed Ickes and President Roosevelt whose concern for the security of the Caribbean was increasing as war approached.[98] So Ickes sent an investigator, a man named Kelly, to the Islands who ignored responsible sources, collected gossip from hostile sources, and otherwise behaved maladroitly. Lovett meanwhile allayed the fears of Ickes who thereupon refused to see Schiffer again and dismissed the indiscreet Kelly. But Cramer was furious and demanded to see Kelly's report, a request to which Ickes acceded. Ickes was by then willing to drop the whole matter. Nevertheless, after reading Kelly's report, Cramer wrote Ickes an intemperate letter which the latter could not properly ignore. Backed by President Roosevelt, Ickes then asked for Cramer's resignation.[99]

Upon Cramer's resignation, the United Government Employees, at their biennial convention in Washington, passed a resolution calling on President Roosevelt "to appoint a Negro as Governor of the Virgin Islands," and recommended two candidates for the post, both of whom had been prominent in Roosevelt's successful 1940 re-election campaign for a third term.[100] The President, however, chose an old Brooklyn Democrat and former federal judge in the Canal Zone, Charles Harwood, on the recommendation of Bronx political boss Ed Flynn of New York City.

To New Deal faithfuls Harold Ickes, Ernest Gruening, and Rexford Tugwell, the patronage appointment of Harwood marked the end of the New Deal in the Virgin Islands. And within the Virgin Islands and the Department of Interior the appointment was "a crushing blow." Rupert Emerson, for example, who had replaced Gruening as director of Interior's Division of Territories and Island Possessions, wrote to Lovett the following:

> I regret to have to report that my ... conversation with Harwood did not leave me with very optimistic sentiments for the near future of the islands. I hope that time will prove me wrong, but I have no impression that he either knew much about the islands now or would be much

---

98. On September 2, 1940, President Roosevelt completed arrangements with Great Britain to exchange, for U.S. destroyers, military equipment and material, the acquisition of 99-year leases on British territory in the Western Hemisphere for the establishment of U.S. naval and air bases, including those in the Caribbean—on the Bahamas, Jamaica, St. Lucia, Trinidad, and Antigua—and in British Guiana. *United States Department of State Bulletin*, September 7, 1940, pp. 199–200.

99. The Schiffer affair is described by Lovett, *All Our Years*, pp. 293–294, and by Grede, *The New Deal*, pp. 229–233.

100. *The New York Times*, December 16, 1940, p. 26, col. 3.

concerned to find out about them. My general sentiment was that he was an elderly gentleman who looked to this governorship as a means of spending his declining years in some tropical indolence.[101]

Charles Harwood became governor in February 1941. Most of his term was consumed by the war effort in the Islands. President Roosevelt as early as 1935 had personally intervened to establish in St. Thomas a marine corps air base and, in 1939, a submarine base. The need for laborers on these construction and later defense projects rapidly boosted employment which hastened the exodus of workers from St. Croix cane fields and contributed to the decline of VICO projects including homesteading. Alien workers from other islands, particularly from nearby British islands, were attracted by the higher wages in both St. Croix and St. Thomas. In St. Croix, wages for cane cutters increased from $1.04 per day in 1940 to $1.36 in 1942, while military construction work on St. Thomas increased from nine or ten cents per hour before 1940 to twenty cents per hour in 1942.

With local authorities waiving immigration restrictions, the alien flow continued unregulated until Harwood became governor. Harwood not only imposed restrictions on the coming and going of St. Thomas' neighbors from the nearby British Virgin Islands, but he insisted that applications for passports for Virgin Islanders to visit the British possessions be cleared for security purposes through the Federal Bureau of Investigation in Washington, thus causing long delays. Lovett, who had remained as Government Secretary, later complained:

> It was Harwood's conduct toward others that I most resented. He seemed to prefer to disoblige. Especially was this the case when the relations of St. Thomas to our British neighbors were in question. He would never realize that St. Thomas is in effect the capital of the Virgin Islands, both British and American. The boundary line had been almost forgotten under the Danes, and families divided between St. homas and Tortola passed freely back and forth. Indeed, Tortolans had no easy way of reaching the outside world except through St. Thomas.[102]

During the war, a large air base was constructed on St. Croix creating still more employment opportunities. War-time prosperity, however, solved none

---

101. Rupert Emerson to Robert Morss Lovett, January 13, 1941. Lovett Papers, as quoted in Grede, *The New Deal*, p. 247.

102. Lovett, *All Our Years*, p. 296. "The American and British Virgin Islands are in fact one big family—one people. The natives of these islands have intermixed socially and economically all through the centuries." Hill, *Rise to Recognition*, p. 121.

of the basic problems of the Islands. Food shortages, labor problems, and alien immigration combined to worsen living conditions. "The maintenance of public order became acute as clashes developed between American bosses and native workmen and between natives and American white servicemen."[103] The refusal of the armed services to eliminate their segregationist practices aggravated racial tensions.

On May 30, 1945, Governor Harwood approved an ordinance enacted by the Fifth Municipal Council of St. Thomas and St. John, entitled an "Ordinance to Determine the Right of All Persons to Enjoy the Facilities Offered by Public Places and Businesses in the Municipality of St. Thomas and St. John and other Purposes." The stated motives of the Council in passing the ordinance were

> to promote and foster (1) the development and firm rooting in the people of the Municipality of St. Thomas and St. John of the basic principles of a functional democracy; (2) the destruction of Nazi-Fascist practices of racial hatreds and outrages directed against minority groups; and (3) the development of the best understanding among all the residents of the Municipality of St. Thomas and St. John, and of the sense of national unity in our islands.[104]

The ordinance significantly applied "to any agency of the Municipal Government and the officers, officials, agents, employees, or grantees thereof," as well as to the usual organizations within the meaning of the legal definition of "person." The prohibition enacted by the ordinance follows:

> No person shall be denied access to, service, equal treatment or employment in/or at any publicly licensed place of business (including public transportation), or benefits soliciting public patronage in the Municipality of St. Thomas and St. John because of politics, religion, race, color, or because of any other reason not applicable to all persons.

Punishment for violation was a fine of $25 to $100, or imprisonment from ten to one hundred days. Punishment for a second violation was suspension of the person's license. This ordinance set the stage for similar action for all the

---

103. Lewis, *The Virgin Islands*, p. 95.

104. Bill No. 51, The Fifth Municipal Council of St. Thomas and St. John, 1945–1946, May 18, 1945, approved May 30, 1945.

Islands in 1946 by the Legislative Assembly.[105] The last hotel and the last large social club eliminated the "color line" in 1946.[106]

Marking the war period in the Virgin Islands were human rights issues centering separately on two leaders—one a white continental, Government Secretary Robert Morss Lovett, and the other a local black intellectual, J. Antonio Jarvis. In his autobiography, Lovett—a well known liberal—recounted the series of events that brought him before the House Un-American Activities Committee and resulted in the House of Representatives prohibiting the use of public funds for his future salary by means of a rider on a war-time appropriations bill. Implying that Harwood might have secretly initiated this witch-hunt, Lovett became a central figure in a real-life drama that made a mockery of decency and justice. It seemed that Lovett's alleged sins were that at times he had been a member of various associations which also included some communist members, and that he had written a private letter to a friend in 1926 in which he asserted his belief that "all governments are rotten." Little did it matter that he meant, as he explained, that all governments have corrupt elements. Neither Secretary Ickes' support of Lovett ("He has, for the seventy-three years of his life, found it difficult to think ill of any man."), nor the municipal councils' combined support of Lovett ("a man of very high humane qualities, in whom the people have implicit confidence"), could deter Congress from taking its ill-fated action against him. Despite the opposition of the United States Senate (the House refused to yield), and a stinging protest of the President in signing the bill (the President does not have an item veto), the House prevailed. After November 15, 1943, Lovett received no salary but continued to perform his duties. On March 13, 1944, however, Secretary Ickes wrote that in view of the threat to the entire appropriation for his Department, he was obliged to request Lovett's resignation, which Lovett promptly gave.[107]

---

105. Bill No. 6, The Eleventh Legislative Assembly of the Virgin Islands of the United States, Session 1946, An Act to Provide Equal Rights in Places of Public Accommodations, Resorts, or Amusements, December 6, 1946, approved December 16, 1946. Among other war-time measures were: repeal by the Municipal Council of St. Croix of $6 per ton export duty on sugar (Dookhan, *History of The Virgin Islands of the United States*, p. 286); the U.S. taking over of the Danish-controlled West India Company facilities in St. Thomas for the war's duration (*The New York Times*, March 27, 1942, p. 2, col. 7); the extension late in the war of the Selective Service Act to the Islands (*ibid.*, October 27, 1943, p. 11, col. 4, and July 4, 1944, p. 13, col. 2); and organization in the Islands of the "Home Guard" (Lewis, *The Virgin Islands*, p. 93).

106. Blanshard, *Democracy and Empire in the Caribbean*, p. 236.

107. The entire episode is discussed in Lovett, *All Our Years*, pp. 297–309; see, also, his appendices, pp. 341–363, esp. letters from Ickes and the municipal councils supporting Lovett.

Lovett then appealed his case to the Court of Claims which decided in his favor. The case was then heard by the Supreme Court of the United States, which also decided in Lovett's favor by declaring unconstitutional as a bill of attainder the action of Congress that punished Lovett without judicial process.[108]

Meanwhile, Ashley L. Totten, president of the American Virgin Islands Civic Association of New York City, bitterly charged that Governor Harwood "is believed by members of the Legislature and the entire population to be involved in the campaign to smear Lovett." Totten continued:

> So embittered are the people of the Virgin Islands against the removal of Lovett that legislators meeting at St. Thomas made brutally frank statements that Governor Harwood knows that he is not wanted in the islands and if a poll was taken he would receive two votes—his own and that of his naval aide.
>
> Governor Harwood refused to make a public statement for Lovett and is quite resentful over the fact that 99 percent of the people want Lovett as their Chief Executive. Harwood soon became unpopular in the Virgin Islands when he ignored the rights of native preference for governmental jobs as stipulated in the Organic Act, by displacing several of them for his friends on the mainland, who in many instances were inefficient and a definite liability to the Federal Government.
>
> Taking advantage of the islands as a health and pleasure resort, the Governor carried with him a racial feeling introducing segregation and its attendant evils, never before experienced by the natives, who are 99 percent colored people. He has earned for himself the name of the most useless Governor ever sent to the islands. Petitions drawn up by the Legislature to be signed by natives residing in the islands and on the mainland will ask for the immediate removal of Harwood and the appointment of Lovett as Governor.[109]

That Harwood was involved in the campaign against Lovett was never proven. It is true that Harwood never spoke in support of Lovett. In any event, it was Lovett who left the Islands and Harwood who stayed.

J. Antonio Jarvis was the central figure in the other human rights episode of the war period in the Virgin Islands. Jarvis, a man of many qualities, had achieved prominence in literature, art, and journalism. While serving as a local school principal in St. Thomas in 1944, Jarvis' book *The Virgin Islands and Their People* was published. Included was a chapter entitled: "Superstition,

---

108. *United States v. Lovett*, 328 U.S. 303 (1946).
109. *The New York Times*, July 17, 1943, p. 7, col. 6.

*Governor Charles Harwood of the Virgin Islands
speaking at a Red Cross meeting, 1941*

Witchcraft, and Necromancy Undermine Health and Morals." It was this chapter that became a center of controversy. Ashley Totten of New York City was again involved, but in a much different role from the Lovett affair. In a press release, Totten charged that Jarvis wrote the book "to hold up the native people generally to disgrace and ridicule." On December 19, 1944, the Legislative Assembly passed a resolution branding the book as "full of untrue, grossly immoral and corrupt material that is unfit for adult reading and disastrous for youth consumption." The resolution called for banning the book from Virgin Islands schools and libraries and petitioned the Governor to direct the School Board to dismiss Jarvis from the public payroll. The resolution was adopted nine votes to one, with Valdemar Hill the lone dissenter. Apparently, the legislators perceived no inconsistency between this resolution and their recent support of Lovett, for a local newspaper reported:

> Hill's argument that freedom of the Press was being interfered with, and the provision to remove Jarvis from the payroll was similar to that which the people of the Virgin Islands objected in the Lovett case were of no avail. Hon. Ralph Paiewonsky declared that Virgin Islanders had protested the Lovett ouster not on account of the constitutional principle involved, but because of his own personal qualities.[110]

Morris de Castro, who succeeded Lovett as Government Secretary, was serving as Acting Governor in Harwood's absence from the Islands. Acting Governor de Castro refused to direct the School Board to remove Jarvis because the right "to speak and write as he thinks is one which has been jealously guarded by our forefathers and which we must be careful to preserve untarnished and inviolate for future generations."[111]

To Harwood's credit, he proved effective in obtaining funds from Washington, but in so doing he contributed significantly to the permanence of the Virgin Islands economic dependence on the Government of the United States. Indeed, Harwood spent more time in Washington than he did in the Islands. According to Lovett, whenever Secretary of Interior Ickes "tried to 'punish him'"—Harwood's own expression—by keeping him in the Islands, he could arrange for a summons to Washington from his political friends in Congress.[112]

Harwood was in Washington at the end of 1944 and obtained, through his friends in Congress, an appropriation of $10 million for an extensive public works program in the Islands providing for slum clearance, fire protection, water sup-

---

110. Hill, *Rise to Recognition*, p. 89, quoting *Daily News*, December 20, 1944.
111. Hill, *Rise to Recognition*, p. 90.
112. Lovett, *All Our Years*, pp. 295–297.

ply, highways, sanitation, and medical facilities. With construction of defense projects in the Islands then completed, the appropriation came just in time to prevent a more serious reaction from the end of the war-time construction boom.[113] The appropriation, however, merely delayed the coming post-war recession.

The First Black Governor

On May 18, 1946, William H. Hastie became the first black Governor of the Virgin Islands, and thus the first black governor in American history, upon appointment by President Truman who promised Virgin Islanders "an ever increasing degree of self-government as the people demonstrate their capacity to govern themselves."[114] Married to a native Virgin Islander, Hastie had already distinguished himself as a judge, administrator, educator, and one of the "most effective leaders in the long struggle to better the lot of the colored people and to establish their civil rights."[115] Norman Manley, leader of the People's Nationalist Party of Jamaica, hailed Hastie as the first Negro Governor of a colony in the West Indies.[116]

Governor Hastie, with President Truman's active support, initiated a public campaign to increase the degree of self-government in the Virgin Islands. For his part, Truman spoke out on every appropriate occasion for more rights and self-government for Virgin Islanders—in his budget message of 1946,[117] in his message to the 1946 West Indian Conference in St. Thomas stating that this basic U.S. policy was "in line with the Charter of the United Nations,"[118] in his

---

113. *The New York Times*, December 22, 1944, p. 6, col. 6.

114. *The New York Times*, May 18, 1946, p. 20, col. 7.

115. Beverly Smith, "The First Negro Governor, *Saturday Evening Post*, April 17, 1948, p. 16.

116. *The New York Times*, January 16, 1946, p. 10, col. 5.

117. *The New York Times*, January 22, 1946, p. 18, col. 6.

118. "The West Indian Conference is believed to be the first international convention from non-self-governing territories. Two delegates from each of the fifteen Caribbean territories are participating in this second session. The delegates represent territories of Great Britain, France, the Netherlands and the United States; that is, the Bahamas, Barbados, Jamaica, Trinidad, British Guiana, British Honduras, Leeward Islands, Windward Islands, Curacao, Dutch Guiana, Martinique, Guadeloupe, French Guiana, Puerto Rico, and the Virgin Islands. The Caribbean Commission was created in 1942 as an Anglo-American group to improve conditions in the region and was expanded last December to include France and the Netherlands. The West Indian Conference was organized under the auspices of the commission in 1944." *The New York Times*, February 22, 1946, p. 5, col. 4.

President Harry Truman and Governor William Hastie at Emancipation Garden, St. Thomas, February 22, 1948

1948 civil rights message,[119] and during his visit to the Islands in 1948.[120] Indeed, Hastie was so convinced of Truman's commitment to civil rights that he took an unprecedented leave of absence in 1948 to campaign for the President's election—a wise move in that he was rewarded the following year with being named by Truman as the first black judge on a federal circuit court of appeals.

When Hastie became Governor, he found a "preponderance of factors tending to create economic depression," including collapse of the rum market, increasing unemployment, and "all the evils of inflation … exceeding those on the mainland." But he hoped for greater employment under the new public works program and for normal weather following the 1946 drought.[121]

Looking backward over the "century of freedom" in the Virgin Islands, the Governor noted the decline of sugar, lack of natural resources, recurrent drought, poor soil, and continuing dependence on the outside world for the necessities of life. "Today the total assessed valuation of all real property … in the Virgin Islands is only about $11,000,000." Hastie advocated three complementary approaches: the development of tourism, the diversification of crops, and the development of new industry.[122]

By the end of his term in 1949, Governor Hastie reported "significant advancement" in all three directions, although he admitted that "the Virgin Islands still have practically no industry." He was placing his trust, nevertheless,

---

119. *The New York Times*, March 8, 1947, p. 1, col. 7. By Executive Order 9808, December 5, 1946, Truman had created the President's Committee on Civil Rights, which issued its report in 1947. Other than the recommendation that Congress enact legislation granting citizenship to the people of Guam and America Samoa, the President's Committee did not concern itself with the status of civil rights or the need for positive action in the territories and possessions of the United States. The Committee did make approving reference, however, to Articles 55 and 56 of the Charter of the United Nations concerning the promotion of "the principle of equal rights and self-determination of peoples." The Report of the President's Committee on Civil Rights, *To Secure These Rights* (New York: Simon and Schuster, 1947), p. 111.

120. Anthony Leviero, "Truman is Hailed in Virgin Islands as Rights' Backer," *The New York Times*, February 23, 1948, p. 1, col. 1. "Welcomed warmly here today as a champion of human rights, President Truman promised the Virgin Islanders to seek wider self-rule for them and to work for freedom from fear and want on a global scale through the United Nations." *Ibid.* The National Platform of the Democratic Party of 1948 urged "the maximum degree of local self-government for the Virgin Islands." *The New York Times*, July 14, 1948, p. 9, col. 1.

121. *Annual Report of the Governor of the Virgin Islands, 1947*, pp. 2–3.

122. *Annual Report of the Governor of the Virgin Islands, 1948*, p. 3.

in the rechartered VICORP, local legislation providing for tax exemptions for new industries, and more federal funds.[123] Predicting that "large-scale tourism and business promotions of various types are ahead," Hastie warned: "The community and its leadership will be tested as never before to maintain values of character, integrity, and human dignity in the Virgin Islands."[124]

As early as 1942, the Legislative Assembly petitioned Congress to authorize, the same as it had for Puerto Rico, a resident commissioner to represent the Virgin Islands in the House of Representatives in Washington.[125] In 1944 Secretary Ickes endorsed this proposal and added he favored a native for Government Secretary.[126] Morris de Castro became the first "native" Virgin Islander in 1945 to be named Government Secretary.

Within a year after becoming Governor, Hastie, stating that "the people of the Islands have demonstrated a real capacity for self-government," called for a resident commissioner in Washington elected by the people of the Virgin Islands, and declared that "the people should elect their own Governor, as is done in all democratic societies."[127] The Governor also testified before Congress that the separation of the three islands into two municipalities each with a complete and separate administrative organization was unjustifiable, and that he favored only one legislature and one administrative system in the three islands.[128]

---

123. *Annual Report of the Governor of the Virgin Islands, 1949*, pp. 2–3.

124. *Annual Report of the Governor of the Virgin Islands, 1948*, p. 15.

125. *The New York Times*, October 5, 1942, p. 3, col. 5.

126. *The New York Times*, June 22, 1944, p. 3, col. 1.

127. *The New York Times*, February 3, 1947, p. 12, col. 6.

128. *The New York Times*, February 16, 1947, p. 40, col. 4. For example, the Organic Act of 1936 did not mention education, perhaps because educational organization in the Virgin Islands was primarily on a municipal basis, each municipality having its own school system. This scheme was the subject of much criticism. Important differences in the ability of the municipalities to support public schools motivated the President's Advisory Committee on Education to recommend, in 1939, that the federal government "give consideration to placing the support of public education in the Virgin Islands on an insular rather than on a municipal basis." L. E. Blauch and C. E Reid, *Public Education in the Territories and Outlying Possessions*, prepared for the President's Advisory Committee on Education (Washington, 1939), p. 162. This recommendation had not been followed by 1947 when the United States Government reported to the United Nations that "the problem of finance is a major difficulty with respect to the municipality of St. Croix." and that of the total of 33 public schools in the Islands, St. Croix had only 9 despite the fact that more than half of the total population of the Islands inhabited St. Croix. *The Virgin Islands of the United States, Information on the Virgin Islands of the United States Transmitted by the United States to The Secretary-General of the United Nations Pursuant to Article 73 (e) of the Charter*, prepared by the Department of Interior in cooperation with the Governor of the Virgin Islands (Washington: 1947), pp. 22, 24; hereafter cited as *U.S.V.I. Report to the U.N. (1947)*.

Governor Hastie was proud of the new merit system installed and of the fact that of the twenty-two principal officers in the executive branch of the central government of the Virgin Islands, seventeen were Virgin Islanders[129]— a fact conveyed by the Government of the United States in its 1947 report to the United Nations.[130] In a letter to this writer in 1949, Governor Hastie observed that "Luther Evans' view that the retaining of policy-making officials on the Central Administration Federal payroll is a device to maintain Washington control ... is not correct." Hastie explained:

> These officials remain on the Federal payroll only so long as the local government is unable to add their salaries to the local budget. As a matter of fact we are constantly resisting pressure of the Bureau of the Budget to relieve the Federal Government of these positions. Local sentiment favors a transfer of such positions to the local budget, but the funds will not be available at least for several years.[131]

The first black governor of the Virgin Islands, however, enjoyed no more success than his white predecessors in dealing with local legislators. Not only did the 1949 Legislative Assembly defy Hastie's postponement of its session by meeting beforehand, but a strong Assembly faction assailed Hastie for not submitting his federally-funded appointees to the Assembly for its approval. They also charged that Hastie showed favoritism in his selection of men for these posts.[132]

Results of the first referendum ever held in the Virgin Islands, in November 1948, must have been a severe disappointment for Governor Hastie. Although the referendum revealed that an overwhelming majority favored representation in Washington by an elected resident commissioner in Congress, they rejected the popular election of their own governor and political unification of the Islands in place of the two existing municipal jurisdictions. Rejection of unification and an elected governor was interpreted as a repudiation of Hastie who, however, noted that "more than 40 percent of the voters who took part in the general elections

---

129. *Annual Report of the Governor of the Virgin Islands, 1948*, p. 2.

130. *U.S.V.I. Report to the U.N.* (1947), p. 7.

131. Hastie to Boyer, June 2, 1949. See Appendix for the full text.

132. See, *The New York Times*, April 4, 1949, p. 9, col. 5 and April 5, 1949, p. 31, col. 7. "The Merit System Law met with stiff opposition from the Progressive Guide, which was the dominant party, and thereby controlled political patronage jobs, whereby they increased their membership ... The introduction of the Merit System Law and creation of the classification plan in 1948 therefore contributed greatly to the decline of the Progressive Guide." Creque, *The U.S. Virgin Islands and the Eastern Caribbean*, pp. 128–129.

did not cast referendum ballots."[133] Whatever the explanation, the referendum caused Congress to postpone the granting of more self-government to the Islands.

There was one vital proposal for which Hastie hoped to secure Congressional approval—the return to the insular treasury of revenues collected on products, including sugar and rum, of the Virgin Islands in the continental United States—a proposal often made in the past but never passed.[134] In testimony before Congress, Governor Hastie referred to recent investigations in the Islands made by the appropriations committees of the House and Senate, and by the Public Administration Service of Chicago, from which both reported that an annual sum of approximately $800,000 was needed, in addition to that which could be raised by local taxation, to make the Virgin Islands self-supporting. The fact that the Organic Act forbade the Islands from incurring bonded indebtedness was pointed out. "What are we to do when we have major capital improvements to make?... We have to do one of two things: Either come to Congress and ask for money ... or build up some reserve of our own funds ... to make the capital improvements as we go along." Hastie then detailed the burdens under which the insular government was operating. Vacated Army and Navy airfields had to be taken over by the municipal governments to insure the expanding tourist trade. ("They are our connection with the outside.") Likewise, a naval submarine station and a marine air station had to be taken over. "At the present time," he continued, "the rum market is in bad shape." Both Puerto Rico and, formerly, the Philippines, had the system the Virgin Islands were asking for. The system of being dependent upon Congressional committees for annual appropriations "indicates the precariousness of the situation in which the question of our police force, ... our hospitals, ... our sewers, ... and the fundamental local services that the community must have are concerned." The cost of living is very little less than that of the United States, he said, but salaries are lower in the Islands. Consequently, the best educated of the young people leave the Islands and go to the United States, and, for the same reason, "the demoralization of our public servants" presents a very serious problem. Also, something had to be done about the water system:

> We have no permanent streams, and no underground water, but we hope with the efforts of the Soil Conservation Service and our own we will be able to hold the run-off in the hills and force more of it underground and thereby ... make the most of our meager water supply.

---

133. *Annual Report of the Governor of the Virgin Islands, 1949*, p. 16; *The New York Times*, November 12, 1948, p. 20, col. 5.

134. See, *e.g., The New York Times*, June 3, 1949, p. 5, col. 5, and July 16, 1947, p. 15, cols. 2–3.

Hastie noted that the federal grant-in-aid acts and the Federal Highway Act were not extended to the Islands, and although one title of the Social Security Act was extended, the public assistance titles did not apply to the Islands. Finally, the insular government gave $5 each month to 1,000 indigent inhabitants, and there was an extensive free medical service. Governor Hastie closed his testimony requesting that the legislation be passed returning revenues on local products to the insular treasury. "You are certainly a good advocator," said the committee chairman.[135]

Unfortunately, the desired legislation was not passed. It was probably killed by the joint reservation of the sponsors of the bill, Senator Hugh Butler and Representative A. L. Miller, that the return of taxes on rum could increase the production of sugar when diversification of agriculture was "absolutely necessary."[136]

Added to Hastie's other disappointments was his failure to move the Islands closer to financial self-sufficiency and stability. He was ready, therefore, to accept Truman's appointment in 1949 to the Third Circuit Court of Appeals in Philadelphia which had appellate jurisdiction over the Virgin Islands.

The First Native Governor

Upon President Truman's nomination of Hastie to the Circuit Court, the Virgin Islands Legislative Assembly cabled Truman urging him to nominate Morris de Castro for Governor, thus reflecting "stubborn and vocal opposition ... against any but a Virgin Islander."[137] Curiously, the supervisory board of the Virgin Islands Civic Association of New York City was against replacing Hastie

---

135. *Hearing before House Committee on Ways and Means on H.R. 4979*, 80th Cong., 2d sess., (1948), pp. 5–23.

136. *Ibid.*, p. 45. "These tax moneys, which in normal times amount to upward of $1,000,000 a year, would make all the difference. Added to the local tax revenues, they would support the islands' government, with something left over for necessary capital improvements." *Saturday Evening Post*, April 17, 1948, pp. 156–157. On May 4, 1948, the Legislative Assembly of the Virgin Islands petitioned Congress, in the form of a resolution, to pass the legislation. The resolution recognized that "a state of emergency now exists in the Virgin Islands," and "the hopes of everyone concerned with the solution of this problem are almost entirely dependent upon the granting of the return of some part of the internal revenues." Protesting the fact that the bill had been tabled by the House Ways and Means Committee, the resolution criticized Congressional "inability to finance its institutions in their basic functions." 94 *Congressional Record* 5602 (1948).

137. *The New York Times*, October 19, 1949, p. 18, col. 4.

with a native Virgin Islander, and sent a telegram to President Truman urging him not to give consideration "to politically-minded native job-seekers whose amateur leadership is best judged by their failure to make sacrifices for the islands and their people."[138] Truman bowed to the legislators and nominated de Castro who became Governor on March 24, 1950.

Although Morris F. de Castro was born in Panama, that technicality did not bar him from being considered the first native Virgin Islander to become Governor of the Virgin Islands of the United States. His family, of Jewish descent, lived in St. Thomas, and he was born while his mother visited relatives in Panama. He had impressive credentials for the position, having been a career official of thirty years government service in the Islands and the Government Secretary since 1945.

Soon after becoming Governor, de Castro went to Washington to tackle the same problems that remained unresolved by Hastie's administration. Stating his commitment for increasing independence, self-sufficiency, and self-government for the Islands, de Castro sought return of the tax on rum, an elective Governor, and a resident commissioner,[139] objectives that were not to be achieved during his tenure.

In his first annual report, he noted some signs of progress, including extension to the Islands of the federal Vocational Education Act and the public assistance provisions of the Social Security Act, completion of the highway from the Harry S. Truman Airport to the city of Charlotte Amalie named the Charles Harwood Highway in honor of the Governor "who initiated the public works program," institution of a "modern system of post-audit of governmental accounts," and an increase in the total population of 1,765—from a total of 24,889 in 1940 to 26,654 in 1950. Reporting that during the previous year fifteen cruise ships had called at St. Thomas, de Castro lauded the considerable expansion of the tourist industry ("which holds great promise for the improvement of the economic stability of the islands") and the near completion of "a modern 130-room luxury hotel in St. Thomas."[140] Regarding the construction of this first luxury hotel in the Virgin Islands, Edward O'Neill, in his book *Rape of the American Virgins*, commented:

> To build this hotel … the broad beach at Brewer's Bay, about two miles from the site, was stripped of its sand. The builder of the hotel

---

138. *The New York Times*, November 1, 1949, p. 16, col. 4.
139. *The New York Times*, April 30, 1950, p. 61, col. 5.
140. *Annual Report of the Governor of the Virgin Islands, 1950*, pp. 2–3, 5, 18.

owned the beach, didn't he?, some people argued at the time. Development, Virgin-Islands style, had begun.[141]

Only seven cruise ships visited St. Thomas the following year, a decline which de Castro attributed to the "increase in competition among the Caribbean islands for the tourist trade."[142] At the time, few tourists chose the Caribbean over Florida, Bermuda, or the Bahamas. Within the Caribbean, moreover, Cuba and Puerto Rico were favored, and transportation connections to the Virgin Islands were still difficult. Nevertheless, the number of large cruise ships visiting St. Thomas increased to twelve in 1952 and twenty in 1953, and the number of air flights "in the peak season was increased to the point where additional flights were not necessary because there was not additional bed capacity."[143]

Although the Virgin Islands could not yet be described as a travel mecca, a trend was evident, and the apprehension was growing among Virgin Islanders that the developing tourism industry would bring discrimination to the Islands. Indeed, Governor de Castro anticipated this problem in his inaugural address, when he said:

> Here in the Virgin Islands we have been accustomed to welcome people of all races and of all nationalities to our shores. We have been accustomed to treat man as a man, without preference as to race, religion or nationality. We pride ourselves on being a cultured people. Our culture is based on the recognition and respect of human rights. There is an anti-discrimination law on our statute books. It may need to be strengthened as the occasion arises.[144]

In September 1950, the Legislative Assembly of the Virgin Islands strengthened its 1946 anti-discrimination act by adopting what was called "the strongest … civil rights bill under the American flag," the expressed intent of which was "to prevent and prohibit discrimination in any form based upon race, creed, color, or national origin, whether practiced directly or indirectly, or by subterfuge in any and all places of public accommodation, resort, or amusement." The law not only covered the usual places of public accommodation, but also any place "where food or drink is sold or rooms rented" in-

---

141. Edward A. O'Neill, *Rape of the American Virgins* (New York: Praeger Publishers, 1972), p. 60.

142. *Annual Report of the Governor of the Virgin Islands, 1951*, p. 32.

143. *Annual Report of the Governor of the Virgin Islands, 1953*, pp. 26–27.

144. Quoted by Jean Deveaux, "Virgin Islands' Anti-Discrimination Act," *The New York Times*, October 8, 1950, sec. 2, p. 17, col. 5.

cluding every private club which was annually required to file its list of officers and members plus an affidavit attesting that "there is no discrimination in such sales, renting or use." Penalties provided for each violation were $500, or ninety days in jail, or both. "Every day of violation shall constitute a separate offense," it was stipulated, and additional penalties included loss of business license.[145] The law was bitterly opposed by resort and club operators, who maintained it would harm the tourism industry, but their opposition soon dissipated."[146]

One reason why Virgin Islanders feared white tourists would infuse the Islands with discriminatory practices was the bitter experience of Virgin Islanders in the U.S. armed services on the mainland during the Second World War. Approximately nine hundred men had been inducted into the armed forces from the Virgin Islands, about six hundred of whom returned after the War.[147] Darwin Creque recounted how the Puerto Rican and Virgin Islands G.I.s were "the victims of discrimination in all its forms."

> Non-whites were expected to perform certain extra-duty chores which the whites were not required to do. These and other discriminatory practices often resulted in dissatisfaction among the colored troops, and on several occasions led to near mutiny.... On the buses and streetcars they were forced to sit in the rear in areas designated by signs which read "FOR COLORED PATRONS."[148]

Returning to the Virgin Islands, these veterans of the segregated armed forces of the United States were determined to work for human rights and not to suffer again such humiliation. Among them were Walter Hodge and Louis Brown of St. Croix who aroused rural Crucians to exercise their political power. "The old groups of the town burghers and landed gentry were thus displaced, politically, by the rising colored talent,"[149] and the Progressive Guide Party gained strength in St. Croix.

When Gordon Skeoch, representative of the old landed Crucian gentry, was appointed in 1951 the new president of VICORP, racial bias was charged because the office of vice president, held by Axel Schade, a black, was abolished and Schade was not appointed president by the board of directors of VICORP chaired by Secretary of Interior Oscar Chapman. Thus, Schade's connection with

---

145. *Ibid.*, and *The New York Times,* September 18, 1950, p. 25, col. 4.

146. *The New York Times,* December 10, 1950, sec. 10, p. 17, col. 7.

147. *U.S.V.I. Report to the U.N.* (1947), p. 25.

148. Creque, *The U.S. Virgin Islands and the Eastern Caribbean,* pp. 115–117; see, also, Hill, *Rise to Recognition,* pp. 99–101.

149. Lewis, *The Virgin Islands,* pp. 324–325.

VICO/VICORP, for which he had worked fifteen years, was abruptly ended. Meanwhile, Governor de Castro was asked by the irate Virgin Islands Assembly to report to it what had taken place at the board of directors meeting that resulted in Skeoch's appointment. When de Castro refused, the Assembly broke up in disorder.[150]

Charging the Assembly and municipal councils with encroaching into the sphere of executive functions, Governor de Castro took up the gauntlet by asserting:

> The policy of the present Governor, announced at the inception of his administration and strictly adhered to since then, of drawing a clear line of demarcation between the function of the legislature to make laws and the function of the executive to execute them has not met with approbation.

The Governor attributed the problem to the lack of a single legislature, in place of the three existing legislative bodies, and the failure to develop a two-party system. "The absence of a clearly defined political opposition within the legislative halls has been a strict deterrent."[151]

An attempt had been made in 1948 to organize an opposition party, called the Liberal Party, by a dissident group of the Progressive Guide Party—spearheaded by Earle B. Ottley and Valdemar Hill—but the new party failed in the 1948 elections. By 1952, the Progressive Guide Party was virtually defunct, and its liberal nucleus, which had formed the short-lived Liberal Party, created the insular Virgin Islands Unity Party, while others reorganized the old Democratic Club into a nationally affiliated Democratic Party to sponsor candidates for election. Thus, a two-party model seemed to be taking shape, and Valdemar Hill later recalled:

> The Unity Party was identified by the Mortar and Pestle symbol, very familiar in the native kitchen, indicating that it was a grass roots party, in the same manner in which the Popular Democratic Party in Puerto Rico under Luis Munoz Marin had adopted the hat of the "jibaro" as a political symbol. The Democrats in turn adopted the traditional Donkey as its symbol. These symbols were to become very important in the development of the political parties in the Islands.[152]

---

150. *The New York Times*, October 19, 1951, p. 20, col. 1, and October 23, 1951, p. 17, col. 1.

151. *Annual Report of the Governor of the Virgin Islands, 1951*, p. 3.

152. Hill, *Rise to Recognition*, p. 103.

Establishment of an embryonic two-party system, however, did not result in the improved executive-legislative relationships hoped for by de Castro. In his last annual report, in 1953, Governor de Castro observed that during the preceding year he had found it necessary to veto three bills passed by the Legislative Assembly, seven bills passed by the Municipal Council of St. Thomas and St. John, and four bills passed by the Municipal Council of St. Croix. "Unfortunately," remarked de Castro, "the executive and the legislative branches of the government of the Virgin Islands have not seen vis-á-vis on many public issues of transcendent importance." He concluded his last report: "This situation can be improved only after strong political parties are organized in the islands, assuring the executive of a voice in the legislature, which does not now exist."[153]

---

153. *Annual Report of the Governor of the Virgin Islands, 1953,* pp. 35–36.

Women in a northern St. Croix village, 1941

A Farm Security Administration borrower and his wife in their homestead house constructed with FSA aid in Christiansted, 1941

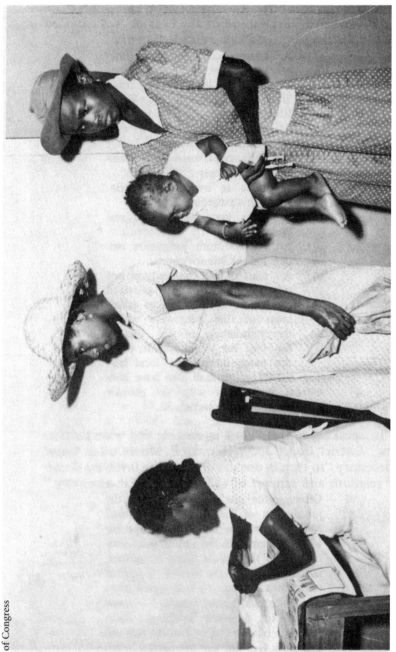

At the health clinic in Frederiksted, St. Croix, 1941

Cultivating sugar cane on Virgin Islands Company land, St. Croix, 1941

A French fisherman and his wife in "Frenchtown," St. Thomas, 1941

Puerto Rican family in a St. Croix village reconditioned by the Virgin Islands Company, 1941

Class in Christiansted high school, 1941

Photographs courtesy of Library of Congress

The police chief of St. John, 1941

Court day in Frederiksted, St. Croix, 1941

The St. Croix Municipal Council in session, Christiansted, 1941

Photographs courtesy of Library of Congress

*In the Government House rum distillery of the Virgin Islands Company
near Christiansted, 1941*

Cooking dinner on coal pots in a district of Charlotte Amalie, 1941

Photographs courtesy of Library of Congress

Alton Adams directing his U.S. Navy Virgin Islands band, 1941

The slaughterhouse in Charlotte Amalie, 1941
In the distance is the "night soil" dump.

Collecting garbage from an open sewer in Christiansted, 1941

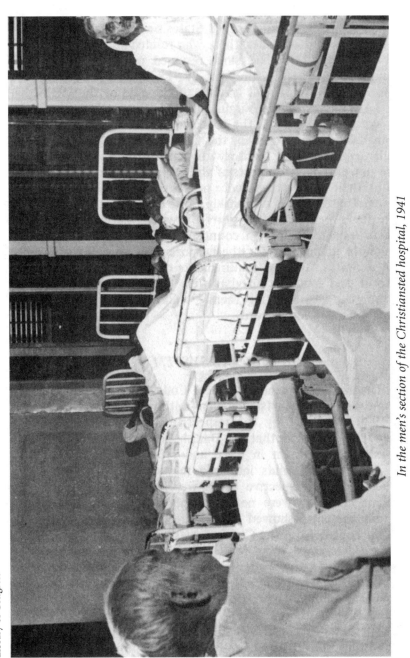

In the men's section of the Christiansted hospital, 1941

An alien inmate of the insane asylum at the Charlotte Amalie hospital, 1941

An inmate of the insane asylum, St. Thomas, 1941

Part III

Tourism Syndrome: 1954–1980

9

Penury to Prosperity

Governor de Castro's conflict with local legislators was not unique. Almost every Virgin Islands governor had experienced similar difficulty, for executive-legislative schism became a consistent theme in the political history of the Virgin Islands. In the 1950s, the schism appeared accentuated not only because of continuing federal paternalism marked by Presidential appointment of the governor, but also because of persisting poverty that plagued de Castro's administration and those of his two successors.

Persistence of Poverty

The end of the wartime construction boom, as well as the end of the wartime demand for rum and the closing of the submarine base, brought about economic recession that was to extend well into the 1950s. For example, revenue collected from all sources in 1950 by the municipality of St. Thomas and St. John was over $250,000 less than the total collected in 1945.[1] Testifying before visiting Congressmen in 1952 that local wages were the lowest of any American territory, St. Thomas labor leader Percival Reese complained: "Our minimum hourly pay is 40 cents ... a laborer in the field in St. Croix receives about $300 to $400 a year.... The workers on these islands are not living, but merely existing. Unemployment is at its peak."[2] Five years later, Governor Gordon attributed persisting poverty to the "comparatively low" wage rates; 40 cents per hour was still the minimum wage, and the government worker averaged only $2,000 per year.[3] Legislation dating from 1949, providing tax exemptions and subsi-

---

1. *Hearings before the House Subcommittee on Territories and Insular Possessions on H.R. 2644*, 82nd Cong., 2d sess., (1952), p. 57; hereafter cited as: *Hearings ... on H.R. 2644* (1952).

2. *Ibid.*, p. 59.

3. *Hearings before the House Subcommittee on Public Works and Resources, Activities of Virgin Islands Government and the Virgin Islands Corporation*, 85th Cong., 1st sess., December 10, 1956, pp. 110, 112; hereafter cited as: *Hearings ... Activities.*

dies for new industries, remained unused for a decade except for establishment in 1951 of a small button factory with a maximum of eighty employees that fell to twenty-five in 1955.[4]

Congressman Earl Chudoff, chairman of a visiting House subcommittee, told Governor Gordon in 1956 that slum districts of St. Thomas are "far worse than anything I have ever seen in the United States." Almost 40 percent of all dwellings in the Virgin Islands were reported unconnected to sewerage lines; they were still serviced by "night soil" removal, because in many instances "the dwelling is such a slum structurally that the cost of sanitary facilities would exceed the cost of the dwelling itself."[5] Governor Gordon admitted that "there are school buildings I have been in where the floors are so weak I am fearful the children will fall through."[6]

Local commissioner of health, Dr. Eric O'Neal, lamented to Chudoff's subcommittee that he had no funds to repair or rehabilitate buildings at the home for the aged nor funds to buy drugs for the treatment of tuberculosis at the hospital. Only 22 cents a day per patient was available for the cost of food. Indeed, former health commissioner Dr. Roy Anduze testified he resigned for the reason, among others, that a 1956 budget freeze caused grievous health conditions. In desperation, Dr. Anduze wrote Governor Gordon of his "most disturbing experience" when tuberculosis patients at the Knud Hansen Memorial Hospital complained of hunger and lack of medicine and other supplies.

> We are practically out of all intravenous solutions needed for the treatment of shock, nausea, dehydration, and other conditions. We have been without flour to make bread for 4 days. We have been without safety pins for weeks, and gowns for infants, and Dr. Smith, the head of the MCH and CC, has paid personally for these items.
>
> We have no hot water because both boilers are broken. We are out of cotton balls, tongue blades, many suture materials and bandages, knife blades, and certain surgical gloves, as well as other essential items too numerous to mention.[7]

Dr. Anduze testified he never received an answer.

Voicing a refrain from the pre-war past, local legislators warned in 1951 that the Virgin Islands were bordering on bankruptcy and "if something is not done soon the three hospitals, the jails and the mental hospital may have to be

---

4. *Ibid.*, p. 113.
5. *Ibid.*, pp. 91, 97, 98.
6. *Hearings ... Activities*, May 1, 1957, p. 769.
7. *Ibid.*, December 11, 1956, pp. 237, 253, 274.

closed." The situation was so bad that "if our people could get off the Islands they would all leave."[8] Their remedy—return to the Virgin Islands "as is done in Puerto Rico" revenue derived from U.S. internal revenue taxes on Virgin Islands rum and other local products. Such legislation would provide self-sufficiency, they claimed, and "We would never need to appear before Congressional Committees annually in the light of beggars."[9]

Organic Act Revision

As early as 1944, eight years after the Organic Act of 1936, local legislation created the Organic Act Reform Committee, which recommended in 1946 the return of internal revenues to the treasury of the Virgin Islands on goods exported from the Islands to the United States, a benefit enjoyed by Puerto Rico since 1917. Its other proposals for revision of the Organic Act were the subject of a referendum in 1948, as noted before, the year of the Emancipation Centennial. Curiously, despite the fact that Puerto Ricans were granted the right to elect their governor in 1947, Virgin Islanders overwhelmingly rejected an elected governor. They also rejected a single legislature, but strongly endorsed a resident commissioner in Congress.

A second Organic Act Reform Committee, created in 1950, held public hearings throughout the Islands, and its draft of a new organic act was approved in 1951 by resolution of the local Legislative Assembly. Its important proposals were: an elective governor, a resident commissioner, a single legislature, and return of internal revenue collections.[10] A bill incorporating these points was introduced in the House of Representatives, and the House Subcommittee on Territories and Insular Possessions held hearings on the bill in the Islands in 1952.[11]

Isidor Paiewonsky, as representative of the liquor dealers of St. Thomas, stated before the Subcommittee:

> Puerto Rico is separated from the Virgin Islands by 60 miles of water. Every time Puerto Rico exports a gallon of rum to the United

---

8. *The New York Times*, July 28, 1951, p. 9, col. 5.

9. Letter to the Editor from Omar Brown, et. al., Members of the Legislative Assembly of the Virgin Islands, October 1, 1951, in *The New York Times*, November 11, 1951, sec. 4, p. 10, col. 5.

10. For the 1951 report of the Organic Act Reform Committee and the draft act approved by the Legislative Assembly, see: *Hearings … on H.R. 2644* (1952), Appendices II and III, pp. 135–152.

11. See, H.R. 2644 in *ibid.*, at pp. 4–12.

States, $10.50 internal revenue tax is returned to the treasury of Puerto Rico. When we export rum from the Virgin Islands to the United States, the internal revenue tax is deposited in the Federal Treasury at Washington, D.C. When it is realized that Puerto Rican and Virgin Island rums compete in the United States market, this inequality of Federal treatment takes on serious proportions. It is exactly as if the Federal Government subsidized the wheat grower of Kansas, then expected the unsubsidized wheat grower of Iowa to go struggle for himself in the same market. This inequality becomes more serious if the federally and lavishly helped grower uses his subsidized condition and assets, at any time, to remove his unsubsidized competitor from the market.[12]

Local legislator Henry Rohlsen claimed that import duties on Virgin Islands rum averaged about $6,000,000 per year, thus enriching the U.S. Treasury by over $64,000,000 through the years—a total in excess of the money spent by the U.S. government in support of the government of the Islands since 1917. Congressman Samuel Yorty cautioned, however, that Puerto Rico had a population of two million whereas the Virgin Islands had only 27,000. "So on a per capita basis," he concluded, "the money which we would be returning to you would be very much greater than to Puerto Rico."[13]

A few conservative businessmen testified against greater self-government for the Islands for the reason that the people were not ready for greater political responsibilities. Most witnesses testified in favor of the bill, with frequent references to the inequality Virgin Islanders suffered in comparison to neighboring Puerto Ricans. Their bid for equality with Puerto Ricans, on the other hand, did not extend to granting the franchise to Puerto Rican citizens living in the Virgin Islands.

The bill before Congress provided merely that "The franchise shall be vested in residents of the Virgin Islands who are citizens of the United States, twenty-one years of age or over." The draft approved by the Legislative Assembly retained the added qualification in the 1936 Organic Act: "and able to read and write the English language." By imposing English as a qualification for voting, Spanish-speaking Puerto Rican residents of the Islands would continue to have been disfranchised. Alva C. McFarlane, chairman of the Legislative Assembly, was extensively questioned by the Subcommittee on this proposed qualification. The following exchange is illustrative:

---

12. *Ibid.*, p. 32.
13. *Ibid.*, p. 92.

MR. MILLER. I believe there are about 4,000 Puerto Ricans engaged in farming on the island.... The thought that you have ... is to see that they didn't vote; isn't that right?

MR. MCFARLANE. I have no objection to their voting ... but I wish and members of the Legislative Assembly wish that they would conform to the standards that have been set in the Virgin Islands.

MR. BENTSEN. Are there any Puerto Ricans in the legislative assembly who would be interested in that decision?

MR. MCFARLANE. There are no Puerto Ricans in the assembly. There have been in the municipal council.

MR. POULSON. Are you opposed to discrimination?

MR. MCFARLANE. Definitely.... I don't subscribe to any form of discrimination. I believe they should adjust themselves to the standards we set.... We have no desire to lower our standards in these islands.[14]

Isidor Paiewonsky was more candid about prevalent local attitudes toward Puerto Ricans, as reflected in the following exchange:

MR. PAIEWONSKY. What seems to have happened recently is that a strict and sudden enforcement of Federal immigration laws to the Virgin Islands has created an artificial iron curtain between the American and British Virgin Islands, disrupting an interdependence of interisland connection that has existed for more than a century and a half....

MR. MILLER. Why do you not get workers from Puerto Rico? They are excellent. Look what a fine job they are doing in St. Croix. How could the economy of St. Croix get along without them?

MR. PAIEWONSKY. The Puerto Ricans are to be admired for ambition and enterprise, but to the Virgin Islander, the Puerto Rican represents a different culture. He speaks a different language and is inclined to be clannish to a marked degree. The native Virgin Islander feels that assimilation will be difficult—that clashes occur because of the above-mentioned differences. On the other hand, the British Virgin Islander represents an identical culture and assimilation is immediate.[15]

---

14. *Ibid.*, pp. 72–73.
15. *Ibid.*, pp. 35–36.

The Subcommittee decided that an elected governor and a resident commissioner in Congress should be postponed until Virgin Islanders had an opportunity to "exercise the increased measure of autonomy" proposed in its pending bill providing for return of revenues as well as a single legislature.[16] That bill was passed by the House in 1952, but died in the Senate.

Results of another local referendum conducted in 1953 showed voters favored a single legislature and treasury, an elected governor, and a resident commissioner in Congress. Although only 1,820 of 6,348 registered voters participated in the referendum,[17] several bills again were introduced in Congress to revise the Organic Act of 1936.

Once again Congressional hearings were held in the Islands, this time under Senator Hugh S. Butler, chairman of the Senate Interior and Insular Affairs Committee. As in the past, native political and labor leaders testified in favor of more self-government, whereas local business leaders—including white continentals—opposed more self-government but favored more financial benefits from the government in Washington. One who testified was former district attorney, Crucian James A. Bough, then United Nations chief of the Caribbean division of non-self-governing territories. Bough proposed an elective governor, a resident commissioner, elimination of the Presidential veto, a single legislature of eleven members with a maximum session of sixty days, a single treasury, and return of revenues.[18]

Senator Butler proved to be no friend of the Virgin Islands. In an early 1954 letter to Governor de Castro, he expressed his conviction that the depressed economy of the Islands was a result of the lack of industry and initiative of Virgin Islanders.[19] Many Virgin Islanders complained that Butler's bill was discriminatory and would deny the pledged self-rule.[20] Butler rejected the claim of unequal treatment in comparison to Puerto Rico for the reason among others that the budget of Puerto Rico, with ninety-odd times the population of the Virgin Islands, is only forty times greater than that of the Virgin Islands.[21] Replying to critics of his bill in a letter to *The New York Times*, Senator Butler wrote disparagingly of Virgin Islanders, as follows:

---

16. *The New York Times*, March 12, 1952, p. 24, col. 8.

17. *The New York Times*, May 2, 1953, p. 15, col. 1.

18. See discussion of the hearings in: Hill, *Rise to Recognition*, pp. 141–143 and Creque, *The U.S. Virgins*, pp. 147–149.

19. See reference to this letter in: Lewis, *The Virgin Islands*, p. 108.

20. See, *e.g.*, Letter to the Editor from Valdemar A. Hill and Herbert H. Heywood, Delegates to the Virgin Islands Assembly, May 13, 1954, in *The New York Times*, May 23, 1954, sec. 4, p. 10, col. 7.

21. *The New York Times*, May 17, 1954, p. 26, col. 2.

While the mainland taxpayer was contributing ... millions to the Virgin Islands, no citizen of the Virgin Islands was making any contribution whatever to the Federal Treasury....

In general, S.3378 provides the people of the Virgin Islands with the opportunity to attain a far greater degree of true self-government—the independence that comes from standing on one's own feet and facing up to the responsibilities of American citizenship as well as demanding all of its privileges and rights....

Enactment of S.3378 ... is necessary for the Governor to do the job that must be done if the people are ever to progress beyond the stage of being, in substance, wards of the Federal Government.[22]

Roger Baldwin of the American Civil Liberties Union disputed Butler's claim that the bill provided greater self-government. Baldwin replied:

He did not specify the way in which this bill provides more self-government for the Virgin Islands. We submit that he did not because he could not; the simple truth being that the bill deprives the elected representatives of the people of the Virgin Islands of many rights and powers which they enjoyed for the past eighteen years—rights extended to them under the 1936 Organic Act.[23]

Differences between House and Senate bills were resolved by conference committee and President Eisenhower signed the Revised Organic Act on July 22, 1954.[24] Whereas the Organic Act of 1936 represented an historic advance toward democratic self-government for the Virgin Islands, no such claim could be made concerning the Organic Act of 1954. Indeed, after closely comparing the two acts, James A. Bough concluded that the Revised Organic Act of 1954 represented "a throwback to more administrative control by Washington."[25]

---

22. Letter to the Editor from Senator Hugh Butler, Chairman, Committee on Interior and Insular Affairs, Washington, May 29, 1954, in *The New York Times*, June 5, 1954, p. 16, cols. 5–6.

23. Letter to the Editor from Roger N. Baldwin, American Civil Liberties Union, New York, June 8, 1954, in *The New York Times*, June 16, 1954, p. 30, col. 6.

24. 68 *Stat.* 497 (1954). The main provisions of the Act are printed as amended in Bough and Macridis, *Virgin Islands*, pp. 59–78.

25. James A. Bough, "Is Commonwealth Status the Next Step?" *The Virgin Islands Bar Journal* (Summer 1974):7.

Revised Organic Act of 1954

Although one could surmise from the earlier insular cases that the Virgin Islands were an unorganized and unincorporated territory of the United States until the 1936 Organic Act, and an organized and unincorporated territory thereafter, not until the 1954 Act did Congress define the status of the Islands to be "unincorporated." This provision signified the intention of Congress to withhold from the Islands incorporated status and eventual statehood.

A bill of rights section was continued in the Act, but—reflecting the mainland paranoia about communism then being abetted by Senator Joseph McCarthy's campaign—a provision was added that no person could hold office in the Islands "who advocates or belongs to any organization which advocates overthrow by force or violence of the Government of the Virgin Islands or the United States." With regard to Puerto Rican residents, the Act added a prohibition against any language requirement to the prior prohibitions against income or property qualifications to vote.

Most significant was the lack of any provision for an elected governor or resident commissioner in Congress. In place of the separate legislatures, one legislature of eleven members was established including six at-large members. The added stipulation that each voter could vote for only two of the six at-large members evoked this comment from James Bough:

> The justification for this innovation, according to the report of Senator Butler, was to insure minority representation in the legislature. It is interesting to note the injection of racial considerations from Washington because, while on the mainland "the minority" is known to refer to nonwhites, in the Virgin Islands context the minority are the whites of the community.[26]

The 1954 Act provided for the separation of powers between executive, legislative and judicial branches, but authorized the governor to "recommend bills to the legislature" and to fill vacancies in the legislature by appointment. For the first time since 1936, his item veto was limited to bills other than appropriation bills, but the Act retained the Presidential veto of bills vetoed by the governor which two-thirds of the legislature has overridden. Regular legislative sessions were limited to sixty days and special sessions to fifteen days. Legislators were to be paid $600 per year, and the legislature was authorized for the first time to issue public improvement revenue bonds, but limited to

---

26. James A. Bough, "General Introduction to the Constitutional Evolution of the Virgin Islands," in Bough and Macridis, *Virgin Islands*, p. 124.

ten million dollars.[27] The Secretary of Interior was authorized by the Act to appoint a government comptroller for a fixed, non-renewable, term of ten years to audit accounts and to call attention to failures to collect revenue and to the existence of expenditures which are "extravagant, excessive, unnecessary, or irregular."

The most important advance for the Virgin Islands consisted of a complicated fiscal formula established by the 1954 Act consisting of three parts. First, permanent residents could pay federal income taxes on income from all sources of revenue, both within and outside the Virgin Islands, into the treasury of the Virgin Islands. Second, and most significant, on a dollar-for-dollar matching basis, an amount equal to the income due the federal treasury each fiscal year from internal revenue collected on articles produced in the Virgin Islands (mostly on rum) would be paid into the treasury of the Virgin Islands, but not in excess of the amount of local revenue raised by the government of the Virgin Islands. The third component of the fiscal formula provided for an additional fund—of $1,000,000 or the balance of such internal revenues, whichever was greater, but not in excess of $5,000,000 annually—payable each fiscal year to the government of the Virgin Islands to be expended for "emergency purposes and essential public projects only."

Expenditures from both matching funds and this surplus balance, however, required the "prior approval of the President or his designated representative." James Bough claimed that the required prior approval—after Presidential delegation to the Secretary of Interior and subdelegation down the "colonial ladder"—means that a Presidential responsibility is discharged by a "political bureaucrat" with perhaps a status of not even a "corporal." He called attention to the fact that no such clearance restrictions were imposed on federal funds granted to pre-Commonwealth Puerto Rico. "Why this difference in federal colonial policy," asked Bough, "with respect to two territories of the United States in the same Caribbean area?"[28]

---

27. According to Darwin Creque, the salary of $600 fixed in 1954 "brought a halt to the abuse of legislative privileges employed by members of the municipal council of St. Thomas and St. John, who held several daily caucus meetings at $5.00 per member per meeting. This resulted at times in netting some members up to $400 per month, much to the displeasure of the Governor, who was powerless to intervene." Creque, *The U.S. Virgins*, p. 150. The 1954 Act cut the basic pay of legislators from $1,800 to $600 a year. See *The New York Times*, June 23, 1954, p. 4, col. 6.

28. Bough, "Is Commonwealth Status the Next Step?" pp. 10, 11. To encourage establishment of manufacturing firms in the Virgin Islands, the 1954 Act raised the foreign raw material content of Virgin Islands manufactured products to enter the United States free of customs duty from 20 to 50 percent.

Bough also was critical of the provision requiring the governor, within a year of the Act, to reorganize and consolidate the many existing administrative agencies of the Virgin Islands government into not more than nine executive departments. It further required that before the governor or legislature could create any other administrative agency it was necessary to secure the prior approval of the Secretary of Interior. This provision not only limited the powers of the legislature and strengthened the power of the governor, but as Bough observed:

> Clearly, instead of an increase in self-government as Senator Butler had proclaimed, this provision ... took away from the Virgin Islands and re-deposited into the hands of the bureaucracy in Washington a large measure of control over the territorial governmental machinery.[29]

Archie Alexander

Since the governor served at the pleasure of the President, Dwight Eisenhower could have replaced Governor de Castro as soon as he became President, but perhaps because of preoccupation with the Korean War[30] he waited until February 1954 to nominate a new governor who took office in April while Congress was finalizing its Organic Act revision.

President Eisenhower chose Archibald Alphonso Alexander whom Senator Butler termed an "excellent" choice.[31] He became the first Republican gover-

---

29. Bough, "Is Commonwealth Status the Next Step?" p. 9. The 1954 Act also provided that the President appoint a United States attorney for the Virgin Islands to "conduct all legal proceedings, civil and criminal," to which the Government of the United States or the government of the Virgin Islands is a party. Since this gave the U.S. Attorney exclusive jurisdiction to prosecute all felonies, the attorney general of the Virgin Islands thereby was limited to prosecuting misdemeanors, unless otherwise permitted by the U.S. Attorney. The establishment of this dichotomy in criminal prosecutions whereby felonies are prosecuted by a federal official, and misdemeanors by a territorial official, constituted, according to James Bough, still another "substantial limitation" on the powers of the government of the Virgin Islands. *Ibid.*, p. 11.

30. A small detachment of Virgin Islands soldiers served in the Korean War as part of the 65th Puerto Rican Regiment of the Third Division. *The New York Times*, September 8, 1952, p. 2, col. 2.

31. Senator Butler commented: "I do believe that S. 3378 will be a substantial help to the excellent Governor chosen by President Eisenhower." Letter to the Editor from Senator Hugh Butler, Chairman, Committee on Interior and Insular Affairs, Washington, May 29, 1954, in *The New York Times*, June 5, 1954, p. 16, col. 6.

nor to serve since Paul Pearson, and the second black governor. A wealthy Republican and construction engineer from Iowa, Archie Alexander became unpopular with Virgin Islanders even before he took office.

During his nomination hearing before Senator Butler's Committee, Alexander referred to Virgin Islanders as "mendicants" and "wards of the United States" who came to Congress "to get vast sums of money every year," but "if the people could tighten their belts and go to work, they would solve their problem."[32] Alexander's testimony rankled Virgin Islanders who had never forgotten President Hoover's similar "poorhouse" remarks. In addition, many Virgin Islanders resented Congress' failure to provide an elective governor, resentment deepened by failure to appoint a native "who has some knowledge and understanding of the islands." A statement by the American Virgin Islands Civic Association of New York City characterized Archie Alexander as being "not only a total stranger to the islands and their people, but one who apparently has no knowledge of or experience in the science of colonial government." Virgin Islanders were "victims of political expediency," and Alexander was chosen "to gratify a political debt."[33]

Alexander, however, was no stranger to the Islands. He had made ten prior visits to the Islands, and had organized—and served as president of—the American Caribbean Contracting Company, a group of contractors who had bid unsuccessfully on construction of the sewer system in the Virgin Islands. Although he promised Senator Butler's Committee during his nomination hearing that his group would not seek work in the American areas of the Caribbean during his governorship, in order to avoid any conflict of interest,[34] he was later to resign amidst such a conflict-of-interest controversy involving his business partners.

Shortly after taking office, Alexander created many enemies. He reorganized the administrative machinery of the government into eight executive departments, as directed by the 1954 Act, by abolishing and consolidating many agencies. He proceeded to replace incumbent administrators with close friends and greatly increased their salaries from 30 to 100 percent. The Chamber of Commerce of St. Thomas complained that "the reorganized government is more

---

32. *Hearing before the Senate Committee on Interior and Insular Affairs, Nomination of Archie A. Alexander*, 83rd Cong., 2d sess., March 10, 1954, p. 5, hereafter cited as: *Hearing ... Archie A. Alexander*.

33. *Ibid.*, p. 13. Upon assuming office, Alexander commented: "Due to the recent Puerto Rican Nationalist uprising in Washington, we've room on these islands but for one flag, the American flag." *The New York Times*, April 10, 1954, p. 34, col. 7.

34. *Hearing ... Archie A. Alexander*, p. 4.

costly than the old."[35] Among charges of wrongdoing made against Governor Alexander, according to a Congressional document, were the following:

(a) He spent island government funds illegally for travel money and entertainment for friends and cronies and government officials, amounting to thousands of dollars.

(b) He misused funds donated for vocational education to bring the pay of the acting commissioner of education up to $11,000 after the legislature refused to confirm his appointment as commissioner.

(c) He entered into excessive and ridiculous contracts for the study of the water problem and of the assessment problem without any public notice of any kind....

(d) He brought friends to the islands as consultants, paying them $50 and $65 a day while living at government house, eating at government expense and using government cars.

(e) He vetoed all items in appropriation bills, leaving only the total amounts and then allocated the funds without regard to the legislative intent. He created positions not authorized or contemplated by the legislature and paid exorbitant salaries.

(f) He issued an executive order prohibiting employees from testifying before the legislature's finance committee, which had been authorized to investigate the expenditures of each and every department.

(g) He vetoed the legislative appropriation bill leaving the legislature without funds to pay its employees.

(h) He transferred funds between departments in violation of the appropriation acts.

(i) Officials appointed by the Governor furnished their homes with furniture and articles belonging to the government. In one case, a commissioner took a Frigidaire, chairs, silverware, dishes, etc., bought for the new high school and not yet used by the students.

(j) The Governor was often rude and obscene and used vile language and threats. He threatened to fire relatives of a legislator unless the latter supported his program.[36]

The first legislature elected under the Revised Organic Act of 1954 convened in January 1955. Of 121 bills considered, it passed 101 of which Governor

---

35. Memorandum to Members of the Public Works and Resources Subcommittee, from Earl Chudoff, chairman, March 28, 1956, in *Hearings ... Activities*, Appendix A, p. 814.

36. *Ibid.*, p. 815.

Alexander approved 40 and vetoed 41.[37] It was inevitable that the 67-year-old Governor would become embroiled in "one of the bitterest executive-legislative encounters in local history."[38] Even the Government Secretary, who becomes acting governor during the governor's absence, had cause for complaint against Governor Alexander. Government Secretary Charles Claunch was felled by a heart attack on March 26, 1955 causing him to be bedridden for nine weeks. Nevertheless, Governor Alexander left the Islands for an extended vacation the day after the attack.[39]

Alexander's principal opponent in the legislature was 32-year-old Earle B. Ottley, chairman of the legislature's finance committee, newspaper publisher, and labor leader, who had been a leading advocate for more self-government. Both Daniel Ambrose, president of the Democratic Club, and Roy Gordon, Republican national committeeman from the Islands, joined in a bipartisan campaign demanding that President Eisenhower recall Alexander.[40] On July 26, 1955, Senator Ottley led a large crowd on a march to Government House demanding the recall of Governor Alexander and the repeal of the Revised Organic Act of 1954.[41] Ottley accused Alexander of "favoritism, incompetence and disregard for the desires of the people."[42]

Meanwhile, Alexander became involved in a scandal that allegedly became the real reason for alarmed Interior officials to quietly urge his resignation. Congressman Earl Chudoff later recounted the events leading to Alexander's resignation, as follows:

> In connection with the St. Thomas waterfront highway, a half-million-dollar job, it is alleged that Ex-Governor Alexander made private arrangements with his business partners, who formed a new corporation, to allow them to use Virgin Islands government equipment and to furnish them with crushed rock at low cost. These arrangements were not offered to other potential bidders. Consequently, the Governor's partners were the low bidders. When another bidder protested, all papers were removed by the Interior Department in Washington where they have been kept since.

---

37. Creque, *The U.S. Virgins*, p. 155.
38. Lewis, *The Virgin Islands*, p. 109.
39. *Hearings ... Activities*, December 10, 1926, p. 132.
40. *The New York Times*, April 11, 1955, p. 24, col. 3.
41. See, *Daily News*, July 27, 1955.
42. *The New York Times*, August 18, 1955, p. 24, col. 3.

The Interior Department canceled the invitation to bid and Governor Alexander resigned....

It was also alleged that the Governor entertained his partners lavishly and gave them the run of Government House and of the Governor's facilities.[43]

Finally on August 17, 1955, the White House announced Governor Archie Alexander's resignation because of "poor health." Alexander explained that he was resented personally mainly because he symbolized the Revised Organic Act which provided for an appointed, instead of an elected, governor.[44]

Charges and Countercharges

Walter A. Gordon, a black attorney from California, was sworn in as governor on October 7, 1955 by his close friend, Chief Justice Earl Warren, with whom Gordon had played football when both were students at the University of California. Although milder in personality than Alexander, Gordon had the same determination as his predecessor, observed one local political leader, "to put the natives in their place."[45] Accordingly, Gordon fared no better in dealing with the local legislature and populace. Perhaps any appointed mainland governor would have courted at the time the same disfavor.

At its 1956 regular session, the legislature refused to approve Governor Gordon's budget and to appropriate funds for the operation of two of his executive departments. For two other departments, funds were appropriated for only six months. Of 129 bills considered, the legislature passed 119 of which Governor Gordon approved only 55 and disapproved 62. Six bills vetoed by Gordon were overridden by the legislature, but all six vetoes were sustained by President Eisenhower.[46] Rent with conflict in almost every facet of public affairs, the functioning of the government of the Virgin Islands during most of Governor Gordon's tenure was chaotic. Once again, top officials were replaced with the Governor's own appointees, and Gordon forbade them to appear before the finance committee of the legislature. The legislature retaliated by withholding funds necessary for the proper functioning of the government comptroller appointed by the Secretary of Interior. This led the General Accounting

---

43. *Hearings ... Activities*, pp. 814–815.
44. *The New York Times*, August 18, 1955, p. 24, col. 3.
45. Hill, *Rise to Recognition*, p. 144.
46. *Annual Report of the Governor* of *the Virgin Islands, 1956*, p. 2.

Office to recommend withholding of federal matching funds in an amount sufficient to staff his office.

Meanwhile, the financial system of the government of the Virgin Islands was in a shambles. No central accounting system existed. Bank statements of government funds remained unreconciled. The government was spending more money than it was raising. In fiscal years 1956 and 1957, the legislature appropriated considerably more funds than were available for appropriation, possibly because of little communication between the executive and legislative branches. Gordon was thus forced to make cutbacks based on his own priorities against the wishes of the legislature. Income was accounted for on a calendar-year basis, while expenses were recorded on a fiscal-year basis. Federal income taxes remained uncollected for some two thousand to three thousand taxpayers because, claimed tax administrator Reuben Wheatley, his office was understaffed. No tax maps locating taxable property existed, and the local tax review board repeatedly changed property assessments without communicating with the tax assessor.[47]

Although the Federal Internal Revenue Code applied to the Islands, it was administered by employees of the insular government. To provide encouragement for establishment of new business, local legislation authorized— without Congressional provision—income tax relief in the form of 75 percent refunds to firms qualifying as new businesses. Though this legislation applied to new business only, it was made retroactive to 1947. "A true appraisal of the financial condition of the government as of July 1, 1956," concluded the government comptroller of the Virgin Islands, "is one of bankruptcy."[48]

Many of these conditions, of course, were inherited from past administrations by Governor Gordon. Now, however, the situation had greatly changed because, under the Revised Organic Act of 1954, for every dollar the Virgin Islands raised in revenue, the United States would match with an equal dollar. Accordingly, continuing deficiencies in financial administration now caused severe losses in federal matching funds, as the following exchange between a General Accounting Office official and Congressman Earl Chudoff made clear:

> MR. MUHONEN. As a result, we have been unable to determine the financial position of the government of the Virgin Islands at any year end or the results of the fiscal operation for any year during the 5 years that the activities of the insular government have been sub-

---

47. See, *Hearings ... Activities*, esp. pp. 222, 223, 308, 359, 381, 385–395, 451.
48. *Ibid.*, esp. pp. 449–450, 454, 459.

ject to comprehensive review ... by the General Accounting Office. We believe that the present condition of the accounting records and internal controls in the insular government, in addition to causing serious operational difficulties, has resulted in noncompliance with section 18 of the Revised Organic Act which specifically requires the Governor to establish and maintain a satisfactory system of accounting and internal control....

MR. CHUDOFF. The purpose of the Revised Organic Act is to try to get the government of the Virgin Islands to legislate proper tax laws and administer those laws in a proper fashion so the more money they take in locally, the more money they will get from Washington.

MR. MUHONEN. That is correct. I believe there should be an incentive to assess themselves fairly.[49]

Financial administration continued to deteriorate under Governor Gordon. The government comptroller of the Virgin Islands resigned, leaving that office vacant, and Interior Secretary Fred Seaton warned that "the people of the Virgin Islands must attain full financial responsibility before they could expect further progress on their way to self government."[50]

Threatened with financial disaster, Gordon finally turned his attention to improving financial administration. At the end of the 1958 fiscal year, he was able to furnish a statement of the financial condition of the insular government. "All obligations incurred and expenditures made," reported the Governor, "were within the limits authorized and allotted."[51]

Troubles abounded in other areas of public concern. Of one hundred and eighty-four public school teachers in 1955, only fifty-five were college graduates, while ninety-four were high school graduates. Costs of health care remained excessive with four hundred and twenty employees staffing a less than two hundred bed government-run hospital which never billed any juvenile ward patient "regardless of whether his father has a million dollars."[52] Pan

---

49. *Ibid.*, pp. 449–452. The General Accounting Office also found "certain deficiencies in the general and financial management" of the Virgin Islands Corporation, and recommended "transferring the financing and, ultimately, the management of the ... Corporation to the Government of the Virgin Islands when the latter has demonstrated its ability to satisfactorily assume this responsibility." *Ibid.*, p. 448.

50. *The New York Times*, December 8, 1956, p. 20, col. 1.

51. *Annual Report of the Governor of the Virgin Islands, 1958*, pp. 16, 18.

52. *Hearings ... Activities*, pp. 106, 320, 350.

American Airways shifted its flights from St. Thomas to St. Croix because St. Thomas airport's short runway could not accommodate larger aircraft.[53]

Gordon's most difficult problem was the persisting water shortage, particularly on St. Thomas. When drought occurred, the problem became severe, and demand for water steadily increased as housing projects, new schools, hotels and hospitals were brought into operation. After firing his commissioner of public works, Gordon finally resorted to barging water into St. Thomas from Puerto Rico, which did not really abate the shortage.[54]

If the small size of the Virgin Islands with a population of only thirty thousand suggested that effective management of public affairs would have been within easy reach of the insular government, this was clearly not the case. Governor Gordon and other mainlanders tended to blame insular problems on Virgin Islanders—that they were lazy and unwilling to work—as the following colloquy between California Congressman H. Allen Smith and Governor Gordon reveals:

> MR. SMITH. I want to ask a couple of questions. I get the impression from this whole hearing that the Virgin Islands is not an asset to the United States, everybody is lazy, you have trouble getting people to cut cane, that they like to sit in hotels, and things like that....
>
> GOVERNOR GORDON. They don't like to cut sugarcane, and they don't mind telling you that. That is one of the things that handicaps us. Vicorp has to import Puerto Ricans. Every week, I sign papers to bring in labor from the outside ... from the British Virgin Islands and the people from the French islands, Antigua. That does worry me. It gives me a lot of concern, just looking at the economic future of the islands, particularly the Puerto Ricans, because as American citizens they come over and stay and right now they number between four and five thousand on the Virgin Islands, out of a population of 30,000. The Virgin Islanders don't like to cut sugarcane. They don't like to do other chores. Why? I would rather they describe it than for me to give my evaluation....
>
> MR. SMITH. It looks like to me we are running around in a circle. If we bring in more water at more costs for more tourists, we will have to have more water, and more people working in the hotels,

53. *Annual Report of the Governor of the Virgin Islands, 1956*, p. 3.
54. *Hearings ... Activities*, pp. 65, 408–419, 569–615.

and nobody cutting sugarcane, so we might as well sell the Virgin Islands back to Denmark.[55]

On the other hand, Virgin Islanders blamed perduring insular problems on the intrusive presence of mainlanders. Thus, Senator Earle B. Ottley retorted it was insulting to blame Islanders for inefficiency "when the government is substantially in the hands of non-Virgin Islanders."

> Because of our size and lack of influence in the national scheme of things, we know how ineffective are the protests we make against the campaign to discredit and ridicule Virgin Islanders before the Congress and to hold us out as a bunch of irresponsible, softbrained people who need to be held by the hand and guided until kingdom come.[56]

Claiming that "we enjoy considerably less self-government than we did in 1936," Virgin Islanders renewed their demands for the right to elect their own governor, to be represented in Congress by a resident commissioner, and to legislate on internal matters. Their campaign was fueled in 1958 by the formation on January 3rd of that year of the British West Indies Federation comprised of ten Caribbean island units—Jamaica, Trinidad and Tobago, Barbados, Grenada, St. Vincent, St. Lucia, Dominica, Antigua, St. Christopher (St. Kitts)-Nevis-Anguilla, and Montserrat. Established to prepare their more than three million inhabitants to move as rapidly as possible toward the attainment of independence within the British Commonwealth, American Virgin Islanders invidiously compared their own continuing colonial status with the grant of comprehensive self-government to their British neighbors.[57]

On January 29, 1958, a demonstration of three thousand Virgin Islanders—led by Valdemar Hill, President of the Virgin Islands Unity Party, and Senator Ottley—marched on Government House petitioning the removal of Governor Gordon "because of his incompetence, abuse of powers, and bad administration," and declaring their readiness for "the responsibilities of self-government."[58] The immediate event that triggered the march was the aftermath of a

---

55. *Ibid.*, pp. 897–809.

56. *Ibid.*, pp. 892–893.

57. Letter to the Editor from Earle B. Ottley, Chairman of the Virgin Islands Organic Act Commission, Charlotte Amalie, St. Thomas, V. I., January 4, 1958, *The New York Times*, January 12, 1958, sec. 4, p. 10, col. 7. The National Democratic Party Platform of 1956 had promised "increased self-government" for the Virgin Islands and other U.S. territories. *The New York Times*, August 15, 1956, p. 12, col. 7.

58. Hill, *Rise to Recognition*, pp. 144–145. Only 1,500 marchers were reported in *The New York Times*, March 16, 1958, p. 52, col. 4.

fire which destroyed the newly constructed redwood home of a friend of a visiting assistant secretary of the Interior Department who apparently insisted that heads must roll. The morning after the fire the chief of police, who was on leave at the time of the fire, and the commissioner of public safety were both summarily dismissed, whereas the fire chief who failed to save the house was spared. The local public was "incensed ... over this apparent injustice."[59]

Washington officials registered disapproval of the demonstration, and Congressman Claire Engle of California, Chairman of the House Interior and Insular Affairs Committee, irately responded: "In the event any sizeable group of Virgin Islanders demands self-government and independence from the United States, I stand ready to introduce legislation to achieve that status."[60]

Eight months after the demonstration, Governor Gordon resigned, whereupon he was appointed federal judge of the United States District Court of the Virgin Islands to succeed Herman E. Moore who retired after twenty years in that post. Crucian John Merwin was nominated by President Eisenhower to succeed Gordon, was unanimously confirmed by the Senate, and took office as the Virgin Islands first native-born governor on September 25, 1968. At thirty-seven, he became the youngest governor since the Islands came under American rule.[61]

Tourism to the Rescue

A 1957 survey revealed the Virgin Islands were registering the third highest growth in tourism of all Caribbean islands.[62] The number of cruise ship visits to St. Thomas increased from forty-eight in fiscal year 1956–57 to one hundred and fifty-seven in 1960–61 when 247,700 visitors came to the Islands. Estimated gross tourist expenditures nearly doubled in those four years, from $13,170,000 to $25,817,000.[63] A number of factors combined to foster this spectacular jump, including an increasingly active tourism promotion cam-

---

59. Creque, *The U.S. Virgins*, pp. 165–166.

60. Hill, *Rise to Recognition*, p. 145. Interior Secretary Seaton vigorously defended Governor Gordon's administration, declaring it "has been characterized by forward-looking policies and sound governmental practices." *The New York Times*, March 16, 1958, p. 52, col. 5.

61. *The New York Times*, September 26, 1958, p. 23, col. 2.

62. Jeanne Harman, "Virgin Islands Rate Reduction," *The New York Times*, April 7, 1957, sec. 11, p. 3, col. 5.

63. *Annual Report of the Governor of the Virgin Islands, 1961*, pp. 60, 61; and *ibid., 1958*, p. 55.

paign conducted by the local government, the advent of the jet airliner, and the cut-off of Castro's Cuba as an American tourist haven with the severance of U.S.-Cuban diplomatic relations.

Along with the spurt in tourism, other economic indicators began to show progress. At the end of the 1956–57 fiscal year, the Virgin Islands Corporation showed a profit for the first time.[64] Construction shot up. Employment was reported in 1958 to be at an all-time high with "more jobs than people." To alleviate a severe labor shortage, the U.S. Immigration Service permitted two thousand alien workers to be brought in, mostly from neighboring British islands.[65] "The jobs now held by aliens in the Virgin Islands," reported Governor Merwin, "have achieved a permanence far beyond the intent of the program." The Governor projected that total local revenues were approaching a figure which in two years should balance the insular budget without the need of federal matching funds. "Consideration may now be given," therefore, "to meeting the aspirations of the people for a greater voice in their government when they are self-supporting."[66]

By the end of fiscal year 1959–60, thirty-three small businesses and nineteen hotels were operating under the local tax exemption program, but Merwin acknowledged serious Congressional objections to tax loopholes in the program that must be closed. Much credit for the economic upsurge he attributed to the bolstering funding provisions of the Revised Organic Act of 1954 and he predicted further stimulation of business and tourism by airport improvement and harbor dredging projects underway in St. Thomas and St. Croix and by construction of a new pier in Frederiksted. The legislative and executive branches have "worked in harmony and accord," work was progressing on surveying and mapping of all real property for development of an equitable assessment system, and the Islands were at "the peak of an era of unprecedented prosperity." Governor Merwin concluded his last annual report with the warning:

> The people of the islands should not expect that local revenues will continue to increase in the same proportion as they did during fiscal year 1960. A period of leveling-off must inevitably follow in the new or succeeding year.[67]

Neither Merwin's prediction of approaching self-sufficiency nor of an imminent leveling-off period would prove accurate. Economic gains during his

---

64. *The New York Times*, September 2, 1957, p. 39, col. 2.
65. *The New York Times*, April 6, 1958, p. 41, col. 1.
66. *Annual Report of the Governor of the Virgin Islands, 1959*, pp. 57, 62.
67. *Annual Report of the Governor of the Virgin Islands, 1960*, pp. 1, 7, 61.

administration would prove in retrospect modest compared with the boom to come. As his governorship neared an end, the 1960 census figures were released. Their analysis portended latent ethnic problems to come. The total population of the Islands had increased by over 20 percent in a decade, from 26,665 in 1950 to 32,099 in 1960. Most significant were the percentage increases since 1950, in terms of "nativity and place of birth," registered by those labeled "Foreign" (from 3,084 to 5,279 or a 71.17% increase), "Continental U.S." (from 1,034 to 2,574 or a 148.93% increase), and "Puerto Rico" (from 2,874 to 3,897 or a 35.59% increase). In other words, nearly 37 percent of the total population of the Virgin Islands in 1960 (up from 26% in 1950) were non-natives. Clearly, should this trend continue, native Virgin Islanders were destined to become a minority in their own homeland, as one obvious price of a tourism-induced economy. Another price could well be an end to the long-time ethnic harmony enjoyed by the people of the Virgin Islands.[68]

Merwin's tenure as Governor ended in 1961 with a per capita income—higher than in Puerto Rico and the Caribbean generally—and without the internecine hostility that marked the administrations of his two predecessors.[69] He had served in the insular legislature and as Government Secretary prior to his appointment as Governor. Not only was Merwin himself a native-born Virgin Islander, but so also was his Government Secretary, Roy W. Bornn. Most conducive to relatively harmonious executive-legislative relations, however, was Governor Merwin's appointment of an all-native cabinet, accounting for the fact that all successful candidates elected to the legislature in 1958 had campaigned on a pledge to support his administration, including a native Puerto Rican-the first successful candidate of a new political party started by Puerto Rican residents in St. Croix.[70]

Although Governor Merwin supported an elected governor and resident commissioner in Congress, he was against having an elected resident com-

---

68. See, *Annual Report of the Governor of the Virgin Islands, 1961*, p. 4.

69. *The New York Times*, January 9, 1961, p. 125, col. 3.

70. *Annual Report of the Governor of the Virgin Islands, 1959*, pp. 1, 62; and *The New York Times*, November 9, 1958, p. 50, col. 4. Governor Merwin did incur the wrath of the legislature, however, by vetoing two bills, upheld by President Eisenhower over the legislature's override, which would have given government employees the right to appeal dismissals, suspensions and declassifications to the Government Employees Service Commission. Senator Earle B. Ottley complained: "The right of a Governor of a territory to fire a Government employee in the civil service and then to sit as judge to make the final decision as to whether or not the firing was fair and just is a farce and a mockery of our democratic system." Letter to the Editor from Earle B. Ottley, Senator-at-large, Virgin Islands Legislature, Charlotte Amalie, V. I., October 4, 1960, in *The New York Times*, October 12, 1960, p. 38, col. 6.

missioner while the governor was still appointive, because such an arrangement "could put me on the spot," he said, especially in his relations with the
insular legislature. Both President Eisenhower in his 1960 and 1961 budget
messages and Interior Secretary Fred Seaton, as well as Puerto Rican Resident
Commissioner Antonio Fernós-Isern, announced their support for a non-voting delegate in Congress. The 1960 national platform of the Republican Party
added its endorsement to the earlier endorsement by the Democratic Party.
Before the United Nations, U.N. Delegate Senator Wayne Morse proclaimed the
death of colonialism under the American flag by noting that Guam had acquired its first indigenous governor, while in the Virgin Islands there had been
a native-born governor for "some time."[71]

Despite growing external support for a non-voting delegate, including
unanimous approval by a Congressional subcommittee, continuing demands
by Virgin Islanders for more self-government[72] were not to succeed for several years.

Rockefeller's Resort

Even before the sudden rise in tourism and business, visitors began to express concern "that most of the natural beauty and scenic charm of St. Thomas
and St. Croix are being destroyed."[73] No such concern was expressed about the
smallest and "most virgin" of the three major islands in the territory, unde-
veloped St. John, which had long been neglected and all but ignored in the
various governors' annual reports to the Secretary of Interior. Its population
had steadily declined from a high of 2,555 in 1841 to 746 in 1950, because the
end of slave labor after 1848 made plantation agriculture unprofitable. In 1955,
only 56 of its 12,160 acres comprised land in cultivation, with most of the remainder—85 percent of the total—covered by bush and second-growth tropical forest. In 1939, Harold Hubler of the National Park Service had made a study
and a report recommending that a national park be established on St. John to

---

71. See, *The New York Times*, November 6, 1955, p. 11, col. 2; January 19, 1960, p. 22,
col. 3; February 23, 1960, p. 63, col. 1; January. 17, 1961, p. 22, col. 3; Jul. 25, 1960, p.
14, col. 3; October 15, 1960, p. 21, col. 3; and *Annual Report of the Governor of the Virgin
Islands, 1958*, pp. 16, 18.

72. See, *e.g.*, *The New York Times*, August 5, 1960, p. 6, col. 3; November 26, 1960, p.
18, col. 8; and March 28, 1961, p. 28, col. 3.

73. Morris Kaplan, "L. S. Rockefeller Offers United States a Virgin Islands Park," *Daily
News*, November 20, 1954.

prevent the island from becoming despoiled, but the onset of World War II intervened and his plan was shelved.[74]

After the War, multimillionaire philanthropist Laurance Rockefeller cruised around the area every winter for six years, and concluded that the island of St. John had "the most superb beaches and view" of any place he had ever seen, and was "the most beautiful island in the Caribbean."[75] In the early 1950s, Rockefeller bought at bargain prices almost half the island. At Caneel Bay—the site of an historic plantation on the northwest shore—he established a "get-away-from-it-all" resort "where a very few of the well-connected rich could relax in surroundings of expensive simplicity."[76] Rockefeller meanwhile discovered Hubler's report and decided to donate his holdings toward conversion of about two-thirds of the nine-by-five-mile island into a national park. He later commented:

> I just started out to preserve a limited area as a business, and develop a unique resort for people who work hard and want peace and loveliness on their vacations. But it developed into a larger concept of a national park so all America could preserve it forever. The resort will be nonprofit now.[77]

---

74. Harold Hubler, "Proposed Virgin Islands National Park," *National Parks*, July–September 1955.

75. *Hearing before the Senate Subcommittee on Territories and Insular Affairs on S. 1604, Virgin Islands National Park*, 84th Cong., 1st sess., May 19, 1955, p. 22, hereafter cited as: *Hearing . . . on S. 1604* (1955).

76. O'Neill, *Rape of the Virgin Islands*, p. 140. Laurance Rockefeller apparently was not the first to consider establishing "a rich man's club" at Caneel Bay. In 1940, a former Yale hockey coach who had spent considerable time in the Virgin Islands as a visitor and businessman, charged that since Germany had taken over Denmark, the Danish West India Company in St. Thomas intended to repatriate its profits to Denmark in support of Germany's war effort (Holcombe York, "Danish Owned Monopoly Dominates Virgin Islands At Heavy Cost to U.S.," *New Haven Register*, June 16, 1940, p. 10). In refuting this allegation in a letter to Rupert Emerson, Director of the Division of Territories and Island Possessions, Department of Interior, Governor Lawrence Cramer wrote: "Incidentally, Mr. York came to the Virgin Islands originally to take over the Caneel Bay development and to establish a rich man's club there. It was a good idea but he did not have the capacity to put it over. He made several other efforts at promoting one thing or another in the Virgin Islands and failed in all of them. Finally, he was hired by the Virgin Islands Board of Business and Tourist Development as Secretary for the organization and in my estimation, contributed little or nothing to the accomplishment of the Board's objectives. He was let out because of the general feeling that he was accomplishing nothing." NARS, RG 126, File 9-11-2 (Part 4); Cramer to Emerson, August 15, 1940.

77. "Laurance S. Rockefeller: Plan for Paradise," *The New Mirror*, December 12, 1954.

Rockefeller's proposal for a national park was endorsed by Governor Archie Alexander, the Interior Department, the member of the insular legislature representing St. John—Julius Sprauve, the legislature itself, the *St. Croix Avis*, and the St. Thomas *Daily News* which predicted that St. John "should boost the tourist program to large proportions," and "will also attract a better type of visitors."[78]

A bill drafted by the Interior Department to create the Virgin Islands National Park was introduced in Congress which held hearings in 1955. The Park was to take up nearly three-fourths of the island of St. John. The total size of the Park was to be limited to 9,450 of the total 12,860 acres, plus 50 acres on the east end of St. Thomas for a docking and parking area. Rockefeller had already acquired 5,000 acres for the Park, and the remaining 4,450 acres were to be acquired over time with additional funds to be donated, presumably by Rockefeller. Establishment of the Park, however, was not to await acquisition of the balance of 4,450 acres.[79]

Testimony before a Senate subcommittee sought to establish that Rockefeller's "whole purpose is a gift to the public and that there is no personal profit involved," and that no one would be displaced nor would any resident on the island be adversely affected. Meanwhile, Rockefeller's money was being used to expand the Caneel Bay resort facilities from fifty to one hundred rooms to be available at rates from $15 to $22 per day per person including all meals.[80]

In anticipation of establishment of the Park, Rockefeller transferred the title to all his St. John holdings, including the six hundred acre Caneel Bay resort, to a nonprofit corporation, the Jackson Hole Preserve, Inc., to acquire the land for the purpose of donating it to the Government. A subsidiary of the Jackson Hole corporation, the Caneel Bay Plantation, Inc., was established to operate the resort, all earnings of which were to revert—after payment of taxes to the Government of the Virgin Islands—to Jackson Hole for "nonprofit, park purposes."[81] The extent of Rockefeller's gift, in terms of dollar-value, was considerable, as witness Rockefeller's early 1956 comments that $3,000,000 had already been spent on land and facilities "with considerable future development to be done."[82]

78. *Daily News*, November 22, 1954: *St. Croix Avis*, November 27, 1954; *Hearing ... on S. 1604* (1955), p. 13; and O'Neill, *Rape of the Virgin Islands*, p. 140.

79. *S. 1604*, 84th Cong., 1st sess., (1955).

80. *Hearing ... on S. 1604* (1955), pp. 5, 14, 33.

81. *Ibid.*, pp. 5, 11–12.

82. John Scofield, "Virgin Islands: Tropical Playland, U.S.A.," *The National Geographic Magazine*, 109 (February 1956): 232.

With no testimony offered against the proposal, Congress easily passed the bill and the National Park Service opened the Virgin Islands National Park in August 1956, consisting of the more than 5,000 acres donated by Laurance Rockefeller. Other properties were acquired and by June 1958 the Park encompassed over two-thirds of the island of St. John, with still more acquisitions planned.

By the terms of their sale agreements, householders living in the Park area were allowed to remain on their land for the duration of their lives. They were obliged, however, to the surprise of some, to abide by the rules and regulations enforced by "stiff-brimmed" U.S. Park Service rangers.[83] Although the Caneel Bay resort as part of the Park was now open to the public, it remained so exclusive that in 1958 Virgin Islands Senator Walter Hodge called it "a millionaire's lodge protected by the Federal Government." Alleged incidents of racial discrimination at the resort moved Hodge to complain that "as long as there is a National Park, no person of color or low means will be able to establish a single home in that area." Senator Theovald Moorehead, St. John's only representative in the insular legislature, added:

> Unfortunately, the gift horse we have accepted is permanently installed in our stable asking for more and more room and threatening, it seems, to kick us off the island entirely if we don't "cooperate." And "cooperate" means, we have learned, simply to agree to whatever is presented.[84]

The "misunderstandings" brought Laurance Rockefeller to visit the island to assure residents that he would buy no more land on St. John, and to answer charges that his agents interfered in areas outside the Park and tried to dictate the development of roads and telephone service, and the improvement of Cruz Bay, St. John's only village and port. Finally, after a long meeting, Senator Moorehead grudgingly subscribed to a joint statement declaring that neither Mr. Rockefeller nor Jackson Hole Preserve, Inc., "ever had any intention of interfering with or attempting to direct the construction of roads, installation of telephone service, community planning or other public interest developments on St. John." It added that they were "anxious, as in the past, to cooperate in any efforts to aid in these matters."[85] Thus ended the first chapter, but not the last, of the Virgin Islands National Park on somnolent St. John.

---

83. O'Neill, *Rape of the Virgin Islands*, p. 140.

84. Lawrence Fellows, "Trouble Invades Island Paradise," *The New York Times*, May 18, 1958, p. 10, col. 1-2.

85. *The New York Times*, June 2, 1958, p. 52, col. 3.

*Governor Ralph Paiewonsky congratulates arrival of
first jet airline, June 9, 1962*

10

Development Decade

The election of John F. Kennedy in 1960 to the Presidency of the United States signaled the advent of phenomenal political change and economic growth in the Virgin Islands. A Democrat in the White House meant a Democrat in Government House and the end of Republican stewardship.

Kennedy's new Interior Secretary Stewart Udall sent Washington consultant Maurice Rosenblatt to the Islands to canvass possible local prospects for the governorship. Rosenblatt recommended wealthy Connie B. Gay, a native North Carolinian who was a legal resident of the Islands. Concerning another wealthy prospect, a white native of Jewish descent and long-time local Democratic leader—rum-maker Ralph Paiewonsky, Rosenblatt reportedly concluded that "With Paiewonsky as Governor, the Virgin Islands would once again become a happy pirate kingdom rivaling the days of Sir Henry Morgan, Blue-beard, and Blackbeard." Ralph Paiewonsky nevertheless was nominated. It was rumored that the President's father, Joseph F. Kennedy, had intervened because of his "connections" with Ralph's father, Isaac, in the liquor business over the years.[1] It was Ralph Paiewonsky's involvement in the liquor (rum) business, however, that caused the Senate Committee on Interior and Insular Affairs, during its hearings on his nomination, to closely question Paiewonsky on possible conflicts of interest.[2]

At issue was Paiewonsky's past involvement through his family business, A. H. Riise Distillers Corporation, with the Virgin Islands Corporation ever since 1949 when Congress ended VICO's rum manufacture upon chartering VI-CORP. VICORP's inherited distillery was at first leased and then sold in 1954 to Riise Distillers. The sale was conditioned by the agreement that VICORP would sell 70 percent of its molasses to Riise Distillers at two cents below mar-

---

1. For a more detailed account of Paiewonsky's selection, see: O'Neill, *Rape of the American Virgins*, pp. 65–68.

2. *Hearings before the Senate Committee on Interior and Insular Affairs, Nomination for Governor of the Virgin Islands*, 87th Cong., 1st sess., March 10, 11, and 14, 1961, esp. pp. 4–34, 132–150; hereafter cited as: *Hearings … (Paiewonsky's) Nomination* (1961).

ket prices, which meant in effect that Paiewonsky's production of rum was subsidized by a federal government corporation.[3] As Governor, he would by law become a member of VICORP's board of directors.

Also at issue before the hearings were various other charges and expressed concerns, among which were the following: that the insular legislature voted an "Emergency Molasses Fund" to further subsidize Paiewonsky's business; that Paiewonsky had fraudulently avoided paying $1 million in U.S. tariffs by importing Cuban rum and shipping it to the U.S. as Virgin Islands rum; that he shipped mislabeled rum to the U.S.; that Riise Company fraudulently received a 75 percent income tax exemption; that the Company refused to pay VICORP for its molasses in 1959; and that the Paiewonsky family sold at enormous profits acreage fronting on Skyline Drive in St. Thomas after large sums of public money were used to pave that road.

Paiewonsky refuted each charge point-by-point. In addition, much testimony was presented showing widespread popular support for his appointment, citing his long record of public service in the Islands. Paiewonsky's successful rum business generated substantial financial support of the insular government through the federal taxes on Virgin Islands rum sold in the United States that were returned to the Islands on a dollar-for-dollar matching basis under the Revised Organic Act of 1954. This fact alone was enough to evoke the gratitude of many Virgin Islanders.[4] He also had helped found and organize in 1954 the West Indies Bank and Trust Company which ended the monopolistic control of the Virgin Islands National Bank. Active in local politics since 1936, Paiewonsky served as a member of the municipal council from 1936 to 1946 and as Democratic national committeeman for the Virgin Islands from 1940 to 1960.

---

3. Isaac Dookhan, "The Virgin Islands Company and Corporation: The Plan for Economic Rehabilitation in the Virgin Islands," *The Journal of Caribbean History*, 4 (May 1972):60.

4. At the time when few other export industries existed, this tax rebated to the insular government amounted to two to three million dollars per year. Puerto Rico, on the other hand, had about $100 million a year rebated to it on rum sold in the U.S. in the mid-1950s. In the words of Congressman Chudoff: "The only difference between Puerto Rico and the Virgin Islands, the Virgin Islands gets half, but Puerto Rico gets all." — meaning that Puerto Rico had returned to its treasury all federal taxes on rum *plus* a sum equal to that amount. For this and detailed testimony explicating Paiewonsky's arrangements with VICORP, see the testimony of VICORP President Kenneth A. Bartlett in *Hearings before the House Subcommittee on Public Works and Resources, Activities of the Virgin Islands Government and the Virgin Islands Corporation*, 85th Cong., 1st sess., March 5, 1957, pp. 514–527, esp. pp. 518, 524. This testimony included allegations about mislabeled 8 and 12-year-old rum; *ibid.*, pp. 525–527.

A number of local political leaders testified in support of Senate confirmation of Mr. Paiewonsky, including former Governor de Castro and Walter Hodge, president of the Virgin Islands legislature. Most interesting, in the light of later events, was the endorsement of Paiewonsky as "the best man in the islands for the position" by local legislator Ron de Lugo, who had defeated Paiewonsky in 1960 in the election for Democratic national committeeman.[5]

Paiewonsky made three promises to the Senate Committee: (1) he would dispose of all stock in his family enterprises; (2) he would work to make VICORP self-sufficient; and (3) he would hold down the costs of government. Concerning this last point, he said:

> I think right now we have enough government. And I do not feel that
> we want to extend and create a more expensive type of government.
> I think we want to have a more efficient type of government. And
> maybe it can be done by less government rather than more government.[6]

The Senate confirmed the nomination, and on April 5, 1961 Ralph Paiewonsky was inaugurated. Assistant Secretary of the Interior John A. Carver used the occasion to announce a new and major policy direction for the federal government in its relationship with the government of the Virgin Islands. In recognizing the federal government's continuing responsibilities to the people of the Virgin Islands, Carver emphasized the federal government would look to the people to identify their problems and to express their hopes and aspirations including "a free choice as to their ultimate form of relationship with the United States."

> In conclusion, let it be said that it is not the intention of the Department of the Interior to impose "administration." Governor Paiewonsky is an appointee of the President of the United States, confirmed by the United States Senate. He is not a subordinate of the Department of the Interior. Your legislature was elected by free people. The Organic Act conveys governmental powers to the Governor and the Legislature, and under the framework of that Act they owe special accountability to laws, not to men who may administer bureaus or departments in Washington.[7]

At the outset, therefore, Governor Paiewonsky was given an unprecedented degree of freedom to run the Virgin Islands without much fear of federal in-

---

5. *Hearings ... (Paiewonsky's) Nomination* (1961), p. 86.
6. *Ibid.*, pp. 4, 28, 133.
7. Carver's entire address at Paiewonsky's inauguration is reprinted in *ibid.*, pp. 675–677.

terference. A month later, President Kennedy's nominee for Government Secretary, Cyril E. King—a native black Crucian, assumed that office. King was a protégé of, and former Senate assistant to, Senator Hubert Humphrey.

Paiewonsky's Progress

Within a month of his inauguration, Governor Paiewonsky, according to one news account, "stirred up more activity than the Virgin Islands have seen in ten years." To attract American investment capital, the tax incentive program was remodelled. A stalled ten-million dollar bond issue to build three new hotels was revived. Acreage was acquired to pave the way for a new public housing development. A food distribution program was expedited. Plans to build a new jet airport on St. Thomas were scrapped in favor of improving the existing Harry Truman Airport. Progress in other areas included a land utilization survey, establishment of a new Department of Commerce, reorganization of the Public Works Department, and paving and beautification of the Veterans Drive Highway along the harbor waterfront of Charlotte Amalie.[8]

Paiewonsky's first months in office coincided with an economic take-off unprecedented in the history of the Islands, and the new Governor happily took credit for the boom. By the end of 1961, the insular government reported the Islands had the highest per capita income in the Caribbean. In 1961, more than four thousand vessels had called in St. Thomas, reminiscent of harbor activity of one hundred and fifty years before. Many were laden with tourists whose business increased $1,000,000 over the previous year. Exports soared $11,000,000 for the same period. Of seven hundred and thirty-one business concerns, only two failed during the year. Bank deposits climbed 30 percent in 1961, and customs collections jumped $300,000. The fifty-four tax exempt businesses covered a wide range, including

> investment firms, stone quarries, heavy equipment, rental, manufacturers of water repellant cloth, industrial belting, watches and watch bracelets, clothing, jewelry, clinical thermometers, linen, fire hose, universal joints, shoe laces, wool yarn, ... silk screened fabrics, vodka, a winery, cannery, and the blending of whisky and other liquors.[9]

---

8. *The New York Times*, April 30, 1961, p. 52, cols. 3–6.

9. Jeanne P. Harmon, "Industry Prospers in the Virgin Islands," *The New York Times*, January 8, 1962, p. 138, col. 1.

At the end of his first fiscal year in office, Governor Paiewonsky reported to the Secretary of Interior still other major accomplishments: completion of a new salt water distillation plant on St. Thomas providing over 275,000 gallons of fresh water daily; signing of a contract with the Harvey Aluminum Company to build a $25 million plant in St. Croix, to process bauxite into alumina, that would employ four hundred persons on a permanent year-round basis; and announcement that the College of the Virgin Islands would open a year hence on July 1, 1963 as a junior college offering a two-year program that would accommodate about one hundred students. The overall growth of the economy during the fiscal year was attributed by the Governor to the "cooperation and understanding" between the insular executive and legislative branches which were "at an all-time high." The only negative was VICORP's reported annual loss of an average $378,000 over the preceding five years. "The sugar operation in St. Croix cannot justify itself," concluded Governor Paiewonsky.[10]

Not reported by the Governor to the Interior Secretary were incidents of alleged racial discrimination in the Islands, namely: attempts to create "white only" residential areas in St. Croix and St. Thomas by white continental immigrants, the operation of two "white only" private clubs in St. Croix, "one instance of reneging on a land sale to a white man when his wife was reported to be colored," and instances of racial discrimination at the Rockefeller-financed Caneel Bay resort on St. John. Despite the fact that Governor Paiewonsky was reported to have felt this problem was "blown out of proportions," the Virgin Islands Legislature created a civil rights commission composed of senators, administrators, and private citizens to investigate complaints of discrimination.[11]

In June, 1961, the Legislature passed a comprehensive "Civil Rights Act" the intent of which was

> to prevent and prohibit discrimination in any form based upon race, creed, color, or national origin, whether practiced directly or indirectly, or by subterfuge in any and all places of public accommodations, resort, or amusement, and in all sales of real estate, goods, articles, accommodations, commodities, or services, and in the employment of persons, or their working conditions, or obtaining union membership, and to prohibit clubs from establishing a private clien-

---

10. *Annual Report of the Governor of the Virgin Islands, 1962*, pp. 2–7.
11. *The New York Times*, May 4, 1961, p. 19, col. 2, and May 7, 1961, p. 130, cols. 3, 4.

tele of either members or guests, which they have selected, and with which persons alone will they transact their business and commerce.[12]

The new Act was based on the Anti-discrimination Act of 1950, but it extended that law to include labor organizations and real estate, and it sought to strengthen the prohibitions against discrimination by private clubs. Maximum penalties were increased from $500 to $2,000 in fines and from ninety days to six months imprisonment. It also provided for any aggrieved person to recover punitive damages up to $5,000 in a civil action.

Condemnation without Representation

The alleged incidents of racial discrimination in 1958 at St. John's Caneel Bay resort, plus other "misunderstandings," had been defused by Laurance Rockefeller's pledge not to buy any more land for the Virgin Islands National Park nor to interfere with community development interests of St. John residents outside the boundaries of the Park. At that time, the Park encompassed over two-thirds of the island of St. John, and it appeared—in view of Rockefeller's promise—that more planned acquisitions by his agents were never to be realized.

In 1962, however, St. John once again became a center of controversy, provoked by a bill before Congress entitled: "An Act to Revise the Boundaries of the Virgin Islands National Park." The bill provided in part for enlargement of the Park through "condemnation" of privately owned lands, and had the approval of the Interior Department, whose Assistant Secretary—John A. Carver—stated: "Authority is needed whereby these lands ... may be acquired by condemnation at their fair market value."[13]

Although the bill had passed the Senate, there incredibly was no evidence that anyone in the Virgin Islands had known of its existence. St. John resident Sabra Holbrook, in her 1969 book, *The American West Indies*, recalled how St. John's 959 residents by chance discovered what Laurance Rockefeller and Congress were intending.

> At six o'clock on the morning of September 1, 1962, George Simmons, the government administrator of Saint John, tuned his radio as usual to an English-speaking station in Puerto Rico and waited for the news. What he heard he could hardly believe. The commentator insisted that the House of Representatives of the United States Congress

---

12. Civil Rights Act, June 9, 1961, Title 10, Chapter 1, par. 1, *Virgin Islands Code*.
13. Quoted by O'Neill, *Rape of the Virgin Islands*, p. 144.

was about to authorize the National Park Service to acquire by *condemnation* another third of Saint John. The condemnation would let the park take not all, but almost all the usable land on the island.[14]

The bill included a provision for appropriation of $1.25 million to acquire St. John property, a sum apparently predicated on an agreement that Rockefeller would offer a matching gift of another $1.25 million. Accordingly, a total of $2.5 million would have become available to compensate land owners refusing to sell, through condemnation if necessary, for enlargement of the Park by 3,300 additional acres, thus permitting the Park to occupy three-quarters of the Island's 12,000 acres.[15]

Within three days after St. John residents first became aware of the bill, they organized their protest and exercised their First Amendment right "to petition the government for a redress of grievances."

Trunk Bay, St. John

14. Sabra Holbrook, *The American West Indies, Puerto Rico and the Virgin Islands* (New York: Meredith Press, 1969), pp. 94–95.

15. *The New York Times*, September 30, 1962, p. 50, cols. 2–3.

Immediately, we all—literally all—wrote, cabled, telephoned or signed petitions as our means afforded. Our one and only representative, Senator Theovald Moorehead, sent 700 signatures to Washington under a plea for a hearing. Our 200 infants were the only non-signers.[16]

The Islanders adopted the slogan—"No Condemnation without Representation!" One resident charged: "What they're doing is just what Castro did. They're appropriating our property. It's not a democratic thing to do."[17]

Former Senator Julius Sprauve, who—representing St. John—had introduced the bill in 1956 in the Virgin Islands Legislature approving the Park, wrote plaintively to Congressman J. T. Rutherford, chairman of the House subcommittee on national parks, that Rockefeller had agreed to eliminate condemnation "as a firm promise forever"; otherwise, the bill would never have been introduced nor approved.

> I consider the recent contrary actions a serious breach of faith and of contract. These islands are our home. We share their beauty gladly. But they are our only happy heritage from an unhappy past. Land ownership is tangible proof of our changed condition. Why should the homes and heritage of nearly a thousand people of Saint John be sacrificed for the brief gratification of short time ... Park visitors who have their own safe homes to return to on our mainland? We too are "natural objects," as Park signs say. We merit at least equal protection as such.
>
> I am particularly grieved by Mr. Rockefeller's offer of matching money for condemnation. I cannot understand the distortions in human thinking that make such philanthropy somehow expressive of the love of man. It comes hard at my age to learn that Saint John has been made the victim of a powerful financial and bureaucratic team-up with a different morality than our own.
>
> I wish to make it clear that I have no objection if owners wish to sell their land. But I shall do all I can in my declining years to prevent the use of force on those not desiring to sell.[18]

Governor Ralph Paiewonsky and the Virgin Islands Legislature joined the protest. Irate Virgin Islanders flew to Washington. Finally, Congressman Ruther-

---

16. Letter to the Editor from Charlotte Dean Stark, St. John, V. I., September 7, 1962, *The New York Times*, September 15, 1962, p. 24, col. 5.

17. Anthony Lukas, "A Grandmother Fights Congress," *The New York Times*, September 10, 1962, p. 19, col. 1.

18. Quoted by Holbrook, *The American West Indies*, p. 98.

ford made a hurried trip to St. John, accompanied by a lawyer representing Laurance Rockefeller. There Rutherford assured St. Johnians that he would move to delete the condemnation provision from the bill. The Islanders were also assured that Mr. Rockefeller, himself, no longer favored condemnation, and, indeed, he had urged from the beginning that condemnation proceedings shall never be invoked.[19] Edward O'Neill in his book, *Rape of the Virgin Islands*, later reflected:

> It might have been more accurate to say that Rockefeller had decided that the proposal had caused too much trouble and had withdrawn his matching $1.25 million.... Why should Laurance Rockefeller, sitting in his office at 30 Rockefeller Plaza, have the power, denied to him in this instance only by a fluke of Capitol Hill reportage, to use the democratic processes of the U.S. legislature to take over the people's homes, however environmentally protective and philanthropic his motives? ... Particularly disturbing is Congress's nearly automatic reaction to the Rockefeller offer, without even bothering to send a committee staff assistant to look into the situation. And even more disturbing is the eager support given the project by Assistant Secretary Carver, under whose jurisdiction the Office of Territories and hence the Virgin Islands came, without so much as sounding out St. Johnian opinion.[20]

With Rockefeller's demurrer, together with the organized protests of St. Johnians, the bill finally passed without the condemnation provision and appropriation of government funds. "Saint Johnians had proved," recounted Sabra Holbrook, "that democracy works if people work."[21]

Impact of Tourism

Aside from sun, sand, and surf offered to tourists in St. John, St. Thomas, and St. Croix, other factors induced tourists to visit the Virgin Islands in ever increasing numbers since the Second World War. The Danish heritage in a West Indian setting was of unique historic interest. All but the largest cruise vessels could use the excellent docking facilities of Denmark's West India Company, in the scenic harbor of Charlotte Amalie, that continued to operate since the

---

19. Lukas, "A Grandmother Fights Congress."
20. O'Neill, *Rape of the Virgin Islands*, pp. 147–148.
21. Holbrook, *The American West Indies*, p. 103.

days of Danish rule. The decline of agricultural activity—particularly sugar cane production—made the Islands more receptive to tourism. Economic growth on the U.S. mainland greatly increased leisure time, early retirement, and disposable personal income—developments that could only spur tourism. The Virgin Islands profited from the revolution in air travel—direct jet service from New York to St. Croix beginning in 1962, and to St. Thomas in 1966. Increased trans-Atlantic air travel released many passenger ships for Caribbean cruises including visits to the Virgin Islands.[22]

The six percent ad valorem duty on all foreign goods entering the Islands, assessed since Danish times, caused imported luxury goods to be available in the Islands at substantially lower prices than on the mainland, thus permitting the misnomer of "free port" to be applied to the Islands when, in fact, they comprised simply a low customs duty area attractive to tourists. Since the closing of Havana to American trade and tourism in 1959 and the special additional customs exemption granted U.S. territories in 1961, St. Thomas became the most popular and busiest cruise port in the Caribbean. The number of cruise ships visiting the Islands increased from one hundred and twenty-six in 1960 to five hundred and seven in 1970, and the estimated tourist expenditures during the development decade increased from $25 million in 1960 to over $100 million in 1970.[23] Together with greatly increased tourism promotion and facilities in the Islands, these various factors combined by 1965 to make tourism the prime source of phenomenal economic development of the Islands.

It is not overstatement to suggest that practically every aspect of Virgin Islands life was affected appreciably—either directly or indirectly—by the impact of the tourism boom of the 1960s. No literature existed specifically concerning the social, economic, and cultural impact of tourism on the Virgin Islands until Martin Carson Orlins completed his 494-page doctoral dissertation on this subject at Columbia University in 1969. Orlins' dissertation, which was never published, examined tourist impact up to 1966.[24]

Heavily economic in analysis and emphasis, Orlins attributed to tourism the following direct and indirect consequences in the Islands: dependence on

---

22. For detailed discussion of factors inducing tourism in the Islands, see: Martin Garson Orlins, *The Impact of Tourism on the Virgin Islands of the United States* (unpublished Ph.D. dissertation, Columbia University, 1969), pp. 83–132.

23. "United States Virgin Islands Comparative Growth Statistics, 1960–1977," *Daily News*, June 16, 1978, p. 12.

24. Orlins, *The Impact of Tourism*. See, also, Gordon K. Lewis, "The U.S. Virgin Islands: Prototype of the Caribbean Tourist Economy," in T. G. Mathews and F. M. Andic, eds., *Politics and Economics in the Caribbean* (Rio Pietras, Puerto Rico: Institute of Caribbean Studies, University of Puerto Rico, 1971), pp. 217–243.

imports for material goods; inducement of construction and some manufacturing; increasing labor and land costs and hence increasing cost-of-living; increasing income and standard of living; full employment and employment opportunities in excess of the insular labor supply; importation of alien workers who already constituted half the local labor force in 1966; greatly increased insular government revenues and expenditures and government employment of native Virgin Islanders; increasing population and changing population composition; changing economic and political power structures; changing land ownership; observance of more holidays; changes in the general tenor of island life; construction of transient tourist facilities and "resident tourist homes"; the growth of "suburban occupance"; and the appearance of "certain hostility ... between some of the island population and some service employees on the one hand and tourists on the other."[25]

Orlins defined native Virgin Islanders as those born in the Islands who are "the Negro and mulatto descendants of the former Island slaves and of the Negroes and mulattos who have migrated to the Islands, particularly from the British Caribbean." Orlins estimated that at the beginning of the tourist era (about 1950), native Virgin Islanders constituted about two-thirds to three-quarters of the total insular population, but by 1965 they comprised less than half the total. The following table, adapted from Orlins' dissertation, illustrates dramatic population changes, particularly in the five-year period, 1960–1965:[26]

Table 6. Estimated Composition of Virgin Islands Population by Groups, 1950, 1960, 1965

	1950	1960	1965
Native	19,600	20,000	22,000
Alien	1,000	2,000	10,000
Puerto Rican	3,000	6,000	9,700
Old French	1,500	1,500	1,500
Continental	1,500	3,900	6,500
Total	26,600	33,400	49,700

Source: Martin Carson Orlins, *The Impact of Tourism on the Virgin Islands of the United States* (unpublished Ph.D. dissertation, Columbia University, 1969), p. 331.

If Orlins' figures are approximately correct, then 1965 may be regarded as a watershed year in the cultural history of the Virgin Islands. By that year, every population group in the Islands constituted a minority group. Native Virgin Is-

---

25. Orlins, *The Impact of Tourism*, pp. 1–3.
26. *Ibid.*, pp. 324–325, 331.

landers had lost, seemingly forever, their majority position in their own home-land, and a certain xenophobia was born. Orlins catalogued the following "re-sentments, or reactions, against the growing continental group" harbored by "many" natives:

(a) The benefits of economic growth have gone mainly to the continen-tals who virtually monopolize all modern and large businesses in con-trast to the few native business successes.

(b) Continentals are accused of being mercenary, on the Islands only for the gains they can make, and will depart when they can no longer profit.

(c) Continentals have caused land values to rise making it very difficult for the average native to own his own home.

(d) While the few early continental residents mixed with natives, now that their numbers are greater they tend to limit themselves to their own group. (The luxurious developments, which resemble enclaves, en-courage this resentment.)

(e) Continental children go to private and parochial schools to keep away from native children.

(f) The Islands are being changed and physical and political control is being taken from the natives.[27]

Far from predicting a dire future for natives and other groups, however, Orlins was an optimist. Although acknowledging that tourists create problems for their hosts, he considered that "the views of the professional sociologists tend to be narrow and inflammatory."

> While the problems resulting from the reactions of poor Negroes to serving affluent whites are inescapable, a brighter future lies in a more lucid and wider appreciation in host areas of the economic necessity for tourism, and of pride rather than humiliation in occupational service. The possible crime, juvenile delinquency, and illusory values which may result from the introduction of large numbers of affluent visitors into poor host areas are the "industrial hazards" of tourism as silicosis is of certain mining operations. With knowledge and under-standing these problems may be minimized.[28]

Orlins' disdain of sociologists was not shared by the headmaster of St. Dun-stan's school on St. Croix, Father Charles Hawes, an Episcopalian priest, who described St. Croix life in the 1960s, as follows:

---

27. *Ibid.*, p. 339.
28. *Ibid.*, p. 381.

Your whites live *here*. Your Crucian blacks live *here*. Your West Indian blacks live *here*. Your Puerto Ricans live *here*. And your continental whites live at the east end. Any sociologist looking at this exclusive grouping by culture and background would laugh at the notion that there is no problem. It is a terrible problem. A Crucian said to me, "The white man came to St. Croix and he took our beaches and in return he gave our women pink hair curlers."

I was appointed by the governor [Governor Ralph Paiewonsky] to a Human Relations Commission. It folded almost as soon as it was called. This was because we thought the hearings ought to be made public and the power of subpoena be given. We wanted to bring up a well-known citizen to testify. This ended it. This was a man widely known for the way he intimidated alien workers. He is not alone in doing this. There are plenty of others. The method is simple. if the alien bonded worker offends in any way, his bond is canceled and he must leave the island. Of course, the most common "offense" is to ask for the promised raise to the legal minimum. This is a polite form of slavery. There is really no use talking to people who do this. You get nowhere....

The economic side of the power here is white. The hotels are white-owned, white-managed. The two major industries here were expected to employ the local labor force. Yet their plants are highly automated and almost run themselves. The workers they require are semi-skilled to skilled labor. The management is white. The home offices are in the States. There is not much autonomy there. Tourism and industry are the chief economic determinants. They are controlled by a very small number of white people. You look at the other side of the picture: government and the vote. All appears well because the government is basically black and native. To what extent is this black government controlled well beyond where it ought to be by the small white economic oligarchy?[29]

Harvey and Hess

After the Second World War, Virgin Islanders were less willing to continue agricultural work, with the result that the Virgin Islands Corporation increas-

---

29. Quoted by Ellis Gladwin, *Living in the Changing Caribbean* (New York: "The Macmillan Company, 1970), pp. 64–66.

ingly resorted to importing agricultural labor to St. Croix from the British West Indies. Accordingly, VICORP—originally (as VICO) established to provide employment for Crucians—paradoxically found itself in the anomalous position of importing foreign workers to harvest sugar cane at substantial losses. These annual losses were covered by federal deficit funding. Thus the federal government was subsidizing an unprofitable enterprise for the benefit of foreign workers.[30]

Although Congress in 1958 extended VICORP's charter for ten years to 1969, Congress intended that period to be one of gradual liquidation of VICORP. The disposition of VICORP's land holdings was completed by 1965, and its electric power and salt water distillation facilities were sold to the insular government to be managed by the newly-created Water and Power Authority. The Harry S. Truman Airport and submarine base in St. Thomas were also transferred to the Virgin Islands government to be managed by the new Virgin Islands Development Authority.[31]

The tourism boom of the 1960s facilitated VICORP's demise. Although VICO/VICORP had thwarted starvation and ameliorated the most abject conditions of poverty accompanying periods of acute depression, and had even contributed to economic development of the Islands, the economic base of the Islands had shifted from agriculture to tourism. Along with the abandonment of sugarcane production, therefore, VICORP was officially ended on June 30, 1966—three years before its charter was due to expire. The federal corporation had served its purpose and no longer could be justified. Thus ended one of the most extreme examples of socialism ever experienced anywhere under the American flag.[32]

To cushion the shock of agricultural decline and the end of VICORP activities, the insular government revised and extended its industrial incentives program to attract private industries to the Islands. In addition, special provisions of the U.S. tariff laws permitted shipment duty-free from the Virgin Islands to

---

30. For testimony revealing Congressional frustration and discontent concerning federal subsidy of VICORP's foreign workers, see, *e.g.*, *Hearings ... Activities, supra*, ch. 9, n. 3 at pp. 496–502, 808–810.

31. For the rise and fall of VICO/VICORP, see: Dookhan, "The Virgin Islands Company and Corporation," pp. 54–76.

32. That VICO/VICORP represented a socialist-type enterprise depends on the definition of socialism as government ownership and administration of the means of production.

33. Division of Trade and Industry, Department of Commerce, *Facts About Doing Business in the U.S. Virgin Islands* (Government of the Virgin Islands, 1974), p. 16.

the mainland of manufactured goods to which at least 50 percent of value had been added by processing in the Islands.[33]

The Virgin Islands Tax Incentive Act was amended every year inclusively between 1961 and 1965 to promote the establishment of private enterprise. Not only were new businesses eligible for ten-year exemptions from local real estate and excise taxes, but they were also eligible for ten-year non-taxable subsidies equal to 90 percent of federal duties on imports into the Islands of materials needed for industrial production or manufacturing, and equal to 75 percent of federal income taxes.

Two important conditions were imposed by the Act on a tax exempted or subsidized industry or business, namely: (1) not less than 75 percent of all its employees were required to be "legal residents of the Virgin Islands," and (2) "the employer agrees not to discriminate against any employee because of race, religion or color."[34]

Taking advantage of the U.S. tariff and local tax incentive laws were fifteen watch companies (eleven on St. Croix and four on St. Thomas) and five textile mills (four on St. Croix and one on St. Thomas). In 1964, eleven local watch companies assembled approximately nine percent of all watch movements consumed in the United States.[35]

Administration of the insular Tax Incentive Act was vested in the Virgin Islands Industrial Incentive Board, except that the Governor was specifically authorized by the amendment of 1962 "to extend similar tax exemption and subsidy benefits" to industries "locating new enterprises in the Virgin Islands ...

---

34. *Virgin Islands Tax Incentive Act*, Reprinted from Title 33 *Virgin Islands Code* (Office of the Government Secretary, St. Thomas, Virgin Islands, 1965) sections 4051, 4052, 4061, 4071.

35. Survival of the Islands watch assembly industry was threatened in 1965–1966 by an investigation by the U.S. Federal Trade Commission which uncovered abuses of the tariff 50 percent clause whereby watch parts processed in other countries were exported duty free into the U.S. The watch industry of the Islands also was fast becoming "a serious threat to the U.S. watch industry and labor." Congress finally passed a law in 1966 establishing an import quota for the Virgin Islands watch industry of one-ninth of the U.S. total yearly consumption of watches. *Annual Report of the Governor of the Virgin Islands, 1966*, pp. 29–32; U.S. Congress, Public Law 89-805, November 10, 1966. Local legislation authorized the Governor to assign similar quotas for the control of the flow of woven woolen yard goods through the Virgin Islands into the United States because "any substantial increase ... would create a most difficult situation." *Ibid.*, p. 26, and *ibid.*, *1967*, pp. 32–35.

36. *Virgin Islands Tax Incentive Act*, section 4092. In *Virgo Corporation v. Paiewonsky*, 259 F. Supp. 26 (1966) Judge Walter Gordon of the Virgin Islands District Court held that Governor Paiewonsky's refusal under this section to grant tax benefits and subsidies to the Virgo Corporation because of "its substantial profit return" was invalid. "It ... is quite clear that the Legislature intended the Governor to use his discretion only to determine if the busi-

and having … effect upon the economic development of the Virgin Islands, such extension of benefits to be subject to the approval of the Legislature."[36] By virtue of this special authorization to the Governor, extraordinary benefits were extended with the approval of the legislature to two giant industries— Harvey Alumina Company and Hess Oil Company—to build and operate industrial establishments on St. Croix, the first heavy industries ever attracted to the Virgin Islands.

The introduction of two sizable transnational corporations into the fragile St. Croix environment was contemporaneous with accelerated investment enterprise during the 1960s of American-based global corporations in less developed countries throughout the world. The Virgin Islands were to share with those countries most of the attendant problems experienced by poor countries from the exogenous intrusion of international business enterprises—problems borne of ambivalent suspension between overwhelming economic dependence and the quest for integrity, dignity, and self-determination. The major difference between dependent countries elsewhere and the Virgin Islands, of course, was the fact that the latter (along with the two multinationals) were under the American flag. But this fact only enhanced the leverage of the multinationals and the Islands' dependence on them. In short, Virgin Islanders were no match for Harvey and Hess whose power, wealth, and manipulative skills procured for them investment deals among the most generous ever negotiated from a host polity.

In January 1962, Harvey Alumina was authorized by the Virgin Islands government to construct a $25 million alumina processing plant on the south shore of St. Croix and to develop a contiguous port for the importing of bauxite from which the plant would extract alumina. The government's justification was that Harvey would "alleviate underemployment." The Corporation, however, would never meet the government's condition that at least 75 percent of its employees would be "legal residents" if this condition were interpreted to mean they had to be Virgin Islanders, which obviously was the intent. Only twenty of four hundred and seventy-one persons employed by the company in 1970 were reported to be Virgin Islanders, most of the remainder being imported aliens while others were white continentals. Harvey stored its bauxite in piles, and Crucians soon complained of the red dust blown by the tradewinds over neighboring areas. The extractive process produced a caustic red mud that polluted

---

ness will promote the public interest by economic development of the Virgin Islands." *Ibid.*, at p. 28.

37. O'Neill, *Rape of the Virgin Islands*, pp. 117–118.

nearby waters. Although Martin-Marietta bought control of the company from Leo Harvey in 1970, despoilation of the Island's ecology continued.[37]

The agreement with Harvey provided a model for the 1965 agreement with Hess. It was reported that banker David Rockefeller induced Leon Hess to build his oil refinery on St. Croix.[38] There were a number of favorable circumstances to minimize risk. During the 1960s, the quota on the import of heavy oil into the United States was raised, and the major oil companies rushed to the Caribbean to establish refining facilities. Whereas Exxon went to Aruba, Royal Dutch/Shell to Curacao, and Texaco to Trinidad, Leon Hess decided in 1965 to build his refinery—which would become the world's largest—next to Harvey's plant on the south shore of St. Croix. Not only was it cheaper, because of lower wages, to build a refinery and to process oil in the Caribbean than on the mainland, but Hess had the advantage under the Stars and Stripes on St. Croix to be classified as a domestic rather than a foreign refinery—an advantage with respect to U.S. import quotas. The Jones Act, moreover, specifically exempted the Virgin Islands—the only such favored area under U.S. jurisdiction—from the requirement that only U.S. vessels be used for transportation between U.S. ports. Accordingly, Hess could use foreign tankers, at 25 to 45 percent lower rates, to carry oil to U.S. ports.[39]

Many Crucians opposed the introduction of heavy industry into St. Croix, but the Paiewonsky-Ottley machine prevailed. Governor Paiewonsky's rationale was that St. Croix attracted only about one-third the number of tourists visiting St. Thomas, and that heavy industry would help alleviate the economic distress of Crucians now that sugar cane production was ending.[40]

During Paiewonsky's governorship, the insular legislature passed nine laws and two resolutions in support of the Hess proposal to invest $70 million in St. Croix, including a $30 million petrochemical plant (that was never to materialize). Hess was given permission to build its own port, and was granted since September 1, 1965 a return of 75 percent of income taxes (a benefit also extended to Virgin Islanders on dividends from their investments in Hess stock) plus complete exemption from paying: the 6 percent ad valorem duty on all im-

---

38. *Ibid.*, p. 119.

39. Tad Szulc, "Playing for High Stakes in the Virgin Islands," *Forbes*, August 1, 1977, p. 53.

40. Virtually all cruise ships in the 1960s stopped only at St. Thomas, and very few visited St. Croix, with the result that the tourist industry in St. Croix was "not as evident as in St. Thomas." Orlins, *The Impact of Tourism*, pp. 107–109. For Crucian opposition to heavy industry, see Florence Lewisohn, *St. Croix Under Seven Flags* (Hollywood, Florida: Dukane Press, 1970), pp. 397–401.

ports, all real estate taxes, all excise taxes on building and raw materials, and the gross receipts tax of 2 percent. All tax exemptions were to remain in effect until 1981.[41]

For its part, Hess promised that at least 75 percent of its employees would be "legal residents of the Virgin Islands." This provision of the Tax Incentive Act was never to be enforced in the Virgin Islands. Although Hess steadfastly refused to divulge the origins of its employees, only about 10 percent of its 1970 workforce were reported to be native Virgin Islanders. Hess also shared with Harvey many complaints about air and water pollution. With its 1969 merger with the huge Amerada Petroleum Corporation, Amerada-Hess figured to assume an even more commanding role on St. Croix.[42]

Donkeycrats and Unicrats

Governor Paiewonsky's effectiveness in winning consistent support for his policies and proposals from a pliant legislature, including generous inducements for Harvey and Hess, was attributable to the alliance he formed with Senator Earle Ottley—leader of the so-called Unity Party—which assured predictable majority votes of the legislature. The Paiewonsky-Ottley alliance during most of the 1960s represented an unprecedented and unparalleled period of executive-legislative cooperation in the history of America's Virgin Islands. It was a painfully procured and sustained alliance, however, because it split the Democratic Party, fostered a vituperative opposition, and presaged political realignments that were to change the insular political system.

From the inception of American rule, the heavy weight of Washington-based bureaucratic power had deterred and delayed the maturation of extra-bureaucratic political institutions in the Islands, including the legislature and political parties. This familiar legacy of colonialism, of course, would be experienced by most developing countries emerging from colonial status after the Second World War.

During Navy rule of the Islands, local political clubs were formed to agitate for self-government, and these clubs gained strength as nascent political parties after the 1936 Organic Act broadened the suffrage. These parties, however, were virtually private clubs with dues-paying members. Something akin to an embryonic two-party system had emerged during the 1950s in the for-

---

41. Szulc, "Playing for High Stakes."
42. O'Neill, *Rape of the Virgin Islands*, pp. 126, 128.

mation of two factions of the Democratic Party—the Unity Democrats (Unicrats) under the leadership of Senator Earle B. Ottley, with the Mortar and Pestle as its symbol, and the Donkey Democrats (Donkeycrats).[43]

After enactment of the 1954 Revised Organic Act and a unified legislature, control of the legislature had vacillated between a coalition of Donkeycrats and Republicans on one side and Unicrats on the other side, with a few Independents switching between the two factions. The strength of the Donkeycrats was in St. Croix and of the Unicrats in St. Thomas—a distinction that both reflected and sharpened the historic rivalry between the two islands. Meanwhile, Ralph Paiewonsky, identified with the Donkeycrat faction, had served from 1940 to 1960 as the territory's representative on the Democratic National Committee, only to be defeated for that post by Crucian Donkeycrat Ron de Lugo in 1960, a defeat that Paiewonsky never forgave despite de Lugo's strong endorsement of Paiewonsky for the governorship during his Senate confirmation hearings in 1961.

As a result of the 1962 election, the legislature in 1963 comprised a narrow six to five working majority for the Unicrats. Governor Paiewonsky's decision to align himself with Unicrat leader Ottley set the stage for the Unicrats' attempt to take over control of the Democratic Party.

The Paiewonsky-Ottley alliance succeeded in taking control of the Democratic Party through a series of extraordinarily convoluted and highly dubious moves, including: (1) adoption of a new election code, (2) stripping Government Secretary Cyril King of his powers, (3) expropriation of the Democratic Party label, (4) adoption of a controversial "loyalty oath," (5) swelling the number of government employees loyal to the Paiewonsky-Ottley alliance, (6) declassification and dismissal of disloyal employees, and intimidation of others, (7) open violation of the Hatch Acts, and (8) the practice of election irregularities. All of these practices were fully documented in the seven hundred and thirty-seven pages of the 1967 Congressional hearings.[44]

The Election Code of 1963 provided for the legal recognition of political parties through nominations by primary elections in place of conventions,

---

43. For development of political parties and factions in the Islands, see, *e.g.*: Hill, *Rise to Recognition*, pp. 91–109; Lewis, *The Virgin Islands*, pp. 320–343; O'Neill, *Rape of the Virgin Islands*, pp. 54–100, 153–173; and Creque, *The U.S. Virgin Islands*, pp. 184–189. For the period 1960–1967, the best source is: *Hearings before the House Subcommittee on Territorial and Insular Affairs, Election of Virgin Islands Governor*, 90th Cong., 1st sess., Parts I and II (1967), esp. pp. 21–32, 46–62, 86–122, 250–283, 295–298, 416–417: hereafter cited as: *Hearings, Election of ... Governor* (1967).

44. *Hearings, Election of ... Governor* (1967).

granted each registered voter the privilege to enroll in a political party, and provided for the election of territorial committees by party members. Administration of the election machinery was vested in a new supervisor of elections—appointed by Paiewonsky and approved by the Unicrat-controlled legislature—a power previously vested in the Government Secretary. Cyril King obviously was being punished for his continued loyalty to the Donkeycrat faction. Other powers removed from King by the machine included his authority over: the Division of Personnel in 1962, the Industrial Incentive Program in 1965, the Board of Tax Review in 1966, and the Division of Licensing of Businesses and Occupations in 1967.[45]

Under the new election code, the Unicrat leaders formally dissolved the Unity Party when they filed a petition signed by one hundred and sixty-five voters with the supervisor of elections registering the Unity Party under the name of the Democratic Party of the Virgin Islands. Although the Donkeycrats had already filed under the Democratic Party label with the supervisor, and the election code required the supervisor to hold a hearing in such a situation "to determine which petition shall be accepted," Supervisor Henrita Todman refused to hold such a hearing. The result was that candidates of both factions contested for election to the Territorial Committee of the Democratic Party with Unicrats winning sixteen seats (twelve at-large and four from St. Thomas) and Donkeycrats winning the remaining six (from St. Croix and St. John). Donkeycrats brought suit against Supervisor Todman in the District Court of the Virgin Islands charging that the Unicrats had unlawfully taken

---

45. *Ibid.*, pp. 26, 279. In a series of extraordinary open letters, the first two addressed to Senator Ottley and the last to Governor Paiewonsky, Judge Albert B. Maris, Senior judge of the U.S. Court of Appeals for the 3rd Circuit, stated his objections to the revised Election Code of 1963, summarized as follows: "(1) that he was of the opinion the Government Secretary would be a better officer to supervise the elections; (2) that he was concerned by the changes ... with respect to the definition of a political party ... because the Supervisor of Elections would be the one to determine which parties would be recognized; (3) that the presently existing parties who actually supported candidates in the 1962 election should be given the right to use their present names; (4) that it will not help the Virgin Islands to secure greater home rule to precipitate a bitter contest between the two leading parties as to which one would use 'democratic' in their name ... ; (5) that it should be necessary for a person to be enrolled as a party member before that person could participate in voting in a party primary or serve as an officer of that party; and (6) that the elimination from the act of the Corrupt Practices Act which would limit and regulate the expenditure of money at the primaries and elections" was in error because such provision "is a necessary feature of a good election law." *Ibid.*, pp. 144–145. Judge Maris' three letters appeared verbatim in the *Daily News*, February 19, March 12, and March 28, 1963.

over the Democratic Party. The immediate ensuing events after election of the Territorial Committee were recited by the Court as follows:

> The election for the Territorial Committee … was held on November 1, 1963…. But at the first meeting, the six members of the plaintiff refused to sit at the meeting. As a result thereof the six members of the Unity Party who were defeated in the primary election took their places with the remaining sixteen members of the Unity Party to comprise the Territorial Committee of the Democratic Party of the Virgin Islands which had been wrongfully certified by the Supervisor of Elections.
>
> The twenty-two members who were nominated by the plaintiff to the Territorial Committee … then proceeded to hold meetings and at all times thereafter considered themselves as the governing body of the Democratic Party.
>
> At no time was there communication between the plaintiff and the Unity Party. Neither group invited the other group to join and participate in the opposing group's activities. Each group at all times considered itself a separate and distinct entity.
>
> To further its scheme to take over the plaintiff party, the Unity Party through the wrongfully constituted Territorial Committee, drafted certain rules and procedures. Included in these rules was a provision which abolished all Democratic Clubs. Other rules were promulgated which stated that no group could form a club in the Democratic Party of the Virgin Islands, unless approved by the Territorial Committee…. This clever device would expel all members of the plaintiff from its clubs and would complete the takeover by the Unity Party of the plaintiff.[46]

Departing from the usual practice of American jurists of stating the facts of a case objectively, District Judge Walter Gordon set forth the facts in this case in a manner obviously prejudicial to the Unicrats. Six years beforehand, he had resigned the governorship after Unicrat leader Ottley led three thousand demonstrators calling for his removal "because of his incompetence." Apparently, it did not occur now to Gordon to disqualify himself from hearing this case for reason of bias against the Unicrats. Concluding that the Unity Party "through a fraudulent, collusive and conspiratorial scheme" took over the Democratic Party, Judge Gordon enjoined the Unicrats from continuing as mem-

---

46. *Alexander v. Todman*, 231 F. Supp. 368, 371 (1964).
47. *Ibid.*, pp. 374–376. See, also, *Alexander v. Todman*, 231 F. Supp. 365 (1964).

bers of the Territorial Committee and ordered Supervisor of Elections Henrita Todman to certify the Donkeycrat nominees "as the only valid Territorial Committee of the Democratic Party of the Virgin Islands."[47]

The Unicrats promptly appealed to the Third Circuit Court of Appeals in Philadelphia which reversed Judge Gordon's decision on the ground that there was a lack of conclusive evidence that the Unicrats committed "fraud and deceit" in achieving control of the Democratic Party.[48] Darwin Creque hailed the Unicrat triumph as "the most momentous judicial decision affecting the political future of the U.S. Virgin Islands."[49]

Finally in complete control of the Democratic Party of the Virgin Islands, Unicrats proceeded to win as Democratic Party candidates six of the eleven seats of the legislature in the 1964 election, relegating the remaining five seats to Donkeycrats who had to run as Independents now that the Democratic Party label was denied them.

Unicrats nevertheless feared that the Donkeycrats would once again form a coalition with the Republican Party, as they did in the late 1950s, to run in the general election of 1966. Accordingly, the Unicrat-controlled legislature amended the Election Code to stop this coalition. First, the legislature legislated the Republican Party out of existence by requiring that no political party shall be recognized, any at-large candidate of which had not polled at least five percent of the total votes cast in the last preceding election. Since no Republican at-large candidate had received five percent of the ballots cast in the 1964 election, Republican Party candidates would not appear on the ballot for the 1966 election. Fortunately for Republicans, however, "pressure from Washington" allegedly induced the legislature to once again amend the Election Code to legally recognize "the officially recognized" political party affiliate in the Virgin Islands of either of the two major national political parties.[50]

Next, to prevent Donkeycrats from running in the 1966 general election, Governor Paiewonsky submitted a bill, which the legislature approved on August 13, 1966, further amending the Election Code—this time to implement party symbol voting and to require voting for all primary candidates on an at-large basis, which would have given the well-disciplined Paiewonsky-Ottley majority all the seats of the legislature. Two weeks later, however, Congress in effect repealed this short-lived measure by amending the 1954 Revised Organic

---

48. *Alexander v. Todman*, 361 F.2d 744 (1964).

49. Creque, *The U.S. Virgin Islands*, p. 186.

50. *Hearings, Election of … Governor* (1967), p. 146.

51. Public Law 89-548, sec. 1, 80 *Stat.* 371, August 30, 1966. The term of office of each senator remained two years, but Congress raised each senator's compensation from $600 to $6,000 per year in 1966 and to $9,000 in 1967.

Act to increase the number of legislative seats from eleven to fifteen, effective for the upcoming general election of 1966, and designating five senators from St. Croix, five from St. Thomas, one from St. John, and four at large.[51]

Undaunted by setbacks, the Unicrats meanwhile enacted, by a six to five vote in the legislature, a loyalty oath requiring every person, who sought to be a candidate of a political party for public office in the 1966 primary election, to sign an oath of allegiance to that political party, as follows:

> I, _____, do solemnly pledge that I will espouse and pursue the principles and policies of the _____ Party of the Virgin Islands and that I will support every candidate of the _____ Party who is nominated for public office at the 1966 primary election and I will not support any candidate or any other political party or body or any independent candidate for public office at the 1966 general election.[52]

Refusal to sign the oath barred appearance of a person's name on the primary election ballot. Republican Party officers immediately challenged the loyalty oath's legality in the local U.S. District Court where two Unicrat senators admitted that the purpose of the loyalty oath was to frustrate and interfere with any coalition between Donkeycrats and Republicans in the forthcoming 1966 general election.[53]

The nomination petition of the Territorial Committee of the Republican Party nominating fifteen candidates had been filed with the supervisor of elections who refused to accept the petition without the prescribed party loyalty oath. Judge Walter Gordon, for the District Court, ordered the supervisor to accept the petition. Since no other nomination petitions for Republican candidates were filed, he reasoned, the fifteen petitioners became the Republican nominees without the need for holding a Republican primary election. There was no necessity for determining the legality of the loyalty oath, therefore, because it was applicable only for candidates in primary elections.[54]

On appeal, speaking for the Circuit Court of Appeals, Judge Maris agreed. Although he, too, did not pass on the oath's legality, there was no question what he thought of it. The oath might be regarded as a "political test" in violation of the Revised Organic Act, Maris observed.

---

52. *Canton v. Todman*, 259 F. Supp. 22, 24 (1966).
53. *Hearings, Election of ... Governor* (1967), p. 57 at n. 1.
54. *Canton v. Todman*, 259 F. Supp. 22, 24 (1966).

Here the pledge to pursue indefinitely the principles and policies of a political party, presumably those principles and policies announced from time to time by the party organization, would tend to bind the legislators to the party leaders without individual freedom of thought or independence of action, tied up and delivered like bunches of beets. This is what happens in totalitarian countries where legislators vote like automatons as their party leaders tell them to, but it is not the practice in free America where our democratic heritage can best be preserved if legislators are free to employ in the discharge of their duties their own individual views and judgment in the light of their own personal responsibility as representatives of the whole community.[55]

Meanwhile, a purportedly disgruntled Republican challenged the legality of the same petition because the fifteen candidates endorsed by the Republican Territorial Committee included "so-called 'Donkey-Crats', thereby permitting alleged Democrats to seek election under the aegis of the Republican Party." Both District and Circuit Courts held, however, that the challenge was made too late.[56] Accordingly, all means to keep the Donkeycrats off the ballot in 1966 failed. The ballot, itself, depicted a veritable "political zoology" that became the wonder and despair of visiting Congressmen.[57]

Departing rather sharply from the nonpartisan role of previous governors in past elections, Governor Paiewonsky campaigned vigorously for the Ottley-supported Unicrats against the Republican-Donkeycrat coalition. The result was another victory for the Paiewonsky-Ottley ticket, with Unicrats (appearing on the ballot as "Democrats") winning nine seats of the newly-expanded legislature of fifteen members, including all four at-large seats and the five St. Thomas seats. The coalition candidates (all of them Donkeycrats appearing on the ballot as "Victory-66" candidates) won the five St. Croix seats and the single St. John seat.

---

55. *Canton v. Todman*, 367 F.2d 1005, 1008–1009 (1966).

56. *Williams v. Todman*, 367 F.2d 1009 (1966). There was some speculation that plaintiff Earl Williams' financing of this litigation actually was provided by Unicrats. *Hearings, Election of ... Governor* (1967), p. 59.

57. *Hearings, Election of ... Governor* (1967), p. 104. Congressman Burton of Utah observed: "I have never seen such a fouled-up ballot in my life as this one used in the November 8, 1966 election down there.... To look at this ballot, I wouldn't know who I was voting for if I didn't know the people involved." *Ibid.*, pp. 570–571.

58. *Ibid.*, p. 89. At the Congressional hearings of 1967, allegations of a number of unlawful and unfair practices on the part of Unicrats were put forward, including: dismissal of key government employees who remained loyal to the Donkeycrat faction; transfer of certain positions from classified to unclassified status to deny dismissed career employees

Ron de Lugo, Donkeycrat chairman and himself a defeated at-large candidate in the 1966 election, charged before a Congressional subcommittee that the election was rigged and many voting irregularities occurred, especially on St. Croix. He claimed that an "army of unclassified political appointees" campaigned at the taxpayer's expense in violation of the Hatch Act.[58] Curiously, Governor Paiewonsky not only acknowledged violation of the Hatch Act, but he admitted that twenty-five of the twenty-six members of his 1966 election campaign committee were government employees. He explained, however, that this issue had never been raised before, and in all previous elections "every local government employee took a most active part in the campaigning and in the electioneering for positions for the legislature."[59]

With regard to Senator Ottley, de Lugo claimed:

At the present time the real political power in these Virgin Islands resides in one man's hands and one man's only, and that is Senator Earle B. Ottley, the president of the legislature. He chooses who shall be the supervisor of elections. He decides who shall be the members of the board of elections. He decides who shall be the election officials on election day. I could go on and on.[60]

Ottley's failure to testify before the Congressional subcommittee, supposedly because of illness, was greatly resented by some Congressmen.[61] Paiewonsky's testimony sought to tag a "sour grapes" label on Donkeycrats as poor losers "in an orderly and honest election."

It has been the consistent strategy of the so-called "Independent Donkey Democrats" to deny the existence of the duly recognized Democratic Party. Essentially it is the diehard notion of the Donkey group that at some point in time they preempted in perpetuity the philosophy, platforms, name and all other rights appurtenant to the Demo-

---

the right to appeal; creation of many new unclassified positions to reward Unicrat supporters; intimidation of career employees with threats of dismissal and denial of salary increases and promotions of those who failed to subscribe to Unicrat policies; threats of government reprisals against employees of firms enjoying benefits of the tax incentive program; illegal threats and pressures against residents of public housing projects; and failure to give equal rights, staff, and other support to Donkeycrat legislators. *Ibid.*, pp. 60–61, 250–260, 277–279, 311–323, 365, 591–593, 618–624.

59. *Ibid.*, pp. 499, 500.
60. *Ibid.*, p. 110.
61. *Ibid.*, p. 554.
62. *Ibid.*, p. 414, 416.

cratic Party, and no amount of popular votes to the contrary can ever change that fact.[62]

Still not satisfied, Unicrats devised a 1967 reapportionment scheme to add another senator to their majority by proposing that one senator represent both St. John and the east end of St. Thomas in place of the senator exclusively representing St. John. The Committee to Save Saint John's Representation in the Virgin Islands Legislature strenuously objected: "While the stateside problem is to prevent a minority from usurping the rights of a majority—*the Virgin Islands problem is to prevent a majority from eliminating the minority.*"[63] St. John retained its seat. In the absence of a court ruling that the 14th Amendment of the U.S. Constitution required the one-man-one-vote principle be followed in the territories as well as in the states, the Virgin Islands legislature was unlikely to take away the senate seat that Congress had given St. John.

Pressure from the Press

Conflict with insular governing authorities was a well established tradition among Virgin Islands journalists. D. Hamilton Jackson, J. Antonio Jarvis, and Rothschild Francis had enriched this tradition with notable contributions to a fiercely independent press in the Islands. Local newspapers had long wielded much political influence, abetted by the political proclivity of Virgin Islanders.

The three major newspapers during the 1960s were *The St. Croix Avis*, founded in 1844, the *Home Journal*, founded in 1951, and the *Daily News*, founded in 1930. Canute Brodhurst, editor and publisher of *The St. Croix Avis*, was the successful defendant in the famous press freedom case of 1945. Senator and labor leader Earle Ottley was the founder and publisher of the *Home Journal*. No journalist, however, could make a better claim to wear the mantle bequeathed by Jackson, Jarvis, and Francis than Ariel Melchior, Sr., publisher and editor of the *Daily News*. It was Melchior who chose to engage the Paiewonsky-Ottley machine in political combat, not by standing for office himself, but by mobilizing the full resources of his newspaper in the effort to unseat Governor Paiewonsky.

Reasons for the Melchior-Paiewonsky feud are not clear. An allegation was made to a Congressional subcommittee that when Paiewonsky moved into the governor's office, he found an open telephone line to Melchior's office, an allegation which former Governor Merwin and Melchior both denied, and which

---

63. *Ibid.*, p. 287.

Paiewonsky himself neither confirmed nor denied. The following sworn testimony of Governor Paiewonsky (labeled "false" by Melchior) before the subcommittee, however, is illuminating:

> MR. CAREY. Were you requested to provide that kind of service to the publisher of the Daily News?
>
> GOVERNOR PAIEWONSKY. I was requested that I would get a good press if I did provide certain types of service directly to consult with the editor of the Daily News before policy decisions are made.
>
> MR. CAREY. In other words, in advance of policy decisions you conduct as the Governor, if you would review those decisions with the publisher of the Daily News?
>
> GOVERNOR PAIEWONSKY. This is correct. I said my appointment is hanging here from the President. I do not see your name on it, and if you want to share the responsibilities of government with me—I have the sole responsibility to the President of the United States and I am not sharing it with anyone. If this means blackmail, I have never succumbed to blackmail in my life and I do not intend to today. And ever since then I think you can see what has happened, happening in the Daily News....
>
> MR. BURTON OF UTAH. Governor, was this proposition made to you directly by the publisher of the Daily News?
>
> GOVERNOR PAIEWONSKY. In my office....
>
> MR. BURTON OF UTAH. And this would be Mr. Melchior?
>
> GOVERNOR PAIEWONSKY. Right. Senior.[64]

Whatever the reasons for the feud, Melchior published thirty-four charges against Paiewonsky and his administration in the *Daily News* of June 3, 1967, which were reprinted in a half-page advertisement in the *Washington Post*. Before the subcommittee, he refused to divulge the names of the contributors who paid for the advertisement. Melchior urged that Congress "first make a thorough investigation into the conduct of the government" before approving a bill providing an elective governor for the Islands.[65]

---

64. *Hearings, Election of ... Governor* (1967), pp. 494–495. Ariel Melchior, Sr., in a letter to Congressman Hugh Carey dated July 22, 1967, labeled this testimony of Governor Paiewonsky as "wholly and deliberately false." Former Governor Merwin's affidavit of September 19, 1967 categorically denied the existence of such a telephone line to the *Daily News*. *Ibid.*, pp. 671–673.

65. *Ibid.*, pp. 334–335.

Most of Melchior's thirty-four charges alleged various conflicts of interest and that there were too many government employees. As he had refuted so effectively the charges against him at his nomination hearing, Governor Paiewonsky now replied point-by-point to each charge once again, and this he did under oath before the subcommittee. With regard to the number of government employees, he replied that the total work force of the Virgin Islands increased by 130 percent from 11,334 to about 25,000, in the period 1961 to 1967, while the local government work force of regular employees increased only about 106 percent, from 2,074 to 4,269. Meanwhile, he added, the population had almost doubled, from 33,000 to 60,000, not counting the many tourists, while local government revenues more than tripled, from $15,500,000 to over $50,000,000.[66] Chairman of the parent House Committee on Interior and Insular Affairs, Congressman Wayne Aspinall, commended Governor Paiewonsky in a statement echoed by Hugh Carey, Chairman of the subcommittee. Said Aspinall: "I commend you once again, Governor, on the way that you have handled the matters in the Virgin Islands and on the way that you have conducted yourself in light of the great criticism that you received."[67]

Some of Melchior's charges, nevertheless, were not without foundation. Audit reports of 1964 and 1965 by Peter A. Bove, Comptroller of the Virgin Islands, had confirmed "excessive and unnecessary" increase in government employment and in expenditures for professional and consulting services, plus a high rate of absenteeism.[68] A chairman of the Democratic Party of the Islands was later to assert that "the government bureaucracy was really created by Senator Ottley," with Paiewonsky's help, "to give Virgin Islanders jobs. Thus, he created a 'monster' since none could be fired nor would they take jobs elsewhere in the Virgin Islands."[69]

---

66. *Ibid.*, p. 477.

67. *Ibid.*, pp. 445, 530.

68. "The employees of the Department of Public Works have increased from 866 to 1,109 or 28% during the past three years. In spite of this overall increase we have seen no appreciable improvement in road construction and maintenance, garbage collection, and other public works services." Letter from Comptroller Bove to Governor Paiewonsky dated January 29, 1965. See also, *ibid.*, August 27, 1964. Both letters are reprinted in *Hearings, Election of ... Governor* (1967), pp. 654–656.

69. Interview of Jeffrey L. Farrow, Publisher and Editor, *Virgin Islands Post*, Charlotte Amalie, St. Thomas, July 23, 1977.

Toward More Self-Rule

Since the advent of American rule in 1917, agitation for more self-government never ceased in the Islands. The Revised Organic Act of 1954 was a severe disappointment for home rule advocates. Economic progress during the first years of Governor Paiewonsky's tenure as Governor emboldened the Virgin Islands legislature to pass a bill in 1964 establishing the first Constitutional Convention to draft a Second Revised Organic Act of the Virgin Islands. The 14,076 qualified electors were authorized to elect twenty-two delegates to the Constitutional Convention of 1965, consisting of twelve elected at-large and ten elected by districts. With the eleven members of the legislature also serving as delegates, the total of thirty-three delegates produced a Proposed Second Revised Organic Act, the major proposals of which were the following:

1. an elective Governor and Lieutenant Governor for a four-year term;
2. the abolition of the limitation on voting for legislative members at large;
3. representation in the U.S. Congress through a Resident Commissioner or Delegate to the House of Representatives;
4. the right to vote for the U.S. President and the Vice President;
5. abolition of the veto of local laws by the President;
6. a comptroller to be appointed by the Governor with the advice and consent of the Legislature for a ten-year term;
7. the Organic Act to be amended by the Legislature or by popular initiative (referendum) or by a constitutional convention; and
8. the Legislature to be authorized to fix salaries of its members, effective upon the election of a succeeding legislature.[70]

These proposals were directed to Congress for its consideration. To allay any apprehension on the part of Congress that approval of any of these proposals would be tantamount to a Congressional "commitment to statehood" for the Islands, the Constitutional Convention adopted a Resolution on Status which stated:

1. The People of the Virgin Islands are unalterably opposed to annexation of the Virgin Islands by any State of the Union as a county, city

---

70. James A. Bough, "Is Commonwealth the Next Step?" *Virgin Islands Bar Journal*, 5 (Summer 1974):12.

71. Thus, before a Congressional subcommittee, Assistant Attorney General of the Virgin Islands James A. Bough testified in 1970: "This declaration should remove from the minds of the Congress any concern that the grant of a resident commissioner will in any way

or precinct, or to any commonwealth or other territory under the jurisdiction of the United States.

2. The People of the Virgin Islands are unalterably opposed to independence from the United States of America.

3. The People of the Virgin Islands desire to have the Virgin Islands remain an unincorporated territory under the constitutional system of the United States with the fullest measure of internal self-government and in the closest association with the United States of America, and the Virgin Islands shall hereafter be designated an "autonomous territory."[71]

Congress chose to address the matter of more self-government for the Virgin Islands on a piecemeal, rather than a package, basis. Bills providing for an elective governor of the Virgin Islands passed both houses of Congress in 1966 but the differences between the two were too substantial for a conference committee to reconcile the two versions. Meanwhile, the struggle for power between Unicrats and Donkeycrats did not inspire Congressional confidence in the political maturity of Virgin Islanders. On October 18, 1966, Congressman John P. Saylor of Pennsylvania, ranking Republican member of the Committee on Interior and Insular Affairs of the House of Representatives, commented:

> Conferees of the two bodies cannot possibly reconcile the differences between the two versions Possibly we were premature; within ... two months a series of events have taken place in the Virgin Islands which make me wonder if certain members of the legislature and the appointive Governor are power hungry; perhaps they're realizing that in order to maintain their positions, they must resort to political shenanigans that they have introduced into the Islands.
>
> With the connivance of the Governor, a six to five majority in the Legislature have tried to confuse and frustrate the voters, so that on November 8th, they will find it almost impossible to cast their ballots in a free election.[72]

---

be a commitment that the Virgin Islands are on the way to statehood." *Hearings before the House Subcommittee on Territorial and Insular Affairs, Nonvoting Delegates—Guam and the Virgin Islands*, 91st Cong., 2d sess., May 18 and 19, 1970, pp. 75, 76.

72. Quoted by Hill, *Rise to Recognition*, pp. 150–151. In a letter to Congressman Saylor, Gustav A. Danielson replied: "You have permitted party politics to interfere with a complete people's right to vote. Your knowledge of the Caribbean possessions appears as weak as your archaic colonial attitudes are strong." *Virgin Islands View*, 2 (November 1966):8.

73. *Hearings, Election of ... Governor* (1967), p. 527.

In 1967 bills again were introduced in both houses and extensive hearings again were held, leading one member of the House Subcommittee on Territorial and Insular Affairs, Congressman Laurence Burton of Utah, to observe: "we have probably devoted more time to the Virgin Islands in the past year than ... any other committee of Congress has in history."[73]

Despite desperate efforts by Governor Paiewonsky to secure passage in time to hold the first election for governor in November of 1968, thus enhancing his prospect of becoming the first elective governor, the Elective Governor Act did not become law until August 23, 1968—to become effective in the 1970 elections when, for the first time, Virgin Islanders would elect their own governor and lieutenant governor for four-year terms.[74]

The Act also abolished the Presidential veto of territorial legislation, and authorized the legislature to override the governor's veto by a two-thirds majority vote. Certain other provisions related to strengthening the office and powers of the government comptroller. Finally, the Act specifically extended to the Islands the following provisions of the U.S. Constitution: (1) Article 1, section 9, clauses 2 and 3—guaranteeing the writ of habeas corpus and prohibiting bills of attainder and ex post facto laws; (2) Article 4, sections 1 and 2, clause 1—the full faith and credit provisions; (3) the First through Ninth Amendments—the Bill of Rights; (4) the Thirteenth Amendment—abolishing slavery; (5) the Fifteenth and Nineteenth Amendments—prohibiting denial of the right to vote on account of race, color, previous condition of servitude, or sex; and (6) the second sentence of section 1 of the Fourteenth Amendment—the provision that would prove most significant for the rights of aliens in the Islands—which reads as follows:

> No State shall make or enforce any law which shall abridge the privileges and immunities of citizens of the United States; nor shall any State deprive any person of life, liberty, or property, without due process of law; nor deny to any person within its jurisdiction the equal protection of the laws.

Efforts to secure a resident commissioner or delegate to Congress from the Virgin Islands commenced in 1945, but twenty years later no progress seemingly had been made. Congress intermittently had considered the matter, but

---

74. Public Law 90-496, 73 *Stat.* 569 (1968). The main provisions of the Act are reprinted in Bough and Macridis, eds., *Virgin Islands*, pp. 103–111.

75. Section 39 of the Foraker Act of 1900 (31 *Stat.* 158) provided that the electors of Puerto Rico "choose a resident commissioner to the United States, who shall be entitled to official recognition by all Departments...." A seat with non-voting privileges was granted first

its inaction was always rationalized in terms of the small size and population of the Virgin Islands in comparison with the states or Puerto Rico. Alaska had been granted a delegate to Congress six years before it was even incorporated. Other territories that had delegates in Congress before they became states were Arizona, Colorado, the Dakota Territory, Hawaii, Idaho, Montana, New Mexico, Utah, and Washington. Congressional representation was granted Puerto Rico and the Philippines when their residents were not even U.S. citizens. Indeed, Puerto Rico was granted a resident commissioner in Congress over thirty years before it was granted in 1947 an elective governor.[75] In light of the territorial history of the United States, therefore, it was curious that Congress should have granted both Virgin Islanders and the people of Guam the right to elect their own governor before granting them the right to elect a non-voting delegate to Congress.[76]

Following the example set by the legislature of Guam in 1964, the Virgin Islands legislature acted in 1968 to provide for a Washington Representative of the Virgin Islands to be elected for a two-year term, who would serve—should Congress so authorize—only until a representative to Congress would be seated.[77]

---

through a House resolution in 1903 and later by Rule 12 of the Standing Rules of the House of Representatives. See, *Hearings, supra*, n. 70 at pp. 45–46, 50.

76. Guam came under American rule as a result of the War with Spain in 1898, and then remained under military rule until passage of its Organic Act in 1950 when it became an organized and unincorporated territory of the United States. With a 1970 population of more than 100,000, the people of Guam in 1968 also were granted the right to elect their own governor. See, *e.g.*, Arnold H. Leibowitz, *Colonial Emancipation in the Pacific and the Caribbean, A Legal and Political Analysis* (New York: Praeger Publishers, 1976), pp. 105–117. See, also, Arnold H. Leibowitz, "The Applicability of Federal Law to Guam," *Virginia Journal of International Law*, 16 (Fall 1975): 21–63.

77. Virgin Islands Legislature, Act No. 2257, approved June 28, 1968.

78. Gordon K. Lewis attributed racial considerations for the reconciliation centering on removal of Governor Paiewonsky from the scene. "The reconciliation was further made possible by the removal of former Governor Paiewonsky from the scene, insofar as one item of the merger agreement was that the first elected governor would have to be a native-born Negro, thereby making it possible for those Donkeycrats who had become mortal Paiewonsky foes to return to the Democratic fold without entirely losing their political dignity. It is even possible, indeed, that the agreement can be interpreted as an effort on the part of the colored political oligarchy to close its ranks in the face of the growing political power of the white transplanted mainlanders, that is, to reaffirm the carefully nurtured thesis that birth in the islands gives the colored native a preferential legacy in politics and government. That, if correct, would be a sort of conservative application of the 'black power' ideology." Lewis, *The Virgin Islands*, p. 331.

Former Senator Ron de Lugo, leader of the Donkeycrats who had lost his seat in the legislature as a coalition candidate in 1966, was now welcomed into the Democratic Party to which the Paiewonsky-Ottley alliance had been given full title by the courts. The *quid pro quo* for reconciliation was the Party's backing of de Lugo who became in 1968 the first elective Washington Representative.[78]

Some recalcitrant Donkeycrats, however, refused to follow de Lugo. Failing to make any inroads in the 1968 Democratic Party primary, these dissidents formed a new political party—the Independent Citizens Movement (ICM). The ICM fielded a partial slate of candidates in the 1968 general election. Although the new party won no seats in the legislature, it garnered a surprising 33 percent of the vote, thus assuring its place on the 1970 ballot as a full-fledged political party.

The Republican Party, meanwhile, continued to remain weak, and its future looked bleak, indeed. Its 1968 vote-getting potential had received a severe jolt by former Republican Governor Merwin's "extremely detrimental" recommendation that, because "the local economy is overheated," the Virgin Islands ought to be brought into the customs boundaries of the United States, even if this would result in the overnight elimination of the watch industry in the Islands. Legislator David Hamilton, noting that the watch industry employed over eight hundred persons, commented: "When statements of this type are made, the Republican image takes a licking."[79]

Republicans accounted for only seven percent of the 1968 vote. All 15 seats of the legislature were won by the Democrats. The Republican Party would have been destined for further oblivion except for one very important development. Republican candidate Richard Nixon had been elected President of the United States—an event that presaged Governor Paiewonsky's resignation and the appointment of a Republican governor.

Ralph Paiewonsky could have remained as Governor until his successor would take office. Instead, Governor Paiewonsky resigned in early 1969, ostensibly at Nixon's suggestion, and Government Secretary Cyril King—titular leader of the new Independent Citizens Movement—became Acting Governor for four and one-half months. This was a chance for King to gain some retribution for the long vendetta waged by the Paiewonsky-Ottley machine against him, ever since as Senator Hubert Humphrey's protégé he was appointed Government Secretary in 1961 by President Kennedy. King's brief tenure as Acting Governor, during which he sought to demonstrate his leadership abilities, served to launch him as a prospective candidate looking toward the 1970 election for governor.

---

79. See, *Hearings, Election of … Governor* (1967), pp. 231, 598.

The principal actors clearly were beginning to take their places and to posture themselves on the political stage that was being set for the coming first election of a Virgin Islands governor. Still, amidst the burgeoning economy, political fervor, and the excitement and enthusiasm presaging more self-rule, there were ominous signs of trouble.

Ominous Signs

During the development decade, 1960 to 1970, the total number of annual tourists visiting the Virgin Islands increased from 210,000 to 1.5 million, an average annual growth rate of over 18 percent. The rapid growth of tourism and tourism-related enterprise was accompanied by an average annual rate of growth of manufacturing of over ten percent, from 1960 to 1970. Together with the introduction of heavy industry by Harvey and Hess (by 1970, crude oil accounted for approximately 75 percent of the total value of insular exports to the U.S.), the economy of the Virgin Islands was marked by astonishing transformation. By 1970, the tourist sector employed nearly half the territory's working force and accounted for nearly 60 percent of the Islands' income. Another 30 percent of the labor force was employed by the insular government (almost all of them natives), the budget of which had increased from $12 million in 1960 to $124 million in 1970. Meanwhile, per capita income in the Islands had increased an amazing 120 percent, from $1,100 in 1960 to $2,400 in 1970 which was twice that of Puerto Rico and five times that of the Caribbean region as a whole.[80]

This tapestry of progress in the 1960s had been rapidly and radically woven. Inevitably, the fabric in places would become taut, and was destined to begin to tear, rip, unravel, and shred. This was plainly happening to the insular social fabric as the development decade neared an end.

A dominant characteristic of the insular economy of 1970 was the massive presence of mainland investment, encouraged by the tax incentive program, and resulting in an economy marked by white-owned and managed enterprises based on cheap imported labor from other Caribbean islands. This pattern of growth left out the native population. Few natives by 1970 owned, controlled,

---

80. For discussion of economic growth indicators in the Islands for the period 1960–1970, see, *e.g.*: Peter Pardo de Zela, *The Impact of Change and Political Leadership, The Case of the U.S. Virgin Islands* (unpublished Ph.D. dissertation, Tulane University, 1978), pp. 80–89 and sources cited; and *Annual Report of the Governor of the Virgin Islands, 1960–1970*.

or were employed in, the private sector. The result was the intrusion of racially and ethnically based discrimination that was to create deep fissures in Virgin Islands society.

In his book published in 1970 on changing life in the Islands, Ellis Gladwin observed: "Almost before the local people realized what had happened, nearly all of the beach front land on St. Croix was in the hands of the continentals." He wrote of the increasing crime, the poverty of alien workers, the "irresponsible racism" as cited in a local editorial, "the anger felt by many local people because the continentals own, or control, most of the businesses," and the fear of "a serious explosion" (St. Thomas and St. Croix "are like smoldering volcanoes"). Noting that few white continental children attended public schools, resulting in "de facto segregation," Gladwin concluded: "It is foolish to deny that there is social tension in the Virgin Islands."[81]

Alienation of the land by white continentals was not an unforeseen problem. As early as 1961, Ron de Lugo in testimony before a Congressional committee said: "In Puerto Rico the government owns all the beaches. We are quite concerned with that problem. I would not be surprised if legislation is introduced by myself to try to do something about it."[82]

Thomas Mathews identified three main problems confronting the Virgin Islands at the end of the 1960s. They were: (1) the restless youth of the Islands; (2) the notable influx of outsiders, including Puerto Ricans, unskilled workers from the English-speaking islands, and continentals ranging from "vagrant outcasts" to "highly affluent and gifted people"; and (3) the "blanket adulation and imitation of all things American" with the result that "the Virgin Islander has turned his back on the past."[83]

Testifying before a Congressional committee, Republican Party Chairman Lloyd W. Joseph blamed several Unicrat candidates for injecting "racism" into the 1966 campaign, but he added that "whites" were responsible initially for implanting racial prejudice in the Virgin Islands where little had existed in the past.[84]

---

81. Ellis Gladwin, *Living in the Changing Caribbean* (New York: The Macmillan Company, 1970), pp. 18, 94–95, 118–119, 127, 128, 187, 188. Governor Paiewonsky accused black power militants from the mainland of trying to stir up "racial trouble" in the Islands. "A few of these crazy people have come down from New York to stir up the natives," he said. He did not identify them. *The New York Times*, May 4, 1968, p. 23, col. 2.

82. *Hearings ... (Paiewonsky's) Nomination* (1961), p. 81.

83. Thomas Mathews, "Social Configuration and its Implications, in Bough and Macridis, eds., *Virgin Islands*, pp. 168–173.

84. *Hearings, Election of ... Governor* (1967), p. 28.

In extraordinary letters to Governor Paiewonsky in 1967, the Office of Territories of the Department of Interior registered a number of serious complaints against his administration. Acting Director John J. Kirwan charged that the economic development of the Virgin Islands, fostered by federal funding and concessions, was purchased at the price of exploiting "the modern version of slave labor—the alien laborer." The Paiewonsky administration has registered "zero effort" in response to this problem, claimed Kirwan, despite the fact

> that there is a very basic and causal relationship between the fact that the Virgin Islands has an *alien* labor force of between 1/3 and 1/2 of its entire labor force, that it has very great housing and medical and public facilities problems, and that it has … a scandalous gap between the low wage and living conditions level of the bottom of the work force, and the increasing affluence of the entrepreneurial segment of the tourist and export industries.[85]

In other correspondence, the Office of Territories chastised the Virgin Islands government for its "tax effort" being less than that of any one of the fifty states. The Office asserted a connection between this low tax effort and the continuing problems of water supply and water pollution. Thus, a 1967 Interior Department report stated that raw sewage was being dumped into the streams and shore waters of the Virgin Islands in such quantities that pollution had reached a critical stage.

> Unless reforms are put into effect immediately, the befouled water will create a health menace and undermine prosperity.… The problem in the Virgin Islands is due to local indifference. For the past several years, $1.4 million in Federal money to help construct sewage plants has gone unclaimed because the Virgin Islands has failed to put up the necessary matching funds.[86]

In a series of three controversial feature articles of *The New York Times* of September 27, 29, and 30, 1969, Martin Waldron trumpeted the theme that prosperity was costly to the Virgin Islands in terms of numerous conflicts of interest, alleged government corruption, special interest legislation, and in-

---

85. Copy of letter from Kirwan to Paiewonsky, dated August 16, 1967, reprinted in *ibid.*, pp. 701–703.

86. *Ibid.*, pp. 710–717, esp. pp. 711, 717.

87. Martin Waldron, "Prosperity Costly to the Virgin Islands," *The New York Times*, September 28, 1969, p. 73, col. 1.

creased racism. With regard to conflicts of interest and corruption, Waldron reported, for example, that one local senator bought a plot of land for $60,000 and sold it to the insular government a few days later for $490,000, and that one hundred and thirty-two consultants—many of them relatives of government officials—were being paid under contracts through the Governor's office.[87]

With regard to increased racial tensions, Waldron reported the starting of a black militant movement at the College of the Virgin Islands whose stated purpose was to wrest control of the Islands' commercial enterprises from white people. He also reported "an increasing number of attacks by Negroes on whites," especially the rape of white women, that "Negro gangs" posing as plainclothes policemen were raping white women, that few arrests had been made, and that—to protect themselves—whites had formed "vigilante" groups and often carried pistols.[88]

Waldron included not one item favorable to the Virgin Islands in his long litany of insular ills. It was obvious that his intent was to do a "hatchet job" on the Islands, and reaction was swift to come. Although one letter to the editor of *The New York Times* claimed Waldron's articles were "accurate,"[89] others categorically denied his report that gangs of blacks were raping white women. One of these was a letter from former Governor Paiewonsky who also countered that Waldron had been "brainwashed" by the "political smut" of the then caretaker Governor Cyril King in terms of "the same old refrains and recriminations."[90] Still another letter intimated that although Waldron may not have been "absolutely" accurate, "there is corruption and there are racial problems and it needed to be told."[91]

"The political implications are clear," wrote Peter de Zela.

---

88. Martin Waldron, "Racism Increases on Virgin Islands," *The New York Times*, September 30, 1969, p. 72, col. 1. Dr. Roy Anduze, chairman of the Governor's Commission for Human Resources, claimed in 1968 that the growth rate of crime in the Virgin Islands was double that of Puerto Rico. A government youth spokesman, Ed Penn, added that youth crimes constituted a 1,000% increase. *Virgin Islands View*, 3 (April 1968):25.

89. Letter to Editor from Frank McLaughlin, St. Thomas, V. I., dated October 1, 1969, *The New York Times*, October 7, 1969, p. 46, col. 1.

90. Letter to Editor from James McWilliams, Assistant Attorney General, St. Thomas, V. I., dated October 3, 1969, *The New York Times*, October 7, 1969, p. 46, col. 6; Letter to Editor from Ralph M. Paiewonsky, St. Thomas, V. I., dated September 29, 1969, *The New York Times*, October 11, 1969, p. 36, col. 6.

91. Letter to Editor from Dianne D. Lyons, Christiansted, V. I., dated October 2, 1969, *The New York Times*, October 11, 1969, p. 36, col. 6.

92. De Zela, *The Impact of Change*, p. 94.

On the one hand, there appears to be a strong relationship between the patterns of economic change and the emergence of a new "nationalism" in the Virgin Islands. Such questions as "white economic power" and the "alienation of precious resources" have become part of the local lexicon, as indeed in many parts of the Caribbean. On the other hand, aspects of that growth raise important questions concerning the real meaning of increased self-government. As someone remarked, are there on both a macro and micro level "new masters at the moment a new freedom is proclaimed?"[92]

In the short span of the development decade, the Virgin Islands had experienced a bewildering and burgeoning growth of population contained in a diminutive and non-expanding territory, an influx of outsiders many of whom took almost all the jobs in the private sector and some of whom acquired ownership and control of almost all private enterprise and choice land, and the inception of a seemingly permanent minority status of its native population.[93] Indeed, all members of this micropolity had become members of minority groups—natives, aliens, Puerto Ricans, and continentals alike. It was evident by the end of the 1960s that the Virgin Islands had become a troubled homeland for aliens and the alienated.

---

93. Professor Marilyn Krigger of the College of the Virgin Islands (CVI) attributed the onset of a serious identity crisis in the late 1960s among black Virgin Islanders, particularly those among students at the College, to the wave of migration to the Islands "overwhelming the Virgin Islander, numerically and culturally." New problems which caused Islanders to become "introspective about their identity" were a CVI faculty "comprised mainly of white mainland Americans" and public school teachers many of whom "were unfamiliar with local history, traditions, foods, and other areas from which one usually draws examples in teaching young children." And Professor Krigger added: "As the white population grew larger, various invidious patterns and practices began to become evident. Private schools were organized which, because of extremely high fees, tended to have almost all white students. Some almost-all-white residential areas came into being, and it was popularly known that many of their residents desired them to remain that way. Some business establishments were known to employ wage and position differentials with respect to black and white employees. A couple of private clubs which excluded Blacks and Jews from membership were formed. There came to exist within ... the Virgin Islands ... two separate societies—one white and one black, and the distrust, misunderstandings, and hatreds which such separation breeds." Marilyn F. Krigger, *Thoughts on the Identity of Black American Virgin Islanders*, unpublished paper presented at the National Endowment for the Humanities Summer Seminar on "The Black American Experience: Insiders and Outsiders" (xeroxed, Boston: Brown University, August 1976), pp. 5, 10–11.

11

Aliens and the Alienated

Richard Nixon moved into the White House in January 1969. Governor Paiewonsky resigned in February,[1] and Acting Governor Cyril King held the post while President Nixon sought a Republican to appoint, who would serve as Governor until the Elective Governor Act would become effective and the new Governor would take office in January 1971. Presumably, this last appointed Governor would be aided by his brief incumbency in becoming the Islands' first elective Governor. The new President, however, nominated a continental, Peter Bove of Vermont, for the position—an unlikely choice later to win election in view of the now seemingly well-established precedent of the successive appointments of natives Merwin and Paiewonsky. Moreover, Bove—who had been U.S. comptroller in the Islands for eleven years—was white, and many Virgin Islanders assumed the Elective Governor Act "meant the certainty of a colored chief executive in Government House."[2]

Questioning of Bove at his Senate nomination hearing was rather benign except in two respects. In response to Senator Burdick's question as to what should be done regarding the presence of so many alien workers, Bove replied that they should be treated "as first-class American citizens," and they "should have all of the privileges that American citizens have," because they were in the Islands "by necessity, and they comprise a majority of the work force." This answer was hardly calculated to advance Bove's popularity among Virgin Islanders. Possibly more damaging was Senator Allott's introduction into the hearing of news columnist Drew Pearson's published reference to a charge that Bove as comp-

---

1. Just hours before he left office, Governor Paiewonsky signed sixty-six bills into law, appointed one hundred and twenty persons to government agencies, and by executive order classified all political (unclassified) government jobs into the civil service. One of the new laws created the Virgin Islands Port Authority, which Secretary of the Interior Stewart Udall had approved four days before he, himself, left office. The Port Authority was given extraordinary governmental authority and Ralph Paiewonsky became its first chairman. Many of its initial powers, however, were later curbed. See, O'Neill, *Rape of the Virgin Islands*, pp. 102–104.

2. Lewis, *The Virgin Islands*, pp. 331, 337.

troller allegedly had made "improper advances" to girls in his office, a charge which Bove denied as "scurrilous."[3]

Whether because of the effort to smear him or because he suffered a heart attack, or both, Peter Bove withdrew from public life, compelling Nixon to cast about for another candidate. President Nixon's second choice was cardiologist Dr. Melvin H. Evans who, as a Democrat, had served as Paiewonsky's commissioner of health, but had become disgruntled with the Democratic machine, returned to private practice in his native St. Croix, and changed his registration to the Republican Party just two months prior to the 1968 elections. Evans was to play a very prominent role in the political life of the Islands for several years to come.

At his Senate nomination hearing, in contrast to Bove, Evans took a much less charitable view of the presence of alien workers. Without any supporting evidence, he charged before the Senate committee that "an outstanding percentage ... of the most serious crimes committed in the islands are committed by people who had overstayed their leave and are there illegally."[4] Dr. Evans became the last appointed Governor of the Virgin Islands on July 1, 1969, succeeding Cyril King who had held the post as Acting Governor for the preceding four and one-half months.

Nixon's new Secretary of the Interior, Walter Hickel, appointed Howard L. Ross of Tennessee to succeed Peter Bove as the U.S. comptroller for the Virgin Islands. Ross, who had served as comptroller and in other capacities for twenty years for the American St. Gaubain Company of Tennessee, had no prior governmental experience to qualify him for this position. The fact that he was a cousin of John Ehrlichman, a principal aide in Nixon's White House, may have been a factor. In any event, Comptroller Ross's first annual report, for the fiscal year ended June 30, 1969, was not only critical of the preceding Paiewonsky-Ottley machine, but must also rank as one of the most political, intemperate, and vituperative audit reports ever directed to any government.

In his report, Ross claimed that existing problems resulted from "the long-time control of politics by a relatively small group." Pointing his finger at Senator Earle Ottley, now that Paiewonsky was gone, Ross described Ottley in unflattering terms as the majority leader of the Legislature's only party who was responsible for a government contract for advertising given to his newspaper, who leases office space to the government in his newspaper building built on government land, and who also heads the labor union of government

---

3. *Hearings before the Senate Committee on Interior and Insular Affairs, Interior Nominations*, 91st Cong., 1st sess., March 14 and 18, 1969, pp. 34, 38.

4. *Hearing before the Senate Committee on Interior and Insular Affairs, Interior Nominations*, 91st Cong., 1st sess., June 17, 1969, p. 11.

*Dr. Melvin H. Evans, President Nixon's nominee to be
last appointed Governor, July 1, 1969*

employees which negotiates their contracts with the government. Under the guise
of "humanitarianism," Ross claimed, the granting of special favors and an excessive number of government jobs perpetuated the small group's control.

> Little did the recipients of unnecessary jobs realize the ultimate effect
> of getting paid for doing nothing or of having two people do the work
> that could be accomplished by one. There is grave danger of serious
> future problems when the level of the Government payroll now uses
> 70% of total local income.

Although the Industrial Incentive Law was passed to stimulate the economy and to provide employment of natives, Ross noted, less than five percent of the employees in the hotel industry were native Virgin Islanders, about six percent of Harvey Alumina Company employees were natives, no more than ten percent of Hess's employees were natives, and only seven of 42 graduates of Hess's vocational school were natives. Ross labeled this a "deplorable" situation arising from the government creating unnecessary jobs highly valued by native Islanders while frequently better private industry positions must be filled by outsiders. Were more natives employed by private industry, Ross reasoned, the government would have less need for a "humanitarian" policy of swelling its payroll, and hence fewer aliens would be present to create demands for already critically inadequate public services.[5] In February 1972, Comptroller Ross choked on a piece of meat while dining in a St. Thomas restaurant and died.

Influx of Aliens

The phenomenon of the influx of thousands of alien workers into the Virgin Islands during the 1960s should properly be assessed in the context of a world-wide development with deep historic roots. After all, the United States itself is a nation of immigrants and the descendents of immigrants, and this is true of the Virgin Islands wherein foreign workers from other Caribbean islands (and even on one occasion from as far away as India) intermittently had been imported, notably to work in the cane fields of St. Croix after the end of slavery and to work in the construction boom of St. Thomas during World War II.

During that War, many alien workers entered illegally with the encouragement of, and without interference by, government authorities.

> The word drifted down through the West Indies that "The Government" needed workers in St. Thomas, Virgin Islands, and people from the nearby British and French possessions began to converge upon the Virgin Islands in the early months of 1941. They came in schooners, motor boats, sloops and rowboats....

---

5. H. L. Ross, U.S. Government Comptroller for the Virgin Islands, *Annual Report of the Government Comptroller of the Virgin Islands on the Government of the Virgin Islands, Fiscal Year Ended June 30, 1969* (Report No. 328-69-00, Office of Territories, U.S. Department of the Interior, June 26, 1970), pp. 3–10.

Needless to say, these aliens could not enter legally. They could not understand how the Government could deny them entry on the one hand, and on the other, beckon them to enter to work at wages which, to them, were unbelievable.[6] Approximately one thousand alien workers remained in the Islands, many of them illegally, after the War.[7]

On the mainland, during and after the Second World War, between 1942 and 1964, over four million Mexican farmworkers were brought into the southwest of the United States on a temporary basis. This so-called treaty-based "Bracero Program" was unilaterally terminated by the United States in 1964 because of pressure from American organized labor. Meanwhile, the "magnet effect" of the Bracero Program induced a parallel inflow of illegal Mexican workers which, in 1954, resulted in "Operation Wetback," the expulsion of over one million illegal Mexican aliens—the greatest mass expulsion of illegal aliens in American history.[8] Since the end of the Bracero Program, the continuing presence of illegal Mexican workers in the southwest quantitatively assumed such importance in the mainland as to dwarf, in comparison, the problem of alien workers in the Virgin Islands and elsewhere under the American flag. Accordingly, Virgin Islands authorities remained fearful that U.S. policy would be directed to the Mexican problem and hence would neglect the special circumstances prevailing in the Islands.

Not only may the influx of alien workers into the Virgin Islands during the tourism boom be viewed as a part of such U.S. mainland developments, as well as part of the rural-to-urban migration characterizing major population change throughout the post-colonial world since World War II, but it is also contemporaneous with very similar developments in Europe.

During the early 1960s, the governments of France, Switzerland, and Germany established programs to import workers, primarily from the Mediterranean Basin, to reduce labor shortages in their rapidly expanding economies. According to Professor Mark Miller, it was assumed that the guestworkers would be temporary—an assumption that appeared correct so long as the

---

6. John M. Bonds, "History of Service Activities in the Virgin Islands," *Immigration and Naturalization Service Monthly Review*, 4 (December 1946): p. 77.

7. *A Special Study of the House Subcommittee on Immigration, Citizenship, and International Law, Nonimmigrant Alien Labor Program on the Virgin Islands of the United States*, 94th Cong., 1st sess., October 1975, p. 5; hereafter cited as: *Nonimmigrant Alien Labor Program* (1975). See, also, Mark J. Miller and William W. Boyer, "Foreign Workers in the USVI, History of a Dilemma," *Caribbean Review*, 11 (Winter 1982) 1: 48–51.

8. Mark Miller and David J. Yeres, *A Massive Temporary Worker Program: Solution or Mirage* (unpublished study prepared for the Interagency Task Force on Immigration Policy, Washington, D.C., February 1979), pp. 5–9.

economies of these three host nations were booming, but which proved incorrect after the economic slowdown beginning in 1973 occurred, partly because of the growing dependence on guestworkers to perform work that became unacceptable to native workers. "Unforeseen social and political integration problems of guestworkers and their dependents also proved vexing to the Western Europeans."[9] Miller concluded that the Western European experience suggests that "guestworkers" are likely to become permanent residents instead of remaining "temporary" workers, and he warned that "the creation of an alien workforce that cannot or will not accede to citizenship is likely to result in domestic political turmoil."[10]

Virgin Islanders never recognized their connection with the broader world in these respects. They continued to consider their problems concerning alien workers as discrete and unique. In broad outline, what was happening in Europe was being replicated in the Virgin Islands. In terms of proportionate impact of alien workers, on the other hand, the Virgin Islands experience was indeed discrete and unique. "The problems attendant to the alien labor program are perhaps the most significant social and economic problems confronting the U.S. Virgin Islands," and are "the most complex immigration problems facing the United States."[11]

A number of circumstances combined to induce the import of thousands of alien workers into the U.S. Virgin Islands during the economic boom. The usual "push" and "pull" factors inducing major population migrations were operative in the Caribbean. The growth of the tourist industry was combined with an apparent unwillingness of many native Virgin Islanders to work in many jobs associated with tourism. Natives generally preferred government jobs. Not only did the local government respond to such preference, but it consciously pursued policies to import alien workers from poverty-stricken West Indian islands.

The federal Immigration and Naturalization Service (INS) cooperated with the local government. Under procedures effective in 1956, British subjects in the nearby British Virgin Islands were permitted to enter as "nonimmigrant temporary workers" under section 101 (a) (15) (H) (ii) of the Immigration and Nationality Act, commonly known as the "H-2 provision." The prospec-

---

9. Interagency Task Force on Immigration Policy, *Staff Report* (Departments of Justice, Labor and State, Washington, D.C., March 1979), p. 37.

10. Mark Miller, *A Comparative Evaluation of Western European Guestworker Policies and Practices in View of Present Circumstances in the United States* (unpublished study prepared for the Interagency Task Force on Immigration Policy, Washington, D.C., December 1978), p. 41.

11. *Nonimmigrant Alien Labor Program* (1975), pp. III, 51.

tive employer was required to file a separate petition for each worker with INS, the approval of which was conditioned upon the employer posting a bond guaranteeing that the worker would not become a public charge, and that he would maintain his status and depart at the end of his authorized stay. Workers could be admitted for a period of a year, with additional extensions of one year each. At the end of each year's employment, workers were required to depart from the U.S. Virgin Islands for at least one day before returning to resume employment. The initial requirement of a bond is the source of the term "bonded aliens" commonly applied to the temporary alien workers of the Islands, although the practice of requiring bonds was discontinued in 1959. In that year, at the behest of Governor Merwin, the British Virgin Islands program was extended to the British, French, and Netherlands West Indies.[12]

The program was not only reminiscent of indentured servant arrangements in eighteenth century America, but in the Virgin Islands it recalled the "free-colored" labor contracts before the end of slavery and the annual contracts under the pernicious labor law of 1849 that ended with the St. Croix rebellion of 1878.

By 1970, the population of the Virgin Islands as reported in the U.S. census totaled 62,468, almost double that of 1960. Thirty percent, or 18,928, were foreign born who had not attained U.S. citizenship. All observers agree, however, that the Virgin Islands numbered many more than counted by the 1970 census, because the census did not include illegal aliens who numbered at least 8,000. The number of nonimmigrant workers were reported to have increased from 5,741 to 13,288 from 1964 through 1968 when an estimated 45 percent of the 27,000 labor force were nonimmigrant aliens who held 90 percent of the construction jobs and 60 percent of the service jobs.[13]

The sudden doubling of the number of alien workers between 1964 and 1968 was the result of a conscious policy of the local government to import foreign workers to foster economic development of the Islands. Although many Puerto Ricans and continentals had migrated to the Islands during the early 1960s, many of the latter group were itinerant, and there was still a labor shortage particularly in menial, construction, and service jobs. Moreover, along with native Virgin Islanders, Puerto Ricans and continentals were reluctant to work for the low wages so willingly accepted by the poorer islanders of the Lesser Antilles. One local observer conjectured that Senator Ottley feared that blacks

---

12. Extension of the program to islands other than the British Virgin Islands was originated by "an administrative error," followed by the intervention of Governor Merwin. *Ibid.*, p. 14.

13. *Ibid.*, p. 15.

would become a minority with the inflow of Puerto Ricans and white continentals, so the decision was made to bring in workers from the other islands to do the work.[14] It is not true that native Virgin Islanders shunned menial and service work, because they willingly performed such work on the mainland. To undertake such work in their homeland, however, would have resulted in the loss of status, especially in light of the continuing influx of alien workers who comprised the lowest class in the socio-economic hierarchy.[15]

The grievous problems of alien workers in the Virgin Islands virtually were ignored by local authorities, and were exacerbated by "a policy of drift" and "administrative neglect" on the part of federal authorities. In 1966, the local legislature responded to their presence by enacting a requirement that resident workers be given preference (over any H-2 workers) in employment in the Islands for which they are qualified and available. "Nonresident workers shall be employed only to supplement the labor force of available and qualified resident workers." The Commissioner of Labor was specifically empowered to order an employer to terminate a nonresident worker whenever the Commissioner ascertained that there was an occupationally qualified worker available to fill the position. This law added to the insecurity of the alien worker who already was subject to deportation upon termination of his employment. Finally, in 1977, the U.S. Court of Appeals in Philadelphia declared this employment preference law in conflict with the authority of the federal Immigration and Naturalization Service and, therefore, invalid under the Supremacy Clause of the U.S. Constitution.[16]

Not until the end of 1966 was any attention given by the Virgin Islands community to the growing problems of alien workers. Under federal funding, the College of the Virgin Islands conducted a conference entitled "The Alien Worker and His Family" attended by one hundred persons including a number of alien workers. The conference took the form of a series of workshops on these sub-

14. Interview, Senator-elect Michael Paiewonsky, Hassel Island, St. Thomas, November 20, 1978.

15. "The 'alien problem,' as it is called here, has deep historical roots. The Danes established a rigid hierarchical system in which Government officials ranked at the top of the social scale and cane choppers and laborers at the bottom. Thus, most native Virgin Islanders have regarded manual labor—agricultural or commercial as degrading. Above all, they want a Government job.... Governor Paiewonsky ... from 1961 until 1969 ... more than doubled the Government payroll—to 7,500, one-tenth of the estimated population." J. Anthony Lukas, "The Plaint of the Virgin Islands," *The New York Times*, April 8, 1971, sec. 6, part I, p. 102.

16. Section 4 (a), Act No. 1670, To Amend Title 24, *Virgin Islands Code*, Approved April 4, 1966, was declared invalid in *Rogers v. Larson*, 563 F.2d 617 (1977).

jects, respectively, concerning the alien worker: immigration, employment, health, housing, social welfare, and education.[17]

One result of the conference was the consciousness raising of certain elements of the Virgin Islands community about the plight of aliens. Accordingly, the conference led to two federally funded studies of the conditions of alien workers in the Islands.[18] These studies pointed to the facts that aliens were denied social services, public schooling for their children, and adequate housing and wages, that they were the source of serious health problems, and that aside from these two studies evidence did not exist that any agency or institution in the Virgin Islands was particularly interested in the problems of the aliens. "Aliens present a unique situation … they represent about half the labor force," stated one of the studies, without adding that this condition alone probably was unparalleled in the world. The same study described the typical alien worker of 1969 in the Islands, as follows:

> The typical alien is a male in his 20's or early 30's. (sic!) He is not married, but living with a woman. He has been in the Virgin Islands about five years and came from St. Kitts. He has not been in trouble with the police. He has applied for permanent residency. Chances are he will never receive it in the foreseeable future, but if he does, he will probably migrate to the continent. He is fairly well educated, at least in terms of Virgin Islands standards. He visits his home island two or three times each year and sends home about $28 per month.
>
> He works in construction at a salary of $1.50 per hour. He does not belong to a labor union. He lives in a small shack consisting of about 100 square feet, is likely to have an outside privy with no running water, but an electrical system. His rent is about $40 per month. His health is good.
>
> He has two children of whom one was born in the Virgin Islands and one "off island." If his children are in the Virgin Islands, the chances are they go to a private school—if at all.

---

17. College of the Virgin Islands, *The Alien Worker and His Family* (St. Thomas, January 1967).

18. The two studies, both sponsored by the College of the Virgin Islands, and funded under Title I of the Higher Education Act of 1965, were conducted by the Social, Educational Research and Development, Inc. (SERD) of Silver Spring, Maryland, entitled: *Aliens in the United States Virgin Islands: Temporary Workers in a Permanent Economy* (January 1968); and *A Profile and Plans for the Temporary Alien Worker Problem in the U.S. Virgin Islands* (August 25, 1969).

His contacts with and the services he has received from public and private agencies are minimal. For the most part his relationship with organizations and agencies has been with those agencies handling alien problems.[19]

In response to the College of the Virgin Islands (CVI) conference, and the follow-up studies, the Alien Interest Movement (AIM) was formed in October 1968 for the noncitizens of St. Thomas and St. John "to organize in common association to promote, protect, and seek, our just and reasonable interests." The basic aims of AIM were to seek alleviation of the distressing conditions of alien workers, and status adjustment of those H-2 workers who had resided in the Virgin Islands for five or more years to that of permanent resident aliens.[20] Far from being "largely crying-towel organizations," as labeled by Edward O'Neill,[21] AIM and its counterpart United Alien Association and successor organizations on St. Croix continued to stand between aliens and their complete alienation. Together with various other alien-oriented associations, representing respectively workers from their home islands (e.g., St. Lucia Association, St. Kitts Association, etc.), these organizations generated a measure of hope and aspiration in the place of despair.

Last Appointed Governor

The period of four and one-half months was an unusually long time for Cyril King to serve as an Acting Governor, between the resignation of Governor Paiewonsky on February 11, 1969 and the inauguration of Dr. Melvin Evans on July 1, 1969. Peter Bove's withdrawal extended the interim and King made good use of it to boost his stock for a 1970 bid to become the first elected governor. Being the leader of the Independent Citizens Movement (ICM), and a former protégé of Hubert Humphrey whom Nixon had just defeated for the

---

19. SERD, *A Profile and Plans*, pp. 1–3.

20. Interview, George Goodwin, President, Alien Interest Movement, Charlotte Amalie, St. Thomas, July 25, 1977. A community organizer employed by SERD helped form AIM, which was described by SERD's president, John McCollum, as an "alien community union" or "social protest group" similar to the Congress of Racial Equality on the mainland. "But they're nonmilitant in the sense as some of our domestic civil rights groups. They are militant in the Caribbean sense, though, because they challenge authority. On the islands, there is no strong tradition of aggressiveness. The tempo is lower." *The New York Times*, August 29, 1969, p. 13, col. 8.

21. O'Neill, *Rape of the American Virgins*, p. 182.

Presidency, King knew he had no chance to be appointed Governor by Nixon for the one and one-half years remaining before an elective governor would take office. King moved quickly to remove Paiewonsky appointees from higher offices, initiated improvements of major roads and the garbage disposal service, and acted to remove government waste including excessive rentals for government offices and excessive use of government consultants—actions that outraged his Democratic opponents in the legislature.

Compared to King's brief tenure in the office, Melvin Evans could look forward to sixteen months in the office as the last appointed Governor to prove himself to voters before the first gubernatorial election in November 1970. A number of developments occurred during this period that spelled trouble for Governor Evans and the Virgin Islands, notably—the founding of a militant black organization on the Islands, a significant increase in crime, legislation permitting alien spouses and children to join H-2 workers in the Islands, and a court decision admitting such children to the public schools.

In January 1970, a young, fiery, Crucian of a prominent family, Mario Moorhead, formed on St. Croix the United Caribbean Association (UCA). Moorhead, a self-proclaimed "revolutionary," announced a program of independence for the Virgin Islands, removal of all forms of white exploitation, and unification of all black people in the Caribbean. Moorhead's short-lived political career was interrupted by his imprisonment in May 1970 for a 1967 holdup of a grocery store in Washington, D.C., but not before a wave of hysteria about a "black power movement" swept over St. Croix. Meanwhile, St. Croix's crime rate soared alarmingly, particularly violent crimes such as murder, rape, and armed robbery most of which were committed "by blacks against whites, particularly elderly white tourists." The Department of Public Safety was "reluctant to release statistics for fear of what they would do to the tourist trade."[22] Governor Evans, however, on nationwide television disputed allegations that anti-white crime and racial tensions had increased in the Virgin Islands.[23]

On April 7, 1970, Congress enacted Public Law 91-225 creating a new "H-4" visa classification permitting the alien spouses and children of H-2 workers to accompany or join such workers. Had Congress been fully informed of the probable impact of this provision on the Virgin Islands, it is questionable that it would have taken this course. This is particularly true in view of the timing of the legislation, which was enacted on the eve of the major policy announcement by the U.S. Department of Labor, in May 1970, providing new

---

22. Lukas, "The Plaint of the Virgin Islands," pp. 108–109.
23. *The New York Times*, October 9, 1969, p. 47, col. 1.

procedures for certification of H-2 workers in the Islands. These new procedures provided, in effect, that all aliens working in the Virgin Islands as of December 31, 1969 would henceforth be considered a part of the permanent work force. They were issued indefinite certifications for employment in the Islands as nonimmigrants, and were free to change employers provided the new jobs were approved by the U.S. Labor Department, and that no more than 60 days elapsed between approved jobs. Previously, such workers had been required to leave the Islands within five days after termination of their employment. These two provisions together, therefore, operated to swell on a lasting basis the number of legal aliens in the Virgin Islands. According to a 1975 U.S. Government report:

> Probably the most significant impact of the H-4 provision was on the Virgin Islands, where its effect was to promote family reunification on a massive scale. Present estimates of the number of H-4 aliens on the U.S. Virgin Islands range from 20,000 to 30,000.[24]

The May 1970 policy in effect provided the right to certified nonimmigrant alien workers and their families to remain indefinitely in the Virgin Islands.

Although the Virgin Islands had a compulsory school attendance law applying to "all children," alien children virtually were excluded from the public schools by the following regulation of the local Department of Education:

> Noncitizens of school age may be enrolled in public elementary and secondary classes, provided that the enrollees:
> (1) are in good health;
> (2) present necessary school records or take a placement test;
> (3) do not cause the number of pupils in any class to exceed prescribed standards;
> (4) shall be given preference if their parents have worked legally in the Virgin Islands for at least two consecutive years and expect to remain in employment;
> (5) present satisfactory evidence of the inability of the off-island guardians to supervise them.
>
> It is further provided that the above conditions shall not apply to special education and multi-graded classes.[25]

---

24. *Nonimmigrant Alien Labor Program* (1975), p. 31.

25. Sec. 103-1, *Regulations of the Department of Education*, Government of the Virgin Islands, as quoted in *Hosier v. Evans*, 314 F. Supp. 316 (1970), n. 8 at pp. 321–322.

Few alien children could meet these qualifications. In an agreement of September 1969, however, with the Office of Economic Opportunity, the Department of Education agreed to admit sixteen alien children for each of eight VISTA volunteers provided by OEO as classroom teachers.[26] Four VISTA volunteers were dismissed the following December for organizing aliens into a "power group" to pressure the local government to admit all alien children to the public schools.[27]

On June 26, 1970, in the case of *Hosier v. Evans* before the United States District Court of the Virgin Islands, Judge Almeric Christian held that alien children are unquestionably "persons" within the meaning of the equal protection clause of the Fourteenth Amendment of the U.S. Constitution, made applicable to the Virgin Islands by the Revised Organic Act of 1954, and that they had a right to "free and unrestrained public education." Against the argument that the cost of educating alien children in the public schools would create an undue burden on the Government of the Virgin Islands, Judge Christian responded that "fundamental rights guaranteed by the Constitution may be neither denied nor abridged solely because their implementation requires the expenditure of public funds." For such purposes, asserted the Judge, the Government must raise the funds. Christian declared the regulation of the Department of Education null and void as imposing "unreasonable and invidious discrimination on alien children."[28]

The *Hosier* decision, in combination with the 1970 "1-1-4" legislation admitting dependents of alien workers, had an immediate and drastic impact on the already overcrowded Virgin Islands public schools. In the fall of 1972, 80 percent of new enrollees were alien children. As of December, 1974, noncitizen enrollment numbered a staggering 7,587 or 32.5 percent of the total enrollment of 23,343.

Racial issues, violent crime, and the so-called alien problem were not new to "America's Paradise" in 1970, but their troubling dimensions provided a heated political setting as Virgin Islanders prepared to choose their first elective governor.

First Elected Governor

When it became apparent that Senator Earle B. Ottley did not aspire to become Governor, a native of St. Croix, Senator Alexander Farrelly, announced

---

26. George Goodwin, *The Alien As a Minority Group in the U.S. Virgin Islands* (unpublished paper, typewritten, AIM, Charlotte Amalie, St. Thomas, May 14, 1970), p. 8.

27. *The Home Journal*, St. Thomas, December 5, 1969, p. 1.

28. *Hosier v. Evans*, 314 F. Supp. 316 (1970) at pp. 320, 321.

his candidacy in September 1969 for the Democratic nomination for that post.[29] Cyril King made his announcement in December for nomination by the Independent Citizens Movement, while incumbent Governor Melvin Evans remained silent about his intentions. All three were duly nominated by their respective party conventions in the summer of 1970, thus assuring that the first elective governor would be a Crucian—a reflection of the fact that political power was shifting to the most populous island of St. Croix.

With the preliminaries completed, the parties by October 1970 girded for political battle. It was a three-way contest, with Senator Farrelly and Elmo Roebuck—former Commissioner of Housing and Community Renewal—heading the Democratic ticket, incumbent Governor Evans and Government Secretary David Maas—a white continental in St. Thomas since 1945—leading the Republican ticket, and Cyril King and Hugh Smith—formerly with the Virgin Islands Security Agency—at the top of the ICM ticket. All contenders for the governorship were Crucians, and all candidates for Lieutenant Governor were St. Thomians, and all were black natives except Maas. The Democrats, of course, were favored, because the Democratic Party held all fifteen Senate seats and claimed over 70 percent of the registered voters, whereas ICM had only seven percent, and the Republicans only about five percent, with the remainder registered with no party.

As a result of the *Hosier* decision, all three gubernatorial candidates listed education as the most pressing problem in the Islands. Both Farrelly and King attacked Governor Evans on the issue, because construction of three new schools was not yet completed, and the Evans administration had not figured what to do with all the new pupils. According to one of King's aides:

> King had dug deeply into Comptroller Howard Ross's 1969 report of the peccadilloes and shortcomings of the Paiewonsky regime and played them back to the electorate with embellishments. He also tried to tie Evans to the shortcomings of the Nixon administration in Washington and, taking a word from the civil rights vocabulary, accused him of "tokenism" in his approach to government.[30]

Moreover, the Democrats warned that the election of Evans would "put a white man a heartbeat away from the governor's chair." A whispering campaign begun in the white community of St. Croix branded King a "black power advocate."

---

29. For lucid accounts of the 1970 elections, see: O'Neill, *Rape of the Virgin Islands*, pp. 153–173; and Hill, *Rise to Recognition*, pp. 155–164.

30. O'Neill, *Ibid.*, p. 164. O'Neill was a speech writer for King during the campaign.

It was quite a spirited and sometimes vicious campaign abetted by the three leading newspapers splitting three ways in their editorial support. *The St. Croix Avis* backed Evans; the St. Thomas *Daily News* supported King; and Ottley's *Home Journal* on St. Thomas predictably backed Farrelly.

Nearly 80 percent of the 19,756 registered voters went to the polls November 3, 1970, and when the votes were counted the next day it was clear that the Democratic Party had suffered a resounding defeat. King led the field with 5,422 votes; Evans was second with 4,926; and Farrelly was last with 4,634 votes. In the legislature, ICM elected six senators, the Democrats elected six, and the Republicans garnered three. In other words, the totally Democratic legislature had lost nine of the fifteen seats. Under the 1968 Elective Governor Act, a runoff election between the two top contenders was necessary since no candidate had won a majority.

The runoff was scheduled two weeks later, November 17. The defeated Ottley Democrats now made a deal to support Republicans Evans and Maas, and the new coalition promptly was dubbed "Republocrats." Previous namecalling was revived, with Evans himself now terming King a "racist" and Democrats spreading the word among government employees that if elected King would "swing a meat axe" in all government departments. Meanwhile, King advocates revived the Democrats' warning that Evans' election would put a white man (Maas) "a heartbeat away from the governor's chair." When the votes were counted after the runoff election, Evans received 8,259 to King's 7,452. The last appointed Governor, Dr. Melvin H. Evans, thus became the first elected Governor of the Virgin Islands.

Roundup of Illegals

Melvin Evans was inaugurated as the Islands' first elected Governor in January 1971. Crime and traffic in dangerous drugs continued to increase, especially in St. Croix, including assaults upon visiting elderly people.[31] Unemployed youth were blamed. Wilburn Smith, representing the Manpower Commission, stated that among the greatest problems was the reluctance of Virgin Islands youth to take advantage of available opportunities. He complained that in vocational classes in the various schools, capable of handling classes up to twenty-five or thirty, "you find only about five persons in the class."[32]

---

31. *The St. Croix Avis*, February 13 and 17, 1971, p. 1.
32. *The St. Croix Avis*, February 6, 1971, p. 1.

Hoping for more cooperation from the legislature than he had received previously, Governor Evans submitted bills that would have reduced from sixteen to fourteen years the age from which juveniles accused of committing felonies could be transferred from the juvenile court to the U.S. District Court for trial, required the establishment and maintenance of juvenile detention facilities, authorized police to fingerprint juvenile offenders between ages twelve and eighteen, provided a "no-knock law" whereby police with a warrant could search for narcotics or dangerous drugs without giving prior notice, and instituted a crash program "to reduce the scourge of drug abuse."[33]

In late February 1971, the body of a missing Puerto Rican girl of eight years of age was found in St. Croix, and three young alien men—two from St. Lucia and the other from Antigua—were arrested and charged with her kidnapping and murder.[34] A parade of five hundred to seven hundred St. Croix residents, all of Puerto Rican descent, marched on Government House in Christiansted demanding "action now" and carrying placards that showed gallows and empty nooses, with the names of the three arrested men beneath.[35]

Two days after the arrest of the three alien men, on February 25, 1971, the Immigration and Naturalization Service (INS) began a massive sweep of the Islands to round up and deport illegally present aliens. All apprehended aliens— men, women, and children—who could not produce papers or documents attesting to their legal presence in the Islands were briefly detained and summarily deported to their home islands. Estimates of the number deported or leaving voluntarily between late February and the end of June, when the roundup ceased, ranged from seven thousand to fifteen thousand.

Crucian Attorney Mario de Chabert, in April 1971, wrote an account of the sequence of events, as follows:

> During the first few months prior to ... the round-up ... there existed a wave of crime, mostly of the mugging and burglary type and mostly directed at tourists. Because of the dependency of the Virgin Islands on the tourist trade and our sensitivity about ruining it, many pressures were brought on the Evans Administration to clamp down on crime. No one seemed to know where to start in the eradicating process. Some seemed to feel that we should have started with the Department of Public Safety ... Others thought that per-

---

33. *The St. Croix Avis*, February 13, 1971, pp. 1, 20.
34. *The St. Croix Avis*, February 23, 24, and 25, 1971, p. 1.
35. *The St. Croix Avis*, March 3, 1971, p. 14. Attorney Albert Sheen, named to represent one of the defendants, withdrew from the case after receiving threats. *Ibid.*

haps the drug problem should be attacked.... Unfortunately, there was a slight rise in the unemployment rate during this period since this year's tourist season isn't up to expectation. But, nevertheless, the blame for this was placed on the alien who occupied a job and was here illegally. Our local manpower ... apprenticeship program had difficulty placing its people and this too was blamed on the alien who was here illegally and occupying a job. Then someone got the bright idea and decided to blame the alien who was here illegally for over fifty percent of the crime regardless of whether he was a working man with a family, a man with a substantial bank account, or an outright criminal.

The year's most brutal crime has now been committed. Three aliens are arrested and allegedly beaten. Two days later, Immigration moves in with a task force, beefed up by Texan Border Patrols and local policemen. Hundreds of aliens walking the streets are picked up and the Governor makes a public appearance accusing and blaming illegal aliens with over 50% of the crime. Of 56 prisoners sentenced and incarcerated ... March 15, 1971, 23 are Puerto Ricans, 18 aliens, 5 from the U.S.A., 1 from Colombia and 9 Virgin Islanders.[36]

Journalist Edward O'Neill called the roundup "Evans swoop." A U.S. Government study, also attributing the roundup to the Governor's initiative, asserted that Evans "appealed to the Deputy Attorney General regarding the need for additional personnel" in the local INS force to conduct the roundup.[37] George Goodwin, President of the Alien Interest Movement on St. Thomas, claimed that the naturalized citizens among voters did not support victor Evans in the 1970 election. "When election results showed this," said Goodwin, "retribution by Evans led to the 1971 alien roundup."[38] George Richards, a leader of the Concerned West Indians Movement of St. Croix, considered the roundup a direct reaction to the arrest of the three aliens accused of murdering the eight-year-old girl.[39]

Evans, himself, later estimating that at least twelve thousand illegals were rounded up in 1971, denied that he initiated or was responsible for the action.

---

36. Mario N. de Chabert, *Report on the Alien Dilemma* (unpublished, mimeographed, Christiansted, St. Croix, April 1971), pp. 7–8.

37. O'Neill, *Rape of the Virgin Islands*, p. 182; *Nonimmigrant Alien Labor Program* (1975), p. 43.

38. Interview, George Goodwin, July 25, 1977.

39. Interview, George Richards, Member of the Executive Committee, Concerned West Indians Movement, Inc., Christiansted, St. Croix, August 2, 1977.

The Immigration and Naturalization Service did it, but they talked to me about it. We did cooperate with INS, but when their methods prompted reports of the abuse of civil rights, I personally ordered my attorney general to look into these charges. In any event, there should never be any illegal aliens in the Virgin Islands. There is no way the Virgin Islands can become the educational and social reservoir for the Caribbean.[40]

Leaders of the alien associations in the Virgin Islands did not dispute the need to apprehend and deport if necessary illegal foreign nationals, but they protested vigorously the alleged "brutal" and "inhuman" treatment meted out by authorities. Reported *The San Juan Star*:

Increasing reports are reaching the public that the detained aliens are allegedly beaten and handcuffed, given little or no time to pack their belongings, are herded "animal-like" into police vehicles and bedded down in unsanitary and overcrowded quarters with no chance to contact their families.[41]

In response to reports of brutal treatment of illegal aliens, St. Croix leaders called for an island-wide boycott. A leaflet, circulated throughout St. Croix, proclaimed the demonstration, as follows:

Aliens are a vital part of the Virgin Islands economy, we amount to some 30 to 40 thousand residents participating in building the Islands economy. The Government of the Virgin Islands has for many years tacitly accepted the presence and services of all aliens, those legally or illegally here as fulfilling the need for labor and other valuable services needed. After many years of blood, sweat and tears it is the order of the same government that has used us in building the Islands to have some twenty thousand of us picked up like the Jews were in Nazi Germany and sent off the Islands within the next two months. This boycott is called in order that we may demonstrate and make known our feelings towards the Government's attitude and make our presence felt by every segment of the Virgin Islands community.

We urge all our alien brothers and Virgin Islanders in sympathy with our cause to refrain from buying in all stores and to stay away from all jobs for 24 hours Thursday March 4th.[42]

---

40. Interview, Congressman Melvin H. Evans, Washington, D.C., June 14, 1979.
41. *The San Juan Star*, San Juan, Puerto Rico, March 5, 1971, p. 24.
42. De Chabert, *Report on the Alien Dilemma*, p. 30.

On March 4th, hundreds of aliens walked off their jobs in St. Croix, and organized a motorcade that tied up traffic in Christiansted. A number of tourist hotels and other businesses had to close down.

The Virgin Islands Amalgamated Workers Union and the United Alien Association cabled President Nixon protesting the "seize and remove" tactics being employed as "reminiscent of slavery days." Basic human rights guaranteed by the United Nations Charter were also being "flagrantly violated," said the cable.[43]

In a letter to Governor Evans, Cephus Rogers, Acting President of the United Alien Association, stated:

> Eye witnesses have reported to us that these people are picked up from the street, from their jobs and dragged from their homes. They are herded like cattle and taken to Richmond Penitentiary where they are not even allowed to see their relatives or advised of available legal assistance.
>
> Many have been residing here from five to ten years and own property here. Many have children who are U.S. citizens.
>
> In many cases the ones who should be punished are the unscrupulous employers who have exploited these people and forced them into their illegal status by repeated promises of securing a bond.[44]

Local businessmen were dismayed and angered by the roundup, representing as it did a severe cut in the labor pool. As a result of the deportation of so many employed persons, bank deposits declined precipitously, tourist hotels became understaffed, occupancy of apartments plunged, and a number of business establishments—including even the Paiewonsky-owned Apollo movie theater on St. Thomas—closed down.

Most of the deportees were citizens of the British West Indies, and their treatment was properly the concern of the British Consul in the Virgin Islands, Henry O'Neal, who commented:

> In 1971, approximately 7,000 aliens were rounded up and sent home. I was not happy with the manner in which this was done, because many were imprisoned, crowded into jails, their basic human rights denied, and their human dignity offended. Notwithstanding they were here illegally, they were not given sufficient time to gather

---

43. *The Trinidad Express*, March 16, 1971, p. 1.

44. Letter to Governor Melvin H. Evans from Cephus N. Rogers, Acting President, United Alien Association, dated February 28, 1971, reprinted in *The Home Journal*, St. Thomas, March 10, 1971.

their personal effects. They were not given any hearings; neither was my office informed. Not only were their human rights violated, but this action was a direct contravention of the consular convention existing between the British Government and the U.S. Government. When I attempted to visit some of these people under detention, I was told I would need a letter of authority to do so from the INS. Because of their lack of an educational background, they did not understand INS regulations. They had been exploited by unscrupulous people who were only interested in making money and had no interest in them otherwise.[45]

The roundup and banishment to British islands evoked a number of protests from Caribbean leaders, two of whom chose to visit the Virgin Islands—Premier Robert Bradshaw of the Associated State of St. Kitts-Nevis-Anguilla, and newly-elected Premier George Walter of Antigua.[46] At the behest of Premier Walter, a delegation of the West Indies Associated States met with U.S. officials on July 8, 1971 to negotiate the terms and conditions under which the employment of nationals of the Associated States in the U.S. Virgin Islands was to be continued.[47]

Despite a plethora of complaints of inhumane treatment of illegal aliens in the Virgin Islands, and the many expressions of concern, officials of the Virgin Islands Government denied their validity as "wild rumors" and Governor Evans dismissed them as "baseless."[48] "We are not blaming aliens in general for crime," said Governor Evans, "but we do know that a disproportionate rate of crime is being committed by illegal aliens."[49] The three young alien men accused of murdering the little girl in St. Croix were convicted, but the submission of new evidence proved their innocence and they were acquitted in late 1972. In 1975, the federal District Court awarded them damages for injuries they sustained due to "personal or even racial considerations" during their incarceration and questioning by Puerto Rican police officers in St. Croix.[50]

---

45. Interview, Henry O'Neal, M.B.E., British Consul in the U.S. Virgin Islands, Charlotte Amalie, St. Thomas, July 22, 1977.

46. *The St. Croix Avis*, March 10, 1971, p. 14; *The Home Journal*, St. Thomas, March 17, 1971, p. 1.

47. *Nonimmigrant Alien Labor Program* (1975), p. 44.

48. *The St. Croix Avis*, March 5, 1971, p. 14.

49. *The San Juan Star*, March 5, 1971, p. 24.

50. *The St. Croix Avis*, July 20, 1975, p. 2.

Alienation of the Land

Most black native Virgin Islanders never owned any land. Throughout the Danish period, and well into the American period, a small number of white families—planters and merchants—owned nearly all the land and property aside from that owned by government. The intent of the homestead program of the early 1930s was to break up old sugar plantations of St. Croix and subdivide the land into homesteads for the tillers of the soil. The program was unsuccessful. "We remember very well," recalled William C. Dowling, "the homestead lands which were supposed to go to the poor people. But through some quirk or government agency, the only people who ever got them were the political people in the island, in the legislature."[51]

Other land deals of subsequent years were at least as highly questionable. After the Second World War, Navy lands and property on St. Thomas, that had been used for defense purposes, were no longer needed and were turned over to the U.S. Department of the Interior for management. The Interior Department, in turn, delegated to the local government its authority with respect to the properties. Through lease arrangements, the local government "permitted private persons to occupy and use lands ... for varying periods of time and for varying amounts of compensation." Finally, in October 1963, the U.S. Senate's Interior Committee voted unanimously to conduct an investigation. At the subsequent hearing, John J. Kirwan, then assistant director of Interior's Office of Territories, claimed that there never was any "legal basis for such leases."[52]

The leasing of U.S. Government-owned land for private development and profit was not confined to the old Navy properties. The fourth U.S. Virgin Is-

---

51. *Hearings before the Senate Subcommittee on Territories and Insular Affairs, Leasing of Naval Properties in the Virgin Islands*, 88th Cong., 1st sess., October 29 and 30, 1963, p. 106.

52. *Ibid.*, pp. 1, 144. The so-called "Gramboko property" was leased by the Government of the Virgin Islands (GVI) which received an annual rent of $8,000, whereupon "the GVI (Department of Education) subleased the property from the lessee at an annual rent of $72,000 for use as a grammar school," even though the GVI could have acquired the property "through condemnation procedures." *Annual Report of the U.S. Government Comptroller for the Virgin Islands on the Government of the Virgin Islands, Fiscal Year Ended June 30, 1974* (Office of the Secretary, U.S. Department of the Interior, June 27, 1975), p. 41. The Gramboko affair still remained an issue at the end of the 1970s. Interview, E. Charles Downs, Desk Officer, Guam and the Virgin Islands, Office of Territorial Affairs, U.S. Department of the Interior, Washington, D.C., August 14, 1979. See, also, "A Statement from Eleanor Heckert About Gramboko," *Daily News*, September 4, 1979, p. 36.

land in size and the largest within the harbor of St. Thomas—two-miles-long Water Island—belonged to the U.S. Army which began building an Army base there, Fort Segarra, during World War II. Construction ceased when the war ended, and the Army discontinued use of the Island in 1950, whereupon it leased the Island to the Development Authority of the Municipality of St. Thomas and St. John. Even though the Authority had only a five-year lease, which the Army could cancel at any time, the Authority nevertheless subleased the whole Island to the Water Island, Inc., a Virgin Islands corporation formed by a white continental, Walter Phillips, for the purpose of commercially developing the Island. Congress transferred Water Island from the Army to the Interior Department in 1952 which promptly gave Phillips' Water Island, Inc., a long lease with firm rights of renewal.

The lease granted to Phillips was a rare example of an extraordinarily generous lease of U.S. public land without competitive bidding to a private party for private profit. The entire Island of five hundred acres, "including all improvements and personal property located thereon and beaches and riparian rights appurtenant thereto," was leased by the Secretary of Interior to Walter Phillips for a term of twenty years with an option renewable by Phillips—not the Secretary—for a further period of twenty years, or, in other words, a forty year nonrevocable lease until 1992.

Concerning the facilities left by the U.S. Army, the Secretary not only granted Phillips the right to occupy all government "improvements"—structures, docks utilities, etc.—on the Island "without obligation on the Lessee for maintenance or repair," but also he granted Phillips the right "to make such alteration and additions" or to effect "the removal" of such improvements. "The Lessee shall have a possessory interest in all improvements made or acquired by it." The Interior Department's interest, according to the lease, was that the Island "might be developed in such a manner as to contribute effectively to the economy of the Virgin Islands." The lessee and sub-lessees, nevertheless, were specifically exempted from paying property taxes to the Virgin Islands Government. Upon termination of the lease, they were to be reimbursed at "fair value" by the Interior Department. For his part, Phillips was required to pay an annual rent of $3,000 plus three percent of "gross receipts" in excess of $200,000 and four percent in excess of $300,000. Thus, Phillips gained control of one of the oldest geologic formations and choicest pieces of real estate in the Caribbean. Thereafter, a resort hotel and permanent and vacation homes and villas were built on the Island.

Edward McArdle acquired part ownership in Phillips corporation in 1965, and J. Edward Bishop gained control of the Island in 1978 to further develop it as a resort. In her 1975 doctoral dissertation, Hazel McFerson described this fourth largest of the Virgin Islands as a "de facto apartheid ... all white enclave for the sixty-five white property owners.[53]

One of the most valuable and historic sites in the Virgin Islands is Hassel Island (before 1860 an isthmus) which also guards the spectacularly scenic St. Thomas harbor. Much of Hassel Island was acquired by the Paiewonsky family in the 1930s chiefly to provide water for the family's distilleries. The Paiewonsky family acquired more of the Island in the 1940s from the Interior Department for restoration purposes, until the family owned one hundred and twenty-five of the Island's one hundred and thirty-five acres. From this point onward, the development of Hassel Island departed significantly from that of Water Island.

Ralph Paiewonsky wanted to develop the Island commercially, with construction of condominiums and tourist-related facilities. Indeed, the controversial Korean cleric, Reverend Sun Myong Moon, offered the Paiewonskys $3 million for the property, and a group of German bankers offered $5 million to build condominiums on the Island. Isidor Paiewonsky, however, was committed to the preservation of the Island's natural setting and as an historic site. Accordingly, these lucrative offers were declined.

Finally, the two brothers reached a compromise decision to turn the Island into a national park. In 1978, Congress authorized the Secretary of Interior to acquire Hassel Island by paying to the owners "the fair market value" for the Island and to make it a part of the National Park System. Whatever compensation ultimately accrued to the Paiewonsky family, it was much less than the amount they could have realized by commercially developing or selling the Island. Indeed, Isidor Paiewonsky boasted that his family is "giving 50 percent of the land for the Park as an *outright gift* to the National Park System."[54] He

---

53. Hazel M. McFerson, *The Impact of a Changed Racial Tradition: Race, Politics and Society in the U.S. Virgin Islands, 1917–1975* (unpublished Ph.D. dissertation, Brandeis University, 1975), p. 133. The lease to Phillips, dated December 10, 1952, was termed "a bad lease" in an interview by E. Charles Downs, Desk Officer, Guam and the Virgin Islands, Office of Territorial Affairs, U.S. Department of the Interior, Washington, D.C., August 14, 1979. A copy of the lease was obtained during an interview from Robert Bowles, Solicitor's Office, U.S. Department of the Interior, Washington, D.C., August 14, 1979. Bowles indicated that the Department was making inquiries in 1979 of the Virgin Islands Government's possible interest in acquiring jurisdiction and ownership of Water Island from the Interior Department. See, also, Donald Janson, "A New Retreat in the Virgin Islands," *The New York Times*, December 3, 1967, sec. 10, p. 15, col. 1; and Freck Hart, "Water Isle Resort Begins Anew as Sugarbird," *San Juan Star*, Travel News, December 31, 1977; and "Water Isle Investors Plead for Extension," *Daily News*, March 27, 1979, pp. 1, 6.

54. Letter to the Editor from Isidor Paiewonsky, St. Thomas, V. I., dated July 18, 1978, *Daily News*, July 19, 1978; see, also, Mary Munroe, "Report from Washington," *Daily News*, May 18 and July 8, 1978; Penny Feuerzeig, "Hassel Restoration: 'Labor of Love,'" *Daily*

predicted that it "is quite likely" that the island park would become a tourist attraction.

However commendable may have been the altruism of the wealthy Paiewonsky family, their disposition of Hassel Island permanently removed it from possible habitation by other Virgin Islanders. The same could be said, of course, of Laurance Rockefeller's disposition of the Island of St. John. Despite past intermittent assurances to native residents of St. John that the Virgin Islands National Park would not seek to acquire more land, especially after the "condemnation" fiasco of 1962, Congress continued to appropriate millions for further acquisitions.[55] Not everyone viewed Rockefeller's ventures on St. John with equanimity, as witness one of Jack Anderson's 1978 columns revealing wealthy Laurance Rockefeller as "quietly cashing in" on two federal government energy grants totalling $211,191 to install solar equipment at "two of the poshest, most exclusive hotels in North America—the Woodstock Inn in Vermont and the Caneel Bay Plantation on St. John Island in the Caribbean."

> The Rockefeller grants puzzled Rep. Richard Ottinger, D.-N.Y., who fired off a private letter to Energy Secretary James Schlesinger, informing the energy czar that he was "flabbergasted" by the hefty grants, which he described as "ludicrous."
>
> At Rockefeller's Caneel Bay Plantation, wealthy guests pay up to $150 a day to frolic in the sun and sand. Few average Americans can afford a trip to the elite resort, which is directly benefitting from taxpayer funds.
>
> Ottinger also noted that developer Rockefeller cannily rode the crest of the conservation wave to build at least one of his resorts—the Caneel Bay Plantation—and assured its exclusivity by getting the adjacent property designated as part of the Virgin Islands National Park.[56]

The introduction of heavy industry into St. Croix effectively alienated thousands of acres of land, an arrangement engineered through a secret deal by insular politicians, and imposed with duplicity upon a reluctant St. Croix—"the most galling and controversial of all the issues to arise during the Paiewonsky

---

News, March 30, 1977, pp. 1, 22. Interview, Senator-elect Michael Paiewonsky, Hassel Island, St. Thomas, November 20, 1978. See, 92 *Stat.* 494, Public Law 95-348, August 18, 1978.

55. See, *e.g.*, Page Stull, "Park to Expand by $2 Million," *Daily News*, November 16, 1977.

56. *Daily News*, March 20, 1978, pp. 6, 23. "Prices for a double room in season ... range from $155 to $175 a day." Robert W. Stock, " 'Perfection'—at a Price," *The New York Times*, December 26, 1976, Travel Section, p. 1.

administration," according to Florence Lewisohn. The pending deal was shrouded in secrecy leading to Crucian demands for a public hearing. Those in opposition to an alumina processing plant were not given the floor at the hearing. Recounted author Lewisohn:

> In the ensuing shambles, the government supporters declared the opposition was "racist" and that the local white and colored upper class wanted to keep the mass of black Cruzans economically depressed. One of the points through which the government spokesmen were attempting to get approval for the idea of the projected plant was on the basis of benefits to local employment. Since St. Croix was importing thousands of aliens to fill jobs for which there were not enough Cruzans to go around, this, and the red-herring of the racial issue, only confirmed the local Cruzan leaders in their suspicions. Altogether the so-called 'public hearings' constituted perhaps one of the most undemocratic episodes ever occurring on the island in all its history.
>
> It was soon discovered that the contract for the plant had been approved by the Senate and signed by the governor before the 'public hearing' had been held. The Legislature, dominated by the St. Thomas Unity-Democrats, had confirmed the governor's arrangement with the company in secret session.[57]

Accordingly, Harvey Alumina Company was given free approximately 1,200 acres of government-owned land, and subsequent efforts to challenge the contract terms in court failed.

Leon Hess, in contrast to Leo Harvey, paid for the thousands of acres on which his company refinery was built. "There was little left to object to," wrote Lewisohn, "as the 'damage was done' and the Cruzans knew when they had lost a fight to save their wild and beautiful south shore and lagoon area."[58]

In mid-island St. Croix, about two thousand acres of former VICORP land was put up for private sale by the Virgin Islands Government on condition that it be utilized for agriculture. A subsidiary of the alumina processing company, Harvlan Properties, Inc.—a Harvey family enterprise, acquired the property in 1968. "Harvlan never fulfilled the condition; they never grew anything on the land," lamented Crucian Attorney Mario de Chabert. "They bought it cheaply (maybe $600 per acre)." In 1979, it was proposed that the Virgin Islands Government buy back this land for approximately $10 million. "It is scan-

---

57. Lewisohn, *St. Croix Under Seven Flags*, pp. 397–398.
58. *Ibid.*, p. 401.

dalous," commented de Chabert. "This is the most agriculturally fertile land in the Virgin Islands."[59] Meanwhile, much of the former VICORP acreage reserved by the Virgin Islands Government for public benefit remained fallow and unused.

This growing corporate ownership was part of the general takeover of the Islands' economy by continental interests. Although there was no data on business ownership by race, one close observer of this subject observed: "The 'fact' that mainland whites control the local economy is something 'everybody knows.'" And he added that "at least 75 to 80 percent of the large businesses on the Virgin Islands are continental-owned."[60]

On both St. Croix and St. Thomas, the landscape became dotted with condominiums, hotels, "unbelievably ugly housing developments," expensive houses of continentals perched on hillsides affording expansive ocean views, and beachfront tourist facilities of every description. Professor Macridis observed in 1970:

> The majority of whites work in the tourist industry, own firms, provide managerial skills, or simply live in the sun.... They also own a great deal of land. While the whites constitute not more than one-fourth of the population, they own more than half of the land, whose value has been skyrocketing.[61]

The issue of public access to and use of the beaches of the Virgin Islands has been one of the most contentious conflicts in modern Virgin Islands' history, and one fraught with racial overtones. Throughout Danish rule and American rule as well, into the 1950s, the people of the Virgin Islands enjoyed unobstructed use of the beaches.[62] The Virgin Islands Legislature expressed its intent "to preserve what has been a tradition and to protect what has become a right of the public."[63] Nevertheless, Ellis Gladwin described the situation in St. Croix in 1970 to be the following:

---

59. Interview, Attorney Mario N. de Chabert, Christiansted, St. Croix, July 5, 1979. See, also, Lewisohn, *St. Croix Under Seven Flags*, p. 403.

60. William Jay Kruvant, *Socio-economic Development in the U.S. Virgin Islands: An Historical Materialist Approach* (unpublished Ph.D. dissertation, American University, 1976), pp. 324, 332.

61. Roy C. Macridis, "Political Attitudes in the Virgin Islands," in Bough and Macridis, eds., *Virgin Islands*, p. 194.

62. See, *e.g.*, Eva Lawaetz, *The Applicability of the Danish Law Concerning Public Right to Traffic and Use of Beaches as a Common and Public Access* (typewritten, Christiansted Public Library, Department of Conservation and Cultural Affairs, Government of the Virgin Islands, May, 1971).

63. Title 12, *Virgin Islands Code*, Section 401.

Many who owned land running to the beach had sold their property without realizing that they had also sold their beachright. This may seem naive, but to the Virgin Islander the beaches were his birthright. When he realized that the wealthy white man from the States had made the beach in front of his land his private property, he bitterly resented this takeover. For the first time ... "Keep Off" and "No Trespassing" signs appeared.[64]

On every other island throughout the Caribbean, the beaches belonged to the public who had free access to them. "One of the major mistakes made in the Virgin Islands," wrote Gladwin, "was the sale of beaches to individual property owners."[65] The courts of the Virgin Islands in the 1970s held, however, that submerged lands in the Virgin Islands up to the mean high water mark are owned by the United States Government, and fences erected to obstruct the free access of the public to beaches of the Virgin Islands (from the high water mark on sandy areas to 50 feet inland) were in violation of the Virgin Islands Open Shorelines Act of 1971 and must be removed.[66] The highly tense issue of access to beaches from the landward side was not raised in these cases and remained still unresolved at the end of the 1970s. Enactment of the proposed Coastal Zone Management Act that would provide for such access appeared to be a viable solution. "Beach access across otherwise private property," observed Peter de Zela, "has not been a sticky question in any other jurisdiction under the American flag."[67]

In 1964, David and Laurance Rockefeller purchased forty-four hundred picturesque acres of northwest St. Croix, including portions of the north shore Davis Bay area, the rain-forested northwest mountains, and the rolling land to the south of the mountains on which they developed the champion-caliber Fountain Valley Golf Course. The eighteen-hole golf course (the first in the

---

64. Ellis Gladwin, *Living in the Changing Caribbean* (1970), p. 18.

65. *Ibid.* See, also, McFerson, *The Impact of a Changed Racial Tradition*, pp. 132–134.

66. *United States v. St. Thomas Beach Resorts, Inc.*, 11 V.I. 79, 386 F. Supp. 769 (1974); *Red Hook Marina Corp. v. Antilles Yachting Corp.*, 9 V.I. 236 (1971). See, also, Virgin Islands Open Shorelines Act, Title 12, *Virgin Islands Code*, Chapter 10.

67. Penny Feuerzeig, "What Happened? Coastal Zone Management Bill," *Daily News*, August 1, 1977, p. 20. In the Turquoise Bay Area, St. Thomas, marked with "Private Beaches" signs, a youngster was shot by a condominium "entrepreneur" for swimming and sitting on the beach. See, letter to the Editor from Darwin A. King, dated February 23, 1977, *Daily News*, February 28, 1977, pp. 7–8. For the decades-old battle over the collection of "admission fees" to Coki Point on St. Thomas, the site of Coral World—a major tourist facility, see *Daily News*, July 7 and 26, 1978, p. 1.

Virgin Islands) and beach facilities were opened in 1966.[68] The Rockefeller brothers formed in 1967 Rockresorts, Inc., to manage these enterprises among others. In August 1978, Rockresorts, Inc., in New York issued a "directive" to close the access road to the beach at Davis Bay.[69]

The unquenched avarice for more and more tourists' dollars, mixed with the ever-present inter-island rivalry, prompted St. Thomas' business and political leaders not only to propose building a new jet airport on the east end of St. Thomas equal to that of St. Croix—a goal never achieved by Ralph Paiewonsky, in part because of conservationist Isidor's opposition—but also to propose development of St. Thomas' own first-class golf course. During February and March 1978, almost every daily issue of St. Thomas' newspapers carried reports and discussions of the proposal to construct an eighteen-hole championship golf course and an adjacent condominium development complex, called Mahogany Run, on St. Thomas' north central side. Those who opposed the project were labeled "advocates of economic underdevelopment" by one local newspaper.[70]

The verdant, breeze-swept, Fountain Valley Golf Course, cupped on three sides by hills, offered varied terrain and a scenic setting to attract many affluent tourists from the States. Some were prominent golf addicts who bought property on St. Croix. A St. Thomas monthly magazine reported in February 1967: "Former Vice President Dick Nixon secured two and a half acres in the wilds of northwest St. Croix, near the Rockefeller's Fountain Valley golf course."[71] Spiro Agnew and his wife owned a fashionable condominium near Christiansted from 1967 to 1976.

In the 1970s the local business and political establishment were willing to consider almost anything to attract even more continentals and their money to the Islands, ranging from "quickie divorces" and casino gambling to construction of a mammoth and costly St. Croix convention center with 100 more condominiums on beach-front land.

Already, by the end of the 1960s, alienation of the land, including almost all of the beaches of St. Thomas and St. Croix, had proceeded under the guise of "development" to the extent that one author was prompted to write a book entitled *Rape of the Virgin Islands*. In a more academic vein, Professor Jerome McElroy of the College of the Virgin Islands wrote in 1975:

---

68. Orlins, *The Impact of Tourism*, pp. 100–101, 438–440.

69. *The St. Croix Avis*, August 17, 1978, p. 1.

70. Editorial, *Daily News*, March 1, 1978.

71. *Virgin Islands View*, February, 1967, vol. 2, no. 9, p. 12. There is no record of this purchase under Richard Nixon's name in the Recorder of Deeds Office in St. Croix.

Finally, perhaps the major structural incompatibility is the exploitative parasitism that develops between an open, metropolitan-connected, aggressive economy and a fragile, passive, unprotected environment. The basic outcome of this functional imbalance is that scarce resources are rapidly depleted for substantially nonresident beneficiaries.[72]

Fountain Valley

According to U.S. census data,[73] the population of the Virgin Islands almost doubled from 32,099 in 1960 to 62,468 in 1970. The latter figure represented a serious undercount, however, because of the tendency of aliens to avoid contacts with civil authority, including census workers. The Virgin Islands Government's own estimate was around 83,000 to 84,000 for 1970.

The 1970 U.S. census counted only 4,014 Puerto Ricans, but this figure did not include those born in the Virgin Islands. Those who were Puerto Ricans or of Puerto Rican descent represented an estimated 25 percent of the total population, most of whom were in St. Croix. The 1970 census counted a total white population of 11,339, more than double the 1960 figure of 5,373. Most whites were continentals, although the two French communities on St. Thomas together numbered an estimated 1,500, and the white population also included a sprinkling of Danish descendants, particularly on St. Croix. The Virgin Islands Government's own estimates in 1975 counted a total population of 92,430 of whom 46,330 were in St. Croix, 43,910 in St. Thomas, and 2,190 in St. John, the total comprising a white population of 20,519 and a nonwhite count of 71,911.[74] Congressman Ron de Lugo estimated in 1972 the total number of aliens in the Islands to be 55,000,[75] which seemed high in view of the 1971 roundup and deportation of illegals. Even if aliens totaled 40,000 to 45,000, however, they represented nearly half the total population.

---

72. Jerome L. McElroy, "Tourist Economy and Island Environment: An Overview of Structural Disequilibrium," *Caribbean Educational Bulletin* (Association of Caribbean Universities, San Juan, Puerto Rico), 2 (January 1975): 54.

73. Bureau of the Census, U.S. Department of Commerce, *1970 Census of Population. General Population Characteristics, Virgin Islands of the United States.* PC (1)-B55 (Washington: Govt. Print. Off., 1972).

74. See, Table P-1, *Population by Age, Virgin Islands and Each Island: 1975*, and Table P-2, *Population by Age, Race, and Sex, Virgin Islands: 1975* (St. Thomas: Bureau of Vital Statistics, Government of the U.S. Virgin Islands, 1976).

75. *The San Juan Star*, San Juan, Puerto Rico, December 3, 1972, p. 3.

Nobody knew which figures were accurate. Two conclusions were apparent, nevertheless, from the official U.S. census: (1) for the first time since the 1940s St. Croix recorded more inhabitants than did St. Thomas; and (2) for the first time, native Virgin Islanders were in the minority. With the aliens and the continentals added to the Puerto Ricans, Crucians found themselves in a numerical minority on St. Croix.

The atmosphere of their island was changing. Indeed, St. Croix was no longer *their* island. Tourist facilities and condominiums, heavy industry, the duty-free shops, the golf course, were all built with white capital and alien labor, and "the difference between boss and worker increasingly became the difference between white and black."[76] Crucians saw their island society disintegrating. Norwell Harrigan put the matter this way:

> They saw the juxtaposition of vacationing whites and laboring blacks as a manifestation of a built-in prejudice-confirming factor and a perpetuation of the old-style subservience and the traditions of slavery, in which the role of the black man was to serve the white. And this fact was trumpeted to the whole world through brochures, advertisements, and television commercials in which they were identified in their own lands as waiters, cleaning maids, bartenders and cabdrivers.[77]

From the midst of this Crucian malaise reappeared Mario Moorhead. Imprisoned at Lewisburg Penitentiary on the mainland, Moorhead spent his time writing letters to local editors in the Islands and a type of Third World Marxist critique of the Virgin Islands. The critique was later published locally as a book entitled *Mammon vs History*. Meanwhile, portions were circulated among his Crucian friends through late 1971 and early 1972.

It was Moorhead's thesis that the Virgin Islands had become dominated by continental whites constituting an alien ruling class. He rejected the contention that the native-controlled government could be relied on to curb the ruling class or that any solution could be found by working within the system. In the preface of his book, dated August 3, 1972, he wrote that "once the society becomes oppressive to the masses of people's productive ability, honest but ignorant leadership can only be in the interest of the ruling class."[78] In the text of his book, Moorhead described the present Virgin Islands as "totally domi-

---

76. Calvin Trillin, "U.S. Journal: St. Croix, American Virgin Islands, Indigenous Population," *The New Yorker*, February 25, 1974, p. 113.

77. Quoted in *ibid.*, p. 114

78. Mario C. Moorhead, *Mammon vs History* (St. Croix: Square Deal Printer, 1973), p. xiv.

nated" by foreign capital and white-owned businesses, with blacks working either for the government or in "subservient" positions.

> Who else but the ignorant native leaders can be responsible for this situation! When a white man opens a business, hires white executive personnel and black menial workers, then builds a home on the beach and raises his no-trespassing signs, we must remember that it is the foreign capital invited by our leaders that made this possible.
>
> Racial discrimination permeates the entire Virgin Islands society for all to see. As in most black colonies with white colonizers, the specious political power of natives would seem to negate the existence of racial discrimination. However, the government is not the ruling class; it is an instrument fashioned by the ruling class for its justification, protection and survival.... And as long as the relations of production place the owners of the means of production in an alien colonizer society, no amount of propaganda to the contrary can make the government other than subject to that alien ruling class. The alien ruling class being white and the natives of the colonized society being black, racial discrimination is an obvious corollary as wet earth from rainfall.[79]

Mario Moorhead, albeit a leader and intellectual among his peers, reflected—rather than contributed to—the growing resentment and radicalization of the Crucian younger generation. These were the young men and women who chose not to take government jobs. They were the alienated—alienated from the government that had made all the deals, and alienated from the white dominated society that had resulted. Their frustration and anger provided the setting for what U.S. Attorney Julio Brady termed "the most heinous crime in the history of the Virgin Islands and one of the most vicious in the annals of western civilization."[80]

There were sixteen persons gathered in the clubhouse area of the Fountain Valley Golf Course in midafternoon of September 6, 1972. They included seven white persons and nine blacks. The whites were two vacationing couples from Miami—the Meisingers and Griffins, a part-time model managing the pro shop—Patricia Tarbert, a Massachusetts-born greenskeeper—John Gulliver, and an electrician—Nicholas Beale. The blacks included Aliston Lowery—

---

79. *Ibid.*, pp. 158–159.

80. *Government's Reply Brief to Defendents' Rule 25 Motion to Reduce Their Sentences, Government of the Virgin Islands v. Beaumont Gereau et al.*, In the District Court of the Virgin Islands, Division of St. Croix, No. 97-1972, undated, pp. 8–9.

Beale's assistant, and eight employees. The atmosphere was relaxed and friendly as usual. Suddenly, five masked gunmen in green Army fatigues entered the clubhouse from different directions, ordered at gun point the two couples to stand at the bar, Mrs. Tarbert to kneel, and Gulliver, Beale and Lowery to lie face down. The gunmen then proceeded to rob the tourists, the bartender, and the cash register for a total of approximately $800.[81]

U.S. Attorney Julio Brady later described the ensuing events as follows:

> The killings started almost casually. The record reflects that Ishmael LaBeet walked over to the Meisingers and the Griffins and said words to the effect, "I hate those white motherfuckers" ... and, at point blank range, with a .45 caliber machine gun shot one of the male tourists, Charles Meisinger. Almost simultaneously either LaBeet or one of the other defendants barked words to the effect, "Don't sorry for them and don't leave no one on the floor" ... The awful clatter of the machine gun and the Luger automatic pistol, the roar of three shotguns dominated the scene. Pandemonium broke loose. Those eight persons who had not directly been held at gun point scattered to save their lives. In the process four of them were shot and wounded....
>
> Of the sixteen persons trapped in this scene of terror only four escaped unscathed by the deadly fire power unleashed by these defendants.
>
> An examination of the scene confirmed that all eight of the victims who were fatally shot were in the same positions that they were in when the shooting began.... Each of the victims, except John Gulliver, sustained multiple gunshot wounds fired from one or more weapons, and each victim suffered at least one gunshot wound in the hack or the back of the head.[82]

After the murders of the seven whites and one black, the five gunmen, according to Brady, "were seen casually strolling from the scene of their carnage."

The killings immediately became headline news throughout the United States.[83] To supplement local police, thirty-four agents of the Federal Bureau

---

81. *Ibid.*, pp. 3–5. For the first eyewitness press accounts, see: Gene Miller and Don Bohning, "Anatomy of a Massacre—8 Minutes to Live," *The Miami Herald*, September 12, 1972.

82. *Government's Reply Brief*, pp. 5–9.

83. See, Robert W. Vaughn, *The Virgin Islands of the United States: Social, Economic, and Political Conditions Referred to in Recent Periodical Literature* (Christiansted, St. Croix: Aye-Aye Press, 1974), pp. 25–35.

of Investigation (FBI) converged on St. Croix. Arrested and charged within days of the slayings were five young black men, all from well known native families—Beaumont Gereau, Ishmael LaBeet, Warren Ballentine, Meral Smith and Rafael Joseph. All five were in their twenties, and three were Vietnam War veterans. The FBI gathered evidence linking the five to the murders.[84] Heading up their defense was William Kunstler, the radical lawyer who ran the defense of the Chicago Seven conspiracy trial and also was representing H. Rap Brown on criminal charges. Detention of the defendants and pre-trial proceedings through the next ten months were marked by intermittent outbursts, courtroom disruption, assaults, scuffles, and shouted obscenities involving the prisoners and authorities. Kunstler tried unsuccessfully to induce U.S. District Court Judge Warren Young to disqualify himself from presiding. Judge Young was white and had been assigned the case by Chief Judge Almeric Christian, a black.

The extraordinary string of pre-trial motions delayed jury selection and opening of the trial. Meanwhile, the accused charged they were the victims of torture by Virgin Islands police officers—allegations which prompted Attorney Kunstler to try to prove their confessions were coerced. In the duty-free shops of Christiansted, young Crucians distributed printed leaflets claiming that "genocide" was being committed "upon our five native sons."

> They have been tortured, condemned and now harassed and threatened by certain government officials, foreign marshals, along with local lackeys.... These evil Gestapo acts will not be tolerated if they are further carried out upon the five brothers.[85]

Meanwhile, Judge Young undertook certain extraordinary preparations for the trial. He arranged for the showing of a film to various lawyers depicting Judge Hoffman's behavior at the Chicago Seven trial, which helped Young to steel himself against insults from the defendants. Next, he read everything he could find concerning conjugal rights for prisoners. The only precedents he could find pertained to conjugal rights for prisoners incarcerated after conviction. He questioned what rights other than liberty should be deprived the accused pending their trial, and he wondered whether the five defendants would have caused outbursts and courtroom disruption had they been granted conjugal rights.[86]

---

84. *Report of the FBI Laboratory, FBI File No. 62-115300* (Federal Bureau of Investigation, Washington, D.C., October 3, 1972).

85. Jon Nordheimer, "Torture Alleged in St. Croix Case," *The New York Times,* May 5, 1973, P. 23, col. 4.

86. Interview, Judge Warren H. Young, U.S. District Court, Christiansted, St. Croix, July 3, 1978.

Accordingly, Judge Young ordered that conjugal rights be permitted the defendants "as a privileged right and arranged discreetly and in a circumspect manner by those in charge of the special Anna's Hope Detention Center." This was an unprecedented action. Pre-trial detainees had never before been granted conjugal rights by a U.S. federal court, but Judge Young justified his order by referring to treatment of prisoners that approaches constitutional dimensions, including visitations with family and friends, consultation with lawyers, and edible board and habitable room.

> I have not listed "conjugal rights," but why not? Is it because the good people on the outside would be shocked or aghast? I believe, initially that the conservative people might. There are plethora of treatises and volumes of books now being written by psychologists, sociologists and penologists as to the physical, psychological and the societal effect in the prisons of the deprivation of this one human right in post-conviction imprisonment.[87]

When Judge Young later learned that conjugal rights were being exercised by defendants in the presence of each other, he replaced local police at the detention center with federal marshals. He considered the defendants "better behaved" for a time thereafter, until they found he would not suppress certain evidence whereupon they reverted to their previous hostile behavior.[88] Meanwhile, Judge Young was severely criticized for his order granting conjugal rights.[89]

Finally a jury of eleven blacks and one white was impaneled, and the trial of the so-called "Fountain Valley Five" commenced. The trial was frequently interrupted by defendants' outbursts and shouted obscenities, and at one point the trial proceeded without the presence of the defendants who "boycotted" the proceedings. The trial lasted a month before the case went to the jury.

After two reported deadlocks and eight days of deliberation, a unanimous jury found the defendants guilty on eight counts of murder, four of assault with intent to kill, and two of robbery. The sentencing took place in a court-

---

87. Order by Warren H. Young, *Government of the Virgin Islands Beaumont Gereau et al.*, In the District Court of the Virgin Islands, Division of St. Croix, Cr. No. 97/72, May 30, 1973, p. 2.

88. Interview, Judge Young, July 3, 1978. Judge Young had one of his own television sets installed in the recreation cell of the defendants. When Defendant Meral Smith learned that the set belonged to Judge Young, he smashed it—thus provoking a fight with Defendant Rafael Joseph. *Ibid.*

89. See, *e.g.*, *The St. Croix Avis*, June 1, 1973.

room so tense that the defendants were shackled and marshals stood guard armed with shotguns.

Judge Young, before imposing eight consecutive life terms on each of the defendants, asked the defendants to come forward. A struggle with the deputy marshals ensued, and the defendant Gereau shouted: "Fuck you, Young, you stinking motherfucker!" Defendant Ballentine echoed Gereau with similar shouted obscenities. The court record continued: "At this time a melee was caused by several, essentially female, spectators and joined in by the defendants." Defense Attorney Kunstler charged that one of the defendants was "blackjacked." The defendants were then ordered removed from the courtroom, and sentence was imposed on each defendant, one by one, while he stood silently with his back to the judge.[90]

Almost immediately after the jury was discharged, some of the jurors were exposed to improper influence by certain St. Croix citizens. Senator Claude A. Molloy, President of the Virgin Islands Senate and a friend of four of the five defendants, contacted Myron Allick who had served as foreman of the jury. Molloy then talked to John Ross and Mario Moorhead (who had been released from prison December 4, 1972) about Allick's expressed inclination to recant his verdict. Ross and Moorhead proceeded to solicit an affidavit from Allick which read as follows:

> I'm a concerned citizen writing to you on the verdict of guilty voted by the twelve jurors. I was one of the twelve, and I have to say that the verdict I turned in was not from my free will. It was involuntary and due to pressure of information carried in and out of the jury room. Because I am concerned about the justice system in these Virgin Islands that I am writing this letter. Sincerely, Myron Allick.[91]

Ross and Moorhead pressured another juror, Lionel Rodgers, to sign a similar affidavit, leading Judge Young to remark:

> I cannot point to any evidence that John Ross and Mario Moorhead are friends of the defendants, but the record of the District Court shows that Mario Moorhead has been convicted of a felony and I would surmise from their interest in getting affidavits from jurors Rodgers and Allick that they are sympathizers of the defendants.

---

90. Verdicts and Sentences, *Government of The Virgin Islands v. Beaumont Gereau et al.*, District Court of the United States, Division of St. Croix, Cr. No. 97/72, August 13, 1973.

91. Memorandum Opinion and Order, *Government of the Virgin Islands v. Beaumont Gereau et al.*, District Court of the United States, Cr. No. 97/72, September 20, 1974, p. 25.

Judge Young found that both jurors "were coerced by Messrs. Ross and Moorhead" into making the affidavits and that "the affidavits were involuntarily made out of fear by which both Allick and Rodgers were possessed." And Judge Young concluded: "Conduct threatening jurors on account of a verdict … is universally condemned and proscribed as obstruction of justice."[92] He therefore denied defendants' motion for a new trial, which was upheld by the U.S. Circuit Court of Appeals in Philadelphia.[93]

Thus ended the most publicized and sensational trial in the history of the Virgin Islands. As events would prove, however, issues relating to the Fountain Valley Five seemingly would never end.

A Crescendo of Crime

The Fountain Valley tragedy was the most cataclysmic event in the modern history of the Virgin Islands. Its effects were seismic. As with "Watergate," a place became an event. "Fountain Valley" became synonymous with the slayings. Even at the end of the 1970s, it was common for residents to refer to past events as happening before or after "Fountain Valley." This watershed perception of the murders was sharpened by subsequent events.

In November 1972, gunmen held up the Brauhaus, a roadside bar-restaurant in St. Croix, and as the outlaws were leaving, they shot two white workers in the back, killing them, and wounded another. Seven young Crucian men were later arrested and charged with the "Brauhaus Murders," but five were released for lack of sufficient evidence by District Court Judge Almeric Christian and the other two were tried and acquitted.[94]

The Brauhaus murders were followed by others. Within nineteen days of late July and early August 1973—while the Fountain Valley trial was still going on—

---

92. *Ibid.*, pp. 26, 33–34. Besides the issue of "verdict tampering," in the same memorandum, Judge Young considered various other issues raised relating to alleged improper influence of the jury while it was impaneled and sequestered. See, also, *The New York Times*, July 15, 1973, p. 15, cols. 2–6, and July 16, 1973, p. 15, col. 1.

93. *Government of the Virgin Islands v. Beaumont Gereau et al.*, 523 F.2d 140 (1975); Certiorari denied, 96 S. Ct. 1119 (1976); see, also, 502 F.2d 914 (1974).

94. *The New York Times*, August 29, 1973, p. 9, col. 1. Many local people interpreted the Brauhaus acquittals as atonement for the Fountain Valley convictions. Others felt the acquittals demonstrated the innocence of the Fountain Valley defendants. Interview, Attorney Thomas A. Elliot, Legal Services of the Virgin Islands, Christiansted, St. Croix, June 30, 1978.

five more whites were slain on St. Croix. A total of fifteen whites and one black had been murdered in St. Croix in a period of eleven months. Other crimes—vandalism, muggings, burglaries—and racial incidents sharply increased on both St. Croix and St. Thomas. A new spate of alarmist stories filled the mainland press. On both islands, hotel occupancy rates plunged, duty-free shops emptied, real estate prices dropped almost in half, and unemployment soared. The Virgin Isle Hilton Hotel (two hundred and thirty-five rooms) on St. Thomas closed on March 6, 1974. St. Croix whites became gripped with fear and a siege mentality. Tension consumed the whole Island, as whites armed themselves.[95]

On August 16, 1973, three days after sentences were imposed on the Fountain Valley Five, Governor Melvin Evans summoned a force of federal marshals from the mainland, because the St. Croix police no longer could handle the situation.[96] Three more whites nonetheless were slain in St. Croix in early October.

Throughout his term as Governor, Melvin Evans denied that the slayings were racially motivated. He accused the mainland press of exaggerating the racial angles. "If these articles do not stop, we will never recover," he said.[97] In February, 1974, Governor Evans released statistics showing that since January 1971, twenty whites, twelve blacks, and six Puerto Ricans had been killed on St. Croix, and he emphasized that nine of the whites had been killed in group murders—at Fountain Valley and the Brauhaus. He acknowledged that without Fountain Valley, nobody would have paid much attention to St. Croix's crime rate.[98]

Evans always would deny that crime in the Virgin Islands was anti-white or racial in character. He explained later, in a 1979 interview, that the mainland

95. For a representative sample of alarmist news stories in the mainland press, see, *e.g.*: Jon Nordheimer, "Economic Future Clouded by Virgin Island Slayings," *The New York Times*, September 11, 1972, p. 1, cols. 1–2; "The Virgin Islands—A Troubled Paradise," *U.S. News & World Report*, November 5, 1973, pp. 79–81; Austin Scott, "St. Croix Problems: Tourists and Crime," *The Washington Post*, March 3, 1974, p. 33. See, also, "St. Croix: A Fear-Gripped 'Paradise,'" *The San Juan Star*, August 19, 1973, p. 22.

96. Earl Caldwell, "Marshals Called to Tense St. Croix," *The New York Times*, August 17, 1973, p. 1, cols. 1–3.

97. Earl Caldwell, "Virgin Island Governor Says Press Overplays Racial Role in Killings," *The New York Times*, October 16, 1973, p. 22, col. 7. Judge Warren H. Young agreed that the Fountain Valley Five were not racially motivated. "They were just looking for money," he explained. Interview, November 23, 1979.

98. Anthony Lukas, "Murder in Paradise: The Case of St. Croix," *The New York Times*, February 10, 1974, sec. X, p. 17, "After Fountain Valley, the hotels in St. Thomas were emptied. Before that, they were filled to about 80–90 percent capacity. People just picked up and left." Interview, John Collins, Night Manager, Sheraton Hotel, St. Thomas, July 29, 1977.

press had "played up" crimes against whites while ignoring those against blacks. The disadvantaged went after "the affluent"—white and black, and most whites in the Islands are affluent. Asked why so many crimes were not solved in the Virgin Islands, Evans responded:

> A poor police force is the main reason why culprits are not apprehended. When I was Governor, I recruited 289 new policemen and I sent many of their officers to the States for training. But at the same time, the population was rapidly increasing. We were at the tail end of the Vietnam War and many young men were returning without marketable skills.[99]

Governor Evans no longer could blame illegal aliens for committing a disproportionate number of crimes. Reported Calvin Trillin:

> It is agreed by all shades of opinion that virtually all of the young men feared as troublemakers and harassers of whites and maybe worse are not aliens but native Crucians. And it is also agreed by just about everyone that being native Crucians is part of their problem.[100]

Even in the absence of statistics or other evidence to the contrary, it was highly unlikely that illegal aliens in the Virgin Islands constituted a major source of crime as formerly implied by Melvin Evans. A 1978 U.S. Government report explained that immigration and other authorities generally agree that illegal aliens do not contribute significantly to the national crime rate and, except for their disregard of immigration statutes, are law-abiding residents.

> The common explanation for this behavior is that illegal immigrants do not want to risk arrest, imprisonment, and formal deportation by coming to the attention of the authorities. Through their relative success in the labor market, they gain a sufficient stake in our society to blunt whatever incentive there may be to commit a crime.[101]

Whether the upsurge of crime in the Virgin Islands was in fact directed essentially against whites, or was not racial in character as Evans and other natives claimed, certain consequences nevertheless were indisputable: (1) many whites in St. Croix and many whites on the mainland—rightly or wrongly—believed most crimes were racially motivated; (2) the tourism-supported econ-

---

99. Interview, Congressman Melvin H. Evans, Washington, D.C., June 14, 1979.

100. Trillin, "U.S. Journal," p. 112. Most crimes committed by aliens are "crimes of passion" or involving relatives. Interview, Judge Warren H. Young, July 3, 1978.

101. *Report of the House Select Committee on Population, Legal and Illegal Immigration to the United States*, 95th Cong., 2d sess., December 1978, p. 45.

omy suffered a severe and relentless decline which took five years to recover, and (3) the crescendo of crime beginning in 1972 would remain the Islands' number one problem and would continue undiminished through the end of the 1970s.

A King for Governor

In the midst of his term, in January 1973, Governor Evans was confronted not only with the fall-out from the Fountain Valley and Brauhaus murders and frightened white residents but also with the resignation of Lieutenant Governor David Maas. His selection as Evans' running mate in 1970 was viewed as a concession to the Islands' white minority, most of whom were Republicans and had voted for Evans. Maas cited as his reason Evans' failure to utilize fully his services—a complaint frequently voiced by almost every government secretary of previous years. The timing was bad for Evans, coming as it did when whites perceived a growth of anti-white feeling in the Islands, and after the resignation of Donald Tonkin as Attorney General, the only other white in Evans' cabinet. Governor Evans chose Verne A. Hodge, a black, to replace Tonkin, and, surprisingly, Democrat Senator Athniel (Addie) Ottley, Vice President of the Virgin Islands Legislature, to succeed Maas. After some wrangling, Ottley was confirmed by the Legislature, thus giving Evans an all-black cabinet without representation by either the white or Puerto Rican communities.

Evans' support from the white community, which was now feeling beleaguered, was further eroded by Attorney General Hodge's controversial address of November 1973 to St. Thomas' Chamber of Commerce. Attributing the main problems of increased racism and crime to a "negative attitude," Hodge cited these examples of "what sticks in the craw of our people and feeds this negative attitude": (1) the establishment of white schools "in the midst of our predominantly black community," (2) paying local executives less than whites holding similar positions, (3) anti-social and monopolistic conduct of certain businesses, (4) segregated white housing which "is a fact of life," (5) discrimination in inter-personal relations, and (6) "discrimination in death," namely "the general practice of burial at sea for whites! Is there any particular reason why the … cemetery cannot be used? Why the distinction?" Hodge ended his address with this warning:

> The recent outcry for independence is not accidental. It is a natural avenue for those who are convinced that the objectives of the whites are incompatible with the objectives of the natives, and that there can be no reconciliation under the present system.

> This outcry should not be ignored, for as in any movement toward independence, there are those who stray from the mainstream of the movement and engage in terrorism on the erroneous premise that the end justifies the means.[102]

Certain white residents fiercely reacted to the speech, accusing Hodge of being "anti-white." Now it was the whites' turn to feel alienated, as expressed by a local resident:

> For the first time in our experience some whites are publicly charging that they are the victims of "reverse" discrimination, that in many areas of concern they are completely "white-listed" and that the discrimination is so imbedded that black officials practice it while loudly proclaiming their belief in the equality of the races.[103]

Attorney General Hodge's comment about an independence movement was in reference to Mario Moorhead's new United People's Party (UPP)—a manifestation of Moorhead's decision to try to work after all within the system. The new party surfaced with its first mass rally in Frederiksted on October 24, 1973, at which Moorhead called for "political, economic, and social independence," proclaimed his book *Mammon vs History* to be UPP's "manifesto," and vowed success as "the only party capable." Campaigning by issuing a lively weekly publication entitled *Alt Deh UP* (a Creolism meaning literally "Up With People"), holding mass rallies, and conducting "political education classes," Moorhead's UPP hoped to field a full slate of candidates for the 1974 elections.

Meanwhile, Governor Evans faced widespread criticism for not delegating authority and for resulting inefficiency. Watergate and the slide and resignation of President Nixon did not augur well for Republican Evans' re-election. Also, his alienation of white support, the crime wave, economic recession, growing unemployment, the enmity of an increasing number of naturalized citizens who blamed Evans for the 1971 roundup, and the confrontation of formidable opponents, combined to reduce his chances of repeating his 1970 victory.

Melvin Evans was eliminated in the three-man election on November 5, 1974, with Evans ranking third behind ICM's Cyril King who ranked second after the Democrat's Alexander Farrelly, who was the frontrunner. King's running mate was Senator Juan Luis—a Crucian Puerto Rican—and Farrelly's

---

102. Verne A. Hodge, Attorney General, *Remarks to Chamber of Commerce*, xeroxed, St. Thomas, Virgin Islands, November 20, 1973, pp. 3–6.

103. R.W.P., "Political Stuff," *Daily News*, December 9, 1973. See, also, Letter to Editor from A Reader, undated, *Daily News*, December 7, 1973.

was Senator Ruby Rouss, thus assuring an all-Crucian winning ticket whoever would win the runoff. The King-Luis ticket was elected in the runoff by a vote of 10,388 (53%) to the Democrats' 9,154 (47%). The Democrats succeeded, however, in re-electing Ron de Lugo, who had become the Islands' first elected non-voting Congressman in Washington in 1972 after having served as Washington Representative—an elected post authorized by the Legislature. The Democrats also succeeded in electing nine of the fifteen seats in the Legislature, while King's ICM party elected five senators, the Republicans only one, and Moorhead's UPP none.

Thus Cyril King became the second elected Governor of the Virgin Islands in January 1975. In his campaign, he had promised he would be "Governor of *all* the people." Now, in his first State of the Territory message before the Legislature, he called for "the help and cooperation of all the people of the Virgin Islands." He declared "a massive war on crime," promised three new interlocking programs—"Operation Recovery, Operation Diversification, and Operation Exploration"—to reverse "plummeted" tourism and the "unprecedented" economic crisis. Stating that "we have reached a watershed ... a moment of truth, a point of decision," Governor King called for a "spirit of unity and self-sacrifice," so that "we can ... in time bask in the warmth of recovery and greet the dawn of a new era, a new beginning for these, our Virgin Islands."[104]

---

104. *Daily News*, February 21, 1975, p. 10.

12

Political Culture

Lest it be assumed that the Virgin Islands constituted a simmering cauldron in the midst of a tranquil and somnolent Caribbean, problems besetting other troubled islands were not less disquieting. There was no end to the chronicle of ills suffered by other Caribbean polities in the late 1970s, from Jamaica and Haiti in the west, to the Lesser Antilles in the east, and to Trinidad and Guyana in the south.

Even in another direction, a few hundred miles north of the Virgin Islands, Britain's Bermuda—another polity dependent on American tourists—could catalog many of the same problems contemporaneously experienced by America's Virgin Islands. While Virgin Islanders were reeling from Fountain Valley and subsequent murders, Bermudians were shocked by remarkably similar circumstances, beginning with the killing of their Chief of Police in September 1972, and followed in March 1973, with the assassinations of their Crown-appointed Governor and an aide and, four weeks later, the murder of two whites. There, too, the island experienced a consequent sudden decline in tourism. Bermuda's troubles also continued through the end of the decade, centering on natives' resentment of white economic domination and of alien workers in their midst.[1]

No other locale in the Caribbean, however—or elsewhere in the world for that matter—had undergone such radical and rapid ethnic and economic change in the 1960s as that experienced by America's Virgin Islands. With the highest per capita income in the Caribbean ($4,743 in 1977) and a population of about 100,000 in the late 1970s, the annual budget of the Government of the Virgin Islands ($130 million) was yet larger than that of the city of San Juan, Puerto Rico, with a population of almost one million. The uniqueness of the

---

1. For a perceptive analysis of Bermuda, see: Suzannah Lessard, "Profiles: A Close Gathering," *The New Yorker*, April 16, 1979, pp. 43–112. See, also, John P. Roche, "A Word Edgewise: Multiracial Challenge," *The St. Croix Avis*, March 29, 1978, pp. 12, 20; Juan O. Tomayo, "Bermuda Riots Spark Independence Debate," *The San Juan Star*, December 12, 1977, p. 6; and *Daily News*, January 25, 1978.

Virgin Islands, however, did not detract from an increasing awareness that the Islands' destiny was linked to other Caribbean entities.

Virgin Islanders, of course, felt very close to Puerto Rico. St. Thomas and San Juan were only thirty minutes apart by plane. About 38 percent of all U.S. tourist arrivals in the Virgin Islands were "day-trippers" from Puerto Rico. The population of St. Croix was becoming increasingly Puerto Rican in ethnic composition. Many Virgin Islanders spent weekends in San Juan and, conversely, Puerto Ricans visited the Virgin Islands in increasing numbers.[2]

At least 70 percent of the Puerto Rican community in St. Croix descended from Vieques and Culebra, Puerto Rican islands situated between St. Thomas and the Puerto Rican mainland, although in recent years more migrated from Puerto Rico itself.[3] The Puerto Ricans in St. Croix comprised at least two distinct classes—a blue-collar working class of lower incomes and a business class of middle or upper income levels. Many of the former worked in the Public Works Department of the Government of the Virgin Islands. Government pay was higher in the Virgin Islands than in Puerto Rico. The fact that many "Afro-Puerto Ricans" migrated from Vieques and Culebra helped their absorption into St. Croix where intermarriage with native blacks was not unusual. Other factors inducing peaceful assimilation of Puerto Ricans were: (1) Vieques and Culebra were geographically very close to St. Thomas and were isolated from metropolitan Puerto Rico itself, (2) radio and other communications media were common to the Virgin Islands, Vieques, and Culebra, (3) St. Thomians were dependent on Puerto Rico for barged water, and (4) many Virgin Islanders could speak some Spanish, and, conversely, many Puerto Ricans could speak some English in spite of minimal bilingual education in the Virgin Islands.[4]

---

2. See, *e.g.*, Ronald Walker, "Islands Bridge the Gap," *The San Juan Star*, August 18, 1978.

3. Interview, Felix Pitterson, Realtor, Fredericksted, St. Croix, July 4, 1978. See, also, Clarence Senior, *The Puerto Rican Migrant in St. Croix*, mimeographed (San Juan, Puerto Rico: Social Science Research Center, University of Puerto Rico, 1947); and Lewis, *The Virgin Islands*, pp. 207–216.

4. Interview, Luc Cuadrado, Frederiksted, St. Croix, July 4, 1978. Although 26 percent of the children of the Virgin Islands whose second language is English are being helped by the Education Department's Bilingual Program, the purpose of the Program has been to develop facility of the non-English-speaking child in the English language as the medium of instruction rather than to maintain a dual or parallel curriculum in English and in another language (*e.g.*, Spanish for Puerto Ricans or French for St. Thomas' French). Eleanor B. Bennewith, "The Virgin Islands Experience in Bilingual Education," *A Report on the First Territorial Conference on Bilingual Education* (St. Croix: Virgin Islands Department of Education, Grapetree Bay Hotel, November 3–6, 1977), Appendix A, pp. 1–4. See, also, "English Presents Problem for Some on St. Croix," *The San Juan Star*, October 30, 1977, p. 24.

As between the Eastern and the Western Caribbean, however, the American Virgin Islands in the 1970s had a closer affinity with the islands to the east. This was true even with respect to St. Croix's ties to Puerto Rico. "Cultural and historic ties between St. Croix and Puerto Rico are more tenuous, the latter being a part of the Hispanic Caribbean as opposed to the Afro-Caribbean."[5]

In response to the Virgin Islands' perceived shared interests with the rest of the Caribbean, Governor Cyril King undertook initiatives unprecedented for a Virgin Islands' Governor. On the one hand, he proposed the formation of an "off-shore governors' conference" consisting of governors of American territories, including Puerto Rico, "to promote our common interests more effectively in Washington."[6] On the other hand, King proposed to make official visits to several Eastern Caribbean islands, in consultation with the U.S. State Department, "not only to convey expressions of good will, promote cultural exchanges and encourage trade, but to discuss problems and approaches peculiar to small entities experiencing the process of rapid change."[7]

Affinity with the East

One of the smallest and most conspicuous ethnic groups in the Virgin Islands consisted of two French-speaking "almost ghetto-like" communities in St. Thomas, together numbering in the 1970s about fifteen hundred Caucasians, except that a small percentage had some black admixture. One of the two communities, an old fishing village, was known as Carenage, Frenchtown, or somewhat derisively as "Cha-Cha Town," located on the western side of Charlotte Amalie's spacious harbor. The other community was known simply as "North-

---

"Looking … at school marks, the most frequent reason given for Puerto Ricans' low achievement is their language problem." Margaret Alison Gibson, *Ethnicity and Schooling: A Caribbean Case Study* (unpublished Ph.D. dissertation, University of Pittsburgh, 1976), p. 160. Accordingly, "Americanization" continued to contribute to "functional disequilibrium" of public education in the Virgin Islands. Charles Wesley Turnbull, *The Structural Development of a Public Education System in the Virgin Islands, 1917–1970: A Functional Analysis in Historical Perspective* (unpublished Ph.D. dissertation, University of Minnesota, 1976).

5. Gibson, *Ethnicity and Schooling*, ibid.

6. Senator John L. Maduro had earlier proposed creation of "a national association of American flag-lands and peoples for mutual cooperation." *Virgin Islands Post*, June 23, 1976, p. 2A. Not to be outdone by Governor King, Congressman Ron de Lugo proposed that President Carter establish a Presidential Commission to investigate and make comprehensive recommendations on the "unique economic and social problems of the off-shore territories." *Daily News*, March 8, 1977.

7. *Daily News*, February 27, 1977, pp. 1, 22.

side" because its inhabitants farmed and settled on the northern slopes of the island.

These communities did not receive the scholarly attention—anthropologically, sociologically, or otherwise—that their anomalous existence seemed to merit. Accordingly, that "French" was the means of communication of over one percent of the Virgin Islands' population was a little known fact outside the Islands. More obscure, even in the Islands, was the fact that the two communities spoke two distinct dialects of archaic West Indian French, a curious phenomenon considering the inhabitants of both were descendants from a very small island of only 9.5 square miles east of the Virgin Islands, St. Barthelemy, commonly known as "St. Barts." The answer to this riddle of ultimate ethnocentricity, according to Professor Arnold Highfield, was that the two communities descended from different linguistic areas of tiny St. Barts. "The regional particularism so evident in St. Barts is kept alive by the two communities at St. Thomas, which to this day have little to do with one another." Little social mixing or intermarriage occurred between the two groups.[8]

Emigration to St. Thomas had begun around 1863 to 1875 when economic conditions greatly worsened in St. Barts. The exact year when the emigration began is uncertain. On the one hand, few in St. Thomas' French communities could relate anything about their past other than "some vague notions about Norman origins." On the other hand, St. Thomas' French always maintained close contact with St. Barts and frequently visited their ancestral home.[9]

Historically, the St. Thomas French were considered the lowest economic and social class in the Virgin Islands. Discrimination against them accounted in part for their low socio-economic status. Although this situation changed dramatically in recent years, with the inflow of alien workers from other islands, Professor Highfield explained that "class discrimination, linguistic and cultural differences, lack of education and self-imposed isolationism" have prevented the French from becoming fully integrated into St. Thomas society. Accordingly, many have emigrated to the mainland where they meet with no color prejudice, unlike darker West Indians, find jobs and easily assimilate.[10]

While those of Puerto Rican descent in the Virgin Islands maintained their orientation to Vieques, Culebra, and Puerto Rico, and St. Thomas' French

---

8. Arnold R. Highfield, *The French Dialect of St. Thomas, U.S. Virgin Islands: A Descriptive Grammar with Texts and Glossary* (Ann Arbor: Karoma Publishers, 1979), chap. 1, esp. p. 18. See, also, Highfield, "The French Child in the Classroom," *A Report ... on Bilingual Education* (1977), Appendix A, pp. 36–38.

9. Lewis, *The Virgin Islands*, p. 200.

10. Highfield, *The French Dialect*, p. 14.

had never forsaken their ties to St. Barts, most Virgin Islanders were Afro-Caribbean in ancestry and culture, related to the British islands of the Lesser Antilles, and comprised the largest groups—natives and aliens—in the multicultural Virgin Islands. The term "native" was not racially exclusive, since it included white descendants of "old" Virgin Islands families. Gordon Lewis, however, explained:

> Whereas it is not applied to French, Puerto Ricans, or continentals, even
> if their parents are born locally, it does extend to Tortolians and British
> West Indians, with whom there exists an extensive relationship spring-
> ing out of the massive migratory movements of the Antillean region.
> These outsiders are accepted as family members and thus become na-
> tives after a passage of time: lower-class individuals after two genera-
> tions, upper-class individuals after three generations, it is sometimes
> surmised.[11]

The closest foreign jurisdiction to the American Virgin Islands are the British Virgin Islands (BVI). The BVI are a British colony located immediately adjacent to the east and north of St. John, separated at their nearest point by only one or two miles. The colony consists of about sixteen inhabited islands and forty-five uninhabited islets covering a total land area of fifty-nine square miles with a population of about 24,500 of whom some 75 percent live on Tortola.[12]

On October 29, 1977, a few days after England's Queen Elizabeth II visited the British Virgin Islands, BVI Governor Walter Wallace led two hundred and twenty-five British Virgin Islanders to St. Thomas to celebrate the Sixth Annual U.S. Virgin Islands-British Virgin Islands Friendship Day. The site of the event alternates yearly between the two jurisdictions. "The ties between the two groups of islands are strong and, in some cases, are even family ties," said a St. Thomas editorial.[13] This was understatement, for an estimated 60 percent of the population of St. Thomas were BVI-descended or related in the late 1970s. The British Virgin Islands even use the U.S. dollar as their currency.[14]

---

11. Lewis, *The Virgin Islands*, pp. 155–156.

12. For the history of the British Virgin Islands, see: Isaac Dookhan, *A History of the British Virgin Islands* (St. Thomas: Caribbean Universities Press, College of the Virgin Islands, 1975); and Norwell Harrigan and Pearl Varlack, *The Virgin Islands Story* (Epping, Essex, England: Caribbean Universities Press, Bowker Publishing Company, 1975).

13. Editorial, *Daily News*, October 29, 1977.

14. For discussion of the BVI-US Treaty, see: Marshall J. Langer and Gustav A. Danielson, *The British Virgin Islands—A Low-Tax Base with Treaty Benefits* (Englewood Cliffs, N. J.: Prentice-Hall, 1978).

Aside from the British Virgin Islands, foreign workers in the U.S. Virgin Islands were drawn principally from the British-connected islands of the Eastern Caribbean—Anguilla, Antigua, Dominica, Grenada, Montserrat, Nevis, St. Kitts, St. Lucia, St. Vincent, and Trinidad. The contributions of the Eastern Caribbean to the social, economic, and political culture of the Virgin Islands, through this alien community, cannot be overstated. Carnival, the steel bands, cricket, soccer, certain foods and beverages originated in the Eastern Caribbean. Foremost, of course, was the economic dependence of the Virgin Islands on foreign workers for most of the employment outside of government.[15] As the 1970s were coming to a close, the most important impact of the "downislanders" appeared to many Virgin Islanders to be political—rather than social or economic—especially with regard to the future. It was the fear that downislanders would eventually wrest control of the political system that most worried native Virgin Islanders.

Increasingly, during the 1970s, aliens were becoming naturalized citizens and hence voters whose favor Virgin Islands' politicians sought. Naturalization was spurred by developments that tended to transform "temporary" alien workers into permanent residents. The issuance of new "H-2" visas was virtually stopped by 1971, except to holders of H-4 visas who were already present in the Islands, thus almost halting the legal inflow of foreign workers. The threat of deportation was indefinitely postponed for alien workers unemployed for more than sixty days through application for "suspension of deportation." Permanent resident status was aided further by the substantial raising of immigration quotas as home islands of nonresidents from the Eastern Caribbean became independent, and by the tripling to six hundred annually of the number of immigrant visas available to people from each dependent area.[16]

Meanwhile, alien organizations in the Virgin Islands pressed for "status adjustment" through special legislation by Congress that would ease the way for aliens to acquire permanent residence "green cards," and would grant "amnesty" to overstayed and illegal alien workers and their dependents. The Virgin Islands Government generally opposed such legislation and insisted that it ought to be given jurisdiction over immigration matters in the Islands, despite the facts that the Governor's task force on immigration policy had met only twice and

---

15. See, *e.g.*, unpublished xeroxed papers authored by George Goodwin, President, Alien Interest Movement, St. Thomas: *Contributions of Immigrant Aliens to Virgin Islands Community* (March 21, 1979), and *The Alien Labor Program in the U.S. Virgin Islands* (June 19, 1979).

16. Richard W. Miller, *The Economy of the Virgin Islands* (Washington: Office of Territorial Affairs, Department of the Interior, June 20, 1979), pp. 10–13.

had yet to make its recommendations,[17] and that immigration theretofore always had been ruled by the U.S. Supreme Court as being exclusively within the jurisdiction of the United States Government.[18]

"Concerned Virgin Islanders"

The post-Fountain Valley economic recession in the Islands, with increasing unemployment, heightened resentment of native Virgin Islanders toward aliens. In June 1974, several hundred Virgin Islanders formed the Organization of Concerned Virgin Islanders for Action whose initial news release stated:

> Virgin Islanders have now organized themselves to demand their inherent and inalienable rights in their own homeland. The Organization appeals to our Governor, our Washington Delegate, our fifteen Senators, our United States Government and, even, if necessary to the United Nations, to urgently assist Virgin Islanders in the struggle to overcome and survive continued acts of injustice being perpetrated against us in our own homeland.
>
> Since we are presently faced with finding a solution to our own collapsing economy, we see no reason why the Government of the Virgin Islands, as well as the Federal Government, should be expected to assume responsibility for solving the economic and social problems of other Caribbean Islands.
>
> We Virgin Islanders are patient, understanding and hospitable, but our supply of these virtues are rapidly becoming exhausted, and we have now replaced them full force with our recognition of the inherent and inalienable rights of Virgin Islanders in these Virgin Islands. We will no longer tolerate the lack of concern of our elected officials and apparent lack of understanding on the part of certain Federal of-

---

17. See, *e.g.*, John P. Collins, *Statement of John P. Collins, Member of the Governor of the U.S. Virgin Islands' Immigration Policy Task Force to the Immigration Policy Workshops, Community Relations Service, U.S. Department of Justice* (unpublished, xeroxed, Washington, D.C., June 2, 1978); Copy of Letter from Juan Luis, Governor of the Virgin Islands of the U.S. to Congressman Joshua Eilberg, Chairman, Subcommittee on Immigration and International Law, U.S. House of Representatives, xeroxed, dated September 14, 1978; and Juan Luis, *Statement of the Governor of the Virgin Islands on S. 2252, 95th Congress, A Bill "To Amend the Immigration and Nationality Act and for other purposes" to U.S. Senate Committee on the Judiciary* (xeroxed, May 17, 1978).

18. See, *e.g.*, *Fong Yue Ting v. United States*, 149 U.S. 698 (1893), and *Hines v. Davidowitz*, 312 U.S. 52 (1941).

ficials in the territory who are witnessing our gradual social, economic and cultural annihilation. If the present trend is permitted to continue our children and grandchildren will become strangers in their own homeland. We do not intend to stand idly by any longer and watch our rights being constantly infringed upon while certain non-resident members of this community continue to demand more and more rights and privileges which can be only at our expense.[19]

The new organization undertook a variety of activities to thwart the influence of alien residents, including petitions and letters to Congress, letters to editors and officials, news releases, protests of visits by the Governor to the Eastern Caribbean, calls for review and restriction of alien certifications, calls for expulsion of unemployed aliens, protests against the issuance of food stamps and other public benefits to alien residents, and even a visit to the United Nations in New York. Before a special committee of the United Nations, members of the Concerned Virgin Islanders delivered in April 1975 their "Declaration of Concern and Appeal for Assistance to the United Nations" making the charge, among others, that increasing naturalization would result by 1986 in thirty thousand citizens of alien extraction in the Islands "completely overwhelming the native Virgin Islander and, conceivably, determining the political destiny of this territory."[20]

Polarization between concerned citizens and alien residents dominated much of the insular politics in the 1970s. Grenada columnist Alistair Hughes wrote in 1975 that such feelings were growing to the point where resident aliens in the Virgin Islands, estimated to be as much as one-third of the population, faced possible expulsion. Should that happen, "it will mean near catastrophe" for Grenada and other eastern Caribbean islands to absorb these thousands back into their "job-scarce communities." "People are losing their jobs," wrote Hughes. "And as conditions worsen, native Virgin Islanders are questioning, with growing emphasis, the presence of large numbers of aliens in their midst."[21]

Social Infrastructure

In a 1979 analysis by the Office of Territorial Affairs of the economy of the Virgin Islands, economist Richard Miller wrote of the many indications of in-

---

19. Organization of Concerned Virgin Islanders for Action, *News Release No. 1* (Charlotte Amalie, June 12, 1974).

20. Organization of Concerned Virgin Islanders for Action, Inc., *Declaration of Concern and Appeal for Assistance to the United Nations* (St. Thomas, April 25, 1975), p. 9.

21. Quoted in "Possible V. I. Expulsion of Aliens Feared," *The San Juan Star*, April 1, 1975.

adequacies of the Virgin Islands' social and economic infrastructure that serve as a powerful disincentive to private investment, offsetting fiscal incentives offered by the government. The major shortcomings in social infrastructure he identified as education, health, and crime prevention. Water supply, electric power, and port facilities he identified as the major problem areas in economic infrastructure.[22] Miller painted a bleak picture of a small economy that consumed a large quantity of imported goods paid through tourism, export earnings and funds from the U.S. Government. The infrastructure never had caught up with population growth, which Miller estimated to be 118,960, citing a 1978 Economic Policy Council household survey. Unemployment, virtually unknown in the 1960s, climbed steadily to a peak of 10.8 percent in 1977, not including sizeable unemployment among aliens that remained unreported, according to Miller, because of their fear of deportation.[23]

According to standardized tests, achievement of public school students in the Virgin Islands ranked far below national norms in the 1970s.[24] More than half the students entering the public high schools dropped out and failed to graduate.[25] Public schools were plagued with vandalism and violence.[26] Overcrowding led to serious problems including bomb threats, assaults on teachers, and hoodlumism.[27] Teacher shortages and structurally defective schools formed only parts of the problem.[28] Lack of parental guidance and the presence of

---

22. Miller, *The Economy of the Virgin Islands*, p. 16.

23. *Ibid.*, pp. 5, 9, 15.

24. In 1976, 92 of 100 public high school graduates in the Virgin Islands failed the 1976 English entrance examination at the College of the Virgin Islands. *Daily News*, December 7, 1976, p. 2. Some 2,000 public school pupils on St. Thomas and St. John, one-sixth of the total, failed promotion in 1977, including 37 percent of seventh graders and 31.6 percent of eighth graders who ranked about four grades behind the national norm in reading and writing skills. Penny Feuerzeig, "New Promotion Rules Will Hold Back 2,000," *Daily News*, June 7, 1977, p. 1; and *Virgin Islands Post*, October 6, 1977, p. 1.

25. Page Stull, "Half of '73 Entering 9th Grade Quits," *Daily News*, January 19, 1978, p. 3.

26. See, *e.g.*, Ben Stubenberg, "Special Ed. School Plagued by Vandals," *The St. Croix Avis*, March 29, 1978, p. 1; Arnold Highfield, "On Vandalism and the Schools," *The St. Croix Avis*, August 7, 1978, p. 11; and Penny Feuerzeig, "'Lack of Discipline' Blamed as Schools' Biggest Woe," *Daily News*, August 3, 1979, p. 1.

27. Twenty percent of public school students in the Islands were on double session in 1977, and there were nearly twice as many public school students in St. Croix as there were classroom seats. *The St. Croix Avis*, August 4, 1976; and *Daily News*, May 10, 1977, p. 1. Assaults and threatened rapes of teachers led to job actions and the assignment of policemen by the Governor at some schools. *Daily News*, January 26 and 28, 1978, p. 1.

28. "More than half the teachers in the V.I. public school system have quit their jobs in the last three years." Page Stull, "Greener Pastures Lure Teachers," *Daily News*, April 9, 1978,

some three thousand children and unemployed youths without homes and families aggravated the situation. Board of Education member Michael Paiewonsky predicted in 1978 that the children born to single juveniles would become the problem youth of the next decade and that the social costs to both child and mother and the community costs would be "unimaginable."

> Twelve-year-old girls are having babies regularly. We were recently reported to have as many as 3,000 children with no family at all....
> We do not yet have programs that reach the children in need early enough. Our incredible crime rate is a reflection of this failure in the past. Sixty-one percent of all major reported crime in the islands is committed by juveniles. Our local aggravated assault is ten times higher than U.S. mainland rates.[29]

It became common for many native Virgin Islanders in the 1970s to blame all social ills on the influx of aliens, including educational problems attributed to the swelling of school enrollments after the *Hosier* decision. "However, the problems predate this decade," commented Richard Miller, "and they have not yielded to rising levels of Federal spending on education programs."[30]

Clearly, whatever the explanation, education in the public schools of the Virgin Islands loomed such a momentous problem area as to dwarf other educational problems, such as failure to provide public education for handicapped children on St. Croix, development problems of the College of the Virgin Islands, and the quality of education in private and parochial schools which had enrolled for many years a large proportion of school-age children of the Islands.[31]

---

p. 1. One architectural consultant stated with respect to public school buildings in the Islands that "the problem of poor construction is a continuous thorn in our side." Emily Tynes, "Education Board Irate Over Bovoni Project," *Daily News*, April 25, 1978, p. 16.

29. *Daily News*, February 13, 1978, p. 3.

30. Miller, *The Economy of the Virgin Islands*, p. 16. For an historical review of studies of educational problems of the Islands, see: Turnbull, *The Structural Development*, esp. pp. 42–60.

31. U.S. District Court Judge Warren H. Young chastised public school authorities on St. Croix for not providing an adequate special educational program for physically handicapped children, in *Harris, et al. v. Kean, et al.*, U.S. Dist. Ct., Div. of St. Croix, Civil No. 76/323, September 15, 1976. A total of 2,122 persons were enrolled in the fall of 1976 in the College of the Virgin Islands, including 481 full-time undergraduates on the St. Thomas campus, and 93 on the St. Croix campus. *Daily News*, November 19, 1976. Predictions were made of a total student body of 4,000 to 5,000 in 1990. Editorial, *Daily News*, December 30, 1976. See, also, Ezra A. Naughton, *The Origin and Development of Higher Education in the Virgin Islands* (unpublished Ph.D. dissertation, Catholic University of America,

There were forty-three public schools in the Islands and twenty-five private or parochial schools in 1976.[32] Gordon K. Lewis attributed the rise of the private school to "parental reaction to the low standards of the public school." Thus, a dual educational system is created with all inequities of a lower class public school as compared to an affluent middle-class private school. The public school, moreover, becomes overwhelmingly black and Puerto Rican, while the private school becomes predominantly light-skinned and white. "The result is that the ordinary Virgin Islands child attends what is in effect a segregated school," Lewis concluded, "obtaining an education that is shaped by factors of skin-color, language, and parental income."[33]

The fact that public educational policy making in the Islands was split between an elected board of education, a department of education whose commissioner was appointed by the elected Governor, and the education committee of the elected legislature did not foster agreement on possible solutions to public school issues.[34]

Closely linked to educational problems and unemployed youth, who had dropped out of school or had graduated without adequate skills, was the still growing crime problem. In mid-1978, a local editorial asserted that "the crime rate has reached almost absurd proportions."[35] In the first half of that year, eight people were murdered in St. Thomas and five in St. Croix.

Although only one in three local victims reported crime, the territory led the entire country in reported violent crimes. Yet, the Virgin Islands had half again as much manpower working in the criminal justice system as the average of U.S. states and localities. The territory had 32 percent more police officers per ten thousand population and an 80 percent higher per capita expenditure for police and corrections than the U.S. average. "The problem most seriously threatens to tear apart the very fabric of our society here in the

---

Washington, D.C., 1973); and Norwell E. Harrigan, *Higher Education in the Micro-State: A Theory of Raran Society* (unpublished Ph.D. dissertation, University of Pittsburgh, 1972).

32. *The 1976–1977 Settler's Handbook* (Christiansted, St. Croix: Prestige Press, 1976), pp. 47–48, 54, 62. Total school enrollment of 32,335 (25,426 in public and 6,909 in nonpublic schools) as of June 1, 1979 was reported. Letter to Editor from Dr. Robert V. Vaughn, *The St. Croix Avis*, September 13, 1979, p. 8.

33. Lewis, *The Virgin Islands*, pp. 275, 276.

34. See, e.g., "Education Decision Making," Editorial, *Virgin Islands Post*, July 26, 1978. A CVI professor of education recommended that all control of public schools should be vested in "an elected non-partisan Board of Education." Herbert A. Hoover, "Observations and Recommendations Concerning Public Education in the United States Virgin Islands," *The Journal of the College of the Virgin Islands*, 2 (May 1976): 71.

35. *Virgin Islands Post*, July 5, 1978.

Virgin Islands," acknowledged Congressional Delegate Ron de Lugo. "In all of our neighborhoods, our people live in fear." And he added: "The truth is that nearly all major crimes go unsolved and unpunished."[36]

A 1978 report of the Virgin Islands Legislature called for a "housecleaning" of the Department of Public Safety, and attributed the "crime wave" to a shortage of funds, inept administration, and—"at the core of the Virgin Islands crime problem"—juvenile delinquency. Up to 75 percent of Virgin Islands crime was "the work of juveniles."[37] Eighty percent was reported to have been committed by persons between the ages of fifteen and twenty-five.[38]

Among this age group, especially after the murder of a St. Croix policeman in 1977, Crucian police singled out youthful followers of the growing Rastafarian religious cult as responsible for much of the crime in St. Croix. Rastafarians theoretically eschewed violence, and all other aspects of capitalist society they called "Babylon," for a peaceful and healthful back-to-nature existence. Many lived in the rain-forested area of northwest St. Croix. In point of fact, among the alienated youth of the Islands, there was a growing number who affected the life style and appearance—such as arranging their hair in "dred locks"—of "Rastas," but nevertheless engaged in criminal activity at variance with the ideals and tenets of Rastafarianism. Crucian police—allegedly acting on appearances only—were accused of violating the rights of many Crucian youths in 1977.[39]

---

36. *Virgin Islands Post*, August 13, 1978, p. 1, and August 23, 1978, pp. 1, 3.

37. Standing Committee on Public Safety, *Report to the Twelfth Legislature of the Virgin Islands of the United States of an Investigation … of the Operations of the Department of Public Safety with Recommendations* (Charlotte Amalie, January 10, 1978), pp. 7, 10, 18.

38. Kay Howard, "20–30 Yr. Old Males Most Likely Targets of Criminals." *Virgin Islands Post*, July 26, 1978, p. 1. See, also, Klaus de Albuquerque, *Juvenile Delinquency in the U.S. Virgin Islands*, and Jerry McElroy, *Crime in the U.S. Virgin Islands: A Socio-Historical Perspective* (unpublished xeroxed papers presented at the Fifth Annual Caribbean Studies Conference, Fort-de-France, Martinique, May 28–30, 1979).

39. See, e.g., Steve Bornn, "Pair Say Rastas' Rights Violated," *Daily News*, August 2, 1977, p. 3; "Rastas: Who Are They?" Editorial, *Virgin Islands Post*, July 23, 1977; "Rastafarians: Where Do We Go From Here?" Editorial, *The St. Croix Avis*, August 3, 1977; James Cuchiara, "Rastafarian Cult Wins Adepts in Virgin Islands," *The San Juan Star*, March 17, 1978, p. 10; Peter Goodwin, "Rastas Misunderstood; 'Ganja' Is Main Reason," *Virgin Islands Post*, April 3, 1977, p. 1; Patricia Blake, "Rasta-type Fruit Vendors Closed Down by Police," *Virgin Islands Post*, April 27, 1978. For the Jamaican origins of Rastafarianism, its tenets, and its spread in the Caribbean, see: Rex M. Nettleford, *Mirror Mirror: Identity, Race and Protest in Jamaica* (Jamaica: William Collins and Sangster Ltd., 1970); Leonard E. Barrett, *The Rastafarians: Sounds of Cultural Dissonance* (Boston: Beacon Press, 1977); and C. Gerald Fraser, "Two Portraits of Rastafarians: Violent or Upright and Artistic," *The New York Times*, June

The criminal justice system of the territory also suffered from inadequate detention programs and facilities not only for convicted adults but also for youthful offenders. A detention center for juvenile offenders had existed in the Islands since 1944. A 1968 study revealed that 82 percent of the detained children were members of "unstable, disrupted families" and that a majority of their parents had never married. Of those parents who were married, 27 percent of their homes "were broken by separation, divorce or death."[40] A decade later, an estimated three thousand homeless children were roaming the Islands, two hundred and fifty to three hundred of them representing "hard core" offenders chiefly responsible for the spiraling incidence of crime.[41] In 1975, Governor Cyril King nevertheless had closed as inadequate the territory's lone juvenile detention center at Anna's Hope on St. Croix. Plans were formulated and funds committed to upgrade the center. By the end of the 1970s, however, the facility had yet to become fully operable, partly because of repeated vandalism by inmates, with the result that most convicted juveniles remained unincarcerated and free to become repeat offenders, while some of those found guilty of major felonies were imprisoned with adults.[42]

Although the modern Golden Grove Adult Correctional Facility had been in operation in St. Croix since 1974, replacing the obsolete Richmond Penitentiary, U.S. District Court Judge Warren Young of St. Croix received "multifarious complaints" and "civil rights actions" filed by prisoners in the new facility, lead-

---

21, 1977, Sec. II, pp. 1, 58. For the influence of Marcus Garvey, see *e.g.*, John Henrik Clarke, ed., *Marcus Garvey and the Vision of Africa* (New York: Random House, 1974).

40. Robert H. Dalton, *Childhood Behavior Problems in Social Focus, A Study of the Insular Training School, United States Virgin Islands* (St. Thomas: Division of Mental Health, Virgin Islands Department of Health, July 1968), p. 11.

41. One of every five Virgin Islanders between the ages of 13 and 17 had at least one felony arrest during 1976. *Memorandum from Troy Chapman, Administrator, to Law Enforcement Planning Commission of the Virgin Islands*, St. Thomas, V.I., dated May 5, 1977, p. 1. See, also, Letter to Editor from Jim Tillett, dated June 13, 1978, *Daily News*, June 16, 1978, p. 6. Public Safety Commissioner Charles Groneveldt commented: "Since Fountain Valley, a group of hard-core malcontents have developed. Today, this group is fractured, but in general organized in their belief that law and order does not apply to them. These groups are armed and also deal in narcotics." *Virgin Islands Post*, June 22, 1978, p. 3A.

42. Complaining that young habitual offenders are released almost as soon as they are picked up, "because there is no place to put them," Public Safety Commissioner Charles Groneveldt pointed out that the Anna's Hope youth facility was designed to hold only twenty "hardcore youth" at a cost of $3.2 million. *Daily News*, July 29, 1978, p. 1. The Youth Services Administration was created in 1978 to undertake ambitious programs and services to help prevent juvenile delinquency. Penny Feuerzeig, "Youth Services Bill Is Passed by Senate," *Daily News*, March 30, 1978, pp. 1, 20.

ing him to appoint an investigating commission in 1976 composed of three citizens and two inmates. From the commission's report, Judge Young concluded that conditions at Golden Grove constituted "constitutional deprivations" and "deficiencies" in violation of the U.S. Constitution's Eighth Amendment, prohibiting cruel and unusual punishment, and of the Due Process and Equal Protection Clauses, protecting prisoners against arbitrary and capricious treatment by prison officials.

> I am in complete sympathy with the victims of the scourge of senseless crimes which has troubled these islands in recent years. We are all victims in the sense that the quality of life is diminished by living in a community where crime is the rule, rather than the exception....
>
> No one gains, however, by sending an individual who is already alienated from society to a place which will only serve to enhance his hostility.... It makes no sense to incarcerate these persons under conditions which qualify them to be nothing other than repeat offenders.[43]

Specifically, Judge Young found no rehabilitation efforts or organized activities taking place at Golden Grove, glaring deficiencies in health care including no psychiatric care, no inmate classification procedure, and unevenly administered discipline that "rarely ... comports with due process." With regard to food, Judge Young found very little effort "to meet the special dietary requirements of such groups as the Muslims and the Rastafarians." Should the territory's authorities refuse to comply with his specific orders, to meet constitutional standards at Golden Grove, Judge Young threatened to recommend that all sentenced offenders be sent to mainland institutions for incarceration. If noncompliance still continued, then he threatened to refuse to incarcerate "all non-dangerous offenders," to resentence and set free "all non-dangerous persons who had been sentenced within the prior 120 days," and, as a last resort to close down Golden Grove as long as the constitutional rights of its inmates are disregarded. Finally, Judge Young threatened contempt proceedings against responsible administrators.[44]

Despite Judge Young's intervention, neither conditions at Golden Grove nor at Fort Christian in St. Thomas—the territory's other prison facility—had shown marked improvement by the end of the decade. Indeed, the entire criminal justice system in the Islands appeared to continue to deteriorate, with police "sickouts," during which rampant crimes including murder were committed, and seeming indifference on the part of police in apprehending wrongdoers.

---

43. *Barnes v. Government of the Virgin Islands*, 415 F. Supp. 1218, 1224 (1976).
44. *Ibid.*, p. 1230.

"There is something wrong," cried *The St. Croix Avis*, "when police officers say 'We know who they are,' but no arrests are made."[45]

Charging that young criminals "enjoy a protected status," St. Croix Senator Sidney Lee added: "We all keep hearing rumors that one reason for the failure of the police to arrest suspects is because those suspects are members of prominent families in 'high places.'"[46] According to one local businessman, "The cops ... don't want to arrest the kids of their own relatives, neighbors or friends."[47] Lest tourism be hampered, civic leaders were particularly sensitive about local crime reports appearing in stateside newspapers, as for example a report in *The Washington Post* that the Chamber of Commerce in St. Croix protested the "near-anarchy" on that island.[48]

Considering the deplorable conditions of the territory's prisons, which still lacked rehabilitation programs at the end of the 1970s, it seemed curious indeed that Senior District Court Judge Almeric Christian ordered the return in 1978 of Ishmael Muslim Ali, formerly known as Ishmael LaBeet, the reputed leader of the Fountain Valley Five, from his stateside prison. Christian, however, had no discretion in the matter. LaBeet had filed a petition alleging that he was facing "cruel and unusual punishment" in the federal prison, and the U.S. Court of Appeals in Philadelphia ruled in favor of the petition overturning a 1976 ruling by Judge Christian.[49] Accordingly, LaBeet was returned to the Virgin Islands for a hearing on his petition and was held in St. Thomas' 17th Century Fort Christian jail, one of the oldest prisons in the Western Hemisphere.

At the hearing, corrections director Rudolf Sims testified that the Golden Grove facility could not handle individuals like Ishmael LaBeet, but LaBeet produced a number of witnesses who testified that he had been subjected to cruel treatment in the federal prison.[50] The hearing ended in early July 1978, whereupon LaBeet asked permission to remain in the Islands pending a decision on his

---

45. "Editorial: Something Wrong," *The St. Croix Avis*, July 5, 1978, p. 10.

46. *The St. Croix Avis*, August 16, 1978, p. 16; *The San Juan Star*, August 25, 1978, p. 10.

47. Pieter Van Bennekom, "Juvenile Crime Wave Hitting the Virgin Islands," *The San Juan Star*, June 12, 1977, p. 7.

48. James Cuchiara, "St. Croix Plagued by a Crime Wave As Holidays Near," *The Washington Post*, December 21, 1977, p. A 16; "UPI Story Cites V. I. 'Near Anarchy,'" *Daily News*, December 21, 1977; Page Stull, "Crime Continues to Haunt V.I. in Mainland Press," *Daily News*, March 14, 1978, p. 7.

49. Penny Feuerzeig, "Fountain Valley 5's Return Allowed," *Daily News*, April 4, 1978, pp. 1, 16.

50. See, *e.g.*, *The San Juan Star*, July 6 and 7, 1978; *Virgin Islands Post*, July 6, 1978, p. 1; *The St. Croix Avis*, July 11, 1978, p. 1.

petition. Amidst protests of a number of citizens and the territorial government alike, Judge Christian granted permission.

As the decade was nearing an end, Judge Christian had yet to rule on LaBeet's petition. At stake was a farsweeping issue concerning the right of the Islands' convicted lawbreakers to be incarcerated in their homeland rather than in federal prisons on the mainland. The reputed Fountain Valley leader meanwhile remained in the Fort Christian jail where, paradoxically, reports indicated "there exists overcrowding on a chronic scale, beatings, insufficient security arrangements, and insufficient funds to correct any deficiencies."[51]

Besides education and crime prevention, health comprised a third major apparent shortcoming in social infrastructure, according to economist Richard Miller. "Health care facilities in the Virgin Islands are inadequate to meet present or projected needs," reported Miller in 1979.[52] Unlike the mainland, nearly all the territory's health facilities and services were publicly owned and administered by the insular Department of Health, the second largest government department. Two general hospitals existed in the Islands, the Charles Harwood Memorial Hospital on St. Croix and the Knud Hansen Memorial Hospital on St. Thomas. In addition, clinics were located at Frederiksted in St. Croix and at Cruz Bay in St. John.[53]

Although Virgin Islanders were charged only about half the hospital fees charged by mainland hospitals, they were characterized, nevertheless, in 1978 as being "infamous for their reluctance to pay for the medical bills they owe." The health department was reportedly in arrears more than $10 million in overdue bills for medical care delivery, half of which was considered uncollectable.[54]

The "deplorable hospital conditions," however, were attributed mainly to "archaic" procurement and personnel systems. According to a 1976 statement by St. Croix health employees:

> Our frustrations include: Inadequate food and eating utensils; inadequate supply of wash cloths, towels, bed sheets, etc.; three and four patients crowded into a two-patient room; free-roaming mental

51. Editorial, "The Landmark Effect," *Daily News*, August 16, 1979, p. 8. See, also, the three-part series feature stories on the conditions of the Fort Christian jail by Steve Bornn in the *Daily News*, July 27, 28, and 29, 1976; Cathleen Cogswell, "Life Inside Fort Christian," *Daily News*, October 11, 1979, pp. 16–17.

52. Miller, *The Economy of the Virgin Islands*, p. 16.

53. See, *e.g.*, Commission for the Study of Nursing Needs and Resources in the United States Virgin Islands, *Study of Nursing Needs and Resources in the U.S. Virgin Islands* (St. Thomas: College of the Virgin Islands, 1976), pp. 58–59.

54. "Hospital Costs Half of U.S. Charges," *Daily News*, January 19, 1978.

patients on the medical ward, and no hospital staff psychiatrist; major pilferage of food and supplies; frequent shortages of medicines; salary levels too low to attract and fill vacancies; supply and property and procurement policies so complex and slow to cause the strongest to cry in anguish.[55]

It was not surprising, therefore, that accreditation of both general hospitals in the territory was withdrawn in 1979 by the national Joint Commission on Accreditation of Hospitals.[56] Health Commissioner Dr. Roy L. Schneider blamed loss of accreditation on local press coverage of criticism of hospital conditions by local physicians whom Schneider labeled "idiots."[57] On the bright side was Congressional authorization of $52 million to build two new hospitals in the Islands, scheduled for construction in the early 1980s.[58]

Economic Infrastructure

The economic development of the Virgin Islands—including expansion of tourism and industry—was hampered greatly by inadequate water supply, electric power, and port facilities. Inadequate water supply competed with crime as the most grievous problem facing the Virgin Islands in the 1970s— both problem areas adversely affecting tourism upon which the local economy was so dependent.

Periodic water shortages, particularly in St. Thomas, had required since 1957 the intermittent barging of water from Puerto Rico. The installation with much fanfare of the Islands' first sea-water desalination plant in St. Thomas in 1962 and the subsequent addition of three more plants were not enough to alleviate the problem. Economic and population growth during the 1960s and 1970s simply outpaced available water supply. Indeed, the costly desalination plants raised false expectations that the problem was solved when, in fact, their

---

55. Editorial, "Health Care 'Frustrations.'" *Daily News*, July 14, 1976; see, also, Penny Feuerzeig, "Spark of Hope at Knud-Hansen," *Daily News*, August 9, 1976, pp. 1, 17, 23.

56. See, *e.g.*, Harry Turner, "Appeal of 2 V.I. Hospitals for Accreditation Rejected," *The San Juan Star*, August 9, 1979, pp. 1, 18; Jack Hillhouse, "Hospitals' Accreditation Deficiencies Recurred," *Daily News*, August 21, 1979, pp. 1, 12.

57. Cathleen Cogswell, "Health Commissioner Blames Press for 'Crippling' Governmental Agencies," *Daily News*, August 17, 1979, pp. 1, 12; see, also, "Doctor Responds to Schneider's Attack," *Daily News*, August 18, 1979, p. 1.

58. "Hospital Funding Measure Gets Sweeping Approval," *Daily News*, June 7, 1978, p. 1.

existence contributed to the abandonment of hillside catchments, and the neglect of other supply sources such as construction of cisterns and development of ground and well water systems. For example, a local law requiring catchments and cisterns on all new construction was not enforced. Far from being the panacea with which they were regarded, the desalination plants were afflicted with gross mismanagement as study after study attested. Most studies agreed that "desalination is too costly a method to be practical as a major source of potable water."[59] But these studies and their recommendations and proposed remedies were ignored by local authorities.[60]

Water and electricity were supplied by the Virgin Islands Water and Power Authority (WAPA) which, like the Port Authority, Housing Authority, and the College of the Virgin Islands, were independent instrumentalities of the insular government run by boards appointed by the governor. The insular government, in turn, was WAPA's largest customer, creating a major conflict of interest. Chief among WAPA's ills in the 1970s were heavy corrosion of plants, little or no preventive maintenance, six executive directors in four years, poorly trained personnel and middle management, lack of expertise, inadequate record keeping and billing, and scandalous waste. An estimated one-half of all potable water pumped into the Islands' pipe system could not be accounted for, according to a "revelation" by the new Public Works Commissioner in mid-1979.[61] A 1976 audit found that the expenses of potable water supply and distribution exceeded income by 74 percent.[62]

Given these chronic conditions, Virgin Islanders should not have been surprised when all four of the Islands' desalination plants were forced to shut down for emergency repairs in November 1977. On November 29, 1977, as the tourist season was about to begin, St. Thomas was totally without potable water, and intermittent rationing and severe water shortages were to persist through the end of the decade.

---

59. Benita Cannon, "Reports Come and Go, Water Problems Stay," *The St. Croix Avis*, March 13, 1978, p. 1. "In December, 1963, St. Thomas was ... down to nearly one day's supply of water ... from the distillation plant and from barge sources." F. W. Morrissey, *The Virgin Islands Economy* (mimeographed, St. Thomas, June 5, 1964), p. 26.

60. See, *e.g.*, Benita Cannon's many articles detailing various studies of the myriad problems afflicting the Virgin Islands Water and Power Authority featured in *The St. Croix Avis*, November 29, 30, December 1, 1977, January 19, 20, 21, 23, 25, 30, February 3, 4, 6, 7, 8, 24, 25, March 4, 13, 16, 17, 18, 22, 25, 1978. See, also, U.S. Department of Interior, *Water Resources Task Team Report on Recommended Actions to Relieve Water Supply Problems-St. Thomas, V. I.* (December 12, 1977).

61. Editorial, "Another Revelation," *The St. Croix Avis*, June 30, 1979, p. 8.

62. Miller, *The Economy of the Virgin Islands*, p. 17.

Desalination plant, St. Croix

Meanwhile, WAPA's solution to this crisis was to acquire still other desalination plants, a decision that was to create a storm of controversy that would continue into the 1980s.

In early 1978, Robert E. Grimshaw left Connecticut to become executive director of WAPA. After a visit to Israel to inspect desalination plants manufactured by the Israel Desalination Engineering (IDE) company, which paid for his trip, Grimshaw recommended, and WAPA's board accepted, IDE's bid to build three new desalination plants in the Virgin Islands, even though it was higher than other bids and $4 million higher than the bid of Aqua Chem, a Wisconsin-based firm. Charges of bias by U.S. Senator William Proxmire of Wisconsin, who threatened to vote against future appropriations for the Islands, and by a local "whistle-blowing" senatorial candidate, John P. Collins,[63] prompted the U.S. Comptroller for the Virgin Islands—Darrel E. Fleming—to conduct an audit of WAPA's procedures in the matter. Fleming's audit report concluded:

---

63. *Daily News*, September 3, 1978, p. 6.

The overall conclusion of our review is that the contract was awarded to one bidder without sufficient consideration of other qualified bidders. Also, the selected bidder did not meet all of the requirements of the bid solicitation; nor was the bidder required to meet the specifications of the legislation governing the procurement. The contract signing was approved by the board of directors. In our opinion, however, the board had not been furnished all pertinent or factual information necessary to make that decision. In addition, many major aspects of the procurement procedures used were seriously deficient.[64]

Fleming, therefore, recommended that the IDE contract not be funded and that the procurement should be rebid. In January 1979, while vacationing in the Virgin Islands, Middle East authority Dr. Alfred M. Lilienthal joined others in claiming "Zionist influence" caused awarding the contract to IDE.[65]

Fleming's audit, in turn, was called a "hatchet job" by Senator Addie Ottley and was termed politically motivated by three other local senators. On the mainland, Eisenberg and Company, a New York firm serving as general agent for IDE, complained about Fleming's audit to New York's two U.S. Senators, Jacob Javits and Daniel Moynihan. Javits accused Fleming of "following highly irregular procedures" in attempting to block the IDE contract, and both Senators requested the U.S. Government's General Accounting Office (GAO) to review Fleming's audit. Without waiting for results of the GAO review, the Virgin Islands Legislature voted on May 8, 1978 to appropriate $15.1 million bond proceeds to WAPA for the three desalination plants. Only two members

---

64. Office of the U.S. Comptroller for the U.S. Virgin Islands, *Audit of Water and Power Authority Procurement Actions for Desalination Plant, U.S. Virgin Islands* (Audit Report No.: 546-78-99. Charlotte Amalie, St. Thomas, December 20, 1978), p. 5.

65. Penny Feuerzeig, "'Zionist Influence' Charged in WAPA Contract Award," *Daily News*, January 3, 1979, p. 1. In his book, Lilienthal wrote: "The St. Thomasite Zionists raised a vast sum of money during the 1973 war, largely through the donation of a free ad in the local paper. The Arab merchants were denied an equal opportunity to appeal to the populace. They were simply told by the newspaper that their fund was 'political, not humanitarian,' and therefore could not be run free." Alfred M. Lilienthal, *The Zionist Connection, What Price Israel?* (New York: Dodd, Mead & Co., 1979), p. 216. Among Jewish contributors to U.S. Senator Henry Jackson's losing Presidential bid of 1972 was oil millionaire Leon Hess who reportedly channeled $225,000 to Jackson's campaign "by disguising his secret donations under the names of other persons, according to records of the Senate Watergate committee. Mr. Hess ... used the same method to mask $250,000 he gave President Nixon in 1972 while an oil refinery in the Virgin Islands belonging to his corporation was under investigation by the Interior Department." *The New York Times*, August 8, 1974, p. 25, col. 6.

of the Legislature—Senators Hector Cintron and John Maduro—opposed the appropriation. Both had pleaded in vain to their Senate colleagues to await the GAO review.[66] On May 30, 1978, GAO's Comptroller General Elmer B. Staats announced that GAO's review upheld Fleming's audit in all respects, that Fleming had not exceeded his authority, that his audit conformed to GAO standards, and that the GAO supported Fleming's findings, conclusions, and recommendation.[67]

Despite GAO's vindication of Fleming's audit, WAPA Director Grimshaw made another trip to Israel after which WAPA and IDE signed a Memorandum of Understanding that evoked serious misgivings from the chief auditor of the Virgin Islands Legislature, Hans Loeffler. Referring to rumors of a "Sweetheart Deal" and of "'under the table' payoffs of certain government officials," Senator Elmo D. Roebuck, President of the Virgin Islands Legislature, publicly asked: "Why are WAPA and some of our senators openly promoting this one firm and resisting all attempts to review this matter properly?"[68]

In late 1979, a number of investigations of the IDE controversy were in progress. Governor Juan Luis had initiated two investigations—one by Comptroller Fleming of WAPA's operations and management "in view of recent intensification of persistent and widespread rumors of gross mismanagement and waste"—and the other by the Islands' Attorney General, Ive Swan, into alleged "under-the-table payoffs to public officials during the course of the efforts of Israel Desalination Engineering Ltd. to sell water desalination plants to the Virgin Islands."[69] A third investigation by the Federal Bureau of Investigation (FBI) of "possible bribery" in awarding the IDE contract was initiated by Comptroller Fleming who said: "Anytime we feel there is the possibility of criminal involvement, we will definitely call the FBI in."[70]

WAPA's difficulties in management and operations brought about a succession of electric power outages during the summer and fall of 1979 causing a serious deterioration in the quality of life of St. Croix and St. Thomas occasioned by damages ranging from many dollars in spoiled food to ruined appliances

---

66. *The San Juan Star*, June 6, 1979, p. 10.

67. Memorandum (B-191654) to Jacob K. Javits and Daniel P. Moynihan, United States Senate, from Elmer B. Staats, Comptroller General of the United States, xeroxed copy, dated May 30, 1978.

68. *Daily News*, August 1, 1979, p. 10.

69. *The San Juan Star*, August 9, 1979, p. 12.

70. *The San Juan Star*, September 27, 1979, p. 16; and Diana Pearson, "FBI Confirms Probe of WAPA," *Daily News*, September 26, 1979, p. 1.

and even heavy losses in many businesses.[71] The Amerada-Hess refinery and the Martin Marietta aluminum factory provided their own power and water facilities, but to many inhabitants of Frederiksted, the second city of St. Croix, the power crisis meant no water for nine days. A popular tee shirt carried the message: "God said let there be light, WAPA said no."[72] WAPA's executive director, Robert Grimshaw, admitted: "It would be difficult to attract industry to the Virgin Islands right now. Every industry wants a reliable source of power."[73] And St. Croix's Chamber of Commerce director, Larry Kavanaugh, cited this unreliability as the major obstacle in attracting new industry.[74] In retrospect, the demise of the so-called South Shore Plant was incomprehensible.

A new electric power plant in Christiansted was first conceived in 1970. In 1972, it was decided—without any long-term planning—to build the plant on the south shore of St. Croix adjacent to Hess and Martin Marietta operations, despite the facts that no transmission lines existed near that location and that the Christiansted site would have required $500,000 less to operate annually from savings in manpower alone. Indeed, the additional cost of the South Shore Plant was variously estimated at four to five million dollars.

Construction of the South Shore Plant commenced in late 1972. In July 1976, WAPA's Board decided to sell the facility—then 85 percent completed—and halted construction. WAPA's engineers estimated that there would be no need for additional power generating capacity on St. Croix before 1988. After an expenditure of over $15 million, WAPA sold its "white elephant plant" in December 1977, for $9.25 million to the Dominican Republic. Attorney Gustav A. Danielson, hearing examiner for the Islands' Public Services Commission, estimated in March 1979 that the "combined loss on disposal of the plant becomes close to eight million dollars." After an extensive rate investigation hearing of WAPA, Danielson concluded that the decision to build the plant was an "imprudent" investment based on "inadequate" analysis that failed to consider costs of putting the plant on line and comparative costs of operating two locations, instead of one.

Even after the July 1976 decision to dispose of the plant, 4.5 million dollars of unused debt bearing loans were kept in certificates of deposit

---

71. Editorial, "The Quality of Life," *The St. Croix Avis*, October 10, 1979, p. 8.

72. "Visitor Comments on St. Croix," *The St. Croix Avis*, September 16, 1979, p. 11.

73. *The St. Croix Avis*, June 26, 1978, p. 1.

74. Interview, Larry Kavanaugh, Executive Director, St. Croix Chamber of Commerce, Christiansted, St. Croix, July 6, 1979.

until April 1977.... Finally, the decision to dispose of the plant was based upon inadequate information. The failure to use future forecasting and the reliance solely upon past patterns to predict future growth has contributed greatly to the utility's woes, as has the reluctance to retain outside expertise to conduct adequate studies.[75]

Without any additional power generating capacity for the 1980s, St. Croix faced a dark future. A former senator commented: "If General Motors were run like the Virgin Islands government it would go bankrupt."[76]

Facing problems similar to WAPA, the Virgin Islands Port Authority had a cumulative deficit of $6.5 million on June 30, 1977.[77] The Authority was responsible for operating the airports on St. Croix and St. Thomas, the latter of which was undergoing a long-delayed major expansion in 1979, and for the maintenance of several docks. The need for substantial improvements of the docks at Frederiksted in St. Croix and Cruz Bay in St. John still remained at the end of the 1970s.

Far from paying its own way, the Authority depended on annual legislative appropriations to cover the costs of operations until Governor Cyril E. King in 1975 ordered the Authority to become self-sustaining. Finally, in 1979, the Port Authority reported a profit, for the first time, of $160,000.[78] Nevertheless, the Authority was the target of criticism that year from Senator Michael Paiewonsky and Comptroller Darrell Fleming. The latter criticized the Authority for spending $18,000 to send seven delegates to a European conference for sixteen days in June 1979. Fleming's audit found the expenditure "excessive compared to the benefits realized," that the trip was not "prudently planned," that some costs benefited the delegates or their spouses personally, and—most revealing—that delegates were reimbursed for both expenses and per diem in violation of the law which specified that one or the other could be paid but not both.[79] In October 1979, Senate President Elmo

75. Gustav A. Danielson, *Hearing Examiner's Report. Public Services Commission Docket 170, Virgin Islands Water and Power Rate Investigation* (Charlotte Amalie, St. Thomas, March 12, 1979), pp. 33–84. See, also, Benita Cannon, "Voice Strong Reaction Sale South Shore Plant," *The St. Croix Avis*, December 10, 1977, pp. 1, 3.

76. Editorial, "Why Was It Ever Bought?" *Daily News*, May 10, 1977.

77. Miller, *The Economy of the Virgin Islands*, p. 18.

78. A Statement from the Virgin Islands Port Authority," *Daily News*, August 21, 1979, p. 11.

79. Penny Feuerzeig, "Port Authority Travelers Rapped," *Daily News*, October 9, 1979, p. 1.

D. Roebuck announced that he was calling for a "full-fledged investigation" by the Legislature of reports of misappropriation of Port Authority funds and property.[80]

Meanwhile, major port facilities in the Virgin Islands were privately owned. Hess and Martin Marietta had constructed their own ports, and Hess—under an agreement with the Virgin Islands Government—planned to build a container port to he turned over to the Port Authority for operations.

The 1917 treaty of sale with Denmark had continued that country's West India Company ownership and operation of Charlotte Amalie's major port facility which was to become one of the busiest cruise ship docks in the world. Under that agreement, the United States Government had guaranteed the West India Company's right to dredge and reclaim the submerged land in the harbor. The Company's application in 1977 to dredge the harbor and to create 29 acres of new land was questioned by the Virgin Islands Conservation Society and the Gift and Fashion Shop Committee of the St. Thomas-St. John Chamber of Commerce, the latter group stating that "the possible consequences are horrifying."[81] By the end of the decade, no action had been taken on the project.

Economic Development

Insofar as all true knowledge may he comparative, the Virgin Islands suffered in the 1970s from comparisons with the mainland that concluded Virgin Islanders were not receiving the quality of public services other Americans were receiving, from Third World perspectives concluding that the territory suffered a serious trade imbalance and other economic woes shared with less developed countries, and from the "new nationalism" and socialist perspectives characterizing the Islands as an example of colonial exploitation by an imperialist power. On the other hand, evidence existed that Virgin Islanders were not paying their fair share of the cost of government, that insular officials themselves preferred to compare local living standards adversely with the mainland to demonstrate relative deprivation and hence the need for more federal assistance, and that residents of other Caribbean islands continued to view the Virgin Islands as offering fulfillment in terms of a decent income and a better life. Different perspectives produced different comparisons and conclusions. According to economist Richard Miller:

---

80. Penny Feuerzeig, "Roebuck Calls for V.I. Port Authority Probe," *Daily News*, October 10, 1979, p. 3.

81. *Daily News*, November 28, 1977, pp. 3, 24, and December 10, 1977, pp. 1, 16.

Market Place, Charlotte Amalie, St. Thomas

Economists and statisticians are faced with a difficult task in analyzing the territorial economies and making meaningful comparisons with the mainland and foreign countries. The difficulties are both statistical and conceptual. Data collection methods vary and statistics may mean different things in different contexts. For example, Virgin Islands per capita income in 1976 was $4,596, compared to $6,393 in the United States as a whole, $4,575 in Mississippi, and $1,248 in Barbados. In money terms, the average Virgin Islander is worse off than the average Mississippian and much better off than other Caribbean islanders. But money comparisons cannot take into account significant differences in income distribution, living costs, climate or lifestyle.[82]

Virgin Islanders were estimated to have spent in 1976 at least 25 percent more for food, shelter, utilities, clothing, and transportation than spent by residents of Washington, D.C. Food alone cost about 27 percent higher. Average weekly earnings in the territory, moreover, were below average mainland earnings by about 12 percent, meaning that the ability of a Virgin Islander to purchase goods and services was approximately 37 percent below that of the mainlander. In addition, the lack of adequate public transportation forced many Virgin Islanders to purchase private vehicles; the lack of adequate medical services prompted many to travel to Puerto Rico or the mainland; and inadequate public education induced many parents to send their children to more expensive private and parochial schools. These statistics and seeming inequities, however, did not ac-

82. Miller, *The Economy of the Virgin Islands*, p. 4.

count for substantial benefits accruing to residents of the territory—no heating expenses, apparel worn year around, and quality of life considered by many to be superior to that on the U.S. mainland.[83]

These benefits, of course, helped to offset the many drawbacks in attracting industry to the Virgin Islands. Also important were the prospects of cheap alien labor, generous government investment incentives, customs exemptions, tax breaks, and other financial inducements.

Tourism continued to be the mainstay of the economy, although many native Virgin Islanders saw little benefit from tourism development.[84] Tourism had declined precipitously between 1973 and 1976, most significantly because of the economic slow-down on the mainland and widely publicized crime beginning with the Fountain Valley murders. But tourism in the Islands was better than ever at the end of the decade. In 1972, a peak of slightly over one million tourists had spent almost $150 million. In the first half of 1979 alone, over 1.6 million visitors had spent almost $275 million.[85]

A large proportion of tourist expenditures, however, was for imported goods rather than for local goods and services.[86] Accordingly, economic development depended greatly on the territory's capacity to attract and keep new industry. Key to this effort was the insular government's Industrial Development Program.

The origins of the Industrial Development Program dated from the original tax incentive act of 1949. Major revisions were made in 1957, 1961, 1972,

83. Page Stull, "Virgin Islands Purchasing Power 37% Below Mainland," *Virgin Islands Post*, March 23, 1978, pp. 1, 3.

84. Some native Virgin Islanders engaged in "tourists-go-home" demonstrations in St. Croix in 1979. Led by Leona Watson—self-styled preserver of Crucian culture—the demonstrators, much to the distress of local business and political leaders, greeted the 1,100 passengers of the cruise ship "Caravelle" (which docked at Frederiksted every Thursday) with posters proclaiming "No more hospitality—Prepare for hostility," "Down with tourism—Up with agriculture." and similar sentiments. Diana Pearson, "Demonstrators Disturb Ship Passengers at Frederiksted," *Daily News*, August 24, 1979, pp. 1, 13. See, also, Gabrielle Hall, "St. Croix Silhouette—Leona Watson," *The St. Croix Avis*, July 12, 1979, p. 9.

85. "Tourists Spending More Than Ever in the V.I.," *Virgin Islands Post*, August 9, 1979, p. 5.

86. "The majority of tourists stay in the Virgin Islands only one day and purchase no accommodations locally. These are cruise ship passengers whose benefit to the local economy is limited mainly to the purchase of imported 'duty-free' goods. According to a survey in 1977, the average cruise ship passenger spent $68 per one-day visit, while the average air arrival spent $382 in 8 days (7 nights). Although the sale of merchandise to cruise ship passengers has become an important business, it contributes much less to the local economy than an equivalent expenditure on food, lodging or entertainment." Miller, *The Economy of the Virgin Islands*, p. 32.

and 1975. The latest revision in 1975 granted incentives to firms for locating in the Islands of complete exemption from property and gross receipt taxes and from excise taxes on construction materials, plus 90 percent subsidies on excise taxes on raw materials, customs duties, and income taxes. The length of time of the benefits varied, at the firm's option, from ten years at 100 percent of these benefits to twenty years at 50 percent of benefits. Renewal of tax incentive grants could be granted up to an additional five years at 100 percent of benefits to ten years at 50 percent.[87]

As noted previously, the Amerada Hess oil refinery and the Martin Marietta aluminum facility received even greater benefits through special legislation. As their benefits were nearing expiration at the end of the decade, the insular government renegotiated the terms of benefits accorded Martin Marietta, but had yet to come to terms with Hess.[88]

Although Hess Oil's benefits, in effect since 1965, were not to expire until 1981, renegotiation began in December 1976—a process marked with much controversy and drama—representing a classic confrontation between a powerful and wealthy multinational corporation and a weak and dependent host polity.

Faced with a fiscal crisis and the need for increased revenues, Governor Cyril King initiated the renegotiation process with Hess in an effort to obtain advance payments in taxes. "We have to begin," acknowledged King, "by admitting they're in the driver's seat."[89] That Leon Hess had used his wealth to get what he wanted in the Islands had long been widely rumored. U.S. Senator Russell Long alluded in March 1976 to the possibility of involvement of "some political corruption" in the building of the refinery in the Virgin Islands.[90] And Leon Hess, an otherwise reclusive man who personally ran the Company,[91] admitted in April 1976, that he had made a "series" of questionable or illegal "payments, substantial in the aggregate, to a foreign government official."[92]

The insular government proposed to extend the original agreement with Hess until 1991 if Hess would give it $15 million at once against future taxes and $14

---

87. Act No. 3748, Virgin Islands Legislature, approved September 23, 1975.

88. See, Christine Redman, "Martin Marietta Taxes, Royalties Quadrupled," *Daily News*, October 8, 1979, p. 3; Dee Kratovil, "Formal Government Talks with Hess Oil Beginning Soon," *Daily News*, October 3, 1979, p. 3.

89. Penny Feuerzeig, "Committee Sets Plan for Hess Oil Taxes," *Daily News*, December 30, 1976, p. 1.

90. "Long Hostile Toward V.I. Refinery Interest," *Daily News*, March 31, 1976, p. 1.

91. See, "Why Leon Hess Is Oil's Quiet Man—Profit From the Best of All Worlds," *Business Week*, July 16, 1979, pp. 64–70.

92. William D. Smith, "Amerada Hess's Chairman Tells of Payments Abroad," *The New York Times*, April 10, 1979, p. 35.

million annually in new royalties. After the proposal met with severe criticism,[93] Leon Hess called off the deal. "Could it have been," asked Tad Szulc of *Forbes* magazine, "that the wily Hess used the criticism as an excuse to hold out for a better deal?"[94] Hess, indeed, held an impressive trump card. He concluded an agreement in mid-1977 to build another refinery on five hundred and thirty acres of nearby St. Lucia, and threatened either to close the St. Croix plant or to shift a substantial portion of its capacity to that newly independent island nation.[95]

During the succeeding months, Hess Oil proceeded to lay off one hundred and twenty of its St. Croix employees, and to cut production almost half at its huge St. Croix refinery. "Has the Virgin Islands killed the goose that has been laying the golden eggs on St. Croix?" asked a local editorial.[96] Labeling itself a "corporate citizen and neighbor," Hess Oil blithely explained in a full-page newspaper advertisement that the reductions had "nothing to do with anything but the lower demand for refined products."[97]

By June 1978, the workers laid off before were back at work and the Hess refinery was restored to full production. Demand for oil had dramatically increased. A world-wide oil crisis in 1978 and 1979, wrought in part by spiraling oil prices and production cut-backs, occasioned by the ongoing Iranian revolution, helped spur enormous profits for oil companies including Amerada Hess, the nation's 16th largest oil company. With its St. Croix refinery—reputedly the world's most productive—fully operating, Hess reported a 300 percent second-quarter gain in profits in 1979 over the corresponding quarter in 1978, and a 290 percent jump over the third quarter of 1978—the greatest percentage gains among major oil firms in the nation.[98]

After the socialist-leaning St. Lucia Labor Party came to power in July 1979 and demanded that the Hess agreement with the St. Lucian government be renegotiated, some of Hess Oil's leverage in its ongoing renegotiations with

---

93. See, *e.g.*, *Daily News*, July 29, 1977, pp. 1, 16; Mildred Wallace, "Speakers Denounce Proposed Hess Pact," *Daily News*, July 30, 1977; pp. 1, 16; and Letter to Editor from 39 Concerned Citizens of St. Croix, *Daily News*, July 1, 1977.

94. Tad Szulc, "Playing for High Stakes in the Virgin Islands," *Forbes*, August 1, 1977, p. 53.

95. "Hess Threatens to Close StX Refinery," *Virgin Islands Post*, June 21, 1977, p. 1.

96. Editorial, "Have We Killed the Golden Goose on St. Croix?" *Virgin Islands Post*, December 15, 1977, p. 1.

97. *The St. Croix Avis*, March 20, 1978.

98. *The Philadelphia Inquirer*, July 21, 1979, p. B3, col. 8. "Amerada Hess said its profits in the third quarter were $119.2 million, up from $30.6 million in last year's third quarter." *The News Journal*, Wilmington, Delaware, October 27, 1979, p. 1. See, also, *The Washington Post*, July 26, 1979, p. C1.

the Virgin Islands Government was reduced. "Everything's been changed. We haven't moved anything to St. Lucia. We will not," said Leon Hess. "The Virgin Islands will maintain its status quo."[99]

In August 1979, Hess Oil finally broke ground to construct the long-promised $18 million container port to make St. Croix a major Caribbean cargo point that would eliminate the costly and time-consuming transshipment of goods through San Juan, Puerto Rico. In exchange, the insular government was to grant Hess a ninety-nine year lease on government-owned lands that Hess needed for a pipeline. Some local officials feared Hess would use the project to obtain still more favorable terms in renegotiating its "tax holiday" agreement with the government. "The container port has no bearing whatsoever on our tax negotiations," averred Leon Hess. "But I am concerned with the fiscal situation in the Virgin Islands and I'm doing everything I possibly can to work something out."[100]

Meanwhile, approval of a second oil refinery on St. Croix stirred familiar controversy between those natives who viewed more industry as a means to free them from dependence on tourism and natives and white continentals who feared more despoilation of the land and pollution of the environment. It was the kind of knotty problem clouding economic development of most Caribbean islands. "To what extent can the islands absorb heavy industry without inflicting lasting damages to the fragile beauty of land and sea," asked journalist Jon Nordheimer, "thereby jeopardizing a tourist industry that in many instances has been the sole support for islands barren of other natural resources?"[101]

Construction of a second oil refinery on 700 acres of St. Croix's south shore by the Virgin Islands Refinery Corporation (VIRCO), a private firm, was approved by the Legislature and Governor in January 1973 in special legislation extending tax concessions similar to those extended to Hess Oil. VIRCO purchased three hundred and fifty-six acres for nearly $10 million from the de Chabert family, the same family that had sold acreage to Leon Hess. A taxpayers' suit to void the enabling legislation failed,[102] but a succession of federal environmental regulations prohibited commencement of construction of the

99. Terry Galvin, "Hess Oil Scraps St. Lucia Move," *Daily News*, October 4, 1979, p. 1.
100. Cynthia Sheps, "Cruzan Port Could Cancel Costly P.R. Connection," *The San Juan Star*, August 12, 1979, p. B9.
101. Jon Nordheimer, "Virgin Islands Asks If Its Tourist Industry Can Live With a 2d Oil Refinery," *The New York Times*, December 20, 1972, p. 49.
102. *Holmes v. Government of the Virgin Islands*, Virgin Islands Reports, D.C.V.I., St. Croix, January 31, 1974, p. 365.

oil refinery until those requirements should be satisfied. VIRCO's refinery was still "in limbo" in the late 1970s.[103]

A case could have been made that government tax incentives were unnecessary to attract a second oil refinery, particularly in the context of the incipient energy crisis and insufficient U.S. refining capacity of the early 1970s. Both Delaware and Maine had passed environmental protection laws effectively closing two of the four to six deep-water ports on the east coast of the U.S. capable of servicing super oil tankers. Inasmuch as the Virgin Islands were singularly exempt from the "American flag" requirements of the Jones Act, moreover, VIRCO stood to realize substantial savings through less expensive foreign flag shipments from its St. Croix refinery to U.S. ports, savings not available to refineries located in the U.S. or Puerto Rico.[104]

In any event, United States Comptroller Darrell Fleming produced data in 1978 that raised the question whether the Industrial Development Program was not much too generous. For fiscal year 1978, Fleming estimated that 52 percent of total revenues and 48 percent of total expenditures of the territorial government were related to the Industrial Development Program. Subsidy payments alone totaled $175.7 million in fiscal year 1978 and $863.9 million since the program began in 1949, whereas Fleming estimated exempted taxes at $146.6 million for fiscal 1978 and $689.2 million since 1949. Hess Oil, as expected, benefited the most from the Program, with Martin Marietta the next largest participant followed by approximately seventy smaller firms. But the dominance of Hess in the Program was overwhelming. The total of all subsidy payments and exempted taxes combined since 1949 was $1,553.1 million of which $1,419 million, or over 91 percent of the total, represented benefits accorded Hess Oil alone, even though its refinery dated only from 1965. The direct monetary benefits paid to the territorial government by all participating firms since 1949 totaled a miniscule $147.1 million of which Hess accounted for $97.5 million or only 66 percent of the total.

---

103. Kay Howard, "VIRCO Refinery In Limbo As Deadline Approaches," *Virgin Islands Post*, July 23, 1978, p. 1. See, also, Diana Pearson, "Hadary Discusses VIRCO Future," *Daily News*, December 18, 1979, pp. 3, 20.

104. Threats by Congress in 1976 to remove the exemption of the Virgin Islands from the 1920 Jones Act, forbidding the use of foreign flag vessels between U.S. ports, and again by President Carter in 1979, aroused much consternation among insular officials who mobilized lobbying efforts opposing such action. See, *e.g.*, Harry Turner, "King Predicts Jones Act May 'Devastate' V.I.," *The San Juan Star*, February 26, 1976, p. 23: Dee Kratovil, "Defense Organized For Jones Act Shipping Exemption," *Daily News*, September 17, 1979, pp. 1, 22.

Fleming also disclosed serious deficiencies in the administration of the Program by the territory's Industrial Development Commission, notably—no formal written procedures manual, no approval and implementation of proposed rules and regulations, no preparation and submission of required quarterly reports, and no cost/benefit analyses performed for any applicant to determine if new or extended benefits should be granted and at what level.

> Further, the Industrial Development Commission had almost no capability to review the commitments made by grantees regarding employment, capital investment, and specific manufacturing commitments. For example, although grantee firms employ approximately 5,300 persons, the Commission does not have reliable information as to how many of these persons are legal residents and how many were imported by the firms from off-island.[105]

In the covering letter of his report, Fleming recommended:

> While we acknowledge the need for fiscal incentives, we believe that the Industrial Development Program should be viewed as a potential source of additional Government revenues in future years. If the Territorial Government, upon renewal of existing tax incentive grants, were able to reduce the benefits given to firms by even a small percentage (about 5–10%), we believe that sufficient funds would become available to meet current operating expenses without the need to institute many of the tax increases discussed elsewhere in the report.[106]

Fiscal Uncertainty

When the Naval Appropriations Act of 1922 proclaimed that United States tax laws likewise applied to the Virgin Islands, except that their proceeds were to be paid into the insular treasuries (constituting 100 percent revenue sharing),[107] it also created, according to tax lawyer, Gustav Danielson, "what may be the world's most confusing tax system."[108]

---

105. U.S. Comptroller for the Virgin Islands, *Report to the Secretary of Interior on the Requirements of Public Law 95-348* (Charlotte Amalie, St. Thomas, June 1979), pp. 15–20 at p. 19.

106. *Ibid.*

107. 48 *United States Code* 1397.

108. Gustav A. Danielson, *Business Operations in the U.S. Virgin Islands* (Washington, D.C.: Tax Management Inc., 1978), p. A1.

The so-called "mirror system" of taxation was achieved by a "cavalier treatment of nationality" whereby the U.S. Internal Revenue Code was transformed into a Virgin Islands taxing statute by substituting the words "Virgin Islands" for the words "United States" wherever the latter appeared in the Code. Not only did this mirror theory presume that the Virgin Islands and the United States were jurisdictions foreign to one another, insofar as the two jurisdictions looked upon each other's citizens, residents, and entities as foreign, but it also made the Virgin Islands (and Guam) peculiarly and inadvertently vulnerable to machinations of international politics and economics as reflected by trade war and balance-of-payments changes in United States income tax statutes. Congress usually forgot its insular possessions when making such changes.[109]

Besides local tax incentives and federal duty exemptions, the mirror system also made it possible, in the opinion of Danielson for the Virgin Islands to be used as a tax haven for investment in overseas operations. "It may be possible to avoid income taxation completely," wrote Danielson, "repatriate profits to the United States tax free, and avoid Controlled Foreign Corporation status." He explained:

> Personal Holding Company provisions may be sidestepped if the stockholders are not inhabitants of the Virgin Islands. Risks attach to the use of the Virgin Islands as a tax haven since such schemes are untested by judicial review. Nonetheless, the strange administrative interpretation of the Internal Revenue Code in the Virgin Islands provides unique tax opportunities which may be well worth the risks.[110]

In 1976, Congress granted $8.5 million to the Virgin Islands to offset losses caused by the Tax Reduction Act of 1975 and authorized the Virgin Islands Legislature to levy a ten percent surtax on the income tax obligation.[111] Instead of levying any surcharge, however, local authorities in the 1970s annually importuned a compliant Washington to fund deficits incurred by the local government.

Even a ten percent surcharge would have left aggregate Virgin Islands income tax rates below those paid by most Americans, because the over-all tax effort in the Virgin Islands was among the lowest under the American flag. In Fiscal Year 1977, for example, Virgin Islanders paid roughly half ($985 per capita in taxes) of that paid by other Americans ($1,955 per capita). Virgin Islanders were quick to point out, however, that their cost-of-living was between

---

109. *Ibid.*, pp. A1, A62.
110. *Ibid.*, pp. A1; see, also, pp. A90–A91.
111. Public Law 94-392, August 19, 1976.

20 and 30 percent higher than on the mainland. Although the tax burden remained fairly constant in the 50 states during the period of Fiscal Years 1971 to 1977, in the Virgin Islands the tax burden declined 16 percent during the same period. Chief among the reasons for this disparity were the post-Fountain-Valley recession and the fact that the Virgin Islands income level did not grow as fast as that on the mainland, while local taxes were not increased at all during the period.[112]

Meanwhile, the Virgin Islands received federal grants-in-aid (for purposes such as public housing, child nutrition, and medicaid, to mention three of the largest) amounting, for example, to $652 per capita in Fiscal Year 1977 or 51 percent above the per capita grants to all states and local governments. Another source of federal financial assistance consisted of the matching fund paid into the insular treasury under the Revised Organic Act consisting of all taxes collected under United States laws on articles produced in the Virgin Islands (such as rum) and transported to the United States. In addition, substantial federal assistance for capital project expenditures in the Islands was authorized by Congress in the late 1970s.

The most contentious and crisis-ridden category of federal financial assistance consisted of the annual Congressional appropriations of the late 1970s to cover the territorial government's annual deficits, justified to compensate for "shortfalls" in income tax collections resulting from federal tax reductions. Beginning with the $8.5 million provided in 1976, $14 million were authorized in 1977, and about $1.9 million were expected for the shortfall in 1978. The Revenue Act of 1978, for the fourth successive year, lowered federal income tax rates, once again causing tax losses in the Islands under the mirror system. A bill that would have provided offsetting compensation to the Islands was passed by Congress, but much to the dismay of local authorities it was vetoed by President Carter on the grounds that it represented a piecemeal approach and failed to address underlying problems.[113]

Carter's veto was a signal to the insular government that Washington intended to watch closely insular fiscal activities. Unfortunately, local authorities remained indifferent to that signal, thus inducing a precipitous deterioration in Washington's financial relations with the Islands as the decade neared an end.

For Congressman Philip Burton, chairman of the House subcommittee on territories, the year 1979 became "far and away the most difficult year I've ever

---

112. See, U.S. Comptroller, *Report to the Secretary*, pp. 3–5; and Miller, *The Economy of the Virgin Islands*, pp. 42–43.

113. Miller, *The Economy of the Virgin Islands*, p. 46.

experienced with respect to the Virgin Islands." In early 1979, newly-elected Republican Congressional Delegate Melvin Evans, representing the Virgin Islands in the House of Representatives, alienated many Washington liberals by his surprising and deciding vote in committee that defeated the Carter administration's major environmental bill, the Alaska lands bill, which would have preserved great tracts of Alaskan land from private development. Allegedly, Evans had agreed to support the bill until his unexplainable and sudden reversal. Whatever his reasons, Evans' vote ended the "quiet success" enjoyed by the Virgin Islands in its Congressional relations. "We were able to do reasonably well before and no one had a sense of being crowded," commented Congressman Burton. "By and large, decisions were made in a kind of easy going context. Now we literally have votes and arguments on virtually every item."[114]

Spearheading the defeat of a 1979 bill to grant $20 million to the Virgin Islands, to offset losses sustained by still another tax decrease voted by Congress in 1978, was Senator J. Bennett Johnston, a Louisiana Democrat, who apparently had done his homework on the Virgin Islands. On the floor of the Senate, Senator Johnston complained of the low tax effort in the Islands, and the failure of the territory's Legislature to enact the 1976-authorized surcharge while voting its members in 1979 a 66 percent pay increase that evoked a letter of protest from President Carter's inflation fighter, Alfred Kahn, about these and other raises for the Governor, Lieutenant Governor, and other government employees, all in substantial excess of President Carter's guidelines. Citing a letter from the Secretary of Interior, stating that granting the $20 million would do nothing to encourage the territory's government to solve its fiscal problems, Johnston also printed in the *Congressional Record* Comptroller Fleming's 1978 findings detailing "serious weaknesses in the entire system" of financial management in the Islands.[115]

---

114. Quoted by Penny Feuerzeig, "'Most Difficult Year' for Islands in Washington," *Daily News*, November 1, 1979, p. 3.

115. 125 *Congressional Record* S8335–S8343 (June 25, 1979). Annual reports of the U.S. Comptroller for the Government of the Virgin Islands throughout the 1970s repeatedly cited increasing deficits, substantial loss of revenues, unnecessary costs, poor accounting and information systems, and wasteful financial and procurement procedures and practices, with little having been done to improve financial management. The result was that the territory's government faced "virtual bankruptcy" at the end of the decade. See, *e.g.*, U.S. Government Comptroller for the Virgin Islands. *Financial Condition of the Government of the Virgin Islands of the United States, Fiscal Year 1978* (Charlotte Amalie, St. Thomas, July 20, 1979). Among other habitual practices of the Virgin Islands Government to balance its budget annually were the overestimation of revenues and the "robbing-Peter-to-pay-Paul" method of financing whereby the Government transferred capital or other segregated funds

The refusal by Congress in 1979 to appropriate $20 million to the Virgin Islands appeared to mark the end of Washington "bailouts," and the onset of "get-tough" policies, with respect to the Virgin Islands. In short, Washington's patience toward the territory's government had worn thin. Congressional Delegate Ron de Lugo and his administrative assistant, Janet Watlington, theretofore had been quick to claim credit for passage of the annual subsidies. Now, de Lugo's successor, Republican Melvin Evans, was widely blamed for the reversal, and many Virgin Islanders speculated that either Democrats de Lugo or Julio Brady, former U.S. Attorney, would defeat Evans in the 1980 election.[116]

No longer able to rely on Congressional subsidies to cover its deficits, the Virgin Islands Government attached added significance to its suit against the Secretary of Treasury, following the lead of a similar suit by the Government of Puerto Rico. The Virgin Islands Government contended that the matching fund provisions of the Revised Organic Act required the U.S. Government to pay to the Virgin Islands the amount of U.S. duties collected on *all* U.S. imports from the Virgin Islands including petroleum products, and that the Act also required payment of U.S. taxes on the sale of gasoline refined in the Virgin Islands the same way that the excise tax on rum is paid to the Islands. Considering the mammoth production of the Amerada Hess refinery on St. Croix—an industry unforeseen by the framers of the Revised Organic Act in 1954—the Virgin Islands anticipated that a favorable decision in the courts would result (although estimates varied) in retroactive payments through 1978 totalling possibly $375 million, and $70 million annually thereafter. A U.S. district court decided in 1978 that revenues from U.S. gasoline taxes be paid into the treas-

---

from autonomous agencies for use as operating expenses, often illegally. See, *e.g.*, Editorial, "Time To Be Self-Supporting," *Daily News*, March 28, 1978. Local newspapers frequently reported evidence: of businessmen defrauding the Government of millions of tax dollars annually (See, *e.g.*, Editorial, "The Great Tax Ripoff," *Virgin Islands Post*, June 25, 1978); of doctors, lawyers, politicians and other notables who were delinquent in payment of property taxes (See, *e.g.*, Michael Scuilla, "Local Notables Owe Real Property Taxes," *Daily News*, March 29, 1978); and of abuse of sick leave among government employees who comprised 35 percent of the workforce in the Virgin Islands—totaling a loss of $3.5 million per year, or 75 percent higher than what the cost would have been "if sick leave were used only by those too ill to work." (Penny Feuerzeig, "Govt. Sick Leave Cost: $3.5 Million Per Year." *Daily News*, June 24, 1977, p. 1).

116. Jan Watlington had defeated Brady in the 1978 Democratic primary to become the Party's nominee for Delegate, but Evans won the seat in the general election. In 1979, the territory's government created a new office to represent it in Washington and appointed Brady to head it, thus giving credence to speculation that Brady was being primed to replace Evans as Delegate. It was de Lugo, however, who ran in the 1980 election and defeated Evans.

ury of the Virgin Islands, but the Supreme Court had yet to finally dispose of the case at the end of the decade.

In light of the recent hostile mood of Congress toward the Virgin Islands Government, it was entirely possible that Congress might override a decision ultimately favorable to the Virgin Islands, by amending the Revised Organic Act, or that Congress might otherwise tie future assistance to the eventual outcome of the suit. It was strongly felt in some quarters that should the Virgin Islands prevail in the courts on this gasoline tax issue, Congress would act promptly to change the law at least to prevent the Virgin Islands retroactively—and perhaps even prospectively—from receiving such revenues.[117]

Meanwhile, legislation was introduced in Congress and was passed by the House of Representatives in April 1979 to provide in part for federal collection of all customs duties and U.S. income taxes in the Virgin Islands, and for the U.S. Government to administer and enforce collection of all other taxes covered into the treasury of the Virgin Islands under the Revised Organic Act. Governor Juan Luis hotly resisted this move as a "return to colonialism," in testimony before the Senate Committee on Energy and Natural Resources.

> We view the prospect of direct Federal intervention in the administration of a program which has been wholly administered by the Government of the Virgin Islands for nearly forty years as a genuine threat to a thoughtfully conceived, carefully nurtured, and highly valued, amicable Federal-Territorial relationship, as well as a major setback in our quest for increased self-government and self-determination.[118]

Not all local political figures, however, disfavored federal collection, "I believe that federal collection of Virgin Islands taxes is a capital idea," said Senator Ruby Rouss of the Virgin Islands Legislature, "because the federal government will collect the taxes without fear or favor." Lieutenant Governor Henry Millin

---

117. Interview, Attorney Gustav A. Danielson, Charlotte Amalie, St. Thomas, November 16, 1979. See, *e.g.*, Harry Turner, "V.I. Awarded Full Retroactivity," *The San Juan Star*, October 12, 1978, pp. 1, 18; and Mary Munroe, "Territory's Federal Suit Appears Headed To Trial," *Daily News*, November 12, 1979, pp. 1, 22.

118. Juan Luis, Governor, *Statement of the Governor of the Virgin Islands on H.R. 3756, 96th Congress, A Bill "to authorize appropriations for certain insular areas of the United States, and for other purposes" to United States Senate Committee on Energy and Natural Resources*, xeroxed copy, October 10, 1979, p. 3. See, also, David Shapiro, "Federal Collection Opposed," *Daily News*, October 12, 1979, p. 1.

also favored federal collection for the reason that local revenues would increase. St. Croix Senator Hector Cintron disputed Governor Luis' contention that federal collection would represent a return to colonialism. "Virgin Islands politicians," he observed, "were not waving the red herring of colonialism over welfare and food stamps," a reference to important federal programs in the Islands.[119]

In the late 1970s, reports by U.S. Comptroller Fleming severely criticized local tax collection efforts, a refrain echoed by U.S. Treasury Department studies in 1979 which also called for overhauling the territory's tax system to close loopholes in federal tax laws that permitted corporations to operate in the Virgin Islands free of U.S. income tax on their territorial source income, while permitting the Virgin Islands to administer companion tax incentive programs. One study commented:

> The relief from Federal tax and the rebate of territorial tax on territorial source income encourages profit shifting ... and generates numerous and severe transfer-pricing problems for the Internal Revenue Service.[120]

Still another development reflecting federal scrutiny of the insular government was the initiation of an investigation by the Federal Bureau of Investigation in late 1979 of possible misuse of funds by certain local legislators. A rumor that the investigation involved some fifty FBI agents prompted speculation that a far more extensive probe of the Virgin Islands Government was underway. St.

---

119. Interviews: Senator Ruby Rouss, Anna's Hope, St. Croix, November 21, 1979; Lieutenant Governor Henry Millin, Charlotte Amalie, St. Thomas, November 19, 1979; and Senator Hector Cintron, Christiansted, St. Croix, November 23, 1979,

120. *Territorial Income Tax Systems: Income Taxation in the Virgin Islands, Guam, the Northern Mariana Islands and American Samoa* (Washington: Department of the Treasury, October 1979), p. 4, See, also, *Second Annual Report: The Operation and Effect of the Possessions Corporation System of Taxation* (Washington: Department of the Treasury, June 1979), pp. 87–99. See, *e.g.*, Emily Tynes, "U.S. Audit Criticizes Govt's Bill Collecting," *Daily News*, April 12, 1978, pp. 1, 20. Relating to growing Congressional concerns that tax collections lagged while demands for federal financial assistance by the Virgin Islands increased was the dismissal of "whistle-blower," and 25 years an internal revenue officer, Liston Monsanto from the Virgin Islands Department of Finance allegedly in retaliation for his exposé of bribery and other fraudulent practices in the Department's tax division. See, *e.g.*, Patricia Blake, "Monsanto Firing Appeal Decision Expected in 14 Days," *Daily News*, November 8, 1979, p. 3. In an interview, Monsanto emphasized that the Government of the Virgin Islands had no external auditor except the U.S. Comptroller who cannot investigate the Department of Finance unless invited, and that there is no one to check the internal audit unit in Finance. Interview, Liston Monsanto, Charlotte Amalie, St. Thomas, November 16, 1979.

Croix Senator Ruby Rouss expressed her belief that the FBI was looking into the entire WAPA operations, including the IDE contract and the sale of the South Shore Plant, and also into "wrongdoings" of Public Works and other departments of the insular government as well as the legislature. She observed:

> There is no place in the world where there is so much waste, misuse, and abuse of government funds, as there is under this canopy of heaven. The government officials of the Virgin Islands seem to believe there is a bottomless well in Washington and that the money in that well can never dry up.[121]

The cumulative effect in the late 1970s of Washington's growing disenchantment with local financial chicanery, and of federal "get-tough" policies, was to increase fiscal uncertainty in the Virgin Islands and, according to some observers, to call into question the basic relationship of the Virgin Islands to the United States Government.

Personalistic Politics

Commensurate with fiscal uncertainty in the 1970s was uncertainty in the highly charged atmosphere of local politics. Increasingly since the 1936 Organic Act, with the advent of popular suffrage and genuine political parties, Virgin Islanders exhibited a passion for politics rarely found elsewhere, marked with an obsession with what goes on and is said in Washington concerning the Islands, as if the Virgin Islands ranked very high on the nation's public agenda.

---

121. Interview, Senator Ruby Rouss, November 21, 1979. Senator Rouss described one dimension of federal-territorial relations as follows: "The officials of the Government of the Virgin Islands are expert in the art of fooling federal officials who come to the territory for the purpose of oversight of many of the federal programs in the territory. First, they are met at the airport and are treated with great deference. Then they are taken to Government House where their photo is taken with the Governor. This is guaranteed to please the average federal visitor because he will have something special in his scrapbook to show the folks back home. He is next whisked to the top of the highest mountain overlooking Charlotte Amalie where he is literally overcome by the breathtaking view. Then he is treated to an elegant luncheon or dinner in one of the spectacular tourist hotels. All of this is cleverly orchestrated to dull the wits and the acumen of the federal official. By this time the purpose of his visit has gradually faded into the back of his mind, and he begins to believe that maybe he should not do as much digging as he had intended lest he offend the nice people he has met along the way. This is one of the reasons why we rarely receive factual, hard-hitting, reports from federal officials." *Ibid.*

Matters other than politics loomed relatively remote and unimportant within the communal consciousness of Islanders.

Writing at the beginning of the 1970s, Gordon Lewis commented that "the degree of personal investment in political talk and activity" in the Islands "is one of the highest, literally, in the world," characterized by "a politics of personality rather than of principles."[122] This assessment remained valid decades later.

The inflated importance of government and politics in the lives of Virgin Islanders was reflected daily in the local media—newspapers, radio, television— by the non-stop publicity of political actors and events. Perhaps for the lack of other distractions common on the mainland, political actors seemed constantly at center stage in the Virgin Islands drama, novel-like characters posturing themselves before the public while engaged in Byzantine intrigues behind the scenes. The insular character of these small entities—a simmering cauldron of growing tension and discontent—intensified the vituperative and volatile nature of Virgin Islands politics.

Through the 1970s, political discourse in the Islands frequently was laced with strong, bitter, all-out denunciations that crossed all lines—principally between the governor and the legislature, between legislators from St. Croix and those from St. Thomas, between the governor and the Congressional delegate, and between the governor and the lieutenant governor.

Executive-legislative clashes and inter-island rivalry comprised consistent historical themes, dating from 19th century Danish rule and continuing unabated (except for Governor Merwin's tenure followed by the Paiewonsky-Ottley machine of the 1960s) through the 1970s despite an elected governor and a single unicameral legislature. Complaining about the "constant infighting" and "petty arguments," one local editorial in 1979 voiced a familiar refrain by lamenting the lack of "give and take" between the two branches and the absence of "any willingness to negotiate, to compromise, to work out problems amicably."[123] Vetoes and overrides abounded, and every year budget time became an elongated crisis between the two branches.

It was not unusual during the 1970s for St. Croix senators to walk out of the legislature. When they were not fighting among themselves, they frequently voted as a bloc. Often they advocated that St. Croix, given a slightly larger population than St. Thomas and St. John, should have a majority in the fif-

---

122. Lewis, *The Virgin Islands*, p. 320, the increase in the number of "independent" candidates during the 1970s aroused some local misgivings, One newspaper commented that "we are playing havoc with our political system," because "we have gone 'independent,' and/or 'No party' crazy," Editorial, *The Virgin Islands Post*, September 26, 1978.

123. Editorial, "Politics Over Public Service," *Daily News*, October 31, 1979, p. 7.

teen-member legislature and even a separate budget. In this, St. Croix senators simply reflected popular Crucian opinion that St. Croix existed as a kind of colony within the St. Thomas-dominated government, that it was always being "short-changed" and suffering inequities. "All of the important offices of government are headquartered on St. Thomas," observed *The St. Croix Avis*, "and St. Croix gets mighty short shrift from any of them."[124]

Meanwhile, it was claimed, St. Croix was assigned the "dirty work" functions for the Islands, not St. Thomas, such as the major prison and polluting heavy industries. With this popular mind-set, it was understandable that those St. Croix senators making the most strident "pro-St. Croix" demands stood to gain re-election. Many St. Thomians condescendingly regarded such Crucian attitudes as "paranoia." Whether Crucian grievances were more imagined than real did not diminish the persistence of inter-island rivalry that had its roots deep in Virgin Islands history, when St. Croix was the agricultural breadbasket of the Virgin Islands while St. Thomas was a cosmopolitan world port.[125]

Expectations that the territory's two top elected officials—the governor and Congressional delegate—would cooperate, to the extent of presenting a united front in Washington for the sake of territorial interests, were seldom realized during the 1970s. Relations between Governor Cyril King, elected as head of the Independent Citizens Movement (ICM) in 1974, and Delegate Ron de Lugo, a Democrat re-elected that year, were at first cool but correct. Soon thereafter, however, they were engaged in a scurrilous attack on each other with de Lugo accusing King of lying and being a "political dummy" and King doing "his best back home to knife de Lugo." Much to the embarrassment of constituents and members of Congress alike, this stormy and counterproductive relationship proceeded so far that both men ignored each other before Congressional committees, each pretending the other was not present.[126]

Not only Congress, but also the White House and Interior Department, were aware of this constant squabbling. Fred Zeder, Director of Interior's Office of Territorial Affairs, warned in 1976 that fighting among Virgin Islands

---

124. Editorial, "We Don't Want To Be Touchy, But," *The St. Croix Avis*, November 25, 1977. See also, *e.g.*: Liz Wilson, " 'St. Croix Short-Changed Again,' Say Lawmakers," *The St. Croix Avis*, March 21, 1978, p. 1.

125. See, *e.g.*, Ronald Walker, "V.I. Split—Sound and Fury, or More?" *The San Juan Star*, September 7, 1977, p. 17.

126. Harry Turner, "Would Benitez and Romero Work in Tandem?" *The San Juan Star*, April 26, 1976, p. 15, See, also, Editorial, "Embarrassment in Washington," *Daily News*, February 27, 1976.

politicians over petty issues ("They're issues of emotion, not substance") was giving the Virgin Islands a bad image in Washington. Seeing himself as having to play the role of "peacemaker," Zeder said: "At times I've felt like Henry Kissinger in the Middle East." Local legislators protested Zeder's comments as an intrusion in Virgin Islands affairs. In a letter to Secretary of Interior Thomas Kleppe, Senate President Elmo Roebuck and Majority Leader Lloyd Williams retorted that Zeder's warning appeared to reflect a new policy "contrary to the best interests of the people of the Virgin Islands."[127] That Zeder's warning had little effect was further evidenced by verbal diatribes against de Lugo during 1977 uttered by Peter de Zela, Governor King's chief assistant, who publicly labeled de Lugo variously as being: a "monumental jackass," an "intellectual disaster," "allergic to ethics," and a candidate for "Grand Messiah."[128]

During the years of appointed governors and government secretaries, the territory's chief executive "ignored, overlooked and humiliated" his separately appointed colleague who was supposed to be the number two officer of the executive branch and acting governor when the governor was away from the territory.[129] Many Virgin Islanders had assumed that electing the governor and lieutenant governor—who replaced the government secretary—on the same party ticket would effectively end the long experience of enmity between the territory's top two executive officers. Such was not the case.

David Maas, the first elected Lieutenant Governor, resigned in midterm in 1973 because Governor Melvin Evans ignored him. When Cyril King replaced Evans as the second elected Governor in 1975, and King's running mate on the ICM ticket, Juan Luis, became Lieutenant Governor, it was speculated that King's bitter memory of his own experience as Government Secretary of being ostracized by the Paiewonsky-Ottley machine would now influence him as Governor to work with Luis in a cooperative spirit. Indeed, public sympathy acquired by King from ill-treatment he received from Governor Paiewonsky helped boost his political stock. Moreover, King was indebted to Luis, himself of Puerto Rican extraction, for helping to deliver the Puerto Rican vote on St. Croix where an estimated half the population was Puerto Rican. Luis, however, soon began to feel that he was being left out of policy making, and in August 1977. *The St. Croix Avis* commented: "The rift between Governor King

127. See, Harry Turner, "Virgin Isles Advised to Halt Spats, Bickering," *The San Juan Star*, May 28, 1976; and "Protest Interior's 'New Policy,'" *Daily News*, June 17, 1976, p. 1.

128. See, "De Zela Confirms Calling de Lugo a 'Jackass,'" *Daily News*, July 8, 1977, p. 1; Editorial, "De Zela's Mouth in Gear Again," *ibid.*, October 13, 1977; and Editorial, "Excesses in Differing," *The St. Croix Avis*, October 20, 1977.

129. Editorial, "Unforgivable Attitude," *Daily News*, August 30, 1977.

and Lieutenant Governor Juan Luis is deeper and much more serious than anyone would dare imagine."[130]

Juan Luis became Governor upon the death of Cyril King in January 1978. In November 1978, Luis was elected Governor in his own right for a full four-year term as an independent, having abandoned the ICM label. Elected with him on this no-party ticket as Lieutenant Governor was St. Thomian Henry Millin. A registered Democrat, Millin nevertheless had lashed out at his Democratic opponents by terming them "rapists" and "vultures" in what one local newspaper called "the dirtiest contest in years."[131] A large, expansive, and dynamic man, it was unlikely that Millin would be ignored by Governor Luis, or by anyone in the Islands for that matter. Rumors of a rift between the two, however, circulated during the last few months of 1979, especially after the local press aired Millin's first public disagreement with Governor Luis.[132] Millin denied any frayed relations with Luis, attributing such rumors to their differences in style, age, and experience.[133] The rift between them, nevertheless, deepened to open hostility in the early 1980s.

The death of ICM leader Governor King and the election of Luis and Millin as no-party independents virtually doomed the Independent Citizens Movement. A similar fate had been previously forecast for the territory's Republican Party which remained dormant after its candidates were trounced in the elections of 1974 and 1976. Richard Nixon's campaign and election as President in 1968 had created hundreds of "instant Republicans" in the Islands, including former Democrat Melvin Evans, the first elected Governor. Crossing party lines and changing party membership were practices perhaps not as common in the Islands as in India and in some other "developing" polities, but certainly more common than on the mainland of the United States. Governor Evans' failure to win re-election in 1974, plus the election of only one Republican to the Legislature in 1976, seemed to have reduced the Republican Party to almost a nullity. The redoubtable Evans, however, rebounded in 1978 to win election as Congressional Delegate, thus reviving Republican hopes.

---

130. Editorial, "Cooperation at the Top," *The St. Croix Avis*, August 25, 1977. See, also, Editorial, "How Not to Run a Government," *ibid.*, August 30, 1977; Ronald Walker, "How Will Juan Luis Act As Acting Governor?" *The San Juan Star*, August 10, 1977, p. 7, and "Will Don Luis 'Reign' End When King Returns?" *Ibid.*, August 28, 1977, p. 18.

131. Editorial, "The Dirtiest Contest in Years," *The Virgin Islands Post*, September 28, 1978.

132. See, *e.g.*, Penny Feuerzeig, "Public Works Leads to First Millin-Luis Public Split," *Daily News*, October 17, 1979, p. 1.

133. Interview, Lieutenant Governor Henry Millin, Charlotte Amalie, St. Thomas, November 19, 1979.

As for the territory's Democratic Party, its strength was more cosmetic than substantive in the 1970s, having never elected a governor and lieutenant governor under its label. Even the popular de Lugo was defeated soundly by Luis in 1978. Senator Earle B. Ottley called the Democratic Party a "hydra-headed monster" in 1977, not one party but several. Gone were the days of acting in unison. "There are a great many individualistic approaches to problems," said Ottley, "but no party approach any more." The Democratic caucus in the Legislature had become "meaningless." Ottley explained:

> Very few have been held because most of us realize it is a waste of time. There is no confidentiality, and you may make a decision in caucus but by the time you hit the floor, five or six guys may renege on it.[134]

Simply put, party labels were no predictors of political behavior in the Virgin Islands. There were no ideological differences among the territory's three major parties. In 1979, journalist Ronald Walker commented:

> To really understand Virgin Islands politics, you have to forget party labels or conventional political wisdom. It is one thing to acknowledge that the Democrats have the overwhelming lead in voter registrations in the Virgin Islands (the ICM runs a poor second, and the Republicans well back). But it is another thing to automatically concede all elections to the Democrats. In fact, there has not been a Democrat elected governor since Virgin Islanders began voting for the chief executive in 1970.... At the same time, however, voters have always returned Democrats to control of the 15-member, unicameral legislature by healthy majorities.
>
> The reason for all this split voting is that the Democratic Party itself is a Balkanized, everybody-for-himself confederation of individuals who are loyal to one or another prominent personality within the party—not the party itself. Time and again, Democrats have gone outside the fold to vote for other candidates.[135]

Formation of a new political party was announced in St. Croix in November 1979. It was named the "Freedom City Political Party," because the city of

---

134. As quoted by Penny Feuerzeig, "Politics," *Daily News*, July 30, 1977.

135. Ronald Walker, "Gov. Juan Luis of the Virgin Islands," *The San Juan Star*, Sunday Magazine, February 18, 1979, p. 3. As the 1970s came to a close, political candidates in the Islands still were not required by law either to disclose campaign contributions or expenditures. "Virgin Islands political candidates have to date enjoyed a freedom from the public's right to know about them rarely heard of elsewhere in this country," Editorial, "Campaign Disclosure," *The St. Croix Avis*, December 3, 1979, p. 8.

Frederiksted on the west coast of St. Croix had long claimed the historic honor of being the "freedom city" of the Islands. The new party was formed in Frederiksted, according to the announcement, because "the Democratic, Republican and the ICM parties have failed in their obligations to one of the most important yet blighted areas of the Virgin Islands." Intending to run a full slate of candidates for the 1980 elections, the new party appeared to be too narrowly based to become a major territorial party.[136]

At the end of the 1970s, the Virgin Islands shared a condition common to civic cultures of most Third World countries. The territory had yet to develop a viable multi-party system.

The Status Issue

As the 1970s ended, prospects for political and economic stability of the Islands appeared more than ever to be related to increased self-determination. Proposals of the Constitutional Convention of 1965—for the right to vote for the U.S. President and Vice President, and for the right to locally select the comptroller—seemed no nearer to being accorded. As noted before, however, Congress had eventually enacted the other 1965 proposals calling for an elective governor, lieutenant governor, and Congressional delegate, authorization for legislators to fix their own salaries, and abolition of the Presidential veto of local laws and of the voting limitation for at-large legislators. And Virgin Islanders meanwhile had never recanted the 1965 Constitutional Convention's on-record rejection of independence, of annexation to any state of the Union, or of any change in the Islands' status as an "unincorporated territory."

A Second Constitutional Convention was authorized by the Virgin Islands Legislature in 1971. The resulting proposed constitution and federal relations act were submitted to the voters at the general election in 1972. Although more voters endorsed than rejected the two documents, a large number of blank ballots meant that the votes in favor totaled less than a majority of the votes cast. Accordingly, the two documents were not submitted to Congress.[137] In-

---

136. Katrina White, "New Political Party Formed in St. Croix," *The St. Croix Avis*, November 21, 1979, p. 1.

137. See, *Constitution of the Territory of the United States Virgin Islands* (1972); and *Proposed Virgin Islands Federal Relations Act as approved by Second Constitutional Convention of the Virgin Islands* (August 10, 1972). See, also, James A. Bough, "Is Commonwealth Status the Next Step?" *Virgin Islands Bar Journal*, 5 (Summer 1974): 18.

stead, Delegate de Lugo introduced legislation in Congress in 1974 to authorize the people of the Virgin Islands to organize a government pursuant to a
constitution of their own adoption.

Congress passed the enabling legislation in 1976, providing for submission
of the proposed constitution by the governor to the President for his review,
approval by the Congress, and finally approval by a majority of voters in a local
referendum. Congress empowered the Constitutional Convention to deal with
such areas of self-government as the taxing power and the jurisdiction of the local
courts, but Congress expressly specified that the constitution must provide for
a republican form of government and contain a bill of rights. Most significant,
perhaps, was the failure of enabling legislation to permit consideration of the
territory's political status or relationship with the federal government.[138]

After failing on two previous attempts through local initiative, the Virgin Islands Legislature—this time pursuant to Congressional action—provided for
a Third Constitutional Convention of sixty elected delegates.

Among its significant proposals, the Third Constitutional Convention of
1978 provided: a seventeen-member legislature, a revised judicial system with
a locally appointed supreme court replacing the U.S. District Court, a system
of local governments to be known as "administrative districts" with elected
mayors and district assemblies, an elected comptroller general, protection of
"Virgin Islands culture, language, traditions, or customs," and stipulation that
all beaches and shorelines "shall be public and open to public use."[139]

When the proposed constitution finally was submitted to the voters in March
1979, less than 38 percent turned out, and of these 56 percent voted to reject it.[140]

As an unincorporated territory, along with Guam, the Virgin Islands occupied the lowest rung of the American colonial ladder, a status that obligated the
United States Government to make yearly reports to the United Nations. Not
until 1977 did the United States Government permit the United Nations decolonization committee to send a mission to visit the Virgin Islands. After its
visit, the U.N. mission noted in its eighty-seven page report that the Congressional enabling legislation for a locally adopted constitution "does not en-
able the people of the Territory to effect any changes in their constitutional
relationship with the administering Power." The U.N. mission, therefore, urged
the U.S. Government, in consultation with the Government of the Virgin Islands, "to hold open and meaningful discussions of all available political op-

---

138. P.L. 94-584 (1971).
139. Special Constitution Edition, *Daily News*, May 9, 1978.
140. *The New York Times*, March 11, 1979, sec. 4, p. E5, col. 1.

tions to the Territory" and then "to ascertain the political aspirations of the people through a referendum or plebiscite under observation of the United Nations."[141]

Such discussions of political options, as urged by the U.N. mission, were commenced in late 1979 by the White House's Interagency Territorial Policy Review Task Force. In response to the Task Force reports relating to the status of U.S. territories, Governor Juan Luis asserted that the Government of the Virgin Islands seeks "freer association, similar to the status of Puerto Rico," that it endorses "the initiation of political status discussions with Congress, supports voting representation in Congress and participation in national elections," and it welcomes "Federal support of Territorial efforts to draft a Constitution to replace the Organic Act."[142]

While the status dialogue continued, the United States Government was in the process of according its Pacific trust territory, Micronesia, greater autonomy and self-determination than ever envisaged for the Virgin Islands or Guam. One Interior official explained this seemingly ignominious situation as arising from the fact that the United States Government was bargaining with an area over which it could claim no sovereignty, and, therefore, Micronesia had "more bargaining chips on the table" than had either the Virgin Islands or Guam.[143]

---

141. United Nations General Assembly, Special Committee on the Situation with Regard to the Implementation of the Declaration on the Granting of Independence to Colonial Countries and People, *Report of the United Nations Visiting Mission to the United States Virgin Islands, 1977*, A/AC.109/L.1198, English Edition (New York: United Nations, September 1, 1977), pp. 75–76.

142. *Comments of the Governor of, the Virgin Islands on the Reports of the Interagency Territorial Policy Review Task Force* (Charlotte Amalie, St. Thomas, U.S. Virgin Islands: Office of the Governor, October 12, 1979), xeroxed, p. 4. Governor Luis responded to a preliminary draft, xeroxed, of *Reports of the Interagency Territorial Policy Review Task Force* released by the White House, September 17, 1979.

143. Sixteen northern islands of Micronesia, after years of negotiation with the United States and a referendum in 1975, became the Commonwealth of the Northern Mariana Islands on January 9, 1978—the first new territory (184 square miles) added to the United States since the purchase of the Virgin Islands in 1917. *International Herald Tribune*, Zurich, Switzerland, January 10, 1978, p. 5, col. 5. Negotiations to end U.S. trusteeship over the remainder of Micronesia resulted in three proposed agreements in 1978 for creating a new form of relationship to be called "free association" between Micronesia and the U.S. whereby Micronesians would run their internal affairs while the U.S. would be responsible for defense and foreign affairs. Robert Trumbull, "Micronesia Heads for a New Era As 3 Semi-Independent Nations," *The New York Times*, December 10, 1978, p. A16. For U.S. administration of its Pacific trust territory, see, *e.g.*: David Nevin, *The American Touch in Micronesia* (New York: W.W. Norton & Co., 1977): Arnold H. Leibowitz, *Colonial Emancipation in the Pa-*

Meanwhile, some Guam political figures were screaming for independence as a strategy for increasing that territory's leverage in extracting concessions from Washington, although it was doubtful that there was much popular sentiment in Guam for independence. Virgin Islanders had consistently rejected independence as a possible option. It appeared that they were now wary of adopting such a Guamian strategy, for they had recently learned from Caribbean neighbors that screaming for independence could become an irreversible and self-fulfilling reality.[144]

A Community in Trouble

As Virgin Islanders faced the eighth decade of the Twentieth Century, they were preparing to convene a Fourth Constitutional Convention, but still another attempt to frame a constitution did not offer any prospects of curing local social ills or of reducing mounting tensions in the Islands. Symptomatically, John Collins, in November 1979, moderated the nightly radio call-in program—"Night Line"—for the last time, forced by the radio station management to relinquish the controversial talk show allegedly because of intemperate utterances of callers. In his farewell comment, Collins said:

> I think there are a number of people in this community who don't want to listen. I listen and I'm very disturbed by what I hear. I hear a community that's in trouble—a lot of angry, frustrated, and alienated people who don't feel their just needs are being addressed by the community in general, the government in particular.[145]

---

cific and the Caribbean, A Legal and Political Analysis (New York: Praeger Publishers, 1976); Donald F. McHenry, Micronesia: Trust Betrayed (New York: Carnegie Endowment for International Peace, 1975); and Carl Heine, Micronesia at the Crossroads, A Reappraisal of the Micronesian Political Dilemma (Honolulu: University Press of Hawaii, 1974).

144. That the pace of decolonization and the consequent creation of new leftist ministates in the Eastern Caribbean was gaining the increasing attention of Washington, after years of comparative neglect, see, e.g.: Tad Szulc, "Radical Winds in the Caribbean," The New York Times Magazine, May 25, 1980, sec. 6, pp. 16–19, 56–72: Tad Szulc, "U.S. Adrift, Foundering in the Caribbean," The San Juan Star, September 6, 1979, p. 20; Lindsay Mackoon, "Leftists Show Power Gains in Caribbean," The San Juan Star, July 30, 1979, p. 10; and Graham Hovey, "U.S. Paying New Heed to Caribbean," The New York Times, December 7, 1977, p. 5.

145. Quoted by Cathleen Cogswell, "Catching Up," Daily News, November 24, 1979, p. 12.

Several developments were unfolding to heighten the sense of alienation of the people of the Virgin Islands. St. Johnians complained about the alienation of still more land including the $4 million sale of St. John property by the wealthy Lockhart family to the National Park Service, while others complained about "secrecy" surrounding the sale of Hassel Island to the National Park Service by the Paiewonsky family.[146] Even more controversial, however, was the decision, disclosed in October 1979, of David and Laurance Rockefeller to sell for $10 million their 4,085-acre Estate Fountain River that covered one-tenth the area of St. Croix including Davis Bay Beach and the tax-exempt Fountain Valley Golf Course. While a public debate raged in the local press between those advocating private purchase and development of the Estate and those advocating purchase by the Virgin Islands Government for its preservation for the benefit of the people, Crucian Senator Hector Cintron questioned why the sale was not publicized until after $690,000 had been appropriated in the 1980 road fund for construction and improvement of roads leading to the property.[147]

Other events in the fall of 1979 served to emphasize the fragility of insular life and economic conditions. The revelation through declassified documents that the U.S. Army secretly conducted biological and chemical testing on Water Island and in St. Croix in the 1940s and 1950s left many residents wondering "whether any harmful effects resulted or remains."[148] Once again, Leon Hess threatened in December 1979 to cut operation of his St. Croix refinery—this time in half—unless the federal government helped replace blocked imports of Iranian oil.[149]

Adding to Crucian apprehensions about the future was the announcement by Commerce Commissioner Almadeo Francis that, although St. Croix almost doubled its number of tourists in 1979, this dramatic increase represented only 9.9 percent of the territory's cruise ship passengers and 33.9 percent of airline customers, Commenting that two-thirds of the territory's government activity is concentrated on St. Thomas. Francis added: "The re-

---

146. See, e.g., "Politics," *Daily News*, October 9, 1978, pp. 7–8; *ibid.*, November 30, 1979, p. 20; *The San Juan Star*, December 1, 1979, p. 10; *Virgin Islands Post*, December 3, 1979, p. 3; and Editorial, "Look Around St. John," *ibid.*, December 6, 1979.

147. See, e.g., *Daily News*, October 19, 1979, p. 1; *ibid.*, November 12, 1979, p. 9; Editorial, "Mixed Reactions," *The St. Croix Avis*, October 25, 1979, p. 8; Barry Micklewright, "Fountain River: Government or Public?" *The San Juan Star*, November 21, 1979, p. 23; and *ibid.*, October 27, 1979.

148. *Daily News*, November 29, 1979, p. 24.

149. Terry Galvin, "Hess May Cut Back Operations," *Daily News*, December 15, 1979, p. 1.

sult of this maldistribution of tourist and government activity and the disjointed structure of agriculture and industry is that the Crucian economy continues to noticeably lag behind the progress achieved in St. Thomas-St. John."[150]

The comments of the highly regarded former Commissioner of Commerce, Dr. Auguste E. Rimpel, Jr., seemed somehow connected to a declining sense of dignity and self-worth of Virgin Islanders. Voicing dismay about "the image" created by the Virgin Islands "continually going to Washington to beg for money," Rimpel warned that unabated dependence on federal help was "a step backwards" in the march toward increasing self-government for the Islands.[151]

Alienation of Virgin Islands youth continued to be the territory's most grievous problem. In October 1979 the territory's mental health director, Dr. Chester Copemann, stated that mental illness among young native Virgin Islanders was rising at a "phenomenal" rate, accountable in part to environmental factors such as overcrowding, high unemployment, and a high student dropout rate. Pointing to the facts that 90 percent of Virgin Islands residents institutionalized in Washington's St. Elizabeth's Mental Hospital are native Virgin Islanders, and 90 percent of all Virgin Islands prisoners are native-born, Copemann attributed part of the problem to the high percentage of working mothers in the Virgin Islands—59 percent as compared to the 40.8 percent national average—and the consequence of unattended children.[152] Some four thousand Virgin Islands children were estimated in late 1979 to have twenty-three hundred absent parents, almost exclusively fathers who contributed nothing to their financial support.[153]

That many of these children and youth became main contributors to the territory's horrendous crime rate was an inevitable conclusion. Violent crimes appeared destined to continue undiminished in the 1980s. In late January 1980 a prominent architect and his wife were murdered at their home in St. Croix a few hours after a jeweler was shot to death in the same neighborhood. All the victims were white. During one week of the same month, St. Thomas experi-

---

150. Quoted by Terry Galvin, "Crucian Visitors Almost Double," *Daily News*, December 21, 1979, pp. 1, 26.

151. Penny Feuerzeig, "'Concerned Virgin Islander' Sees Need for Leadership," *Daily News*, September 7, 1971, pp. 5, 12.

152. See, Cathleen Cogswell, "Doctor Says Mental Illness Rising At Phenomenal Rate," *Daily News*, October 30, 1979, p. 3; Lawrence Joshua, "Mental Illness A Youth Problem," *Virgin Islands Post*, November 19, 1979, p. 3; Editorial, "What's More Important Than Children?" *ibid.*, October 22, 1979; and Editorial, "Our Mentally Ill," *The St. Croix Avis*, November 28, 1979, p. 8.

153. Bernita Akin, "Abandoned to Poverty," *Virgin Islands Post*, October 18, 1979, p. 1.

enced one murder, fifty-two robberies, and twenty-three assaults. The Islands as a whole had experienced a total of six homicides in just nineteen days.[154]

Concerned citizens of St. Croix proclaiming a "Day of Mourning" publicly stated: "There are none among us who have not had at least one relative or close friend burglarized, raped, or senselessly murdered."[155] Public Safety Commissioner Milton C. Branch told a mostly-white crowd of two hundred and fifty people: "There is no need for panic; there is no need for hysteria." Branch explained that there was no evidence that the murders were racially motivated. Of the 1.5 million tourists who visit the Virgin Islands in a year, Branch said that only six hundred and four are the victims of any crime, or four in ten thousand. "I defy any stateside community to have a safer climate for their visitors," he asserted.[156]

Douglas Schwartz, Assistant U.S. Attorney for St. Croix, responded, however, that it was impossible to rule out racial motivations "as a possible primary motive."[157] St. Thomian Senator Lloyd L. Williams agreed. "Even if the crimes themselves start out as burglaries or robberies," said Williams, "the senseless killings, raping and humiliation of the mostly white victims reek with racial overtones." He explained:

> The business community and the well-to-do perceive to some extent the local residents as generally lazy, shiftless, unmotivated, unreliable, untrainable, uneducated, wanting only the clean and easy jobs and, in general, the easy way out.
>
> On the other hand, the locals perceive the business community as leeches, taking everything out without making any significant contribution in return; not committed to the territory but who would leave the minute things get rough; who import white stateside employees to fill available jobs, and are not paying their fair share of taxes.[158]

While the truth "lies somewhere in the middle," Senator Williams called for greater mutual understanding, reduction of the big gaps between rich and

---

154. Diana Pearson, "Three St. Croix Residents Murdered," *Daily News*, January 29, 1980, pp. 1, 15; Michael Goodwin, "3 Murders in St. Croix Inspire Fear in Whites and the Tourist Trade," *The New York Times*, January 31, 1980, pp. A1, A12.

155. *Daily News*, January 31, 1980, p. 9.

156. Diana Pearson, "Branch Sees Drugs, Not Race Tied to Crime," *Daily News*, February 2, 1980, pp. 1, 18.

157. Terry Galvin, "Assistant U.S. Attorney Has Other Views," *Daily News*, February 2, 1980, pp. 1, 18.

158. Quoted by Penny Feuerzeig, "Racism Crime Motivator—Williams," *Daily News*, February 5, 1980, pp. 1, 18.

Cruise Ships in St. Thomas harbor

poor, more jobs for the young, and marked improvements in youth services and the criminal justice system.

Whether the rash of murders was racially motivated could not be determined until the killers were apprehended. One fact was indisputable—unlike the aftermath of the Fountain Valley slayings, most hotels in the Virgin Islands experienced few reservation cancellations after the January 1980 homicides.[159]

Perhaps, then, history was not to repeat itself. Perhaps, Virgin Islanders had reached the depths of alienation and agony and had reaped the last spoils of uncontrolled growth. It was not too late for them to reverse direction. Obviously, the Islands were not yet a "tropical ghetto." After all, millions of tourists still considered the Virgin Islands to be "America's Paradise." Many Puerto Ricans, continentals, and downislanders preferred to live and work in the Virgin Islands, and many native Virgin Islanders were learning to share their Islands with the latecomers. By no means had all—or perhaps most—of the more able and better educated native Virgin Islanders moved to the continent.

---

159. Terry Galvin, "Tourist Cancellations Few Following St. Croix Crimes," *Daily News*, February 4, 1980, p. 1.

Part IV

Persisting Problems:
1980–2010

13

Constitutional Conundrums

According to the 1980 census, the territory's population reached a total of 96,589. Many of these Virgin Islanders were well aware of their persisting problems, and they realized that their long struggle to gain control of their own destiny would continue to challenge them.

Virgin Islanders, as discussed in the last chapter, had failed to gain approval of a constitution on three previous occasions. They first approved a constitution in 1964, but Congress failed to approve it. They approved another constitution in 1972, but the margin of approval was so small that it was not submitted to Congress. As we have noted, a third constitution was resoundingly rejected by 56 percent of only 38 percent of the eligible voters who turned out for a referendum in 1979. The Third Constitutional Convention president, Alexander Farrelly (later to become governor), was reported to have commented that the "St. Thomas vs. St. Croix split" was an issue permeating nearly every debate of that convention.[1]

The Fourth Constitutional Convention

The Fourth Constitutional Convention convened in March 1980. Its first draft stipulated that the governor must be a "native" of the Virgin Islands, but this provision was removed making many native-born islanders unhappy. However, the final draft defined a Virgin Islander as a person either born in the territory or who had at least one parent born in the territory. Although such a person would have no special privileges, the mere inclusion of this definition was an emotional issue making many newcomers unhappy.

The ensuing constitutional debate was both lively and heated, reflecting many anxieties in a small finite territory that had grown so rapidly—a so-called "community of minorities" wherein "native-born islanders" were com-

---

1. Quoted by Shirley Lincoln, "V.I. Constitutional Conventions: Background," *St. Croix Source*, May 24, 2009, p. 3.

peting for influence with large numbers of "newcomers." According to John Collins, himself a transplanted mainlander and one of three convention delegates refusing to sign the final document, "A unique culture and history are being overwhelmed by outsiders.... There are Puerto Ricans, down-islanders and continentals living here, and it has created a schizophrenic atmosphere. We only have 100,000 people, and they all want their interests catered to. The rights and privileges of the natives should be preeminent."[2]

Despite the strong backing by Governor Juan Luis, legislators and civic groups, only 47 percent of the territory's registered voters turned out on November 4, 1981 for the single-issue ballot, with 7,157 voting against the proposed constitution and 4,821 voting for it. Governor Luis, lamenting that it was a mistake to put the constitution before the voters in a non-election year, pledged to ask the legislature to take immediate steps toward a fifth attempt.

Senator Ruby Rouss—the first female president of the legislature—as well as diverse others who had opposed this draft constitution, agreed that it was more important to first address the status question of whether the Virgin Islands should remain an unincorporated territory governed by the 1954 Revised Organic Act or choose some other status. "The Virgin Islands needs to get a clear understanding with the Federal Government as to our relationship," said Rouss. "Whether we can control customs and immigration matters— these are the things we need straightened out first."[3]

Virgin Islands Nonimmigrant Alien Adjustment Act of 1982

A momentous development in 1982, however, was to postpone for some years consideration by local authorities of, first, the status question and, much later, an attempt to convene a fifth constitutional convention. This development was an act of Congress granting permanent residence to the thousands of nonimmigrant H-2 aliens and their H-4 families in the territory—that would pave the way for them to become U. S. citizens and Virgin Islands voters in the years to come.[4]

---

2. "Virgin Islands Resoundingly Reject Fourth Draft of Constitution," *The New York Times*, November 5, 1981, p. B19.

3. *Ibid.*

4. Pub. L. 97-271, 96 Stat. 1157, Sept. 30, 1982. H. Akia Gore was in error in stating that "the approved legislation became known as the Virgin Islands Non-immigrant Alien Adjustment Act of 1981" whereas it did not become law until September 30, 1982; see Gore,

House Subcommittee Chairman Romano Mazzoli opened the June 18, 1981 hearing on this proposed legislation by stating that it "is premised on the belief that long-term H-2 workers have become a permanent part of the social and economic structure of the Islands and that the Federal Government has a moral obligation to resolve the uncertain status of these aliens."[5]

It became apparent during the hearing that the bill H.R. 3517 had actually been drafted as a joint proposal by Governor Juan Luis and Delegate to Congress Ron de Lugo and unanimously endorsed by the Virgin Islands Legislature following a series of public hearings at which witnesses from all three islands overwhelmingly endorsed it. This circumstance moved H. Akia Gore to comment in his 2009 book that the hearing was "the first time that the Governor, Senators, and the Delegate to Congress were unanimous in their decision on ... the need to adjust the immigration status of H-2 workers and their families."[6]

Among the territory's delegation in support of the bill were: David Iverson, Attorney of the St. Thomas Legal Services; George Goodwin, President of the Caribbean Development Coalition (formerly the Alien Interest Movement); and Senator Gilbert Sprauve, Vice President of the Virgin Islands Legislature. Iverson testified that the genesis of the situation occurred through violation of pertinent laws and regulations by government agencies—a history of the H-2 program in the Islands "well described in previous House Reports ... and the paper ... by Mark Miller and William Boyer, University of Delaware."[7] Goodwin asserted that "Passage of this Bill will assist greatly in eradicating the social stigma; it will remove the shackles of bondage that presently afflicts us; it will remove the wall that divides the people of the Virgin Islands; it will provide a humane solution and ... bring an end to the plight and discriminatory acts on our people." Sprauve noted that the proposed legislation addressed a most delicate and potentially explosive issue, namely that "a very large segment of the Virgin Islands populace ... are subjected daily to the terrifying fear

---

Garrote: The Illusion of Social Equality and Political Justice in the United States Virgin Islands (New York: Wadadli Press, 2009), p. 410.

5. Hearing on H.R. 3517 before the Subcommittee on Immigration, Refugees and International Law of the Committee on the Judiciary, House of Representatives, 97th Congress 1st Session, June 18, 1981, pp. 1, 12.

6. H. Akia Gore, *Garrote* (2009), supra, n. 4, at p. 393.

7. Specifically, Iverson was referring to: *Non-Immigrant Labor Program of the Virgin Islands of the United States*, 94th Congress, 1st Session, 1975; and Mark J. Miller and William W. Boyer, "Foreign Workers in the USVI: History of a Dilemma," *Caribbean Review*, Winter 1982, Vol. 11, No. 2, pp. 48–51; in Hearing on H.R. 3517, supra, n. 5, at p. 78.

of mass deportation and the spectre of a fate rivaling that of the 'boat people' in and around Miami."[8]

The only opposition to the bill in the hearing appeared as a statement of an organization—"Virgin Islanders for Action, Inc."—which was buried in small print on the very last pages of an appendix to the hearing. Five prominent Virgin Islanders signed the statement, three of whom had served as delegates of previous constitutional conventions. Their argument is apparent from the following excerpts:

> We believe this bill will profoundly impact on the Virgin Islands, a small territory with limited resources and land mass and a society with a fragile culture presently experiencing extreme stress and strain because of rapid growth and overpopulation....
>
> Fear has also been expressed by some Virgin Islanders that the ultimate political destiny of the territory and its future relationship to the United States could be determined by outsiders in clear violation of our great Nation's commitment to self-determination....
>
> We recognize the contributions of aliens in the building of America as well as the Virgin Islands. However, please realize that the same formula devised for a gigantic nation on the vast continent of North America cannot and should not be imposed on a small territory like the Virgin Islands....
>
> Gentlemen, we say enough is enough and implore you not to be a party to a short-term politically expedient solution which we sincerely and strongly believe will back fire and create a long-term nightmare that will haunt the Virgin Islands and the United States of America for the rest of this century.[9]

The 1982 law, passed without difficulty by both houses of Congress, ended the temporary bonded workers program in the Islands. It would be easy thereby to dismiss the influence of opponents were it not for the fact that the legislation portended the addition of thousands of new voters from the Eastern Caribbean. If anything, this act of Congress stiffened and extended opposition by many so-called "native" Virgin Islanders. They "found themselves as a minority in their homeland," according to local Professor Frank Mills, "and

---

8. See testimony by Goodwin and Sprauve in Hearing on H.R. 3517, supra, n. 5, at pp. 64 and 31, respectively.

9. Hearing on H.R. 3517, p. 83.

with this there emerged an increasing degree of xenophobia."[10] They were most worried that "down-islanders" would eventually wrest control of the local political system. Results were to delay voting on possible status options for a few more years and to postpone convening a fifth constitutional convention until the first decade of the next century.

The Political Status Referendum of 1993

By 1965 over half the work force of the U.S. Virgin Islands—itself an Eastern Caribbean polity—comprised nonimmigrant workers from the British islands of the Eastern Caribbean. Considering its affinity with the English-speaking Caribbean, it was little wonder then that the U.S. Virgin Islands became vitally affected by the wave of independence that swept the former British colonies of the Caribbean between 1962 and 1983. During this brief span of 22 years, a total of 12 new nations had been born in the Caribbean Basin—beginning with Jamaica and Trinidad-Tobago in 1962; followed by Guyana and Barbados in 1966; Grenada in 1974; Suriname in 1975; Dominica in 1978; Belize, St. Vincent and the Grenadines, St. Lucia, and Antigua-Barbuda from 1978 through 1982; and St. Kitts-Nevis in 1983. All except Belize, Jamaica, Guyana, and Suriname are in the Eastern Caribbean, and all but Suriname were former British colonies. In short, the U.S. Virgin Islands was experiencing a growing identity crisis over the issue of "self-determination," which the dictionary defines as "the right of a people to decide upon its political status or form of government without outside influence."[11]

---

10. Dr. Frank L. Mills, Professor of Social Sciences, University of the Virgin Islands Isaac Dookhan Lecture, "Historical Foundation of the Immigrant Culture and Modes of Its Incorporation in the U.S. Virgin Islands," presented at the University of the Virgin Islands, St. Thomas campus, Nov. 12, 1998, and at St. Croix campus, November 13, 1998, unpublished, p. 27.

11. See: William W. Boyer, "The United States Virgin Islands and Decolonization of the Eastern Caribbean," *The Review of Regional Studies* (Special Issue on Caribbean Studies, ed. by William R. Latham III), Vol. 14, No. 3, Fall 1984, pp. 34–46; published for the Southern Regional Science Association by the Strom Thurmond Institute of Government and Public Affairs at Clemson University. This article was adapted and revised from the Distinguished Scholar Lecture "Self-Determination for the U.S. Virgin Islands—Myth or Reality?" presented at the College of the Virgin Islands, St. Croix campus, December 2, 1982, and St. Thomas campus, December 3, 1982, by the author while serving as Visiting Professor of Social Sciences.

Whereas there had been a total of four attempts before 1982 to draft a constitution for the Islands, there were to be three attempts to address their political status. The first attempt to consider the issue of political status was motivated by U.S. President Jimmy Carter's February 1980 message to Congress that: "In keeping with our policy of self-determination, all options for political development should be open to the people of the insular territories...." This was followed by his strongly worded statement in June 1980 to the Democratic Party Platform Committee that the United States "must be firmly committed to self-determination for Puerto Rico, the Virgin Islands, Guam, American Samoa and the Northern Mariana Islands and vigorously support the realization of whatever political status aspirations are democratically chosen by their people."[12]

In response to President Carter's initiative, the Virgin Islands Legislature established in late 1980 the Virgin Islands Status Commission and chose former Senator Earle B. Ottley as its executive director. President Carter's failure to win re-election in November 1980, followed by the indifference of the Reagan Administration, effectively ended the flurry of excitement about self-determination. Moreover, President Reagan's so-called Caribbean Basin Initiative failed to include any prospect of self-determination for the U.S. Virgin Islands. For his part, Ottley soon resigned his position, lamenting: "There is no interest in building a consensus, and because no one sees any immediate political gain to be achieved from status determination, interest among political leaders has been low."[13] Perhaps an October 1980 article in the London-based *Economist* portrayed some of this waning interest:

> The main political problem ... is immigration. The islands' population has almost quadrupled since 1960. Many of the new arrivals have been sucked in from the Virgin Islands' poorer neighbours, mostly ex-British colonies. But the greater resentment among the black community has been caused by the unlimited immigration from the United States. The proportion of whites has been climbing rapidly in the past few years as Americans have been attracted by the cheapness and climate of the islands; whites now account for a fifth of the population. This community, wealthy and isolated, is predictably the one most

---

12. See: "Federal Territorial Policy," Message to Congress, February 14, 1980, Administration of Jimmy Carter, 1980, *Weekly Compilation of Presidential Documents*, Monday, February 18, 1980, vol. 16, no. 7, p. 319; and Statement by President Jimmy Carter to the Democratic Party Platform Committee, June 12, 1980, pp. 61–62.

13. Earle B. Ottley, *Trials and Triumphs: The Long Road to a Middle Class Society in the U.S. Virgin Islands* (St. Thomas, USVI: Earle B. Ottley, 1982), p. 428.

against self-government, particularly for such things as the administration of justice. It has taken over the shops, pushed up the price of
property and increasingly dominated the economy. It is the colonial
knot that both the United States and the Virgin Islands will find hardest to untie.[14]

The second attempt to consider status options was the Fifteenth Legislature's creation in 1984 of the "Select Committee on Status and Federal Relations" under the chairperson of longtime Senator Lorraine L. Berry. The
Sixteenth Legislature, however, failed to continue the Select Committee.

The third attempt was protracted, to say the least. The United States Virgin
Islands Commission on Status and Federal Relations was established by the
Seventeenth Legislature and signed into law by Governor Alexander Farrelly
on March 4, 1988. The Commission was composed of fifteen members, two
of whom served as chairpersons—longtime Senator Lorraine Berry and history professor Dr. Marilyn Krigger—both residents of St. Thomas. Appointed
as executive director was Gerard Emanuel of St. Croix. The Commission sought
to hold a referendum on November 14, 1989 for voters to choose from among
seven status choices, that were mandated for the Commission by a committee
of the territory's legislature headed by Senator Berry, namely: (1) Commonwealth, (2) Compact of Federal Relations, (3) Free Association, (4) Incorporated Territory; (5) Independence; (6) Statehood; and (7) Status Quo—
Unincorporated Territory. The Commission stipulated that "If none of these
seven options receives more than 50% of the vote, a run-off election will be held
on November 28, 1989, at which time voters will choose among the two options that received the highest and second highest number of votes."[15]

Within the night and morning of September 17 and 18—two months before the referendum could be held—Hurricane Hugo raged through the Virgin Islands, causing more than $1.5 billion in losses, 7 deaths, and on St. Croix
alone, according to one estimate, the damage or destruction of 90 percent of
all structures followed by massive looting and unrest.[16]

---

14. "Virgin Islands: Time to Loosen the Knot?" *The Economist*, October 11, 1980, p.
42. (no author listed).

15. U.S.V.I. Commission on Status & Federal Relations, *Brief Descriptions of the Seven
Political Status Options* (St. Thomas: Bureau of Public Administration, University of the
Virgin Islands, 1988).

16. For overall destruction from this Category 5 hurricane, see "Hurricane Hugo," *Wike-
pedia* (1989), http://en.wikipedia.org/wiki/Hurricane_Hugo (accessed July 30, 2009). For
an eyewitness account of the hurricane on St. Croix by a well-known local historian, see Arnold
Highfield, "Notes From the Eye of a Storm," in Gloria I. Joseph and Hortense M. Rowe,

Accordingly, the Status Commission had little choice but to suspend its operations into 1990, whereupon it engaged in renewed comprehensive activity to educate the voters about the meaning and significance of the political status choices they were to face in a postponed referendum. Meanwhile, various notables contributed articles in the local media publicly explaining their respective choices. For example, former Governor Ralph Paiewonsky opted to continue the *status quo*; both former Senator Adelbert Bryan and planning director Keith Richards chose *independence*; Professor Linda White Benjamin preferred *commonwealth*; and Republican chairwoman Charlotte Poole-Davis explained *statehood* was her preferred option.[17]

The first political status referendum in the history of the Virgin Islands was finally held on October 11, 1993. To legitimize the result of the referendum, the law required a turnout of at least 50 percent of the eligible voters. However, only 27.4 percent voted, rendering the referendum null and void and leaving by default continuance of the status quo.[18]

The question of why such a low percentage of the electorate voted in the referendum was to remain unanswered. As a matter of conjecture, however, it was possible that two large groups of the populace were most responsible—white mainlanders and down-islanders. Many eligible voters from both of these sizeable population sectors had strong motives to withhold their participation. The segment quoted above from the 1980 *Economist* article contended that whites, then comprising one-fifth of the territory's population, were "predictably the one most against self-government."

---

eds., *Hell Under God's Order: Hurrican Hugo—Disaster and Survival* (St. Croix: Winds of Change Press, 1990), pp. 131–152. Concerning the post-Hugo looting on St. Croix, William Boyer said that "given the ... disaffection of natives who are against people outside taking over their island, I'm not surprised by the instability caused by the hurricane" as quoted by columnist Alexander Cockburn, "For St. Croix, Hugo Was Just the Latest in 200 Years of Battering," *The Wall Street Journal*, September 28, 1989, p. A23. For St. Croix a year after Hugo, see: Mireya Navarro, "Year Later, St. Croix is Coming Back, And Trying to Bring Tourists With It," *The New York Times*, September 23, 1990, Section 1, Part 1, p. 26.

17. These various articles appeared in three issues of *The Voice* published in St. Thomas: the summer issues of 1989 and 1992, and the issue of 1993, No. 2.

18. Hal Hatfield, "Status Issue Dies As Voters Stay Home," 1993: The Year In Review, *Daily News*, January 4, 1994, p. 6. Dr. Carlyle Corbin, former Minister of State for External Affairs of the Government of the Virgin Islands, is generally regarded as the territory's most knowledgeable authority with regard to political status issues. See Corbin, *Adoption of a (US)Virgin Islands Constitution and Its Implications for Status* (St. Thomas: The League of Women Voters, US Virgin Islands, April 22, 2006) http://www.vihumanities.org/papers.htm (accessed July 30, 2009).

For their part, many down-islanders withheld their participation because they feared any status option that might threaten their future. They felt, according to H. Akia Gore in his 2009 book, "The Referendum ... would eventually lead to a state of political affairs ... which would take immigration and residency functions from the Federal government and bestow those functions on native Virgin Islanders." In his extensive 1997 interview with Gerard Emanuel, who had served as the Status Commission's executive director, Gore quoted Emanuel as stating:

> The fundamental reason for the referendum was to grant the people ... who could trace their roots back to the time when the islands were bought, an opportunity to finally have a say about their futures.... they are the ones whose ancestors were disaffected.... the Referendum.... called for all registered voters to participate.... However, only native Virgin Islanders had the right to decide on the status question. Not people from the Eastern Caribbean, not people from the United States mainland, no one else should make the Status decision.

Whereas Gore in his book began his discussion of the referendum by asserting it "has been one of the most politically polarizing activities the Virgin Islands has ever witnessed, second only to the mass roundup and repatriation efforts of the 1970s," he ended his book by stating that:

> many Eastern Caribbean immigrants withheld their participation, and those that voted selected the Status Quo, thus depriving the process of the fifty plus one votes required to affect [*sic*] any proposed change.... The astronomical growth of the white mainlander population.... added appreciably to the existing fears of native Virgin Islanders, who are concerned that one day soon they will become the governed, rather than the government.[19]

Given the fact that Guam and the Virgin Islands had failed to adopt constitutions, as authorized by Congress in 1976, the governments of both of these unincorporated territories continued to operate under federal revised organic acts of the 1950s. It became apparent during subsequent Congressional hearings that failure to adopt a constitution was caused in part by uncertainty about the effect a constitution would have on the right of self-determination. Guam's government petitioned Congress in 1997 to add a new section as an amendment to the 1976 authorization that would make clear that the adoption of a

---

19. See: Gore, *Garrote* (2009), pp. 419, 423, 425, 427.

constitution would not affect the territories' right of self-determination by stating: "Establishment of local constitutional self-government would not preclude or prejudice the further exercise in the future by the people of Guam or the Virgin Islands of the right of self-determination regarding the ultimate political status of either such territory." Accordingly, Congress in 2000 added this exact language to its 1976 law.[20]

The deep emotions, misinformation and uncertainty aroused during the status discussions in the Virgin Islands were followed by a vacuum of dialogue on issues of political development. The only exception was a petition in 2003 originated by *The St. Croix Avis* calling on the U.S. Congress to amend the 1954 Revised Organic Act to allow St. Croix to secede from the Virgin Islands— an initiative that reflected years of continuing Crucian resentment toward St. Thomas. A surprising number of more than 7,000 of St. Croix's 27,000 registered voters were reported in 2009 to have signed the petition.

The Virgin Islands non-voting Delegate to Congress, Donna Christensen, responded that change must come through adoption of a new constitution. For his part, Governor Charles Turnbull rejected secession and declared in 2003 that another attempt be made to draft a constitution. Accordingly, it was not until 2004—some eleven years after the political status referendum—that a local bill was enacted to create the Fifth Constitutional Convention.[21]

The Fifth Constitutional Convention

The Fifth Constitutional Convention did not get down to business until mid-2008, and not with intensity until the following year. As their deadline of May 31, 2009 approached, the delegates met with a frenzy in plenary sessions day and night, as they were running out of time and money, frantically trying to reach a consensus. A divisive stalemate between two factions continued between those who supported certain controversial exclusive rights for so-called "native" Virgin Islanders and those opposed. Former Governor Charles Turnbull, the only delegate to have served in all five constitutional conventions, re-

---

20. See: *Virgin Islands and Guam Constitutional Self-Government Act of 2000*, adding a new section 6 to Public Law 94-584 (90 Stat. 2899) of 1976; and Report 106-745 to accompany H.R. 3999, 106th Congress, 2nd Session, July 17, 2000.

21. See, *e.g.*: Mireya Navarro, "St. Croix Hopes Gambling Will Bring Back Tourists," *The New York Times*, January 4, 1999, A12; Nancy Cole, "Push for St. Croix Secession from V.I. Spotlights Frustration But Lacks Support," *Daily News*, March 19, 2003; and Mat Probasco, "St. Croix Committee Seeks Federal Audit of V.I. Finances," *St. Croix Source*, April 23, 2009.

minded his fellow-delegates in vain that the Fourth Constitutional Convention's document failed approval by voters because of the issue of native Virgin Islanders. Suggestions to ask the Senate for more money and time to reach a consensus, and to finalize a draft, in the end failed.[22]

A controversial article was added at the last minute to the draft calling for creation of a political status advisory committee of 11 members within two years of the constitution's enactment. The committee would spend one year educating the people about different status options after which a status election would determine which status relationship with the United States the territory would pursue. The article stipulated that all committee members and all voters in the special status election would be limited to native Virgin Islanders (those born in the Virgin Islands) or "ancestral" Virgin Islanders (those who could trace their bloodlines to people living in the Virgin Islands prior to June 28, 1932). Delegate Gerard Emanuel, the prime architect of the article, explained the importance of limiting the status election to people born in the Virgin Islands or having deep roots in the Virgin Islands; whereas all other residents chose to live in an unincorporated territory and thus chose that political status, native Virgin Islanders were born in a colony. "The Virgin Islands is a colony," Emanuel said. "Self-determination is a decolonizing activity." And he asked, "If you are not among the colonized, why would you want to be a part of a decolonization effort?"[23] Other hotly contested provisions in the final draft would require the governor and lieutenant governor to be native or ancestral Virgin Islanders, and would exempt ancestral Virgin Islanders from paying any property taxes.

Finally, 20 of the 30 delegates voted on May 26, 2009 to approve a draft—just five days before the deadline, thus barely meeting the convention's own ruling requiring a two-thirds majority for approval. Faced with the imminent deadline, it was obvious that some delegates who opposed certain key provisions nevertheless voted their approval so that the process could move forward through the Governor, President, Congress and ultimately to the territory's

---

22. See, *e.g.*: Megan Poinski: "Constitutional Convention Marred by Loud Shouting, Personal Insults and Delegates Storming In and Out," *Daily News*, March 30, 2009, pp. 4–5; "Controversial Measures Doom Draft," *ibid.*, May 15, 2009, pp. 6–7; Verdel L. Petersen: "They Do Not Deserve More Time and Money," *St. Croix Source*, May 20, 2009; "Little Hope Left that Delegates Can End Divisiveness…," *Daily News*, May 21, 2009; and Ananta Pancham: "An Unconventional Meeting for Constitutional Convention," *St. Thomas Source*, May 15, 2009; "Convention Fails to Pass Proposed Constitution," *St. John Source*, May 18, 2009.

23. Quoted by Megan Poinski, "Last-minute Addition to Constitution Calls for Vote on Virgin Islands Status—by Natives Only," *Virgin Islands Daily News*, May 27, 2009, p. 2.

voters. All five delegates who voted against the draft constitution claimed that they would have voted for it had it not contained the native rights provisions.[24]

Failure of the Fifth Attempt

In an editorial entitled "We Deserved Better," the territory's leading newspaper vilified the delegates:

> The convention has ended in hopeless capitulation to desires for division.... It is a document written in the vitriol of vengeance ... fashioned to be a sword that divides and punishes ... that enshrines a culture of victimhood. It is unworthy of the diverse people of the Virgin Islands, who deserve equal treatment in a constitution that should heal, not hurt; that should give, not take; that should relieve, not burden.[25]

The federal law authorizing a constitution outlined an elongated process to be followed, namely that it be submitted to the Governor who within ten days will submit it to the President who, in turn, would have about two months to consider and comment on the draft before submitting it to Congress for its review. Congress then would have 60 days to modify or amend the document before returning it to the territory's voters to ratify or reject it. Accordingly, the document was duly submitted to Governor John deJongh Jr. as the first step in the process.

Much to the dismay of many Virgin Islanders, Governor deJongh refused to forward the document to President Barack Obama. "I will not forward this document to the President of the United States," deJongh asserted, "that both fails to recognize the supremacy of the Constitution of the United States and is additionally and clearly inconsistent with basic civil rights and protections contained in the U.S. Constitution." The Governor explained that the provisions granting special rights to "native" Virgin Islanders clearly violated the Equal Protection Clause, and he added: "Surely no one should expect me, one of only three African American Governors in our Nation—and by the way, a Native and Ancestral Virgin Islander—to forward a Proposed Constitution that is clearly un-

---

24. Megan Poinski: "V.I. Constitution Is Approved by Delegates," *Virgin Islands Daily News*, May 27, 2009, p. 3; "Controversy in the Constitution: Deadline Pressure Drove Delegates to Approve Hot-button Provisions that Doomed Earlier Drafts," *ibid.*, May 28, 2009, p. 2; and "Dissenters Explain Their Votes on Constitution Draft," *ibid.*, May 28, 2009, p. 3.

25. "We Deserved Better: The Fifth Constitutional Convention Has Failed the Virgin Islands," *Daily News*, May 28, 2009, p. 16.

constitutional to our Nation's first African American President, who happens to also be a constitutional scholar and a former law professor."[26]

Governor deJongh's rejection paradoxically fostered further division within the territory. There were those opposed to his decision because they thought the law did not permit him to exercise such discretion but required him pro forma to forward the draft constitution to President Obama. According to the Constitutional Convention President Gerard Luz James II:

> He's just a conduit to send the document to the president. It's not open for his opinion. His opinion can come out when the document comes back to the people for a vote. But with this decision, the governor played judge and jury at the midnight hour with the people's business.[27]

Retired St. John school teacher Oswin Sewer said Governor deJongh was trying "to play God."[28] On the other hand, there were those who lauded the governor for his decision to stop the process.[29]

Dr. Charles Turnbull belonged to the critics who opposed his fellow-Democrat deJongh's decision. Turnbull was the territory's governor (1999–2007) preceding deJongh and was the only elected delegate to serve in all five constitutional conventions. Although Turnbull had opposed the controversial provisions about native Virgin Islanders, he nevertheless was instrumental, as the deadline was approaching, in influencing other critics among the delegates to join him in voting approval of the document, in order to move the constitutional process forward. Thus the former governor shared deJongh's reservations. But Turnbull interpreted the law pertaining to the constitutional process as requiring the governor to forward the draft to the President within the stated ten days, and therefore Governor deJongh had no such discretion to interdict the process. Turnbull regarded the substance of the draft constitution to be a matter for the President and the Congress to review and change any of its provisions or otherwise to determine its fate. Governor Turnbull acknowledged that the controversial provisions regarding native rights were included in the draft

---

26. "Gov. John deJongh Jr.'s Comments on the Proposed Constitution Drafted by the Fifth Constitutional Convention," *Daily News*, June 12, 2009, pp. 6–7.

27. Quoted by Megan Poinski, "Delegates Blast Governor, Vow Lawsuit," *Daily News*, June 12, 2009, p. 5.

28. Interview of Oswin Sewer, retired St. John school teacher of social studies, in Charlotte Amalie, St. Thomas, June 24, 2009.

29. "Gov. John DeJongh Jr. Lauded for Rejecting Proposed Constitution for the Virgin Islands," *Daily News*, June 15, 2009, p. 19.

constitution because the convention was not representative of all the people of the Virgin Islands—no delegates were down-islanders from the Eastern Caribbean.[30]

Former Governor Turnbull with the author in St. Thomas, 2009

Within a day after Governor deJongh's rejection of the constitution drafted by the Fifth Constitutional Convention, the Convention's President Gerard Luz James II and Secretary Mary Moorhead filed a lawsuit on behalf of the Convention's delegates to compel Governor deJongh to forward their proposed constitution to Washington, D.C. But ten days passed and deJongh did not budge. Pending the unlikely event that the lawsuit would be successful, it appeared that the constitutional process was dead.[31]

Thus, five attempts to create a constitution, together with three attempts to choose a political status, appeared to have failed, as Virgin Islanders were reach-

30. Interview of Dr. Charles Turnbull, former Governor of the USVI (1999–2007), in Charlotte Amalie, St. Thomas, June 18, 2009.

31. See articles by Megan Poinski: "Delegates File Suit to Force deJongh to Forward Draft," *Daily News*, June 13, 2009, p. 3; "Constitutional Convention Delegates Oppose Lawsuit," *ibid.*, June 19, 2009, p. 2; and "Constitution Drafters Take Case to Superior Court," *ibid.*, July 16, 2009.

ing toward the end of the first decade of the twenty-first century. Pessimism was trumping optimism. Foremost among reasons for the assumed failure of the Virgin Islands to achieve a semblance of self-determination appeared to be the continuing hostility between the two major population groups—native Virgin Islanders versus down-islanders.

Natives versus Down-Islanders

Every resident of the U.S. Virgin Islands in 2010 was a member of a minority group. In other words, no ethnic group constituted a majority in the territory, and this had been increasingly the case at least since 1980. Of an estimated total population in 2003 of 110,740 in the territory, the two major population groups by birth were 49,007 (44.3%) native Virgin Islanders, and 35,037 (31.6%) down-islanders. The total population since 1980 had become increasingly diverse, with the influx of growing numbers of the non-native population, comprising Puerto Ricans particularly on St. Croix, and persons from the Dominican Republic, Arabs from the Middle East, and continental Americans particularly on St. Thomas-St. John. Altogether, the non-native population's impact on the territory's politics and economics became much greater during 1980–2010 than before that period.[32]

In separate interviews, St. Croix educator Gerard Emanuel claimed in mid-2009 that native-born Virgin Islanders comprised the highest number of registered voters in the Islands,[33] whereas the long-time leader of down-islanders, St. Thomas accountant George Goodwin, claimed that down-islanders represented 54 percent of the territory's voting population.[34] Who was correct remained unresolved, just as the decades-old rift between their respective followers was likely to continue much deeper into the twenty-first century. Indeed, the "ferment" between the two population groups, according to University of Virgin Islands Pro-

---

32. See Dr. Frank L. Mills, Project Director, *2003 United States Virgin Islands Community Survey*, particularly "Table 1-3. Place of Birth by Island and Race, U.S. Virgin Islands: 2003," (St. Thomas, USVI: Eastern Caribbean Center, University of the Virgin Islands, June 2004). The number of 24,714 natives in St. Croix (22.3%) was slightly greater than the 24,293 natives in St. Thomas-St. John (21.9%), whereas the number of 20,832 down-islanders (18.8%—Eastern Caribbean and Dominican Republic) was significantly greater than the 17,206 down-islanders in St. Croix (15.5%); *ibid.*

33. Interview of Gerard Emanuel, Assistant Director, Cultural Education Division, Government of the U.S. Virgin Islands, in Christiansted, St. Croix, June 30, 2009.

34. Interview of George Goodwin in St. Thomas, June 16, 2009.

fessor Malik Sekou, had never been greater than it became in 2009 after the assumed demise of the fifth attempt to develop a constitution for the Islands.[35]

Gerard Emanuel became a leading spokesperson for native rights during and after the 1990s. Somewhat of a modern-day Thomas Paine, he was the author of several lengthy and lucid essays he intended to publish in a book. In an interview, he acknowledged that not all, but a "large number," of native Virgin Islanders share his views that in sum call for: (1) "redress for past and current discrimination against natives"; and (2) "compelling governmental interests to preserve our culture." Mr. Emanuel stressed that the ancestors of native Virgin Islanders suffered greatly during the period of the Navy's military rule of the territory (1917–1931) when marines and sailors oppressed the natives, and whose leaders were vilified and imprisoned for advocating basic freedoms. He asserted that the Fourteenth Amendment of the U.S. Constitution granted U.S. citizenship to all persons born in the states, but it took an act of Congress in 1932 to grant citizenship to all natives of the Virgin Islands. Therefore, "the U.S. Constitution still does not follow the flag!"[36] With regard to the writing and adoption of a constitution, therefore, some Virgin Islanders questioned whether Virgin Islanders are fully U.S. citizens whose rights can not be taken away, because their citizenship was conferred by Congress—not by the U.S. Constitution. Others insisted that because no Virgin Islander can ever meet the requirement in the U.S. Constitution that a President must be a "natural born citizen" (this issue has never been decided by the U.S. Supreme Court), there is ample justification that a governor of the U.S. Virgin Islands must be a "native" Virgin Islander.

The following excerpt from one of Gerard Emanuel's essays illustrates the vehemence of his argument:

> In the V.I., … the 14th amendment's equal protection clause … should be applied in favor of natives. This has been lacking since the purchase of these islands by the U.S.… Therefore the persons in the V.I. whose right to equal protection has been historically, deliberately and consistently violated here are the Ancestral Native Virgin Islanders. THAT IS A FACT!!! Natives deserve justice. The fact is that there … never will be true and lasting peace and unity in the V.I. without first

---

35. Interview of Dr. Malik Sekou, Professor of Social Sciences, University of the Virgin Islands, in St. Thomas, June 19, 2009.

36. Interview of Gerard Emanuel, supra, n. 33. For insights of Virgin Islands culture and "the mentality" of natives, Mr. Emanuel recommended two books of fiction by Mario Moorhead of St. Croix: *Who Feels It Knows It: A Crucian Tale* (St. Croix: Mario Moorhead, 1994); and *He and Me* (St. Croix: ABS Printing, 2008).

satisfying the pre-condition of justice for the Natives. Until all our fellow citizens realize and respect the need for this, we will always have problems. It must be remembered that <u>EVERYONE</u> HAS THE RIGHT TO EQUAL PROTECTION — NOT JUST NON-NATIVES. (emphasis included)[37]

A leading spokesperson for the down-islanders, on the other hand, emerged contemporaneous during the immediate aftermath of the ending of the 5th Constitutional Convention, with the appearance in the territory's bookstores of Dr. H. Akia Gore's 2009 book about the injustices experienced by the Eastern Caribbean workers in the U.S. Virgin Islands. In late June 2009, many Virgin Islanders rushed to bookstores to buy Gore's somewhat sensational diatribe. In his "prologue" Gore stated:

> This book tells the story of Eastern Caribbean Nationals and their experiences ... living in the United States Virgin Islands. The story is about their struggles to achieve social, economic and political equality in that U.S. possession.... The history of mistreatment of the immigrant workers was a collective effort, involving succeeding generations of political and law enforcement authorities, in collusion with their native publics. The cruel treatment of these people represents the most horrific and painful experiences ever suffered by any group of people that lived in the Caribbean sub-region since the annihilation of the native Caribs, Arawaks, Siboney, and Tiano by the Europeans, and the atrocities that were committed against the African slaves during the plantation era.[38]

A comparison of the above quoted excerpts from Emanuel's and Gore's writings reveals unambiguously the depth of the implacable conflict that separates natives and down-islanders in the territory. Much of Gore's book is a litany of perceived injustices experienced by down-islanders, most notably the 1971 "roundup" and deportation of illegal aliens initiated, according to Gore, by Governor Melvin Evans for whom the major East-West road in St. Croix is named. Although Gore acknowledged the economic and political gains increasingly experienced by "Eastern Caribbean nationals" since the 1980s, including the election of five of the fifteen senators of the 25th Legislature of the territory, he ended the last chapter of his book of 454 pages with this lament:

---

37. Gerard Emanuel, "5th V.I. CONSTITUTION FACT AND FICTION," June 19, 2009, p. 6 (unpublished emailed copy).

38. H. Akia Gore, *Garrote* (2009), p. viii.

"Clearly, the negative attitudes and behavior that have been exhibited by native Virgin Islanders toward the aliens over the years have created deep scars in the immigrant persona, scars that remain open."[39]

---

39. *Ibid.*, p. 437.

14

Cacophony of Conflicts

During the 1980–2010 period, the territory experienced a plethora of persisting problems. The continuing conflict of natives versus down-islanders was a major problem likely to thwart approval of a constitution and/or a different political status for the foreseeable future. Other major problems of the past also threatened to make a mockery of the territory's motto—"United in Pride and Hope." Foremost among these was the systemic crime enmeshing Virgin Islanders.

Crime and Law Enforcement

Politician Earle B. Ottley authored two memoirs about the politics and government of the Virgin Islands—one published in 1982 and the other in 1994. He ended his first book with this observation:

> There are scores of desperate, misguided youth on the streets who are pursuing careers of crime.... Young people who are headed toward juvenile delinquency, crime and associated mischief, must have a radical change in outlook.... What will be the consequences for the Virgin Islands if they reach maturity with the same, hostile, anti-social attitudes they hold today? If we fail in this vital area, the future for the Virgin Islands will be dark indeed.[1]

Twelve years later, Ottley ended his second book even more emphatically:

> Criminal activity in the islands has become so rampant that many officials are ... concluding that more prisons and heavier sentences are the only solutions.... Drug use is a problem that is spreading like

---

1. Ottley, *Trials and Triumphs* (1982), p. 438.

wildfire among the youth, triggering other serious problems.... Once
they are caught and sent to prison where mandatory sentences expose
them to ... hardened criminal elements, they are locked into a lifetime cycle of crime, and by then most are beyond salvation.... An entire generation is at great risk.[2]

Unfortunately, Ottley's dire forebodings were to prove all too true. Unchecked
crime became a horrendous reality on all three islands. The 1990s became particularly stressful across the territory because of the increasing level and frequency
of violence among youth throughout the territory. Drug abuse and violent
street crime had already become ubiquitous in 1990, so much so that U.S. Attorney Terry Halpern said: "We are losing, if not have lost, a generation of
young Virgin Islanders." He added: "Approximately seven of 10 defendants we
now see are drug abusers; the crimes are much more violent."[3]

In December 1999, a St. Thomas newspaper reported that "The number one
cause of death among young men is murder." A decade later, the situation if
anything had become even worse, prompting a St. Croix editorial to declare:
"Our streets run red with the blood of our children, gunned down before
they have had a chance to make something of themselves, to give back to their
community."[4]

In June 2003, the University of the Virgin Islands (UVI) released an 83-page
study of juvenile offenders in St. Thomas and St. Croix that was replete with
statistics aimed at pinpointing "risk identifiers" pertaining to juvenile delinquency. Among the findings, approximately 50 percent of juvenile offenders lived
in a household with their mother, but without their natural father.[5] Some of
the 2006 statistics, comparing children indicator rates for the USVI versus national rates, were particularly ominous: juvenile violent crime arrest rate (499%
vs. 283%); child death rate (30.8% vs. 19.5%); teens who are high school
dropouts (13.8% vs. 7%); teens not attending school and not working (22.8%
vs. 8%); children in poverty (29.5% vs. 18%); and children in single female par-

2. Earle B. Ottley, *The Hardball Years: A Chronicle of Politics, Progress, and Pain In the
U. S. Virgin Islands* (St. Thomas: Earle B. Ottley, 1994), pp. 458–459.

3. Quoted by John Shaw, "Drug Problem Runs Deep," *Daily News*, August 1, 1990, p.
D-12.

4. See: "100 Years in the Virgin Islands: Time Line," *Daily News*, December 1999; and
"Editorial: Time to March," *The St. Croix Avis*, July 3–4, 2009, p. 8.

5. Frank L. Mills, Director, *A Study of Juvenile Offenders in St. Thomas and St. Croix, USVI*
(St. Thomas: Eastern Caribbean Center, University of the Virgin Islands, June 2003), p. xii.

ent households (40.5% vs. 32%).[6] UVI Professor Malik Sekou in 2009 attributed the rise of crime to a number of factors as, for example: the lack of early intervention programs for youth; a lack of marriages; absentee fathers; a very active drug culture; and the alarming and tragic trend of youth not acquiring skills to assure future income.[7]

Of the 323 students graduating in 2005 from the University of the Virgin Islands, 255 or 78.9 percent were females. The gender gap in 2006 was even greater; of 354 graduating students, 290 or 81.9 percent were females. Actually, the gender gap is observable throughout the territory's public school system, leading one authority to observe: "Too many boys are dazed on the street like walking zombies. Somewhere between elementary school and high school they became slaves to drugs. Unperceptive of the subtleties of culture domination and psychological conditioning, too many boys choose to 'live large' behind the barrels of guns."[8]

By mid-July 2009, the Virgin Islands had recorded 32 murders, a rate of homicides five times the national average and, according to the FBI's *Uniform Crime Report*, the territory was on a pace whereby "the toll could mount to 69 by year's end clearly ranking the territory as among the most murder-ridden communities in the world." On September 1, 2009, the territory's murder count already had reached 47 making the year 2009 the deadliest in the history of the Virgin Islands, with four more months to go.[9]

A total of eight police commissioners served the territory during the period of 1980 through 2003. Accordingly, one scenario repeated intermittently through the years had been for the governor to appoint a new police commissioner to implement a crime-fighting plan, an initiative demonstrating that the gover-

---

6. See: Table 2, *U.S. Virgin Islands Kids Count Data Book 2008* (Charlotte Amalie, St. Thomas: Community Foundation of the Virgin Islands, 2008), p. 6; and Fiona Stokes, "Kids Count Report Shows Some Gains and Setbacks," *Daily News*, June 18, 2009, p. 3. Note that Kids Count data were compiled from community surveys conducted by the Eastern Caribbean Center of the University of the Virgin Islands and from government.

7. Interview of Dr. Malik Sekou, Professor of Social Sciences, University of the Virgin Islands, in St. Thomas, June 19, 2009.

8. Whitman T. Browne, "The Dilemma of Virgin Islands Boys," *Caribbean Perspectives*, January 2009, pp. 12–20, at p. 13. See also: Prospero E. A. Lewis, "The Success of Young Black Males in Virgin Islands High Schools," *Ibid.*, pp. 3–10; and Lawrence R. Sewer, "Strategies for Success of Young Black Males," *Ibid.*, pp. 21–24. Note that *Caribbean Perspectives* is a publication of the Eastern Caribbean Center of the University of the Virgin Islands.

9. See: Barbara Birt, "Bullets And Words Fly As Feds Head for Sidelines," *St. Thomas Source*, July 15, 2009; and Corliss Smithen, "St. Thomas Slaying Pushes V.I. Homicide Count to Record Number," *Daily News*, September 1, 2009.

nor was doing something important regarding rising crime in the territory. Governor John deJongh followed his predecessors by unveiling such a plan in 2007. He appointed new Police Commissioner James McCall who had considerable mainland experience as a troubleshooting supervisory special agent. Among the crime-busting measures in the plan was expansion of the police force. McCall's Assistant Commissioner was Novelle Francis who had two decades of law enforcement experience in the territory. St. Croix was to be the center of the anti-crime initiative. The pristine image of St. John was tarnished, to say the least, when Governor deJongh also pointed to violent crime in that island over recent years.[10] Two years after McCall's appointment, however, events prompted a repeat of the scenario with Governor deJongh appointing Francis as Commissioner in May 2009 to replace McCall. Once again, deJongh pledged increasing the number of police officers. For his part, new Police Commissioner Francis pledged to end police corruption by applying "one code of ethics" across the board. And he announced:

> We will disempower those who inflict harm on the people of this territory. No more will we allow children to be caught in the crossfire; no longer are law-abiding residents to be hostages in their homes, and not one more traveler is to become active on an unwarranted battlefield.[11]

One conclusion was inescapable—the appointment and rhetoric of new police commissioners did not alter the systemic increase of violent crime in the territory.

Ultimately, of course, juvenile offenders become adult hardened criminals who commit most of the territory's violent crimes that fuel unending problems for law enforcement. Unfortunately, the steady increase in criminal activity during the 1980–2010 period surpassed the capabilities of Virgin Islands police. A comprehensive investigative study of Virgin Islands police, reported by the *Daily News* in December 2003, revealed that of 95 homicides in the territory, during the years 2001 through 2003, only 33 were solved and therefore 66 percent remained unsolved—the worst by far of any police jurisdiction of similar size anywhere in the United States. During the same period, the U.S. average was 38 percent unsolved. Reasons in the Virgin Islands varied. The territory's police department did not have a crime laboratory or a forensics ex-

---

10. Kate Joynes, "Governor Launches Crime Crackdown in USVI," *World Markets Research Centre*, February 23, 2007.

11. Quoted by Ananta Pancham, "Novelle Francis Named New Police Commissioner," *St. Thomas Source*, May 28, 2009.

pert. Moreover, of 85 shootings by Virgin Islands police examined by the study, 65 of the victims were unarmed—a grim history of extrajudicial killings by Virgin Islands police, and an astonishing figure attributable to the lack of police training, leadership and accountability. According to the study, "The V.I. Police Department never has offered training on how to decide when to use force."[12]

Health

Among the persistent problem areas encountered by Virgin Islanders during the 1980–2010 period were those centering on health.

The good news began in October 1982 when new hospitals were dedicated and opened on St. Thomas and St. Croix. The St. John Clinic was also dedicated but did not then open. The three facilities were funded by the federal government at a cost of $64 million. The successful performance of a kidney transplant at the new St. Thomas hospital in 1982 was the first such surgery in the territory—another hopeful sign.

Jumping ahead to July 2009, when the population was estimated to be 109,825, the health of Virgin Islanders in retrospect could be said to have fared well in comparison with the nation as a whole, in so far as longevity of life and the infant mortality rate may be considered major indicators of the general health and overall health care of a populace. Indeed, the territory's life expectancy in 2009 was 79.05 years, slightly higher than 78.1 years for the United States. The territory's infant mortality rate, on the other hand, was 7.56 deaths per 1,000 live births which was slightly higher than 6.26 deaths for the U.S., but much lower than the nation's rate for African Americans and significantly lower than the infant mortality rates in a number of states.[13]

The bad news for Virgin Islanders through the intervening years concerned the difficulties afflicting their hospitals on St. Thomas and St. Croix and their

---

12. Lee Williams, *Deadly Force: A Special Investigative Report* (St. Thomas, The Virgin Islands Daily News, December 30, 2003), pp. 3, 23, 29. Besides violent crime, the territory has also experienced substantial corruption involving high government officials. See, *e.g.*: the special investigative report by journalists Tim Fields and Megan Poinski, "Contracts and Cronies," *Daily News*, January 14, 2005, 20 pp.; and an article by the Virgin Islands Inspector General, Steve van Beverhoudt, "Corruption: A United States Virgin Islands Perspective," *Caribbean Perspectives*, January 2008, pp. 3–4.

13. See: Central Intelligence Agency, *The World Fact Book* (U.S. Virgin Islands), May 24, 2009; and U.S. Census Bureau, *Statistical Abstract: State Rankings* (2009).

412 14 · CACOPHONY OF CONFLICTS

clinic on St. John. Symptomatic of troubles to come were the resignation of three doctors at the St. Thomas hospital within a period of about three weeks in October 1984 that left only one staff pediatrician, and the revelation in April 1987 that the roofs on both the 4-year-old hospitals had been leaking badly, with the roof on the St. Croix hospital partially collapsed. Neither roof had been replaced by the end of that year. Structural, equipment, and staff problems caused both hospitals and the St. John Clinic to close temporarily in August 1988 except for emergency cases. Newly arrived Health Commissioner Deborah McGregor found in 1988 that the territory's two hospitals were crumbling, overworked nurses were threatening to strike, and supplies and equipment were non-existent or not working.[14]

Neither hospital had ever been accredited by the Washington, D.C.-based Joint Commission when Hurricane Hugo struck in September 1989 causing major damage to both St. Croix and St. John hospitals and devastation of the St. John clinic. A 1990 audit by the U.S. Interior Department found that the St. Thomas hospital had 82,000 unpaid patient bills, totaling $44.6 million accumulated between 1981 and 1988.[15]

St. Croix's hospital lost its certification in 1989 by the U.S. Department of Health and Human Services and still was not certified five years later, losing $3 million to $4 million each year in Medicare funding. Renamed the Juan Luis Hospital and Medical Center, the St. Croix facility gained accreditation for the first time in August 1995 by the nation's Joint Commission on Accreditation of Health Care Organizations (JAHC), followed by restoration of Medicare reimbursements, and received accreditation renewal in 2004, only to be downgraded to "provisional" accreditation in January and to regain full accreditation in June 2009.[16] By comparison, the St. Thomas Hospital was not accredited for the first time by JAHC until December 2003. On June 28, 2006, both the

---

14. Crouch, "Emergency Treatment Failed to Cure Health's Many Woes," *Daily News*, January 7, 1989, Special Supplement—1988: The Year in Review, p. 8.

15. See: Ed Crouch, "V.I. Hospitals in Poor Health," *Daily News*, August 1, 1990, p. D-14; Ed Crouch, "1989 in Review: Health Department, Hospitals Beset by Turmoil," *ibid.*, January 10, 1990, p. 10; and "1990 in Review," *ibid.*, January 19, 1991, p. 10; and Kay Johnson, "1993: The Year in Review: Resentment on St. Croix," *Daily News*, January 4, 1994, p. 6.

16. See: Brenda Thompson, "Hospital Regains Accreditation, Community Support," *Daily News*, December 30, 1995, p. 5; Bill Kossler, "Luis Hospital Fails To Gain Accreditation," *St. Croix Source*, November 1, 2008; and Bill Kossler, "Juan F. Luis Hospital Gets Full Accreditation," *ibid.*, June 5, 2009. The Joint Commission on Accreditation of Healthcare Organizations is recognized as the nation's predominant standards-setting and accrediting body on health care.

St. Thomas Hospital and St. John Clinic, renamed the Schneider Regional Medical Center on St. Thomas and the Myra Keating Smith Community Health Center on St. John, temporarily lost their accreditation from JAHC.[17]

The ups and downs of the two hospitals through the years paled in significance compared to the scandals afflicting the Schneider Regional Medical Center (SRMC) in 2008–2009. A Pandora's box of sorts was opened on July 28, 2008 by the *Islands Daily News* publication of its investigative report—"Salaries First, Patients Later"—detailing how SRMC executives enjoyed inflated pay and perks packages, and how former CEO Rodney Miller lied in not disclosing in his job application a former crime conviction and bad discharge from the U.S. Navy. The very next day, the U.S. Interior Department Inspector General and the Virgin Islands Inspector General released their scathing joint audit report of SRMC. They confronted "an alarming degree of secrecy and deliberate concealment of financial records" that required court-enforced subpoenas to reveal their findings of gross mismanagement and lack of oversight and financial viability. Among their "more egregious examples," resulting in referrals to criminal investigators, were: inappropriate retirement fund payments; compensation overpayments to SRMC executives; abuse of credit card privileges; inappropriate cost reimbursements to SRMC executives; and underreporting of executive compensation.[18]

On October 7, 2008, four former SRMC officials were arrested on criminal charges for conspiring, lying, and taking large sums of hospital money for themselves. Those arrested were: former Chief Executive Officer Rodney Miller, Sr. who was later found to have had a mainland criminal past; Chief Financial Officer Peter R. Najawicz who also was later found to have had a mainland criminal past; Chief Operating Officer and Legal Counsel Amos W. Carty, Jr. who previously was President of the Virgin Islands Bar Association; and June A. Adams who was Chairperson of the District Board of SRMC. They were

---

17. Editorial, "Hospital's Lost Accreditation," *Daily News*, June 30, 2006; and "V.I. Year in Review," *ibid.*, January 3, 2007, p. 6.

18. Letter to Governor de Jongh dated July 28, 2008, in: U.S. Department of Interior Office of Inspector General and Office of the Virgin Islands Inspector General, Government of the Virgin Islands, Final Audit Report, *Administrative Functions, Roy Lester Schneider Regional Medical Center, Government of the Virgin Islands* (Report No. V-IN-VIS-0001-2007), July 2008, 20pp. at p. 1–2. The St. Thomas-based newspaper won the 2008 Investigative Reporters and Editors Award and in August 2009 an Editors and Associated Press Managing Editors Public Service Award for its SMRC corruption stories. See: Aldeth Lewin, "Daily News Wins National Journalism Award," *Daily News*, April 2, 2009; and Priya Kumar, "Journalism in Your Face," *American Journalism Review*, August/September 2009: http://www.ajr.org/Article.asp?id=4810 (accessed September 5, 2009).

charged, variously, with a total of 144 "counts" (charges) brought by the V.I. Attorney General before the territory's Superior Court. The first trial on February 2009 took less than 45 minutes for a V.I. Superior Court jury to find Miller guilty of criminal charges, and he faced up to three years in prison.[19]

Public Education

A myriad of problems also confronted public education in the territory during the three decades ending in 2010. Failure to make needed repairs to school buildings plagued the education system throughout the period. In 1985, for example: the auditorium in the Arthur Richards Junior High School in St. Croix was termed unsafe for students; cracking walls made classrooms unusable at the Bertha C. Boschulte Junior High School on St. Thomas; and asbestos was reported in the ceilings of three classrooms at the Edith Williams School, a St. Thomas elementary school. Perhaps most important was the fact that leaky roofs at the Eudora Kean High School in St. Thomas evoked protests from students, parents, and teachers alike in 1985—an uncorrected problem that helped prevent that school from gaining accreditation.[20]

Twenty-three years later, in May 2008, the Middle States Association of Colleges and Schools granted full four-year accreditation to the Eudora Kean High School by virtue of some progress being made at long last, and money was appropriated for completing necessary work. However, the work stopped shortly after accreditation. In May 2009, it was reported that the Kean gym was falling apart, and that: "The sky can be seen through holes in the roof, and the water that leaks into the building during rainstorms has damaged equipment, canceled gym classes and practices and caused the gym roof to buckle and become a dangerous playing surface." President and Executive Director of the Commission on Secondary Schools for Middle States, Henry Kram, responded:

---

19. See: Joy Blackburn and Tim Fields, "Former Hospital Officials Hit with Criminal Charges," *Daily News*, October 8, 2008; Joy Blackburn and Tim Fields, "Secret Pasts," *ibid.*, December 29, 2008; Tim Fields, "Miller Guilty: Hospital Ex-CEO Now Faces Up to 3 Years in Prison," *ibid.*, February 11, 2009; Affidavit of Nicholas Peru, Special Investigator, Office of Virgin Islands Inspector General, October 22, 2008, 37 pp.; and Vincent E. Frazer, ESQ., Attorney General, Virgin Islands Department of Justice, People of the Virgin Islands vs. Rodney E. Miller, Sr., Amos W. Carty, Jr., Peter R. Najawicz, June A. Adams, Amended Information, March 3, 2009, 74 pp.

20. Philip Harrigan, "Failure to Fix Up Schools Tops List of Education Woes," *Daily News*, January 14, 1986, p. R-7.

"Once a commitment is made to do something, then we expect them to follow through and put whatever resources they have available to it."[21]

Meanwhile, staff shortages and teachers strikes became intermittent problems.[22] Hurricane Hugo, in September 1989, damaged schools throughout the territory. More damage six years later from Hurricane Marilyn in September 1995 was not repaired in time for school openings in September 1996. Regardless of massive education spending, whereby the territory spent more per pupil than most states and U.S. possessions, Virgin Islands students were reported in 1996 to have finished last in the nation in every standardized test they took.[23] During 1992 gangs and youth violence had begun to threaten several junior and senior high schools. But this was a problem that was to extend through the following seventeen years.[24]

The host of accumulating problems affecting public education in the territory led to a "bombshell" in November 2001 when the Middle States Association announced it intended to withdraw accreditation from three of the territory's public high schools—Ivana Eudora Kean High School and Charlotte Amalie High School on St. Thomas, and Central High School on St. Croix—because the Department of Education had failed to address key areas: site-based management; improvement of student and teacher attendance rates; and securing an adequate pool of substitute teachers. Meanwhile, other factors contributing to the loss of accreditation were low teachers' pay and lack of basic learning tools and textbooks. Education Commissioner Ruby Simmonds admitted that a reminder from Middle States "fell through the cracks" because she was busy on other matters. She met with Middle States officials to appeal the decision. Finally, on April 30, 2002, Middle States withdrew accreditation from the three high schools after years of unheeded warnings to the territory's Education Department, whereupon Governor Charles Turnbull fired Simmonds. The loss of accreditation threat-

---

21. Quoted by Aldeth Lewin, "Schools Fight to Keep Accreditation Despite Poor Athletic Facilities," *Daily News*, May 11, 2009.

22. See, *e.g.*: Joycelyn Hewlett, "Staff Shortages, Asbestos and Strike Plagued Schools," *Daily News*, January 13, 1987; and Chris Larson, "Top Stories of 2000: Teachers Strike," *ibid.*, January 2, 2001.

23. See, *e.g.*,: Fredreka Schouten, "Virgin Islanders Were Busy Recovering from Hugo," *Daily News*, January 10, 1991, p. 3; Melvin Claxton, "Many Problems in Education Predate Marilyn," *ibid.*, December 31, 1996, p. 5; and Aldeth Lewin, "Education Proposes $197 M Budget," *ibid.*, August 20, 2009.

24. Barrington Salmon, "Schools Fight Back As Violence Escalates," *Daily News*, January 5, 1993, p. 4; Andrea Milam, "Gangs Becoming Prevalent in Schools, Youth Violence Increasing," *St. John Tradewinds*, May 18–24, 2009, p. 4.

ened some V.I. students' eligibility for admission to a number of colleges and universities.[25]

Not until 2005 had all three high schools been granted reaccreditation. After some repairs of school facilities, an increase of teachers' salaries, and longer school days established for secondary schools, 19 of the territory's 33 public schools showed some improvement in students' performance on annual national standardized tests. Given the fact, however, that 82 percent of the territory's schools still ranked in the bottom third of schools nationwide in 2005, based on standardized test results, there was still a long way to go.[26]

In March 2005, after years of waiting for the Virgin Islands government to fix its antiquated financial system, the U. S. Department of Education issued an ultimatum to the V.I. government to either hire a grant manager or forfeit $32 million a year of federal funding for the territory's schools. In addition, not until a grant manager came on board to manage education funding would nearly $57 million be released that was then in the pipeline. The existing system was too cumbersome and lacked enough transparency for federal auditors to track federal grants in the territory. Not until August 28, 2006 did Governor Turnbull announce that an international firm had been awarded a contract to manage the federal education grants.[27] The V.I. Department of Education Fiscal Year 2010 total operating budget of $262.8 million included an estimated $55million in federal funds with the remainder coming from local funds. Public education had about 3,000 employees and served about 15,700 students at 33 school buildings.[28]

In 2008 and 2009, it appeared that progress was being made in the territory's school system. On May 22, 2008, it was announced that the Bertha C. Boschulte Middle School on St. Thomas became the first middle or junior high school in the territory to receive accreditation by Middle States. And on July 1, 2009 the V.I. Board of Education reported it found overall improvement in

---

25. Jennifer Inez Ward, "V.I. High Schools Lost Accreditation," *Daily News*, January 2, 2002, p. 6; "The Year's Top Stories in the V.I.—Schools Lose Accreditation," *ibid.*, January 3, 2003, p. 5.

26. Central High School on St. Croix received a one-year provisional accreditation in 2008, but the school principal was optimistic in late 2009 that it would soon receive a full, four-year accreditation. Cristian Simescu, "Middles States Officials Take Accreditation Tour of Central," *ibid.*, September 15, 2009. See also, "2005: V.I.'s Very Big Year," *Daily News*, January 6, 2006, p. 1.

27. See: *ibid.*, p. 2; and "2006: The Year That Was," *Daily News*, January 3, 2007, p. 7.

28. Aldeth Lewin, "Education Proposes $197M Budget," *Daily News*, August 20, 2009.

the management of the territory's school system. It also became known in 2009 that the National Park on St. John—by swapping land with the National Park on St. Croix—would thereby give up enough acreage for construction of a high school on St. John that would finally end the need for St. John children to travel to and from St. Thomas to receive a public high school education.[29]

Contrasted with the territory's public schools, the news about higher education in the territory was mostly positive. In 1986, the College of the Virgin Islands was renanmed the University of the Virgin Islands, reflecting its growth, diversification, services, and research programs. Also in 1986, the U.S. Congress named UVI one of the nation's "Historically Black Colleges and Universities" (HBCU), the only HBCU outside the continental United States. The University of the Virgin Islands (UVI) did not have a problem with accreditation. On November 15, 2007, the Commission on Higher Education of the Middle States Association of Colleges and Schools reaffirmed its accreditation of UVI until 2016. UVI announced on June 15, 2009 that it was moving closer to the goals set forth in its Vision 2012 strategic plan. More students were full time: 70 percent on St. Thomas and for the first time over 50 percent on St. Croix. Accordingly, 25 percent more daytime classes would be offered in the fall of 2009. Male students had increased from 23 percent in 2006 to 27 percent in 2009. UVI expected to achieve a 75 percent retention rate for the 2009 fall semester, up 2 percent from the fall of 2008.[30]

Politics and Government

The passion for politics exhibited by Virgin Islanders before the 1980s continued unabated through the ensuing three decades. Political discourse was more than part-time. It was the bedrock of the distinctive political culture of the territory. Personalistic politics, in lieu of party politics, became more enhanced. In his 1994 memoir, Earle Ottley lamented that "there are no lasting alliances; the party system exists in name only." He added, "Voters are com-

---

29. "The Year That Was ... Images and Events of 2008," *Daily News*, January 6, 2009, p. 3; Adeth Lewin, "Report Finds Improvements in V.I. Schools," *ibid.*, July 1, 2009, p. 2.

30. "The Year That Was ... Images and Events of 2007," *Daily News*, January 11, 2008, p. 3; Adeth Lewin, "Trustees Receive Year-end Update," *ibid.*, June 15, 2009, p. 4. At a press conference in August 2009, UVI's new president, David Hall, said he hoped to address the low numbers of males applying to UVI. Aldeth Lewin, "New UVI President Introduced," *ibid.*, August 15, 2009.

pelled to support candidates merely on instinct, and not because of any concerted offerings or appealing platforms."[31]

It was not uncommon for many aspirants, whatever their political identities, to vie for election for governor every four years. A list of elected governors illustrates a spectrum of political identifications, as follows:

Melvin Evans	(1971–1975)	Republican
Cyril King	(1975–1987)	Independent Citizens Movement (ICM)
Juan Luis	(1978–1987)	No-Party
Alexander Farrelly	(1987–1995)	Democrat
Roy Schneider	(1995–1999)	Independent
Charles Turnbull	(1999–2007)	Democrat
John deJongh	(2007–)	Democrat

In 2010, Governor deJongh was still in his first term as Governor. Among the other elected governors, only Roy Schneider and Republican Melvin Evans failed to be elected to a second term. Schneider was also a registered Republican, but he chose instead to run as an independent. Accordingly, "In winning in 1994, Schneider attracted substantial numbers of independent voters, as well as members of the ICM, Democratic and Republican parties."[32] The fact that no governor had run as a Republican since 1975 suggested an irreversible decline of that party in the territory.

The Virgin Islands has been a strong-governor polity unlike many weak-governor mainland states. The territory's governors have often clashed with the legislature, by casting vetoes of legislation many of which have been overridden by the legislature. The power of incumbency of a governor has been a huge advantage by dangling a wide range of patronage, jobs, commissions, and offering a variety of other favors. Comparatively, the legislature continued to be weaker.

---

31. Ottley, *The Hardball Years* (1994), pp. 389, 452.

32. "Supporters, Foes Look at Schneider As He Approaches Mid-Term in Office," *Pride*, November 1996, p. 18. Schneider's failure to win a second term was attributable to a number of factors: the burgeoning of government debt; the resignation of an all-time high of 20 cabinet members most of whom were women: and the economic plight of St. Croix in particular. See, *e.g.*: Luance Rake, "V.I. Deficit Burgeoning," *Daily News*, December 31, 1997, p. 5; Eunice Bedminister, "High Cabinet Turnover Plagues Administration," *ibid.*, p. 7; and "Turnbull Elected Governor," *ibid.*, January 2, 1999, p. 7. Note also that Gore considered Schneider "one of the worst governors in the history of the Virgin Islands" for "his contempt of up-islanders ... with origins in the Eastern Caribbean ... rivaled only that of Melvin Evans, an avowed anti-alien political official." *Garrote* (2009), p. 156.

Composed of 15 senators, each serving two year terms, the turnover in the legislature since 1980 has been a continuing saga, compared with governors who usually serve two four-year terms. Moreover, party identification has been no predictor of legislative behavior as party discipline has been virtually non-existent. Sectionalism has predominated instead, by virtue of the fact that seven senators are elected from St. Croix, and seven from St. Thomas. St. John has only a single representative in the legislature who is elected "at large" throughout the territory.[33]

Increasingly since 1980, after each biennial election, a flurry of activity has ensued among members to put together a majority from which a senate president and committee chairs are chosen. Party identifications have tended to mean little in forming a coalition. The process has involved personalistic politics, crossing party and sectional lines, deals, promises, and even threats. Often, a losing minority will pressure or entice one or more majority member(s) to defect to it so that a new majority is formed. It has not been uncommon for the process to be laced with vituperation, swing voting, and even chaos lasting through the two-year term. In the extreme, the fed-up voting public has sometimes replaced most members at the next election.[34]

In 2002, a local political writer—whose pseudonym was I. C. Keen—had this to say about party politics in the territory:

> There was once a time when anyone wanted to play ball in the political arena, you had to be a player in one of the three major political parties in the territory: the Democratic Party, the Republican Party, or the Independent Citizens Movement. However, within the last two decades, the landscape and criteria for acceptance into these parties has shifted from a position of platform to one of popularity. Consequently,

33. Oswin Sewer of St. John has complained: "The St. Thomas/St. John district services favor St. Thomas. We pay property taxes that are three times more than we receive in services from the government. We have only one representative in the territory legislature, but he is elected at large. Senators from St. Thomas are supposed to be representative of both St. Thomas and St. John, but we only see them at election time. None of them has any staff member posted at St. John." Interview of Oswin Sewer at St. Thomas, 24 June 2009.

34. See, e.g.: Bernetia Akin, "Senate Takeover Came After Months of Minority Effort," *Daily News*, January 19, 1984, pp. R4–R7; and Hal Hatfield, "Senate Disinegrates in Intramural War," *ibid.*, January 5, 1993, pp. 1, 2. In the 1984 election, only 5 of the 13 senators who sought re-election were returned to the Legislature. "Most apparently were victims of a public perception of the Legislature as a group whose members made deals with one another ... and was short on decorum and long on nepotism and cronyism." Bernetia Akin, "Year's Top Story: The Election Rout," *ibid.*, January 10, 1985, p. R-1.

many first-time aspirants choose to run as independents or "no party" candidates....
The Democratic Party has ... more than 30,000 registered members. There are 3,100 registered Republicans and 2,160 registered ICMs. There are more than 5,300 voters registered as "No Party."[35]

It was no surprise, therefore, that the territory's 25th Legislature, elected in November 2008, numbered 9 Democrats, 4 Independents, and 2 ICMs. This meant that the Virgin Islands Legislature was "the only partisan legislature of its kind in the U.S., where the Republican Party has no legislative representation."[36]

Gubernatorial feuds between the territory's two top executives have been the rule rather than the exception since the advent of U.S. rule in 1917. Even before 1970, when Virgin Islanders began electing their own governors and lieutenant governors, appointed governors and government secretaries usually did not get along with each other. By 2010, there were a total of seven elected governors, only two of whom—Alexander Farrelly and John deJongh—whose administrations were relatively free of hostility or squabbles with their lieutenant governors. Governor Farrelly (1987–1995) had tried to groom Lieutenant Governor Derek Hodge to succeed him, whereas Governor deJongh (2007–) had served only three years with Lieutenant Governor Gregory Francis by 2010.

Governor Charles Turnbull (1999–2007) and Lieutenant Governor Gerard Luz James had a conflicted relationship, leading Turnbull to select Vargrave Richards, an "old friend," as his second term running mate. An historian and former governor, Dr. Turnbull attributed traditional conflicts between the territory's two top executives to a number of factors, prominent among which are: "personality conflicts"; usually one is from St. Thomas and the other from St. Croix, reflective therefore of long-time rivalry between the two islands; each having his own staff and the same territory-wide constituency fosters competition between them; and when the governor is away from the territory, the lieutenant governor actually acts as governor—a situation that can lead to conflict.[37]

During the three decades stretching from 1980 to 2010, the Virgin Islands government expenditures exceeded its income, which meant that the govern-

35. I.C. Keen, "Election 2002: The Status of Party Politics in the Territory," *VI Chronicles*, Vol. 1, Issue 4, August 2002, p. 8.

36. "Election of the 25th Legislature, November 4, 2008," *Wapedia-Wiki: Legislature of the Virgin Islands.* http://wapedia.mobi/en/Legislature_of_the_Virgin_Islands (accessed August 16, 2009).

37. Interview with Dr. Charles Turnbull in Charlotte Amalie, St. Thomas, June 18, 2009. See also: "Frequent Clashes over Years between VI. Govs. & Lt. Govs." *Pride*, October 1996,

The author with Governor Farrelly at Government House, St. Thomas

ment funded the difference by borrowing money that caused an increasing deficit. Prior to 1983, money was initially borrowed through inter-fund transfers—"robbing Peter to pay Paul" so to speak—and later through selling bonds. Borrowed money was used not only for operating expenditures but also to pay for short-term debt service that more than doubled from 6.7 percent of the total budget in 1983 to 14.5 percent in 1984. Thus a worsening cash flow problem was set in motion, to which the government responded by deferring payments for: payroll contributions (employees' retirement, social security, and health insurance); income tax refunds; and vendors.[38]

At the beginning of his administration in January 1987, Governor Farrelly proposed a number of cost-cutting measures to defray a deficit of $80 million that had accumulated since 1982. A generally improving economy wrought increasing revenues that erased the deficit by the end of the fiscal year in Sep-

---

pp. 13, 28; and I.C. Keen, "Incompatibility in Government House: A Long-standing Trend," *VI Chronicles*, Vol. 1, Issue 5, September 2002, pp. 10, 27.

38. See Arnold H. Leibowitz, *Defining Status: A Comprehensive Analysis of United States Territorial Relations* (Dordrecht, The Netherlands: Martinus Nijhoff Publishers, 1989), p. 301.

tember 1987 with a $7 million surplus, allowing the government to pay thousands of its employees retroactive pay increases.[39]

The good news was short-lived, however, as Hurricanes Hugo in 1989 and Marilyn in 1995 wreaked havoc with the territory's economy. More than 40 businesses closed on St. Croix alone, while tourism plummeted on St. Thomas and St. John. A federal audit reportedly put the territory's deficit at close to $600 million at the end of 1996.[40] The territory's government issued $268 million in new bonds in 2003, while leaving spending untouched. The government's bonded indebtedness totaled $742.7 million at the end of 2003. "When have we not been in a fiscal crisis?" asked Richard Moore, a University of the Virgin Islands economist. "The best indicator of the future is the recent past, and the recent past is that we have been in a perpetual fiscal crisis."[41]

Sectionalism, in the form of inter-island rivalry, continued to play an important role in the territory's politics and government during the 1980–2010 period. Regardless of the fact that the Revised Organic Act of 1954 ordained St. Thomas to be the seat of the territory's government, the headquarters of the Virgin Islands National Guard Joint Force are in St. Croix. However, St. Croix partisans, after fierce battles, were unsuccessful in having the newly established Supreme Court located on St. Croix. Even though the 1954 Act replaced the municipal councils of St. Thomas, St. John, and St. Croix with one unified legislature located on St. Thomas, many Virgin Islanders have favored a return to local government for each of the three islands. For example, many St. John residents have felt their interests have not been adequately represented, or have been subsumed, in the Senate by their representative who is elected at large throughout the territory.[42] And though the secessionist movement on St. Croix ultimately faltered, as noted before, it was surprisingly supported by many Crucians and should be taken seriously as symptomatic of widespread antipathy toward St. Thomas. As the first decade of the 21st century was ending, it appeared that inter-island rivalry was not diminishing.

---

39. Bernetia Akin, "Deficit Disappearance Meant Back-pay Checks," *Daily News*, January 8, 1988, p. 3.

40. Hal Hatfield, "V.I. Economy Tops Headlines," *Daily News*, December 31, 1996, pp. 1, 4.

41. Quoted by Jeremy W. Peters, "Virgin Islands Top Story of 2003: Financial Reforms Missing from Turnbull's Budget," *Daily News*, December 31, 2003, p. 5.

42. See *supra*, note 33.

Tourism

For all its problems, there are few places in the world that can match the bountiful beauty of sun, sand, and surf that nature has created in America's Virgin Islands. Its geography and balmy weather are ideal for attracting tourists. Its beaches at Magens Bay on St. Thomas and Trunk Bay on St. John are ranked among the most beautiful in the world. But there are many other white beaches surrounding the territory's three main islands that also offer tranquil and exotic vacations to thousands of tourists throughout each year. The sustainability of tourism in the Virgin Islands, and throughout the Caribbean, is of course vulnerable to hurricanes and the ups and downs of the global economy. The devastation wrought by Hugo and Marilyn drastically curbed the number of visitors and hence the territory's economy. To some extent, the same was true of the economic downturn in the early 1980s and the "Great Recession" of the late 2000s. Loosening restrictions on U.S. travel to Cuba in 2009, and planned tourist activity in Aruba, were also developments watched closely by local business leaders.[43] Regardless of such occasional externalities, the economy of the Virgin Islands from 1980 to 2010 continued overwhelmingly to depend on tourism. Tourism had long been the primary activity in the U. S. Virgin Islands, accounting for 80 percent of GDP and employment in 2009. The territory hosted 2.6 million visitors in 2005, up from 1.9 million the year before Hugo struck in 1989.[44]

Preponderant dependence on tourism explained why the territory had gone to great lengths to promote it since 1980, such as the lengthening and modernizing of airports on St. Thomas in 1992 and St. Croix in 2000, the 1993 purchase of the Danish-owned cruise ship dock in St. Thomas, and the opening in St. Croix of casino gambling in 2000.[45] By 2002, the Caribbean had become the single most important cruise destination in the world, accounting for 45 percent market share followed by Europe at 20 percent. And St. Thomas had long enjoyed being one of the busiest cruise ports in the Caribbean. For example, within the typical week of June 13–20, 2009, well after the height of the tourist

---

43. See, *e.g.*, Eric Schmitt and Damien Cave, "Obama to Loosen Restrictions on Policy with Cuba," *The New York Times*, April 5, 2009, p. 9.

44. See: Central Intelligence Agency, *The World Fact Book* (U.S. Virgin Islands), September 1, 2009.

45. See, *e.g.*, Hal Hatfield, "King Airport Complete after 14 Years," *Daily News*, January 5, 1993 p. 4; Hal Hatfield, "$48 Million Buys Last Vestige of Colonialism," *ibid.*, January 4, 1994, p. 3; and Devin Carrington, "The Influence and Impact of Gaming in the Virgin Islands: A Synopsis," *Caribbean Perspectives*, January 2005, pp. 3–8.

season that ended in May, six cruise ships had dispatched a total of 17,175 passengers to feast and shop along the streets of Charlotte Amalie.[46]

Accommodation of ever larger cruise ships in scenic St. Thomas harbor became a priority through the summer of 2009 that caused waves of discontent within the tourist industry itself. At issue was a plan to dredge the St. Thomas harbor to allow the largest cruise ship in the world—Royal Caribbean's Oasis of the Seas—to begin calling with its 5,400 passengers on St. Thomas in December 2009. The total cost of the project was reported to be $12 million provided by Royal Caribbean. About 162,000 cubic yards of dredged spoils would then be dumped into an old dredged hole in nearby Lindbergh Bay from which sand was removed in 1935 to create a land base for the adjacent airport. A tranquil palm-fringed beach, with three resort hotels and a restaurant, looked out at the scenic bay. Together with the Coalition to Save Lindbergh Bay, they filed an appeal with the Board of Land Use against the plan approved by the Coastal Zone Management Committee, Governor deJongh, and the Senate. Another appeal was filed by the National Wildlife Federation, the Virgin Islands Conservation Society, and the Environmental Association of St. Thomas-St. John. Moreover, many members of the community voiced their intense disapproval about the science used to support the project, the accuracy of the environmental assessment, and what the action would do to both the tourism industry and the marine life of Lindbergh Bay. One opponent suggested that the dredged material be dumped half-way between the 40 miles separating St. Thomas and St. Croix in the deepest part of the sea. Meanwhile, the fate of beautiful Lindbergh Bay had yet to be determined by the fall of 2009. The Army Corps of Engineers had not yet given its required approval, and no hearing date had been scheduled for either appeal.[47]

National attention concerning the incidence of intermittent crime against tourists in the territory continued to be a vexing issue since the mid-1980s.

---

46. Edward E. Thomas, "Developing the Caribbean Cruise Ship Industry for 21st-Century Technology," *Caribbean Perspectives*, January 2002, pp. 17–18; "Cruise Ships," *Virgin Islands Daily News*, June 13, 2009, p. 5.

47. See these articles by Aldeth Lewin in the *Daily News*: "CZM Unanimously Approves Dredging," May 6, 2009; "Senate Delays Vote on Dredging," May 28, 2009, p. 3; and "Coalition Appeals CZM Permit Allowing Dredge Spoils Dumping in Lindbergh Bay," August 6, 2009. See also: Augusta Johns, "Lindbergh Bay Hearing Betrayed Trust," *ibid.*, June 25, 2009, p. 16; CJ and Mac Hardy, "Don't Stop Fighting to Save Lindbergh Bay, *ibid.*, July 1, 2009, p. 23; Eddie Donoghue, "WICO Did Not Do Cost/benefit Analysis on Dredging for Megaships," *ibid.*, October 2, 2009; and Sean McCoy, "Dredging for Cruise Ship Tourism Threatens Virgin Islands Reefs," *Cyber Divers News Network*, August 31, 2009. http://www.cdnn.info/news/ecoo/e090831.html (accessed September 24, 2009).

For example, Victor Borge, a world-renowned pianist and comedian, had his pocket picked in St. Thomas in 1988. Two Iowa travel agents were robbed in St. Thomas in 1990. A world-renowned swimming instructor of infants was slain in St. Thomas in 1994 causing cruise ships to warn visitors to be cautious and the U.S. Navy to cancel port calls. The shootings in St. Thomas of three tourists from the mainland in one week of January 1996 caused turmoil, with Governor Schneider ordering roadblocks, searches, and a nighttime curfew for youths. Two Carnival-owned cruise lines pulled out of St. Croix in 2002, citing crime against passengers and crew members. Some upturn for St. Croix appeared with announcements that both Royal Caribbean and Disney cruise ships planned to begin port calls in 2009–2010. However, St. Croix continued to lag behind St. Thomas and St. John in every aspect of the tourist industry, from air arrivals to cruise ship passengers and to hotel occupancy.[48]

---

48. See, *e.g.*, Larry Rohter, "Slaying in St. Thomas Stains Image of an 'American Paradise,'" *The New York Times*, April 19, 1994, p. A17; "Police in Virgin Islands on Alert After the Shootings of 3 Tourists," *ibid.*, January 28, 1996, section 1, p. 22; and "Travel Advisory; Two Cruise Lines Cancel St. Croix Calls," *ibid.*, July 28, 2002, section 5, p. 3.

Epilogue

During late December 2009 through the first three months of 2010, certain events occurred to suggest that the Virgin Islands might change direction in a number of important respects.

The dredging of St. Thomas harbor and dumping the spoils in Lindbergh Bay was scrapped until an alternative plan could be developed. Meanwhile, the new "megaship" Oasis of the Seas docked at Crown Bay on March 30th helping to break the St. Thomas record of 20,000 cruise ship passengers in one day.

At the end of March, the territory's homicide count stood at 20 (9 in St. Thomas and 11 in St. Croix)—a projected pace of 80 homicides for 2010 that would shatter the already deadliest all-time record of 56 homicides in 2009 (a rate of 51 of every 100,000 people compared with only 5 of every 100,000 on the mainland). Considering the fact that the national trend in 2009 showed a ten percent decline in homicides, there was some hope that the Virgin Islands could also reverse its trend—albeit unlikely in 2010.

Perhaps the most significant event was the December 23rd 2009 ruling by Presiding Virgin Islands Superior Court Judge Darryl Donohue ordering Governor John deJongh to send the draft constitution, submitted by the Fifth Constitutional Convention, to President Barack Obama. Accordingly, Governor deJongh's decision to kill the draft merely delayed the process of review by first the President, then the Congress, and finally by a referendum of Virgin Islands voters. Governor deJongh forwarded the draft on December 31st to President Obama who, in turn, requested review by the Department of Justice. Among the Justice Department's foremost recommendations was the removal from the proposed constitution of those provisions "conferring legal advantages on certain groups defined by place and timing of birth, timing of residence, or ancestry...." The draft was formally submitted to the Congress by President Obama on March 17, 2010.

Although Congress had the power to modify the document, curiously both opponents and supporters of the proposed constitution from the Virgin Islands testified before Congress that the draft should be sent back to the territory's people for a final vote without a single word changed. Among those testifying who opposed the draft were, of course, Governor deJongh, as well as two convention delegates who had voted against the document—Eugene Peterson and Douglas Brady. Those testifying in support of the proposed constitution included Constitutional Convention President Gerard Luz James II, along with two convention delegates who had voted for the document—Adelbert Bryan and Gerard Emanuel.

It remained to be determined—whatever modifications, if any, Congress should make—whether enough Virgin Islanders who support the proposed constitution would avail themselves to vote at the last stage of the process, a referendum.

Arnold H. Leibowitz, a long-time legal scholar of U.S territories and counsel to the Virgin Islands Third Constitutional Convention, was the author of a monumental book published in 1989 that comprehensively analyzes United States territorial relationships.

After devoting seventy-eight pages to a legal and political discussion of the Virgin Islands, Leibowitz concluded: "To treat the issue of long-term discontent, the U.S. must seriously address status moving toward full economic and political participation for the U.S. citizens in the Virgin Islands: namely, Statehood."[1] Dr. Marilyn Krigger, Emerita Professor of History of the University of the Virgin Islands and co-chairperson of the territory's former Commission on Status and Federal Relations, considered statehood as not a realistic option and, for that reason, "most Virgin Islanders, rightly or wrongly, do not want a big change in status; they prefer an improved variation of their current relationship."[2]

Assuming Dr. Krigger's assessment is correct, and given the wave of decolonization and independence that has engulfed almost all of the Caribbean Basin, a legitimate question is why most Virgin Islanders prefer retaining their status quo or a similar relationship with the United States. Without administering a poll of most Virgin Islanders, an answer to this question may not be forthcoming. Responses to such a poll would probably highlight benefits of having U.S. citizenship, such as freedom to travel to and from the mainland. However, it is likely also that financial benefits accrued from the territory's relationship to the federal government would be paramount, such as: the so-called mirror system of taxation and consequent federal revenue sharing, an overall low Virgin Islands tax effort, federal grants-in-aid, annual Congressional appropriations, and other federal financial benefits.

---

1. Leibowitz, *Defining Status* (1989), pp. 233–311, at p. 311.

2. Telephone interview of Dr. Marilyn Krigger, Charlotte Amalie, St. Thomas, June 28, 2009.

A former doctoral student of history at George Mason University in Virginia, was author of an article in 2007 covering the period 1917–1936 of federal administration of the Virgin Islands in which she concluded that during this twenty-year period:

> the United States expended more money and energy than it intended and the islanders made significant economic and political gains. This period also provided a foundation for growth over the next century.... Tourism, fostered during this period of early American rule, has become the breadwinner for the isles."[3]

Notwithstanding financial and economic benefits gained by Virgin Islanders during almost a century of federal suzerainty, their struggle to enjoy a full measure of self-government is still not over. The so-called territorial clause of the United States Constitution—Article IV, section 3, clause 2—states: "The Congress shall have Power to dispose of and make all needful Rules and Regulations respecting the Territory or other Property belonging to the United States...." This clause has been used to justify Congressional and executive action predicated on the assumption of absolute federal discretion with respect to U.S. territories. As long as this unilateral authority exists, the Virgin Islands can not be considered self-governing by the United Nations. Moreover, the basic principles governing the federal-state relationship—namely, equality of treatment and limitation of federal power—are not extended to the territories. They should be.

In terms of the example of America's Virgin Islands, assurance of civil liberties of the people of the Virgin Islands is no longer the key issue. All civil liberties in the U.S. Constitution, except indictment by grand jury, likewise protect residents of the Virgin Islands. Today the issues are participation in the national political system and territorial control over territorial affairs. The territory of the Virgin Islands does not participate as an entity in Congress because it has only a single nonvoting representative in Congress. Citizens of the Virgin Islands are not granted the right to vote for the President and Vice President and therefore are not represented in the national political system in any meaningful capacity. They should be.

The right of self-government is more important than the manner in which that right is exercised. Even should the people of the Virgin Islands govern themselves badly, they should have the right to do so. This means that once Vir-

---

3. Stephanie Hunter McMahon, "You Pay for What You Get: The U.S. Virgin Islands, 1917–1936," *The Journal of Caribbean History*, Volume 41: 1 & 2 (2007), p. 130.

gin Islanders have created a territorial constitution that has been approved by Congress, Congress should not have the power to override its provisions. The status of that constitution should be accorded the presumptive equivalent of the Tenth Amendment of the U.S. Constitution. Just as the Tenth Amendment constitutionally restricts national intrusion upon the reserved powers of the states, so also would the Constitution of the Virgin Islands restrict national government intrusion upon the powers exercised under its provisions. Once the Constitution of the Virgin Islands is approved by Congress and by the people of the Virgin Islands, Congress should use the territorial clause of the U.S. Constitution only to advance the development of the Virgin Islands.[4]

Should these principles be observed, then long-time aspirations such as Casper Holstein's plaintive wish of 1934 will not have been expressed in vain. Holstein said: "We want to be the same as every member of this American nation, and we are entitled to that privilege."[5]

---

4. For similar analysis, see, Arnold H. Leibowitz, "United States Federalism: The States and the Territories," *The American University Law Review*, Volume 28 (Summer 1979), pp. 479–482.

5. Report of a mass meeting, Casper Holstein presiding, held under the auspices of the Virgin Islands Congressional Council and Allied Virgin Islands Societies at Frederick Douglas High School, No. 139, 140th Street, New York City, November 25, 1934, in NARS, RG126, File 9-11-2, Part 3 (1934).

Appendix

Letter from Governor Hastie to the Author
June 2, 1949

Mr. William W. Boyer, Jr.
108 Monroe Park
Madison, Wisconsin

Dear Mr. Boyer:

Thank you very much for the opportunity to read your Master's thesis entitled "Civil Liberties in the Virgin Islands of the United States." I very genuinely enjoyed the thesis. The style is interesting and it brings together a single conception of civil liberties a body of information nowhere else conveniently available in a single place.

I hesitate to ask whether I might keep the copy which you so very genuinely permitted me to read. If, however, this copy is additional to your needs for other purposes, I would like very much to keep it. Otherwise I will return it as soon as I hear from you.

The observations which I have to make of a critical nature are relatively minor but may interest you.

First of all, I believe the verdict of history will be that Governor Von Scholten seized the events of early July 1848 as a justification for the emancipation which he had wished to accomplish for a considerable period. He had been with the faction in Denmark, including the Queen, which had urged emancipation strongly. Von Scholten's arrest and conviction following the emancipation also strongly indicates that the course he followed was deliberate.

On page 84 you suggest that the American Presidents have not taken a personal interest in Virgin Islands affairs. As a matter of fact, President Truman has taken a very lively personal interest in Virgin Islands matters. He spent two days with us, February 22 and 23, 1948, and we are quite hopeful that he will return this year. His interest in the Virgin Islands Company as a development agency for this territory has been very keen. In his budget message to Congress this year he dealt with the subject specifically. Last June in approving a bill temporarily continuing the existence of the Virgin Islands Company he wrote quite sharply to Congress concerning the failure of the legislature to set the company up in such a manner as to carry out a long-range development program. The White House has on several occasions made specific representations to the Bureau of the Budget or to leaders of Congress with references to Virgin Islands matters. During recent months the President invited the new Chairman of the House Sub-committee on Territories to the White House, and it is understood that the President expressed his personal concern that Congress act upon pending legislation concerning the political status of several of our possessions as well as the pending Virgin Islands Company legislation.

On page 92 you refer to Luther Evans' view that the retaining of policy-making officials on the Central Administration Federal payroll is a device to maintain Washington control. This is not correct. These officials remain on the Federal payroll only so long as the local government is unable to add their salaries to the local budget. As a matter of fact we are constantly resisting pressure of the Bureau of the Budget to relieve the Federal Government of these positions. Local sentiment favors a transfer of such positions to the local budget, but the funds will not be available at least for several years.

On page 130 you speak of the original PWA grant of one million dollars to the Virgin Islands Company. You will probably be interested in the story of this grant. Governor Pearson, Secretary Ickes and others had worked vigorously for a long time in an attempt to get the money necessary to start the Virgin Islands Company program. They were not successful. Several appeals direct to the President failed. Finally they convinced him that he should act, and he scribbled in long hand on a piece of note paper addressed, as I remember, to Harry Hopkins, the words "Give Virgin Islands one million dollars."

I hope you enjoyed writing this thesis, as I am sure many will enjoy reading it if they only know of its existence. Again many thanks for the opportunity to read your work.

Sincerely yours,

Governor
William H. Hastie

Selected Bibliography

Anderson, John L. *Night of the Silent Drums, A Narrative of Slave Rebellion in the Virgin Islands.* New York: Charles Scribner's Sons, 1975.

Anstey, Roger. *The Atlantic Slave Trade and British Abolition, 1760–1810.* Atlantic Highlands, New Jersey: Humanities Press, 1975.

Armstrong, Irene. *Robert Skeoch: Cruzan Planter.* Christiansted, St. Croix: Armstrong, 1971.

Barrett, Leonard E. *The Rastafarians: Sounds of Cultural Dissonance.* Boston: Beacon Press, 1977.

Beisner, Robert L. *Twelve Against Empire: The Anti-Imperialists 1898–1900.* New York: McGraw-Hill Book Company, 1968.

Berkhofer, Robert F., Jr. "The Northwest Ordinance and the Principle of Territorial Evolution." In *The American Territorial System,* ed. John Porter Bloom. Athens, Ohio: Ohio University Press, 1973.

Bestor, Arthur. "Constitutionalism and the Settlement of the West: The Attainment of Consensus, 1754–1784." In *The American Territorial System,* ed. John Porter Bloom. Athens, Ohio: Ohio University Press, 1973.

Blanshard, Paul. *Democracy and Empire in the Caribbean.* New York: The Macmillan Company, 1947.

Blauch, L. E., and Reid, C. F. *Public Education in the Territories and Outlying Possessions.* Prepared for the President's Advisory Committee on Education. Washington: Government Printing Office, 1939.

Bonds, John M. "History of Service Activities in the Virgin Islands." *Immigration and Naturalization Service Monthly Review* 4 (December 1946).

Bonsal, Stephan. *The American Mediterranean.* New York: Moffat, Yard and Company, 1912.

Bough, James A. "Is Commonwealth Status the Next Step?" *The Virgin Islands Bar Journal* 5 (Summer 1974) 1: 1–21.

Bough, James A., and Macridis, Roy C., eds. *Virgin Islands, America's Caribbean Outpost—The Evolution of Self Government.* Wakefield, Mass.: Walter F. Williams Publishing Co., 1970.

Boyd, William M. *The Administration of Territories and Island Possessions by the United States*. Ph.D. dissertation, University of Michigan, 1944.

Boyer, William W. *Civil Liberties in the U.S. Virgin Islands 1917–1949*. St. Croix: Antilles Graphic Arts, 1982.

Boyer, William W. "From Territory to State: The Historical Record, the Constitution, and Unincorporated Territories Today." In Paul M. Leary, ed., *The Future Political Status of the United States Virgin Islands*. St. Thomas: University of the Virgin Islands, 1989.

Boyer, William W. "Rothschild Francis and Freedom of the Press in the U.S. Virgin Islands." *Caribbean Affairs* (Trinidad). Vol. 4, No. 4, 1991, 129–43.

Boyer, William W. "The First 130 Years of United States Colonial Policy, 1787–1917." In Paul M. Leary, ed., *Recent Developments in United States-Offshore Areas Relations*. St. Thomas: University of the Virgin Islands, 1988.

Boyer, William W. "The Navy and Labour in St. Croix. U.S. Virgin Islands, 1917–1931." *The Journal of Caribbean History*, (Barbados: University of the West Indies) 9 Vol. 20.1 (1985–6), 78–104.

Boyer, William W. "The United States Virgin Islands and Decolonization of the Eastern Caribbean." *The Review of Regional Studies*, Vol. 14, No. 3, Fall 1984.

Campbell, Albert A. *St. Thomas Negroes—A Study of Personality and Culture*. Psychological Monographs, vol. 55, no. 5, Evanston, Ill.: The American Psychological Association, Inc., Northwestern University, 1943.

Canegata, D.C. *St. Croix at the 20th Century, A Chapter in its History*. New York: Carlton Press, Inc., 1968.

Caron, Aimery. *Inventory of French Documents Pertaining to the U.S. Virgin Islands 1642–1737*, St. Thomas: Bureau of Libraries, Museums and Archeological Services, Occasional Paper no. 3, 1978.

Caron, Aimery, and Highfield, Arnold R. *Jean-Baptiste DuTertre on the French in St. Croix and the Virgin Islands: A Translation with Introduction and Notes*. St. Thomas: Bureau of Libraries, Museums and Archeological Services, Occasional Paper no. 4, 1978.

Clarke, John Henrik, ed. *Marcus Garvey and the Vision of Africa*. New York: Random House, 1974.

Commission for the Study of Nursing Needs and Resources in the United States Virgin Islands. *Study of Nursing Needs and Resources in the U.S. Virgin Islands*. St. Thomas: College of the Virgin Islands, 1976.

Coudert, F. R. "Evolution of the Doctrine of Incorporation." *Columbia Law Review* 36 (1926) 832.

Creque, Darwin D. *The U.S. Virgins and the Eastern Caribbean*. Philadelphia: Whitmore Publishing Co., 1968.

Curtin, Philip D. *The Atlantic Slave Trade: A Census.* Madison: University of Wisconsin Press, 1969.

Dalton, Robert H. *Childhood Behavior Problems in Social Focus, A Study of the Insular Training School, United States Virgin Islands.* St. Thomas: Division of Mental Health, Virgin Islands Department of Health, 1868.

Danielson, Gustav A. *Business Operations in the U.S. Virgin Islands.* Washington, D.C.: Tax Management Inc., 1978.

de Booy, Theodoor. *Archeology of the Virgin Islands.* New York: Museum of the American Indian, 1920.

de Booy, Theodoor, and Faris, John T. *The Virgin Islands, Our New Possessions and the British Islands.* Philadelphia and London: J. B. Lippincott Co., 1918, and Westport, Conn.: Negro Universities Press, 1970.

Department of Education, Government of the U.S. Virgin Islands. *Profiles of Outstanding Virgin Islanders.* St. Thomas, 1976.

Department of Interior, *Annual Reports of the Governor of the Virgin Islands, 1951–1970.*

de Zela, Peter Pardo. *The Impact of Change and Political Leadership, The Case of the U.S. Virgin Islands.* Ph.D. dissertation, Tulane University, 1978.

Dookhan, Isaac. *A History of the Virgin Islands of the United States.* St. Thomas: College of the Virgin Islands, Caribbean Universities Press, 1974.

Dookhan, Isaac. "The Virgin Islands Company and Corporation: The Plan for Economic Rehabilitation in the Virgin Islands." *The Journal of Caribbean History* 4 (May 1972): 54–76.

Eblen, Jack Ericson. *The First and Second United States Empires.* Pittsburgh: University of Pittsburgh Press, 1968.

Egan, Maurice Francis. *Ten Years Near the German Frontier.* New York: Hodder and Stoughton, 1918.

Elkins, Stanley. *Slavery, A Problem in American Institutional and Intellectual Life.* Chicago: University of Chicago Press, 1959.

Evans, Luther H. *The Virgin Islands from Naval Base to New Deal.* Ann Arbor, Mich.: J. W. Edwards, 1945.

Evans, W. *The Virgin Islands, A General Report by the Governor.* Washington, D.C.: Navy Department, 1928.

Freyre, Gilberto. *The Masters and the Slaves, A Study in the Development of Brazilian Civilization.* New York: Alfred A. Knopf, 1946.

Garner, J. W. "The Right of Jury Trial in the Dependencies." *American Law Review* 40 (1909) 340.

Geigel, Wilfredo A. *Salt River in St. Croix: Columbus' Landing Site?* Santurce, P.R.: El Libro, Inc., 2005.

Gibson, Margaret Alison. *Ethnicity and Schooling: A Caribbean Case Study.* Ph.D. dissertation, University of Pittsburgh, 1976.

Gill, Pat. *Buddhoe, The Man Who Shaped the History of St. Croix.* New York: Wentworth Press, 1976.

Gladwin, Ellis. *Living in the Changing Caribbean.* New York: The Macmillan Company, 1970.

Gore, H. Akia. *Garrote: The Illusion of Social Equality and Political Justice in the United States Virgin Islands.* New York: Wadadli Press, 2009.

Gould, Lyman Jay. *The Foraker Act, The Roots of American Colonial Policy.* Ph.D. dissertation, University of Michigan, 1958.

Goveia, E. V. *The West Indian Slave Laws of the 18th Century.* Barbados: Caribbean Universities Press, 1970.

Grede, Frederick. *The New Deal in the Virgin Islands, 1931–1941.* Ph.D. dissertation, University of Chicago, 1963.

Green, James W. *Social Networks in St. Croix, United States Virgin Islands.* Ph.D. dissertation, University of Washington, 1972.

Green-Pedersen, Svend Erik. "The History of the Danish Negro Slave Trade, An Interim Survey Relating in Particular to its Volume, Structure, Profitability and Abolition." *Revue Française d'Histoire d'Outre-Mer* (Paris: Société Francaise d'Histoire d'Outre-Mer, Librarie Orientaliste Paul Guenthner, 1975): 196–220.

Green-Pedersen, Svend Erik. "The Scope and Structure of the Danish Negro Slave Trade." *The Scandinavian Economic History Review* 19 (1971) 2: 149–197.

Haas, William H., ed. *The American Empire.* Chicago: University of Chicago Press, 1940.

Hall, Neville. "Anna Heegaard—Enigma." *Caribbean Quarterly* 22 (June–September 1976): 62–72.

Hall, Neville. "Slave Laws of the Danish Virgin Islands in the Late Eighteenth Century." In *Comparative Perspectives on Slavery in New World Plantation Societies,* ed. Vera Rubin and Arthur Tuden. Annals of the New York Academy of Sciences, vol. 292 (New York: New York Academy of Sciences, 1977), 174–185.

Hansen, Knud. *From Denmark to the Virgin Islands.* New York: Dorrance and Company, 1947.

Harrigan, Norwell. *Higher Education in the Micro-State: A Theory of a Raran Society.* Ph.D. dissertation, University of Pittsburgh, 1972.

Harrigan, Norwell, and Varlack, Pearl I. "The U.S. Virgin Islands and the Black Experience." *Journal of Black Studies* 7 (June 1977) 4: 387–409.

Harrigan, Norwell, and Varlack, Pearl I. *The Virgin Islands Story.* Epping, Essex, England: Caribbean Universities Press, Bowker Publishing Company, 1975.

Hayward, Du Bose. *Star Spangled Virgin*. New York: Farrar and Rinehart, 1939.

Heine, Carl. *Micronesia at the Crossroads, A Reappraisal of the Micronesian Political Dilemma*. Honolulu: University Press of Hawaii, 1974.

Highfield, Arnold R., in collaboration with Max Bumgarner, comp. and eds. *A Bibliography of Articles on the Danish West Indies and the United States Virgin Islands in the New York Times 1867–1975*. Gainesville, Florida: University Presses of Florida, 1978.

Highfield, Arnold R. *The French Dialect of St. Thomas, Virgin Islands: A Descriptive Grammar with Texts and Glossary*. Ann Arbor: Karoma Publishers, Inc., 1979.

Hill, Valdemar, A., Sr. *Rise to Recognition, An Account of Virgin Islanders from Slavery to Self-Government*. St. Thomas: St. Thomas Graphics Inc., 1971.

Hoetink, Harry. *Caribbean Race Relations: A Study of Two Variants*. London, Oxford, New York: Oxford University Press, 1967.

Hoetink, Harry. *Slavery and Race Relations in the Americas: Comparative Notes on Their Nature and Nexus*. New York: Harper & Row, Publishers, 1973.

Holbrook, Sabra. *The American West Indies, Puerto Rico and the Virgin Islands*. New York: Meredith Press, 1969.

Hoover, Herbert A. "Observations and Recommendations Concerning Public Education in the United States Virgin Islands." *The Journal of the College of the Virgin Islands* 2 (May 1976): 66–73.

Horowitz, Michael M., ed. *Peoples and Cultures of the Caribbean, An Anthropological Essay*. Garden City, N.Y.: The Natural History Press, 1971.

Jarvis, J. Antonio. *A Brief History of the Virgin Islands*. St. Thomas: The Art Shop, 1938.

Jarvis, J. Antonio. *The Virgin Islands and Their People*. Philadelphia: Dorrance & Company, 1944.

Johnson, Robert Amandus, *Saint Croix 1770-1776: The First Salute to the Stars and Stripes*. Bloomington, Indiana: Author House, 2006.

Klein, Herbert. *Slavery in the Americas: A Comparative Study of Virginia and Cuba*. Chicago: University of Chicago Press, 1967.

Knox, John P. *A Historical Account of St. Thomas, V.I.* New York: Charles Scribner, 1852, and St. Thomas: College of the Virgin Islands, 1966.

Koht, Halvdab. "The Origin of Seward's Plan to Purchase the Danish West Indies." *The American Historical Review* 50 (July 1945) 4: 762–767.

Krigger, Marilyn F. *A Quarter-century of Race Relations in the U.S. Virgin Islands, St. Thomas, 1950–1975*. Ph.D. dissertation, University of Delaware, 1984.

Kruvant, William Jay. *Socio-economic Development in the U.S. Virgin Islands: An Historical Materialist Approach*. Ph.D. dissertation, American University, 1976.

Langer, Marshall J., and Danielson, Gustav A. *The British Virgin Islands—A Low-Tax Base with Treaty Benefits.* Englewood Cliffs, N.J.: Prentice-Hall, Inc., 1978.

Lansing, Robert. "Drama of the Virgin Islands Purchase." *The New York Times Magazine* 80 (July 19, 1931) sec. 5.

Larsen, Jens. *Virgin Islands Story, A History of The Lutheran State Church, Other Churches, Slavery, Education, and Culture in the Danish West Indies, now the Virgin Islands.* Philadelphia: Muhlenberg Press, 1950.

Larsen, Kay. *Dansk Vestindien, 1666–1917.* Copenhagen: C. A. Reitzel, 1928.

Lawaetz, Eva, ed., trans., comp. *Free Coloured in St, Croix, 1744–1816.* Christiansted, St. Croix: 1979.

Lawaetz, Eva, ed. and trans. *Oxholm's Report of 1816: A Report from Governor General P. L. Oxholm to the Royal Westindian Chamber in Copenhagen (Det Kongelige Vestindiske Kammer) Dated May 4, 1816, St. Croix.* Christiansted, St, Croix: 1977.

Leary, Paul M., ed. *Major Political and Constitutional Documents of the United States Virgin Islands 1671–1991.* St. Thomas: University of the Virgin Islands, 1992.

Leibowitz, Arnold H. *Colonial Emancipation in the Pacific and the Caribbean, A Legal and Political Analysis.* New York: Praeger Publishers, 1976.

Leibowitz, Arnold H. *Defining Status: A Comprehensive Analysis of United States Territorial Relations.* Dordrecht, The Netherlands: Martinus Nijhoff Publishers, 1989.

Leibowitz, Arnold H. "The Applicability of Federal Law to Guam." *Virginia Journal of International Law* 16 (Fall 1975) 1: 21–63.

Leibowitz, Arnold H. "United States Federalism: The States and the Territories." *The American University Law Review* 28 (Summer 1979) 4: 479–482.

Lewis, Gordon K. *Puerto Rico: Freedom and Power in the Caribbean.* New York: M R Press, 1963.

Lewis, Gordon K. "The U.S. Virgin Islands: Prototype of the Caribbean Tourist Economy." In *Politics and Economics in the Caribbean,* eds. T. G. Mathews and F. M. Andic. Rio Pietras, Puerto Rico: Institute of Caribbean Studies, University of Puerto Rico, 1971, 217–243.

Lewis, Gordon K. *The Virgin Islands: A Caribbean Lilliput.* Evanston, Ill.: Northwestern University Press, 1972.

Lewisohn, Florence. *St. Croix Under Seven Flags.* Hollywood, Florida: The Dukane Press, 1970.

Lewisohn, Florence. *"What So Proudly We Hail," The Danish West Indies and the American Revolution.* St. Croix: Prestige Press, 1975.

Lovett, Robert Morss. *All Our Years.* New York: The Viking Press, 1948.

Macauley, Zachary. *Negro Slavery*. London: Hatchard and Son of Picadilly and J. Arch of Cornhill, 1823.

May, Ernest R. *Imperial Democracy, The Emergence of America as a Great Power.* New York: Harcourt, Brace & World, Inc., 1961.

McElroy, Jerome L. "Tourist Economy and Island Environment: An Overview of Structural Disequilibrium." *Caribbean Educational Bulletin*. San Juan, Puerto Rico: Association of Caribbean Universities, 2 (January 1975) 1.

McFerson, Hazel M. *The Impact of a Changed Racial Tradition: Race, Politics and Society in the U.S. Virgin Islands, 1917–1975*. Ph.D. dissertation, Brandeis University, 1975.

McHenry, Donald F. *Micronesia: Trust Betrayed*. New York: Carnegie Endowment for International Peace, 1975.

McMahon, Stephanie Hunter. "You Pay for What You Get: The U.S. Virgin Islands, 1917–1936." *The Journal of Caribbean History* (Barbados: University of the West Indies) Vol. 41: 1 & 2 (2007).

Miller, Mark J. and Boyer, William W. "Foreign Workers in the USVI: History of a Dilemma." *Caribbean Review*, Vol. 11, No. 2 (Winter 1982).

Miller, Richard W. *The Economy of the Virgin Islands*. Washington, D.C.: Office of Territorial Affairs, Department of the Interior, 1979.

Mills, Frank L. *A Study of Juvenile Offenders in St. Thomas and St. Croix, USVI.* St. Thomas: Eastern Caribbean Center, University of the Virgin Islands, June 2003.

Moore, Herman E. "The Virgin Islands and Its Judicial System." 3 *National Bar Journal* 352 (1945).

Moorhead, Mario C. *Mammon vs. History*. St. Croix: Square Deal Printer, 1973.

Morison, Samuel Eliot. *Journals and Other Documents on the Life and Voyages of Christopher Columbus*. New York: Limited Editions Club, 1963.

Morison, Samuel Eliot. *Second Voyage of Christopher Columbus from Cádiz to Hispaniola and the Discovery of the Lesser Antilles*. Oxford: Clarendon Press, 1939.

Murphy, Patricia Gill. *The Education of the New World Blacks in the Danish West Indies/U.S. Virgin Islands: A Case Study of Social Transition*. Ph.D. dissertation, University of Connecticut, 1977.

Myrdal, Gunnar. *An American Dilemma, The Negro Problem and Modern Democracy*. New York: Harper & Brothers Publishers, 1944.

Naughton, Ezra A. *The Origin and Development of Higher Education in the Virgin Islands*. Ph.D. dissertation, Catholic University of America, 1973.

Nettleford, Rex M. *Mirror Mirror: Identity, Race and Protest in Jamaica*. Jamaica: William Collins and Sangster Ltd., 1970.

Nevin, David. *The American Touch in Micronesia*. New York: W. W. Norton & Co., 1977.

Norregard, Georg. *Danish Settlements in West Africa 1658–1850*. Boston: Boston University Press, 1966.

Oldendorp, C. G. A. *Geschichte der Mission der evangelischen Breuder auf den caraibischen Inseln S. Thomas, S. Croix und S. Jan*, trans.: *History of the Mission of the Evangelican Brethren on the Caribbean Islands of St, Thomas, St. Croix and St, John*. Leipzig, Germany: Barby, 1777.

O'Neill, Edward A. *Rape of the Virgin Islands*. New York: Praeger Publishers, 1972.

Orlins, Martin Garson. *The Impact of Tourism on the Virgin Islands of the United States*. Ph.D. dissertation, Columbia University, 1969.

Ottley, Earle B. *The Hardball Years: A Chronicle of Politics, Progress, and Pain in the U.S. Virgin Islands*. St. Thomas, USVI: Earle B. Ottley, 1994.

Ottley, Earle B. *Trials and Triumphs: The Long Road to a Middle Class Society in the U.S. Virgin Islands*. St. Thomas, USVI: Earle B. Ottley, 1982.

Perkins, Dexter. *The United States and the Caribbean*. Rev. ed. Cambridge, Mass.: Harvard University Press, 1966.

Perkins, Whitney T. *American Policy in the Government of its Dependent Areas— A Study of the Policy of the United States toward the Inhabitants of its Territories and Insular Possessions*. Ph.D. dissertation, Fletcher School of Law and Diplomacy, 1948.

Perkins, Whitney T. *Denial of Empire, The United States and its Dependencies*. Leyden, Netherlands: A. W. Sythoff, 1962.

Pope, Pauline Holman. *Cruzan Slavery: An Ethnohistorical Study of Differential Responses to Slavery in the Danish West Indies*. Ph.D. dissertation, University of California, Davis, 1969.

Postma, Johannes. *The Dutch Participation in the African Slave Trade: Slaving on the Guinea Coast, 1675–1795*. Ph.D. dissertation, Michigan State University, 1970.

Pratt, Julius W. *America's Colonial Experiment*. New York: Prentice Hall, Inc., 1950.

Reid, Charles F., ed. *Bibliography of the Virgin Islands of the United States*. New York: The H. W. Wilson Company, 1941.

Reid, Charles F. *Education in the Territories and Outlying Possessions of the United States*. New York: Bureau of Publications, Teachers College, Columbia University, 1941.

Scofield, John. "Virgin Islands: Tropical Playland, U.S.A." *The National Geographic Magazine* (February 1956): 201–232.

Sekou, Malik. *Nation-state Formation in the Insular Caribbean Before, During, and After the Cold War*. Ph.D. dissertation, University of Delaware, 2000.

Senior, Clarence. *The Puerto Rican Migrant in St. Croix*. San Juan, Puerto Rico: Social Science Research Center, University of Puerto Rico, 1947.

Seward, Olive Risley. "A Diplomatic Episode." *Scribner's Magazine* 2 (November 1887) 5: 585–602.

Sircar, K. K. "Emigration of Indian Indentured Labour to the Danish West Indian Island of St. Croix, 1863–68." *The Scandinavian Economic History Review* 19 (1971) 2: 133–148.

Spingarn, Laurence P. "Slavery in the Danish West Indies." *The American Scandinavian Review* 45 (March 1957) 1: 35–43.

Stephen, James. *The Slavery of the British West India Islands.* London: Joseph Butterworth and Son, 1824; New York: Kraus Reprint Co., 1969.

Tannenbaum, Frank. *Slave and Citizen, The Negro in the Americas.* New York: Alfred A. Knopf, 1947.

Tansill, Charles C. *The Purchase of the Danish West Indies.* Baltimore: The Johns Hopkins Press, 1932.

Taylor, Charles E. *Leaflets from the Danish West Indies.* London: Wm. Dawson and Sons, 1888; reprinted New York: Negro Universities Press, 1970.

Thomas, Hugh. *Cuba: The Pursuit of Freedom.* New York: Harper & Row, 1971.

Toplin, Robert Brent, ed. *Slavery and Race Relations in Latin America.* Westport, Conn.: Greenwood Press, 1974.

Trillin, Calvin. "U.S. Journal: St. Croix, American Virgin Islands, Indigenous Population." *The New Yorker* February 25, 1974, 111–116.

Tucker, Rufus S. *Report on Economic Conditions in the Virgin Islands.* 69th Cong., 2d sess., Sen. Doc. No. 41 (1925).

Turnbull, Charles Wesley. *The Structural Development of a Public Education System in the Virgin Islands, 1917–1970: A Functional Analysis in Historical Perspective.* Ph.D. dissertation, University of Minnesota, 1976.

Tyson, George F., Jr. *Powder, Profits & Privateers, A Documentary History of the Virgin Islands During the Era of the American Revolution.* St. Thomas: Bureau of Libraries, Museums and Archeological Services, Occasional Paper no. 1, 1977.

Vallee, Lionel. *The Negro Family on St. Thomas, A Study of Role Differentiation.* Ph.D. dissertation, Cornell University, 1964.

Van Cleve, Ruth G. *The Office of Territorial Affairs.* New York: Praeger, 1974.

Varlack, Pearl I. *Teacher Education in the Virgin Islands: A Strategy for Curriculum Design.* Ph.D. dissertation, University of Pittsburgh, 1974.

Vaughn, Robert W. *The Virgin Islands of the United States: Social, Economic, and Political Conditions Referred to in Recent Periodical Literature.* Christiansted, St. Croix: Aye-Aye Press, 1974.

Walrond, Eric D. "Autocracy in the Virgin Islands." *Current History* 19 (October 1923) 1: 121–123.

Weinberg, Albert K. *Manifest Destiny.* Baltimore: The Johns Hopkins Press, 1935.

Weinstein, Edwin A. *Cultural Aspects of Delusion: A Psychiatric Study of the Virgin Islands.* New York: Free Press, 1962.

Westergaard, Waldemar. "Account of the Negro Rebellion on St. Croix, Danish West Indies, 1759." *Journal of Negro History* 11 (January 1926) 1: 50–61.

Westergaard, Waldemar. *The Danish West Indies Under Company Rule (1671–1754).* New York: The Macmillan Company, 1917.

Williams, Eric. *Capitalism and Slavery.* Chapel Hill: University of North Carolina Press, 1944.

Williams, Eric. *From Columbus to Castro: The History of the Caribbean 1492–1969.* New York: Harper & Row, Publishers, 1970.

Williams, Eric. "Race Relations in Puerto Rico and the Virgin Islands." *Foreign Affairs* 23 (January 1945): 308–317.

Willis, Jean Louise. *The Trade between North America and the Danish West Indies, 1756 to 1807, With Special Reference to St. Croix.* Ph.D. dissertation, Columbia University, 1963.

Willoughby, William Franklin. *Territories and Dependencies of the United States: Their Government and Administration.* New York: The Century Co., 1905.

Woolbert, R. G. "Rehabilitation in the Virgin Islands." *Foreign Affairs* 17 (July 1939) 4: 799–804.

Index

Abbott, Patricia, xv
ABC Television, xxxiii
Abolitionists, 36, 54
absenteeism, 282
Accreditation of Hospitals, Joint
    Commission, 351
Adams, Sr., Alton, 119, 221
admiralty, 192n
adult education, 164
adultery, 190
Africa, xviii, 2–5, 15–22, 25, 31,
    35, 36, 172n, 347n
African Methodist Church, 132
Afro-Caribbean, 337, 339
Afro-Puerto Ricans, 336
aged, 22, 67, 230
Agnew, Vice-President Spiro, 320
Agricultural Experiment Station, St.
    Croix, 74, 120
Agriculture, 7, 12–14, 16, 24, 53,
    62, 74, 121, 152, 162, 167, 170,
    177, 181, 182, 190, 209, 250,
    264, 267, 268, 317, 360n, 383
Agriculture, US Dept. of, 121
Agriculture, VI, US Dept. of, 121
Ah Deh UP, 332
air travel, 211, 245, 248, 254, 264
airport improvement, 248, 357
Akin, Bernita, 383n
Alaska, 86n, 90, 97n, 105, 126, 285,
    368

Alaskan Code, 126
Alexander, Governor Archibald,
    238–242
Alexander v. Todman, 275n, 276n
Alexis, George, xx
Ali, Ishmael Muslim (Ishmael La
    Beet), 324, 349–350
Alien Interest Movement, xviii, 302,
    309, 340n, 391
Alien Registration Act, 195n
Alien Reunification Act (PL91-225),
    294
alienated, 292–333, 346, 348, 368,
    385
alienation of precious resources,
    291
aliens, xviii, 59, 67–68, 71, 85, 100,
    131–132, 133, 144, 147, 149n,
    170–171, 197, 198, 225, 248,
    249, 265, 267, 270, 285, 288,
    296–302, 317, 321, 333, 335,
    338, 339–344, 390–392, 405,
    406
all white enclave, 315
Allick, Myron, 327
Allied Virgin Islands Societies, 154,
    430n
Allott, Senator Gordon, 293
alumina, 259, 270, 296, 307, 317
ambivalent suspension, 270
Ambrose, Daniel, 241

Amerada Petroleum Corporation, *see* Hess

American Bar Association, 127n, 128n

American Caribbean Contracting Company, 239

American Civil Liberties Union, 128n, 137, 147, 148, 149n, 185, 235

American Consul, in Barbados, 131n

American Consul, in St. Croix, 70

American Federation of Labor, 130

American Historical Review, 77n

American Law Review, 105n

American Molasses Company, 178

American Philosophical Society (Penrose Fund), xvii

American Revolution, 3, 15n, 35, 91

American St. Gaubain Company, 294

American Scandinavian Review, 24n

American University Law Review, 430n

American Virgin Islands Civic Association, 200, 239

Americanization, 123–125, 127, 139, 143, 337n

"America's Paradise," 305, 385

amnesty, 26, 340

Anderson, Jack, 316

Anderson, John L., 32n

Andic, F. M., 264

Anduze, Madeleine, xv

Anduze, Dr. Roy, 230, 291n

Anglicans, 47, 49, 63, 133n, 266

Anglo-American Group, 203n

Anguilla, 246, 312, 340

"Annapolis mentality," 114

Anna's Hope Detention Center, 326, 347

annexation, opposition to, 283, 378

annihilation, fear of, 342

Annual Reports to United Nations, 207, 212n

Anstey, Roger, 36n

anti-colonialism, 165

Anti-discrimination Act of 1950, 260

anti-discrimination law, 211

Antigua, 26, 51n, 67, 71, 162n, 196n, 245, 246, 308, 312, 340

Antigua, Bishop of, 67

anti-imperialists, 94, 97

Antilles, Greater, xxiii, 5

Antilles, Lesser, xxiii, 4, 5, 299, 325, 335, 339

Anti-lynching Bill, Costigan-Wagner, 178n

Antilles Yachting Corp., 319n

Anti-Saloon League, 179

Antislavery protests, 35

Anti-Slavery Society of England, 47

apartheid, de facto, 315

Apollo Theater, 311

Aqua Chem, 353

Aquinas, Thomas, 21, 24

Arab merchants, 354n

Arawaks, xxv, 405

Archeology, 5n

Arizona, 152, 285

Arizona, battleship, 152

armed robbery, 303

armed services, US, Virgin Islanders in, 212

Armstrong, Edwin, xx

Armstrong, Irene, 69n

Army, US, 147n, 208, 314, 382

Arnold, Benedict, 160

art, 115, 172, 200, 372
Articles of Confederation, 90, 105
Aruba, 271, 423
Aspinall, Congressman Wayne, 282
Association of Caribbean Universities, 321n
Atlantic Ocean, xxiii, 18n, 78
At-large council members, 186
At-large members of the Legislature, 236, 277, 278
Attorney General, U.S., 145, 186
Attorney General, V.I., 291, 310, 414
Audain, George E., 131
Austria, 77
autocracy, 120, 127, 132n, 133, 143, 147, 149

Baa, Enid M., xx, 17n, 195
"Babylon," 346
Back-of-All, 117n
Bahamas, 196n, 203n, 211
"bailouts," 369
balance of payments, 366
Baldwin, Hanson, 156n, 159, 160n, 169, 174, 176n, 179n
Baldwin, Roger, 128n, 137, 235
Balkanization, 377
Ballentine, Warren, 325, 327
Baltimore, 79, 97, 128
Balzac v. United States, 105n, 108n
bank deposits, 258, 311
bankruptcy, 13, 230, 243, 368n
Barbary, 11
Barbados, 18, 21, 68n, 71, 131, 132, 170, 203n, 246, 359, 393
Barck, Jr., Oscar T., 106n
barging of water, 245, 351
Barnes v. Government of V.I., 348n
Barrett, Leonard E., 346n

Barrett, R. E., 117, 130
Barrow, Reginald G., 132
Bartlett, Kenneth A., 256n
Bassin, *see* Christiansted
bauxite, 259, 270
Bay of Pigs, xxii
bay rum, 121n, 145n
beaches, 251, 267, 289, 314, 318–320, 379, 423, 424
Beale, Nicholas, 323, 324
Beatty, Harry A., 192, 195
Bederman, Julie, xv
Beccaria, 33
Beisner, Robert L., 97n
Bengal, 68
Benitez, Resident Commissioner Jaime, 374n
Benjamin, Lawrence, Dr., xv
Benjamin, Ulrich, xx
Bennewith, Eleanor B., 336n
Bentsen, Senator Lloyd M., 233
Bentzon, Adrian, 49
Berkhofer, Jr., Robert F., 90
Berle, Jr., A. A., 137, 147
Bermuda, 211, 335
Berne, Emile, 130
Bestor, Arthur, 90n
Bethlehem (Pa), 47
Bicentennial, xix
Bidwell, *see Delima v. Bidwell, Downes v. Bidwell*
"Big Stick" Corollary, *see* Roosevelt Corollary
Bilbo, Senator Theodore G., 193
bilingual education, 336, 338n
Bill of Rights, U.S., 104, 275
Bill of Rights, V.I., 143, 144, 182, 226
bills of attainder, prohibition, 275
biological, chemical testing, 382

Bishop, J. Edward, 314
"Black Moses," *see* D. Hamilton
  Jackson
"black power ideology," 286n
black power militants, 289n
black power movement, 303
Blackbeard, 255
blackmail, 281
Blackstone, William, 105
Blair, Henry C., 111
Blake, Nelson M., 106
Blake, Patricia, 346, 371
Blanshard, Paul, 26, 174
Blauch, L. E., 206
Bloom, John Porter, 90
Bluebeard, 163
Bluebeard's Castle Hotel, 163
Bornn, Steve, 346, 350
Boston, 16, 89, 158, 176, 292, 346
Botanical Experiment Station, St.
  Croix, 74
Bough, Ingrid A., Dr., xv
Bough, James A., 64, 189, 234–236,
  238, 283, 378
Bough, Ralph, 76
Bove, Federal Comptroller Peter A.,
  282
Bovoni Project, 344
Bowles, Robert, 315
boycott, 130, 310
Boyd, William M., 102
Boyer, Barbara Massey, xxi
Boyer, Helen Hoy, v, xv
Boyer, Nancy E., Dr., xv
Boyer, William W., 58, 89, 131,
  136, 177, 297, 391, 393, 396,
  402, 421, 431
"Bracero Program," 297
Bradshaw, Premier Robert, 312

Brady, U.S. Attorney Julio, 323,
  324, 369
Bramson, Leon, 72
Branch, Commissioner Milton C.,
  384
Brandenburg Trading Company, 12,
  16
Brauhaus, 328, 329, 331
Brauhaus murders, 328, 329, 331
Brazil, 13, 23, 78
Brazilian, 13, 23, 437
Bretons, 4
Brewer's Bay, 210
"bribery," 82, 355, 371
Britain, Great, 9, 36, 54, 70, 77, 81,
  196n, 203, 335
British Commonwealth, 246
British Consul, in St. Croix, 68
British Government, 67, 77, 298,
  312
British Guiana, *see* Guyana
British Honduras, *see* Belize, 203,
  393
British occupation, 30, 37, 38, 43
British Virgin Islands, 4, 31, 37, 54,
  73, 170, 171, 197, 233, 245, 296,
  298, 299, 311, 312, 339, 340,
  393
British West Indies, 15, 43, 50, 51,
  53, 58, 162, 170, 246, 268, 299,
  311
British West Indies Federation, 246
Brodhurst, Canute A., 192–195,
  280
Bronx, The, 196
Brooklyn, 196
Brown, H. Rap, 325
Brown, Herbert D., 122, 150, 154
Brown, Henry, 188
Brown, Louis, 212

Brown, Councilman Omar, xx, 188–189, 190n, 231
Browne, Anvil, xx
Browne, Otis, 120
Buchanan, Secretary of State James, 93
Buck Island (St. Croix), xxiii
Buddhoe, "General," *see* Moses Gottlieb, 57, 58, 438
budget, 65, 121, 122, 155, 180, 203, 207, 230, 234, 242, 248, 250, 288, 335, 368, 373, 374, 415, 416, 421, 422
Budget, Bureau of the, 180, 207
Buffington, Joseph, 160
Burdick, Senator Quentin, 293
Burgess, John W., 94
Burgher Council, St. Croix, 30
Burgher Councils, 65
burial at sea, 331
Burnet, August, 117
Burton, Congressman Philip, 367
business failures, 258
Business Week, 361
Butler, Senator Hugh, 209, 234, 235, 238
button factory, 230
"Byzantine intrigues," 373

Calcutta, 67, 68
Caldwell, Congressman Charles P., 113
Caldwell, Earl, 329
California, 30, 93, 242, 245, 247
California, University of, 30, 242
campaign disclosures, 377
Campbell, Albert A., 30, 41, 169
Canaday, Ward, 195
Caneel Bay Plantation, Inc., 252
cannery, 258

Cannon, Benita, 352, 357
Canton, Annice, xv
Canton v. Todman, 277, 278
capital improvements, 155, 208, 209
capitalism, 15, 156
Caravelle, cruise ship, 360
Carenage, *see* Frenchtown, 219, 357,
Carey, Congressman Hugh, 281
Caribbean, 3–5, 8, 12, 15, 17, 21, 23, 26, 28, 29, 31, 39–41, 48–50, 52, 71, 72, 78, 81, 83, 84, 86, 95, 100, 106–108, 111, 114, 115, 124, 125, 131, 136, 151, 165, 170, 171, 174, 177, 186, 196, 199, 203, 207, 211, 212, 234, 237, 239, 246, 247, 249, 251, 256, 258, 264, 265, 267, 271, 284, 286, 288, 289, 291, 296–298, 302, 303, 310, 312, 314, 316, 319, 321, 335–337, 339–342, 346, 358, 359, 363, 381, 391–394, 397, 402, 403, 405, 408, 409, 411, 418, 423–425, 428, 429
Caribbean Commission, 203
Caribbean Educational Bulletin, 321
Caribbean Quarterly, 50
Caribbean Review, 131, 297, 342, 391, 393
Caribs, 3, 405
Carlyle, R. W. & A. J., 22
Carnival, 340
Caron, Aimery, 6
Carrera, Annamaria, xx
Carroll, Dr. Henry K., 98
Carter, President Jimmy, 394

Carver, Assistant Interior Secretary John A., 257, 260
casino gambling, 320, 423
Castro, Fidel, xxiii
catchments, water, 120, 352
Catholics, 21, 26, 63, 156
"cauldron, simmering," 68, 335, 373
Census, xxv, 14, 18, 34, 80, 174, 249, 299, 321, 322, 389, 411
Centerline Road, 13
Central Factory, 68, 70, 73, 74
Century Magazine, 168
certiorari, writ of, 138
Chamber of Commerce, St. Croix, 349, 356
Chamber of Commerce, St. Thomas, 239, 331, 332
Chanca, Dr., 2
Chapman, Interior Secretary Oscar: 177, 212
Chapman, Troy, 347
Charles Harwood Memorial Hospital, 350
Charlotte Amalie, Queen, 58, 85, 431
Charlotte Amalie town, 11, 337
Chautauqua, 153
Chicago, 23, 86, 151, 158, 191, 192, 208, 325
Chicago Seven, 325
child labor, 148, 187
children, homeless, 347
Christian IV, 9
Christian V, 9, 11
Christian VI, 45, 46
Christian VIII, 56
Christian, Elena, 124
Christian, Judge Almeric, 305, 325, 328, 349

Christianity, 38, 46
Christiansted, 5, 14, 38–41, 48, 49, 57, 60, 63, 68–70, 73, 76, 120, 124, 192, 216, 219, 220, 223, 224, 291, 308, 309, 311, 318, 320, 324, 325, 328, 345, 356, 371, 403
Christiansted High School, 219
Christmas, 60, 115, 116
Chudoff, Congressman Earl, 230, 241, 243
Ciboneys, xxv
Cicero, 22
Cintron, Senator Hector, 371, 382
citizens, naturalized, 309, 332, 340
citizenship, Danish, 79, 82, 85, 88, 114, 139
citizenship, U.S., 168, 299, 404, 428
Civic Betterment Assn., 157n
Civic Betterment Club, 157
civil liberties, 92, 105, 128, 133, 137, 147, 148, 185, 235, 429
civil rights, 63, 82, 88, 93, 97, 101–103, 140, 147, 151, 165, 203, 205, 211, 259, 260, 302, 306, 310, 347, 400
Civil Rights, President's Committee on, 205
Civil Rights Commission, V.I., 259
civil rights law, 211
Civil War, American, 77
Civilian Conservation Corps, 166
civilian government, 148, 156
Clarke, John Henrik, 347
class, 7, 34, 38–41, 43, 52, 61, 67, 69, 71, 73, 76, 85, 116, 125, 129, 131, 162, 170, 174, 175, 190, 219, 300, 304, 307, 317, 322, 323, 336, 338, 345, 394
classified system, 161, 278, 279, 293

Claunch, Government Secretary Charles, 241
Claussen, Peter, 30
Clen v. Jorgensen, 126
Clendinen, Vincen M., xx
Cleveland, Grover, 95
clubs, private, 259, 260, 272, 292
Coastal Zone Management Act, 319
coastwise laws, 145, 148, 155
Code Noir, 21
Codes of 1920-21, 126–128, 139
coffee, 7
Cogswell, Cathleen, 350, 351, 381, 383
Coki Point, 319
Colcord, Joanna C., 156, 177
College of Virgin Islands, 5, 11, 17, 48, 49, 121, 125, 170, 259, 290, 292, 300–302, 320, 339, 343–345, 350, 352, 393, 417
Colliers, 179
Collins, John, xx, 329n, 341n, 353, 381, 390
Colombia, 106, 309
Colonial Council, St. Croix, 65, 68, 122, 145, 157, 176, 184
Colonial Council for St. Thomas-St. John, 122, 132, 133, 144, 145, 176, 184, 189, 191n
Colonial Council of 1852, 64
Colonial Councils of 1863, 65
"colonial ladder," 237, 379
Colonial Law of 1852, 64–65
Colonial Law of 1863, 65, 69, 114, 184
Colonial Law of 1906, 66, 114, 123, 126, 144, 155, 174, 184
"Colonial Office, American," 167
colonialism, 3–20, 37, 72, 75, 111, 173, 250, 272, 370, 371, 423

color, 41, 51, 52, 61, 72, 114, 115, 118, 133, 171, 174, 175, 187, 198, 199, 211, 253, 259, 269, 285, 338
"color line," 199
Colorado, 285
Columbia Law Review, 104
Columbia University, 15, 124, 152, 264, 265
Columbus, 3–21, 26, 28, 31, 53, 55, 107
Comenius, 44
Commager, Henry Steele, 89, 106
Commerce, V.I. Department of, 258, 268n
Commission, Offshore, Presidential, proposed creation of, 337n
Commission to Investigate Industrial and Economic Conditions in the VI, USA, Federal, 172n
Committee on Appropriations, House, 208
Committee on Appropriations, Senate, 182n, 208
Committee on Energy and Natural Resources, Senate, 370
Committee on Insular Affairs, House, 185, 282, 284
Committee on Insular Possessions, House, 148
Committee on Interior and Insular Affairs, House, 282, 284
Committee on Interior and Insular Affairs, Senate, 179, 239, 255, 294
Committee on Pacific islands and Puerto Rico, U.S. Senate, 9
Committee on Population, Legal and Illegal Immigration to the U.S., House Select, 330n

Committee on Public Lands, House, 181

Committee on Territories and Insular Possessions, U.S. Senate, 138, 147, 148n, 159n, 161, 165, 185, 186, 313

Committee on the Judiciary, U.S. Senate, 341

Committee on Ways and Means, House, 209

common law, English, 23

common law marriage, 39, 127, 171

commonwealth status, 235, 237, 238, 246, 378

communism, 236

"communists," 189, 195

communists, 189, 195

Community Relations Service, 341

competition, tourism, 211

Compiled Code, 134, 137

comptroller, local, 283, 371

Concerned Virgin Islanders for Action, Inc., 342

Concerned West Indians Movement, 309

condemnation, 260–263, 313, 316

condominiums, 315, 318, 320, 322

Confederate Army, 104

conflict between governor and Congressional delegate, 373

conflict between governor and judges, 184

conflict between governor and legislative branch, 184, 185, 187, 207, 213–214, 229, 241, 242, 249n, 373, 418

conflict between governor and lieutenant governor, 373, 375, 420

conflict of interest, 239, 352

Congress, Act of March 3, 1917, 112, 113, 122, 126, 139, 143

Congress, U.S., 82, 85, 88, 90, 91–94, 95n, 96, 97n, 99, 100, 101, 103, 104, 105, 107, 112, 114, 119, 122n, 137, 139–140, 144, 145, 146, 147n, 148, 149, 150, 151, 155, 160, 161, 179, 180, 185, 186, 187, 199, 200, 202, 205n, 206, 207, 208, 209n, 232, 234, 236, 238, 239, 240, 246, 248, 251, 255, 260, 261, 263, 268, 269n, 273, 276, 278, 280–281, 283–284, 285–286, 289, 303, 314, 315, 316, 340, 342, 351, 364n, 366, 367, 368, 369, 370, 371, 374, 378, 379, 380, 389, 390, 392, 394, 397, 398, 399, 400, 401, 404, 417, 427–430, 432

Congress of Racial Equality, 302

Congressional Record, 97, 100, 101, 113, 186, 209, 368

conjugal rights, 325, 326

Connecticut, 44, 111, 147, 353

consciousness raising, 301

Conservation Society, V.I., 358, 424

consolidation of agencies, 239

constitution, local, 94, 379, 381

Constitution, U.S., 280, 285, 300, 305, 348, 400, 404, 429, 430

Constitutional Convention, First, 282, 389, 393

Constitutional Convention, Second, 282, 378

Constitutional Convention, Third, 379, 389, 428

Constitutional Convention, Fourth, 381, 389, 399

Constitutional Convention, U.S., 104

construction boom, 203, 229, 296

consultants, 240, 290, 303

container port, Hess, 358, 363

contempt of court, 132, 137, 138, 191, 195

continentals, 168, 174, 234, 266, 270, 288, 289, 292, 299, 300, 318, 320–322, 339, 363, 385, 390

Contract Day, St. Croix, *see* Labor Riot of 1878, 68–71, 81, 299

contracts, labor, 68, 71, 148, 299

Controlled Foreign Corporation status, 366

convention center, St. Croix, 320

Coolidge, President Calvin, 132

"coolies," *see* East Indians, 68

Copeman, Dr. Chester, 383

Copenhagen, 9, 11, 33, 35–38, 42, 45, 48, 62, 67, 76, 82, 83, 85–87, 153

Coral Bay, xxiv

Coral World, 319

Corbin, Carlyle, Dr., xv, 396n,

Cordova-Davila, Felix, Puerto Rican Resident Commissioner, 147n

Corner, George W., xvii

Correctional Facility, Golden Grove Adult, 347

corrections, 345, 349

La Correspondencia, 131

corruption, 159–161, 290, 291, 361, 410, 411, 413

Corrupt Practices Act, 274

cost of living, 208

cotton, 4, 13, 14, 163, 230

Court of Appeals, Third Circuit, 133, 192, 209, 276

Court of Claims, 200

Court of the Virgin Islands, US District, xx, 126, 127, 128, 133, 134, 137, 138, 148n, 149n, 159, 174, 186, 191–192, 247, 269n, 274, 277, 305, 308, 312, 323n, 325, 326, 327, 328, 344n, 347, 349, 379

Courtney, W. B., 179

courts, 22, 29, 63, 122, 126, 131, 132, 136, 139, 172, 186, 192, 278, 286, 319, 369, 370, 379

Cramer, Governor Lawrence, 183, 184, 251

Crawford, Richard C, xix

creole dialect, 47, 48

Creque, Darwin D., 31

cricket, 340

Cummings, Homer, 159, 160

Curacao, 40, 41, 83, 203, 271

Current History, 122, 132, 158

Curtin, Philip D., 18

customs duties, 98, 187, 361, 370

customs exemption, 264

customs zone, US, 287

Cyprus, 7

Daily News, Virgin Islands, 58n, 60n, 76n, 115n, 133n, 154n, 166n, 167n, 183n, 186n, 187n, 231n, 240n, 241, 255n, 265n, 270, 271, 297, 303n, 305n, 306n, 309n, 310n, 322n, 325n, 327n, 329n, 333n, 334n, 335n, 336n, 337n, 339n, 340n, 341n, 344n, 345n. 346n, 347n, 349n, 350n, 351n, 353n, 354n, 355n, 357n, 358n, 360n, 361n, 362n, 363n,

Daily News, Virgin Islands, *continued*
364n, 368n, 369n, 370n, 371n,
373n, 374n, 375n, 376n, 377n,
379n, 381n, 382n, 383n, 384n,
385n, 386n, 398n, 399n, 400n,
401n, 402n, 408n, 409n, 410,
411n, 412n, 413, 414n, 415n,
416n, 417n, 418n, 419n, 422n,
423n, 424n
Dakota Territory, 285
Dalton, Robert H., 347
Danes, 9, 12–14, 16, 18, 36, 39, 52,
62, 66, 68, 72, 75, 76, 83, 85,
111, 112, 114, 121, 123, 143,
145, 147, 197, 300
Danielson, Gustav A., 284, 339,
356, 357, 365, 370
Danish Bank, 74, 164
Danish Company, 9, 10, 12–17, 19,
45, 62, 63, 74, 76, 83, 163, 251
Danish Plantation Company, 13, 74
Danish West India Company, 9, 10,
12, 13, 16, 19, 45, 74, 76, 251
Danish West India and Guinea
Company, *see* Danish West India
Company, 9–10, 45, 74, 76, 159,
199n, 251, 263, 358,
Darwinian theory, 15
Davis Bay, 319, 320, 382
Davis, George W., 98
Davis, James G., 122
Davis, John W., 106
Davis, Morris, 130, 156–158, 161
"Day of Mourning," 384
"day-trippers," 336
de Abadia, Mathias, 12
de Albuquerque, Klaus, 346
de Booy, Theodoor, 4, 5, 31
de Castro, Governor Morris, 190,
209, 210

de Chabert, Mario N., 309, 318
de Chabert, Sr., Ralph, 130
de Chabert family, 363
Declaration of Independence, 90,
93, 104, 105, 380
Decolonization, 3, 379, 381, 393,
399, 428
Decolonization Committee, United
Nations, 379
deficits, 65, 75, 81, 121, 163, 179,
366–369
dehydration, 230
Delaware, 89, 362, 364, 391
Delaware, University of, 89, 391
Delima v. Bidwell, 102
de Lugo, Congressional Delegate
Ron, 346, 369
democracy, 26, 54, 95, 116, 143,
144, 174, 188, 198, 199, 263
Democratic Club, St. Thomas, 241
Democrats, 100, 156, 160, 181,
213, 272, 273, 278, 279, 287,
306, 307, 333, 369, 377, 420
Denby, Secretary of the Navy, 132
Denmark, 9–16, 21, 24, 25, 29, 35,
36, 43, 45, 49, 54, 57, 58, 62, 63,
73, 75–86, 88, 89, 111, 112, 120,
126, 145, 184, 246, 251, 263, 358
dependency, 103, 165, 176, 182,
308
de Poincy, Phillipe de Louvilliers,
6–8
depression, 121, 130, 152, 163, 189,
205, 268
de Riencourt, Amaury, 89
de Sales, Chevalier, 8
desalination plants, 351–355
despoilation, 270, 363
destroyers, 196
Deveaux, Jean, 211

developing countries, 176, 272

development, 13, 23, 41, 47, 54, 69, 73–75, 83, 91, 97, 99, 112, 118, 122, 145, 150, 162, 167, 176–178, 180–184, 198, 205, 211, 213, 248, 251–253, 255–292, 296, 299, 301, 313–315, 318, 320, 337, 344, 351, 352, 358, 360, 363–365, 368, 371, 382, 390, 391, 394, 398, 430

Development Authority, V.I., see Port Authority, 268, 293n, 314, 358n

Dewey, George, 113n

"Dewey Islands," 113

de Windt, William, 43

de Zela, Dr. Peter P., xx, 288n, 291, 319, 375, 437

Dickinson, Thomas, 122

dignity, 43, 47, 70, 79, 124, 153, 165, 173, 206, 270, 286, 311, 383

disarmament, naval, 151

discrimination, 43, 115, 187, 211, 212, 233, 253, 259, 260, 288, 305, 323, 331, 332, 338, 404

diversification of crops, 205

Division of Territories and Island Possessions, see Office of Territories

Dober, Leonard, 45

Dolan, Michael J., 131, 132

dollar, U.S., 339

dollar diplomacy, 107

domestic relations, 192

Dominica, 3, 246, 340, 393

Dominican Order, 8

Dominican Republic, 107, 356, 403

donkey, 213, 273, 279

Donkeycrats, 272–274, 276–279, 284, 286

Donkey Democrats, see Donkeycrats

Dookhan, Isaac, xx, 5n, 9n, 13n, 15n, 26n, 31n, 40n, 54n, 55n, 59n, 62n, 63n, 65n, 66, 68n, 69n, 71, 74n, 75n, 80n, 114n, 121n, 123, 124n, 127n, 132n, 144n, 145n, 148, 149n, 158n, 177n, 199n, 256n, 268n, 339n, 393n, 437

Dorr v. United States, 105

double-sessions, school, 343n

Dowling, William C., 313

Downes v. Bidwell, 101, 102, 104

Downing, Councilman Carlos, 188

Downislanders, see Aliens

Downs, E. Charles, 313, 315

Drake, Professor Thomas, xx

"dred locks," 346

drop-outs, high school, 343n

drum dancing, 60

du Bois, M., 5, 7

due process, 128, 148, 285, 348

Dunsmore, Lord, 89

dust, red, 270

Dutch, 5, 6, 9, 10, 13, 16, 17, 21, 22, 45, 47, 62, 63, 203, 271

Dutch Guiana, see Surinam, 203n, 393

Dutch Reformed Church, 45, 63

du Tertre, 6, 8

duty, 6% ad valorem, 271

duty-free shipments to mainland, 268, 269, 322, 325, 329, 360n

Dyer, Jesse F., 129

earthquake, 48

East Indians, 67–68

East Indies, 78
Eblen, Jack Ericson, 91
economic boom, 298
economic decline, 71, 74, 150, 167,
    168
economic depression, 121, 130,
    152, 205, 268
economic development, 73, 112,
    122, 145, 162, 264, 268–270,
    289, 299, 351, 358, 360, 363
Economic Policy Council, Gover-
    nor's, 343
economic rehabilitation, 150, 153,
    176, 177, 256
economic upsurge, 248
education, 44, 47, 49, 50, 55, 56,
    67, 72, 73, 92, 98, 111, 118, 120,
    124, 125, 143, 152, 156, 157,
    164, 175, 188, 190, 195, 206,
    210, 240, 301, 304–306, 313,
    332, 336–338, 343–345, 350,
    359, 403, 414–417
Education, President's Committee
    on, 206
Education, V.I. Department of, 416
Edwards, John H., 154n
Efficiency, U.S. Bureau of, 122, 150,
    154
Egan, Dr. Maurice Frances, 83, 437
Ehrlichman, John, 294
Eighteenth Amendment, 140, 145,
    178
Eighth Amendment, 348
Eilberg, Congressman Joshua, 341
Eisenberg & Co., 354
Eisenhower, President Dwight D.,
    235, 238, 241, 242, 247, 249n
election code, 273, 274, 276
Elective Governor Act, 284, 293,
    307

Election Code of 1963, 273, 274
election irregularities, 273, 278
Elections, Board of, 279
elections, supervisor of, 274, 275,
    277, 279
electricity, 189, 352
Eliot, Thomas A., xix
Elkins, Stanley, 23
emancipation, 3, 35, 38, 44, 47, 49,
    50, 52–54, 57, 58, 60, 61, 72,
    111, 164, 204, 231, 286, 380
Emancipation Centennial, 231
Emancipator, The, 131–133
Emanuel, Charles A., 116
Emanuel, Gerard, xv, 395, 397,
    399, 403–405, 428
Emergency Molasses Fund, 256
emergency purposes, federal fund-
    ing for, 209n, 237
Emerson, Rupert, 196, 197, 251
emigration, 67, 68, 71, 121, 153,
    338
employment, 10, 59, 68, 71, 114,
    152, 162, 163, 178, 197, 198,
    205, 248, 259, 265, 268, 282,
    296, 299–301, 304, 312, 317,
    340, 365, 423
energy crisis, 364
England, 21, 24, 36, 47, 90, 339
Engle, Congressman Claire, 247
English, 5, 6, 8–10, 12, 13, 16–18,
    21, 23, 34, 36, 47, 52, 55, 62, 73,
    124, 140, 170, 187, 232, 336,
    343, 380
English language, 10, 47, 73, 124,
    140, 232, 336
Enid M. Baa Library and Archives,
    xvi, xix
Enright, Edward, 128, 129
environmental regulations, 363

Episcopalians, *see* Anglicans

equal protection, 148, 262, 285, 305, 348, 400, 404, 405

equal rights, 93, 148, 199, 205, 279, 400

equal treatment, 198, 348, 400

ethnic problems, 249

European conference, 357

European guest worker programs, 297–298

Evans, Governor Waldo, 149–151

Evans, Governor Melvin H., 307, 311

Evans, Luther H., 53

excise taxes, 269, 271, 361

executive branch of government, 207

executive departments, 238, 239, 242

executive-legislative harmony, 249, 259, 272

expansionism, American, 89

"Experimental Quaker," 158

exploitation, white, 303

exploitation of aliens, 310–311, 405–406

export duty, 113, 140, 145, 148, 149, 199

export tax, 139, 145, 148, 256

exports, 7, 10, 17, 121, 179, 231, 258, 288

ex post facto laws, prohibition of, 148, 285

Exxon, 271

Fair Labor Standards Act of 1938, 190

Faris, John T., 4, 31

Farley, Dr. R. A., 158

Farley, James, 16

Farrelly, Senator Alexander, 305

Farrow, Jeffrey, 282

fascism, 189n

fascists, 195n

favoritism, 182, 207, 241

Federal Bureau of Investigation, 197, 325, 355, 371

Federal Comptroller, xx, 237, 242, 243, 244, 282, 293–296, 306, 313n, 353–355, 357, 364, 367n, 368, 371

federal funds, 159, 177, 180, 184, 186, 206, 237, 243, 248, 416

Federal Highway Act, 209

federal relations act, proposed, 378

federal-territorial relations, 372

Federal Trade Commission, 269

Fellows, Lawrence, 253

felonies, 238, 308, 347

Ferdinand, King, 5

Fernos-Isern, Resident Commissioner Antonio, 250

Ferö, 10, 11

Feuerzeig, Penny, 315, 319, 343, 347, 349, 351, 354, 357, 358, 361, 368, 369, 376, 377, 383, 384

Fifteenth Amendment, 285

Fifth Amendment, 126

finance committee, V.I. Senate, 240, 241, 242

Finance, Department of, 371

financial chicanery, 372

First Amendment, 106, 194, 261

Fischer, Christian, 47

fishing, 337

flag, American, 94, 100, 122, 126, 146, 211, 239, 250, 268, 270, 297, 319, 364, 366

Fleming, G. James, 76

Fleming, U.S. Comptroller Darrell E., xx, 353–355, 357, 364–365, 368, 371

Flemish, 13

Flood, Henry D., 113

Florence Williams Public Library, xvi

Florida, 211, 271

flour, 230

Flourney, Jr., Richard W., 140

Flynn, Ed., 196

Fong Yue Ting v. U.S., 341

foods, 292, 340

food stamps, 342, 371

Foraker Act, 99–102, 107, 113, 285

Foraker, Joseph B., 99

Forbes Magazine, 362

Foreign Affairs, 25, 39, 94, 177, 380

foreign raw material content, 237

fornication, 190

Fort Christian, 11, 31, 348–350

Fort Christiansborg, 18

Fort Frederiksberg, 18

Fort Segarra, 314

Foster, Janet, xx

"Fountain Valley," 319–321, 323, 326, 328, 329, 331, 335, 347, 349, 350, 360, 382, 385

Fountain Valley Five, 326, 328, 329, 349

Fountain Valley Golf Course, 319, 320, 323, 382

Fourteenth Amendment, 285, 305, 404

France, 7, 9, 12, 21, 24, 70, 79, 81, 92, 203, 297

Francis, Commissioner Almadeo, 382

Francis, Rothschild, 116, 121, 122, 130–133, 136, 138, 144, 147, 148, 155, 280

Francis v. People of the Virgin Islands, 133, 194

Franck, Harry A., 168

Fraser, C. Gerald, 346

Frederick Douglas High School, 154, 430

Frederik III, 9

Frederik VI, 43n, 52

Frederiksted, 5, 41, 57, 68–71, 76, 217, 219, 248, 332, 336, 350, 356, 357, 360, 378

free-black, 39

free colored, 31, 38–44, 49, 50, 52

free-colored militia, 42, 43, 50

"Free Negro Corps," 33

"free port," 40, 264

free speech, 132, 137, 194, 195

free trade, 7, 85, 99

Freedom City Political Party, 377

French, 4–8, 10, 12, 13, 17, 21–23, 28, 31, 32, 36, 62, 67, 89, 91, 92, 174, 203, 219, 245, 265, 296, 299, 321, 336, 338, 339

French, archaic West Indian, 338

French community, St. Thomas, 337

French Consul in St. Croix, 70

French Guiana, 203

French West India Company, 8

French West Indies, 7, 13, 23, 67, 299

Frenchtown, 219, 337

Freneau, Philip, 34

Freyre, Gilberto, 23

Friendship Day, U.S.-British Virgin Islands, 339

functional disequilibrium, 337

functional imbalance, 321

Gaffney, J. J., 128, 131
Galvin, Terry, 363, 382–385
"ganja," *see* marijuana, 346
garbage collection, 282
Gardelin, Philip, 27
Garner, J. W., 105
Garvey, Marcus, 347
gasoline excise tax case, 369, 370
Gay, Connie B., 255
Geigel, Wilfredo A., xv, 4n, 437
General Accounting Office, 243, 244, 354
General Motors, 357
"genocide," 325
Georgia, 168
Gereau, Adolph, 149
Gereau, Beaumont, 323, 325–328
German expansion in Caribbean, American fear of, 83
German propaganda, 117
Germans, 10, 13, 14, 62, 83
Germany, 44, 55, 81, 83, 85, 112, 151, 251, 297, 310
"Gestapo acts," 325
Gibson, Margaret Alison, 72, 337
Giddings, Frank H., 94
"giddy-boys," 189
Gifft, Mrs. Ella, 157
Gift and Fashion Shop Committee, 358
Gilbert and Sullivan, 153
Gill, Pat, *see* Murphy, Dr. Patricia Gill
Gimenez, Jose I., 158
ginger, 7
Gladwin, Ellis, 267, 288, 289, 318, 319
Gold Coast, 16

Goodwin, George, 302, 305, 309, 340, 391, 403
Goodwin, Michael, 384
Goodwin, Peter, 346
Gordon, Councilman Roy, 241
Gordon, Governor Walter A., 242
Gould, Lyman Jay, 99
Gore, H. Akia, 390n, 391, 397, 405, 418n, 438
Goveia, E.V., 21
Government Corporation Control Act of 1945, 180
Government Employees Service Commission, 249
Government House, 100, 118, 151, 160, 190, 220, 240–242, 246, 255, 293, 308, 372, 421
governor, 6–12, 16, 26–32, 38, 46, 48, 49, 58, 60, 62–66, 72, 86, 87, 89, 91, 93, 100, 101, 111, 112, 114, 116–119, 121–124, 127–133, 141, 144–147, 149–155, 157, 158, 161–165, 167, 170, 172, 176–188, 190, 191, 195–198, 200–211, 213, 214, 229–231, 234–252, 254–259, 262, 267, 269–274, 276–291, 293–295, 299, 300, 302, 303, 305–309, 311, 312, 317, 329–333, 335, 337, 339–343, 345, 347, 352, 355, 357, 361, 363, 368, 370–380, 389–391, 395, 396, 398–402, 404, 405, 409, 410, 413, 415, 416, 418, 420, 421, 424, 425, 427, 428
first black, 192, 203, 205, 207
first elected, 240, 286, 302, 305, 307, 333, 375, 376, 418
first native-born, 247, 286

governor, *continued*
  first native, 191, 206, 209, 210,
    249, 322, 389
  last appointed, 293–295, 302,
    303, 307
  second black, 239
  second elected, 333, 375, 418
  third black, 241
governor, elected, 6, 207, 231, 234,
  236, 242, 249, 286, 287, 302,
  305, 307, 333, 345, 373–377,
  401, 418
Gramboko, 313
Granady, Octavius C., 116
Grand Hotel, 150
grand jury, 105, 126, 187, 429
grants-in-aid, federal, 367, 428
Grapetree Bay Hotel, 336
grass roots, 213
Great Negro Trade Commission,
  36, 37
Grede, John Frederick, 151
"green card," 340
Green, James W., 171
Green-Pedersen, Svend, 17, 25
Grenada, 133, 246, 340, 342, 393
Griffin, Richard and Mattie Ruth,
  323, 324
Grimshaw, Robert E., 353
Groneveldt, Public Safety Commissioner Charles, 347
gross receipt taxes, 361
growth rate, 288, 291
growth, uncontrolled, 385
Gruening, Ernest, 154, 167, 176,
  183, 191, 196
Guadeloupe, 6, 8, 203
Guam, 96, 205, 250, 284, 286, 313,
  315, 366, 371, 379–381, 394,
  397, 398

Guantanamo, 106
Guinea, 12, 13, 16–19, 36, 38
Guirty, Geraldo, 115
Gulliver, John, 323, 324
Guyana, 335, 393

H-2 provision, 298
H-4 classification, 303
Haas, William H., 86
habeas corpus, 148, 285
Haiti, 8, 24, 40, 84, 107, 335
Hall, Gabrielle, 360
Hall, Neville, 28, 30, 41, 42, 48–50
Hamburg-American Line, 83
Hamilton, Senator David, 287
Hamilton Law College, 191
handicapped children, 344
Handicraft, 163, 177
Hans Lollik, xxiii
Hansen, George P., 77
Hansen, Governor, 31
Hansen, Knud, 120, 230, 350
harbor dredging, 248, 427
Harding, President Warren, 118
Harlan, Justice John, 104
Harlem, 169
Harmon, Jeanne P., 258
harmony, ethnic, 249
Harrigan, Norwell, 5, 118, 322,
  339, 345
Harrington, Elizabeth, 118, 119
Harris, et al. v. Kean, et al., 344
Harrison, President William, 95
Harry S. Truman Airport, 210, 268
Hart, Freck, 315
Harvard Law School, 192
Harvey, Leo, 270, 317
Harvey Aluminum Company, 259
Harvlan Properties, Inc., 317

Harwood, Governor Charles, 167, 197, 201, 210

Harwood Highway, 210

Hassel Island, 181, 182, 300, 315, 316, 382

Hastie, Governor William H., 58, 177, 182, 203

Hatch Acts, 273

"hatchet job," 291, 354

Havana, 96, 264

Hawaii, 90, 105, 140, 285, 381

Hawaii v. Mankichi, 105

Hawes, Reverend Charles, 266

Hay, John, 85, 94, 96

Hayward, Du Bose, 156

health, 18, 73, 143, 164, 168, 190, 200, 202, 217, 230, 242, 244, 290, 294, 301, 304, 343, 347, 348, 350, 351, 383, 411–413, 421

Health, V.I. Department of, 347n, 350, 412, 437

Hearst, William Randolph, 95, 96

Heckert, Eleanor, 32, 313

Hedman, Christine, 361n

Heegaard, Anna, 49, 50, 52

Heine, Carl, 381

Helweg-Larsen, Christian, 86

Henry, James E., xx

Hernnhut, 44, 45, 46, 55

Herrick, Government Secretary Robert, 191

Hess, Leon, 271, 317, 354, 361–363, 382

Hess Oil, 270, 271, 288, 354, 361–364

Hesselberg, Englebret, 33

Hestres, John B., 127

Heywood, Councilman Herbert H., 234n

Hickel, Interior Secretary Walter, 294

Highfield, Professor Arnold R., xv, xx, 6n, 7, 8n, 338, 343n, 436, 439

Hill, Elroy, xx

Hill, Sr., Councilman Valdemar, 60, 118n, 188, 190, 202, 213, 234n, 246, 439

Hillhouse, Jack, 351

Hines v. Davidowitz, 341

Hinton, Harold B., 159

Hispanic Caribbean, 337

Hispaniola, 4, 8

"Hitlerites," 193

Hodge, Judge Verne A., 331–332

Hodge, Senator Walter, 253

Hoetink, Harry, 23, 24

Hoffman, Judge, 325

Holbrook. Sabra, 260, 261, 263

holidays, 130, 265, 349

Holmes v. Govt. of the V.I., 363n

Holst, Axel, 130

Holstein, Casper, 118, 148, 154, 169, 430

Home Guard, 199

Home Journal, 280, 305, 307, 311, 312

homes, broken, 347

homesteading, 150, 151, 164, 168, 177, 178, 197

Honduras, 107, 203

Hoopes, Townsend, 89

Hoover, Herbert A., 345

Hoover, President Herbert, 151, 166

Hopkins, Harry, 177

Hosier v. Evans, 304, 305

hospitals, new, 245, 351, 411

hospitals, withdrawal of accreditation of, 351, 412, 413
hostility, inter group, 12, 173, 185, 249, 265, 360, 403, 403–406
hotels, 182, 245, 248, 258, 267, 311, 316, 318, 329, 372, 385, 424
Hough, Henry, 133
House of Commons, British, 34
House of Representatives, U.S., 181, 182, 185, 341
housing, 30, 68, 161, 164, 177, 182, 245, 258, 279, 289, 301, 306, 318, 331, 352, 367
housing projects, 245, 279
Hovey, Graham, 381
Howard, Kay, 346, 364
Howard University Law School, 192
Hubler, Harold, 250, 251
Huguenots, 13
Hughes, Alistair, 342
human dignity, 70, 206, 311
Human Relations Commission, 267
Human Resources Commission, 291
human rights, 37, 104, 199, 200, 205, 211, 212, 311, 312
"humanitarianism," 295
Humphrey, Senator Hubert, 258, 287
hurricanes, 54, 422, 423
Hus, John, 44

Ickes, Harold L., 154
Idaho, 93, 285
identity crisis, 292, 393
ideological differences, 377
illegitimacy, 127, 156, 171, 172
Illinois, 92, 179
illiteracy, 98, 125

immigration, 13, 40, 67, 121, 131, 153, 170, 171, 187, 197, 198, 233, 248, 297, 298, 300, 301, 308–310, 330, 340, 341, 390, 391, 394, 397
Immigration and Nationality Act, 298, 341
Immigration and Naturalization Service, 131, 297, 298, 300, 308, 310
Immigration and Naturalization Service Monthly Review, 297
immigration fund, 67
Immigration Policy, Interagency Task Force on, 297n, 298n
Immigration Policy Task Force, V.I., 341
imperialism, 3, 83, 94, 106, 108
import quota on oil, 271
import quota on textiles, 269n
import quota on watch parts, 269n
imports, dependence on, 7, 18, 38, 264–265, 343, 360, 369
income tax, federal, 145, 367
incorporation, doctrine of, 102, 104, 105, 123, 126
indefinite certification, 304
independence, financial, 187
independence from U.S., 210, 247, 283, 303, 331–332, 378, 381, 395, 396, 428
Independent, The, 46, 70, 98, 120, 136, 172, 277, 279, 280, 286, 287, 302, 306, 340, 352, 362, 373, 374, 376, 418, 419
Independent Citizens Movement (ICM), 286, 302, 374, 418
independents, 273, 276, 376, 420
India, 8–10, 12, 13, 16, 19, 22, 45, 50, 57, 61, 66, 67, 74, 76, 77,

159, 199, 251, 263, 296, 358, 376

Indiana, 92

Indians, 3–5, 47, 68, 85, 90, 309, 338, 339

Indians, American, 47

Industrial Development Commission, 365

Industrial Development Program, 360, 364, 365

Industrial Incentive Law, 296

Industrial Incentive Program, 274, 360

Industrialization, 205–206, 229–230, 267–272, 316–318

industry, 121, 150, 152, 176, 178, 182, 205, 210–212, 234, 258, 267–269, 271, 287, 288, 296, 298, 316, 318, 322, 351, 356, 360, 363, 369, 383, 424, 425

infant mortality, 73, 112, 152, 164, 411

inflation, 75, 205, 368

infrastructure, economic, 351–358, 360, 363, 378, 382, 391, 405, 418, 423, 428, 429

infrastructure, social, 342–351, 381, 391, 393, 401, 404, 405, 409, 421

Inner Brass, xxiii

Innis, Randolph A., 116

insane asylum, 128, 225, 226

Institute of Caribbean Studies, 125, 264

Insular Affairs, Bureau of, 147

Insular Cases, 101, 105, 106, 126, 236

insular psychology, 164

integration problems of European guest workers, 297–298

Interior, Department of, 150, 151, 154, 157, 160, 167, 182, 183, 185, 192, 196, 206, 247, 251, 252, 257, 260, 289, 290, 296, 313, 315, 340, 352, 374, 413

Inter-island rivalry, 188, 320, 373, 374, 422

intermarriage, 336, 338

Internal Revenue Code, Federal, 243

Internal Revenue Service, 371

International Herald Tribune, 380

interplay between American and British, V.I., 54, 73, 170, 197, 233, 245, 298, 299, 339, 440

intervention, 46, 84, 89, 95, 107, 108, 150, 299, 348, 370, 409

intervention, federal, 370

investment firms, 258, 365

investment incentives, 343, 360

Iowa, 232, 239, 425

Iranian oil, 362, 382

Iranian Revolution 362

Irish, 13, 62

iron curtain, artificial, 233

Irving, Washington, 4

Isabella, Queen, 5

Isert, Paul, 36

island life, changes in, 265

Island Resources Foundation, xviii

isolationism, self-imposed, 338

Israel, 353–355

Israel Desalination Engineering, Ltd., 355

Iversen, George, 10

Ivins, George H., 157

Jackson, David Hamilton, 75

Jackson, Helen Hunt, 89

Jackson Hole Preserve, Inc., 252, 253
Jackson, Senator Henry, 354
Jacobs, Delita, xx
jails, 230, 311
Jamaica, 23, 71, 196, 203, 246, 335, 346, 393
Janson, Donald, 315
Jarvis, J. Antonio, 115, 123, 172, 188, 199, 200, 280
Javits, Senator Jacob, 354, 355n
Jefferson, President Thomas, 90, 91, 103
Jensen, Merrill, 90
Jensen, Sister Caroline, 73
Jerusalem, 7
Jessup, Philip C., 99
jets, advent of, 148, 264
Jewish refugees from Nazism, 195n
Jews, 10, 13, 49, 63, 292, 310
"jibaro," 213
Jim Crow policy, 175
Johnson, Dr. Mordecai W., 177
Johnson, President Andrew, 80
Johnson, Robert A., xv, 439
Johnston, Senator J. Bennett, 368
Jones, Edward D. W., 157
Jones Act, 107, 108, 139, 271, 364
Joseph, Lloyd W., 289
Joseph, Paul E., 194
Joseph, Rafael, 325, 326
Joshua, Lawrence, 383
Journal of Black Studies, 5, 118
Journal of Caribbean History, 177, 256, 429
Journal of Negro History, 33
Journal of the College of the Virgin Islands, 345
journalism, 95, 200, 413
judicial branch of government, 186

jury trial, 63, 102, 105, 126, 134, 136, 138, 192, 325, 326
Justice Department, U.S., 341
Justinian Code, 22
juvenile delinquency, 266, 346, 347, 407, 408
juvenile detention facilities, 308

Kahn, Dr. Alfred, 368
Kansas, 96, 232
Kansas City Times, 96
Kaplan, Morris, 250
Kavanaugh, Larry, 356
Kennedy, Joseph F., 255
Kennedy, President John F., 258, 287
Kent, James, 105
Kenyon, William S., 133
King, Darwin A., 319
King, Governor Cyril E., 357
King, Helen M., 86
King, Senator William H., 186
Kirwan, John J., 289, 313
Kissinger, Henry, 375
Kittelle, Governor Sumner, 118, 132, 133, 144
Klein, Herbert, 23
Kleindienst, R. A., 154, 157
Kleppe, Interior Secretary Thomas, 375
Knox, John P., 11n, 28n, 25n, 45n. 46n, 56, 58n, 59n, 63, 64n, 439
Knud Hansen Memorial Hospital, 230, 350
Koht, Halvdab, 77
Korean War, 238
Kratovil, Dee, 361, 364
Krigger, Marilyn F., xv, xx, 170, 292, 395, 428n, 439
Krigger, Rudolph ("Rudy"), xv

Krug, Secretary of Interior Julius, 181

Kruvant, William Jay, 318

Kunstler, William, 325

LaBeet, Ishmael, *see* Ali, Ishmael Muslim

Labor, U.S. Department of, 147, 303

Labor, V.I. Department of, 121, 300

Labor, V.I. Federation of, 130

Labor Act of 1849, 59, 69–71

Labor Riots of 1878, St. Croix, 68–71, 76, 81, 299

Labor Union, St. Croix, 76

Labor Union, St. Thomas, 76

Lake, Edgar O., xv

land, alienation of the, 289, 313, 320, 382

land, increasing cost of, 265, 266, 419n

land use, 424

landed gentry, St. Croix, 212

Landsthing, *see* Parliament, Danish

Langer, Marshall J., 339

language requirement, prohibition of, 236

Lansing, Robert, 84

Larsen, Jens, 9, 18, 39, 45

Larsen, Kay, 42

Latin America, 23, 107

Latourette, Kenneth Scott, 89

Law Enforcement Planning Commission, V.I., 347n

Lawaetz, Eva, 38–40, 42, 48, 49, 318

Leary, Paul, xx, 436, 440

leases, 196, 294, 313

leases, base, 196n

Lee, Senator Sidney, 349

leeward islands, 203

Legal Services, 328, 391

Legislative Assembly, 144, 186, 195, 199, 202, 206, 207, 209, 211, 214, 231–233

legislative branch of government, 135

legislature, unified, 273, 422

Legislature, V.I., 249

Leibowitz, Arnold H., 286, 380, 421, 428, 430

leprosy, 73

less developed countries, 270, 358

Lessard, Suzannah, 335

Leviero, Anthony, 205

Levitt, Judge Albert, 174, 191

Lewis, Gordon, 28, 69, 87, 100, 114, 119, 171, 173, 175, 264, 286, 339, 345, 373, 440

Lewisohn, Florence, 5, 15, 271, 317

libel, 127, 131, 133, 134, 136, 138

Liberty Day, 76, 136

Libraries, Museums and Archeological Services, Bureau of, 6, 15

Library of Congress, 215–226

Licensing Division, V.I., 274

lieutenant governor, elected, 375–377

Lightbourn, Jno., 11, 31

Lilienthal, Dr. Alfred M., 354

Lincoln, President Abraham, 78, 94

Lindemark, Governor, 28

Linqvist, June, xx

liquor dealers, St. Thomas, 231

Literary Digest, 178, 179

Loango, xxiii

Lockhart family, 382

Lodge, Senator Henry Cabot, 94

Loeffler, Hans, 355

Long, Senator Russell, 361

Loomis, Francis B., 107
Lorentz, Johan, 16, 26
Lose, E.V., 48
Louis XIV, 8
Louisiana, 86, 92, 93, 103, 104, 193, 368
Louisiana Purchase, 92, 103
Lovett, Government Secretary Robert Morss, 195, 199
Lowery, Aliston, 323, 324
loyalty oath, 273, 277
Lugo, Susan L., xv
Luis, Governor Juan, 341, 355, 370, 375, 376, 380, 390, 391
Luis-Millin rift, 376
Lukas, Anthony, 262, 300, 329
Lusitania, 84
Lutherans, 48
lynching, 81, 85
Lyons, Dianne D., 291

Maas, Lieutenant Governor David, 331, 375
Macauley, Zachary, 22n, 441
Mackoon, Lindsay, 381
Macridis, Roy C., 64, 318
Maduro, Senator John, 337
Mahan, Alfred Thayer, 94
Mahogany Run Golf Course, 320
Maine, battleship, 96
Maine, state of, 364
malaria, 120
Malmin, Lucius J. M., 127
Malta, 6–8
Malta, knights of, 6–8
mandamus, writ of, 127, 174
"Manifest Destiny," 94, 97
Manila, 96
Manley, Norman, 203
Manpower Commission, 307

manufacturing, 181, 237, 265, 269, 288, 365
manumission, 22, 29, 39, 55
Marco Polo, 3
Marden, Michael, xxi
Marine Corps Air Facility, 182
Marines, 76, 95, 106, 115–117, 119, 129, 132, 173, 404
Maris, Circuit Judge Albert B., 193, 194, 274n, 277
Market Square, 188
marketing, 180
marriage, 29, 37, 45, 127, 172
marshals, federal, 326, 329
Martin, Friederich, 45
Martin-Marietta, 270
Martinique, 8, 32, 203, 346
matching funds, 237, 243, 248, 290
Maternal Child Health and Crippled Children, (MCH and CC), 230
Mathews, T.G., 264
matricentric societies, West Indian, 171
matrifocal family structure, 172
matrilineal descent, 172
Matthias, Philip, 133–135
Maupin, Jere, 58
May, Ernest R., 95
medicine, 230
Mediterranean Basin, 297
Meisinger, Charles and Joan, 323, 324
Melchior, Sr., Ariel, 280, 281
Mena, Judge George A., 119n
"mendicants," 239
mental illness, 383
merchants, 9, 18, 20, 34, 62, 66, 75, 115, 122, 131, 134, 144, 153, 156, 157, 159, 184, 188, 190, 313, 354

merit system, 207
Merwin, Governor John, 247–249,
    280, 281n, 287, 293, 299, 373
Messick, Dr. Charles P., xvii
Methodist Episcopal Church, 179
Methodists, 49
Mexican Cession, 86
Mexican farmworkers, 297
Mexico, 93, 107, 124, 285
Miami, 323, 324, 392
Miami Herald, 324
Michigan, 17, 92, 99, 102
Micklewright, Barry, 382
Micronesia, 380, 381
micropolity, 292
Middle East, 354, 375, 403
migratory movements, intra-
    Caribbean, 338–339
Milan, Governor Gabriel, 26
military construction work, St.
    Thomas, 197
Miller, Congressman A. L., 233
Miller, Gene, 324
Miller, Mark J., 131, 297, 391
Miller, Richard W., 340
Millin, Lieutenant Governor Henry,
    370, 371, 376
"millionaire's lodge," 253
Mills, Frank L., Dr., xv, 392, 393n,
    403n, 408n, 441
minimum wage, 229
Ministerial Alliance of Washington,
    D.C., 158n
minority representation, 236
"mirror system," 366, 367, 428
misdemeanors, 238
mismanagement, 352, 355, 413
missionaries in Hawaii, 95n
Mississippi, 193, 194, 359
molasses, 178, 181, 255, 256

Molloy, Senator Claude A., 327
Monroe Doctrine, 81, 83, 107, 108
Monroe, President James, 91
Monsalud, Suzanne, 188
Monsanto, Liston, 371
Montana, 285
Montserrat, 246, 340
Moon, Reverend Sun Myong, 315
Moore, Judge Herman E., 192–195,
    247, 441
Moorehead, Senator Theovald, 253,
    262
Moorhead, George A., 76
Moorhead, Mario, xv, 303, 322,
    323, 327, 332, 404, 441
Moravians, 35, 44, 46–48, 55, 63
More, Thomas, 9, 17, 65, 134, 145,
    190, 239, 258, 322, 336, 351,
    385, 398, 408, 417, 419
Morenga-Bonaparte, Thomas, 133
Morgan, Sir Henry, 255
Morison, Samuel Eliot, 4, 89
Moron, Alonzo G., 155
Morrissey, F. W., 352
Morse, Senator Wayne, 250
mortality rate, 45, 68, 73, 152, 164,
    411
Mortar and Pestle, 213, 273
Moth, Governor Frederik, 26–27,
    46
mothers, working, 383
Moynihan, Senator Daniel, 354,
    355n
Muhonen, Congressman E. W.,
    243–244
multinational corporations, 270,
    361
Municipal Council of St. Croix,
    186, 199n, 214, 220

Municipal Council of St. Thomas-
St. John, 186, 189, 190, 195,
198, 214, 237n, 256, 422
municipal councils, 14, 147, 186,
199, 213, 422
Munoz-Marin, Governor Luis, 213
Munroe, Mary, 315, 370
murder, 46, 157, 192, 193, 303,
308, 326, 329, 335, 346, 348,
384, 408, 409
Murphy, Dr. Patricia Gill, xxi, 44,
58, 111, 120, 124, 438, 441
Muslims, 348
mustee, 50
McArdle, Edward, 314
McCall, Daniel F., 16
McCarthy, Senator Joseph, 236
McCollum, John, 302
McElroy, Jerome L., 321
McFarlane, Councilman Alva C.,
232
McFerson, Hazel, 314, 315
McHenry, Ambassador Donald F.,
381n, 441
McIntosh, Leonard W., 160
McKinley, President William, 95n,
96, 99
McLaughlin, Frank, 291n
McLean, Senator George P., 147
McWilliams, James, 291n

narcotics, 308, 347
Nation, The, 3, 35, 36, 77, 89, 90,
96, 100, 107, 127, 128, 132, 149,
160, 179, 192, 194, 296, 362, 372,
392, 400, 411, 412, 415, 417, 430
National Archives, 112
National Association for the Advancement of Colored People,
178

"National Association of American
flag-lands and peoples for mutual cooperation," proposed creation of, 337
National Bar Journal, 192
national defense, 170
National Endowment for the Humanities, 292
National Geographic Magazine, The,
252
National Park Service, 250, 253,
261, 382
National Parks, 251, 262
nationalism, 3, 165, 291, 358
native preference in employment,
200
native Virgin Islanders, 169, 170,
172, 175, 249, 265, 272, 296,
298–300, 313, 322, 340–342,
344, 360, 383, 385, 392,
397–401, 403, 404, 406
natural resources, lack of, 205
naturalization, 131, 187, 192, 297,
298, 300, 308, 310, 340, 342
Naughton, Ezra A., 47, 118, 344
Naval Appropriations Act of 1922,
365
Navy, U.S., 112, 221, 313, 413, 425
Nazis, 195n, 198, 310
necromancy, 202
Negro World, The, 118
Negroes, federal commission, 146
Netherlands, The, 9, 21, 203, 299,
421
Netherlands and Antilles, 118n, 299
Nettleford, Rex M., 346
Nevin, David, 380
Nevins, Allan, 95
Nevis, see St. Kitts-Nevis
New Day, The, 131, 316

New Deal, 53, 75, 86, 112, 151, 154, 156, 157, 159–163, 165, 167, 168, 170–174, 176–181, 184, 187, 189, 191, 195–197, 307

New Haven Register, 251

New Herrnhut, 46

New International Economic Order, 165

New Mexico, 124, 285

New Mirror, The, 251

"new nationalism," 165, 291, 358

New Orleans, 93

New Republic, 89, 168

New York City, 86, 96, 116, 118, 132, 138, 148, 154, 168, 169, 179, 196, 200, 202, 209, 239, 430

New York City, Virgin Islanders, 118, 168

New York Journal, 95, 96

New York News, 116, 241, 379

New York Times, xx, 76n, 80, 81n, 83, 85-86, 110n, 119, 120n, 125n, 129n, 130, 131, 136n, 137n, 139, 140n, 141n, 144n, 145n, 146n, 148, 149n, 150n, 151n, 152n, 153n, 154n, 155n, 156n, 165, 170n, 172n, 174n, 175n, 176n, 181n, 187n, 196n, 199n, 200n, 203n, 205n, 206n, 207n, 208n, 209n, 210n, 211n, 212n, 213n, 231n, 234n, 235n, 237n, 238n, 239n, 241n, 242n, 244n, 246n, 247n, 248n, 249n, 250n, 253n, 258n, 259n, 261n, 262n, 289n, 290, 291, 300n, 302n, 303n, 315n, 316n, 325n, 328n, 329n, 346n, 354n, 361n, 363n, 379n, 380n, 381n, 384n, 390n, 396n, 398n, 423n, 425n, 439, 440

New York World, 95

New Yorker, 322, 335

News Journal, 280, 307, 362

Newsweek, 161

Nicaragua, 107

"Night Line," 381

"night soil," 222, 230

Nineteenth Amendment, 174, 285

Nitschmann, David, 45

Nixon, President Richard, 287, 376

"no knock law," 308

Nolan, Sharon L., xxi

Nonimmigrant Alien Labor Program, 297, 298, 304, 309, 312

non-self-governing territories, 203, 234

"no party" candidates, 420

Nordheimer, Jon, 325, 329, 363

"Norman origins," 338

Normans, 4

Norregard, Georg, 16, 20, 36

North Carolina, 15

Northern Mariana Islands, 371, 380, 394

oil exports, 288

oil refinery, 271, 354, 361–364

Oldendorp, C.G.A., 29, 30

oligarchy, economic, 267

Oliver, Governor James, 112, 128, 144

Oman, Governor Joseph, 127

one-man-one-vote principle, 280

O'Neal, British Consul Henry, 311, 312

O'Neal, Dr. Eric, 230

O'Neill, Edward, 118, 210, 211, 263, 302, 309

Open Shorelines Act of 1971, 319
Operation Diversification, 333
Operation Exploration, 333
Operation Recovery, 333
"Operation Wetback," 297
opposition to heavy industry, 271
Ordinance of 1787, 90, 92, 94, 103,
   105
Organic Act, first draft, 147, 282
Organic Act of 1936, 188, 191, 194,
   206, 231, 234–236, 372
Organic Act Commission, Virgin Is-
   lands, 246
Organic Act Reform Committee,
   first, 231
Organic Act Reform Committee,
   second, 231
Orlins, Martin Carson, 264, 265
Ottinger, Congressman Richard,
   316
Ottley, Flavius, xxi
Ottley, Lieutenant Governor Ath-
   niel, 331
Ottley, Senator Earle B., 246, 249,
   273, 279, 305, 377, 394
Oulahan, Richard, 152
Outer Brass, xxiii
outsiders, influx of, 289, 292
overcrowding, 343, 350
Oxholm, P. L., 38

Pacific Ocean, 78
Paiewonsky, Governor Ralph, 190,
   254, 255, 262, 267, 287, 396
Paiewonsky, Isidor, 231, 233, 315,
   320
Paiewonsky, Isaac, 181
Paiewonsky, Senator Michael, 357
Paiewonsky-Ottley alliance, 272,
   273, 286

Pan American Airways, 244–245
Panama Canal, 83, 107, 108
Panama, 83, 106–108, 117, 210
paranoia, mainland, 236
parental guidance, lack of, 343
Parliament, British, 36
Parliament, Danish, 82
Parole Board, Federal, 161
parties political, emergency of,
   272–274
passport fees, 187
passports, 140, 197
paternalism, federal, 229
patrilineal descent, 172n
pay increase for senators, 368
payroll, government, 207, 295, 300,
   421
Peabody, George Foster, 151, 178
Pearson, Diana, 355, 360, 364, 384
Pearson, Drew, 158, 165, 293
Pearson, Governor Paul M., 150
Pegler, Westbrook, 195
Penn, Ed, 291n
Pennsylvania, 47, 150, 284
People of the Virgin Islands v. Brod-
   hurst, 192
People's Civic League, 189
People's Nationalist Party of Jamaica, 203
People's Party, 149, 203, 284, 332
per capita income, 249, 258, 288,
   335, 359
per capita tax rate, 367
Perkins, Dexter, 95
Perkins, Whitney T., 91, 122
permanent resident status, 340
Personal Holding Company, 366
Personnel Division, 274
petrochemical plant, 271

Philadelphia, 4, 9, 18, 31, 123, 126,
127, 135, 160, 192, 209, 276,
300, 328, 349, 362
Philadelphia Inquirer, 362
Philippines, 86, 96, 99, 101, 105,
140, 208, 285
Phillips, Walter, 314
Pierce, Franklin, 99
piracy, 7, 8
pirates, 12, 31
Pitterson, Felix, xxi, 336n
Pittman, Senator Key, 138
planters, 6, 7, 14, 17, 20, 26, 29,
32, 33, 37, 45–47, 50, 53,
55–59, 62, 66–68, 75, 76, 87,
129–131, 144, 156, 172, 184,
188, 313
Platt Amendment, 106
Plebiscite of 1868, 79–80
Plebiscite of 1933, 156–157
polarization, 342
police, 30, 42, 57, 60, 63, 68–70,
76, 107, 116, 120, 122, 126–128,
131–135, 146, 55, 157, 158, 191,
192, 208, 219, 247, 301, 308,
310, 312, 324–326, 329, 330,
335, 345, 346, 348, 349,
409–411, 425
policemen, relationships to criminals, 349
political appointees, 278
"political expediency," 239
political maturity, 284
political parties, 188, 213, 214, 272,
273, 276, 306, 372, 419
"political smut," 291
political takeover, fear of, 340–342,
403–405
"political zoology," 278
Polk, Frank L., 140

Polk, President James, 95
pollution, 272, 290, 363
polygamy, 171, 172, 187
"Poorhouse," remark, 151–153
Pope, Pauline Holman, 30
Popular Democratic Party, 213, 279
population increase, 13, 43, 168,
172, 174, 210, 249
Port Authority, V.I., 358
port facilities, 343, 351, 358
Porter, Vice Admiral, 78
Portugal, 9, 13, 21
Portuguese, 3, 13, 16, 17, 22
Post, Louis F., 139
post-colonial era, 298
Postma, Johannes, 17
Poulson, Congressman Norris, 233
poverty, 111–141, 153, 155, 169,
194, 229, 268, 288, 383, 408
Powell, Gordon "Specs," xxi
Prague, 44, 79
Pratt, Julius W., 97
pregnancy, teenage, 344
prejudice, 61, 111–141, 159, 289,
338, 398
Presbyterians, 47, 179n
press, 4, 5, 9, 15, 16, 18, 21, 23, 26,
28, 36, 58, 63, 66, 76, 79, 81, 86,
89–91, 95, 97, 100, 119, 126,
130–136, 148, 152, 158, 170,
172, 192, 194, 195, 202, 261,
271, 280, 281, 324, 329, 330,
339, 345, 346, 349, 351, 376,
381, 382, 391, 396, 413, 417
primary elections, 273, 277
prisoners' rights, 325, 347
prisoners, threat to set free, 348
prisons, mainland, 350
private enterprise, 179, 181, 269,
292

private sector, 288, 292

privateering, 8

Privy Council, Danish, 11, 26, 62

profit shifting, 371

Progressive Guide, Virgin Islands, 188, 207

Progressive Party, 149, 189–191, 207, 212, 213

prohibition, 7, 29, 121, 129, 145, 156, 168, 198, 236

prosperity, 14, 15, 35, 53, 178, 197, 229–254, 290

prostitution, 43, 159, 190

protectionism, 99, 108

Protestantism, 5, 23, 65

protest marches, 241, 246–247, 275, 308

Proxmire, Senator William, 353

Prussia, 77

public access, 318, 319

Public Administration Service, 208

public assistance, 209, 210

public safety, 247, 303, 308, 346, 347, 384

Public Safety Department, 303, 308, 346

public services commission, 356, 357

public utilities commission, 189

public welfare, 121, 155

Public Works Administration, 161

Public Works Department, 160, 258, 282, 336

Puerto Rican nationalist uprising, 239

Puerto Ricans, 85, 98–100, 107, 153, 170, 171, 231–233, 245, 267, 289, 292, 299, 300, 309, 321, 322, 329, 336, 337, 339, 385, 390, 403

Puerto Rico, 4, 6, 12, 25, 26, 28, 39, 84, 96, 98–104, 107, 108, 113, 121, 128, 131, 139, 147, 148, 152, 170, 203, 206, 208, 211, 213, 231–234, 237, 245, 249, 256, 260, 261, 264, 285, 288, 289, 291, 310, 321, 335–338, 351, 359, 363, 364, 369, 380, 394

Puerto Rico elective governor, 285

Puerto Rico representation in Congress, 285

Pulitzer, Joseph, 134

Purcell, William, 43

puritan morality, American, 172

Quakers, 49

Quarterly Review, 69

Queen Elizabeth II, 339

"Queen Mary," 71

"quickie divorces," 320

quotas, employment, 269, 272

quotas, immigration, 340

racial antagonism, 191, 195–196, 198, 289, 303, 306

racial considerations, 153, 236, 286, 312

racism, 114, 118, 119, 131, 143, 173, 288–291, 331, 384

radio, 260, 336, 373, 381

"raising the color," 61, 115

Rankin, Congressman John E., 193

rape, 118, 191, 210, 211, 251–253, 255, 260, 263, 270, 272, 273, 290, 293, 302, 303, 306, 309, 320, 343n, 384

Rappollee, C. E., 128

"Raran" society, 345

Rasmussen v. United States, 105

Rastafarians, 346, 348
Ratledge, Edward, xv
real estate business, 151
real property, 205, 248, 369
reapportionment, 279
recession, post war, 203, 229
Red Cross, 152, 163, 201
Red Hook Marina Corp. v. Antilles Yachting Corp., 319
"Reds," 132
Reese, Senator Percival H., 229
referendum of 1948, 231
referendum of 1953, 234
reforestation, 150, 182
Reformed Dutch Church, 45, 63
refugees, 5, 195, 391
Reglement of 1755, 28, 29
rehabilitation programs, prison, 349
Reid, Charles F., 124, 152
religion, freedom of, 66, 97, 126
remittances back home, alien, 301
representation in Congress, 207, 283, 380
repression, 21–34, 64, 71, 76, 128, 131, 143
Republican Club of St. Thomas and St. John, 119, 149
Republicanism, 91
Republicans, 94, 99, 100, 149, 160, 273, 276, 277, 287, 306, 307, 331, 333, 376, 377, 420
"Republocrats," 307
resentments, native, 341-342, 392, 403–405
return of revenues, 208, 209, 231, 234
Revenue Act of 1978, 367
revenue bonds, public improvement, 236

revenue sharing, 365, 428
Revised Organic Act of 1954, 235, 236, 240, 241, 243, 248, 256, 273, 276, 282, 305, 369, 422
Revised Organic Act, Proposed Second, 283
Reynolds, Frank, xxiii
Rhodes, 7
Rich, Dan, Dr., xv
"rich man's club," 251
Richards, Councilman Henry, 188
Richards, George, 309
Richmond Penitentiary, 311, 347
Riggs, Fred W., 176
Rigsdag, *see* Parliament, Danish
Riise, A. H., Distillery, 181
Rimpel, Jr., Dr. Auguste E., 383
rising expectations, 165
Rivera, Eulalie, 124
road commissioner, St. Croix, 132
road construction, 282, 382
Roberts, James C., 117
Roberts, Lionel, 155, 177, 189
Robinson, George, 160
Robinson, Senator Joseph T., 138
Roche, John P., 335
Rockefeller, David, 271, 319, 382
Rockefeller, Laurance, 251, 253, 260, 263, 316, 319, 382
Rockefeller Plaza, 263
Rockresorts, Inc., 320
Rodgers, Lionel, 327
Roebuck, Senator Elmo, 306, 355
Rogers, Cephus, 311
Rogers, Judith V., xv
Rogers v. Larsen, 300n
Rohlsen, Councilman Henry, 232
Roman Catholic Church, 7
Roman Law, 22

Romero-Barcelo, Governor Carlos, 374n
Roosevelt Corollary, 107
Roosevelt, Eleanor, 151
Roosevelt, President Franklin, 114, 156
Roosevelt, President Theodore, 83
Roosevelt-Garner Democratic Club, 156
"Roosevelt Laboratory," 178
Root, Elihu, 98, 99, 106, 107
Ropes, Blanca, xx
Rosenblatt, Maurice, 255
Ross, Federal Comptroller Howard L., 294–296, 306
Ross, John, 327
round-up of illegal aliens, 307–312
Rouss, Senator Ruby, xxi, 333, 370–372, 390
Rousseau, Jean Jacques, 33
Royal Danish Commission of 1902, 73
Royal Dutch Shell, 271
Royal Mail Steam Packet Company, 40
Rubin, Vera, 28
rum, 10, 15, 41, 121, 145, 153, 156, 163, 168, 176, 178, 179, 181, 182, 205, 208–210, 220, 229, 231, 232, 237, 255, 256, 367, 369
runoff elections, 307
rural-to-urban migration, 297
Russia, 159
Russian Revolution, 3
Rutherford, Congressman J. T., 262

St. Barthélemy, St. Bartholomew, St. Barts, 338, 339
St. Christopher, see St. Kitts

St. Croix, xvii, xxi-xxiii, 2–3, 4n, 5–6, 10–13, 15, 22–23, 31–32, 35–38, 40, 45–46, 49, 53–59, 60n, 62–63, 65–74, 78, 115, 117–118, 121–123, 126–127, 129, 137, 140–141, 146–147, 151–53, 157–158, 163–169n, 172, 174–175, 181, 186–190, 192–193, 197, 201, 208n, 214, 219, 223–224, 229, 233, 245, 248–250, 252, 259, 263–264, 266–274, 276–278, 280, 288, 294, 296, 299, 302–303, 305–313, 316–330, 335–337, 343–347, 349–350, 352–353, 355–357, 360n, 362–364, 369, 371, 373–378, 382–384, 389, 393, 395n, 396n, 398–399n, 403–405, 408, 410–412, 414–420, 422–425, 427, 435–438, 440–444
St. Croix Avis, 7, 61, 81, 158, 192, 252, 280, 307, 308, 312, 320, 326, 335, 343, 345, 346, 349, 352, 356, 357, 360, 362, 374–378, 382, 383, 398, 408
St. Croix Herald, 132
St. Croix Tribune, 158
St. Domingue, see Haiti
St. Dunstan's School, 266
St. Elizabeth's Hospital, 383
St. Eustatius, 6, 68, 71
St. John, xxi-xxiii, 7, 11–15, 25, 29, 31–33, 40, 46, 49, 53–56, 62–66, 73, 78–79, 82, 111, 119, 122, 125, 133–134, 143–145, 149–150, 163, 176, 184, 186, 189–191, 195, 198, 214, 219, 229, 237, 250–253, 259–263, 274, 276, 278–280, 302, 314,

316, 321, 329, 335, 339, 343, 350, 357–358, 373, 382–383, 399, 401, 403, 410–413, 415, 417, 419, 422–425

St. John's Representation in the Virgin Islands Legislature, Committee to Save, 280

St. Kitts-Nevis, 393

St. Kitts Association, 302

St. Lucia, 196, 246, 302, 308, 340, 362, 363, 393

St. Lucia Association, 302

St. Lucia Labor Party, 362

St. Martin, 6, 8, 45, 356

St. Thomas, xxi-xxiii, 5, 6, 9–18, 20, 24–26, 29–32, 40–41, 44–46, 48–50, 52–67, 72–74, 76–80, 82–87, 111–112, 115–119, 121–122, 125, 130–134, 143–146, 149–150, 152–153, 155–159, 163, 166, 168–172, 174–177, 181–182, 184, 186, 188–191, 195, 197–200, 203–204, 210–211, 214, 219, 226, 229–231, 237, 239, 241, 245–248, 250–252, 256, 258, 259, 263–264, 268–269, 271, 273, 274, 276, 278–279, 282, 288, 291, 296, 300–302, 305–307, 309, 311–322, 328–329, 331–332, 336–340, 342–345, 347–352, 354–355, 357, 359, 365, 368, 370–371, 373–374, 376, 380, 382–383, 385, 389, 391, 393–396, 398–399, 401–404, 408–417, 419–425, 427–428

St. Thomas Alamance & Commercial Advertiser, Walloe's, 31

St. Thomas Beach Resorts, Inc., 319

St. Thomas Bulletin, 117

St. Thomas Mail (Notes), 153

St. Thomas Times, 63, 122, 133, 149, 153, 163, 199, 246, 419

St. Thomas-St. John, Municipality, 134

St. Ursula, 4

St. Vincent, 246, 340, 393

"saboteurs," 195

salary of legislators, 236, 276n, 283, 378

Salvation Army, 117

Salt River, 4

sambo, 50

Same v. Williams, District Judge, 133

Samoa, America, 205

San Juan, 6, 100, 101, 131, 310, 312, 315, 321, 329, 335–336, 342, 346, 349, 351, 355, 363, 364, 370, 374–377, 381–382

San Juan Star, 310, 312, 315, 321, 329, 335–336, 342, 346, 349, 351, 355, 363–364, 370, 374–377, 381–382

Saturday Evening Post, 203, 209

Savan, 117n

Saylor, Congressman John P., 284

Scandinavian Economic History Review, 17, 67

Schade, Councilman Axel, 212

Schiffer, Councilman Jacques, 195

Schimmelmann, Ernst, 35, 36

Schimmelmann, H. C., 35

Schlesinger, Energy Secretary James, 316

Schleswig-Holstein, 81

Schneider, Commissioner Roy, 351

scholarships, 164, 169, 190

School Board, 202

schools, poorly constructed, 344n, 414

schools, private, 56, 72, 125, 266, 292, 344, 345, 359

Schwartz, Douglas, 384

Scofield, John, 252

Scots, xxv, 4, 13

Scott, Austin, 329

Scott, Dred, 94, 97

Scribner's Magazine, 78

Scuilla, Michael, 369

Seaton, Interior Secretary Fred, 244, 250

segregation, 41, 43, 72, 200, 289

segregation, de facto, 289

Sekou, Malik, Dr., xv, 404, 409, 442

Selective Service Act, 199

self determination, 165, 205n, 270, 378, 380, 392, 393, 394, 397–398, 399, 403

self-government, 60, 90, 91, 94, 98, 99, 114, 128, 143, 146, 148, 169, 188, 203, 205, 206, 208, 210, 232, 234–235, 238, 241, 246–247, 250, 272, 282–284, 291, 370, 379, 383, 395–396, 398, 429

Senate, U.S., 138, 179, 182, 185, 313, 341

Senate Commission, Joint, 146

Seneca, 22

Senior, Clarence, 336

separation of powers, 188, 236

sessions of legislature, 236

Settler's Handbook, St. Croix, 345

Seward, Olive Risley, 78, 79n

Seward, William H., 77, 78, 79

Sewer, Lawrence, xv

Sewer, Oswin, xv, 401, 419

sewer system, 239

sexual relationships, 115

Shapiro, David, 370

Sheen, Albert, 308

Shelley, Olive D., 179

Shells, Rachelle, xv

Sheps, Cynthia, 363

Sheraton Hotel, St. Thomas, 329

Shipley Samuel S., 149

"shortfalls," 367

sick leave, abuse of, 369

siege mentality, 329

silk screened fabric, 42, 258

Simmons, George, 260

Sims, Rudolf, 349

Sircar, K. K., 67

Sixth Amendment, 134

Sixto, Adolph, 11

Sixty-fifth Puerto Rican Regiment, 238n

Skeoch, Councilman Gordon, 212

Skeoch, Robert, 69

Skyline Drive, 256

slaughterhouse, Charlotte Amalie, 222

slave labor, modern version of, 289

slave trade, 15–18, 20, 25, 35–38, 54, 172

slavery, 3, 5, 8, 15, 21–25, 28, 30, 31, 34–61, 64, 66, 70, 72, 81, 92, 111, 162, 169, 171, 172, 187, 188, 267, 285, 296, 299, 311, 322

slums, 230

smallpox, 120

Smit, Erik Nielson, 9

Smith, Beverly, xv

Smith, Congressman H. Allen, 245

Smith, Sr., Hugh, 306

Smith, Meral, 325, 326

Smith, Dr. Wilburn, 307
Smith, William D., 361
"smoldering volcanoes," 288
smuggling, 7
Smythe, Robert B., 154
soccer, 340
Social, Educational Research and
    Development Inc., 301
Social Science Research Center, 336
Social Security Act, 209, 210
social tension, 289
socialism, 176, 189, 268
socio-economic hierarchy, 300
sociologists, 266, 326
soil conservation, 182, 208
Soil Conservation Service, 208
solar equipment, 316
Soto et al. v. United States, 123
South, the American, 120
South Shore Plant, 270, 271, 356,
    357, 372
Southwest, U.S., 92, 297
Southwest Territory, 92
Soviet Union, xxiii
Spain, 5, 9, 12, 13, 21, 24, 95, 96,
    102, 105, 286
Spanish, 5, 6, 12, 22, 25, 26, 29,
    31, 39, 53, 95, 96, 98, 99, 336
Spanish American War, 94, 95, 101
Spanish language, 336
special education, 304
special interest legislation, 290
Special Study of the House Sub-
    committee on Immigration, Citi-
    zenship and International Law,
    Nonimmigrant Alien Labor Pro-
    gram on the Virgin Islands of the
    United States of 1975, see Non-
    immigrant Alien Labor Program
speech, freedom of, 194

"spies," 188, 195
Spingarn, Lawrence P., 24
Sprauve, Gilbert, Dr., xv, 391
Sprauve, Senator Julius, 262
Staats, U.S. Comptroller General
    Elmer B., 355
standard of living, 73, 129, 173,
    265
Stannard, Dr. Amy, 161
Stark, Charlotte Dean, 262
Starosselsky, D. V., 182
State Department, U.S., 337
state of emergency, 209
State of the territory message, 11,
    333
statehood, 90–94, 97, 98, 103, 236,
    283, 284, 395, 396, 428
status, political, 66, 82, 88, 97, 103,
    112, 140, 141, 180, 237,
    378–380, 393–396, 398, 399,
    402, 407, 428
status, social, 61, 66, 169
status awareness, 61, 169
Steel, Ronald, 89
steel bands, 340
Stephen, James, 22
Stephens, H. Morse, 9n
Stock, Robert W., 316
stock market crash, 149
stone quarries, 258
Story, Joseph, 105
strike, St. Croix general, of 1916,
    76, 117–119, 121, 125, 126, 130,
    134, 155
strike, St. Thomas of 1916, 76
Strong, Josiah, 94
Stubenberg, Ben, 343
Stull, Page, 316, 343, 349, 360

Subcommittee on Immigration and
International Law, House of
Representatives, 341
Subcommittee on National Parks,
House of Representatives, 262
Subcommittee on Public Works and
Resources, House of Representatives, 229n
Subcommittee on Territories and
Insular Possessions, House of
Representatives, 231
Subcommittee on Territories and
Insular Affairs, Senate, 251, 313
submarines, 96, 182, 197, 208, 229,
268
subsidy, 182, 187, 268, 269, 364
suffrage, universal, 107, 144, 148,
188, 190
suffrage, women's, 174, 187
Suffragist League, 157
suffragists, American, 143
sugar, 4, 7, 8, 13, 14, 35, 37, 38,
45, 53–55, 68, 73, 74, 113, 121,
139, 140, 145, 148, 149, 151,
152, 156, 162, 163, 168, 176,
178, 179, 181, 182, 199, 205,
208, 209, 218, 259, 264, 268,
271, 313
Sugarbird Resort, 315
suicide, 19, 25, 31, 32
superstition, 130, 200
Supremacy Clause, 300
Supreme Court, Danish, 58
Supreme Court, U.S., 341, 379, 404
Surinam, 393
surtax, 366
Survey Graphic, 156
Susanna of St. Croix, 50
suspension of deportation, 340
Swan, Attorney General Ive, 355

Swarthmore (Pa), 150, 154n
Swedes, 13, 16
"sweetheart deal," 355
Swenson, Laurits S., 82
Swing, Raymond Gram, 160, 161
Swisher, Carl Brent, 97
Switzerland, 297, 380
Szulc, Tad, 271, 362, 381
Taft, President William Howard,
106, 107
Tamarin, Mingo, 33, 42
Tamarin, Peter, 42
Tannenbaum, Frank, 22
Tansill, Charles C., 79
Tap Huis, *see* St. Thomas, 10
Tarbert, Patricia, 323
Taussig, Charles W., 178
Taylor, Charles E., 28
Taylor, Harry, 158
tax commission, colonial, 146
tax exemptions, 206, 229, 272, 360,
366
tax haven, 366
Tax Incentive Act, 269, 272, 360
tax incentive program, 258, 274,
279, 288, 360
tax, internal revenue, 232, 243, 366
tax loopholes, 248, 371
Tax Reduction Act of 1975, 366
taxes, 43, 122, 155, 156, 184, 187,
209, 231, 237, 243, 252, 256,
269, 271, 314, 361, 364, 366,
367, 369, 370, 384, 399, 419
taxes, federal collection of, 370
television, 303, 322, 326, 373
Teller Amendment, 96, 106
Tennessee, 294
Tennis Club, St. Thomas, 159
Tenth Amendment, 430
territorial policy, 90, 93, 380, 394

Territorial Policy Review Task Force, White House Interagency, 380
territories, American, 90, 92, 95, 97, 101–103, 337, 430
territory, autonomous, 283
terrorism, 332
Texaco, 271
Texas Border Patrol, 309
textile mills, 269
Thatch Cay, xxiii
Third World, 165, 322, 358, 378
Thirteen Colonies, 15
Thirteenth Amendment, 285
Thomas, Hugh, 95
Thomas, Mary, *see* "Queen Mary"
Thompson, Andrew, 192
Thompson, Ralph, 158
Thoron, Benjamin W., 173
threats, 12, 158, 240, 279, 308, 343, 364, 419
Tillett, Jim, 347
time, 5, 8, 17, 21, 24, 28, 29, 31, 35, 37, 41, 45, 47, 50, 60, 61, 64–68, 71–74, , 35576–78, 81, 82, 85, 89, 94, 97, 99, 111, 117, 122, 123, 128–131, 133, 138, 148, 149, 151, 152, 154, 160, 162, 163, 177, 179, 185, 189, 190, 196, 202, 203, 208, 211, 231, 232, 234, 236, 242, 247, 248, 250–252, 256, 260, 262, 264, 275–277, 279, 284, 285, 302, 310, 311, 313, 314, 319, 322, 326, 327, 330, 332, 333, 339, 357, 361, 369, 372, 373, 377, 379, 381, 382, 391, 395, 397–399, 408, 412, 415, 417, 419
Timmons, C. C., 118, 119, 130, 131

Title I, Higher Education Act of 1965, 301
tobacco, 7, 8, 13
Todman, Henrita, 274, 275
"tokenism," 306
Tomayo, Juan O., 335
Tonkin, Donald, 331
Toplin, Robert Brent, 23
Tortola, 12, 32, 54, 131, 197, 339
Toth, Tibor, Dr., xv
Totten, Ashley L., 148, 169, 200
tourism, 150, 175, 182, 205, 206, 211, 212, 227, 247, 248, 250, 263–268, 271, 288, 297, 298, 320, 333, 335, 343, 349, 351, 360, 363, 422–424, 429
tourist expenditures, 247, 264, 360
trachoma, 120
trade imbalance, 358
trade tariffs, 256,
tradewinds, 270, 415
Transfer, of islands from Denmark to U.S., 83–88, 107, 112, 115, 120, 121, 123, 126, 128, 139, 143, 145, 149
transitional society, 61, 175, 176
transnational corporations, 270
transportation, inter-island, 181
Treasury Department, U.S., 371
Treaty between U.S. and British Virgin Islands, 339
Treaty of Cession, *see* Treaty of Sale of 1917
Treaty of 1867, between Denmark and U.S., 77–80, 82, 88
Treaty of 1902, between Denmark and U.S., 80–83, 85, 88
Treaty of 1904, 106
Treaty of Paris, 96–98, 100, 103, 106

Treaty of Sale of 1917, 99, 139, 358
Treaty with France, 92
Trench, Governor Martin E., 119
Trillin, Calvin, 322, 330
Trinidad and Tobago, 246
Trinidad Express, 311
Trollope, Anthony, 134
Truman, President Harry, 204
Trumbull, Robert, 380
Trunk Bay, 261, 423
Trust Territory of the Pacific, 380
tuberculosis, 230
Tucker, Dr. Rufus S., 168
Tuden, Arthur, 28
Tugwell, Rexford, 178, 196
Turnbull, Dr. Charles W., xiv, xv,
    337n, 344n, 398, 401, 402, 415,
    416, 418, 420, 422n, 443
Turnbull, Joel, xv
Turner, Frederick Jackson, 89
Turner, Harry, 351, 364, 370, 374,
    375
Turquoise Bay, 319
two-party system, 213, 214, 272
Tydings, Senator Millard, 159, 161
Tynes, Emily, 344, 371
Tyson, Eugene, xxi
Tyson, Jr., George F., xv, xviii, 15,
    443

Udall, Interior Secretary Stewart,
    255, 293
Ulrich, Anthony, 45
Un-American Activities Committee,
    House of Representatives, 199
"under-the-table payments," 355
Underwood, Senator Oscar W., 113
unemployment, 75, 121, 163, 177,
    205, 229, 309, 329, 332, 341,
    343, 383

unemployment compensation, 177
UNESCO (U.N. Educational, Sci-
    entific and Cultural Orgn.), xix
Unicrats, 272–279, 284
unification, of all black people in
    the Caribbean, 303
unification of the islands, political,
    207
unincorporated territory, 236, 283,
    286, 378, 379, 390, 395, 399
Union of Sleeping Car Porters, In-
    ternational, 169
unions, 127, 128, 171
United Alien Association, 302, 311
United Caribbean Association, 303
United Government Employees,
    196
United Nations, 94, 106, 203,
    205–207, 234, 250, 311, 341,
    342, 379, 380, 429
United Nations, Charter of the,
    203, 205, 206
United Nations Visiting Mission of
    1977, 379–380
United People's Party, 332
United Press International, 349n
United States, 5, 23, 26, 40, 47, 49,
    58, 62, 66, 70, 76–86, 88–108,
    112–114, 120–126, 131–134,
    137–141, 145, 146, 148, 149,
    151–153, 155, 163, 165, 168,
    170, 171, 174, 177, 179,
    184–187, 189, 190, 192, 194,
    196, 199, 200, 202, 203,
    205–208, 210, 212, 230–232,
    236–239, 243, 245, 247, 250,
    255–257, 260, 264, 265, 269,
    271, 281, 283, 285–287,
    296–298, 301, 305, 319, 321,
    324, 327, 330, 341, 345–347,

350, 355, 358, 359, 364–368, 370, 372, 376, 378–380, 391–395, 397, 399, 400, 405, 410, 411, 417, 421, 428–430
United States Attorney, 145, 238
United States Government, 49, 80, 85, 89, 92, 99, 170, 184, 185, 187, 202, 206, 207, 236, 238, 319, 341, 358, 368, 372, 379, 380
United States v. Lovett, 200
United States v. St. Thomas Beach Resorts, Inc., 319
Unity Democrats, *see* Unicrats
Unity Party, 213, 246, 272, 274, 275
University of Puerto Rico, 28, 264, 336
uprisings, slave, 31, 42
urbanization, 62
U.S. News & World Report, 329
Utah, 124, 278, 281, 284, 285
Utopia (Thomas More), 134

vacancies in legislature, filling, 236
vagrant outcasts, continental, 289
Vallee, Lionel, 24, 171, 172
Van Bennekom, Pieter, 349
vandalism, school, 343
Varlack, Pearl I., 5, 118, 124
Vasco da Gama, 3
Vasquez, Bertha S., xxi
Vaughn, Dr. Robert W., 324n, 345n, 443
verdict tampering, 328
Vermont, 293, 316
Vest, George C., 97
Veterans Drive, 258
veto, gubernatorial, 91, 184, 187, 214, 240, 241, 242, 249, 418

veto, line item, 199, 236
veto, Presidential, 234, 236, 283, 285, 367, 378
veto over-ride, 236, 373
Vibaek, Jens, 25
"Victory-66," 278
Vieques, 336, 338
Vietnam, 3, 89, 325, 330
Vietnam War, 89, 325, 330
"vigilante" groups, 291
Vikings, 3
Virgin Islands Amalgamated Workers Union, 311
Virgin Islands Bar Association, 413
Virgin Islands Bar Journal, 192, 235, 283, 378
Virgin Islands Committee, 147, 148, 181, 239, 275, 280, 284, 358, 379
Virgin Islands Company (VICO), 176, 268
Virgin Islands Congressional Council, 154, 430
Virgin Islands Corporation (VICORP), 180, 268
Virgin Islands National Bank, 164, 256
Virgin Islands National Park, 251–253, 260, 316
Virgin Islands Post, 196, 282, 337, 343, 345–347, 349, 360, 362, 364, 369, 373, 376, 382, 383
Virgin Islands Refinery Corporation, 354, 363
Virgin Islands View, 119, 284, 291, 320, 358
Virgin Isle Hilton Hotel, 329
Virginia, 23, 89, 189, 286, 429
Virginia Journal of International Law, 286

Virgo Corporation, 269
visas, immigrant, 340
vocational education, 210, 240
Vocational Education Act, 210
vocational school, Hess's, 296
vodka, 258
Volstead, Andrew J., 121n, 145n
Voltaire, 33
Volunteers in Service to America
    (VISTA), 305
von Prock, Governor Christian, 29
von Scholten, Governor Peter, 30,
    111
von Zinzendorf, Nicholas, 44
vote, naturalized, 340, 342
vote for President, 186, 283, 378,
    429
voting franchise, 64–66, 71, 98,
    114, 143, 144, 147, 155, 185,
    187, 232

Waldron, Martin, 290, 291
Walker, Ronald, 336, 374, 376, 377
Walker, Wendell, xxi
Wallace, Henry, 178
Wallace, Mildred C., xxi
Wallace, Governor Walter, 339
Walrond, Eric D., 132
Walter, Premier George, 312
Walterstorff, E. E., 48
War, between Denmark and Prus-
    sia, 77
War Department, 98
Warden, The (Anthony Trollope),
    134
"wards of the United States," 239
Warner, Arthur, 132
Warren, Chief Justice Earl, 242
Washington, D.C., 112, 118, 158,
    183, 232, 297, 298, 303, 310,
    313, 315, 325, 330, 341, 345,
    359, 365, 402, 412
Washington, State of, 298
"Washington Merry-Go-Round,"
    165
Washington Post, 154, 281, 329,
    333, 349, 362
Washington Representative, Virgin
    Islands, 286
Washington Star, 95, 96, 154, 310
watch industry, 269, 287
water, 19, 30, 54, 68, 78, 112, 120,
    138, 182, 202, 208, 230, 231,
    240, 245, 258, 259, 268, 272,
    290, 301, 314, 315, 319, 336,
    343, 351, 352, 354–357, 382,
    414
Water Island, 78, 314, 315, 382
Water Island, Inc., xxiii, 78, 314,
    315, 382,
Watergate, 328, 332, 354
Watergate Committee, Senate, 354
Water and Power Authority, 268,
    352, 354
Water Resources Task Team, Inte-
    rior, 352
watershed event. 328, 333
Watlington, Janet, 369
Watson, J. C., 131
Watson, Leona, 360
Weaver, Robert C., 192
Weinberg, Albert K., 97
Weinstein, Edwin A., 170
West End News, 158, 194
West India Company, 8–10, 12, 13,
    16, 19, 45, 74, 76, 159, 199, 251,
    263, 358
West India and Guinea Company,
    see Danish West India Company
West Indian Conference, 203

West Indies, University of, 30, 41

West Indies Associated States, 312

West Indies Bank and Trust Company, 256

Westergaard, Waldemar, xviii, 9n, 10n, 13n, 14n, 15n, 16n, 19n, 20n, 26n, 28n, 31n, 32n, 33n, 54n, 62n, 63n, 83n, 444

westward migration in U.S., 89

wheat subsidy, 232

Wheatley, Reuben, 243

whisky, 258

White, Justice Edward D., 102, 103, 104

White, Katrina, 378

White, Walter, 178, 314

"white economic power," 267, 291

"white elephant plant," 356

White House, 180, 242, 255, 293, 294, 374, 380

"white man's burden," 94

white supremacists, 118

Whitehead, Henry S., 119, 120

Whitehouse, Mrs. Norman de R., 143

Wilberforce, William, 36

Wilbur, Interior Secretary Ray Lyman, 152, 154, 156

Williams, Earl, 278

Williams v. Todman, 278

Williams, Prime Minister Eric, 15n, 23, 31, 39n

Williams, George Washington, 128, 131, 133

Williams, Senator Lloyd, 384

Williams, Philip, 117, 119, 122, 128, 130, 145

Williams, R. G., 129, 130

Willis, Jean Louise, 15

Willoughby, W. W., 101, 104

Willoughby, William Franklin, 92

Wilson, Liz, 374

Wilson, Judge T. Webber, 189, 241, 316, 384

Wilson, President Woodrow, 84

Windows of Westminster, The (Joseph Pulitzer), 134

Windward Islands, 203

winery, 258

Wintberg, Estate, 182

Wisby, James, xxi

Wisconsin, 18, 92, 353

witch hunt, 199

witchcraft, 27, 202

Wolters, Raymond, xxi

women, 7, 10, 18, 29, 32, 39, 40, 43, 44, 50, 55, 68, 76, 86, 115, 120, 143, 154, 161, 163, 168, 173, 174, 179, 190, 215, 267, 290, 291, 308, 323, 396, 418

Women's Christian Temperance Union, 179

Women Suffrage Party, 143

Women's Society of the First Presbyterian Church, 179

Woodstock Inn, 316

Woolbert, R. G., 177

Woolley, Judge Victor B., 135, 136, 137

working force, 288

Working People's Committee, 130n

workmen's compensation, 190

Works Progress Administration (WPA), 170

World War I, 75, 151

World War II, 167, 179, 251, 296, 297, 314

Wyoming, 93

xenophobia, 266, 393

Yale University, 251n
Yates, Paul C., 160
"yellow press," *see* press
Yeres, David J., 297
York, Holcombe, 251
Yorty, Congressman Samuel, 232
Young, Judge Warren H., 325, 329, 330, 344
Young Peoples Democratic Club, 157
youth, 202, 289, 291, 307, 344–347, 383, 385, 407–409, 415

Youth Services Administration, 347

Zalinski, Wolf, 191
Zane, William S., 119
Zeder, Fred, 374
Zionist Connection: What Price Israel? (Dr. Alfred M. Lilienthal), 354
"Zionist influence," 354
Zionists, 354